WHEN PARTNERS BECOME PARENTS

CAROLYN PAPE COWAN
and PHILIP A. COWAN

When Partners Become Parents

The Big Life Change
for Couples

 BasicBooks
A Division of HarperCollinsPublishers

Library of Congress Cataloging-in-Publication Data
Cowan, Carolyn Pape.
    When partners become parents: the big life change for couples /
by Carolyn Pape Cowan and Philip A. Cowan.
        p.   cm.
    Includes bibliographical references and index.
    ISBN 0–465–01595–6 (cloth)
    ISBN 0–465–09160–1 (paper)
    1. Parents—United States—Longitudinal studies.
2. Parenthood—Longitudinal studies.   I. Cowan, Philip A.
II. Title.
HQ755.8.C68   1992
306.87—dc20   91–55457
                                                                        CIP

Designed by Ellen Levine

93 94 95 96 CC/CW 9 8 7 6 5 4 3 2 1

With our love and appreciation to our parents and children—
Norman Cowan, Lee Pape
Joanna Cowan White, Dena Cowan, Jonathan Cowan
Kennen White, and Jennifer Cowan

and in loving memory of
Bertha Cowan, Grace Pape, and Ben Pape

CONTENTS

Preface   ix

Acknowledgments   xv

Introduction: Becoming a Family   1

PART I THE NEW PIONEERS

1 Changing Families in a Changing World   15

2 To Be or Not to Be a Parent   31

3 The Pregnant Pause: Nine Long Months   48

PART II CROSSING THE GREAT DIVIDE

4 What's Happening to Me?   75

5 What's Happening to Us?   91

6 Beyond the Doorstep: New Problems, New Solutions   114

7 Legacies from Our Parents   137

8 Parenting Our Children   150

PART III PROTECTING THE HOMESTEAD

9 An Ounce of Prevention: Couples Groups   165

10 Talk to Me: Hidden Challenges in Couples' Communication   184

11 Who Is at Risk and What Can Be Done?   202

   Notes   215

   References   223

   Index   237

PREFACE

BABIES ARE GETTING a bad press these days. Newspaper and magazine articles warn that the cost of raising a child from birth to adulthood is now hundreds of thousands of dollars. Television news recounts tragic stories of mothers who have harmed their babies while suffering from severe postpartum depression. Health professionals caution that child abuse has become a problem throughout our nation. Several books on how to "survive" parenthood suggest that couples must struggle to keep their marriage alive once they become parents. In fact, according to recent demographic studies, more than 40 percent of the children born to two parents can expect to live in a single-parent family by the time they are eighteen (Glick and Lin 1986). The once-happy endings to family beginnings seem clouded with strain, violence, disenchantment, and divorce.

What is so difficult about becoming a family today? What does it mean that some couples are choosing to remain "child-free" because they fear that a child might threaten their well-established careers or disturb the intimacy of their marriage? Is keeping a family together harder than it used to be?

Over the last three decades, sociologists, psychologists, and psychiatrists have begun to search for answers to these questions. Results of the most recent studies, including our own, show that partners who become parents describe an ideology of more equal work and family roles than their mothers and fathers had; actual role arrangements in which husbands and wives are sharing family work and care of the baby less than either of them expected; more conflict and disagreement after the baby is born than they had reported before; and increasing disenchantment with their overall relationship as a couple.

To add to these disquieting trends, psychiatrists' and obstetricians' studies of emotional distress in new parents suggest that women, and possibly men, are more vulnerable to depression in the early months after having a child, and that mothers with children under five and without a supportive partner are at greater risk for becoming clinically depressed than any other group of adults.

Finally, in the United States, close to 50 percent of couples who marry will ultimately divorce. In our longitudinal study of relatively well functioning couples having a first baby, 12.5 percent of the parents had separated or divorced by the time their first baby was one and a half years old. If this figure were to hold up in larger studies, it would mean that at least one-quarter of American divorces occur in households with children who are not old enough to retain the memory of living with two parents.

We believe that children are getting an unfair share of the blame for their parents' distress. Based on fifteen years of research that includes a three-year pilot study, a ten-year study following seventy-two expectant couples and twenty-four comparable couples without children, and ongoing work with couples in distress, we are convinced that the seeds of new parents' individual and marital problems are sown long before their first baby arrives.

Our conviction is bolstered by two findings from our studies: The couples who report the most marital difficulty after having a baby tend to be the ones who were experiencing the most strain in their relationships before they became parents; and the couples who feel that they have productive ways of working out the differences and difficulties that confront them report the least dissatisfaction and distress in the first few years of parenthood.

Our concern about the high incidence of marital distress and divorce among the parents of young children led us to study systematically what happens to partners as they become parents. Rather than simply add to the mounting documentation of family problems, we created and evaluated a new preventive program, the Becoming a Family Project, in which mental health professionals worked with couples during their transition to parenthood, trying to help them get off to a healthy start. Then we followed the families as the first children progressed from infancy to the preschool period to the first year of elementary school, to get a fuller picture of how the parents' well-being or distress affected their children's development at home and at school.

What we have learned from our Project is more troubling than surprising: The majority of husbands and wives become more disenchanted with their relationships as couples as they make the transition to parenthood. Most new mothers struggle with the question of whether and when to return to work. For those who do go back, the impact on their families depends both on what mothers do at work and on what fathers do at home. The more unhappy mothers and fathers feel about their marriage, the more anger and competitiveness and the less warmth and responsiveness we observe in the family during the preschool period—between the parents as a couple and between each parent and the child. The cycle continues as the children of parents with more tension during the preschool years have a harder time adjusting to the challenges of kindergarten two years later.

On the positive side, becoming a family provides a challenge that for some men and women leads to growth—as individuals, as couples, and as parents. For couples who work to maintain or improve the quality of their marriage as they become parents, with or without help, having a baby can lead to a revitalized relationship. Couples with more satisfying marriages work together more effectively with their children in the preschool period, and their children tend to have an easier time adapting to the academic and social demands of elementary school.

When Partners Become Parents describes what happens to men and women, and especially to their relationships as couples, when they have their first baby. In an introductory chapter, we describe how our personal history led to the creation of the Becoming a Family Project, our study examining both stability and change in five major aspects of a couple's life on their journey to parenthood. In part I we begin with a discussion of why the transition to parenthood is stressful even for well-functioning couples. We then explore a couple's preparation for the excursion: their decision-making process about whether and when to have a baby and the issues they face during pregnancy and childbirth.

Part II begins where childbirth preparation classes end. The men and women in our study talk about the changes they experience after their babies are born in their sense of self, in the "who does what?" of family life, in their work outside the family, and in their relationships with their parents and in-laws. We demonstrate that what is happening in the marriage provides a context for the relationship that each parent establishes with the child, and that the preschooler's family environment is influential in his or her academic and social adjustment to elementary school. It becomes very clear that for new parents to maintain the quality of their relationships as partners, they must strike a delicate balance among these competing but essential aspects of their lives.

In the service of stimulating more preventive work with developing families, we focus in part III on the reactions of a randomly chosen set of parents in our study. These couples met once a week throughout the last three months of pregnancy and the first three months of parenthood in small groups led by couples who are trained mental health professionals. Our results show that when sensitive group leaders help men and women focus on what is happening to them as individuals and as a couple during their transition to parenthood, it buffers them from turning their strain into dissatisfaction with each other and seems to keep them from resorting to early separation and divorce. We show how the typical difficulties of keeping marital communication open and intimate can easily become more problematic in the hectic period around the birth of a first child. Finally, we talk about who is most at risk for distress in the early family years, spelling out the implications of our findings for new parents, for health professionals, for family researchers, and for those who make the policy decisions that affect both parents and children.

This book is addressed to several audiences. It is for couples thinking about having a baby as well as for those who have started their families but want to know more about the parts of family making that friends and researchers rarely discuss: Why does becoming a parent have such a powerful impact on a marriage? What can couples do to make the family formation period a time of development rather than decline? From our couples groups we have learned that one of the most difficult aspects of becoming a family is that so much of what happens is unexpected. At the risk of sounding alarmist, we provide some warnings about the dangers that seem to sidetrack couples from the wonderful side of having babies and nurturing their development. We find that helping couples anticipate how they might handle the potentially stressful aspects of becoming a family can leave them feeling less vulnerable, less likely to blame each other for the hard parts, and more likely to decide that they can work it out together.

We believe that our findings have something to say to researchers from various disciplines who study what goes on in families. We want to urge family sociologists, developmental psychologists, and psychiatrists who study the family to look beyond the relationships between mothers and children—to accord fathers their full due as family members and to pay more attention to the effects of parents' marital quality on their children's early development.

In addition to parents and family researchers, this book is addressed to health professionals who are involved with family matters. The experiences of the parents in our study should convince obstetricians, pediatricians, nurse practitioners, and physicians in family practice to be more active in attending to the health of the whole family. If doctors and nurses were to ask more about the well-being of both parents during checkups in the early family years—for example, by asking "How are *the two of you* doing?"—they could encourage parents to seek help for moderately troubling problems before they feel insurmountable.

We hope to begin a dialogue with mental health professionals about the prevention and treatment of family distress. Throughout the book, we demonstrate that our assessments of how the partners are doing during pregnancy as individuals and as a couple can identify a substantial number who are at risk for later distress. We are eager to involve more health professionals in this venture in order to give parents at greater risk a chance to beat the odds before their distress permeates all of the relationships in the family.

We conclude by highlighting our picture of the delicate balance: what it takes for today's fathers and mothers to feel satisfied with themselves as individuals, as parents, and as couples. In the virtual absence of comprehensive government policies to support the development of families, contemporary couples are forced to be pioneers, making the arduous trek to parenthood on their own. Men and women push on, wondering when they will feel less alone, trying to find better ways to take care of themselves, their babies, their work inside and outside the family, and their relationships as partners and parents. How parents approach the rough spots and how satisfied they are with the outcome of their efforts can have profound effects on how they feel about themselves, what happens to their marriage, and how well their children do as they meet the challenges of elementary school.

When Partners Become Parents is not so much a "how-to" book as a "why-it's-so-hard-to" book. Whether you are a new parent, an old hand, a grandparent, or a researcher or clinician who works with families, we hope that the ideas here will help you make more sense of the difficult parts of becoming a family and suggest some new ways to search for the delicate balance that contemporary family making seems to require.

ACKNOWLEDGMENTS

A STUDY AS LONG AND COMPLEX as the Becoming a Family Project can be accomplished only with extremely dedicated and loyal colleagues, and we have had the good fortune to work with many. First, we pay tribute to Trudie Heming, who served as data manager for the entire ten years of the study. In addition to her exceptional ability to keep us and the data on track, Trudie has made invaluable contributions to our thinking about statistical analysis and our conceptualization of the project's direction.

The data set for a longitudinal study is the backbone of the enterprise. We are indebted to Dena Cowan, who entered a major portion of the data into the computer and conducted some of the analyses with patience and a keen eye for detail. Others contributed their time and skill to the painstaking work of entering data as each follow-up of the families was completed: Barbara Epperson, Beth Schoenberger, and Karen Whitmer. Marc Schulz also conducted some of the recent statistical analyses.

For their early collaboration, support, and friendship, we give special thanks to John and Lynne Coie. Together, the four of us developed the initial interviews and questionnaires, interviewed couples in a dozen obstetrical practices, and led the first couples group in the pilot study. During the next five years, we had the good fortune to work with three other wonderful staff couples. Harriet Curtis-Boles and Abner Boles III, and Ellen Garrett and Bill

Coysh, the other interviewers and leaders of the couples groups throughout the first four years of the longitudinal study, met together regularly with us to monitor the process of the groups and refine our ideas about the intervention. When these two couples moved on to begin their personal family projects, Laura Mason Gordon and David Gordon joined us to complete the final follow-ups of the study families. The sensitivity and warmth of these staff couples kept the participants working with us well beyond the two years we envisioned when we recruited them.

We are most grateful for the enthusiastic cooperation of a number of obstetrician-gynecologists and their staff members for believing enough in the project to help us get the word out to potential participants for our studies. Special thanks go to Joe Weick, Linda Robrecht, Hank Streitfeld, Max Bynum, Elijah Hill, Joseph Washington, Ed Blumenstock, Louis Klein, Jeffrey Waldman, and the dedicated staff of each of their practices.

The playroom visits with the children in the preschool and kindergarten periods were conducted with empathy and skill by Sacha Bunge, Michael Blum, Julia Levine, David Chavez, and Marc Schulz. The parent-child and family visits were conducted and rated by Linda Kastelowitz and Victor Lieberman, who helped to develop the rating scales, and Marsha Kline and Charles Soulé, who were instrumental in revising them for the later follow-ups. As the children completed kindergarten, Joanna Cowan White met with each one, administering an individual achievement test and talking with them about their families, their friends, and their experiences at school. The children's delightful responses are a tribute to her skill and sensitivity.

Incredible resourcefulness in convincing kindergarten teachers to rate each child in their classrooms was shown by Elaine Ransom and Laurie Leventhal-Belfer. A new set of rating scales for the family visits when the children were three and a half was constructed under the guidance of Yona Teichman by Joanna Self, Nancy Miller, Christina Whitney, and Juanita Dimas. The family scale items were revised and the kindergarten year visits coded by Jennifer Berland, Eric Gortner, Gwen Lai, and Reni Szczepanski under the able supervision of Elizabeth Owens. Yo Elberbaum, Eve Cumberbatch, Stacy Miller, Karen Spangenberg, and Barbara Zachary devoted hours to searching different aspects of our interviews with the couples for patterns of change and stability, and Isabel Bradburn and Joan Kaplan prepared detailed case studies of two of the families. Thanks also to Jamie McHale and Juanita Dimas for additional help in reviewing the literature on the family-to-school transition.

A number of graduate student researchers have contributed to our understanding of the early family-making period. Using the data to make in-depth explorations of some aspect of the becoming a family period, fourteen team members completed studies, a number of them already published: doctoral dissertations by Trudie Heming, Jessica Ball, Abner Boles III, Bill Coysh, Marsha Kline, Julia Levine, Pat Kerig, Elaine Ransom, and Laurie Leventhal-Belfer; Master's theses by Rachel Conrad, Joan Kaplan, Marc Schulz, and Dan Silver; and an undergraduate honors thesis by Barbara Epperson.

We have been most fortunate in having the collaboration of a number of colleagues from afar over the past ten years. Nancy Miller, now at the University of Akron, and Deborah Cohn, now at the University of Virginia, served as Postdoctoral Fellows with us, sponsored by a grant from the National Institute of Mental Health to the Family Research Consortium. In addition to their contributions to data analyses and publication, they contributed a great deal to the life of the project during their two-year tenure. Michael Pratt, from Wilfred Laurier University in Canada, has collaborated with us for a number of years, taking us in new directions with his ideas about children's and adults' cognitive development. Yona Teichman, from Tel Aviv University in Israel, has stimulated our thinking about how to assess family dynamics.

For help with the daily organization and secretarial support of the project, we thank Julia Babcock, Joanna Self, and Bonita Thoreson. Especially during the crunch of preparing grant proposals or conference papers, Jonathan Cowan and Jennifer Cowan offered their considerable talents to do timely editing, reference checking, and data preparation.

We are indebted to the National Institute of Mental Health for ongoing financial and collegial support throughout the ten-year longitudinal study, and to the Spencer Foundation for a year of crucial support as we completed our analysis of the data on the family-to-school transition.

The members of the Family Research Consortium, brought into being by Joy Schulterbrandt at the National Institute of Mental Health, have made ongoing and valuable contributions to our conceptualization of this work. At their regular meetings and summer institutes, we received encouragement combined with the kind of critical feedback that was essential to refining our ideas. The second phase of the project especially shows the influence of discussions with David Reiss, Mavis Hetherington, John Gottman, Irv Sigel, Ross Parke, Shep Kellam, Bob Cole, Elaine Blechman, and Gerry Patterson.

The Institute of Human Development at U.C. Berkeley has supported our work with allocations of research space and video equipment to record the family visits. Over a period of five years, the Interdisciplinary Faculty Study Group in Family Dynamics, initiated by Ed Swanson, met monthly at the Institute. Our regular discussions of both professional and personal experiences of family life stimulated our thinking and broadened our horizons.

Joanne Wile made helpful comments on an earlier draft of this manuscript. Dan Wile and Hilde Burton provided detailed critiques that contributed immeasurably to the final version. In the early years of the project, Hilde Burton also served as our consultant, helping us to sort out all of the couples' issues—our own, those of the group leaders, and those raised by the couples in the study. We are most appreciative of her warmth, her insightful observations, and her ongoing support of our work over the years. For their patience and encouragement as we completed this project, warm thanks to Audrey Cole, David Burton, Gene Rosenberg, Pat Miles, Kit Naftzger, Naomi Lowinsky, Rhona Weinstein, Harvey Weinstein, R. Jay Engel, and Pam Hamilton.

The people at Basic Books have been wonderful to us. Judy Greissman initially signed us on and encouraged us. Susan Arellano served as Senior Editor, taking us through the evolution of the manuscript, and going beyond the call of duty by initiating her own family project. Linda Carbone, Development Editor, understood what we were trying to say and, with the deft surgical strokes of her blue pencil, helped us say it more economically. It has been our pleasure to have Senior Editor Jo Ann Miller shepherd us through the last phase of the project. Her knowledge of the ropes and her unswerving support have been invaluable.

And, finally, we owe our greatest debt to the devoted families who have participated in the Becoming a Family Project. By giving us so many hours of your time—talking to us in the interviews, visiting our project playroom, completing our questionnaires year after year—you have made it possible for us to take an inside look at what it means to be partners and parents today. It has been a truly humbling and inspiring experience for us and our staff to have the opportunity to get to know so many wonderful families in the making.

WHEN PARTNERS BECOME PARENTS

INTRODUCTION

Becoming a Family

OUR DECISION to undertake a study of what happens when partners become parents was triggered by the collision of events in our personal and professional lives. We met as teenagers in the mid-1950s and, like many of our contemporaries, were still young when we married, four years later. Carolyn was nineteen and had just signed her first contract to teach elementary school. Phil, twenty-one, was completing his undergraduate degree in psychology. Having worked and gone to school throughout our teenage years, we felt ready to take on the responsibilities of the adult world we had entered.

We began trying to start a family two years after we were married. Carolyn's desire to have a baby was powerful. Because Phil felt unable to articulate his feeling that he was not yet ready to become a father, Carolyn's expressed feelings governed the decision about timing. Over the next few years we would learn the painful lessons taught by making decisions that affect both partners without thoroughly exploring or talking about them.

Carolyn did not become pregnant for eighteen months, by which time both of us were more than eager to expand our family. Joanna was born in 1961, followed by Dena in 1963 and Jonathan in 1965. We felt extremely lucky. All three children were healthy, different from one another in many ways, and a total delight to their parents and grandparents. These were times when a majority of women stayed home to look after the children, and, despite loving her work and having earned a permanent teaching credential, Carolyn eagerly left her position to become a full-time mother.

We spent the early years of parenthood trying to juggle everything so that our lives as parents and partners would match our dreams. We were totally absorbed by the parenting part and worked hard to make everything else in our lives fit around it. With our first child not quite two years old and our second about to be born, Phil's offer of a position at the University of California at Berkeley triggered our move there from Canada.

In our naïveté, we did not consider that moving three thousand miles from our family and friends to a new country and a new job might bring stresses that would challenge our relationship as a couple. In the years that followed, when our children were out of diapers and we began to sort out what had happened to us, one thing became abundantly clear: We had not been prepared for the shifts that had occurred in almost every aspect of our lives—especially in our relationship as a couple. In the midst of the family adventure we had embarked upon, our ten-year marriage began to feel precarious for the first time.

We had expected to feel differently about ourselves once we became parents, but we were startled by what felt like a major upheaval in our sense of ourselves. We had assumed, naturally, that there would be some changes in the "who does what" of our life, but had given little thought to how those shifts might actually feel. We hadn't known that becoming parents might lead us to feel more distant from each other based on our different levels of involvement in work inside and outside the family. We hadn't anticipated that having a baby could revive long-buried feelings of gratitude or disappointment about how loved we had felt as children, or realized that our disagreements about whether the baby needed to be picked up and comforted or left alone to "cry it out" would actually have more to do with our own needs than they did with the baby's. And, having always viewed the important issues of life similarly, we certainly did not anticipate how differently we could see the "same" things. Not only were we unprepared for these conflicts inside or between us but we found ourselves unable to talk about them productively once they surfaced.

By the time our children were in elementary school, there was no avoiding the issue: Our relationship was very strained. The task of dealing with our stress felt all the more daunting because suddenly we were surrounded by friends and neighbors who were looking up after ten or fifteen years of marriage and saying, in effect, "This isn't what I dreamed it would be. I want out!" Couples who had once been full of hopes and plans were dismantling families they had been building for decades. Announcements of separations and divorces became so frequent that a friend joked wryly that someone must have been tampering with the local water supply.

As we listened to the pain and disenchantment that other husbands and wives described in their relationships and struggled to make sense of our own, we began to hear a common refrain. We were experiencing distress now in our relationships as couples, but almost all of us could trace the beginning of our difficulties back to those early years of becoming a family. Our dreams had gotten lost somewhere between our starry-eyed pictures of intimate couples with cuddly babies and the stark reality of juggling the competing needs of growing children and parents.

In our professional roles, too, we realized that we were hearing over and over that when things start to feel shaky, few husbands and wives know how to tell anyone, especially each other, that they feel disappointed or frightened. "This is supposed to be the best time of our lives; what's the matter with me?" a wife might say through her tears. Or a husband would ask: "How can I talk about how scary it feels to have so much responsibility when I convinced her that we could manage our work, our relationship, *and* kids? When she's upset, I feel *I* have to be strong." Without discussing these worrisome thoughts and feelings with others, parents don't get to discover how widely their experiences are shared. They can't see that some of their tension may be attributable to the conflicting demands of this very complex stage of life, not simply to a suddenly stubborn, selfish, or unresponsive spouse.

As we talked with others about what seemed to be happening to contemporary families, we continued to work at getting our marriage back on track. We came to see that becoming parents had not so much raised new problems as it had brought old unconscious or unresolved issues to the surface. For example, we had grown up in qualitatively different family atmospheres, but we both came to our relationship determined to avoid conflict and fighting. Before children come along, it is possible for a couple to deal with differences or disagreements by avoiding them or by simply accepting the fact that each partner has a different view. But once children are part of the family, most of us discover, certain disagreements have to be resolved on the spot. Crying infants will not wait tolerantly while their parents engage in long-winded discussions about how to respond to them. And, somehow, in these years with so much vulnerability and so much to take care of, differences that have nothing to do with the children can take on a greater urgency.

After some trying and painful struggles, we slowly began to regain some of our balance and our sense of humor—with the help of each other, therapy, some good friends, and the sheer wonder of life with three active, inquiring children. We began to learn how to work out our differences or impasses more productively, which led paradoxically to our feeling both closer *and* more separate. This difficult work took a number of years. We now believe that most couples must undertake this kind of rebalancing of their relationship at certain points in their lives, to accommodate their individual and family growth and change.

We emerged with a stronger marriage and a resolve to "do something" about the stress that so many couples seem to experience in the early family-making years. We wondered whether we could encourage couples to confront their early difficulties rather than sweep them under the proverbial carpet. By this time we were into the 1970s, and had begun to hear about childbirth preparation classes for expectant mothers *and* fathers. In six- to eight-week classes, childbirth educators were instructing couples to use exercises and breathing techniques to cope with the pain of labor and delivery without medication. One of the best parts of this experience, couples told us, was that they attended these sessions together and "went through it" with other couples.

We were struck by a certain irony in this wonderful new intervention. Meeting with calming experts and other expectant couples was clearly reassuring for men and women as they approached first-time parenthood. But the work and support in these groups focus on preparing the couple for one day, the day of their baby's birth, after which they are completely on their own to manage the rigors of the next twenty years. Carolyn began to wonder whether we could create groups for expectant couples in which they could begin meeting with mental health professionals before the birth of their babies and continue talking with them after the babies were born. Not parenting groups and not merely support groups, these would be settings in which professionals could help men and women talk about the disappointments and impasses that we had found so difficult to discuss. Phil had been initiating some preventive programs in local elementary schools to spot some of the problems children were having before they felt overwhelming to the children, their parents, and their teachers. In addition to creating and systematically evaluating our couples groups for expectant and new parents, he suggested that we encase the preventive program in a more comprehensive study, following a larger group of expectant couples who would not take part in groups. We hoped that with this combined longitudinal and intervention study, we would be able to learn more about what happens to men, women, and marriage as families are beginning.

Much of our initial thinking about the question of what to study was stimulated by the preparation for our pilot study with two friends and colleagues from North Carolina, Lynne Coie, then an obstetrical nurse, and John Coie, a professor of psychology at Duke University. They agreed to work on the pilot study with us in 1974–75 while in Berkeley on sabbatical (Cowan et al. 1978). The four of us met regularly for several months, reviewing the existing research literature and talking about our own lives as partners and parents. Slowly, we pieced together a picture of what to look at based on the scant research literature at the time (see Cowan and Cowan 1988) and on what we felt had made a difference to our doing well or feeling under stress as individuals and as couples when we began our own families. We then selected or developed interviews and questionnaires to tap what we believed to be the key aspects of family life for men and women during this major transition.

Over the next few years, we made a number of additions to what we asked about the lives of the study participants, based on our ongoing reading of the relevant research and on influential consultations with a number of colleagues, particularly Gertrude Heming on our own research team, Jay Belsky at Pennsylvania State University, Frances Grossman at Boston University, Christoph Heinicke at UCLA, Shirley Feldman at Stanford University, Joy

Osofsky and Howard Osofsky, now at Tulane University, Susan McHale at Pennsylvania State University, Ted Huston at the University of Texas at Austin, Martha Cox, now at the Western Carolina Center, Mavis Hetherington at the University of Virginia, Ross Parke and Barbara Tinsley, now at the University of California at Riverside, and the members of the Family Research Consortium sponsored by the National Institute of Mental Health (see Patterson 1990; Cowan and Hetherington 1991).

What emerged from this conceptual work is a model describing five central aspects of family life that we expect will affect what happens when partners become parents (see Cowan and Cowan 1990):

1. The inner life of both parents and the first child, with special emphasis on each one's sense of self, view of the world, and emotional well-being or distress;
2. The quality of the relationship between the husband and wife, with special emphasis on their family roles and patterns of communication;
3. The quality of the relationships among the grandparents, parents, and grandchildren;
4. The relationship between the nuclear family members and key individuals or institutions outside the family (work, friends, child care), with special emphasis on the stress and support that these people and institutions provide;
5. The quality of the relationship between each parent and their first child.

We think of this model as a map of five separate but interrelated aspects or "territories" that partners encounter on their journey to becoming a family. As they make their way along the path from pregnancy to parenthood, they cross and recross the borders that mark off their inner lives, their relationship as a couple, their links to other generations, their connections with the world outside the family, and their relationships with their child.

We followed Urie Bronfenbrenner's (1979) admonition to study families in their ecological context. Our model directs us to look for change in family life at different levels, from the small details to the big picture. We zoom in for a close-up by asking what is happening to each individual family member. We move back for a mid-level view of what is happening in the immediate family by examining each of the relationships within it (mother-father, mother-child, father-child, sibling-sibling) and the dynamics of the family as a whole. For a longer shot, we step back to examine the links between family members and key people and institutions in the world outside the family.

Even with all of this information about the critical parts of family life, static snapshots of each of these separate domains of family life miss some essential ingredients of the larger scenario. What we need is a moving picture of how change in any one family domain affects all the individuals and relationships in the family. We use the metaphor of spillover at various points in the book to illustrate the idea that distress in any of these central areas of family life can seep into any of the other areas. Think, for example, of a man who feels anxious about becoming a new father (inner life) and wants to be more involved with his child than his father was with him (quality of relationships in family of origin) but feels pressured by the demands of his job (stress outside the family). Once the baby is born, he may have difficulty negotiating new family roles and decisions with his wife (quality of the marriage). He may begin to attribute the distress he feels at home to problems in his marriage. Although the partners may not be aware that he is experiencing distress in a number of these aspects of his life, both are likely to experience tension *between* them, with the result that one or both feel less confident and more vulnerable about themselves and their relationship as a couple.

Fortunately, spillover can be positive too. When a parent has a wonderful day with the baby or accomplishes a great deal at work, both partners may reap the benefit later when they are together. Support from one spouse who feels satisfied can provide encouragement and energy for the other—to try a new tack with the baby, to think in a different way about a problem at work or with a parent or in-law, or to arrange to spend time together as a couple. Our assumption has been that if we can discover some of the crucial links among the five domains of family life, we will understand more about what leads to progress or difficulties in parents' and children's development.

The design of our study is based on a number of assumptions about families and how they develop over time. Our five-domain model is consistent with the premise of family therapists that the family is a "system" and that we cannot make sense of the well-being or distress of individual family members until we understand something about the characteristics of the system as a whole (Bateson et al. 1956; Bowen 1978; Framo 1981; Haley 1976; Minuchin and Fishman 1981). In other words, to understand more about the children's development we must go beyond observing the relationship between the mother and the child to look at the relationship between the father and the child and at the *combined* influence of both parents and their relationship on the child. We give special attention to the question of how the quality of the parents' marriage may be affecting their child's adjustment, both by influencing the kind of relationship each parent establishes with the child and by providing the child with a model of how to behave in relationships.

In 1957, the sociologist E. E. LeMasters concluded that the transition to parenthood can produce a "crisis" for couples. Although our results are consistent with this notion, we do not view crisis as inevitably destructive in the long run. One of the fathers in our study taught us that the Chinese ideograph for "crisis" combines characters that represent danger *and* opportunity, a particularly fitting way to think of the becoming-a-family period. The transition to parenthood can increase the tension within or between new mothers and fathers, or between either of them and their child, and this can feel very frightening to already vulnerable new parents. But it is equally plausible that becoming a parent will provide the kind of challenge that pushes men and women to develop new insights, more effective ways of solving their problems, and greater feelings of maturity, which can result in their feeling particularly strong and triumphant (P. Cowan 1988a).

Who the Couples Are

For a three-year pilot study of our Becoming a Family Project, we followed sixteen couples becoming parents in 1975 (Cowan et al. 1978). For our ten-year study, we recruited ninety-six couples: seventy-two expectant couples and twenty-four nonparent couples from a range of obstetrics and gynecology practices, both private and clinic, and from announcements in several newsletters in the San Francisco Bay Area.* We followed them from their pregnancies in 1979 or 1980 through their child's kindergarten year (Cowan et al., in press).

Most of the couples (94 percent) were married—anywhere from eight months to twelve years, with an average length of relationship of four years— and several married after they joined the study. They lived in twenty-eight different cities and towns in Northern California within a forty-mile radius of the University of California at Berkeley. Their backgrounds and education ranged widely: All had completed high school and some had extensive training beyond. Over the ten years, we talked with carpenters, teachers, architects, writers, housewives, doctors, nurses, postal workers, professors, lawyers, retail store clerks, mental health professionals, electricians, an airline mechanic, a clothes designer and seamstress, a caterer, and a cable car driver. Their family incomes ranged from $7,000 to $72,500 per year, with an average family income of $22,500 at the beginning of the study in 1979–80. Fifteen percent of the participants were black, Asian American, or Hispanic; 85 percent were Caucasian.

When we first met them, the men and women ranged in age from twenty-one to forty-nine; on the average, the expectant mothers were twenty-nine years old and the fathers were thirty. The average age of the partners not yet decided about having children was one year younger. The age of the expectant parents seemed somewhat high to us for couples expecting a first baby, but it is consistent with the ages of men and women in the other recent longitudinal studies of the transition to parenthood (Belsky, Lang, and Rovine 1985; Grossman, Eichler, and Winickoff 1980; Heinicke et al. 1986; Lewis, Owen, and Cox 1988).

Just how far can we generalize our conclusions based on these ninety-six couples? Certainly, the sample we recruited is not representative of all new families in the United States. It consists of volunteers from a wide, though not randomly sampled, array of communities in Northern California. Our announcements attracted two expectant mothers under twenty years of age, but

*The names and identifying characteristics of the study participants have been changed to respect their privacy.

we decided to limit the sample to women who were at least twenty years old, reasoning that the issues and stresses for teenage parents might be quite distinct from those of adults in their twenties to forties. In addition, we could accommodate only those participants who spoke and wrote English. We did not turn people away based on socioeconomic status, but families on welfare did not tend to volunteer, nor did families from the upper class.

We believe that what we describe in the following chapters applies to a large segment of the population of couples becoming first-time parents, for two main reasons. First, the couples span a wide range of demographic and psychological characteristics. The income differential between the lowest and highest earners is immense. Men's and women's scores on a widely used marital satisfaction measure (the Locke-Wallace Brief Marital Adjustment Test, Locke and Wallace 1959) indicate that their marriages ranged from very happy to seriously distressed. Similarly, men's and women's scores on a symptoms-of-depression scale developed for use in nonclinical populations (Center for Epidemiological Study of Depression Scale, CES-D, Radloff 1977) indicate that at least one-quarter to one-third of the parents in our study were in the clinically distressed range when their children were in preschool and kindergarten. The proportion of couples at risk in our study may vary from the proportion in a large national sample, but the range from well-being to dysfunction in our study families makes it clear that we are describing a wide spectrum of men and women creating new families.

Second, our central findings about what happens to couples' satisfaction with marriage are consistent with those of many other investigators. Scores on the Locke-Wallace marital satisfaction scale typically range from about 40, which indicates serious dissatisfaction, to about 140, which suggests very high satisfaction; average scores are expected to be around 100. In the beginning, the expectant spouses' average marital satisfaction scores were well above 100—121 for the men and 123 for the women—as we would expect from a majority of partners about to have a first baby. Five to six years later, however, when their first children were in kindergarten, the parents' average scores were close to the average score of 100 reported in studies of couples across the entire marital life span.

Over the past ten years, the results of other studies in other locales— Southern California, Texas, Kansas, Pennsylvania—have conveyed similar pictures of couples making the transition to parenthood. At a talk he gave in Toronto in 1990, Jay Belsky, a researcher from Pennsylvania State University who has published a great deal on this topic, said in reference to our study that finding such similar results in working-class parents in the middle of Pennsylvania and working- to middle-class parents in California gives us a pretty solid indication that what we're saying about the transition to parenthood can be taken seriously.

The couples in our study were invited to participate in one of four ways: in groups of couples, as individual couples before and after childbirth, as individual couples after childbirth only, and as couples who have not yet decided whether to have children. We followed the expectant couples from late pregnancy until their children were eighteen months old and tracked the nonparent couples over the same number of months in Phase 1.

COUPLES GROUPS

One of our central goals was to create and evaluate a couples group intervention designed to strengthen the parents' relationship as a couple while they are making the transition from couple to family (discussed at length in chapter 9). We randomly selected one-third of the expectant couples and invited them to take part in a couples group with us or with leaders whom we trained. We set up six groups of four couples with similar due dates to meet with their staff couple every week during the last three months of pregnancy and the first three months after the baby arrived.* Over the course of six months, we talked with these men and women about their dreams and their difficulties as they made the journey to first-time parenthood.

The couples groups provided an experience that we wish we could have had as we became parents fifteen years earlier. In the last few months of pregnancy, the group leaders helped couples take a look at their current lives, anticipate what their lives would be like once the baby arrived, and make explicit some of their unexplored pictures of life as a family. The staff couples provided a safe setting in which husbands and wives could begin to discover where they differed or disagreed, and how they could work together to get their relationship on a more solid base before the babies arrived. The babies joined us in the groups in the first week or two after they were born. It did not take long for us to see how every couple's conversations got interrupted regularly, and how easy it was for partners to get out of touch. Through the tears and the laughter, couples began to see that despite many differences in background, outlook, personality, and economic circumstance, they were experiencing very similar shifts in their relationships. Along with our encouragement to modify the patterns that felt unsatisfying, this feeling of being in the same boat had a powerful impact on the participants.

EXPECTANT PARENTS: BEFORE AND AFTER

A second randomly chosen set of twenty-four expectant couples was interviewed and filled out questionnaires just as the group participants had (during pregnancy and six and eighteen months after birth), but did not take part in our group intervention. We were concerned initially that we were offering less help to these couples than to the group participants, but the couples in our control group in our pilot study (Cowan et al. 1978) told us that thinking and talking about the issues we raised in our regular interviews

*Of the first couples we randomly chose for the groups, 85 percent agreed to participate in a group. We continued to invite every third expectant couple entering the study until we had enough couples to fill six groups, with four participating couples and one staff couple in each group. The two other staff couples were Ellen Garrett and Bill Coysh and Harriet Curtis-Boles and Abner Boles.

and questionnaires proved very helpful to their adjustment to parenthood. Apparently the regular follow-up format with questionnaires and interviews with mental health professionals was operating as an intervention in its own right.

EXPECTANT PARENTS: AFTER ONLY

The third set of twenty-four randomly chosen expectant couples met with us for our standard interview during pregnancy but did not fill out questionnaires until six and eighteen months after their babies were born. By comparing these couples with those who filled out questionnaires before and after they became parents, we had an opportunity to evaluate whether the experience of looking at their lives in detail with our questionnaires before and after having a baby acted as an intervention in itself.*

NONPARENTS

Finally, using the same obstetrics/gynecology practices and community newsletters with which we recruited the expectant parents, we recruited twenty-four couples who had not yet decided whether to have children. These couples had not closed off their options about having children and were not, to their knowledge, infertile. We interviewed each of these couples, too, and asked them to complete our questionnaires at the beginning of the study (comparable to late pregnancy for the expectant couples) and at intervals that correspond to the six- and eighteen-month postpartum follow-ups with the new parents. In the first two years of the study, fifteen of the original twenty-four nonparent couples remained childless. The patterns they described help us distinguish between changes that occur in couple relationships over time and those that are apparently attributable to having a baby.

Couple Relationships and Children's Development

The first two years of the study comprised Phase I, in which we concentrated on the period from late pregnancy until eighteen months after the baby is born. Since we were focusing on men's and women's perceptions and evaluations of their lives, our analysis of the results from Phase I relied heavily on what they told us in the interviews and questionnaires. During Phase II, as we

---

*We did *not* find that the couples who were interviewed and filled out questionnaires in pregnancy were any better off after their babies were born than those who filled out only postbirth questionnaires. However, the couples who did the prebirth questionnaires were more loyal to the study. All of them continued with us at least to the eighteen-months-after-birth follow-up, whereas only 63 percent of the couples who filled out the questionnaires for the first time after they had given birth agreed to do them again one year later.

attempted to understand how the dynamics of family interaction were affecting the children's development and adaptation, we began to rely increasingly on information from our observations of the parents and children to supplement their self-reports.

When we returned to interview the parents of eighteen-month-olds, we saw that many had recovered from the disequilibrium of being the parents of new babies, but now they faced the new challenges of an independent toddler.

Most of the couples were enjoying their babies' development, but a few appeared seriously stressed. Although we did not conduct systematic observations in Phase I, our impression was that there was a strong similarity between how parents handled the dilemmas and strains of the early months of becoming a family and how they responded to their children as toddlers. We noticed that parents who talked about having very conflicted relationships with their own parents described more conflicted relationships with their children. Parents who fought more as a couple said that they were having more difficulty in handling their children. By contrast, parents who got along well with each other tended to describe their relationships with their children in more positive terms.

We also noticed that parents who described positive relationships with each other and their children tended to describe their children's development as proceeding well. They did not spontaneously characterize their children as having or posing severe problems. The idea that parents influence their children's development is not new, of course. Nor is the idea that parenting is influenced by what we carry over and reject from the families we grew up in or by our children's temperaments and how they affect us. What is news, we think, is that the relationship *between* the parents seems to act as a crucible in which their relationships with their children take shape.

When we were interviewing the parents, we could not know whether they were describing their children's development or the parent-child relationship accurately. Virtually all studies of how families socialize children begin after children are born, making it impossible to tease out which parts of the parent-child relationship come from the parents and which from the temperament or personality of the child. Because we had come to know these couples before they had children, we were in a unique position to shed some light on the question of how adaptation in the family before the child is born influences the nature and quality of the relationships between parents and their children. Clearly, eighteen months after becoming a family was not the time to end our investigation of adaptation to family life.

We conducted two more intensive follow-ups of each family, gathering information about the children and parents in the preschool and kindergarten years. To this new round of interviews and questionnaires we added visits to our laboratory playroom in the Institute of Human Development at the University of California at Berkeley. In these visits, members of our research staff worked and played with the children to get a sense of their level of cognitive and social adaptation. We invited each parent separately and then together to work and play with their son or daughter using structured and unstructured tasks and games so that we could observe the range of responses in parents and children.

When the children were in kindergarten, we incorporated their teachers' views of them by asking them to describe every child in the classroom, using a checklist of behaviors that reflect academic, social, and emotional adjustment. This gave us an indication of how the child was doing in relation to his or her classmates. By combining this information from Phase II with the information the parents had given us before their children were born, we could begin to trace the links from how couples adapted to parenthood, to their family patterns during the preschool period, to how the children met the academic, emotional, and social challenges of their lives at home and at school.

Our study is not simply to demonstrate that the transition to parenthood can leave men and women feeling vulnerable about their marriage. We must try to understand why, at such a potentially hopeful time of life, tension and distress tend to intrude on the stability of the parents' relationship as a couple. Our study could not address the special circumstances of parents dealing with abortion, adoption, or single parenthood, although some of the issues we address will be relevant to their lives.

There are warnings here that we hope will help some readers find ways to reduce the tension and distress they are experiencing in their lives as individuals, couples, or parents. Perhaps some of the examples from the couples we interviewed will suggest ways to modify the arrangements in your life to make it more satisfying. Even if the story sounds a little grim at times, we encourage you to read on. Some of the couples' experiences will let you know that you are not alone if your life feels stressful.

It is certainly clear from our own lives, from what our study participants tell us, and from the results of large-scale national surveys of men and women (Fawcett 1988) that despite the strain, most parents are thrilled that they have had children and would make the same decision if they were starting again. Nothing can substitute for the wonders of seeing the world anew through the eyes of a child or watching a tiny human being develop into a curious, independent, self-motivated young person and adult. And the strain that partners experience on becoming parents can propel them to work out some of their unresolved difficulties, either on their own or with help. We have provided examples in each chapter of couples who managed to overcome the unexpected obstacles in their path and to respond to the challenge of being partners and parents with creativity, growth, and a renewed sense of humor and purpose. We hope that they will inspire you with their optimism, as they have inspired us.

PART I

The New Pioneers

CHAPTER 1

Changing Families in a Changing World

SHARON: I did a home pregnancy test. I felt really crummy that day, and I stayed home from work. I set the container with the urine sample on a bookcase and managed to stay out of the room until the last few minutes. Finally, I walked in and it looked positive. And I went to check the information on the box and, sure enough, it *was* positive. I was so excited. Then I went back to look and see if maybe it had disappeared; you know, maybe the test was false. Then I just sat down on the sofa and kept thinking, "I'm pregnant. I'm really pregnant. I'm going to have a baby!"

DANIEL: I knew she was pregnant. She didn't need the test as far as I was concerned. I was excited too, at first, but then I started to worry. I don't know how I'm going to handle being there at the birth, especially if anything goes wrong. And Sharon's going to quit work soon. I don't know when she's going to go back, and we're barely making it as it is.

SHARON: My mom never worked a day in her life for pay. She was home all the time, looking after *her* mother, and us, and cleaning the house. My dad left all of that to her. We're not going to do it that way. But I don't know how we're supposed to manage it all. Daniel promised that he's going to pitch in right along with me in taking care of the baby, but I don't know whether that's realistic. If he doesn't come through, I'm going to be a real bear about it. If I put all my energy into Daniel and the marriage and something happens, then I'll have to start all over again and that scares the hell out of me.

Sharon is beginning the third trimester of her first pregnancy. If her grandmother were to listen in on our conversation with Sharon and her husband, Daniel, and try to make sense of it, given the experience of her own pregnancy fifty years ago, she would surely have a lot of questions. Home pregnancy tests? Why would a woman with a newborn infant *want* to work if she didn't have to? What husband would share the housework and care of the baby? Why would Sharon and Daniel worry about their marriage not surviving after they have a baby? Understandable questions for someone who made the transition to parenthood five decades ago, in a qualitatively different world. Unfortunately, the old trail maps are outmoded, and there are as yet no new ones to describe the final destination. They may not need covered wagons for their journey, but Sharon and Daniel are true pioneers.

Like many modern couples, they have two different fantasies about their journey. The first has them embarking on an exciting adventure to bring a new human being into the world, fill their lives with delight and wonder, and enrich their feeling of closeness as a couple. In the second, their path from couple to family is strewn with unexpected obstacles, hazardous conditions, and potential marital strife. Our work suggests that, like most fantasy scenarios, these represent extreme and somewhat exaggerated versions of what really happens when partners become parents. Our goal in this book is to tell the story behind both the fantasy and the reality of changing families in our changing world.

The Five Domains of Family Life

The responses of one couple to our interview questions offer a preview of how the five domains in our model capture the changes that most couples contend with as they make their transition to parenthood.* Natalie and Victor have lived in the San Francisco Bay Area most of their lives. At the time of their initial interview, Natalie, age twenty-nine, is in her fifth month of pregnancy. Victor, her husband of six years, is thirty-four. When their daughter, Kim, is six months old, they visit us again for a follow-up interview. Arranged around each of the five domains, the following excerpts from our second interview reveal some universal themes of early parenthood.

CHANGES IN IDENTITY AND INNER LIFE

After settling comfortably with cups of coffee and tea, we ask both Natalie and Victor whether they feel that their sense of self has shifted in any way

---

*An extended description of this couple's transition to parenthood can be found in Bradburn and Kaplan (in press).

since Kim was born. As would be typical in our interviews, Mother and Father focus on different aspects of personal change:

> NATALIE: There's not much "me" left to think about right now. Most of the time, even when I'm not nursing, I see myself as attached to this little being with only the milk flowing between us.
>
> VICTOR: I've earned money since I was sixteen, but being a father means that I've become the family breadwinner. I've got this new sense of myself as having to go out there in the world to make sure that my wife and daughter are going to be safe and looked after. I mean, I'm concerned about advancing in my job—and we've even bought insurance policies for the first time! This "protector" role feels exciting *and* frightening.

Another change that often occurs in partners' inner lives during a major life transition is a shift in what C. Murray Parkes (1971) describes as our "assumptive world." Men's and women's assumptions about how the world works or how families operate sometimes change radically during the transition from couple to family.

> NATALIE: I used to be completely apathetic about political things. I wasn't sure of my congressman's name. Now I'm writing him about once a month because I feel I need to help clean up some of the mess this country is in before Kim grows up.
>
> VICTOR: What's changed for me is what I think families and fathers are all about. When we were pregnant, I had these pictures of coming home each night as the tired warrior, playing with the baby for a little while and putting my feet up for the rest of the evening. It's not just that there's more work to do than I ever imagined, but I'm so much more a part of the action every night.

Clearly, Natalie and Victor are experiencing qualitatively different shifts in their sense of self and in how vulnerable or safe each feels in the world. These shifts are tied not only to their new life as parents but also to a new sense of their identities as providers and protectors. Even though most of these changes are positive, they can lead to moments when the couple's relationship feels a bit shaky.

SHIFTS IN THE ROLES AND RELATIONSHIPS WITHIN THE MARRIAGE

> VICTOR: After Kim was born, I noticed that something was bugging Natalie, and I kept saying, "What is bothering you?" Finally we went out to dinner without the baby and it came out. And it was because of small things that I never even think about. Like I always used to leave my running shorts in the bathroom . . .

NATALIE: He'd just undress and drop everything!

VICTOR: . . . and Nat never made a fuss. In fact she *used to* just pick them up and put them in the hamper. And then that night at dinner she said, "When you leave your shorts there, or your wet towel, and don't pick them up—I get furious." At first I didn't believe what she was saying because it never used to bother her at all, but now I say, "OK, fine, no problem. I'll pick up the shorts and hang them up. I'll be very conscientious." And I have been trying.

NATALIE: You have, but you still don't quite get it. I think my quick trigger has something to do with my feeling so dependent on you and having the baby so dependent on me—and my being stuck here day in and day out. You at least get to go out to do your work, and you bring home a paycheck to show for it. I work here all day long and by the end of the day I feel that all I have to show for it is my exhaustion.

In addition to their distinctive inner changes, men's and women's roles change in very different ways when partners become parents. The division of labor in taking care of the baby, the household, the meals, the laundry, the shopping, calling parents and friends, and earning the money to keep the family fed, clothed, and sheltered is a hot topic for couples (C. Cowan and P. Cowan 1988; Hochschild 1989). It seems to come as a great surprise to most of them that changes in some of their major roles affect their feelings about their overall relationship.

In a domino effect, both partners have to make major adjustments of time and energy as individuals during a period when they are getting less sleep and fewer opportunities to be together. As with Natalie and Victor, they are apt to find that they have less patience with things that didn't seem annoying before. Their frustration often focuses on each other. For couples who thought that having a baby was going to bring them closer together, this is especially confusing and disappointing.

NATALIE: It's strange. I feel that we're much closer *and* more distant than we have ever been. I think we communicate more, because there's so much to work out, especially about Kim, but it doesn't always feel very good. And we're both so busy that we're not getting much snuggling or loving time.

VICTOR: We're fighting more too. But I'm still not sure why.

Victor and Natalie are so involved in what is happening to them that even though they can identify some of the sources of their disenchantment, they cannot really make sense of all of it. They are playing out a scenario that was very common for the couples in our study during the first year of parenthood. Both men and women are experiencing a changing sense of self *and* a shift in the atmosphere in the relationship between them. The nurturance that partners might ordinarily get from one another is in very short supply. As if this were not enough to adjust to, almost all of the new parents in our study say that their other key relationships are shifting too.

SHIFTS IN THE THREE-GENERATIONAL ROLES AND RELATIONSHIPS

> VICTOR: It was really weird to see my father's reaction to Kim's birth. The week before Natalie's due date, my father all of a sudden decided that he was going to Seattle, and he took off with my mom and some other people. Well, the next day Natalie went into labor and we had the baby, and my mother kept calling, saying she wanted to get back here. But my dad seemed to be playing games and made it stretch out for two or three days.
>
> Finally, when they came back and the whole period was past, it turned out that my father was *jealous* of my mother's relationship with the baby. He didn't want my mother to take time away from him to be with Kim! He's gotten over it now. He holds Kim and plays with her, and doesn't want to go home after a visit. But my dad and me, we're still sort of recovering from what happened. And when things don't go well with me and Dad, Natalie sometimes gets it in the neck.
>
> NATALIE: I'll say.

For Victor's father, becoming a first-time grandfather is something that is happening *to* him. His son and daughter-in-law are having a baby and he is becoming a grandfather, ready or not. Many men and women in Victor's parents' position have mixed feelings about becoming grandparents (Lowe 1991), but rarely know how to deal with them. As Victor searches for ways to become comfortable with his new identity as a father, like so many of the men we spoke to, he is desperately hoping that it will bring him closer to his father.

As father and son struggle with these separate inner changes, they feel a strain in the relationship between them, a strain they feel they cannot mention. Some of it spills over into the relationship between Victor and Natalie: After a visit with his parents, they realize, they are much more likely to get into a fight.

CHANGING ROLES AND RELATIONSHIPS OUTSIDE THE FAMILY

> NATALIE: While Victor has been dealing with his dad, I've been struggling with my boss. After a long set of negotiations on the phone, he reluctantly agreed to let me come back four days a week instead of full-time. I haven't gone back officially yet, but I dropped in to see him. He always used to have time for me, but this week, after just a few minutes of small talk, he told me that he had a meeting and practically bolted out of the

room. He as much as said that he figured I wasn't serious about my job anymore.

VICTOR: Natalie's not getting much support from her friends, either. None of them has kids and they just don't seem to understand what she's going through. Who ever thought how lonely it can be to have a baby?

Although the burden of the shifts in roles and relationships outside the family affects both parents, it tends to fall more heavily on new mothers. It is women who tend to put their jobs and careers on hold, at least temporarily, after they have babies (Daniels and Weingarten 1982, 1988), and even though they may have more close friends than their husbands do, they find it difficult to make contact with them in the early months of new parenthood. It takes all of the energy new mothers have to cope with the ongoing care and feeding that a newborn requires and to replenish the energy spent undergoing labor or cesarean delivery. The unanticipated loss of support from friends and co-workers can leave new mothers feeling surprisingly isolated and vulnerable. New fathers' energies are on double duty too. Because they are the sole earners when their wives stop working or take maternity leave, men often work longer hours or take on extra jobs. Fatigue and limited availability means that fathers too get less support or comfort from co-workers or friends. This is one of many aspects of family life in which becoming a parent seems to involve more *loss* than either spouse anticipated—especially because they have been focused on the gain of the baby. Although it is not difficult for us to see how these shifts and losses might catch two tired parents off guard, most husbands and wives fail to recognize that these changes are affecting them as individuals and as a couple.

NEW PARENTING ROLES AND RELATIONSHIPS

Natalie and Victor, unlike most of the other couples, had worked out a shared approach to household tasks from the time they moved in together. Whoever was available to do something would do it. And when Kim was born, they just continued that. During the week, Victor would get the baby up in the morning and then take over when he got home from work. Natalie put her to bed at night. During the weekends the responsibilities were reversed.

It was not surprising that Natalie and Victor expected their egalitarian system—a rare arrangement—to carry over to the care of their baby. What is surprising to us is that a majority of the couples predicted that they would share the care of their baby much more equally than they were sharing their housework and family tasks *before* they became parents. Even though they are unusually collaborative in their care of Kim, Natalie and Victor are not protected from the fact that, like most couples, their different ideas about what a baby needs create some conflict and disagreement:

VICTOR: I tend to be a little more . . . what would you say?
NATALIE: Crazy.

VICTOR: A little more crazy with Kim. I like to put her on my bicycle and go for a ride real fast. I like the thought of the wind blowing on her and her eyes watering. I want her to feel the rain hitting her face. Natalie would cover her head, put a thick jacket on her, you know, make sure she's warm and dry.

NATALIE: At the beginning, we argued a lot about things like that. More than we ever did. Some of them seemed trivial at the time. The argument wouldn't last more than a day. It would all build up, explode, and then be over. One night, though, Victor simply walked out. He took a long drive, and then came back. It was a bad day for both of us. We just had to get it out, regardless of the fact that it was three A.M.

VICTOR: I think it was at that point that I realized that couples who start off with a bad relationship would really be in trouble. As it was, it wasn't too pleasant for us, but we got through it.

Despite the fact that their emotional focus had been on the baby during pregnancy and the early months of parenthood, Victor and Natalie were not prepared for the way their relationship with the baby affected and was affected by the changes they had been experiencing all along as individuals, at work, in their marriage, and in their relationships with their parents, friends, and co-workers—the spillover effects. They sometimes have new and serious disagreements, but both of them convey a sense that they have the ability to prevent their occasional blowups from escalating into serious and long-lasting tensions.

As we follow them over time, Victor and Natalie describe periods in which their goodwill toward each other wears thin, but their down periods are typically followed by genuine ups. It seems that one of them always finds a way to come back to discuss the painful issues when they are not in so much distress. In subsequent visits, for example, the shorts-in-the-bathroom episode, retold with much laughter, becomes a shorthand symbol for the times when tensions erupt between them. They give themselves time to cool down, they come back to talk about what was so upsetting, and having heard each other out, they go on to find a solution to the problem that satisfies both of their needs. This, we know, is the key to a couple's stable and satisfying relationship (Gottman and Krokoff 1989).

Compared to the other couples, one of the unusual strengths in Natalie and Victor's life together is their ability to come back to problem issues after they have calmed down. Many couples are afraid to rock the boat once their heated feelings have cooled down. Even more unusual is their trust that they will both be listened to sympathetically when they try to sort out what happened. Because Natalie and Victor each dare to raise issues that concern them, they end up feeling that they are on the same side when it comes to the most important things in life (cf. Ball 1984). This is what makes it possible for them to engage in conflict and yet maintain their positive feelings about their relationship.

Most important, perhaps, for the long-term outcome of their journey to parenthood is that the good feeling between Victor and Natalie spills over to their daughter. Throughout Kim's preschool years and into her first year of kindergarten, we see the threesome as an active, involved family in which the members are fully engaged with one another in both serious and playful activities.

What Makes Parenthood Harder Now

Natalie and Victor are charting new territory. They are trying to create a family based on the new, egalitarian ideology in which both of them work *and* share the tasks of managing the household and caring for their daughter. They have already embraced less traditional roles than most of the couples in our study. Although the world they live in has changed a great deal since they were children, it has not shifted sufficiently to support them in realizing their ideals easily. Their journey seems to require heroic effort.

Would a more traditional version of family life be less stressful? Couples who arrange things so that the woman tends the hearth and baby and the man provides the income to support them are also showing signs of strain. They struggle financially because it often takes more than one parent's income to maintain a family. They feel drained emotionally because they rely almost entirely on their relationship to satisfy most of their psychological needs. Contemporary parents find themselves in double jeopardy. Significant historical shifts in the family landscape of the last century, particularly of the last few decades, have created additional burdens for them. As couples set foot on the trails of this challenging journey, they become disoriented because society's map of the territory has been redrawn. Becoming a family today is more difficult than it used to be.

In recent decades there has been a steady ripple of revolutionary social change. Birth control technology has been transformed. Small nuclear families live more isolated lives in crowded cities, often feeling cut off from extended family and friends. Mothers of young children are entering the work force earlier and in ever larger numbers. Choices about how to create life as a family are much greater than they used to be. Men and women are having a difficult time regaining their balance as couples after they have babies, in part because the radical shifts in the circumstances surrounding family life in America demand new arrangements to accommodate the increasing demands on parents of young children. But new social arrangements and roles have simply not kept pace with these changes, leaving couples on their own to manage the demands of work and family.

MORE CHOICE

Compared with the experiences of their parents and grandparents, couples today have many more choices about whether and when to bring a child into their lives. New forms of birth control have given most couples the means to engage in an active sex life with some confidence, though no guarantee, that they can avoid unwanted pregnancy. In addition, despite recent challenges in American courts and legislatures, the 1973 Supreme Court decision legalizing abortion has given couples a second chance to decide whether to become parents if birth control fails or is not used.

But along with modern birth control techniques come reports of newly discovered hazards. We now know that using birth control pills, intrauterine devices, the cervical cap, the sponge, and even the diaphragm poses some risk to a woman's health. The decision to abort a fetus brings with it both public controversy and the private anguish of the physical, psychological, and moral consequences of ending a pregnancy (see Nathanson 1989). Men and women today may enjoy more choice about parenthood than any previous generation, but the couples in our studies are finding it quite difficult to navigate this new family-making terrain.

Sharon, who was eagerly awaiting the results of her home pregnancy test when we met her at the beginning of this chapter, had not been nearly as eager to become a mother three years earlier.

> SHARON: Actually, we fought about it a lot. Daniel already had a child, Hallie, from his first marriage. "Let's have one of our own. It'll be easy," he said. And I said, "Yeah, and what happened before Hallie was two? You were out the door."
>
> DANIEL: I told you, that had nothing to do with Hallie. She was great. It was my ex that was the problem. I just knew that for us a baby would be right.
>
> SHARON: I wasn't sure. What was I going to do about a career? What was I going to do about me? I wasn't ready to put things on hold. I wasn't even convinced, then, that I wanted to become a mother. It wouldn't have been good for me, and it sure wouldn't have been good for the baby, to go ahead and give in to Daniel when I was feeling that way.

In past times, fewer choices meant less conflict between spouses, at least at the outset. Now, with each partner expecting to have a free choice in the matter, planning a family can become the occasion for sensitive and delicate treaty negotiations. First, couples who want to live together must decide whether they want to get married. One partner may be for it, the other not. Second, the timing of childbirth has changed. For couples married in 1950–54, the majority (60 percent) would have a baby within two years. Now, almost one-third of couples are marrying *after* having a child, and those who marry before becoming parents are marrying later in life. Only a minority of them have their first child within two years. Some delay parenthood for more than a decade (Teachman, Polonko, and Scanzoni 1987).

Couples are also having smaller families. The decline in fertility has for the first time reduced the birthrate below the replacement level of zero population growth—less than two children per family.* And because couples are having fewer children and having them later, more seems to be at stake in each decision about whether and when to have a child. What was once a natural progression has become a series of choice points, each with a potential for serious disagreement between the partners.

Alice is in the last trimester of her pregnancy. In our initial interview, she and Andy described a profound struggle between them that is not over yet.

> ALICE: This pregnancy was a life and death issue for me. I'd already had two abortions with a man I'd lived with before, because it was very clear that we could not deal with raising a child. Although I'd known Andy for years, we had been together only four months when I became pregnant unexpectedly. I loved him, I was thirty-four years old, and I wasn't going to risk the possibility of another abortion and maybe never being able to have children. So when I became pregnant this time, I said, "I'm having this baby with you or without you. But I'd much rather have it with you."
>
> ANDY: Well, I'm only twenty-seven and I haven't gotten on track with my own life. Alice was using a diaphragm and I thought it was safe. For months after she became pregnant, I was just pissed off that this was happening to me, to us, but I gradually calmed down. If it was just up to me, I'd wait for a number of years yet because I don't feel ready, but I want to be with her, and you can hear that she's determined to have this baby.

Clearly, more choice has not necessarily made life easier for couples who are becoming a family.

ISOLATION

The living environments of families with children have changed dramatically. In 1850, 75 percent of American families lived in rural settings. By 1970, 75 percent were living in urban or suburban environments, and the migration from farm to city is continuing.

We began our own family in Toronto, Canada, the city we had grown up in, with both sets of parents living nearby. Today we live some distance from our parents, relatives, and childhood friends, as do the majority of couples in North America. Increasingly, at least in the middle- and upper-income brackets, couples are living in unfamiliar surroundings, bringing newborns home to be reared in single-family apartments or houses, where their neighbors are strangers. Becoming a parent, then, can quickly result in social isolation, especially for the parent who stays at home with the baby.

John and Shannon are one of the younger couples in our study. He is twenty-four and she is twenty-three.

---

*There are indications, however, that the birthrate in the United States is now on the rise.

JOHN: My sister in Dallas lives down the block from our mother. Whenever she and her husband want a night out, they just call up and either they take the baby over to Mom's house or Mom comes right over to my sister's. Our friends help us out once in a while, but you have to reach out and ask them and a lot of times they aren't in a position to respond. Some of them don't have kids, so they don't really understand what it's like for us. They keep calling us and suggesting that we go for a picnic or out for pizza, and we have to remind them that we have this baby to take care of.

SHANNON: All the uncles, aunts, and cousins in my family used to get together every Sunday. Most of the time I don't miss that because they were intrusive and gossipy and into everybody else's business. But sometimes it would be nice to have someone to talk to who cares about me, and who lived through all the baby throw-up and ear infections and lack of sleep, and could just say, "Don't worry, Shannon, it's going to get better soon."

WOMEN'S ROLES

Since we began our family thirty years ago, mothers have been joining the labor force in ever-increasing numbers, even when they have young babies. Women have always worked, but economic necessity in the middle as well as the working classes, and increased training and education among women, propelled them into the work force in record numbers. In 1960, 18 percent of mothers with children under six were working at least part-time outside the home. By 1970, that figure had grown to 30 percent, and by 1980 it was 45 percent. Today, the majority of women with children under *three* work at least part-time, and recent research suggests that this figure will soon extend to a majority of mothers of one-year-olds (Teachman, Polonko, and Scanzoni 1987).

With the enormous increase in women's choices and opportunities in the work world, many women are caught between traditional and modern conceptions of how they should be living their lives. It is a common refrain in our couples groups.

JOAN: It's ironic. My mother knew that she was supposed to be a mom and not a career woman. But she suffered from that. She was a capable woman with more business sense than my dad, but she felt it was her job to stay home with us kids. And she was *very* depressed some of the time. But I'm *supposed* to be a career woman. I feel that I just need to stay home right now. I'm really happy with that decision, but I struggled with it for months.

TANYA: I know what Joan means, but it's the opposite for me. I'm doing what I want, going back to work, but it's driving me crazy. All day as I'm working, I'm wondering what's happening to Kevin. Is he OK, is he doing some new thing that I'm missing, is he getting enough individual

attention? And when I get home, I'm tired, Jackson's tired, Kevin's tired.
I have to get dinner on the table and Kevin ready for bed. And then I'm
exhausted and Jackson's exhausted and I just hit the pillow and I'm out.
We haven't made love in three months. I know Jackson's frustrated. *I'm*
frustrated. I didn't know it was going to be like this.

News media accounts of family-oriented men imply that as mothers have
taken on more of a role in the world of paid work, fathers have taken on a
comparable load of family work. But this simply hasn't happened. As Arlie
Hochschild (1989) demonstrates, working mothers are coming home to face
a "second shift"—running the household and caring for the children. Although there are studies suggesting that fathers are taking on a little more
housework and care of the children than they used to (Pleck 1985), mothers
who are employed full-time still have far greater responsibility for managing
the family work and child rearing than their husbands do (C. Cowan 1988).
It is not simply that men's and women's roles are unequal that seems to be
causing distress for couples, but rather that they are so clearly discrepant
from what both spouses expected them to be.

Women are getting the short end of what Hochschild calls the "stalled
revolution": Their work roles have changed but their family roles have not.
Well-intentioned and confused husbands feel guilty, while their overburdened wives feel angry. It does not take much imagination to see how these
emotions can fuel the fires of marital conflict.

SOCIAL POLICY

The stress that Joan and Tanya talk about comes not only from internal
conflicts and from difficulties in coping with life inside the family but from
factors outside the family as well. Joan might consider working part-time if
she felt that she and her husband could get high-quality, affordable child care
for their son. Tanya might consider working different shifts or part-time if
her company had more flexible working arrangements for parents of young
children. But few of the business and government policies that affect parents
and children are supportive of anything beyond the most traditional family
arrangements.

We see a few couples, like Natalie and Victor, who strike out on their own
to make their ideology of more balanced roles a reality. These couples believe
that they and their children will reap the rewards of their innovation, but they
are exhausted from bucking the strong winds of opposition—from parents,
from bosses, from co-workers. Six months after the birth of her daughter,
Natalie mentioned receiving a lukewarm reception from her boss after negotiating a four-day work week.

NATALIE: He made me feel terrible. I'm going to have to work *very* hard to
make things go, but I think I can do it. What worries me, though, is that
the people I used to supervise aren't very supportive either. They keep

raising these issues, "Well, what if so-and-so happens, and you're not there?" Well, sometimes I wasn't there before because I was traveling for the company, and nobody got in a snit. Now that I've got a baby, somehow my being away from the office at a particular moment is a problem.

VICTOR: My boss is flexible about when I come in and when I leave, but he keeps asking me questions. He can't understand why I want to be at home with Kim some of the time that Natalie's at work.

It would seem to be in the interest of business and government to develop policies that are supportive of the family. Satisfied workers are more productive. Healthy families drain scarce economic resources less than unhealthy ones, and make more of a contribution to the welfare of society at large. Yet, the United States is the only country in the Western world without a semblance of explicit family policy. This lack is felt most severely by parents of young children. There are no resources to help new parents deal with their anxieties about child rearing (such as the visiting public health nurses in England), unless the situation is serious enough to warrant medical or psychiatric attention. If both parents want or need to work, they would be less conflicted if they could expect to have adequate parental leave when their babies are born (as in Sweden and other countries), flexible work hours to accommodate the needs of young children, and access to reasonably priced, competent child care. These policies and provisions are simply not available in most American businesses and communities (Catalyst 1988).

The absence of family policy also takes its toll on traditional family arrangements, which are not supported by income supplements or family allowances (as they are in Canada and Britain) as a financial cushion for the single-earner family. The lack of supportive policy and family-oriented resources results in increased stress on new parents just when their energies are needed to care for their children. It is almost inevitable that this kind of stress spills over into the couple's negotiations and conflicts about how they will divide the housework and care of the children.

THE NEED FOR NEW ROLE MODELS

Based on recent statistics, the modern family norm is neither the Norman Rockwell *Saturday Evening Post* cover family nor the "Leave It to Beaver" scenario with Dad going out to work and Mom staying at home to look after the children. Only about 6 percent of all American households today have a husband as the sole breadwinner and a wife and two or more children at home—"the typical American family" of earlier times. Patterns from earlier generations are often irrelevant to the challenges faced by dual-worker couples in today's marketplace.

After setting out on the family journey, partners often discover that they have conflicting values, needs, expectations, and plans for their destination.

This may not be an altogether new phenomenon, but it creates additional strain for a couple.

> JAMES: My parents were old-school Swedes who settled in Minnesota on a farm. It was cold outside in the winters, but it was cold inside too. Nobody said anything unless they had to. My mom was home all the time. She worked hard to support my dad and keep the farm going, but she never really had anything of her own. I'm determined to support Cindy going back to school as soon as she's ready.
>
> CINDY: My parents were as different from James's as any two parents could be. When they were home with us, they were all touchy-feely, but they were hardly ever around. During the days my mom and dad both worked. At night, they went out with their friends. I really don't want that to happen to Eddie. So, James and I are having a thing about it now. He wants me to go back to school. I don't want to. I'm working about ten hours a week, partly because he nags at me so much. If it were just up to me, I'd stay home until Eddie gets into first grade.

Cindy and James each feel that they have the freedom to do things differently than their parents did. The problem is that the things each of them wants to be different are on a collision course. James is trying to be supportive of Cindy's educational ambitions so his new family will feel different than the one he grew up in. Given her history, Cindy does not experience this as support. Her picture of the family she wanted to create and James's picture do not match. Like so many of the couples in our study, both partners are finding it difficult to establish a new pattern because the models from the families they grew up in are so different from the families they want to create.

INCREASED EMOTIONAL BURDEN

The historical changes we have been describing have increased the burden on both men and women with respect to the emotional side of married life. Not quite the equal sharers of breadwinning and family management they hoped to be, husbands and wives now expect to be each other's major suppliers of emotional warmth and support. Especially in the early months as a family, they look to their marriage as a "haven in a heartless world." Deprived of regular daily contact with extended family members and lifelong friends, wives and husbands look to each other to "be there" for them—to pick up the slack when energies flag, to work collaboratively on solving problems, to provide comfort when it is needed, and to share the highs and lows of life inside and outside the family. While this mutual expectation may sound reasonable to modern couples, it is very difficult to live up to in an intimate relationship that is already vulnerable to disappointment from within and pressure from without.

The greatest emotional pressure on the couple, we believe, comes from the culture's increasing emphasis on self-fulfillment and self-development (Bellah et al. 1985). The vocabulary of individualism, endemic to American society from its beginnings, has become even more pervasive in recent decades. It is increasingly difficult for two people to make a commitment to each other if they believe that ultimately they are alone, and that personal development and success in life must be achieved through individual efforts. As this individualistic vocabulary plays out within the family, it makes it even more difficult for partners to subordinate some of their personal interests to the common good of the relationship. When "my needs" and "your needs" appear to be in conflict, partners can wind up feeling more like adversaries than family collaborators.

The vocabulary of individualism also makes it likely that today's parents will be blamed for any disarray in American families. In the spirit of Ben Franklin and Horatio Alger, new parents feel that they ought to be able to make it on their own, without help. Couples are quick to blame themselves if something goes wrong. When the expectable tensions increase as partners become parents, their tendency is to blame each other for not doing a better job. We believe that pioneers will inevitably find themselves in difficulty at some points on a strenuous journey. If societal policies do not become more responsive to parents and children, many of them will lose their way.

A HAZARDOUS JOURNEY

Unfortunately there are no historical comparative studies to substantiate our claim that the transition to parenthood is more difficult now than it used to be, but the evidence of risks to the parents' marriage and the children's well-being continues to mount. When we began the Becoming a Family Project in 1974, several studies suggested that the early child-rearing years could be stressful, but no one had studied the transition to parenthood by following *couples* from before to after they had their first baby. Today there is a large body of data to suggest that the transition to parenthood is disequilibrating for a majority of men, women, and marriages (see Cowan and Cowan 1988). Edward E. LeMasters's (1957) claim that a majority of new-parent couples experience "moderate or severe crisis" may be a slight overstatement of the case (see Hobbs and Cole 1977), but it is clear that both mothers and fathers are at increased risk for disenchantment or distress in the early years of parenthood. We can expect to find that one in a thousand new mothers will have a full-blown postpartum psychosis, that 7 percent to 15 percent will be diagnosed as clinically depressed, and that 30 percent to 50 percent (some claim as high as 80 percent) will experience "the blues" (Kumar and Robson 1984; O'Hara 1986). Because there are no epidemiological studies of new fathers, we do not have estimates of how many men becoming parents suffer from disabling psychological distress (Zaslow et al. 1981).*

---

*It was sobering to find that in our own study of ninety-six couples, one of the seventy-two men who became a father and one of the seventy-two women who became a mother during

There is consistent evidence from a number of careful longitudinal studies that couples' conflict and disagreement increases after they have a baby (Cowan et al. 1985) and that, on the average, men's and women's dissatisfaction with marriage tends to increase from pregnancy into the early child-rearing years (Belsky, Lang, and Rovine 1985; Cowan et al. 1985; Grossman et al. 1980).

Living in changing families in a changing world, pioneering couples find the trek to parenthood exciting, but surprisingly lonely, stormy, and frightening. Given the mixed messages from the family frontier, couples considering whether or when to become parents face a difficult decision.

---

the first two years of the study experienced a severe emotional breakdown requiring psychiatric care in the first three months after the birth of their first babies.

CHAPTER 2

To Be or Not to Be a Parent

ROB: We thought and thought about whether we should have kids and when would be a good time—a time that wouldn't somehow take away what we've worked so hard to build between us. And the more we thought, and the more we went back and forth about it, the more we discovered that there wasn't a clear answer or a perfect time. So I said, "Let's stop using birth control and see what happens."

JOAN: I was more committed than he was. At first, I was content to let it ride, because I was building my career, but I couldn't let it go forever. I always knew I wanted a child, so if he hadn't at least agreed to try, our marriage would have been in serious difficulty. I mean, I love Rob but I don't know if I could have just given in on this one. I was relieved when he said that I should stop taking the pill. He didn't really agree to "go for it" but at least he was willing to let it happen.

The decision to have a child has been described as the most fateful (Whelan 1975) or important (Bombardieri 1981) choice a couple can make, especially because its consequences are so far-reaching financially and psychologically (LaRossa 1986). There is no question that children are expensive. One husband in our study referred to his and his wife's debate about whether to have a baby as the "million-dollar decision." It was estimated about a decade ago that raising a male child from birth to twenty-five years of age cost at least $214,956 (Olson 1983), and a daughter cost even more (LaRossa 1986). Considering inflation and the state of the economy, not to mention the fact that these days children stay in college or professional training beyond the age of twenty-five, a seven-figure estimate may not be too far off.

The psychological aspects of having children add greater complexity to the debate. Unlike some other family decisions, becoming a parent is irrevocable. This provides a high incentive for couples to make the "right" decision.

As we listened to men and women talk about the choices they made, we heard both the reasons they wanted to have or not to have babies and the process—or the absence of a process—by which they decided what kind of family theirs would be. We began to discover just how important this process can be in determining how couples cope with the consequences of their baby decisions, especially if they fail to resolve serious disagreements between them.

At the time of our initial interview at six or seven months into the pregnancy, nine of the seventy-two expectant couples (14 percent) are still voicing strongly contrasting views about whether they are ready to have a child. In two couples, the husbands are eager to have a baby, but their wives are still facing parenthood reluctantly. Over the next six years these two couples experience serious marital crises but they stay together. In seven couples, the wives are feeling enthusiastic but their husbands have serious reservations about becoming fathers. These seven couples all separate and divorce by the time their first child is six years old.

This startling finding, which we will return to, reinforces one of our central themes. The birth of a baby does not suddenly convert a well-functioning couple relationship into one that is fraught with difficulty. Much of what happens after the birth of a baby is shaped by what is happening in couples' lives before the baby comes along. And one of the most important things that happens in the prebaby period is the way the couple goes about deciding whether to become parents in the first place.

My Choice, Your Choice, Our Choice

Rob and Joan touch on some of the most salient baby-maybe dilemmas that contemporary couples face. Quoted at the beginning of the chapter, they are in their early thirties and have been married for eight years. Like most of the participants in our study, they were initially somewhat ambivalent about becoming parents—if not about whether, at least about when. When two partners agree to live together or get married, they rarely make a firm agreement about whether to have children or when to begin a family (Daniels and Weingarten 1982). Even couples who discuss their family-making timetable before they make a long-term commitment to each other often find that changing circumstances, like career moves or parents who become ill and need to be taken care of, can alter the plans of one or both partners and throw their timetables into conflict. Because couples have to cope with both predictable dilemmas and unexpected events *for each partner,* it is a wonder that they ever arrive at the same conclusion at the same time about this major life step.

By the time we come to conduct our initial interview, about half of the couples have discussed the issues at length, come to a mutual decision, and entered into a deliberate plan that they will or will not have children. By contrast, the other half of the couples seems to have been involved in a rather inarticulate process in which both partners have been teetering between individual soul searching and meaningful conversation. For them, the process of deciding seems muddier and the outcome of their deliberations much less clear-cut. Peggy and Bill, in their mid-twenties, are talking with us in the living room of their small suburban apartment. Peggy is six months pregnant and feeling uncomfortable. Bill is telling us about how they came to be having a baby at this time.

> BILL: Well, you know, we've been talking about it on and off, and it was always, "Do you want one?" "I don't know, do you want one?" And I didn't want to say, "I want one," because I don't want my wife to go through the tremendous changes if she doesn't really want one. And she was afraid to say she wanted one because I might not really want one.
>
> PEGGY: I don't know how we finally decided, really. I got a new job last year, and I felt that it was not right to say "Let's have children" my first year on the job. And Bill was just getting his roofing business going, so we thought we'd probably start next year. And that's why we were so surprised to find we were pregnant.
>
> I wouldn't have minded having children sooner. It's just that I didn't know if he really wanted—you know, if he could put up with the noise they would make. Like, we'd go out to lunch, and there would be kids screaming, "Mommy, mommy, I want . . ." and I could tell by looking at Bill that he was not very happy about all the noise these kids were making. So I didn't really push the matter. To me, it was OK if he didn't want any.

Only a few of the expectant couples describe themselves as having had a consistent stance over time; most report that each partner has shifted positions at least once before meeting with us at our initial interview. We find four patterns in how couples come to be—or not to be—having a baby:

Planners. These couples actively discuss the question and come to an agreement about becoming pregnant.

Acceptance-of-Fate Couples. These partners acquiesce or are pleasantly surprised when they discover that a baby is on the way.

Ambivalent Couples. They have strong feelings pro and con before and after conception and well into the pregnancy.

Yes-No Couples. By late pregnancy, these couples are still struggling, with each other and with the consequences of deciding to go ahead with the pregnancy.

Three of these patterns—Planners, Ambivalent, and Yes-No—are also present in the couples who are not having babies when we meet them at the beginning of the study.

To illustrate how couples in each of the four patterns handle the parenthood decision, we focus on a few representative couples. We show how the partners' reasons for wanting or not wanting to have a child are influenced by who they are, what routes they have taken to arrive at this time of life, and how they feel about their relationship. That is, their histories as individuals and as couples set the stage for whether their family-making discussions will be smooth or rough sailing.

Especially because we do not meet the expectant couples in our study until the seventh month of pregnancy, we are under no illusion that what they describe provides a complete picture of their motivations. What the interviews do reveal, we think, is what couples expect to happen if or when they have children—Will it be wonderful, problematic, or both?—and how they think and feel about making major life decisions when they agree or disagree on a course of action.

Four Decision-Making Patterns

One assumption that seems to be shared by most of the couples in our study, whether they wish passionately to have children or resolve firmly to remain child-free, is that babies will bring change: more closeness, excitement, and joy according to some couples; more distance, frustration, and tension, say others. Almost all of the reasons men and women gave for or against having children focused on one or more of the aspects of family life we had set out to study. Couples who are becoming parents expect their relationship with the child to change their lifestyle; alter their sense of themselves; affect their friendships, work lives, and stress levels; promote a reworking of their relationships with their parents; and have a profound impact on their marriage.

THE PLANNERS

Fifty-two percent of *both* nonparents and expectant couples in our study approached family making in a very deliberate way. By the time they try to conceive, the Planners who want a child have agreed that they do, and most have waited until both spouses agree on when. After extensive discussions, the Planners who are not expecting had decided (1) probably, but not now

(32 percent), or (2) definitely no for now, but the future is unclear (20 percent).

Clearly No   Marty and Evelyn, both twenty-eight, live in a small, comfortably furnished home, which they own. Marty is self-employed as a lawyer with an office nearby. Evelyn is a therapist who also works close to home. After ongoing, serious discussion, they have made a mutual decision not to have children.

> MARTY: The more I think about it, the clearer I get. I don't know if I can love another little being unselfishly. Most of the kids I know are unmanageable, and I don't think I have the patience to deal with that. I just don't have my shit together. Growing up in my family was like being in the middle of a perpetual shouting match. There's no way I can guarantee that it would be different with Evelyn and me.
> EVELYN: Well, my family didn't get the "Little House on the Prairie" award either. I know from what I did when I was growing up that kids can make their parents miserable. I might still be OK as a mother, I guess, but at this point babies would seriously interfere with where I am going in my work.

Wanting to avoid what happened in the families they grew up in is one of the most frequently mentioned reasons men and women give for deciding not have children. Yet, other couples with similarly troubled childhoods feel challenged to make their peace with their pasts by creating new, better-functioning families of their own.

The issues that Evelyn raises about work and career advancement play a major role in both men's and women's decisions about parenthood, but the consequences of the decision appear to be much more serious for women. Studies of women and careers document the fact that those occupying top positions in business and industry tend disproportionately to be single and/or childless (Baum and Cope 1980). It is little wonder, then, that many women are apprehensive about what will happen to their jobs if they become mothers. Since women still maintain primary responsibility for home and child care, even if they work full-time (see chapters 5 and 6 and Hochschild 1989), they wonder how they will be able to handle the demands of work and family without losing professional ground. As Evelyn says, "I'm afraid that I'd be torn in both directions, and not do justice to either one." Men are rarely asked by researchers about this work-family balance, and they rarely raise the issue spontaneously.

Not surprisingly, Marty and Evelyn believe that parenthood would have a negative effect on their marriage, too.

> EVELYN: We've worked very hard to get our marriage where it is. At the beginning, we were scrapping all the time. I hated it. He hated it. We got some help, and it got a little better.

MARTY: But it still wasn't better enough. Finally, we went camping for a
week and talked maybe sixteen hours a day. I said that I wanted to be
with her, but things would have to change. I'd have to give up some of
my critical, angry stuff, and she'd have to pay more attention to me.

EVELYN: And I said I'd be willing to try if he would, and it really has been
getting better ever since. I worry that a kid would shake us up, and I'm
not willing to risk it.

At the time of our interview, Marty and Evelyn are both clear about their
individual choices, and in agreement. Furthermore, they are able to talk
about their emotions directly, without having to hold back on potentially
controversial feelings, such as their fear about what effect children might
have on the solidity of their marriage.

Clearly Yes   Marty and Evelyn raise issues that are familiar to John and
Shannon, but John and Shannon have a very different view of them. John is
a twenty-four-year-old, energetic sports enthusiast who works in a small auto
parts firm. His boss, whom he describes as "crusty," has promised John a
share of the business if he stays on for a few years. Shannon, six months
pregnant, is a year younger than John and works as a secretary in a community college. They can hardly wait to become parents, a goal they worked
toward for more than a year. As they talk to us about why they decided to
have a baby now, their eyes get misty:

SHANNON: Having a child will give me someone to love—someone who
will love me back in a special way. It'll be unlike any other relationship
I've ever had, even with John. I've always wanted to be a mother,
whatever else I do. It's a very important part of me. It's giving me a
greater purpose in life; I don't know how to describe it, but I know it's
going to make my life more meaningful. I'd have been crushed if we
couldn't conceive *(patting her stomach tenderly)*. I was even a little
worried when it didn't happen the first month we tried.

John focuses more on the influence he will have:

JOHN: I see having a child as a chance to shape the life of another human
being—someone who will be very important to me and who I can teach
about my view of the world.

The most frequent reason both men and women gave us for becoming a
parent was their desire for an intimate and special relationship with their
children. Watching them grow and develop would bring parents fulfillment.
Being with them would give grownups a chance to be childish or playful, and
to look at the world anew through the eyes of a child.

The second most frequent reason men and women gave for having a baby, or for remaining childless, had to do with changes they thought parenthood would make in their sense of themselves. As John says, "Becoming a dad now has something to do with my personal development. At twenty-four, I'm running out of ways to be adolescent gracefully."

The idea that having babies means being a "grownup" led about half the couples in our study to decide that it was not wise to become parents until they had reached an appropriate place in their life journey. Lois and Martin Hoffman found this to be true two decades ago: "More than finishing school, going to work, or even getting married, parenthood establishes a person as a truly mature, stable, and acceptable member of the community and provides him access to other institutions of adult society" (1973, p. 47).

Men's and women's relationships with their friends, their jobs, and the larger communities in which they live are the third most frequently mentioned issues. Some couples' decisions about having children are heavily influenced by whether their friends have babies, although friends can also be a source of pressure against having children. When John and Shannon first started talking about having a baby, he was shocked to find that their friends actively tried to discourage them, warning them that it would interfere with their friendship: "They said that we wouldn't be able to go to dinner or play softball or just hang out with them. Some even upped the ante by telling us about couples they knew whose marriages were falling apart now that they have children!"

Neither partner feels that work ambitions will interfere with his or her family plans. Shannon likes her job but is not emotionally invested in it right now. She thinks she will be able to return to a secretarial job in the college if and when she is ready to go back to work. John has the fantasy that his boss may see him as more serious and responsible once he becomes a father, and thus more disposed to offer him a share in the business.

They do not share Marty and Evelyn's assumption that life with children will be full of conflict. Shannon and John expect to have fun with their children. They expect parenthood to enhance their views of themselves and their work. Not surprisingly, their childhood family memories are mostly warm and positive, and their own relationship has been solid since they met.

A number of couples cite their marriage as the reason they want to go ahead and have a child. Beth and Paul are both thirty-four when they decide to have a baby. He is finishing up his doctoral degree, and she is a drama teacher and coach at a local high school. It took him a bit longer than her to make the decision. As he explains it, the change came when he realized that "over time our relationship, which has always been good, has been getting better and better. We've learned so much from each other in the past few years that I feel we're in a really good place to bring a child into the world."

Beth had been more eager to go ahead but felt like she had to wait: "He was willing to keep on talking about it, and I felt that he heard me out even though he wasn't ready to go along. He's really behind it now—I know he didn't just give in. I don't know what would have happened if Paul wanted even more time, what with the biological clock ticking away." She feels that bringing up a baby will give them something special to work on together.

Clearly, Planners do not always begin with unambivalent feelings about having a baby, nor do the partners always agree at the outset. Their conclusion that their relationship is now on good enough footing to handle bringing a child into the world flows naturally from their style of working things out. Each seems to assume that the other is "on the same side." They describe themselves as ready to negotiate, although Beth hints that she might not have been able to accommodate to Paul's timetable much longer. Perhaps the most important aspect of their style of working on this major decision is that both of them have been willing to keep talking about it.

As we follow Paul and Beth over the years of the study, we continue to be impressed with their engaged and thoughtful stance toward their life together. They work very long hours and love their jobs. They travel regularly to visit their parents in another state, where they originally met, and even more often since they learned that Paul's mother has a terminal illness. They continue to work at their relationships with their parents and with each other, and we see them struggling gently over the things they want to change. Beth and Paul's is a very well functioning and satisfying marriage. We rarely found couples like them, who could continue to sail the stormy seas after someone had rocked the boat. Planners as a group have developed a more effective process of problem solving and more satisfying relationships than the couples in the other three groups, whether they remain childless or become parents.

Frustrated Plans: Due Date Surprises and Infertility   Planner couples tend to proceed as if the world were predictable and under their control, but even the most elaborate plans do not always work out. One of our academic colleagues attempted to become pregnant in August so that the baby would be born late the following May, at the end of the spring semester, giving her all summer to be home with the baby. Her carefully thought out timetable began perfectly, but a surprise was in store: She did become pregnant in August, but "the baby" turned out to be twins. The boys arrived early, just before she needed to grade final exams, and the new mother never did complete that academic year.

A much more serious deterrent to family planning is the inability to conceive for months or years after deciding to begin a family. Problems with fertility, which increase the longer a couple waits, remind us that nature can thwart the best-laid plans.

Four of the thirty-seven Planners in our study took at least two years to become pregnant. By the time we interviewed Seth and Karen, their infertility problem had been resolved, but its consequences lingered. Over three years of attempting to conceive had left them careworn from continually coping with the uncertainties and with the monthly evidence that their efforts had failed. They had to face the possibility that they would never be able to have their own biological child. Because the inability to conceive is often experienced by men and women as a failure of their basic masculinity or femininity, infertility can pose a serious psychological challenge. The evidence is beginning to show that those who do not mourn or cope with this loss may suffer serious long-term consequences to their well-being as individuals and as couples (Menning 1977; Shapiro 1982).

Along with scientific advances in the field of reproduction come unforeseen problems. What we hear from couples who have struggled with problems of fertility is that today's high-tech medical procedures, designed to help them have babies, actually bring a combination of possibly false hope and intrusion into what used to be a private and delicate matter. Rigidly scheduling sexual intercourse almost inevitably decreases partners' spontaneity and enthusiasm for lovemaking. After months or years of preoccupation with getting pregnant, many couples say they never get back to normal. Forever trying to catch up with themselves, with their relationship as a couple, and with the child they desperately want, couples who are unsuccessful at conceiving a baby may be at increased risk of marital distress and divorce (Brodzinsky 1987; Snarey et al. 1987).

Of the four couples in our study who had wrestled with infertility before becoming pregnant, two were among the couples who were most satisfied with their marriages, but the other two were among the most unhappily married in the study. Perhaps the crisis of infertility, like so many other crises, presents a challenge that calls forth a successful effort to respond for some couples, but leads for others to deterioration under the strain. Seth and Karen and the other happily married couple had already successfully coped with a crisis or challenge to their relationship before being faced with the possibility of never conceiving. They gathered their strength to face this new obstacle and came out feeling that their relationship as a couple had grown stronger.

By contrast, the two couples whose satisfaction with marriage was low after their battle with infertility had been dealing for years with other issues they could neither discuss nor resolve. For them, the initial failure to conceive placed an added strain on an already overburdened emotional system. To draw more general conclusions about the effects of infertility, we will need systematic information about the state of couples' marriages before infertility becomes a problem, but we can conclude at this point that, regardless of whether they ever have a viable pregnancy, couples with fertility problems face a special emotional stress that can take a toll on their relationship.

THE ACCEPTANCE-OF-FATE COUPLES

One in seven, or 14 percent, of the expectant couples in our study were surprised by the news of their pregnancies but readily accepted the cards fate had dealt them.* In slightly more than half of these couples, both partners

*All the Acceptance-of-Fate couples, most of the Yes-No couples, and about half the Ambivalent couples had unplanned pregnancies—a total of about 35 percent of those participating in our study. So much for the increases in effective methods of birth control described in chapter 1.

definitely wanted to have children, but not yet. These couples generally took the news as a pleasant surprise.

Ariel and Harry had been living together for five years, married for three, when Ariel was in an automobile accident that left her seriously injured. Eighteen months later, still receiving medical treatments that included hormone therapy for a disrupted menstrual cycle, she discovered she was pregnant. They had not even begun to think about family plans:

> ARIEL: I didn't even have a sense of myself as being fertile—I was so shaken from the accident. And there it was. Part of me was saying, "Wait, we haven't really spent enough time together now that I know I'll live." But the more I thought about having this baby, the more excited I became.
>
> HARRY: I got this romantic picture of a pregnant woman, standing at the window, the sun shining in. Of course, I'm worried sometimes about having a child now, but sometimes you just have to trust that it will all work out.

Not all Acceptance-of-Fate couples sounded as glowing as Harry and Ariel. Some had an attitude of quiet welcome, neither joy nor despair. Bart and Sheila had not yet made a firm decision about parenthood, but neither was opposed to having a child: "When it was right it was going to happen. This pregnancy wouldn't have occurred unless we were at a point in our life where it was OK for a baby to come."

In the useful distinction made by Warren Miller (1978), the babies of the pleasantly surprised and quietly welcoming couples are not planned but, once conceived, are wanted by both partners. The reasons they give for their reaction to the pregnancy resemble those of the Planners: They expect a baby to enrich their lives, to enhance their sense of themselves, to bring them closer to their parents, or to add to the good feelings in their marriage. They do not anticipate that having a baby will interfere seriously with their work or their friendships.

Acceptance-of-Fate couples tend to have very strong and positive feelings about their relationships. Their satisfaction with the marriage may have led them to react quickly and resolutely to welcome their unplanned pregnancies, or their ability to cope well with the pregnancy may have led to feeling satisfied with their marriage. It seems plausible that the process works both ways. Furthermore, it is not unreasonable to wonder whether the Acceptance-of-Fate couples' positive involvement with each other may even have contributed to their reluctance to plan a family more deliberately. From what they recount, it seems clear that few, if any, of them became pregnant because of contraceptive failure. Rather, they seem to have been engaged in a partly unconscious or unspoken game of Russian roulette by being less vigilant about their use of contraception or, in several cases, by not using contraceptives at all. And yet, they expressed surprise when the pregnancy occurred.

Bart says: "We never really talked about it, never really discussed it. One day, even though we knew it wasn't a safe day, we were feeling very good about our relationship and life and we went ahead anyway." Sheila has a more fatalistic interpretation: "It just sort of happened. It seemed to be divinely directed."

Given how difficult it is to make a decision with such far-reaching consequences, some couples may need a little help from a higher being, or from their unconscious. This way they "win" whether she becomes pregnant or they remain "free" and "flexible."

THE AMBIVALENT COUPLES

The theme of ambivalence ran through our discussions with nearly all the couples. We placed a couple in the Ambivalent category when both partners expressed positive *and* negative feelings about parenthood, but one leaned more toward one side and the other more toward the other side. It was more common for men to be reluctant to go ahead, but a few women were not at all ready for parenthood. At the beginning of the study we found couples who fit this Ambivalent pattern among the childless group (44 percent) and among the parents-to-be (20 percent).

Rob and Joan, already quoted, live in a rented apartment near the courthouse where Rob works as a court reporter. They described their mixed feelings about what becoming a family could do *for* them and *to* them:

> JOAN: I thought I wanted a baby someday. But then I would think, "What will happen to me? Will I become a boring housewife, able to talk only about kids and diapers?" That would be a big change from my work at the bank.
>
> ROB: I can see two scenarios very clearly. In one I'm the kind of hero-daddy that I hope I'll be, but in the other I'm the wimp that I'm afraid I'll be.

In contrast to Shannon, who is eager to give up her job for now, and Evelyn, who is totally wrapped up in her work, Joan feels stuck at a difficult choice point in her life. She had to decide whether to apply for managerial training at the bank, but was also worried about being "one of those old moms, sort of decrepit when my kids were teenagers *(sighs)*. So I sent in my application to the training program, really worked on it, and got pregnant three days before I was accepted!"

Rob and Joan provide a clear illustration of a couple who has discussed parenthood extensively before the baby "surprises" them. We have the strong impression that for a few women, like Joan, such an unexpected pregnancy can resolve, at least temporarily, an immobilizing dilemma about whether to step onto the family or the career path. While Joan did not consciously plan it this way, her accidental pregnancy provided a solution.

For Rob and Joan, and for many of the Ambivalent couples, a struggle has preceded the realization that both of them have mixed feelings. Seven months into the pregnancy, they report that their negotiations began with strong disagreements: One spouse was eager to have a baby, the other definitely opposed. Unlike the Yes-No couples, to be discussed next, Ambivalent partners were somehow able to tolerate their own and their partners' mixed feelings long enough to come to some joint resolution of the dilemma.

During our first interview with Steve and Yu-Mei, one of the Ambivalent couples who have not yet decided whether to have children, Steve says that he leans toward going ahead with it. Although he secretly shares his wife's fears that having a baby could change their life, he tries to convince her that her fears are unfounded.

But Yu-Mei doesn't want to hear Steve's fantasies about how things will be if they have a baby, even though she sometimes has similar daydreams: "Once Steve hears my positive feelings, he will say 'OK then, let's go ahead,' and I'm just not ready to do that."

Steve and Yu-Mei tell us in our interview that each feels partly ready to go ahead and partly fearful—but in talking with each other, Steve has mentioned only the "yes" and Yu-Mei only the "no." Thus their discussions feel polarized and antagonistic, and they cannot escape the common pattern for couples with important differences of opinion or experience: Instead of trying to resolve the conflict *within* each of them, they get into a struggle with each other. Each tries to reduce the inner turmoil by trying to convince the other to change. Not being aware of this pattern, both partners usually feel misunderstood and hurt. We believe that the marital polarization becomes more painful than it would be to resolve their inner turmoil, but they do not see this as an option. Some never get past the deadlock.

Those who do, including Steve and Yu-Mei, begin to let on that there are really two sides to both their stories. In the protected setting of our personal interview, Steve admits some of his reservations; Yu-Mei says she sometimes daydreams about the two of them with a baby. In the process of talking to each other and answering our questions, they realize that both of them understand and feel both sides of the dilemma; at the same time they each want and fear parenthood. They have shifted from a *decision* to a *discussion* mode in which expressing a feeling for or against having a child does not have to lead to immediate action. When both spouses can talk about both poles of their own inner struggle, it creates the possibility that they will feel they are on the same side and that, whatever the ultimate resolution, it will be based on both partners' needs.

Unfortunately, such an outcome was not achieved by most of the Ambivalent couples in our study. Both expectant and childless couples typically stopped at the polarized stage. It apparently felt less threatening for each partner to remain ambivalent, to back off and suffer in silence. Significantly, the Ambivalent couples tended to feel less positive about their marriages at the beginning of the study than did couples in any of the other groups.

THE YES-NO COUPLES

Ambivalence about having a child is one thing. Strong, unresolved conflict about becoming a family is another. As we mentioned earlier, nine of the original seventy-two couples who were expecting a baby when they entered our study were still in a Yes-No conflict about the wisdom of becoming parents in our initial interview with them in the sixth or seventh month of pregnancy.

A tenth Yes-No couple was one of the twenty-four couples not yet decided about having children. Tom and Valerie had been together for four years. Tom wanted to have a baby but Valerie was definitely not ready for this step. They had even separated over this issue once. In our first interview, Tom said he felt that Valerie had "welched" on their deal. For her part, Valerie made clear that she had always told him she wanted kids *someday*, but that for her someday was still a long way off.

Nine months later, when we called to set up our next interview, we found that Tom and Valerie were living separately again. Two years into the study (equivalent to the eighteen-months-after-birth follow-up of the couples who had had a baby), we reached Tom by telephone. He told us that Valerie had moved to another city to take a job and that they had filed for divorce.

Fourteen percent of the expectant couples and 5 percent of the childless couples fell into the Yes-No category. In two of the Yes-No couples who were expecting a baby, the husbands had been eager for the baby since the pregnancy was discovered but the wives' initial reaction had been negative. Both women came around, apparently without completely resolving their earlier misgivings. Although we could not have predicted from our first interviews which couples would wind up in the most marital difficulty, we know now that the marriage of one of these two couples has been in almost constant turmoil since their baby was born, and the other has been teetering between periods of amicable feeling and talk of divorce. Despite these painful early years as a family, both couples with the initially hesitant mothers were still together at the end of their first child's kindergarten year.

What happens when it is the man who says no, and when the partners' inability to resolve the conflict continues into the late stages of pregnancy? Recall thirty-four-year-old Alice and twenty-seven-year-old Andy from chapter 1. Alice became pregnant when they had been living together only four months. She was determined to have a child, regardless of whether Andy stayed in the picture. He did not feel ready to become a father, and was struggling to come to terms with Alice's pregnancy:

> ANDY: It was the hardest thing I ever had to deal with. I had this idea that I wasn't even going to have to think about being a father until I was over thirty, but here it was, and I had to decide now. I was concerned about my soul. I didn't want, under any circumstances, to compromise myself, but I knew it would be very hard on Alice if I took action that would result in her being a single parent. It would've meant that I'm the kind of person who turns his back on someone I care about, and that would destroy me as well as her.

It is important to understand that Alice and Andy were struggling with more than the dilemmas of impending parenthood. Individually and together, they have had to overcome serious adversities from their youth. Alice told us that she experiences her mother as emotionally aloof, critical, and rejecting. Her close relationship with her father—too close, according to Andy—was very important to her, but he died when Alice was in her early twenties. She had become disoriented for a time after he died, and seems not to have completed her mourning for him. She had been searching for that closeness elsewhere in her life ever since, and her relationship with Andy had made her hopeful of having found it. So, for Alice, having a baby with Andy dovetailed perfectly with where she had been heading on her journey through adulthood.

Andy, however, was working on a different aspect of his adult development. During his teen years, he suddenly realized that his parents were alcoholics. He would come home from school each night to his parents' unpredictable moods, which swung wildly from hilarity to violent anger. No wonder an unexpected pregnancy leaves him in turmoil. Longing for a true family, he is nevertheless troubled by Alice's pregnancy, although he loves her.

Both Alice and Andy are drawn to the tenderness and passion they find together, but Alice is also sometimes frightened by Andy's anger. As he explained: "When I have a few drinks, I tend to get nasty the way my father did. I was hoping to wait until I got that kind of thing under control before becoming a father myself."

Many of the men and women in our study had had unhappy or disturbing experiences while growing up, and these experiences play a part in how each of them envisions family making. Some who are choosing to become parents have been bolstered by the strong conviction that they can create more nurturing families than those they knew as children. A few feel that they are already dealing with all they can manage in the life they have constructed as a couple and cannot risk repeating a destructive pattern. Still others, like Alice and Andy, feel powerful but contradictory feelings about whether it is possible to break the chain of family dysfunction.

Alice longs to have a child now, in part to combat her feelings of insecurity and to make up for the loss of her truly accepting parent. But her need puts her in conflict with Andy, who needs to get himself and his relationship with Alice more comfortably settled before he takes on the care of yet another needy human being. Alice imagines that nurturing the baby that was conceived in a loving relationship will fill some of her longing for tenderness and love. Andy sounds as if he needs that kind of tenderness too, but he was counting on finding it in his new relationship with Alice. In addition to the turmoil within and between Andy and Alice, they must also untangle both the support and pressure from their close friends. According to Andy, his friends are urging him "to run." Alice's friends are very supportive of her having the baby, even if it means she has to be a single parent.

Here is our five-domain model in action. As they begin their journey to parenthood, Alice and Andy come face to face with the other four arenas of their lives: their sense of themselves, their relationships with their parents, and the stress and support provided by close friends. For obvious reasons, the pregnancy is having a dramatic effect on their relationship with each other.

It is difficult to convey the tone of Andy's and Alice's remarks on paper, but we were very moved by their emotion and warmth during our interviews with them. They talked about the pregnancy struggle with insight and understanding, and both sounded sympathetic to the other's point of view, even though the discussion got a bit abstract at times. They almost convinced us that the troubles between them were in the past. Swayed by their moving and articulate descriptions of their feelings, we missed some of the obvious danger signals.

In retrospect, we can see that many critical factors were working against Alice and Andy's relationship as a couple, exacerbating rather than helping to resolve their differences. The most obvious, of course, is that they had not lived together long enough to establish a firm intimate relationship before the pregnancy occurred. Second, each had a different picture of what life with a child would be like, a picture that reinforced their respective feelings about family life. Third, it was not so much the difference in their ages as in their different places in their developmental journeys at the time the pregnancy occurred that increased the intensity of Andy's negative feelings and Alice's determination to have the baby.

Finally, we learned later that there had been very little give-and-take in their discussions. Unlike Steve and Yu-Mei, neither Alice nor Andy experienced ambivalence about what he or she wanted. Their individual needs were so compelling that neither was able to recognize any feelings on the other side of the issue. As a result, their intense discussions remained polarized. Once Alice decided that she was going ahead with the pregnancy regardless of what Andy decided, Andy had a very difficult time coming to terms with his distress. Apparently, in contrast with the warm way they talked to each other in our presence, their private conversations were more like take-it-or-leave-it emotional showdowns, with Alice feeling pressure from both Andy's distress and her own gut feeling of need. She decided that to be true to herself and her needs, she had to have the baby. Andy decided finally that to preserve his self-respect and respond to his own need for intimacy, he had to stay with Alice and give in on the baby question.

We, and they, have learned a good deal since that initial interview in 1980. We can see more clearly now that major decisions with these conflicting, emotionally laden elements are probably destined to be short-run resolutions. For Alice and Andy, this one was to have painful long-term consequences, for both of them and for their daughter, Jessica. For several years, it looked as though there might be a hopeful resolution to their tumultuous family beginning. But, following a number of events over which he felt he had little control, Andy felt compelled to separate from Alice and Jessica when Jessica was three and a half. They tried to work out a life that would satisfy all of them, but one year later Alice and Andy reluctantly filed for divorce.

Decision Making, Problem-Solving Effectiveness, and Marital Satisfaction

We wanted to know more about the couple relationships of the partners in each of our four categories—how they fared in solving more general problems during pregnancy, and how their satisfaction with marriage changed over the next two years as they began to live with the results of their decision. First, we asked partners to choose a recent problem or disagreement and (on separate questionnaires) to explain how they tried to solve it, how they felt about that attempt, and whether they felt satisfied with the outcome. Among the examples they reported, one partner got upset with the other for not turning off the lights when leaving a room; one couple had a conflict about whether the wife should return to work; another argued repeatedly about who should take out the garbage; one spouse got irritated with the other for making an illegal U-turn; and another couple had a misunderstanding about whether one had given the other an unambiguous invitation to make love.

We constructed an overall measure of each partner's view of their problem-solving effectiveness by having our staff members independently rate the husband's and the wife's answers to each question.[1] Our premise was that partners who were able to maintain their individual points of view, understand their partners' points of view, and feel satisfied with the outcome of the discussion would feel more effective as problem solvers. We found that the Yes-No couples' problem-solving effectiveness, rated from both spouses' descriptions, was significantly lower than that of the Planners, Acceptance-of-Fate couples, and Ambivalent couples. These partners' inability to reconcile their views about having a baby appears to be part of a larger difficulty: They do not have a viable process for resolving major or minor problems between them.

Next, we examined changes over time in marital satisfaction (Locke and Wallace 1959). Scores below 100 on this scale are in a "danger zone," indicating that the couple is at risk for serious marital distress. The couples with these low scores are not necessarily heading for divorce, but their descriptions of their relationships are similar to those of couples who have sought therapy for a marriage that is disturbingly conflictful or cold and distant.

As you can see from the figure on the next page, both expectant parents and nonparents describe themselves on the happier end of the continuum at the beginning of the study.* Only the Ambivalent couples who are expecting a baby are significantly less happy than couples in the other groups. Their decision to go ahead with the pregnancy in spite of their ambivalence seems to place a burden on their relationship. To our surprise, the Yes-No couples whose decision-making effectiveness ratings were low in pregnancy began the study at about the same high level of marital satisfaction as the Planners.

---

*Because the trends are so similar, we have averaged the men's and women's marital satisfaction scores in the figure.

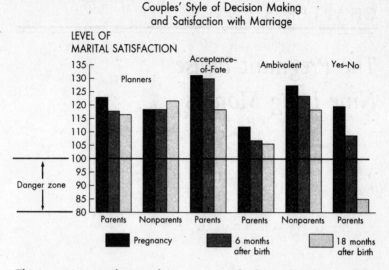

Couples' Style of Decision Making and Satisfaction with Marriage

This is consistent with our early experience with Alice and Andy. One of the reasons we were misled by their initial description of their situation is that their intense struggle, followed by Andy's agreement to go forward, had resulted in a temporarily rosy outlook on how they were doing as a couple.

The Planners, those who become parents and those who do not, show very little change in their feelings about their marriage over the two-year period. Although Acceptance-of-Fate couples show some decline in marital satisfaction, they start at such a high level that they are still satisfied when they are midway into the second year of parenthood. The Ambivalent couples who have become parents show enough of a decline in their satisfaction with marriage that their average scores are now close to the danger zone.

But it is among the Yes-No decision makers that we see the most dramatic changes. By the time they have been parents for six months, their descriptions of their marriages reveal a significant drop in satisfaction from their positive views in pregnancy. One year later, their scores plummet drastically, placing them as a group into the severely distressed range. Since this group is composed primarily of men who were very reluctant to have children, it is not surprising to find that the husbands' scores plunge even more steeply than do their wives'.

As we mentioned earlier, all seven of the couples in the kind of Yes-No deadlock that Alice and Andy described in late pregnancy had separated and then divorced by the time their first child entered elementary school. The sad irony is that when husbands give in reluctantly and resentfully to having a baby in order to preserve the marriage, the child and the marriage may ultimately be at risk.[2]

CHAPTER 3

The Pregnant Pause:
Nine Long Months

When the doctor called with the news that I was pregnant, I was so excited I wanted to run out on the street and tell everybody I met.

One night she had a vivid dream about having a baby. She woke me up, turned to me, and I knew right away that she was pregnant. The whole thing felt like jumping off a cliff.

I felt confused—a mixture of up and down, stunned, in a daze, really.

When the test results came back positive, my reaction was, "Oh no, this can't happen now!"

These variations on a theme remind us that the enthusiastic Planners, the pleasantly surprised or acquiescent Acceptance-of-Fate partners, the dragging-their-feet Ambivalent couples, and the battling Yes-No spouses have traveled very different paths to the milestone of their first pregnancy. We first meet with couples in their sixth or seventh month of pregnancy, some time after their initial reactions of delight, surprise, resignation, or shock in finding out they are going to become parents have settled down. They typically have one of three pictures of pregnancy: They see it as a time of dreadful illness, as a period of refuge, or as a simple inconvenience.

Peggy, twenty-four, and Bill, twenty-seven, described themselves in the last chapter as ambivalent about their decision to have a family. As she talks about how the pregnancy has been going, Peggy's vivid pictures seem to be framed by her dark hair and vibrant eyes.

PEGGY: Well, I'm nauseous, weepy, irritable, and exhausted from making five middle-of-the-night trips to the bathroom. I limp through my day in a fog, and I seem to shift unpredictably from total optimism to buckets of tears without knowing why. I feel more and more dependent on Bill for support. Some of my old worries have come back to haunt me, and they are being joined by some new ones. Other than that, it's been terrific!

BILL: For a while it was scary. Lately the worst parts have tapered off a little, but I'm still worried.

Like medical doctors and some psychiatrists, Peggy and Bill focus on Peggy's debilitating physical and psychological symptoms.

Beth and Paul, the Planner couple with a very positive relationship whom we also introduced in chapter 2, are both thirty-four. They had timed it so that Beth would give birth in the summer, enabling her to return, part-time, to her job as a high school drama coach in the fall. Beth looks radiant when we first meet with her and Paul in their cozy living room. Her hand on her swelling belly, she sways to and fro in the rocker, the picture of health, serenity, and inner confidence.

BETH: There's really no way to describe it. I feel this awe at the magic of this child growing inside me.

PAUL: What about the times that you sit there and worry about what kind of mother you'll be?

BETH: Sometimes I do worry, but mostly I'm just wrapped up in a haze. Nothing else in the world seems important anymore, except you and me and this baby of ours.

In contrast with the medical view, some sociologists and a few psychoanalysts romanticize pregnancy as a protective cocoon in which a woman takes refuge for nine months until she emerges as a mother. Even though pregnancy may raise internal psychological issues and concerns, it is viewed as a time in which the mother, and sometimes the father, focus only on themselves, each other, and the baby.

Sonia and Eduardo are also Planners. From large Hispanic families, they both knew from the beginning that they wanted children. When we meet them, they appear to be taking everything in their stride. Sonia is twenty-four, an energetic woman who works in a small insurance firm. She has so much to accomplish in the next month, she can barely sit still for the interview. Eduardo, twenty-six, is very involved in his job as a technician in a medical laboratory.

SONIA: The pregnancy has been just great. It disrupted my work schedule this week, but not much else. I'm having a lot of fun with it. We went to Japan during my third month. I had to finish writing a report while I was over there, but the only thing that bothered me was the smells. And then, when I was six months pregnant, Eduardo and I went on a two-week hike in the Sierras. That was hard. I wouldn't do it again. But I haven't let the pregnancy stop me from doing anything I really want to do.

EDUARDO: I wanted to plan a camping trip before it turns too cold, but the doctor told us to forget it. I guess we'll just have to find some other weekend adventure so that we can have some fun together before we settle down with the baby.

In this "no big deal" view, pregnancy is normalized to the point of seeming no more than a minor inconvenience for a woman or a couple who lead an active and complex life.

We might be tempted to think of pregnancy as a medical condition when we are talking with Peggy. The thought would hardly cross our minds when talking to Beth and Sonia. The issue is not simply that some women are relatively symptom-free, while others are physically debilitated. As we ask couples entering the third trimester of pregnancy how it has been so far, we are struck by a contradiction between what they report as the most challenging or affecting aspects of pregnancy and the issues to which doctors, hospitals, and childbirth educators direct most of their attention. Expectant parents talk primarily about the psychological and emotional changes they are experiencing and about what is happening to their relationships with the people who are important to them. Doctors and childbirth educators focus primarily on the physical, physiological, and medical aspects of pregnancy and delivery, paying attention to women's emotional reactions only when they are unpredictable or disruptive.

In this chapter we discuss the journey to parenthood, beginning with the physical changes in individual women, and men, during pregnancy and showing that there is much room for disputing the assumption that pregnancy should be considered first and foremost a medical condition. Next, we examine how women's and men's physical and psychological changes play out in the couple's relationship. We then show how pregnancy creates new issues in the relationships between the new parents and their own parents, as well as in their alliances with co-workers and friends. In a final section we summarize how all of these shifts lead to some uneasiness as couples prepare for labor, delivery, and the reality of becoming parents.

Physical Changes in Women—And Men

The typical regime of prenatal care, including regular visits to the doctor and giving birth in a hospital rather than at home, is based on the beliefs that pregnant women need special care and may be at risk for becoming ill during pregnancy, and that preventive care and medical treatment by experts will result in better health for mothers and their babies. Should pregnant women be treated as potentially ill? All of them will undergo rapid changes in weight, size, shape, and hormone-endocrinological balance. One of the most familiar symptoms is nausea, or "morning sickness," which fortunately tends to decrease after the first three months. But backache, indigestion, tiredness, shortness of breath, painful intercourse, swollen ankles, and leg cramps tend to increase as the pregnancy progresses, especially in the last three months.

About half of the expectant mothers we interviewed in the last trimester of pregnancy said, like Beth and Sonia, that it was going very well. They reported few troubling symptoms, even in the first trimester. Data from a detailed British study by Eva Zajicek (1981) and a comprehensive American study by Doris Entwisle and Susan Doering (1981) reinforce the need to rethink pregnancy stereotypes. The women in Zajicek's study, in their seventh month of pregnancy, reported relatively mild symptoms: indigestion (43 percent), lack of energy (68 percent), breathlessness (46 percent), leg cramps (68 percent), backache (48 percent), tired legs (55 percent), and more urgent urination (66 percent). "Many other pregnancy symptoms were conspicuous by their infrequency, and even with the most common symptoms, it was clear that not all women were affected" (Zajicek 1981, p. 45).

A similar conclusion can be drawn from Entwisle and Doering's study of pregnant women in Maryland. Only about half of them experienced frequent nausea or vomiting in the first three months, allegedly a "certain" symptom of pregnancy. It seems clear that a substantial number of women do not fit the picture of pregnancy as a time of heightened physical distress. Those who do, though, suffer a range of severe, often unexpected symptoms.

PEGGY: Before I even knew for sure that I was pregnant, my breasts were sore as hell, I spent mornings for two weeks with my head in the toilet, and my joints hurt so much I couldn't walk downstairs. One day I woke up and said to myself, "Either I'm dying or I'm pregnant."

BILL: It felt like a little bit of both. I read that women are supposed to be sick in the first three months or so, but then they are supposed to get better. I guess Peggy hasn't been reading the same books. I'd say she's still feeling lousy at least part of every day, and she's in her seventh month.

Many self-help books on pregnancy imply that debilitating symptoms are almost universal. One unfortunate consequence of presenting pregnancy in this light is that women who feel well during their pregnancies may begin to worry that they are abnormal. Beth said that she kept phoning her obstetrician: "I wasn't getting any of those symptoms I was supposed to. I kept wondering whether maybe something had gone wrong inside."

In the traditional medical view of pregnancy, the woman goes for regular medical checkups while her partner, who is also expecting a baby and has concerns of his own, waits outside the door. Our study and others, however, reveal that men undergo physical changes in pregnancy too. A number of studies, primarily by English anthropologists, of what is called the *couvade* syndrome document the fact that in some non-Western, nonindustrialized cultures, fathers-to-be experience many of the same physical symptoms as their pregnant spouses do, sometimes to an even more extreme and incapacitating degree (Trethowan and Conlan 1965). While waiting for their babies to be born, these men retire to bed with unremitting nausea and incapacitating back problems, demand to be looked after, and otherwise raise an emotional fuss during the last months of their wives' pregnancies. Some American studies (Curtis 1955; Shereshefsky and Yarrow 1973) suggest that this phenomenon may be part of our culture as well, although there is no specific information on how many men may have such dramatic reactions to their wives' pregnancies.

In our study, men reported gaining weight, growing beards, losing weight, shaving beards, nursing obscure injuries, and other physical and behavioral changes. Some are unconscious of the parallels with their wives' symptoms, but others are quite aware of them. After Beth describes to us the changes that have taken place in her body over the last few months, Paul observes that he underwent "pregnant fathers' weight gain": "It's really funny. Now Beth's eating more than me, and I usually eat a lot. I guess I'm just trying to keep up."

As much as we pushed couples for detail, though, talk about physical symptoms usually ended quickly, while talk about psychological and relationship changes could have gone on long into the night. Perhaps the overshadowing of the physical aspects of pregnancy stemmed from the fact that our first meetings with couples took place after many of the physical surprises had already occurred. We do not think that this is the case, but more detailed psychological studies of pregnancy are needed to settle the matter. Based on our own interviews, and those of the other researchers we mentioned, we conclude that the physical changes associated with pregnancy function as a backdrop against which both spouses' feelings about themselves and each other are played out.

Psychological Changes

What is it about pregnancy that raises the risk of stormy weather for the couple? The men and women we spoke to talked about many issues, but there are five that topped their lists:

Changes in each partner's emotional life are not easy to talk about.

Changes in their sexual relationship leave them feeling vulnerable as a couple.

Partners tend not to share their expectations about the next steps of their journey; when they get to their destination, they are caught off guard by their different pictures of what they thought it would be like.

Both men and women anticipate a much more equal division of household chores and taking care of the baby than actually happens.

As the baby becomes more and more of a reality for both spouses, their balance of independence and interdependence as a couple begins to shift.

These issues become a problem for couples when they cannot find a nonaccusatory way of talking to each other about what they think is happening. Peggy and Bill, for example, cannot avoid blaming each other for their distress. She feels that his poor business decisions have forced him to work extra hours now, just when she could use his help getting the baby's room ready. If she were "the least bit encouraging" about his business, Bill claims, he wouldn't feel that he has to work so late every night.

Pregnancy heightens certain personal issues for men and women, some of which spill over into their relationship as a couple. Emotional changes can exact a particularly high toll. The stereotype of a pregnant woman's emotional state has her riding a rollercoaster that might veer out of control at any moment without warning. We can see from our brief portraits of Peggy, Beth, and Sonia that a more elaborate and differentiated set of metaphors is needed to cover a range of reactions, from virtually no change in women's emotional lives to dramatic mood swings during the course of a day.

WOMEN'S MOODS AND CONCERNS

Researchers attribute pregnant women's moods mostly to how they are feeling physically and psychologically as expectant mothers. But without similar studies of women at other stages of life, we do not know whether we might discover the same range of emotions, for example, in women who have just divorced, who have gone to back to work after many years at home, or whose children have just left the nest.

The common belief is that women's emotional states in pregnancy are a product of hormonal changes. Mary Brown Parlee (1973), in an early extensive review of studies that look for links between women's hormones and mood during the menstrual cycle, in fact failed to find a correspondence between individual differences in women's hormone levels and differences in their emotional states. In a similar vein, P. N. Nott and his colleagues (1976) found no systematic connections between women's pre- and postbirth hormone levels and their moods in early parenthood.

We feel that dismissing pregnant women's mood changes as attributable to "hormones" does them a disservice. Though not focused on pregnancy, findings in new studies by psychologists and endocrinologists suggest that we would do better in trying to understand pregnant women's emotional experiences by looking at the interaction between physiological and psychological reactions. For example, Jason Dura and Janice Kiecolt-Glazer (1991) have shown that during a stressful major life transition like divorce, hormone levels are altered and the immune system functions less effectively, with the result that divorcing and newly divorced women have an increased chance of becoming physically ill. Dura and Kiecolt-Glazer believe that these effects are circular: Psychological stress affects biological functioning, and biological disruptions increase psychological stress.

Most of the third-trimester women we spoke to (about three in five) said they had been worried about the viability of the fetus in the early stages of pregnancy. Understandably, these fears are especially strong in women who have had a miscarriage, who tend to resist becoming involved in the pregnancy until they are well beyond the time when miscarriage occurred in the earlier pregnancy.

By the second trimester, feeling the baby kick and move calms some of the fears, makes the baby seem more real, and leaves both parents feeling excited. During the third trimester, with the fetus's increased size and movement, women's focus shifts (or shifts back) to concerns about whether the baby will be healthy when it is born. Peggy worried about whether her baby would be normal and, if not, how she and Bill would deal with a retarded or deformed child. Some women are particularly haunted by movies and books featuring a child with a birth defect or a life-threatening illness; those images stay with them for a long time.

Another source of anxiety for pregnant women lies in worrying whether they will be good enough mothers. About one-third of the women in our study expressed such concerns. A few worried consciously or unconsciously about whether they would love their child as much as they feel parents ought to. One mother-to-be, Helen, said that her insecurity about being a parent came out while she was asleep: "I keep dreaming that I put the baby in a drawer and then forget about it."

In the late stages of pregnancy, most women report feeling less concern about the health implications of their weight gain (a big early worry) and less bothered by their lack of interest in sex. Their new concerns center on how they will cope with labor and delivery. Despite all the information from childbirth classes, it is not uncommon for a woman to become preoccupied briefly with the thought that she will not know what to do when the time comes: Will I know if my water breaks? What if I'm at work when I go into labor? How will I know when it's time to go to the hospital?

One of our most important discoveries was that couples who grapple with their concerns and the issues behind them seem to do better than those who ignore or deny their uneasy feelings. Whether the pregnancy is unexpected or money is a problem or there is general nervousness about the major change to come, some anxiety during pregnancy can be adaptive (Leifer

1980; Grossman et al. 1980). Husbands and wives who feel no trepidation about bringing a baby home may be in for quite a jolt.*

Beth, the quiet dreamer, and Sonia, who never let the pregnancy interfere with her active life, had some concerns about themselves, the baby, and their family. At the same time, like most expectant mothers (Feldman and Nash 1984; Leifer 1980; Grossman et al. 1980), they felt very positive about their lives and optimistic about the future. Even Peggy took care to set the record straight, emphasizing to us that despite her complaints she was sure it would be worth all the trouble.

MEN'S MOODS AND CONCERNS

About fifty years ago, psychoanalysts became interested in men's inner life during their wives' pregnancy. They focused on emotions at the extremes: depressive reactions, psychosis, mental illness (Zilboorg 1931; Towne and Afterman 1955; Wainwright 1966). As investigators became more systematic and turned to samples of men who were not patients, the picture of men's adaptation to pregnancy brightened (Benedek 1959, 1970; H. Osofsky 1982; Osofsky and Osofsky 1984; Parens 1975). But we still know little about men's emotional experience over the course of the pregnancy. Our impression from our interviews is that a majority of expectant fathers feel that they are doing very well. Some point to positive changes in themselves. Doug told us he seemed to have "mellowed out a little bit. I don't get quite as angry. I give up on my little annoyances a lot faster than I used to—and I think that Josie will vouch for me there." On the other hand, most men acknowledge worries about having the major responsibility of making enough money to support their families—especially during the period when their wives will not be bringing home a salary.

Al is twenty-nine and has been married for two years to Helen, twenty-three. Each of them had chosen to work part-time at a succession of jobs so that they would be free to pick up and travel at a moment's notice. This plan worked well for them until Helen became pregnant, which was an unexpected pleasure. After recounting with some nostalgia their footloose life before the pregnancy, Al becomes serious and determined as he explains: "I need to get my act together here. I've been goofing around with any old job, so that *I* can take time off when I want to and *we* can be spontaneous with

---

*Irving Janis (1958) conducted an intriguing study of patients who were about to undergo surgery in order to understand what people do with their concerns and fears when they are about to experience a stressful event. He found that men and women who "do the work of worrying" before they face the stress of hospitalization actually cope better and have smoother recoveries than people who experience no concerns before the event. This, of course, is one of the notions behind the couples group intervention in our study. By creating a setting in which we can encourage men and women to anticipate how they will handle some of the inevitable stress of having a newborn—at the same time trying to stay in touch as a couple—we hope to help them do some of the work of worrying before the inevitable 3:00 A.M. cries wake them to discover that they have totally different ideas about how to respond.

our travel plans. But now I've got to find something solid and steady. I hope it's not too late."

Like the women, some men worry about being adequate parents. Sometimes their fantasies extend their worries many years into the future:

> AL: There's going to be this other person coming into my life. And things are going to have to change. At first I felt resentment about that. I took a while to sort it out. Today we met the doctor who will be our child's pediatrician, and we were filling out forms at her office. I felt a jolt when I had to fill in the line that said, "Father's name." I had all these visions about report cards and parental problems and permission forms and all these things—and *I'm* going to be the one signing where it says "Father"!

About 15 percent of the men in our study expressed deep concern during their wives' pregnancies. Paul stressed how vulnerable he and Beth felt. Once the pregnancy was under way, there was nothing more they could do: "It's all out of our control." Andy, discussed in chapter 2, had more specific anxieties:

> ANDY: I went through about three months of heavy-duty worrying. I think about two issues: One is the responsibility issue, since Alice won't be working while the baby is young; the other is more of a selfish thing. Things are hitting me deeply. I keep thinking, "I'm a dying creature." Ideas about my own dying have really taken hold.

Recall that Andy and Alice had strong disagreements about whether to continue the pregnancy, which perhaps magnified his brooding about mortality and the darker side of life.

The men in our study were more worried than their wives about certain issues, especially about their wives' aches and pains. In our pregnancy interviews, few men broached their concern about the temptation to be unfaithful. We learned later that several had succumbed.* Both husbands and wives are concerned about the intactness and well-being of the baby during pregnancy, but wives are more concerned about the emotional climate of the family and their adequacy as mothers while husbands more often worry about the economic security of the family. The difference in their concerns is not usually what provokes tension for the couple during pregnancy; rather, it is

---

*In three of the seventy-two couples in our study who were having a baby, the husband had an extramarital affair. In one case, the wife discovered the other relationship early on, discussed it extensively with her husband, and the marriage continued. In the second case, the wife discovered in the first year of their baby's life that her husband had been having an extended affair. They separated and then divorced before the baby was two. A third couple reported that they had agreed to an "open relationship" in which both of them were free to have other sexual partners. This couple stayed together for some years, but were divorced by the time their child entered kindergarten.

the fact that husbands are much less willing than their wives to talk about what worries either of them.

Men are especially reluctant to raise a topic they think may lead to conflict or distress—their own, their wives', or both (Ball 1984; Gottman and Levenson 1989). Although men admitted having worries once they became comfortable talking to us, their wives said that their husbands rarely talked about these concerns to them spontaneously. When we asked Bill and Peggy what "pictures" they had of labor and delivery, for example, it went like this:

> BILL: I'll be there, of course, and it'll be fine. Well, actually, I'm concerned that when Peggy really gets into her pain, I'll find that it's worse than I can handle. And I have this big fear that I'm going to be grossed out by the physicalness of it. I wonder if men ever faint in the delivery room?
>
> PEGGY: Bill, you're so gung-ho in our Lamaze class, I had no idea that you were feeling that way. How come you didn't tell me?

Most of the men we talked to seemed to think there are "rules" for men in relationships with women. Especially when their partners are anxious, men feel that their task is to be calm, strong, and reassuring. Mentioning their own worries, they believe, will increase their wives' distress and reveal themselves as vulnerable at a time when their wives need them to be strong. Men's reluctance to talk about their worries and their motivation to stay calm at all costs create two problems: First, they deprive men of a chance to express their feelings and to learn from others that their fears are understandable and often experienced by others; and second, they prevent women from discovering that their worries are understood and shared by their mates.

Finally, when men keep their worries hidden, they stop talking to their wives about many of the things that matter to them. If one partner does raise a concern, and the other reacts immediately with a denial, a defense, or a more pressing concern of his own, many topics of conversation go undiscussed because they are not considered serious problems. The cost of protecting against upset can be silence or safe, but dull, conversations (Wile 1988). Occasionally, though, even the most vigilant attempts to keep things on an even keel give way to outbursts that are surprising in their intensity. Thus men's attempts to protect their wives—and themselves—from emotions that might stir things up can contribute instead to increased tension and distance, both within and between the partners:

> PEGGY: Bill and I got into a battle about having my mother come when the baby is born. I started to worry about where the baby would sleep when my mother and sister come, but I didn't want to raise it because I know how Bill feels about my mother. Then, one day, it was really on my mind so I mentioned it casually. Bill immediately began saying that it was silly to worry since the baby wasn't even born yet. Then he started suggesting that they should stay in a hotel in town. I got furious, more than

the situation warranted, I think. I was worried about the baby, but I didn't want my family to stay somewhere else. I assumed that I, or we, could eventually figure out an alternative. I just didn't want to bottle it up anymore. We both got really upset until I told him that I didn't want him to *solve* the problem, I just wanted him to let me *talk* to him about it.

BILL: I'm not very good at that. As soon as Peg gets upset, I go into action to try to make her feel better, and she always ends up shouting at me! She never gives me credit for the fact that I am only trying to help.

Not surprisingly, the couples who fare best during these emotional forays are those who can listen sympathetically to each other, without thinking they must talk the other out of his or her worry or come up with a solution immediately.

SEXUALITY

The physical and emotional changes that take place during pregnancy can have a direct effect on a couple's feelings of intimacy. The woman's (and, in minor ways, sometimes the man's) body is undergoing radical changes in size, shape, and maneuverability. "Leftovers" from the way couples decided about whether and when to have a baby inevitably color their perceptions and feelings about themselves and each other. And changes in a couple's sex life can become problematic when one or both partners feel that they cannot discuss them.

Expectant mothers, even those who suffer from physical symptoms, often describe a sense of awe and power in discovering what their bodies can do.

SONIA: I feel a little unattractive and lumpy right now. But, when I'm by myself, I find what's happening to my body fascinating.

BETH: I'm surprised to find what a miracle bodies are. I'm blown away about what's going on and about how it all works. I just can't get over it.

Approximately 25 percent of the pregnant women in our study said that they felt uneasy about their appearance: "awkward," "bloated," "like a blimp." The physical changes of pregnancy and their consequences for how women look and move may be the stuff of cartoons and comedies, but to women they are not amusing. A few, like Peggy, find their swelling bodies deeply disturbing:

PEGGY: I feel fat, ugly, and gross. My self-concept changes from mood to mood. I don't feel good about myself physically and I don't want anyone to look at me—even Bill most of the time. I am more introverted for physical reasons. I still want to talk to people and be part of things, but I really don't want to be seen.

Most of the husbands were supportive, and some were truly proud, of the changes in their wives' bodies as the pregnancy progressed. They were pleased by what they saw and by what their wives' full bodies signified. Eduardo watches his wife maneuver gracefully into a chair during our interview. "The great painters," he says, "tried to show the beauty of a pregnant woman, but when I look at Sonia, I feel they didn't do it justice." Occasionally, though, a husband made a sharp comment about his wife's weight gain. Since, especially in recent decades, women and men have been conditioned to regard thin women as pleasing and desirable, the lumbering expectant mother, and sometimes her partner, may find that her swelling body takes some getting used to. A critical father-to-be can make his pregnant wife very uneasy about her changing shape and size. This is one of those sensitive issues that couples don't talk much about, but their uncomfortable feelings can permeate the atmosphere between them and turn off one or both spouses sexually.

As they look back on it from the sixth or seventh month of pregnancy, couples tend to report a loss of sexual interest and activity during the first three months of pregnancy, an increase in interest in the middle three months, and another, greater loss of interest and activity as they enter the home stretch. They give several reasons for the slow down, or stopping altogether, of their sexual activity. The woman's general physical discomfort and fatigue are mentioned most often, followed by pain or feelings of physical awkwardness. Some men and women are fearful of hurting the baby or stimulating contractions. Men, more than women, feel some psychological inhibitions about physical intimacy with their pregnant wives; some say they "just don't feel like it" or that making love seems awkward "now that she's a mother."

Spouses' feelings about shifts in their relationship before and during pregnancy affect their sex life more often than changes in their sex life affect their relationship. We can hear in the tone of Peggy's and Bill's remarks that they are having a difficult time with the pregnancy and with each other. Their ambivalence about becoming pregnant may be contributing to their sexual difficulties now:

PEGGY: After a long time discussing it, going back and forth, we had been trying to get pregnant for about a year. We had a lot of false alarms. And every month we had to "re-choose." Were we still going to do it? Should we change our minds? It was hell.

BILL: So, the last time, we "unchose." We said no. And then it showed up. Peggy was pregnant, and it was very scary for me. I thought, "Oh my God, I don't know if this is exactly what I had in mind."

PEGGY: Now, the embarrassing part—I'm not sure I want to say this, but it's important. Terrible, but important. Sexuality simply dropped out. The first few months I was *so* nauseous and so tired that I couldn't be bothered. I was probably so nasty that Bill wasn't even interested. My breasts hurt. I was uncomfortable. Sleeping in the same bed with Bill was just horrible. And after that I was embarrassed—about how I looked and how I was shaped.

Now I'm not so embarrassed, but it's not the same. I've had this zillion-year legacy: Mom's aren't sexual, and now I'm a mom, so I'm not supposed to be interested in sex. I have fears that it's going to be like that forever. I'm never going to be a sexual being again, which is a little terrifying, I must say.

BILL: I'm embarrassed too, but I do want to talk about it. We've had a few nice times in bed in the last six or seven months, but only a few. I mean, it's so many things. First, we just couldn't do it after we found out she was pregnant. I think it was the unchoosing part, and the shock. Then I was withdrawn, out the door to work early every morning and staying late at the end of the day. My business has really been in a mess. In the last month or two, as we've gotten used to it, I really feel that there's nothing in the way. And yet, we don't do it. I'm walking around with the idea that many couples have a great sex life in pregnancy, but maybe I'm just making it up.

Very few of the couples spontaneously told us that they were having serious difficulties in their sexual relationships during pregnancy. Many others were probably experiencing sexual problems but did not want to mention it. Significantly, among the couples who did discuss lack of sex, the men were more unhappy about their work than were other men in the study, and the women had the most negative images of their bodies in late pregnancy.

It seems to us that it is often their perception of awkwardness rather than actual physical pain or discomfort that leads to much of the diminished lovemaking in the last months of pregnancy. We hear repeatedly how embarrassing it is for most partners to talk about what they long for, what they worry about, and what they experience in this intimate aspect of their relationship.

We have learned that most couples seem to have an either/or view of sex in pregnancy: Either they are making love as they did before the pregnancy began, or they are abstaining altogether. Many couples were having difficulty finding ways to touch, snuggle, or please each other without necessarily engaging in intercourse. Both men and women told us that they hesitated to make affectionate overtures if they were not sure they were ready to progress to intercourse. The reasoning goes something like this: "If he responds positively to my hug, and reads it as an invitation to make love, I'm afraid that I may not be ready to be aroused. He could see my pulling back as rejection, so it's probably safer for me not to begin in the first place." It is very common for partners to be out of sync in this way, but the problem is intensified because almost none of them feel they can talk about it.

And if they cannot talk about these ambivalent or uncomfortable feelings, they risk moving physically and psychologically farther apart at a time when mutual nurturance and support are especially needed. The couples who do find ways to stay in touch, physically and emotionally, seem much more relaxed about their relationship in the late months of pregnancy, but they are clearly in the minority.

UNSHARED EXPECTATIONS

Couples tell us that they spend a great deal of time before they become pregnant discussing their expectations about how life with a child will be, but a surprisingly large number seem to avoid the topic altogether as their due dates draw closer. Some, like Bill and Peggy, can give detailed fantasies about how they think labor and delivery will go, but when we ask if they have pictured the time when they will first bring the baby home, more than half of the couples look at us blankly.

After the birth of the baby, many partners are surprised to find that they differ on some of their basic ideas about the early phases of family life. Joan and Rob described in one of our couples groups the events around the birth of their son, Chuckie, as he lay quietly in a car seat in front of them:

> JOAN: I had this picture. We would come home from the hospital, and my mom would be there and Dan and Ellen, our neighbors, and my sister Miriam. So, Chuckie's just been born and it's gone really well. I didn't have any anesthetic. I'm tired but wide awake. And Rob is going off to make some of the first phone calls. And I suggest that he invite everybody over. When I told him about what I had pictured that's when we had our first after-baby blowup.
>
> ROB: It still gets me mad just to think of it. All I wanted was to get Joan out of the hospital with all the nurses and orderlies and noise, and bring Chuckie into our bedroom and quietly welcome him home—just our new little family together. And I find out that Joan wants the whole world to be there when we arrive!

It seems not to have occurred to Joan and Rob that they might have discussed their pictures of what would happen after the baby was born *before* Joan went into labor. By encouraging spouses in the couples groups to explore some of these before and after pictures, we wanted to help them anticipate some of the tricky issues that catch most new parents off guard: Should we invite our parents to visit right after the baby is born? Do you pick up a baby whenever she cries, or let her cry for a while if she is fed and dry? What happens if one of us changes our feelings about when the new mother will go back to work? How will we make time for our relationship after the baby is born? Even the most compatible spouses can turn out to have diametrically opposed inclinations on these issues. Since they will be particularly difficult to resolve over the wail of a fussy infant at the end of a busy day, a few tranquil conversations before the baby comes home would be invaluable.

One sign of the successful transition between before and after, we found, is in the connection between how a couple works together to manage the household and prepare for the baby and the level of intimacy they are able to establish in their relationship.

PAUL: The pregnancy has been such a moving experience for me. I feel really committed to Beth and to being a parent with her.

BETH: Certain things that have been issues between us, like sex, have somehow gotten tabled. But I feel a lot of closeness, especially since we started working on the baby's room. And some feelings—like, "Oh my God, if we don't work this out tonight it'll be the end of the world"—seem to be a thing of the past.

PAUL: For me it doesn't feel like our issues are taking a back seat, it feels like they're in perspective. It also seems like we've had to make some heavy decisions. Say about things like money. When we first got married we had separate checking accounts. And separate friends. As we draw closer to having this baby, there is some merging going on. And she's been willing to say to me, "You know, money is not *your* problem. It's *our* problem." I feel like she made it really much easier for me.

BETH: Household stuff, though, has always been pretty easy, but even that's going better. Paul is phenomenal about doing a lot around the house. I think it's been a little more balanced lately. He's been doing all the shopping, and some of the cooking, because I had zero energy, and if someone hadn't put food in front of me, I wouldn't have eaten

PAUL: And the two of us have spent days and days building shelves in the baby's room and getting all the things we need to have it ready.

Paul and Beth's pattern of doing more household tasks together as the pregnancy progresses may be common (Goldberg, Michaels, and Lamb 1985). As we will see in chapter 5, however, their more equal participation in the division of family labor does not tend to continue after the baby comes—and this, too, has implications for how the spouses feel about their overall relationship.

It may be easier to see the connection between intimacy and how household tasks are arranged and carried out by listening to a couple whose debate over who does what is heated. Sharon, whom we met while she was waiting for the results of her home pregnancy test, was worried about Daniel's willingness to do his part in preparing for the baby:

SHARON: It's maddening. I asked him to paint the cupboards in the baby's room. He said he would do it, but weeks went by and nothing happened. I tried not to nag.

DANIEL: Not successfully.

SHARON: Well, I needed to know *if* you'd do it and *when* you'd do it. If you'd just been up front with me and said no, I'd have hired someone or done it myself.

DANIEL: And been angry for a month.

SHARON [*ignoring Daniel's last remark*]: So, one day I come home after visiting my father, who's been sick, and Daniel's painted all the cup-boards—purple! It doesn't go with anything in the room.

DANIEL: It's a bright color, one a baby would like. And I got it done two months before the baby is due. I guess I just can't win with her.

This is not an unusual conversation between parents getting ready for the baby's arrival. The sticking points arise not only around whether someone will do something, but when and how it will get done. Each partner has a different set of priorities, a different timetable, and a different picture of what the end product should look like. The fact that both partners might also be feeling some anxiety about becoming parents does not enter the discussion. This means that it is unlikely that one spouse will think to say to the other, "You know, I didn't mean to fly off the handle about that. I guess I'm actually a little nervous about just what it will be like when the baby comes. I don't want our life together to change totally." Sharon and Daniel might have been able to avoid their fight if they had taken the time to discuss their explicit expectations or pictures about painting the baby's room before Daniel bought the paint. As reasonable as it seems, this kind of discussion is apparently rare.

DEPENDENCE, INDEPENDENCE, AND INTERDEPENDENCE

In dealing with their emotions, their sexual relationships, their expectations, and the nitty-gritty of who does the work of preparing for the baby, couples are grappling with the issues of staying in touch with each other while sometimes being pulled in different directions. Paul and Beth's description of their increasing closeness during pregnancy is echoed by more than half of our sample. As Al put it, "I no longer think of myself as just me, but as us." Although many partners enjoy this increased sense of closeness, some are worried about the accompanying feelings of greater dependency. Al's wife, Helen, admits that "we depend on each other almost totally. I wonder if it's good. Our friends don't do this." When she mentions the possibility of ever losing Al, she begins to cry.

Although the partners may not recognize it, a pregnancy highlights a challenge that is central to any couple relationship: how to balance both partners' individuality or autonomy *and* enough mutuality or "coupleness" to satisfy both of them. Most couples work on this balance throughout their married lives, but pregnancy brings it into bold relief. Both partners are about to add a major new role to their identities as adults, taking a step forward in their individual lives and in their life as a couple. At the same time, the arrival of the baby demands some collaborative work toward the mutual goal of how to nurture a child and create a family.

Many expectant parents struggle with this conflict as though they had to choose between individuality and coupleness. Because this struggle is mostly unconscious, new parents rarely discuss the possibility that more interdepen-dence—some dependence on each other and some independence for each spouse—may make it possible for them to feel secure as individuals and as a couple during the family-making period.

Making, Changing, and Breaking Connections Across the Generations

Pregnancy galvanizes virtually every expectant parent to make connections with their own parents and their in-laws. Regardless of the quality of relationships between the generations, the couple's parents are usually the first to be told about the pregnancy. By the time the receivers are put down, the impending grandchild has begun to alter the relationships among the three families. The news is often received with delight and excitement, but their parents' reactions do not always match what the expectant couple had been hoping for. Joan told us that her mother was thrilled—she rushed right out that day and bought baby furniture. Joan and Rob wished she had consulted them about what kind of furniture they wanted, but they were touched by her reaction. James's mother reacted positively, too—at first: "But then she told Cindy she'd have to give up her work for fifteen years, followed by, 'You're messing up my son's life. Now he won't be able to continue his education.' "

The initial reactions of these expectant grandmothers have more to do with their own dreams than with their children's needs. In time, Joan would feel that she and Rob had to impress upon her mother their need to make the baby theirs. In this important phase, already-grown children must learn to differentiate from their parents once again. James's mother got past her negative reaction to the idea of her son becoming a father, and in fact made frequent visits to baby-sit for her new grandson, giving her son and daughter-in-law some time on their own.

Observing these generational dances as we ourselves approach this time of life has helped us to understand why becoming a grandparent can be a difficult adjustment. The timing is never under the grandparents' control, and it can catch them at a point where they are just beginning to experience a new freedom (Lowe 1991). Although many grandparents may be disequilibrated by the news, the initial shock is often followed by the pleasant realization that a new phase of their development is being ushered in (Tinsley and Parke 1988).

As the grandparent generation of the family begins to redefine their place in the extended family, the expectant parents often find that they are being treated differently by their parents and relatives:

JOAN: After we told my family, they suddenly began to include me in their discussions of the "family secrets." At Thanksgiving, we stayed at the "big table" after dinner, talking with my parents and aunts and uncles, while my sisters, who don't have children, went off with the little kids. I found out that Aunt Maude was married three times before she had

a child with Uncle Harry, and all kinds of other things I ha
known.

The pregnancy also stimulates the expectant parents' memories of their
childhoods. They often relive both old joys and sorrows, resolving to recreate
their early positive memories and to avoid a repetition of the painful experiences with their children.

It was the men in our study who talked most earnestly about doing things
differently. The traditional families these couples grew up in seemed almost
invariably to include a father who was away at work, and somewhat removed
even when he was home. In interview after interview, almost every expectant
father told us of his determination to have more of a presence with his sons
and daughters than his father had with him. This is what men look forward
to about having a baby, and it is what they worry about while they are
waiting:

EDUARDO: My father left when I was twelve and I didn't see him for
twenty-three years. That's not going to happen to my kid.
DOUG: My dad's always felt so distant. I still have trouble talking to him
about anything that matters. My children are going to know me and be
able to talk to me about whatever's on their minds. They're not going
to have any doubt about how I feel about them.

Not all the fathers had been psychologically absent. Sometimes their positive
presence figures influentially in their son's plans:

PAUL: My close relationship with my father is what saved my mental health
growing up. Having a mother who was very ill meant that I had to really
push myself to keep going some of the time. My dad's steady encouragement told me that I was an OK kid, even when I didn't feel that
inside. I want to do that for my child.

While many expectant parents, in answer to our questions, can vividly
describe their families' typical patterns, they continue to hope that their
relationships with their parents and in-laws will change for the better. They
seem to feel that having their baby will somehow set things right—they will
feel closer as a couple, they will take on the care of their home and baby
together, and their parents will be especially warm and nurturant—even if
none of these things were so in their earlier years.

In our couples groups and our work with distressed couples, we try to
capitalize on this tendency to dream of making things better, since it can lead
to renewed attempts to connect the generations. While some couples are
disappointed, especially if their initial overtures to their parents are not well
received, those who do not give up often make some progress toward a better
relationship.

Of course, renewing relationships with parents and in-laws does not always have positive consequences or leave room for optimism. We were moved by the intensity and sadness of Henry and Anna's experience. Henry is a Muslim from Jordan whose grandfather, on his deathbed, made Henry promise that he would never marry an "infidel." Henry moved to the United States, where he went to school, met Anna, an Italian-American woman, and married her. Henry's father, who also moved to the United States, was unhappy about Henry's marriage but did not sever contact with his son. After much urging on Henry's part, his father eventually agreed to meet Anna, with whom he maintained a distant but polite relationship.

Henry and his father had never gotten along well, even at the best of times, and the relationship continued to feel strained. Several years into the marriage, Henry told his father with some trepidation that he and Anna were expecting a child. Henry's father reacted by announcing that he would no longer see Anna. Henry felt that he had to make a choice between his father and his new family. Although there was no question that Anna and the baby came first, Henry's anguish at losing contact with his father is with him every day.

While Henry and Anna's experience with his family is extreme, it highlights a theme that is found among most new parents: Pregnancy tends to intensify already existing patterns in relationships with parents and extended family members. When the relationships are reasonably good, the pregnancy tends to bring the generations closer; when the relationships are troubled, old problems can resurface and feel more complex. If this is a family that busies itself with others' business, relatives may become involved in the pregnancy as if it were theirs. If one or both of the partners' families tend to keep their distance, the expectant parents may get little or no reaction to their news.

If the reaction is positive, the arrival of a grandchild does not magically mend the intergenerational rifts, but it often sets in motion new attempts at understanding and reconciliations across the generations. Naomi Lowinsky (1990, 1992) writes about daughters' efforts to connect with their mothers or grandmothers through the stories from their "motherline"—the generations of women who carry within them the history and biology of a family. If these attempts at reconnection are successful, the grandchildren can become the beneficiaries of strong generational ties. If not, as in the case of Henry and Anna, a legacy of sadness may leave its mark on the early family-making years.

Even successfully renewed relationships between the generations during pregnancy can pose new dilemmas for expectant couples. Already dealing with many new feelings within and between them, they may confront different issues in relating to their parents. One partner may want more closeness and contact with the parents while the other can't get far enough away. Cindy didn't want to go anywhere near James's mother after the remark about his education. When she invited them to dinner the next week, James felt they would hurt her feelings if they turned her down. They went, but Cindy wished James "had the guts to tell her off."

Partners' capacity to empathize with each other's generational dilemmas may become limited as they make the transition from couple to family. Efforts to reconnect or redefine their relationships with their parents and in-laws can create one more arena in which their differences trigger conflict or withdrawal.

Changing Relationships with the World Outside the Family

Pregnancy also has an impact on the relationships with important people and institutions outside the inner family circle. Well-meaning people who would not ordinarily approach a stranger on the street suddenly feel free to pat the protruding belly of a pregnant woman and tell their own stories or offer unsolicited advice about pregnancy and babies. This is a peculiar ritual that intrudes on the privacy of the expectant parents, at the same time drawing them into the larger world of families with children. Once they announce that they are going to be fathers, men also find that neighbors and co-workers they hardly know want to share stories about their experiences with babies and children.

Expectant parents begin to notice that they experience the world around them in new ways. In our interview, Sonia mentioned her new preoccupation with violence—"the random killings and so many missing children on posters and milk cartons."

Both men and women change their relationship to work in ways that are both expected and unexpected. We have already heard about Al's determination to get his work life on track. With similar reasoning, about 10 percent of the men we spoke to changed jobs over the nine months of their wives' pregnancies, and a number of others began planning for changes they would make as their babies grew into toddlers. The expectant fathers who were not changing direction seemed to be rededicating themselves to their work. Even though virtually all of them saw their job changes as a direct response to increased responsibility for providing for their wives and children, their wives tended to see their husbands' investment in work as a form of withdrawal from them and from the family. The gulf between their perceptions only widens as women begin to disengage from their work in the end stages of the pregnancy.

All of the women we interviewed were employed or going to school when they began the pregnancy, and a majority continued to work into the ninth month. But, unlike the men, every one of them planned to take some time off after the baby was born, for periods ranging from weeks to years. So, just as they are moving back into the family to do more of the hands-on care of the baby, their husbands are getting more involved in their work. Although many women formulate their plans voluntarily, early in the pregnancy, some become concerned as the pregnancy ends about what will happen to their jobs or careers:

> ANNA: I used to think that all I wanted in life was four kids and a good vacuum cleaner. But I take my career seriously. I'm an accountant in a busy practice, and I don't know whether my clients are going to wait for me while I get settled. I'm not sure how I'm going to look after my clients, my child, and me at the same time.

In addition to different changes in their work patterns, to the surprise of the couples in our study, their relationships with friends who are not pregnant begin to shift. Couples find themselves spending much more time with recent acquaintances who are expecting babies or who have young children than with old friends who are not parents or parents-to-be. Men, and especially women, described shifts in their engagement with and disengagement from people outside the family. As women withdraw from their jobs and co-workers, their opportunities for talking with adults who may be important sources of esteem and support are reduced. Theoretically, expectant mothers who have left work have more time to visit friends, but there is so much to do in late pregnancy that women are usually too tired. Staying close to home keeps them socially and emotionally isolated.

What we are seeing, then, is an accumulation of changes in the network of relationships that expectant parents have established with their families, their co-workers, and their friends. In essence, women who are expecting a baby come to rely on their husbands for much of their adult company and support. If husbands' social contacts are also reduced, then both partners may feel more dependent on each other for companionship and emotional nurturance. If, in addition, wives begin to feel deprived by their husbands' involvement in work and husbands begin to feel hemmed in by their wives' dependency, the last trimester of pregnancy can draw partners apart emotionally rather than pulling them together to meet the challenges of a new baby.

Pregnancy as an Opportunity for Development

As expectant parents begin to integrate Father or Mother into their identities as men and women, partners and lovers, workers and students, sons and daughters, and so on, they are faced with significant shifts in their relationships to their work, their parents, their friends, and each other. At the same time, both partners are becoming preoccupied with their emerging relationships with the baby. While all this is taking place internally and interpersonally, most expectant parents are also dealing with the medical establishment, which is focusing microscopically on physical changes in the woman's body. They are on their own in managing the psychological shifts that pregnancy stimulates in them as individuals and as a couple. Our recent work is teaching us that this presents quite a challenge, even to men and women in very well functioning relationships.

Despite the inherent difficulties, the kind of disequilibrium that often accompanies this major adult transition can serve as an opportunity for personal development for both men and women. Certainly, for some, expecting a baby can evoke painful memories of difficult or neglectful relationships with their parents when they were babies or young children. For others, the reawakening of conflicts from the past leads partners to begin to work on some of their unresolved conflicts, either on their own or with professional help. In our interviews with each couple over a seven-year period, we heard many examples of new fathers and mothers who felt a new sense of confidence and maturity, often from having successfully tackled the challenges of a very stressful period. Sonia told us she felt more confident about her artistic abilities since she'd become pregnant: "Two months ago I enrolled in an art class, and I'm preparing to have a show of my drawings after the baby comes—something I've always wanted but have been too timid to arrange. I may put some of my poetry in it too. It feels like there's been a transition in me, and somehow I'm beginning to feel like I know what I'm all about."

Her husband, Eduardo, explained that after many years of thinking about his father with bitterness (he deserted the family when Eduardo was a boy), he feels his attitude changing: "Something about the prospect of being a father myself is having this strange effect on me. I haven't forgiven him, exactly, because I don't think that what he did was forgivable. But I'm kind of letting it go now. I'm going to be different with my kid. Maybe I can get on with things without constantly comparing myself to what I remember of my father."

According to Erik Erikson's theory of development (1950, 1959), we experience shifts in our sense of ourselves as we move through life and bump up against each major transition. Even if the change is one we choose and prepare for, it can throw us off balance. We can find that our usual style of coping is not adequate to meet the demands of this new stage of life, and that we do not know how to change or add to our repertoire of coping skills.

Erikson's theory suggests that active grappling with the pain and self-doubt of personal crises is necessary if real development and growth are to occur. If we cannot acknowledge our feelings of uncertainty or anxiety or distress, we are in danger of becoming stalled or fixated at our present stage of development, or in some cases of slipping back to an earlier level of functioning.

Preparing for the Birth

We may need to be reminded about the source of all this excitement, anxiety, and upheaval: A baby is about to be born. Two sets of professionals are involved in helping couples get ready for the big day: Obstetricians and family doctors monitor women's pregnancies in regular checkups, and child-birth educators offer classes for both partners to help them become more active participants in the birth process. Based on what the couples in our study have been telling us, we are concerned that both doctors and childbirth educators are leaving important things out of the preparation package.

During the months of pregnancy, as we have seen, most expectant parents spend relatively little time focusing on physical symptoms and much more time dealing with psychological changes in themselves and in their relationships. Although there are some welcome exceptions, few obstetricians and family practitioners are attuned to these issues in the women they see. Virtually none of them provides opportunities for expectant fathers to discuss their concerns, or for couples to talk about marital issues raised in the course of the pregnancy.*

There is, then, a mismatch between the medical focus of the doctors and the central concerns of their patients. A number of British sociologists, Ann Oakley foremost among them (1980, 1986), have questioned why the medical profession has been allowed to exert so much control over pregnancy and childbirth since it tends to ignore the central psychological issues. This view has led some families to rely on midwives rather than doctors. We would be reluctant to give up all of the hard-won medical advances, especially in complicated pregnancies and deliveries. But we worry that current medical practice fosters the tendency to separate the concerns of women from the concerns of men, thereby contributing to men's and women's separation from each other, a separation that grows wider, as we will see, during the early child-rearing years.

In addition to doctors' visits, an increasingly large number of couples today take part in some kind of formal childbirth preparation.† Nevertheless, many feel surprised by their experience of the delivery. In one couples group, a mother practically shouted, "Why didn't they tell us how painful it would be? That woman we saw in the Lamaze film was *smiling* through it all!"

Time and again the women we spoke to explained that the instructors in their childbirth classes were so intent on convincing them that they could control their pain during labor and delivery that those who, during the event, accepted medication felt they had let down their classmates, their teacher, and themselves. In the excruciating pain of a long or difficult labor, their husbands and doctors may have urged them to ease their suffering, but many of them felt that in succumbing to it they had "failed" at childbirth. As Terrie said, "I keep feeling that if I had just been able to hang in there a little longer, I could have made it without any drugs. Carrie was so sleepy for the first day

---

*Of the obstetrical and clinical offices we worked with in the study, only one had a family-focused preventive orientation. The two obstetricians, the nurse practitioners, and the nutritionist offered a series of evening meetings for expectant couples and time to meet with fathers during regular office hours.

†Between 50 percent and 80 percent of pregnant women in the United States now attend childbirth preparation classes, a major historical shift that has taken place in just one generation (Duncan and Markman 1988).

or so—I can't help thinking that she might have been livelier and easier to nurse if I hadn't had any medication."

The intent of childbirth preparation classes is to demedicalize and humanize the process of giving birth, and it is a welcome and successful change. But as we talked with parents, it became clear that something is missing from these classes. In their efforts to be encouraging and reassuring, instructors tend to cut off discussion of the fears and concerns that every parent-to-be experiences. Women want to know that it will hurt—a lot!—and that drugs may be of great help. Men want to talk about the possibility of suddenly feeling unable to accompany their wives into the delivery room, or of feeling faint when the birth gets under way. Providing psychological support, including recommending that obviously troubled couples seek professional help, may be one of the most effective ways for an instructor to lower men's and women's anxiety and to reduce the incidence of medical complications during labor and delivery (Grossman et al. 1980; Markman and Kadushin 1986; Nuckolls, Cassell, and Kaplan 1972).

In addition, the heavy emphasis on natural childbirth obscures the fact that, for various and controversial reasons, more than 20 percent of deliveries will be performed by cesarean section (Alexander and Entwisle 1988). The almost exclusive focus in childbirth classes on vaginal delivery means that one in five couples will be ill prepared for the physical and emotional shock of undergoing major surgery to deliver their baby.

Despite all the confusion and increased choice—hospital delivery? midwife? home birth?—couples who successfully deliver a child experience a feeling unlike any other they have known. In the new tradition of fathers' participation in the birth of their babies, Jackson helped deliver his son and talked to us of how it made him feel:

> JACKSON: I couldn't have imagined the incredibly powerful feelings that engulfed me when I saw Kevin slip out of Tanya. I was right there, and this was my son! All the next day whenever he began to cry or nurse, I was in tears. I'm still transfixed watching him. It's the most amazing experience I've ever had.

His wife, Tanya, adds her view:

> TANYA: It was a shattering experience. I was huffing and puffing, crying and pushing, and suddenly his head emerged. Then, slowly, out came the rest of him in one long, unbearably painful, wonderful surge. After all of the wait and the worry and the wondering, our son had finally arrived. Later in my hospital room, I remember Kevin in my arms and Jackson holding me with one hand and Kevin with the other. It was magical. Our family!

Moments like these are the end of the nine long months of waiting. But in the journey to becoming a family, they are only the beginning.

PART II

Crossing the Great Divide

CHAPTER 4

What's Happening to Me?

A S THEY BRING THEIR FIRST BABY home from the hospital, new mothers and fathers find themselves crossing the great divide. After months of anticipation, their transition from couple to family becomes a reality. Entering this new and unfamiliar family territory, men and women find themselves on different timetables and different trails of a journey they envisioned completing together. We set the stage for the changes they describe by recounting briefly how they see their lives when their babies are six months and eighteen months old. Then, in this and the next four chapters, we describe changes in each of the five domains in our model of family life.

We begin here with a focus on the view from the inside, as men and women experience the shifting sense of self that comes with first-time parenthood. Using a simple pie chart and a long list of adjectives to describe themselves during pregnancy, and again when their children are infants and toddlers, the couples in our study help us to understand both change and continuity as they settle into family territory. In the next chapter, we show how new mothers' and fathers' shifting sense of self plays out in the day-to-day realities of caring for a baby while trying to maintain their relationships as couples.

After many years of being parents ourselves, and more than fifteen years of working with couples becoming parents for the first time, we understand the impossibility of being fully prepared for parenthood—for the initial feelings of awe at having produced this fragile being, for the constant frantic state during the first months of never-ending feedings, for the maddening regularity of interrupted sleep. For most parents, both those whose labor and delivery went smoothly and those who faced the rigors of cesarean section delivery, the euphoria immediately after birth is followed by weeks of feeling dazed and operating on "automatic pilot." Men and women who were used to anticipating and mastering the complexities of demanding jobs and intimate relationships are overwhelmed by their unexpected and contradictory feelings.

Meeting with couples in their homes when their babies were six months and then eighteen months old, we tended to be treated as members of the family. We were immediately presented with either the latest baby pictures or, usually, with the baby, not yet quite awake from his or her nap or sleepily on the way to bed.

We are sitting in the garden of a small brown-shingle house, talking to Doug and Josie. Doug, thirty-seven, worked for the state for many years, but he has recently opened his own business consulting with corporations on environmental issues. Josie, thirty-six, is uninterested in going back to her former job, and moderately content to stay at home with their son, Zack. At the six-month mark, the shock of becoming a parent has usually subsided:

JOSIE: It's a good thing you didn't come two months ago. We were just about at our wit's end. There was nothing that we could follow through on. Everything was disjointed.

DOUG: Before the baby came, we used to take a walk every evening. We tried to do it about two weeks after Zack was born, but it felt like we were packing for a month-long trip so we gave it up.

JOSIE: Things started to feel better when Zack really became more of a little human being, when he could laugh and babble and you could play games with him. Now it seems like he's a real person, not just an infant lying there and crying and that's all. I really enjoy him. I think he's done wonders for me. He's calmed me down considerably.

From being helpless, totally unpredictable newborns, babies at six months have usually settled into some routines. Most sleep through the night, although that description is misleading because the period of quiet typically lasts from some time after midnight to only 4:00 or 5:00 A.M. The babies are generally still nursing from breast or bottle, and many have begun to eat solid food. Having developed definite "personalities," they have very specific likes and dislikes. There are things that they simply cannot be forced or enticed to do, no matter how hard the parents try.

Some sociologists refer to the six-month-postpartum point as part of the honeymoon period in the life of a new family. This description certainly fits Victor and Natalie, whom we last heard discussing the problem of running shorts on the bathroom floor and Victor's fondness of taking his daughter bicycling in the rain. "After a major adjustment during the first three months, the last three months have been very, very nice. Kim's a delight."

Most parents feel powerfully drawn to their six-month-old babies and love the peaceful times with them. They are relieved at having survived all of the planning and worrying during the pregnancy, and are beginning to experience a new sense of excitement and competence at having learned how to provide for an infant whose needs are continuous but whose ability to communicate about them is limited. At the same time, many couples are showing signs that the *marital* honeymoon is drawing to an end. Sharon, whom you may remember from chapter 1, was initially ambivalent about having a child but got excited by the results of her home pregnancy test. She was also worried that, despite her husband's assurances, there would not be enough collaboration on the home front. Her fears, it seems, are being realized:

> SHARON: We aren't able to pay much attention to each other, because Amy needs so much. She's great, don't get me wrong. But Daniel comes home from work cranky, I'm cranky because I haven't talked to anyone who says anything back to me, Amy's cranky because she wants to eat *right now,* and we don't have time to find out how each other's day went. So I'm making dinner for three cranky people. And as a consequence, we have not been as close as before she came. We're going through a transition and I'm sure it's going to work itself out. We've almost got it down, I think.

Mothers of six-month-olds sound as if they are emerging from a period of total immersion in their infants. In our sample, about 55 percent of the women are back at work, more of them part-time (36 percent) than full-time (19 percent). Fathers talk about their increased feelings of responsibility for their families, mostly in relation to being good providers. It is rare for the men to be centrally involved in the day-to-day tasks of caring for their infants. Many describe themselves as "baby-sitting" for their children while their wives prepare dinner or go out for an occasional evening or weekend morning. Some husbands refer to "helping" their wives by taking their turn getting up with the baby in the middle of the night. New mothers have mixed feelings, not knowing whether to feel grateful or resentful about their husbands' "help."

Men and women clearly have different experiences of being new parents. Especially for partners who managed their lives pretty equally before they became parents and expected that life after baby would retain this quality, the shift in the family balance can be surprising and unsettling.

When we pay our call a year later, when the children are eighteen months old, the scene has changed. A number of the couples have moved to different homes, usually for space, sometimes to live in neighborhoods more congenial to rearing young children. Toys and books are scattered about, mostly on top of parents' unread magazines, mail, and newspapers. Six-month-olds who had stayed put are now explorers on the move—toward light sockets, delicate vases, pets, toilet bowls, open doors, and, of course, our tape recorder. And most of them are talking! Parents who had been mystified because they didn't know what their infants' cries meant now hear incessant commands of "Want 'dat" with every attractive new object or "No!" in reaction to limits.

Our two strongest impressions at this stage are that the parents want us to see how their children have grown, and that some have difficulty putting them to bed. The bedtime routine seems particularly difficult for parents who are away at work for much of the children's waking time. Because their children must adhere to the parents' schedules all day, they try to avoid more conflict in the evening.

Besides, many couples are finding that they have different ideas about what toddlers need in order to feel that life is predictable and secure. Their discussions about how to get their toddler undressed or into bed are sometimes strained. For parents who have been working since the early morning hours, dealing with these differences can be the last straw, stretching the limits of their patience at the end of a wearing day. Some couples react by sweeping their differences under the carpet.

In response to our questions about their experiences of family life, parents sound as though they have climbed up one side of a huge mountain. Our interviews catch many of them at a plateau from which they try to take stock of how far they have come:

> JOSIE: The older Zack gets, the better it is, in terms of me feeling more like a person instead of just his mom. I'm nowhere near as selfish as I used to be. He's really taught me that it's possible to look after someone's needs first, and to feel OK about that. At moments when he's upset, I don't say, "Oh God, what have I done wrong?" I just say to myself, "OK, here we go again." I must have become more easygoing or something.

For parents like Josie, the view from the mountain is fairly peaceful and gratifying. For others whose ascent has been more strenuous, it sounds as if an avalanche could descend at any moment:

> SHARON: I went through this whole stage of feeling very trapped. It seemed like all my waking hours were spent on caring for Amy, caring for Daniel and thinking about him, caring for the house and thinking about the house. There was no time for myself, absolutely none. And I was just really feeling boxed in.

When their children are eighteen months old, 57 percent of the mothers are working outside the home, about the same proportion as a year ago. Now, the employed women are almost evenly divided between part-time (30 percent) and full-time (27 percent), the latter logging up to forty hours a week away from home. Fathers, all employed, work from thirty-two to eighty hours a week. They are not as involved in the daily chores at home as they and their wives expected them to be, but they have become more involved in the care of their children and more psychologically involved in the family than they had been a year before:

DANIEL: Last year, when I came home from work, Sharon would just shove Amy at me so that she could get the dinner done. And that was hard. But now, Amy asks about me when I'm gone, and when I get in the door she runs to me and wants me to read her stories. We play together at night before she goes to bed, while Sharon is cleaning up.

The living environments and routines have altered drastically in one year. Parents now talk about who they are, who they are becoming, and the kind of partners and parents they are striving to be. Josie says her son's arrival has calmed her down and made her less selfish. Her husband, Doug, like many of the new fathers in our study, reports equally positive changes in his sense of himself:

DOUG: Well, it's not that I look in the mirror every morning wondering who's looking back. It's still me. But I'm different since Zack was born. I'm more aggressive in recruiting new business for my consulting firm. I'm more organized at work and at home. But I'm also loosening up a little socially; I even enjoy a party every now and then—I hated them before. I'm enjoying being a father. I'd recommend it to anybody.

Josie and Doug seem delighted with some of the psychological shifts they are experiencing. Other new parents tell us that having a baby has brought them up against some less desirable parts of themselves. Recall Alice and Andy, who were having a difficult struggle deciding whether they could stay together after Alice became pregnant. Their daughter, Jessica, is now eighteen months old:

ALICE: Some days I feel that my brain turned to mush on the day Jessica was born. I can't seem to keep to a decision. I get confused easily. I have a much harder time talking with people than I did before. I guess I'm not much fun to be with. Except with Jessica. When she's nursing, I'm transported to a different place. I feel so different now that I'm a mother.

ANDY: I used to be real spontaneous. I could take unexpected things in my stride. Since I've become a father I don't feel as flexible or resilient as I was or as I want to be.

As they talked to us about both changes and continuities in their characteristic ways of dealing with the world, both men and women reported positive, negative, or mixed feelings about themselves as they moved closer to or farther from their ideal pictures.

Identity Changes: Parent, Worker/Student, Partner

In order to understand how parents integrate Mother or Father as a central component of their identity, we asked them to think about the various aspects of their lives (worker, friend, daughter, father, and so on), and to mark them off on a pie chart[1] based on how large each portion feels, not on how much time they spend "being it." During pregnancy, and again when their children were six months and eighteen months old, we also asked them to fill out a second pie indicating how they would like it to be divided among these important parts of themselves. The size of each pie piece, we thought, would reflect their psychological involvement or investment in that aspect of themselves. Their reactions to this graphic representation took some of the new parents by surprise.

Looking at the chart she had filled in before the baby was born, Joan said: "I see I drew this immense piece and labeled it Mom. I didn't realize that so much of me was already invested in being this pregnant woman about to be a mother. I hardly had enough space left for the other important parts." Indeed, about one-third of her pie was taken up with motherhood. Her husband, Rob, on the other hand, had not even included the role of father in his pie at that time. Were Rob and Joan to remain so out of sync after they had their baby, their ability to communicate effectively would be severely hampered.

People include a variety of aspects of themselves but almost all show pieces that represent parent, worker or student, and partner or lover. The most vivid identity changes during the transition to parenthood take place between pregnancy and six months postpartum. Neither men's nor women's drawings show much change between the time their children are six months and eighteen months old.[2] The part of the self that women call Mother takes up an average of 10 percent of their pictures of themselves in late pregnancy. It then leaps to 34 percent at six months after birth, and stays there through the second year of parenthood.

For some women, the psychological investment in motherhood is much greater than the average. At the six-month follow-up, for example, Peggy drew a wedge that filled almost three-quarters of her pie and called it "mother/child-care person." You may recall that Peggy had a difficult pregnancy, with uncomfortable physical symptoms all the way along. She felt badly about her body and about the high level of conflict with her husband, Bill. With her six-month-old daughter, Mindy, in her arms, Peggy's spirits now soar:

> PEGGY: I can't believe how wonderful this is—how wonderful *she* is. I'm so glad I didn't plan on going back to work. I couldn't pull myself away. Even during the day when she's asleep, I keep coming into her room just to look at her. I feel like a whole different person. I'm not sick anymore. The breastfeeding is going well. If Bill and I could just get it together, things would be perfect.

Bill looks away in some embarrassment and distress. Then, almost as if he's talking to himself:

> BILL: You guys are sure close, all right. Sometimes I wonder if it's too close.
> PEGGY: Too close for what? Sometimes I wonder if you have any idea what being a parent is all about.

Although Bill's critical tone was unusual, he was typical of the husbands we interviewed, most of whom took on the identity of parent more slowly than their wives did. During pregnancy, Father takes half as much of men's pies as their wives' Mother sections do, and when their children are eighteen months old, husbands' identity as parent is still less than one-third as large as their wives'.

Investment in the identity of parent has different meanings for men and women. For example, midway through the child's first year, men with larger pieces of the pie allocated to parent had higher self-esteem as we measured it on the Adjective Check List (Gough and Heilbrun 1980). But women with larger investment in their parent identity tended to have lower self-esteem. What's going on here?

New mothers like Peggy with a great deal of investment in their parent self have very little room for anything else in their inner lives. They may have become highly involved in parenthood as a way of feeling better about themselves. The men with the largest parent pieces are not much more involved in that aspect of themselves than the average woman. It looks like new fathers who feel good about themselves are able to devote more energy to their parent identity without giving up other central aspects of their psychological lives. And what they get back from this relationship helps them to keep their self-esteem on a positive track.

Peggy and Bill are a couple with highly discrepant levels of psychological investment in parenthood. Their interaction suggests that this discrepancy is taking a toll on their relationship as a couple. When we examine the pies of all the couples this way, we find that the larger the difference between husbands and wives in the size of their parent piece of the pie when their babies are six months old, the less satisfied both spouses are with the quality of their marriage, and the more their satisfaction with marriage declines by the time their babies are eighteen months old.[3]

Once they have had a baby, men's and women's sense of themselves as parents is certainly expected to increase. What comes as a surprise is that other central aspects of the self are getting short shrift as their parent piece of the pie expands. In their sixth or seventh month of pregnancy, most women are still in school or working, although some report a declining interest in their jobs. On the average, women show that Worker or Student takes up 18 percent of who they are, probably lower than before they became pregnant. For expectant fathers, Worker claims an average of 28 percent of the pie at our first interview.

By the time their children are eighteen months old, the Mother aspect of

women's identity is twice as large as the Worker/Student part. Even when
women work full-time, their sense of self as Mother is more than 50 percent
greater than their psychological investment in their identity as Worker. This
sits in bold contrast to their husbands' experience. Despite men's increasing
psychological investment as fathers, their Worker or Student aspect of self
remains virtually unchanged. Even at its height, the Father aspect of men's
sense of self is smaller than the Worker/Student part.

The greatest surprise for us and for the couples in the study is what gets
squeezed as new parents' identities shift. Women apportion 34 percent to the
Partner or Lover aspect of themselves in pregnancy, 22 percent at six months
after birth, and 21 percent when their children are eighteen months old.
Men's sense of themselves as Partner or Lover also shows a decline—from 35
percent to 30 percent to 25 percent over the two-year transition period.

The size of the Partner piece of the pie is connected with how new parents
feel about themselves: A larger psychological investment in their relationship
seems to be good for both of them. Six months after the birth of their first
child, both men and women with larger Partner or Lover pieces have higher
self-esteem and lower parenting stress. This could mean that when new
parents resist the tendency to ignore their relationship as a couple, they feel
better about themselves—or that when they feel better about themselves,
they are more likely to stay at least moderately involved in their marriage.

At our eighteen-month follow-up, Stephanie and Art talk about the consequences for their marriage of trying to balance—within them and between
them—the pulls among the Parent, Worker, and Partner aspects of themselves:

STEPHANIE: We're managing Linda really well. But with Art's promotion
   from teacher to principal, and my going back to work and feeling guilty
   about being away from Linda, we don't get much time for us. I try to
   make time for the two of us at home but there's no point in making
   time to be with somebody if he doesn't want to be with you. Sometimes
   when we finally get everything done and Linda is asleep, I want to sit
   down and talk, but Art says this is a perfect opportunity to get some
   preparation done for one of his teachers' meetings. Or he starts to fix
   one of Linda's toys—things that apparently are more important to him
   than spending time with me.
ART: That does happen. But Stephanie's wrong when she says that those
   things are more important to me than she is. The end of the day is just
   not my best time to start a deep conversation. I keep asking her to get
   a sitter so that we can go out for a quiet dinner, but she always finds
   a reason not to. It's like being turned down for a date week after week.
STEPHANIE: Art, you know I'd love to go out with you. I just don't think we
   can leave Linda so often.

Stephanie and Art are looking at the problem from their separate vantage
points. Art is very devoted to fatherhood, but is more psychologically in-

vested in his relationship with Stephanie than with Linda. In his struggle to hold on to his sense of himself as Partner, he makes the reasonable request that he and Stephanie spend some time alone so that they can nurture their relationship as a couple. Stephanie struggles with other parts of her shifting sense of self. Although Art knows that Stephanie spends a great deal of time with Linda when she gets home from work, he does not understand that juggling her increasing involvement as Mother while trying to maintain her investment as Worker is creating a great deal of internal pressure for her. The Partner/Lover part of Stephanie is getting squeezed not only by time demands but also by the psychological reshuffling that is taking place inside her. Art knows only that Stephanie is not responding to his needs, and to him her behavior seems unreasonable, insensitive, and rejecting.

Stephanie knows that Art's view of himself has changed as he has become a parent, but she is unaware of the fact that it has not changed in the same way or to the same degree as hers. In fact, typical of the men in our study, Art's psychological investment in their relationship as a couple has declined slightly since Linda was born but his Worker identity has not changed much. He is proud and pleased to be a father, but these feelings are not crowding out his feelings about himself as a partner and lover. All Stephanie knows is that Art is repeatedly asking her to go out to dinner, and ignoring her inner turmoil. To her, his behavior toward her seems unreasonable, insensitive, and rejecting.

Connections Between Identity and Well-being

These internal changes in each of the new parents begin to have an impact on their relationship as a couple. Art adds Father to his identity but preserves the other central parts of himself. Stephanie adds Mother, a new and even larger part of her sense of self, but loses and then regains her sense of self as a Worker, which absorbs most of her psychological energy so that she has little available for the part of her that is a wife and partner to Art. These discrepancies between his and her shifting sense of self during this major adult transition create a climate in which their transition as a couple is moving through potentially hostile territory.

To put these changes in new parents in perspective, we can compare them with what happened to the childless couples in our study. Among those who were still childless and who stayed together (20 percent became parents; 16 percent divorced), the women showed a decline in their psychological involvement as a Partner, though it is 10 percent higher than that of mothers. There was, however, a large increase in their identity as Worker or Student. The men's identity as Partner and as Worker remained virtually the same over time, creating an even more equal balance between childless partners.

It might have been tempting to conclude that it is natural for psychological involvement in one's identity as a partner and lover to wane over time, had we not had the patterns of the childless men to refute such an assumption. The childless couples also helped us contrast the balance between spouses in these two groups of couples. The husband and wife who do not have a baby experience similar shifts as individuals, and their satisfaction with their relationship as a couple remains stable. In the couples who become parents, he and she begin diverging in terms of their individual changes and, as we will see more graphically in the next chapter, in terms of both their mutual roles and the intimate aspects of their marriage. The costs of making such different shifts appear to borne in the relationship between the spouses.

Let us be clear that remaining childless does not guarantee marital bliss. As we have seen, 16 percent of the couples not having a baby have become unhappy or discouraged enough to separate or file for divorce two years into the study. The couples who stayed together and did not have a baby during the same period appear to have had the option of expanding some of the existing parts of their identities and roles without having to cope with the stress of any major additions to their sense of self. Perhaps the most salient difference between the two groups of women is that the childless women seem to have room, if they choose, to expand their work and career identities while keeping a substantial portion of their psychological energy for their marriages. This is in contrast to what we have seen in the new parents; when women add Mother to their identity, *both* Worker and Partner or Lover get squeezed.

Although parents hope that they will have energy for the old aspects of their identity as they add the new one of Parent, their pie charts reflect the reality that as some parts get larger, there is less "room" for others. The challenge, then, is how to allow Parent a central place in one's identity without abandoning or neglecting Partner. The couples who manage to do this feel better about themselves and their lives.

Changes in Self-esteem

Filling in a pie chart lets men and women give us a global picture of how they are changing as they become parents. A more specific way they can communicate how they think and feel about themselves during this transition is by choosing from an Adjective Check List (Gough and Heilbrun 1980) those words they feel accurately describe them.* Selecting from three hundred adjectives, each man and woman filled out three checklists at each phase of

---

*Examples from the Adjective Check List: active, affectionate, aggressive, dependent, emotional, feminine, intelligent, logical, masculine, mature, nervous, preoccupied, sexy, shy, sociable, stubborn, trusting, zany.

It is reasonable to be skeptical about whether self-descriptions can provide accurate information about real-life behavior, but Gough and Heilbrun have found that the Adjective Check List scales correlate well with other personality tests and with direct observations of people's behavior in both laboratory and naturalistic settings.

the study: one describing "me as I am," a second for "me as I'd like to be," and a third describing "my partner."

Harrison Gough and Alfred Heilbrun constructed these personality scales to assess an individual's tendency to be dominant, aggressive, nurturant, self-confident, masculine, feminine, well-adjusted, and so on. Personality traits remained very stable over time for all of the men and women in our study. We used the discrepancy between each person's description of "me as I am" and "me as I'd like to be" to measure their self-esteem. We assumed, as have Gough and his colleagues (Gough, Fioravanti, and Lazzari 1982), that people who describe themselves very differently from their ideal picture of themselves tend to have low self-esteem: They describe themselves in negative terms, they have little self-confidence, and they have difficulty being active rather than passive in the face of threat and challenge.

We found that one's age seems to make a difference to self-esteem during the transition to parenthood. Remember that the women and men in our study ranged from twenty-one to forty-nine when they entered the study, with the average age of the expectant parents being twenty-nine for the women and thirty for the men. We find different patterns in what happens to men and women who are twenty-nine or younger and those who are thirty or older when they have a first baby. Younger men and women (temporarily) appear to be more at risk for declining self-esteem than those who are at least thirty when they become parents. Younger mothers' self-esteem drops significantly between pregnancy and six months after giving birth. By the time their babies are in their second year, though, these younger mothers bounce back to their earlier level of satisfaction with themselves. Younger fathers' self-esteem declines later than their wives'—between six and eighteen months after they have become fathers. So, just as the wives are on the way up, their husbands are on their way down in terms of how satisfied they feel about themselves.

Mothers in their thirties maintain their satisfaction with themselves throughout the two years from pregnancy to eighteen months after their child is born. In contrast to the younger men whose self-esteem is dropping between six and eighteen months after childbirth, fathers in their thirties and forties describe themselves in even more positive ways during their second year of parenthood.

Even with these age differences in self-esteem, we cannot conclude that later is better than sooner until we consider what happens to the marriages of the younger and older parents. Although the older couples maintain their satisfaction with themselves as individuals during the transition to parenthood, they experience a significantly larger decline in marital satisfaction than the younger couples.

Why would this be so? The older parents have had a longer time to establish themselves, to build up a greater number of accomplishments, and to develop alternative resources for bolstering their self-esteem. At the same time, since they tend to have been married longer before becoming parents, integrating a baby into their lives may present a greater challenge to their established routines, flexibility, and spontaneity as a couple. This is supported by our finding that the older couples felt the reduction in intimacy most keenly, and reported more decline in satisfaction with their relationships as couples than the younger couples did.

The younger couples, on the other hand, seem to be more vulnerable to feeling less competent and less pleased with themselves as individuals once they become parents. Even if they have been working since they were young, as many of them have, taking on the care of a needy infant while maintaining contact as a couple and managing their work outside the family presents a hefty challenge for adults under thirty. Even so, they have not had time to build up as many expectations and to set patterns as a couple to be disrupted by the baby. Their relationships seem more resilient than those of the older parents in the sense that the partners show less dissatisfaction with them over time.

Tanya, twenty-six, and Jackson, twenty-seven, described their sense of themselves from the time their son, Kevin, was six months old to a year later:

TANYA: I was feeling trapped because Jackson was still going out, not only to work but with friends. And there I was, at home taking care of Kevin. Being with Kevin was marvelous, up to a point, but I felt cut off from everything else. Even when Jackson was there, he sometimes created more mess than he cleaned up. But I wasn't feeling nearly as bad about him as I was about me.

JACKSON: The irony was that Tanya was resenting the fact that I was going off to work every day, and I *hated* it. I would've quit two years ago. My job at the post office was not what I wanted to do for the rest of my life. But when Kevin came, I had to dig in and make a go of it. I'd go into work every day and grit my teeth. My boss was critical. Inside, I knew he was right. I was a fraud. I just wasn't the person I wanted to be.

TANYA: About two or three months ago, I got tired of feeling like a victim and realized that it wasn't making sense. Sometimes you just have to tell Jackson gently what needs to be done and he will do it. He just had to snap out of his own funk and realize that there were other people in the family who needed him to get on the stick.

During the months when Tanya and Jackson were having a difficult time, feeling badly about themselves, their connection with each other and their sense of humor helped pull them through. So did Tanya's ability to make some explicit demands for Jackson's involvement in the family. He accepted her complaints as reasonable and became more involved with Kevin, which began to rebalance Tanya's and Jackson's roles in the family. Although we could not tell from our conversation with them, the questionnaire data confirmed that Jackson's self-esteem had not returned to the level it had been during Tanya's pregnancy, but he was more satisfied with his marriage when Kevin was eighteen months old than he had been a year earlier. Having

Tanya's help in drawing him in to the family may have enhanced Jackson's evaluation of his relationship with her.

Marian and Bruce were older when they had their first baby. She is thirty-seven and he is thirty-nine when we visit on a rainy Sunday for our eighteen-month-postpartum follow-up. Bruce is very involved in his small but newly successful window design company. Marian, a lawyer in a large law firm, is working hard to make partner while becoming a parent. Given her complex schedule, we have had difficulty arranging this interview. Their daughter, Gayle, is closer to two years than eighteen months when we finally pin them down. When we ask them about the changes in their sense of themselves they have undergone in the past two years, Marian's initial answer is reminiscent of the responses of many mothers in our study, especially the women in their thirties: She talks more about the baby than about herself.

We get the sense that how Marian feels about herself depends in part on how each day goes with her daughter. But as we talk further, we come to appreciate her overall sense of ease and her ability to put things in perspective. The previous week Gayle had been sick and Marian had to bring her to work with her since they couldn't leave her with the usual day care. One of the senior partners in the firm came into her office and, not noticing Gayle's crayons on the floor, slid right into Marian's desk. "I started to laugh," Marian says, "but Paul was not amused and walked out in a huff. For a minute I thought, There goes *his* vote, but then I thought, Screw it! If I don't make partner because my sick kid is coloring in my office, then I'm working for the wrong firm. What's happened to my sense of myself? I guess I'm feeling pretty good about me. I wish I could say the same about *us.*"

Bruce describes changes in his sense of himself. "If you can believe it, I've gotten nicer," he says, while Marian makes a face of mock disapproval, which he ignores. "My business has really taken off. I feel terrific about Gayle. I'm not home much but when I am, we just hang out together in the park or down in my work room. I've been waiting for my life to come together like this for a long time."

Asked about any changes in their sexual relationship after having a baby, they both laugh and ask, "What sexual relationship?" Bruce explains that Marian is hardly home long enough for them to get together. And when she is home, she's poring over her files, spread out all over the dining room table. This is a common phenomenon, the new mother working at the dining room table because her home office has become the baby's room. They continue to discuss the changes:

BRUCE: We used to have all the time in the world, you know. Reading the Sunday papers. Going out in the middle of the week. I still remember it, and I miss it.

MARIAN: Bruce, you sound like you're totally available and I'm not. It seems to me that you're down in your work room about as much as I'm at the table. But the fact that we haven't made love in months does worry me.

BRUCE: I guess I take the long view. We did have our time. And we'll have

our time again. But right now, we choose to do other things. By the time
we turn around again, Gayle will be grown up. We'll just pick up where
we left off.

MARIAN: I'm just hoping we're not too old, and that we'll have something
left to pick up.

Like other couples in their thirties, Marian and Bruce are feeling pretty good
about themselves, but at least from her point of view, their relationship with
each other is showing signs of strain. Postponing parenthood until partners
are in their thirties may provide a foundation for the development of a
stronger sense of self, one that tends to be maintained or even enhanced after
having a baby. Yet maintaining their growth as individuals, especially with
regard to furthering their careers, may be possible only at some cost to their
marital intimacy and satisfaction.

Continuity Despite Change

It is important to tell the other side of the story, which establishes that for
most men and women who become parents there is not only change but
continuity in their personalities and in their way of being in the world. Even
though the new identity of parent may crowd out some of the other central
aspects of men's and women's sense of themselves, and despite a possible
increase or decline in their self-esteem, there is a core of stability, predictability, and continuity in personality style as people make the transition to
parenthood. Many men and women *feel* that they have changed since becoming parents, but we found no systematic change in their self-described
personality traits from pregnancy through eighteen months after birth according to the Adjective Check Lists.[4] So, despite Doug's feeling that he has
become more aggressive in his business dealings and more comfortable at
social gatherings than he was before becoming a father, overall men and
women show little real personality change in any consistent direction. (Toni
Antonucci and Karen Mikus [1988] reviewed the results of the studies that
followed men and women from pregnancy into parenthood. They found no
evidence of personality change in a systematic direction. This is also consistent with psychoanalytic ideas that "new" conflicts during the transition to
parenthood are usually reawakened conflicts from the past [Benedek 1970;
Osofsky and Osofsky 1984; Wenner et al. 1969]).

In addition to this stability of personality traits, in every family domain,
especially in their views of themselves, we found remarkable predictability
across the transition to parenthood. That is, when we know something about
men's and women's perceptions, opinions, feelings, and behavior before they
became parents, we can predict with some degree of accuracy how they will
see themselves, feel, and behave when their children are six months and
eighteen months old.

Although the size of the Parent piece of the pie in pregnancy does not predict psychological involvement two years later, the Partner, Worker, and Leisure pieces measured in pregnancy are all significant predictors of those aspects of men's and women's identities six months and eighteen months after becoming parents.[5] In the same way, despite the change in their average scores on our measures of well-being or distress, parents who are very satisfied with themselves during pregnancy tend to have higher self-esteem eighteen months after the birth of their first child. Conversely, men and women who are feeling distressed about themselves before the baby comes tend to have lower self-esteem when their children are toddlers. A number of other research teams have found similar continuities in new parents' lives, leading them to conclude that parents' adaptation measured in pregnancy is the best predictor of how well they will function during the first year or two of parenthood (Belsky, Lang, and Rovine 1985; Grossman et al. 1980; Heinicke et al. 1986; Shereshefsky and Yarrow 1973). As we describe in chapter 8, we can predict the reactions of the parents in our study as far ahead as the children's kindergarten year.

The notion of continuity during a time of transition is important for three reasons. First, it adds something essential to our understanding of the impact of becoming a parent on men, women, and marriage. Having a baby does not turn men and women into different people. It does not plunge parents from the heights to the depths of feeling about themselves or their marriage, nor does it rescue a troubled parent or bridge the gap between spouses who were already miles apart. The most important piece of information to forecast how men and women will fare as parents is how they are doing before they begin their journey to parenthood.

Second, the fact that there is continuity during the transition to parenthood makes it possible to identify individuals, couples, and children who are at risk for distress during the early years of family life—essential information if we are ever to develop preventive services for families. In her dissertation based on the Becoming a Family Project data, Trudie Heming (1985, 1987) finds it possible to make fairly good predictions of who will report most depression on our depression symptom checklist (Radloff 1977) when their babies are eighteen months old, based on men's and women's descriptions of themselves during the pregnancy. If couples most likely to be in distress after their baby arrives can be helped earlier on, we may be able to prevent predictable family problems from escalating to a point beyond repair.

Finally, if it is possible to predict who is at risk for later distress, it is also possible for couples themselves to become informed about what might lie ahead in their journey to parenthood. Our information, after all, comes from what men and women have been telling us as we follow them on their journey from couple to family. We can alert expectant couples, and health professionals who are concerned with early family life, that long-term, enduring negative feelings that husband and wives hold about themselves, their partners, or their relationships before they have babies are not likely to disappear after the first flush of excitement of bringing the baby home. At the same time, expectant couples who are worried about what life with a baby will bring can be reassured to know that if they are coping well with the challenges of their lives, they can probably afford to be optimistic about how the becoming a family journey will turn out.

CHAPTER 5

What's Happening to Us?

SHARON: I really thought we'd discussed it before Amy was born—that Daniel was going to be more help around the house. But he just wasn't. I stewed for a long time and felt angry when I could have just said something. He'd never been around anyone who'd had a C-section or any major surgery. He didn't know that he wasn't supposed to let me cart tubs of wet diapers down the hall for the first month. I was feeling so shaky, and before I knew it our whole relationship was on shaky ground.

I finally said something to Daniel when Amy was about four months old. But I've had to *keep* doing it. I'm not very good about saying, "Things are not going well here." I usually give out a couple of hints, and then wait until I get really irritated. I'll sit on it for a couple of months before I come to Daniel and say something like, "Who died and left me in charge of the laundry?"

Sharon and Daniel are describing to us what has happened to their relationship in the six months since Amy was born. Daniel is used to Sharon's humorous but cutting complaints; he says something conciliatory but has some complaints of his own:

DANIEL: Looking back, I can see now that I wasn't as sensitive as I could have been. But what Sharon is leaving out is that I did all the shopping and errands during that time—and some of the housecleaning and all of the dishes and stuff and, of course, I worked all day too. I never got credit for that. All she talked about was how stressed out she was and how things were going wrong.

A combination of the stress of recovering from major surgery and caring for a new baby, along with Sharon and Daniel's holding-it-back-and-then-blurting-it-out style of expressing their feelings, are taking a toll on their relationship. Daniel had apparently not understood what Sharon needed after her surgery. Sharon did not know how to tell him what her needs were until she felt so upset that she angrily accused him of not offering any help. Feeling unacknowledged for what he *has* done, Daniel is unwilling to tell her that he is sorry he missed the cues.

In the last chapter we described changes in new parents' internal sense of themselves. Here we explore how some of the internal shifts in new fathers' and mothers' identity play out in their marriage. We focus on two related issues. First, we take a detailed look at the shifts in couples' division of the daily work of managing a household and family, especially how they share the work of caring for their child. We find that "who does what?" issues are central, not only in how husbands and wives feel about themselves but in how they feel about their marriage. Second, we describe alterations in the emotional fabric of the couple's relationship, showing that how caring and intimacy get expressed and how couples manage their conflict and disagreement have a direct effect on their marital satisfaction.

We find that husbands and wives, different to begin with, become even more separate and distant in the years after their first child is born. The increasing specialization of family roles and the emotional distance between partners who have become parents combine to affect their satisfaction with the overall quality of their relationship. Jessie Bernard (1972) observed that "in every marriage there are two marriages—his and hers." We find that in every transition to parenthood there are three transitions—his, hers, and theirs (Cowan et al. 1985).

Who Does What?

Gustav Geijer, a Swedish historian, said that "the position of women in a society provides an exact measure of the development of that society." If he was right, we are in deep trouble. His observation implies that in more highly developed societies, women's position would not differ from men's. Since the new wave of the women's movement in the 1960s, feminist literature and features in popular news media have made us more conscious of the unequal roles of men and women within the family and in the outside world. These news features have been stimulated in part by the fact that mothers a generation ago felt hemmed in by their constricted family roles (see Friedan

1963) and that today's mothers are entering the work force in increasing numbers. The implication seems to be that as women have become more equally involved in the world of work, men have increased their share of the work at home. But the men and women who have been talking to us over the last fifteen years have made it clear that behind the ideology of the egalitarian couple lies a much more traditional reality.

Scholars in a number of fields have been studying couples' role arrangements for managing the work of the house, bringing home the bacon, and rearing the children (Chodorow 1978; Hoffman and Nye 1974). The results of research over the past fifteen years tell a pretty consistent story about what sociologists call the instrumental tasks of family life (Parsons and Bales 1955): Although more than half the mothers with children under five have entered the labor force and contemporary fathers have been taking a small but significantly greater role in cooking, cleaning, and looking after their children than fathers used to do, women continue to carry the overwhelming responsibility for managing the household and caring for the children (Pleck 1985; Strelitz in Rapoport, Rapoport, and Strelitz 1977; Robinson 1977). Furthermore, studies of many different samples of couples leave no doubt that most women have the primary responsibility for family work even when both partners are employed full-time outside the home (Barnett and Baruch 1988; Hochschild 1989; Stafford, Backman, and Dibona 1977) and even in countries whose official policies dictate an equal division of labor (Szinovacz 1977).

As we discussed earlier, couples whose division of household and family tasks was not equitable when they began our study tended to predict that it would be after the baby was born—not that they expected to split the baby care 50-50, but that they would work as a team in rearing their children. Once their babies are born, however, the women do more of the housework than before they became mothers, and the men do much less of the care of the baby than they or their wives predicted they would.

Like many of the over-thirty parents in our study, Doug and Josie were feeling good about themselves but their marriage was a little strained. Doug tells us about their arrangements to care for six-month-old Zack, explaining how the burden came to fall almost entirely on Josie. When she was breast-feeding, it seemed impossible to have it any other way. He estimates that 95 percent of the labor in taking care of Zack has been done by Josie, then adds: "But I thoroughly enjoy him and don't feel deprived."

Josie, on the other hand, is outraged. All the talk about men and women sharing the responsibility and equal parenting, she says, "is just bullshit! Someone is going off and putting in eight or nine hours every day and the other parent is staying home doing not just the feeding but the constant changing of diapers, the laundry, the meal planning, the housecleaning—everything that keeps this family going! That's where the inequality starts, and it just goes on from there."

Doug describes their changes in theoretical terms, almost as if he were a sociologist explaining how historical trends and societal norms affect what happens in families. Josie, still disconcerted by her realization that she is in charge of most of Zack's daily care and everything else at home, stays focused on what is happening to their family. While Doug appears to be listening to his wife during this interview, he does not know how to respond supportively to her distress: "I would have gone along with the hypothesis of equal parenting right at first, though I admit that I didn't think about it much. But the way it works out, it falls on the mother."

This last sentence of Doug's is a succinct illustration of how couples explain that their egalitarian ideology is not easily put into practice. They talk about their arrangements of work inside and outside the family as if they have happened to them instead of as if they have worked them out. If one partner tries to get the other to look at the difference between their initial expectations and where they have ended up, as Josie does here, the quandary seems too big for the couple to solve alone:

> JOSIE: Last week we had our hundredth talk about my going back to work. But, as Doug says, there's no way I can possibly earn anything close to his salary so that he could consider cutting back on his time.
>
> DOUG: I'd say our discussion was academic. If Josie could go out and make sufficient money to support our lifestyle, I'd be perfectly willing to discuss taking a year off or six months off and staying home with Zack once he's weaned. Perhaps it's just as well that she doesn't, though. I wouldn't want to trade jobs with Josie. On my worst day I wouldn't want to trade jobs with her.

In recent years, the division of labor in the family when partners become parents has tended to be treated as a woman's issue, because the consequences of an unequal division of labor usually fall on mothers. Our findings suggest that who does what becomes an issue for fathers too when children appear because it is then that a couple's role arrangements—and how both the husband and the wife feel about them—become linked with their well-being as individuals and as couples.

Contemporary jokes, cartoons, and situation comedies frequently parody couples' heated disputes about who watches the children or takes out the garbage, reflecting the friction caused by the division of family labor in most couples' lives. Far from being amused by it, new parents are disillusioned and at the same time worried about being petty in complaining about who is folding the laundry, cooking the dinners, taking out the garbage, or getting up with the baby in the middle of the night. These have become hot issues not only for feminists but for all couples trying to raise healthy children, do serious work, and keep up with the soaring costs of housing, food, and medical bills.

Most studies of couples' role arrangements focus on who actually performs the roles, but this ignores how they *feel* about their arrangements and misses the connection between partners' feelings about their family and work arrangements and their satisfaction with their marriage. Arlie Hochschild began to unearth this link in *The Second Shift* (1989). In this chapter we will show how these parts of life become connected as partners become parents.

We expected the California couples who participated in our study, starting the families of the 1980s and 1990s, to be more egalitarian than the couples of the 1960s and 1970s. We were impressed with their pioneer spirit. Hopeful of becoming leaders at the frontier of modern family life, many felt ready to break new ground.

Natalie and Victor were hoping to right the wrongs in their families of origin, and expected to do their family making as a team:

> NATALIE: This family of ours is already different than the one I grew up in. Victor and I work much more closely as a couple than our parents did and we are determined to keep it that way. I'm not going to make our kids my whole existence the way my mother did.
>
> VICTOR: And I'm going to be there for my kids, the way my father *wasn't*.
>
> NATALIE: My mother's sacrifice in staying home to look after us full-time didn't really help. Although she was doing what she thought good mothers were supposed to, she was depressed a lot of the time and we ended up feeling like we had to take care of her. I'm determined that that's not going to happen in this family.

Each time we met with them, couples indicated on our Who Does What? questionnaire (Cowan and Cowan 1990b) how they actually divide the responsibilities for household tasks, family decisions, and the care of their baby, and how satisfied they felt with those arrangements. Couples who were not expecting a baby answered the same questions over the same period of time. A closer look at their responses will help us understand how the division of labor becomes entwined with a couple's intimacy when they try to put the rhetoric of equality to the test.

HOUSEHOLD AND FAMILY TASKS

The first twelve items on the questionnaire ask each spouse to use a 9-point scale to rate their division of responsibility for household and family tasks, in reality and according to their ideal. We assume that the greater the distance between how it is and how they would like it to be, the less satisfied they are with the current arrangements. A rating of 1 indicates that *she* takes all of the responsibility for that task. A rating of 5 means that they divide the task about equally, and a 9 shows that *he* is responsible for managing all of that task. The final question asks outright how satisfied they are with the way they divide these household and family tasks (very satisfied; pretty satisfied; neutral; somewhat dissatisfied; or very dissatisfied).

Simply adding up and taking the average of men's and women's ratings for all twelve household and family tasks at our first visit indicates that, in both expectant and childless couples, spouses are dividing the *overall* burden of family tasks fairly equitably. (The husbands' average rating was 4.8 and the wives' 4.5.) There is little change overall in couples' division of these twelve household and family tasks during the transition to parenthood. But simply averaging the scores for all of these items conceals important realities of life with young babies. In our first interview, almost all the couples agreed that men had more responsibility than women for repairs around the home, taking out the garbage, and looking after the car (6.9, 6.5, and 7.0, respectively, combining his and her ratings). In the last trimester of pregnancy, expectant fathers are also providing more of the family income than their wives are (6.2). Over the next two years, there is virtually no change in the arrangements of these tasks among the couples who remain childless, whereas the new parents begin to divide these tasks in more gender-stereotyped ways.

Six months after the birth, with 45 percent of the women at home full-time, men are providing even more of the family income than they were at the end of the pregnancy (from 6.2 to 7.3). They are doing a smaller proportion of the mounting loads of laundry than they were doing before the children were born, but they show significant increases in preparing meals, cleaning the house, and shopping for food. The average rating of the three household tasks in which men increase their participation never goes higher than 3.9, however, which means that even with men taking on more of the burden women are still doing more of the work. On the new parents' ratings of the other seven tasks, the division remains stable; wives continue to take more of the responsibility than their husbands throughout the transition to parenthood.

Eighteen months after the birth, men have cut back on meal preparation (average scores go from 3.6 to 3.2) and taking out the garbage (6.7 to 6.3), but they are beginning to shop (3.5 to 4.0) and take care of the yard or garden (5.0 to 5.3) more, presumably tasks they can do on the way to and from work or on the weekends.

How do couples react to these shifts? One subtle change is that instead of both partners performing some of each task, a common pattern for childless couples, now he tends to take on a few specific household responsibilities and she tends to do most of the others. So his and her overall responsibility for maintaining the household may not shift significantly after having a baby, but it feels more traditional because each has become more specialized. This leaves some husbands and wives feeling more separate. Given their shifting internal identities and their vows to be different from their parents, this separation can feel disappointing, a little frightening, and somewhat lonely:

> VICTOR: Sometimes I think that our lives are working out great. We have this great kid, and this great marriage, and this great family. It's just that Natalie and I hardly see each other. It seems that while I'm looking after one thing, she's always looking after something else.
>
> NATALIE: I know. I'm so preoccupied with the baby during the day. And I miss our time together as a couple. It takes some getting used to that

by the time each day is over, we just give each other a peck on the cheek and fall into bed like an old married couple.

FAMILY DECISIONS

On a second page of the questionnaire, we asked how family decisions are made on twelve common issues, both actual and ideal arrangements, so that we could calculate the discrepancy between them, and determine how each partner feels about their decision-making pattern overall.

Family decision making was the one arena in our study that came close to the egalitarian idea of equal influence or responsibility. According to both spouses' ratings, men have a little more influence than their wives do on decisions about financial planning, work outside the family, and initiating lovemaking (an average rating of about 6). Women, on the other hand, tend to have a little more influence on decisions about the couple's social arrangements and about participation in community activities and religious organizations (an average rating of about 4). On most of the other issues, such as major expenses, how to spend time at home, and how people should behave in the family, both new parents and childless spouses reported about the same amount of influence and responsibility for deciding.

This pattern of family decision making does not change much from late pregnancy until the children are almost two. Men's and women's satisfaction with their balance of decision making also stays stable for both parents and childless couples.

TAKING CARE OF THE BABY

A third set of items for couples to rate described some of the major tasks involved in caring for a baby.[1] One unique feature of having expectant parents complete this list is that in addition to asking about their current role arrangements, we could ask how they expected to do things after the baby arrived.

Men's and women's ratings in the last trimester of pregnancy show that they predict that the mothers will be responsible for more of the baby-care tasks than will the fathers. Their ratings range from a low of 2.0 (mothers will do most of the feeding) to a high of 3.8 (mothers will do more of the choosing of toys for the baby). Clearly, expectant parents are predicting less than a 50-50 division of the daily care of their babies. Approximately nine months later, when the babies are six months old, a majority describe their arrangements for taking care of the baby as even more Mother's and less Father's responsibility than either parent had predicted. This is the basis of our contention that the ideology of the new egalitarian couple is way ahead of the reality. The fallout from their unmet expectations seems to convert both spouses' surprise and disappointment into tension between them.

Jackson and Tanya talked a lot in one of our couples groups about their commitment to raising Kevin together. Three months later, when the baby was six months old, Tanya explained that Jackson had begun to do more housework than ever before but he wasn't available for Kevin nearly as much as she would have liked:

> TANYA: He wasn't being a chauvinist or anything, expecting me to do everything and him to do nothing. He just didn't *volunteer* to do things that obviously needed doing, so I had to put down some ground rules. Like if I'm in a bad mood, I may just yell: "I work eight hours, just like you. This is half your house and half your child, too. You've got to do your share!" Jackson never changed the kitty litter box once in four years, but he changes it now, so we've made great progress. I just didn't expect it to take so much work. We planned this child together, and we went through Lamaze together, and Jackson stayed home for the first two weeks. But then—wham!—the partnership was over!

Tanya underscores a theme we heard over and over: The tension between new parents about the father's involvement in the family threatens the equilibrium between them.

Among parents of six-month-old babies, mothers are shouldering more of the baby care than either parent predicted on eight of the twelve items of the questionnaire: deciding about meals, managing mealtime, diapering, bathing, taking the baby out, playing with the baby, arranging for baby-sitters, and dealing with the pediatrician. On four items, women and men predicted that mothers would do more and their expectations proved to be on the mark: responding to the baby's cries, getting up in the middle of the night, doing the child's laundry, and choosing the baby's toys.

The fact that mothers are doing most of the primary child care in the first months of parenthood is hardly news. What we are demonstrating is that couples' arrangements for taking care of their infants are less equitable *than they expected* them to be. Shannon, one of the new mothers, said that she and her husband, John, were astounded. They had always shared the chores around the house pretty evenly, but since she has been home with the baby she has assumed almost all of the household and child-care work. John is amazed that they became so traditional so fast.

It's not just that couples are startled by how the division of labor falls along gender lines, but they describe the change as if it were a mysterious virus they picked up when they were in the hospital having their baby; they don't seem to view their arrangements as *choices* they have made. This is why both mothers and fathers of infants show significantly greater discrepancies than do childless couples between "how it is now" and "how I'd like it to be." Since the greater burden of care has fallen to mothers, this is also why, at each follow-up interview during the transition to parenthood, mothers express much less satisfaction than fathers with the sharing of the baby care. The fathers are dissatisfied too—they say they would like to be more involved in the care of their babies, but they cannot figure out how to arrange it.

During the year between their babies' six- and eighteen-month birthdays, men do begin to take on a little more of their care. This increase is evident on eight of the twelve tasks we ask about, including bathing the baby, getting up during the night, and taking the baby out. On the remaining four tasks—playing with the baby, doing the baby's laundry, and arranging for baby-sitters and doctor's visits—fathers' involvement stays fairly constant from the year before. Tanya has noticed this shift in Jackson's involvement with Kevin by the next time we visit, when Kevin is about nineteen months old. Kevin's age makes it much easier for his father to take him out, sometimes for a whole day. But then she explains that by the time she gets Kevin up, feeds him, dresses him, makes him lunch, and so on, she is often too tired to enjoy the peace and quiet.

Despite fathers' increased involvement with their babies during this second year of parenthood, even the item that gets the highest ratings for fathers' participation—playing with the baby—receives average ratings of only 4.1 on our scale, still something mothers do more than fathers. Like the couple's specialization of household and family tasks, the care of their children becomes more specialized; they are less likely to make joint contributions to it. The modest increase in fathers' involvement in the care of their children between six and eighteen months after birth is not, therefore, accompanied by an increase in men's or women's satisfaction with the division of child care.

HIS AND HER VIEWS

Husbands' and wives' descriptions of their division of labor are quite similar,[2] but they do shade things differently: Each claims to be doing more than the other gives him or her credit for.* The feeling of not being appreciated for the endless amount of work each partner actually does undoubtedly increases the tension between them.

In our couples groups, we use the participants' responses to the Who Does What? questionnaire to talk about some of these issues. We soon learn that some couples treat the ratings quite seriously, which can lead to a heated exchange:

JACKSON: What do you *mean,* you take out the garbage more than I do? What score did you give it? Every day when I come home the bag in the kitchen is full, and I take it out to the incinerator.

TANYA: Jackson, how can you say that? Maybe once or twice during the week you do, but I have to ask you to throw out the baby's disposable diapers almost every day. I gave it a 3.

JACKSON: Amazing! I thought it was *really* about 4.5, but I put down 4 because I know you do it when I'm not home.

*Partners tend to agree most about who takes out the garbage, pays the bills, responds to the baby's cries, buys the toys, and plays with the baby. They agree least about how they divide the shopping, the preparation of meals, looking after the car, and taking the child out or arranging baby-sitting and doctor's appointments.

With this last remark, Jackson looked at the rest of us and shrugged as if to say, "Can you believe that couples argue about this petty stuff?" We believe it.

For the childless couples, *overall satisfaction* with role arrangements (household tasks plus decision making) remained stable over the first two years of the study. By contrast, new parents' overall satisfaction with their role arrangements (household tasks plus decision making plus child care) declined significantly—most dramatically between pregnancy and six months after the baby's birth (C. Cowan and P. Cowan 1988). We will discuss in chapter 9 the fact that trends were different for men and women who had been in one of our couples groups than for couples who did not take part in our intervention. When we compared the satisfaction of parents who had been in one of our couples groups and those who had had no intervention, the former *maintained* their satisfaction with the division of household and family tasks. This trend is particularly true for women. Since the actual role arrangements in the group and nongroup participants were very similar, we can see that men's and women's satisfaction with who does what is, at least in part, a matter of perspective.

Fathers' Involvement in Family Tasks

Group trends clearly show that fathers of babies and young children do much less work in the family than mothers do, right from the day they bring the baby home. Given the fact that most new mothers take more time off work than their husbands do, this may be inevitable in the first months. But the inequities continue into the second year of life, long past the time when many women return to work. Arlie Hochschild (1989) has also documented that mothers who work full-time are coming home to a "second shift" in which they do about two-thirds of the family work. Hochschild calls this current state of affairs a "stalled revolution," in reference to the unfulfilled promise of the prevailing egalitarian ideology. In detailed case studies, she demonstrates how the subterranean struggles involved in managing inequitable arrangements are subtly eroding the quality of men's and women's relationships as couples.

Although our data document these imbalances in the division of labor in a majority of families, there is a small cadre of men who *are* taking a significantly more active role in running their households and rearing their children. If we listen carefully to what those men and their wives are telling us, we can see that these men tend to feel better about themselves and about their family relationships than men who are less involved in family work. What's more, their wives feel significantly better too.

THE RANGE OF ARRANGEMENTS

In the 1980s, the popular press delighted in running stories of men who "gave up" their careers to take on the primary care of their children. Who are these unusual men, what leads to their decisions to care for their children, and how do they fare? Researchers have talked with such men in California, Connecticut, Michigan, Sweden, Israel, and Australia (Ehrensaft 1987; Pruett 1986; Radin 1988; Russell 1983). Of course, many men who are widowed (Schwebel, Fine, and Moreland 1988), divorced (Hanson 1988; Loewen 1988), or gay (Bozett 1988) can be primary parents, but here we are focusing on men who take on a major share of the care of very young children when their families are beginning. On the whole these studies show that men who choose to be the primary caretakers of their young children are involved and nurturant parents, although they tend not to continue in this role over the long haul. Only about 20 percent of them are still in the primary parent role two years after they take it on (Radin 1988; Russell 1983).

In our study, two of the seventy-two families having a baby described a reversal of parents' traditional roles during the preschool years: The husband was the primary caretaker of the baby and the wife was the primary wage earner. One of the couples made an active choice to arrange their lives this way. In the other, the father had been laid off for six months and then assigned to the night shift; the couple decided that the mother would keep her daytime job and the father would look after their son during the day until he was two years old. In another six couples, both parents worked full-time and shared the care of the house and children almost equally. In the remaining 88 percent of the families, the arrangements have a more traditional split: She is the primary caretaker and his involvement ranges from very little of the child's care to somewhere less than 50-50 on most of the child-care tasks on our list.

We discussed in the previous chapter our finding that there are advantages for men's and women's self-esteem when men feel more psychologically involved in being a parent. Are there benefits as well when men have more actual involvement in their children's day-to-day care? To answer this question, we correlated his and her ratings of his actual care of the baby, and their satisfaction with their arrangement of family roles, with measures of their well-being as individuals, as a couple, in the parent-child relationship, and with regard to stress outside the family.[3]

In late pregnancy, the wives who predicted that their husbands would be more involved in caring for the baby were more satisfied with their marriage and described their life together as warmer, more expressive, and less conflictful (a more cohesive family) than did other women. Husbands who predicted that they would be more involved in caring for their babies also perceived their family life during pregnancy as more cohesive.[4]

Six months after the birth of their child, when these fathers are actually taking care of their children more, they have higher self-esteem and so do their wives. Both partners describe their marriages as more satisfying, their families as more cohesive, and their parenting stress as lower. They also feel that they have more social support and fewer stressful events in their lives.[*]

When their children are eighteen months old, fathers' involvement in

---

[*]These findings are very similar to the links between men's greater psychological involvement in fatherhood (a larger Parent piece of the pie) and both men's and women's well-being.

caring for their children is no longer related to how they describe their satisfaction with themselves or their marriage, their view of the family atmosphere, or their level of life stress and support. Nevertheless, more involved fathers continue to have lower parenting stress and report fewer symptoms of depression. Men's involvement with the children still makes a difference to their wives' feelings about the quality of marriage and family life. Women whose husbands took more of a role in the care of their child were more maritally satisfied and described their family as having greater cohesion than mothers whose mates were less involved with the children. Parents' satisfaction with the division of the child-care tasks was even more highly correlated with their own and their spouses' well-being than was the fathers' actual amount of involvement (C. Cowan and P. Cowan 1988).

Tanya describes how Jackson's active involvement with Kevin affects her: "When I see Jackson making an extra effort with Kevin, I feel that he's telling me that he loves me. Rationally, I know that he and Kevin have their own thing going, but it makes me feel so good about him. And when we were fighting because Jackson wasn't really doing anything with Kevin, that just felt like a slap in my face."

Victor and Natalie, who share Kim's care and are less stressed than many of the other parents of eighteen-month-olds, also benefit from sharing the load—and seem to realize that their contentment is not typical. Victor told us: "I know that we're supposed to be stressed out now, but frankly we're having a fine time." And Natalie added: "I know things are fine. He's stopped leaving his shorts in the bathroom! But, seriously, when I see how involved Victor is with Kim and then I hear my friends complaining about how their husbands are out to lunch, I'm really thankful."

We cannot really tell which comes first—fathers' involvement in the family or both parents' feelings of well-being. It could be that when partners are feeling good about themselves and their relationship, men are more motivated to get involved with their children. Evidence supporting this view comes from our ability to *predict* which fathers will be more involved with their children's care, using a combination of their self-esteem and satisfaction-with-marriage ratings before their babies are born (Cowan and Cowan 1987a). It is also possible that fathers' involvement has a positive payoff in terms of the quality of the relationship they develop not only with their children but also with their wives; that, in turn, may keep active fathers feeling good about themselves. This view is supported by analyses showing that when fathers are involved in caring for their six-month-old infants, their own satisfaction with marriage, and especially their wives' satisfaction with marriage, tends to go up in the two-year period between pregnancy and eighteen months after their babies are born.[5]

On the distressing side of this equation, the less involved a father becomes with the baby's care, the more likely it is that he and his wife will become disenchanted with their relationship as a couple over the next year. If, in addition, both spouses are dissatisfied with their arrangements for looking after their baby, they and the marriage will suffer. Clearly, the higher fathers' involvement with their children is, the happier they and their wives are. What prevents a large majority of couples from living out this arrangement?

THE OBSTACLES

There are powerful barriers to creating egalitarian family arrangements. Discussions of who does what in the family usually assume that men will do as little child care as they can get away with. Most of the men in our study, however, wanted desperately to have a central role in their child's life. Despite some support for the notion of the new, involved father, powerful obstacles inside and outside the family prevent men from becoming equal participants in the business of raising a family (see also Russell 1983). When couples want to move in the direction of a shared division of family labor, just saying yes is not enough.

1. *It is hard to shake the idea that child rearing is women's work.* Most of today's parents were raised primarily by their mothers. The men have no models of male nurturers, and the women have internalized prohibitions against abdicating their role as primary caretakers of their babies. Even for couples who want to expand the traditional parental roles, these early models and constraints conspire to make it very difficult to create new kinds of family relationships (see Chodorow 1978).

2. *Men clearly expect their wives to be competent with babies right from the start.* We were surprised at how little time fathers allowed themselves for uncertainty, and at how quickly mothers would step in the moment their partner or the baby looked uneasy. Given the frequent male discomfort with feeling incompetent, it takes a minimum of implicit criticism or "help" for them to hand the baby back to "the expert," as many fathers dub their wives. And once men step out, it becomes hard for them to get back in.

3. *The "marital dance" tends to discourage men's active involvement in child care.* No matter how much they want their husbands to establish a wonderful relationship with the child, women who become full-time mothers can feel threatened if their husbands become too active or skilled. As Shannon put it: "I love seeing the closeness between John and John Junior, especially because I didn't have that with my father. But if John does well at his work *and* his relationship with the baby, what's my special contribution?"

The marital dance can be seen clearly in couples' discussions about feeding the baby. Many nurses and doctors emphasize breastfeeding almost exclusively. They may not mention or may actively frown upon the use of supplemental bottles in the early postpartum period. Doug, the "sociological observer," comments sardonically: "Josie has the kid on her breast about every two hours. And then, for ten minutes, I get to clean up the poop and diaper him and put him back to sleep. What's the point? I might as well be out bringing in some more money."

Because holding a squalling infant before feeding, or changing a soggy diaper, do not feel like significant contributions to child rearing, many fathers feel unnecessary or pushed out of a central role with their newborns.

They back away and turn to their work, where they know they can make a visible contribution to their family's welfare. The merits of breastfeeding are not at issue here; but its benefits may have unintended side effects, and couples may want to consider supplemental bottles as a way of encouraging fathers' early involvement.

4. *The more men attempt to take an active role in the care of their children, the more mixed or negative feedback they report from their own parents.* Victor said that every time he told his father about some wonderful thing that Kim had just done, his father asked him a question about work. And when his parents visit, they always ask Natalie about the baby, even though Victor knows as much or more about Kim than she does.

Many grandparents find their children's attempts to establish egalitarian family roles a threat or implied criticism of the "old way" of family making. This intergenerational tension creates a subtle but imposing obstacle to fathers becoming as involved with their children as they had hoped to be.

5. *The economics of the workplace and the lack of quality child care encourage fathers to work and mothers to stay home while children are young.* Maternity leave is available, but often without pay. Paternity leave, if offered at all, is usually short, only teasing both parents with a taste of what it could be like to share the care of their child. When both partners work outside the home, the lack of high-quality, affordable child care drains parents' natural excitement about parenthood and creates anxiety about leaving their children in someone else's care.

For those parents in our study who did overcome social pressures and tried to arrange it so that both could be home more, the marked differences between men's and women's wages often placed an additional financial burden on the new family. These practical realities can be the last straw, forcing partners to assume more traditional parenting arrangements than they had intended (Coysh 1983).

Because of these social realities, many fathers in our study did not accept the prevailing definitions of a father's "involvement" in the family:

> RAY: Most of my responsibility for the family is providing the bread. You know, Daddy is at work, Mommy is at home. Daddy makes the money, Mommy makes the house and takes care of Faith. I get really pissed off at Celie's friends. They're always asking her, "How come Ray doesn't look after Faith more?" Man, I'm looking after Faith six days a week, ten hours a day, busting my ass at the plant.

Despite all the obstacles, some of the men in our study made great efforts to be actively involved in the care of their children, enabling a few couples to make arrangements that approached their ideal. Unfortunately, they are swimming upstream, fighting off a formidable array of forces as they try to make their way forward.

What's Happened to the Marriage?

Ironically, many partners expend enormous energy on deciding and preparing to bring a child into their lives, only to feel that their marriage is shaky once they have become a family. Couples in our study who felt upbeat, the way Victor and Natalie and even Tanya and Jackson did in their first years as a family, were decidedly a minority.

Indeed, almost every study of the transition to parenthood has found that most new parents feel some disenchantment in their marriage. It is tempting to blame this on two related facts reported by every couple. First, after having a baby *time* becomes their most precious commodity (LaRossa and LaRossa 1981). Couples say that there are simply not enough hours in the day to look after the baby, keep the household running, go to work, talk with a co-worker or friend, and have any time left to nurture their relationship.

Second, even if a couple can eke out a little time together, the effort seems to require a major mobilization of forces on the part of both spouses: sitters need to be recruited; bottles must be prepared; instructions need to be left. New parents say that by the time they get out the door, they feel none of the spontaneity that had kept their relationship alive when they were only a twosome.

As we have seen, new parents' sense of themselves is shifting in unexpected directions. He is feeling the responsibility of supporting a family. She is wondering what to do about her job or career. Dissatisfaction with the family division of labor is increasing, and support from parents, friends, and co-workers seems hard to come by. Because most of these changes are unexpected, and because some have different implications for men's and women's lives, partners end up feeling that the balance between them is shifting too. These mounting strains and pressures begin to affect the more intimate aspects of the relationship between them—their caring, closeness, and sexual relationship; the amount of conflict and disagreement; and their feelings about the overall marriage.

EMOTIONAL INTIMACY AND SEX

We asked husbands and wives to describe in an open-ended way what they do to show their partners that they care and what their partners do to show their caring. It soon became clear that different things feel caring to different people—some romantic, others mundane: bringing flowers or special surprises; being a good listener; touching in certain ways; picking up the cleaning without being asked.

Also, husbands and wives often interpret caring differently. Bill says that when Peggy is sick, he tries to stay close by and bring her things. But Peggy says she likes to be left alone when she's not feeling well. She gets irritable when he hovers and fusses over her. Bill is doing "for Peggy" what *he* would find caring if *he* were ill. In many similar examples, the wife intends what she does to be caring, but her husband misses the point. It is as if partners follow the golden rule about caring—Do unto others as you would have them do unto you—only to have it backfire. Understandably, they may then feel hurt, misunderstood, or unappreciated.

New parents describe fewer examples of caring after having a baby compared to before, but as we keep finding in each domain of family life, men's and women's changes occur at different times. Six months after the birth of their babies, new mothers say that they are doing the same number of caring things for their husbands as they did in pregnancy, but their husbands report doing significantly fewer caring things for them. Perhaps not coincidentally, this is the period when wives' overall satisfaction with marriage declines most. This subtle shift in intimacy between the partners may be coloring women's perception of the whole relationship.

Between the babies' six- and eighteen-month birthdays, wives and husbands report that the women are doing fewer caring things for their husbands than the year before. This is the year in which the *men's* overall satisfaction with marriage takes its greatest plunge. We don't know whether the decline in caring contributes to the feeling that the marriage is less satisfying, or whether one partner's increasingly negative view of the marriage leads to less caring behavior. What we do know is that in the parents' natural preoccupation with caring for the baby, they seem less able to care for each other.

Both husbands and wives also report a negative change in their sexual relationship after having a baby. The frequency of lovemaking declines for almost all couples in the early months of parenthood, after having declined for about half of them during the last stages of the pregnancy. Sharon speaks for all new mothers: "It's all I can do to keep my eyes open until nine o'clock. As soon as the baby is down I race for the bed, and I'm asleep most nights before my head hits the pillow."

Couples are about evenly divided between those who report that sex is very good when they do get around to it and those who describe a decline in the quality of their sexual relationship as well. Sharon's husband, Daniel, said that as new parents, neither of them seemed very interested in sex. And when one of them was, the other was usually too busy or tired.

There are both physical and psychological deterrents to pleasurable sex for new parents. Some women have slow-healing scars from an episiotomy, which can make intercourse very painful. Others have temporary breast infections, or are embarrassed by the flow of breast milk when they become aroused. Even without any of these impediments to spontaneity or sensuality, almost all mothers are exhausted during the early weeks and months of what feels like twenty-four-hour-a-day on-call baby care, particularly if they are recovering from the major surgery of cesarean section delivery. A more subtle psychological deterrent, not often discussed but mentioned in chapter 3 with regard to sexual tendencies in late pregnancy, has to do with both partners' shifts in identity and roles. Joan told us that on the few nights when she is wide awake and even thinking about making love with Rob, "I have this little voice that begins to nag at me, saying, 'Parents don't have sex.'" Rob has the same feelings: "You're my wife but you're also a mother now, and it's not OK to turn on to a mother."

Probably the greatest interference with what happens in the bedroom comes from what happens between the partners outside the bedroom. Martin and Sandi, for example, tell us that making love has become problematic since Ellen's birth. To give an example of a recent disappointment, Martin explains that he had had an extremely stressful day at work. Sandi greeted him with a "tirade" about Ellen's fussy day, the plumber failing to come, and the baby-sitter's latest illness. Sandi picks up the story at the point when she asked Martin to take care of Ellen while she finished preparing dinner, which he did without enthusiasm or comment. Dinnertime was tense, and they spent the rest of the evening in different rooms. When they got into bed they watched television for a few minutes, and then Martin reached out to touch Sandi. She pulled away, feeling guilty that she was not ready to make love.

Like so many couples, Sandi and Martin were disregarding the tensions that had been building up over the previous hours. They had never had a chance to talk in anything like a collaborative or intimate way. This is the first step of the common scenario for one or both partners to feel "not in the mood."

Although men and women tend to give similar descriptions of the negative changes in their sexual relationship after becoming parents, they often see the positive changes differently. New fathers report fewer positive changes in their sexual relationship, whereas new mothers describe about the same number of positive changes at each point in the study. This difference in perception is reminiscent of the couple in Woody Allen's film *Annie Hall*. The partners, played by Woody Allen and Diane Keaton, are shown, after a difficult period in their relationship, on a split screen, having separate conversations with their therapists. The woman's therapist asks her how often they are having sex, and she answers, "Oh, constantly. At least three times a week." The man's therapist asks him the same question, to which he replies, "Uh, hardly at all. Only three times a week."

CONFLICT, DISSATISFACTION, AND DIVORCE

We have seen that the changes couples report in their division of labor and in the caring and intimacy of their marriages appear to be affecting how they feel about their relationships as couples. Here we focus directly on the difficulties new parents describe in their relationships: their conflict and disagreement, their dissatisfaction, and, for a small, unhappy group, their discouragement about being able to stay together as a couple.

Ninety-two percent of the men and women in our study who became parents described more conflict and disagreement after having their baby than they had described before they became parents. Using a questionnaire (adapted from one by Sheldon Starr, no date), we asked them to rate the amount of conflict and disagreement (a great deal, a moderate amount, a little, or none) they have as a couple in ten common aspects of family life and to indicate which three issues of the ten are most likely to lead to conflict for them: the division of the workload in the family; the amount of time spent together as a couple; willingness to talk about their sexual relationship; management of family money; the need for time alone; the quality of time spent together as a couple; relationships with in-laws; ideas about how to raise children; willingness to work for improvement in the relationship; or the way they communicate with each other.

From the reports of men and women in both one-job and two-job families, the division of the workload in the family wins, hands down, as the issue most likely to cause conflict in the first two years of family making.[6] This makes it graphically clear that there is a link between shifts in the day-to-day quality of a parent's family life and his or her feelings about the quality of the couple relationship. Art told us that a lot of things that hadn't been important before he and Stephanie became parents suddenly began to cause trouble. They had never kept tabs on who cleaned up after dinner; whoever had the time would take care of it. Now, Stephanie explained, "I know that Art is tired from working all day, but I need to have him get rid of the dishes after we eat. If things aren't in order, I can't start to relax. If he doesn't help me with that, we're likely to start getting cross with one another almost before we realize what's happening."

Most of the couples we spoke to did not, of course, go from a state of shared bliss to one of shouting and carrying on once they became parents. But regardless of their level of disagreement and conflict before they had babies, between pregnancy and eighteen months after becoming parents they described an average increase in conflict of 1 point on a 7-point scale for each item on the list[7]—a small average increase, but one that is reported by almost every new parent in our study.

Given this pervasive increase in marital conflict, our next area of investigation centered on establishing what happens to the marital satisfaction of the couples in our study. We used both partners' descriptions of their marriage from pregnancy to eighteen months after the baby is born on our marital satisfaction questionnaire (Locke and Wallace 1959).[8] Of course, some spouses feel differently about their relationship, but in our study most husbands' and wives' ratings were quite similar.[9]

Let us begin with how the parents who did *not* take part in our couples group intervention described their marriages over time, since they are comparable to most couples having babies with no special help during their transition to parenthood. The typical scores on the questionnaire range from about 40, which would indicate a marriage in serious distress, through 100, which is about average, to 140, which suggests a very satisfying couple relationship. During late pregnancy, the average level of marital satisfaction is quite high in a majority of the expectant parents with no intervention (129 for women, 126 for men), although 9 percent of the women and 14 percent of the men are already in the distressed range.

From late pregnancy to six months after giving birth, the mothers' average marital satisfaction scores decline by eight points, and then drop another seven points between six and eighteen months postpartum—both statistically significant changes. New fathers' marital satisfaction scores drop five points from pregnancy to six months after the birth, then plunge twelve points during the following year.[10] Here we see the now-familiar pattern in which women feel the impact of the transition more strongly during the first six months after birth, and their husbands feel it more strongly in the following year.

The average scores suggest a small downward slide in new parents' satisfaction with their marriages, but still quite positive views. By the time their babies are eighteen months old, however, almost one-quarter—24 percent of new mothers and 22 percent of new fathers—are indicating that their marriage is in some distress. Keep in mind that these figures do *not* include those husbands and wives who separated or divorced during these two years. Among the forty-eight expectant couples who did not participate in our couples groups, 12.5 percent were announcing separations or divorces before their children were eighteen months old and another 3.5 percent divorced by the time their child was three years old. A cumulative total of 20 percent divorced by the end of their first child's kindergarten year.

Although our sample was relatively small, our divorce figures appear to be in line with national trends (Bumpass and Rindfuss 1979). If so, the 12.5 percent divorce rate among parents whose first child is less than eighteen months old suggests that one-quarter (12.5 percent divided by 50 percent) of divorces will have taken place before a child is old enough to remember living with both biological parents. Approximately 40 percent (twenty out of fifty) have taken place by the end of the child's kindergarten year.

Two comparisons help us to place these divorce figures in a broader perspective. First, we compared the divorce rate of the new parents in our study with that of couples who had participated in one of our intervention groups during their transition to parenthood. During the same two-year period, all of the couples in the group intervention were still in intact marriages. (We will see in chapter 9 that this impressive effect did not last forever.) By the time the children were three and a half, only one couple from the intervention sample (4 percent) had divorced. This comparison suggests that some of the marital disruption that occurs very early in the life of a child can be prevented or at least delayed.

A second comparison sample is most enlightening. What happens over the same period of time to the marriages of couples who do not have a baby? Six years after the study began, the divorce rate of the new parents was 20 percent, but the divorce rate of the couples who remained childless throughout that period approached the national average of 50 percent. It seems that having a child decreases, or at least delays, a couple's likelihood of divorce.

At first, these comparisons between parents and nonparents may seem contradictory: How could having a baby be associated with an increase in marital dissatisfaction and a decrease in the rate of divorce in the early family-making years? We are talking about two different aspects of marriage: how partners feel their marriage is working, or marital quality, and whether they stay together, or marital stability. Couples who are satisfied with their relationships will be more likely to stay together, but some will stay married even when one or both partners are unhappy with the marriage (Lewis and Spanier 1979). The marital stability of couples who have preschool children is "protected" (Cherlin 1977). Although new parents may be experiencing increased tension or dissatisfaction as couples, their joint involvement with managing the baby's and the family's needs may lead them to put off, or possibly to work harder on, the problems in their marriage—at least while the children are young.

Where are the bright spots in this somber picture of marital distress? There are a significant number of couples, though they are clearly in the minority, whose relationships feel qualitatively better in the first eighteen months after having a child. In Jay Belsky's study (Belsky and Rovine 1990), about 20 to 35 percent of couples showed "modest positive change" according to different measures, without any intervention or therapy. In our study, about 18 percent of the parents who did not take part in one of our couples groups and about 38 percent of the group participants showed increased satisfaction with their relationships as couples during the transition to parenthood.

Paul and Beth enthusiastically described their life as they tried to find the right balance. Their life with Willie could get "really crazy," they said, but they approached each difficulty as a challenge, and put their heads together to come up with a plan. It helped that Paul was very involved in the day-to-day child care. Beth said, "I appreciate his strength even more than I used to. But I was afraid that he was giving up his own work too much." "Well, I did, some," Paul responded. "But I kept thinking, 'It's hard now, but it won't last forever.' "

Paul and Beth did so well because, when things got difficult or chaotic, they were able to avoid blaming each other for the strain. Somehow they managed to keep working as a team, "on the same side" (Ball 1984), helping each other maintain the perspective that the hard stretches would not last forever. Given many spouses' tendency to blame the other in times of stress, this seems like a heroic achievement for overextended new parents.

WHY DOES SATISFACTION WITH MARRIAGE GO DOWN?

The question we are asked most often by parents, writers, and people from the media is why there is such a consistent finding of disenchantment with marriage among new parents. It begins, we think, with the issue of men's and women's roles, the topic with which we opened this chapter. The new ideology of egalitarian relationships between men and women has made some inroads on the work front, in the sense that mothers are more likely to be employed than they used to be. Most couples, however, are not prepared for the strain of creating more egalitarian relationships at home, and it is this strain that seems to lead men and women to feel more negatively about their partners and the state of their marriage. But why?

The more we thought about this question, the more complicated and elusive it became. Even with sophisticated research and analytic strategies, there is very little systematic information to help us understand the processes or mechanisms that drive marital satisfaction down during the sensitive family-making period. Part of the increase in conflict and the decline in sexual and marital satisfaction after having a baby is self-explanatory. Major life changes, even positive ones, are stressful, and negative ones can exact a high toll on one's sense of well-being (Holmes and Rahe 1967; Lazarus and Folkman 1984). Given the consistent pattern of shifts in a negative direction during the transition to parenthood, we might *expect* to see a decline in satisfaction with marriage; and the more negative the changes, the greater the decline in marital satisfaction should be. But our results do not support this hypothesis. In fact, we found very little correlation between declining marital satisfaction and any single negative change reported by new parents—the loss of the lover aspect of self, the more traditional division of family work, declines in role satisfaction, changes in ideas about parenting, declining social support, or shifting work patterns. Although each of these aspects of life is related to how partners feel about their marriage *at a given time,* when things become increasingly problematic from one period to the next there is not a corresponding decline in satisfaction with marriage. How, then, can we explain the drop in satisfaction with marriage for a majority of the couples who have had a baby?

First, as we described in chapter 2, couples enter the transition to parenthood with very different attitudes and decision-making processes. We saw that those different decision-making patterns led to different patterns in the parents' feelings about their relationships as couples from pregnancy to almost two years after having their babies. The Planners and the Acceptance-of-Fate couples continued to feel quite happy with how their relationships as couples were feeling once they became parents. The Ambivalent and Yes-No couples, on the other hand, described feeling less enthusiastic—or very distressed—about their marriages in the first years of parenthood. Some of the decline in marital satisfaction, then, must be attributed to the couples who did not embark on their journey to parenthood wholeheartedly in the first place.

We also noted that childbirth preparation classes seem to set the stage for couples to think about parenthood as a joint venture. The increased visibility of prepared childbirth classes, most of which include mothers and fathers, says to men, in effect: Preparing for the baby's arrival is for fathers, too. What we are hearing is that men's increasing involvement in the preparation for the *day* of their baby's birth leads both spouses to expect that he will be involved in what follows—the ongoing daily care and rearing of the children. How ironic that the recent widespread participation of fathers in the births of their babies has become a source of new parents' disappointment when the men do not stay involved in their babies' early care. We know now that both parents' disappointment about his involvement can have consequences for the marriage. In our study, when there was a larger discrepancy between the wives' expectations of their husbands' involvement in looking after the baby and the husbands' *actual* involvement, the wives showed a greater decline in marital satisfaction between late pregnancy and eighteen months after giving birth (Garrett 1983). (Belsky and colleagues [Belsky, Ward, and Rovine 1986] report a similar finding.)

Third, as we have described with a number of critical aspects of couples' lives, a husband and a wife have different experiences of becoming parents. In our interviews and couples group discussions, husbands and wives kept emphasizing different things: She's the one carrying the baby; he's the one who has to go to work early every morning; he thinks they should let the baby cry; she can't stand to hear the baby crying. Almost all of these differences were being recounted as stimulators of friction between the parents. It seemed clear that the differences between husbands' and wives' experience of the transition were leading to their feeling distant, which stimulated conflict, which, in turn, affected both partners' satisfaction with their overall relationship.

In several important respects, men and women are changing in different directions while becoming parents: in the division of household tasks and child care, in social support outside the marriage, in work life, and so on. Furthermore, those differences grow larger along the journey to parenthood. In some couples, the increased difference between the partners is modest, but in others the growing differences become marked. The more different he and she become from each other in their descriptions of themselves, their role arrangements, their sexual relationship, their ideas about parenting, and the families they grew up in, the more they report increases in conflict between them.

As we suspected, couples with the greatest increases in both differences and conflict from pregnancy to six months after they have a baby showed the greatest decline in marital satisfaction over the two-year period from pregnancy to eighteen months after the birth.[11] Clearly it is difference *and* conflict, rather than conflict alone, that explains most about the partners' declines in satisfaction with marriage once they have become parents.

Recall Peggy and Bill, whose difficulty began with their ambivalence about having a child, extended through Peggy's very difficult pregnancy, and continued after their daughter, Mindy, was born. Eighteen months after the birth, this is how they described their relationship:

BILL: I thought we were doing OK. I was pitching in at home. We'd started to make love again, after all that difficulty when Peggy was pregnant. But mostly she's just mad before I go to work in the morning and mad as soon as I get back at night.

PEGGY: Well, I know we're making love more often, but it still hurts about half the time, from that terrible episiotomy. And we've got very different ideas about your "pitching in." I don't consider changing a diaper once a month and feeding Mindy when you've got nothing else to do much of a "pitch." What's really getting to me, though, is that we hardly ever agree about how to handle her. I think you're too rough and you think I'm spoiling her, and neither of us wants to change. I know your business problems are bugging you, but that's no excuse to take out your frustrations on Mindy and me.

Peggy and Bill have different perceptions of the "same" events. They have different sets of physical and emotional stresses both within and between them. They have different ideas about what to do with Mindy. They perceive that they are moving ever farther apart. It is not difficult to see how this has begun to take its toll in greater dissatisfaction with each other and with their relationship.

Of course, we cannot be sure that these differences *caused* the conflict in Peggy and Bill or in the sample as a whole. But experience and research data suggest that marital tensions are more likely to erupt when fathers and mothers become polarized (cf. Block, Block, and Morrison 1981). Because our culture still promotes gender-stereotyped family and work arrangements, the transition to parenthood heightens the differences between men and women, and these differences threaten the equilibrium of their marriage.

Perhaps Ray best captured, in his typically humorous style, both the complexity and the dramatic simplicity of what happens to marriage when partners become parents. His and Celie's daughter, Faith, was three and a half years old when we asked him what had been the *hardest* part of becoming a family. His answer: "The changes in our relationship as a couple." And the *best* part of becoming a family? He grinned. "The changes in our relationship as a couple!"

CHAPTER 6

Beyond the Doorstep:
New Problems, New Solutions

WOMEN MAKE MANY DIFFERENT KINDS OF CHOICES about whether, when, and under what conditions they will return to work after having a baby. We found a substantial number who were relatively happy with their choice to stay home while their babies were young, and others who felt sure that they and their children were benefiting from their decision to return to work. Whatever their ultimate work/family arrangements, *every* woman we talked with continued to think about the possibility that perhaps she made the wrong choice. "In my mom's day they said, 'To be a full-fledged woman, you've got to be a mother and not a career woman,' and now it's switched. I'm expected to have a career and *not* be a mother. Or be a mother, but keep my career on track. So I'm at home looking after little John, but I keep wondering whether I ought to be at work. Meanwhile, my friend Abby is back at work feeling desperate because she feels she ought to be home!"

We are talking to Shannon and John when their baby is six months old. One of the most up-beat women in our study, Shannon is in a couple who were Planners (chapter 2) and had a fairly serene pregnancy (chapter 3). Despite their surprise at how "traditional" their arrangements of who does what have become, John and Shannon are still feeling quite positive about their relationship as a couple (chapter 5). Compared to other couples in our study they are feeling less strain, yet Shannon's deliberations about staying home or going back to work were echoed in some form by every woman in our study.

Balancing family and work life after the baby comes is one of the major tasks that couples face when they come up for air and turn their attention to the outside world. A second task to be accomplished, whether or not women return to their jobs, is finding acceptable, affordable caregivers when neither parent is available to look after the child. These tasks are part of an ongoing challenge for new parents. Following families over the past fifteen years, we have discovered that it is typical for couples to make not one but several major shifts in their lives during this period of family formation. Some are undertaken voluntarily, others are out of their control. But almost all of them increase a couple's strain. A couple might move to larger or more congenial quarters, which usually means higher expenses and being farther away from the people they count on for support. A partner loses or gives up a job. A grandparent or one of the new parents themselves becomes seriously ill. During the course of our longitudinal study, at least six of the new parents suffered serious illnesses—postpartum depression, a severe back injury, lupus, multiple sclerosis, rheumatoid arthritis—while countless others grieved for a parent who had become ill and died.

When life changes and the stresses they bring loom large, as they inevitably do during the transition to parenthood, couples must look to their personal resources and their network of support, people they can turn to for advice, financial backing, empathy, or emotional sustenance. The theory is that social support can buffer or reduce the impact of life stress (Crnic et al. 1983; Crockenberg 1981). In this chapter we follow couples as they turn from adapting to the unexpected shifts in themselves and their marriage to coping with changes in their worlds outside the family.

In chapter 4 we listened to Art and Stephanie's struggle about whether she would agree to get a baby-sitter so that they could spend some time together as a couple. It seemed like a typical inside-the-family issue. As we listen more closely, however, we hear how pressures from outside the family are contributing to the strain in Stephanie and Art's relationship as a couple.

A few months before our eighteen-months-after-birth conversation, Stephanie had returned to her job in the dental office four days a week and Art had been promoted from teacher to principal of an experimental elementary school. In addition to these major shifts, they had also moved to a new community in order to be closer to his school. Stephanie said it had taken six months of phone calls, letters, and meetings to convince the dentist she worked for that she could do the job on a four-day-a-week schedule: "It is too good a job to give up, but I was ready to tell him to stuff it until he finally gave in. He's a good guy, but he just doesn't understand. He's got a wife at home full-time, and his kids have grown up. He gets everything at home taken care of by her, and at the office by me, and he just assumes that that's what women do."

It doesn't help, she tells Art, that his work is so demanding that she and Linda hardly see him during the week. Art knew that working long hours

made him miss some of the most important times in Linda's life: "But I don't
know how to manage it all with this new job. I obviously couldn't turn down
the promotion, and I just can't do it on a nine-to-five schedule. It's for you
and Linda, too. I wish you'd back off a little."

Although couples themselves can take a long time to recognize that
pressures from the outside world spill over into their relationship, we see
here how difficult it can be for them to juggle the demands of the job and
the needs of the baby and still have energy and time for each other. As if this
task were not difficult enough, Stephanie goes on to other serious concerns.
She doesn't know where the local child-care facilities in her new neighborhood are. She has not met any neighbors yet, and their new home is too far
away from their old one to see much of their former next-door neighbors,
who had become close friends.

Three of the most common outside-the-family challenges are how to find
a balance between work and family life; how to find adequate child care; and
how to find stable sources of support in a world that seems to be dominated
by change. Each unresolved challenge becomes a source of increased stress,
each challenge successfully met, a source of added support. Despite all the
talk about stress, struggle, and obstacles, these negative-sounding conditions
do not necessarily lead to unhappy outcomes. In fact, if parents are to keep
changing and growing as their children develop, some challenge may be
necessary. An important case in point, as we will see, is that when women
with young children do juggle work and family roles successfully, they tend
to feel better about themselves and their marriages, even if they are breathless at times.

Work

Although every one of our interview questions is addressed to both members
of the couple, when we ask about returning to work after the baby is born,
it is the women who tend to answer. Men do not think that this question is
meant for them. There is a little variation in *when* new fathers plan to go back
to work: Some arrange to stay home for several days after their babies are
born; a few might take more than a week off. But the basic assumption is so
automatic that it is never stated directly: Fathers do not quit or cut back on
their jobs once the baby comes home. It is mothers who must decide whether
or when to return to their work outside the family.

Despite the cultural shift in ideology toward a more egalitarian stance,
gender-stereotyped attitudes have crept into the framing of most researchers'
questions about mothers' work. Early studies focused on identifying the
potentially harmful consequences of mothers' work outside the family, especially for young children. We can hear that parents have been affected by
knowing about journalists' and researchers' writing about this issue. Does
working increase a woman's stress or depression? Does it create problems in

her marriage? Does a mother's working deprive her husband and children of nurturance and support? (Here we are reminded of the man in Gail Sheehy's *Passages* [1976] who said that ever since his wife went back to work, their family had had no butter and no desserts!) No one thinks to ask a father what his wife and baby might miss when *he* goes back to work.

There are advantages *and* drawbacks to both parents working when children are young. When all of the findings are toted up, the balance appears to be generally positive, especially for mothers and daughters (Greenberger and Goldberg 1989; Moorehouse in press). Perhaps even more important, our results suggest that when fathers and mothers manage to balance family and work to their satisfaction, there is positive spillover for the wife's satisfaction with herself, for the quality of the relationships both parents develop with their children, and for *both* spouses' satisfaction with their marriage.

PARENTS' WORK/FAMILY ARRANGEMENTS AND SATISFACTION

The majority of mothers with children under three are working outside the home, and this will soon be true of mothers of one-year-olds. Given these rapid historical shifts and the powerful competing ideologies about how men and women should balance work and family life, we expected to find a variety of work/family arrangements in the couples in our study. The patterns in our sample seem to match the national demographics fairly closely. When their infants were six months old, 55 percent of the mothers were back at work, 36 percent part-time (less than twenty hours a week) and 19 percent working between twenty and forty hours a week. One year later, when the children were one and a half, 57 percent of the mothers were employed, 30 percent part-time and 27 percent full-time.

These apparently stable averages over time hide an important fact. About one-third of the women are making shifts in their work arrangements over the year between their babies' six- and eighteen-month birthdays—some entering the labor force, some leaving it, others increasing their work hours from part-time to full-time, and others cutting back from full-time to part time. Even within two-worker families, "full-time" work can mean different things for mothers and fathers. The mothers working full-time in our study were employed between thirty-two and forty hours a week during their children's toddler years, but some of the fathers were away from home as many as fifty to eighty hours a week. Any way we look at these figures, they spell potential strain for a couple with very young children. A discussion of four common work/family arrangements will help show that each alternative involves trade-offs.

Mom is home, but anguished. When we meet them in late pregnancy, Gail and Michael describe themselves as happily married.* As a couple, they are

---

*An extended case study of this couple can be found in a chapter by Bradburn and Kaplan (in press).

feeling closer together than ever before, but both worry about what will happen when they try to balance work and parenthood after their child is born. Gail has decided to stay home for a while but is concerned about how they are going to manage: "How guilty am I going to feel not working? How guilty am I going to feel working? How are we going to arrange child care and all that?" Michael's job demands intense involvement. His worries center on how much his work will take away time he could be spending with the baby: "I've made the resolution that I want the child to be uppermost."

When we visit Gail and Michael six months after their daughter, Sarah, is born, we find that, just as they had feared, juggling family and work is creating a good deal of stress for both of them. Michael's job as a medical researcher does offer flexible hours, so he takes care of some of the morning and evening routines with Sarah. But recently work has become hectic and he has had to put in about sixty-five hours a week:

> MICHAEL: I'm used to working in the evenings, but now, either I don't get to do it at all or I finish and I'm exhausted. I'm in a bind. I miss watching every detail of Sarah's development. But if I really want to build my career and get off on a solid footing, now's the time to do it.
> GAIL: I'm in a bind, too. I feel restless being at home all the time. I've been thinking that a part-time job would be good for me, doing something practical, something other than being a mother. But at the same time I feel guilty at the thought of leaving Sarah with strangers. I firmly believe that children should stay at home with one parent.
> MICHAEL: I really disagree with Gail about child care. I think it would be good for her to work, and good for Sarah, too. Others find good part-time day care, and I know we can, too.
> GAIL: We could sure use the extra money, but it seems that what it costs for decent child care would take everything I can earn.

As we follow Gail and Michael over the next five years, there is little resolution of this issue. When their second child, Jason, comes along, Gail continues to feel ambivalent about working or arranging any regular day care for the children. Michael's work becomes even more demanding, the typical pattern for men in the family-making period. Gail says that she is longing for a career direction but pursues it "halfheartedly" because of her conflict about leaving the children with someone else. She eventually finds part-time work that she can do at home.

As they struggle with these conflicts between family and work—within and between them—Michael and Gail describe more conflict and distance in their relationship as a couple. When Sarah is about three years old, they seek couples therapy to see whether they can recapture their earlier closeness. Although most couples do not look for professional help for their marital strain, this is a typical example of how outside-the-family pressures begin to play out in the marriage.

There are many reasons for Michael and Gail's work choices and their subsequent distress about them, but several stand out. Gail has been truly confused about how to get on with her own career and still be with the children during the period when they need her regular care and attention. Since she has not been able to understand what is fueling her confusion, she feels unsure about her competence as a mother and a professional, especially when she looks at Michael's rising career. Husbands' support for their wives' work is important, but Michael's "support" for Gail finding a job has not been helpful because it fails to recognize the underlying emotional dilemmas that pull her to stay home. To complicate matters further, the combination of Michael's increasingly demanding work schedule and his direct involvement with the children leaves him little time and energy for his relationship with Gail, so the marriage feels a little shaky to both of them.

Finally, like most of the couples in our study, Michael and Gail use what to us is a curious approach to calculating the financial "costs and benefits" of a mother's going back to work. For some reason, the common assumption is that the cost of child care should be subtracted from the *wife's* salary. This line of reasoning ignores the fact that if parents must work, *someone* must look after the children. If the husband works outside the home and the wife looks after the children, part of his salary could be thought of as subsidizing that choice. By the same logic, if both the husband and wife work outside the home, part of each of their salaries could be earmarked for the care of the children. Locked into a traditional view of a mother's role, however, most parents assume that if the wife chooses to work, *she* should pay for someone to look after *their* child. So even if both parents acknowledge that the wife's work is important to her, she can become discouraged from resuming her job if she cannot earn more than the cost of their children's care. It is important to reexamine the price of this kind of logic—in actual dollars and in emotional toll—on the wife, the husband, the marriage, and the children.

Mom planned to continue working, but changed her mind. Sharon is one of the mothers who decided not to go back to work as early as she had planned. This is how she explained it to us six months after Amy was born:

SHARON: It was understood that I would take six months off work. I took one month off before she was born, so that left five. Then, as the end of the fifth month approached, I realized that I didn't want to go back to work. Boy, we went through a lot at that point. Can we survive on just one salary? I really didn't want to leave Amy with anybody. I had no idea I would be so possessive. It was about that time that I heard on the news that a child-care center had caught fire, and that somebody had kidnapped somebody else's baby, and I'm saying, "I'm not sending my child anywhere!"

So I asked for an extension to my leave, and I figured I'd get Amy a little more self-reliant because she was still strictly a breast-fed baby. At the same time, Daniel went through a job change and got a large bonus. So he told me that I didn't have to go back to work for a while.

Regardless of how well-thought-out their plans are, few couples can predict how the women will feel about going back to work after the baby is born. Many women tell us that their feelings about being with their babies and about the importance of their work alter dramatically once they become mothers. Some say that work simply doesn't feel as important as it used to, and others say that they are so much more drawn to their babies than they had anticipated. Thus, decisions that seemed firm before they became mothers become "unmade." This pattern is consistent with the results of a recent study of new mothers by Karen Harber (1991), who found that 75 percent of the mothers felt significant conflict between wanting to work and wanting to be with their babies in the first months of motherhood.

Women's uncertainty does not disappear as their babies grow older. When we talk with Sharon and Daniel again a year later, her plans about returning to full-time work have changed again. Like Gail, Sharon has been reluctant to leave her daughter and argues that the wages and commuting costs—taken, of course, out of *her* salary—will not result in much more money for the family. Still, because she is determined to use her working skills before she loses them, Sharon has taken a job with a cosmetics firm where she can set her own hours: "I don't work *for* anyone. It's the first time having a job has been fun. Amy goes to the baby-sitter twenty hours a week. If I'm not out doing a demonstration or a facial, I have time for catching up around the house. And then she comes home and has a nap, and then her father comes home. It works out well as long as I get back early. If Daniel and I come home at the same time—watch out!"

Women like Sharon are going to great lengths to make adjustments in their work outside the family so that their family lives will feel more nurturant and less frantic. By contrast, when fathers make shifts in their jobs, it is to keep them moving up the career ladder. These moves feel especially important, the men say, now that they are supporting a family.

Mom is a student, but is always frazzled. Cindy and James have been fighting a lot lately. He is working as a chemist in a paint company between his undergraduate and graduate training in chemistry so that Cindy can complete her studies in economics and business. They are frustrated with juggling so many hours of work, rushing to complete their education, and trying to spend "quality time" with their son, Eddie. Their stress is aggravated by Cindy's one-hour commute to and from school each day. She must get Eddie to a sitter near her college at 7:30 A.M. and pick him up at 4:30 P.M.:

CINDY: I feel like I don't have a moment's peace. In the morning I have to rush Eddie, rush James, get everybody moving, get ready, drive like mad, take the time to get Eddie settled at day care, and get to classes. When I sit down in the quiet of the library to begin my assignments, I find myself thinking about Eddie and what he's doing. Or thinking about the last fight that James and I had, and what we're going to do about it. Trying to get my reading and assignments done before I leave to pick Eddie up at the end of the day is like being in a Charlie Chaplin movie. By the end of the day, I'm really uptight. And then in the late afternoon, we replay the whole scene in reverse. By the time everything stops moving and Eddie's in bed, my head is already into what I have to face at school tomorrow.

Cindy and James's pace is more frenetic than that of the typical new family, but we see variations on this theme in every family with two parents who work or have full-time school schedules. It is not surprising that, when the days begin and end with parents and children feeling rushed and frazzled, thoughtful and tender moments between the parents are rare.

Mom is at work and pleased about her situation, sort of. Natalie and Victor, you may recall, have been doing well as a couple. Their daughter, Kim, is eighteen months old, and Victor's and Natalie's sense of humor and flexibility seem to be pulling them through the early challenges of parenthood.

Reflecting on the fact that her mother's sacrifice in staying home did not make her a satisfied woman, Natalie has been determined since the beginning of her pregnancy to return to her job, which she loves. This she does, although, like Stephanie, she finds herself engaged in complex negotiations with her company to reduce her schedule to four days a week. Victor, wanting to be available to his child in a way that his father was not for him, is taking a very active role in Kim's daily routines. Although he was working for his father when we first met him, he has recently taken an interim job in which he can set his own hours and earn a decent salary while he sorts out "what I really want to be when I grow up." When his and Natalie's work hours overlap, Kim's two sets of grandparents, who live nearby, take turns looking after her. It seems as if Natalie and Victor have the kinds of support that couples need to manage the stress of the early family years.

But these "solutions" leave Natalie feeling uneasy a lot of the time. Although she realizes that she and Victor share work and family time more equally than most other couples, and have the extra benefit of grandparents who love to care for Kim, she has mixed feelings about her work/family balance: "On one hand, I'm feeling more and more independent, able to take business trips without feeling guilty. Feeling good that I can put a limit on my work time. But I'm still uneasy about leaving Kim, even though she's with Victor or our parents. I want to be with her *and* be at work. The dilemma does not feel totally resolvable right now." Natalie is not alone: Even when they are reasonably contented with how their lives are shaping up, *not one* of the employed mothers in our study was entirely satisfied that she was devoting enough energy to her work outside the family or that she had chosen the best way to be with the baby.

The compelling ideology of the egalitarian family has saddled new mothers with two major decisions: *whether* to work while their children are young, and *how* to arrange their work so that their children will feel loved and secure. The pressure of making arrangements so that men and women will have more equal roles at work and at home affects the emotional atmosphere in the family much more than it affects couples' behavior. And work/family arrangements clearly exact a greater toll on women's progress in their jobs and careers than on men's. Many women say that this state of affairs would probably be acceptable if it lasted just for the first family-making year. But most are concerned that any substantial impediment to increasing their earning power could put them and their children at risk if anything were to happen to their husbands or their marriages. Their fears are not assuaged by reading the shocking statistics about how women's and children's standard of living plummets when families are torn apart by death or divorce (Wallerstein and Blakeslee 1989; Weitzman 1985).

PARENTS' WORK PATTERNS

Just as we found that the impact of a new baby on parents depends on how they were doing before the baby came along, so we learned that couples' decisions about how to balance work inside and outside the family after having a baby stem from attitudes in the workplace and from the partners' work and family histories, especially those of the wife.

Women's Work History and Well-being During Pregnancy   A woman's decision about working after her baby is born is influenced by how invested she was in her job or career before. We noted that Gail has been ambivalent about going out to work since her children were born. If we go farther back in her preparenthood history, we find that she was torn about "who she was going to be" even before she became a mother. Gail says that her sense of a work or career direction has been cloudy since she completed her schooling. Even when she had the luxury of time, her search for work was not very serious. Not surprisingly, it remained so after Sarah came along.

Working outside the home appears to play a role in women's well-being. The mothers in our study who had returned to work by the time their children were eighteen months old reported slightly but significantly fewer symptoms of depression. Was this because new mothers who are less depressed are more likely to be motivated to return to their work outside the family, or because the time spent working and the feelings of self-worth that jobs can promote lower the probability that mothers will feel depressed? If we go back to what the women told us about themselves during pregnancy, we know that both self-esteem and marital satisfaction in late pregnancy predicted women's level of depression when their children were eighteen months old (Heming 1985, 1987), although they did not predict whether women went back to work. Nevertheless, women who had returned to work part- or full-time by the time their child was a year and a half reported fewer symptoms of depression, whereas those who remained at home full-time reported more depression than their well-being during pregnancy had led us to expect.

It does not seem to be the case that feeling less depressed makes it more likely that mothers return to work. It looks as if going back to work helps to protect them against feeling depressed.[1]

These results make more sense of Gail's symptoms of depression. Not only was she discouraged about her career direction before she became a mother but she had not had the advantage some mothers have of finding their sense of competence in a job they are invested in. Some of her husband's encouragement is based on his knowledge of Gail's skills and his belief that work will help her feel better about herself, but she has not felt ready to take this step.

Attitudes and Practices in the Workplace   How new parents make and manage their work choices is influenced partly by their work histories and attitudes, and partly by their general level of distress or well-being before they become parents. Clearly, attitudes and practices in the working world play a significant role too. Only the United States and South Africa, of all the world's industrialized countries, lack a national policy for maternity leave (Steinberg and Belsky 1991).

Most of the women in our study know all about the maternity leave or family policies where they work. At most, women are allowed up to six months' leave, usually without pay, if they are employed in a business that has at least twenty workers. Self-employed women—writers, therapists, and freelance workers, for example—are on their own in figuring out whether they can afford to take time off to recuperate from giving birth and to spend the first weeks or months with their infants. Marian, a thirty-seven-year-old attorney, tells us about the double messages she feels from her colleagues: "I did take the six-month maternity leave my firm offers. But I'm feeling that behind their smiles, the partners think that any woman who would actually take time off from the practice of law is not 'partner material.' "

We hear stories like Marian's from men, too, although they are less likely to be familiar with, or to take advantage of, their employers' paternity or family-leave policies. Tom, who describes himself as a troubleshooter for a firm that makes computers, is astonished at his boss's attitude when he returns to work immediately after his daughter's birth: "My buddies at work were full of congratulations when I came back in on a Friday to announce that Kristin had just been born. Then my boss, Alec, pops into my office, offers me a cigar, and says, 'Congratulations, Tom! I hear it's a girl. By the way, I'll need that report of yours on my desk on Monday morning.' That's it—and he's out the door!"

Juggling Work and Family   Researchers have worried that the strain of juggling work and family life may contribute to family stress, particularly for women. Yet systematic studies of women's work and home lives find that women who manage multiple roles actually feel better about themselves and their lives (Baruch, Barnett, and Rivers 1983).

A critical question about the impact of both partners having jobs, as we discussed in chapter 5, is what happens to the division of work at home (Hochschild 1989). Our study and others (Pleck 1985) indicate that husbands whose wives are employed do a little more housework and caring for the children than husbands whose wives do not work outside the home.[2] In our study, the more fathers were involved in the day-to-day tasks of running the family, the more satisfied both parents were with themselves and their marriage. When mothers are employed, then, the impact of their work on the family depends not only on what they do outside the family but on what their husbands do inside.

For many modern couples, coordinating a number of work and family roles that they consider important represents a challenge and an opportunity to show their competence. Managing it all can be hectic for both parents, but when they feel that they are part of a team that is managing it all successfully, there seem to be benefits for how they both end up feeling about themselves and their marriage. Part of the excitement of the journey for pioneers is mastering the hardships they encounter.

Some couples tell us that life runs more calmly and smoothly in the early family-making period when one parent stays home to care for the baby while the other functions as the breadwinner—of course, the stay-at-home parent is almost always the mother. In theory, the parent at home should have more time to be responsive to the baby's unpredictable fluctuations in schedule and mood, to get through the laundry, cleaning, and cooking on a more relaxed schedule, and to greet the breadwinner on his or her return. Indeed, for a small number of couples, like Shannon and John, this is exactly what they describe: a relatively satisfying traditional division of labor both inside and outside the family.

But both practical and psychological considerations seem to get in the way of homemaker/breadwinner arrangements being satisfying for most of the single-earner families we saw. As the at-home parent described it, the traditional way of doing things demands a considerable balancing act, too. To begin with, in order for one partner to stay home with the children, both must feel that they can manage on one income. For the couples in our study, considerations other than finances play an even more salient role in such decisions. Parents' notions about what a baby needs to feel secure and cared for are central in their decisions about "mother or other care." But ideas about what babies need are colliding with the new ideology about what men and women *ought* to be doing inside and outside the family. Particularly in a culture that values accomplishments that are rewarded with a paycheck, the stay-at-home parent must feel very strongly about the baby's and family's needs to feel satisfied with the more traditional arrangements of the previous generation.

What Is the Impact on Children?   The women in our study worried about the potentially negative impact of their working on their children. There is little we can say yet, positive or negative, about the direct links between mothers' work and how their children are developing (see Bronfenbrenner and Crouter 1982; Hoffman 1989; Moorehouse in press). We will have a more realistic picture of what works best for parents and children when we can assess how fathers' and mothers' work and family relationships play out in the parents' feelings about themselves, their marriage, and their relationships with their children.

There is at least one consistent finding in the research on the effects of mothers' employment on children: Whereas preschool-age sons of working mothers are sometimes found to be more distressed than sons of mothers at home full-time, daughters of working mothers appear to benefit in both their cognitive and social development compared to girls whose mothers stay home. What could account for this gender difference?

Studies of the way parents socialize their sons and daughters show that parents tend to encourage boys' independence and girls' dependence (Block 1984; see also chapter 8). Perhaps when mothers are at home full-time, they have a tendency to help and protect their daughters more than working mothers do, which may leave these daughters less room than daughters of working mothers to develop self-reliance, independence, and competence. Mothers who must manage a household and a job outside the family may expect their children to do more for themselves, which could encourage more self-reliance as well as providing a model of both competence and achievement for their children to emulate, a model that might be especially important for their daughters.

What gets set in motion when a couple decides whether the mother will return to work? One intriguing finding from our study suggests that spouses' disagreements about this issue may reverberate throughout the family (Schulz 1991). Husbands and wives who disagree about who should be bringing in the family income[3] are more likely to be angry and competitive with each other while they are working and playing with their children in our playroom. Such parents are less warm, responsive, structured, and limit setting with their three-and-a-half-year-old preschoolers. Finally, the preschoolers whose parents disagreed about their work/family arrangements were rated two years later by their kindergarten teachers as more shy and withdrawn. What we are seeing here is that the parents' feelings about their work/family arrangements play out in their relationship as a couple. This finding is quite consistent with Arlie Hochschild's (1989) study, in which she finds negative effects on the couple's relationship of women doing the second shift at home after working outside the family. What our data add is that when husbands and wives disagree about their arrangements of family and work, the effects of their differences are felt in their marriage, in their relationships with the child, *and* in the child's social development.

Child Care

More than half of the preschool children in the United States spend a substantial part of the work week being cared for by someone other than their parents. Recent estimates show that even though 35 million American children under fourteen years of age have mothers who work, there are only 5 million places available for them in before- and afterschool care centers

(Quindlen 1991). The psychologist Sandra Scarr has made a thorough investigation of the child-care shortage and concluded that it is a "national scandal" (1984, p. 224).

Scarr's judgment is based on the premise that child-care resources are a necessity. During the late 1970s and early 1980s, influential reviews of the research on the impact of child care on young children's development (Belsky and Steinberg 1978; Belsky, Steinberg, and Walker 1982) were generally reassuring to working mothers. Not only were researchers finding no negative effects of day care on children's intellectual development; their results were suggesting that children might actually reap advantages in their social development by being in a reasonably good child-care setting while their parents were at work. In a startling reversal, Jay Belsky and his colleagues (Belsky 1986, 1988; Belsky and Rovine 1988), citing their own and others' research, recently expressed concern that infants who are in "nonmaternal care" for more than twenty hours a week before they are one year old might be at risk of developing insecure attachments to their parents: Having been separated and then reunited with Mother or Father, such children might be more likely to avoid the parent or to respond angrily, and less likely to use the parent as a "secure base" when they are anxious or distressed.

We cannot reassure parents who avail themselves of day care in this situation that Belsky's view is mistaken, although some important and thoughtful reviews by other researchers raise serious questions about his conclusions (Clarke-Stewart 1989; Phillips et al. 1987). We can point out, though, that simple comparisons of young children who are or are not in child care can give a distorted picture of a very complex issue. First, we must not lump all child-care arrangements together when evaluating their impact on children: Obviously, they are not all alike, and within each type are wide variations in the quality of care (Phillips and Howes 1987). Second, as we have seen in our discussion of women's work, we cannot simply evaluate the impact of outside-the-family care without considering the influence of family processes on the parents' choice of whether to seek child care and what kind of care they seek. Belsky himself, in an excellent review and rethinking of this issue (1990), agrees that we must include information about family processes in any study of the effects of day care.

DO WE CHOOSE CHILD CARE?

At the six-months-after-birth follow-up, 6 percent of the babies are being cared for primarily by both parents and approximately 45 percent primarily by their mothers. The families are divided almost equally into those who do and those who do not place the child in the care of a nonfamily member for more than five hours per week. By the time the children are one and a half, the proportion of babies being cared for primarily by one or both parents has declined to 32 percent, and by the time they are three and a half, only 17 percent of the parents are doing the primary care.

Obviously, considerations about both parents' wanting or needing to work top the list of whether and when to use child care. Second, questions of child-care costs and availability affect couples' decisions. In talking about whether they use child care regularly, couples in our study mention three additional considerations that affect their decisions: their beliefs and feelings about whether it is helpful or harmful for young children to spend time in the care of someone else; their experience of how easy or difficult it is to be separated from their child; and the legacies of attitudes from their parents that can make outside child care feel like a positive or a negative option.

It does not take much historical or anthropological research to realize that what is regarded as normal—in this case, children reared primarily by their parents—has not been common throughout the course of human history. In other times and cultures, and in much of the world today, extended family members, nonrelated adults, and older children in the community take care of the young. But modern couples have grown up with a powerful message that mother care is optimal and any other care is a poor substitute.

This opinion has been reinforced by a number of influential psychoanalytic theorists (A. Freud 1965; Mahler, Pine, and Bergman 1975) and child-rearing experts. Until very recently, the most widely quoted pediatricians and developmententalists in North America and England stated clearly that babies need their mothers to be with them to assure their optimal development. Benjamin Spock and Berry Brazelton held this view early on but have revised it in recent years. Burton White and Penelope Leach still advise mothers to stay at home with their young children. Beyond these views of the "experts," a number of the parents we spoke to were being swayed by their own experience of having felt abandoned as children when their parents were away at work. This leaves parents in a serious bind if they want or need to work.

Laurie Leventhal-Belfer (1990) asked the parents in our study to write down their thoughts and feelings about the child-care choices they made. One mother responded:

> I don't enjoy staying at home all day long with our child, but I don't think I could allow myself to use any other child-care arrangement. It also is not economically feasible for us to do something different, because good child-care alternatives are so expensive. So I've just stayed home. I've even taken care of other people's children five days a week from 8:30 to 6:00 to earn a little extra money because of my husband's reduced salary. It's hard to believe, isn't it?

This mother's painfully honest response gives us pause. Her beliefs about who should bring up children, in combination with her economic circumstances, have led her to create a twenty-four-hour-a-day role in which she is clearly not invested. We feel concern for her well-being, her child's and that of the other children who spend their day with her. Clearly, we cannot assume that a parent will always provide better care than a child-care provider, especially if the parent wants to be somewhere else.

At the other end of the spectrum are those women who find it difficult to spend any time away from their children. While some fathers talk about how much they miss their child during the day, and about occasionally wanting to come home early to see them from an evening out or a weekend away, such feelings are expressed most powerfully by mothers.

Gail describes this feeling vividly when she mentions her confusion about going to work. She feels guilty about the thought of leaving Sarah and Jason "with strangers," but her feelings seem to be based on deeper concerns. She has strong ties to both of her children, so strong that she identifies with what she imagines are *their* feelings based on her own early distressing experiences. "I think I'm Sarah. I think I'm Jason. And I think they're me. I think Sarah's exactly like I am, with all my anxieties, and I think I deal with her based on that. It's like I turned into her, and she turned into how I was as a kid."

Gail conveys the notion that placing their children in someone else's care will be a personal loss to *her*. Indeed, the more hours babies spend in alternative care when they are six months and eighteen months old, the more likely the mothers in our study were to draw smaller Mother pieces on their pie charts.[4] It may be that for women like Gail, who have not settled on who else they are besides Mother, the prospect of giving the children over to someone else's care is too threatening. For other women whose psychological and actual involvement as Mother is less than average, there seem to be positive trade-offs in that their identity as Partner or Lover can expand. We have seen that this is one of the "pieces" that Gail and Michael are trying to put back into their lives.

Although most discussions about work and child care focus on what children need, parents' needs are an important part of the equation. As Nancy Chodorow argues eloquently in *The Reproduction of Mothering* (1978), women are much more susceptible than men to powerful feelings of connectedness, especially in relation to their roles as mothers. Their feeling that women must do the mothering is certainly reinforced by attitudes and arrangements in our society that make it almost impossible for men and women to make equal and independent choices about balancing work and family life.

It is also reinforced by the example of new parents' parents. From the information we gathered about the relationships of the parents we studied with *their* parents, we learned that Gail's mother had also felt guilty about leaving Gail when she was young. This also goes some way toward explaining Gail's unrelenting ambivalence about work and motherhood. The tendency to repeat generational patterns, especially those that have to do with a parent's anxiety or anger, seems to have Gail in its grip. We discuss this in more detail in the next chapter.

We have been moved in following Gail in her struggle to keep from replaying the painful part of her own and her mother's history. Several years after becoming a mother, Gail begins to discover that this part of the pattern from her childhood has not served her well. Something about her own growing up has left her feeling stalled in her development as an adult, and it is also beginning to get in the way of her being able to allow her children to have their own experiences, separate from hers. These revelations lead Gail to seek professional help in an effort to understand and modify this pattern in her relationship with her children.

Becoming a mother has led to a personal crisis for Gail, although it took some years for her to articulate it that way. The support of getting her relationship with Michael back on track gives her the strength to begin facing the conflict she has been feeling about her life. And, as Victor uses the support of his wife, Natalie, to shift his troubling work situation, Gail uses Michael's encouragement to begin some part-time work that will help her to spend some time separate from the children. At the same time, she and Michael work on reestablishing the intimacy of their relationship as a couple.

By the time Sarah is in kindergarten, Gail has begun to talk with her mother about why she was reluctant to leave Gail in someone else's care. This seems to be helping Gail put her own anxiety about this into a broader perspective. As Naomi Lowinsky (1990, 1992) suggests, when women make opportunities to hear the stories from their own "motherline," the women in their extended families, they can often begin to come to grips with a fuller sense of themselves as mothers, daughters, wives, and fully conscious women. We are confident that Gail's explorations into the source of her confusion will eventually shed more light on what has kept her in conflict about finding her career direction, being a mother, and maintaining an intimate relationship with Michael.

In Gail's example we see the twin meanings of crisis: danger and opportunity. When she experienced danger, she was frightened for a time and different parts of her life felt shaky. But she has been able to use the occasion of her children's growth to move on with her own development by confronting some of the unresolved fears and problems from her past (P. Cowan 1988a). While it is too soon to be sure about how her story will end, Sarah is now in the fifth grade and doing well, Jason is in second grade, and both parents feel that they are getting back on track as individuals, as a couple, and as a family.

WHAT KIND OF CHILD CARE?

Some couples begin their search for child care with an image of a smiling middle-aged woman who takes a few children into her comfortable old house. Others believe that only pert and energetic young women in clean and tidy child-care centers will take adequate care of their child. Some parents want a child-care person who will be actively involved in stimulating their child's intellectual development, while others are equally or more concerned about fostering their children's social relationships and giving them room to play in a relaxed setting.

Even after extensive searching, parents rarely find a day-care arrangement that completely fits their initial hopes. As one mother wrote: "It's difficult to accept that no child-care arrangement is as perfect as I fantasized before we confronted the real world." Only a few couples feel they were lucky enough to have found the "perfect situation." Beth and Paul are thrilled with Margo, who provides just the kind of loving care for Willie that they want. Paul refers to her as "part of our family team." Most are more like Tanya and Jackson. In addition to assuming most of the responsibility for the household and looking after Kevin, Tanya has also taken the major role in finding someone to care for Kevin when she returns to work. She is clearly distressed:

> TANYA: I found this one place that looks great. It's close to my work and I could easily drop Kevin off, but it's $20 a day. That might not sound unreasonable, but it's $5,000 a year that we don't have—it didn't cost me $5,000 a year to go to college! There's this other place that's great and it's cheaper, but it's all the way across town. A third place is cheap, but I wouldn't leave any kid there for a minute.
>
> JACKSON: As I see it, the most important thing we have to figure out is what will be best for Kevin.
>
> TANYA: But you *don't* see it, Jackson. You haven't visited *one* of these places. And I'm the one who's going to take Kevin every day and pick him up. The other possibility is a day-care center that's a little big, but the staff seems great, the equipment is brand-new, and it costs only a little more than I think we can afford. I'd really hoped to have Kevin in a small place, with a loving, motherly person, but I just don't think that's going to work.

With a few notable exceptions, it was the mothers in our study who gathered all the information about child-care resources, made most of the visits, and spent hours worrying about alternatives. Then, usually in consultation with their husbands, they would make the final decision. Even though most of the women seem to assume that this is their job, many resent the responsibility, particularly because the choices are so difficult and seem to have such far-reaching consequences.

Although the task of figuring it out is considered "women's work," men's feelings about their child-care decisions and arrangements make a difference to both parents. A few fathers have serious reservations about using any major outside child care during their baby's first year. In light of modern notions about male-female equality, some of the fathers are almost apologetic in suggesting that they really prefer their wives to stay home with their child.

One intriguing finding (Leventhal-Belfer 1990; Leventhal-Belfer, Cowan, and Cowan in press) is that the family's actual day-care arrangements—mother care or other care—are not related to either parent's well-being or distress (their marital satisfaction, self-esteem, depression, or parenting stress), but that *wives'* well-being or distress is related to their *husbands'* satisfaction with the child-care decision. If the fathers are satisfied with the child-care arrangements, the mothers report less parenting stress and fewer symptoms of depression. Furthermore, mothers' satisfaction with their arrangements for the children's care is related to their perceptions of their husbands' support for their role in them.

Husbands' involvement is important not only in the major decisions about child care but also in the occasional baby-sitting arrangements. Again, wives are stuck with most of the work in finding baby-sitters, even when husbands are insistent that the couple needs to go out. Remember Stephanie and Art's arguments about this issue? They told us that their discussions eventually led them to decide to go out together at least once every two weeks. This has given them more time alone together but has not solved the problem entirely:

STEPHANIE: Art thinks that somehow sitters just magically appear when you need them. Last week I made fifteen calls and then at the last minute I got a sitter I didn't know, and I really didn't like her very much. I keep wondering why he can't do some of the calling.

ART: I know I should. And I've tried. But every time I phone one of those girls' houses, a voice asks suspiciously exactly who I am and what I want. And then I talk to the girl, and she doesn't know whether she can come or not. It's like asking for a date. I find it humiliating and embarrassing.

From the large dilemmas of child care to the small ones, men and women must deal with a set of complex issues. They arrive at different conclusions through very different processes. Some of them feel good about their choices, and others are in mild or severe distress over them. Their problems are intensified by the frustrating ambivalence on the part of politicians and business people who make, or neglect to make, policies that affect the families of workers. The reluctance to take a stand that would support parents with young children puts families in a classic double bind. On one hand, the economy continues to depend on women workers; on the other, government and business policies support neither dual-worker families nor child-care facilities, especially for parents of preschool children. Parents are caught in this squeeze and they and their children feel the effects of the strain. The unresolved threads of these important work/family issues are weaving their way into the fabric of family life.

Social Support

It is not always possible to reduce or eliminate the stress involved in coping with life inside and outside the family. One way that new parents can feel better about themselves and make their lives more manageable is to find additional sources of support. People or situations that provide new parents with satisfaction, challenge, understanding, or direct advice and services can help them solve specific problems, stop worrying so much about their family responsibilities, relax and have some fun, and feel emotionally connected with others.

Where do new parents find support? Although we have emphasized the strain of trying to balance work and family and find the best care for their children, these can be sources of support and satisfaction as well. The stimulation of a meaningful job and co-workers can bolster a parent's confidence. Similarly, a caring child-care person can provide essential support for parents: instrumentally, by facilitating their ability to earn more income for the family; emotionally, by relieving anxiety about their child's care. Most of the parents in our study longed for or actively sought support from four other sources as they made their journey to parenthood: friends, members of their extended families, organized support groups, and health professionals.

FRIENDS

We asked about each partner's support from others with a questionnaire about the key people who provide it (Curtis-Boles 1979). Partners were asked to name four people who are important in their lives and to tell how far away they live, what kind of support they provide, and how satisfying their support feels.[5] One finding from the parents' responses on this questionnaire surprised us, but perhaps we could have expected it. About 20 percent of the expectant and new fathers told us that they did not have four people they could list. This seems to reflect the fact that in our society, men are much less likely than women to be part of a network of relationships with people in whom they can confide.

Most of the couples in our study live far from their parents and the communities in which they grew up. In contrast with their parents' generation, they have not come of age at a time when young people routinely marry and start families in lock step in their early twenties. The friends they spent time with before becoming pregnant often have no children themselves. As a consequence, when couples start having babies and facing some of the changes we have been describing, they can feel out of step with their close friends and may find themselves rushing to make new friendships, or strengthening old ones, with other parents. Shannon said that from the day she told people she was pregnant, their friends who had children began to call more often, offering advice as well as baby clothes and furniture. She and John received it all gratefully, but "could have lived without some of the war stories—things about rough times with each of their kids." They spent more and more of their free time with friends who were parents, and by the time little John was born their relationships with single or childless friends began to feel strained.

We heard similar stories over and over. In part, of course, new parents simply have less time to socialize than they used to. A few nonparent friends may make an active effort to take on the mantle of a favorite uncle or aunt to the new baby and to keep up their interest in the new parents, but more often such friendships, especially with friends who are single, begin to go through a period of disengagement. New parents often feel hurt or insulted when their childless friends suggest a spontaneous get-together, neglect to invite the baby, and "forget" that the parents can't respond without making complex arrangements for their baby.

As the babies grow, most of the couples are surprised to find how much of their social life they are spending with couples who are parents. These are the people they can talk to about things that hold little interest for their childless friends but are essential to them: cloth versus disposable diapers, the safest car seats and strollers, pediatricians, baby foods, nursery schools. If these friends are new, they can provide important information and support but cannot replace the shared history that makes old friends so comforting to be with, leaving parents to feel the loss of those more intimate relationships.

EXTENDED FAMILY

There seems to be a great nostalgia for earlier times when couples lived close to their extended families and could get help from them in times of joy, sorrow, and strain. The truth of the matter is that then was probably not so different from now (Skolnick 1991). For some couples, having extended families close by while they are becoming parents is truly a blessing. Family gatherings feel warm and welcoming to both the new parents and the baby. For others, the advice and visits of relatives and parents can be a burden.

Beth mentions that she felt close to her mother when she was young. A period of strain between them began in her late teens and extended through her college years. As a new mother, she is trying to reconnect: "We still have some tense times, but it's been good to visit her and talk about what it was like when I was growing up. I'm learning more about *her* struggles as a mother and wife. And I've gotten closer to my brothers and sisters too."

Bill and Peggy have a harder time with family togetherness:

BILL: Each Sunday and holiday, there's a "command performance." We have to show up at Peggy's folks' and Mindy has to "perform." Last year, I said to Peggy, "Hey, it's Father's Day at our house, too. What do you say we celebrate it at home?" She said her father would be crushed if we didn't go, so we went.

PEGGY: I sympathize with Bill, but I can't seem to get out of it. I think it would be OK if it was fun when we got there. Being with my parents and my sister and her family. My sister's mission in life seems to be to make me feel stupid. Her kids are teenagers now, and she thinks that makes her the expert. All I hear when we are there is what I'm doing wrong with Mindy, and what I could do different. By the time we leave, I'm ready to scream.

MOTHERS' AND FATHERS' SUPPORT GROUPS

About one in eight of the mothers in our study attend a mothers' group regularly. Some are led by a trained leader, while others are informal meetings for mutual support and conversation. At some, there are provisions for the children to play while the mothers talk. At first, almost all of the women find the groups invaluable. As Shannon said, "I don't think I could have survived without it. Every time I went, I would have a concern or worry that I thought was silly, and every week I would find that I wasn't the only one. It was so reassuring to know that my worries weren't way out of line." But after a while, some women say, several kinds of issues begin to pose problems that make the groups feel less productive. Sometimes a child's uncontrollable behavior creates tension. Mothers who work may feel indirect criticism about having decided to return to their jobs, while mothers at home may feel challenged by the women who are back at work. The topic of husbands comes up often, and, though most women find solace in expressing irritation with their husbands, the group leaders are rarely able to help the mothers make headway on what is troubling them because the men are not there in the group.

We were both puzzled and saddened by what we heard about groups for fathers. In contrast with mothers' groups, which meet regularly over an extended period of time, sometimes for several years, groups for fathers tend to be offered once or at most twice on successive weekends, with rare exceptions (Bittman and Zalk 1978; Levant 1988). It is difficult to know whether this is what group leaders believe men need, or whether it is all they think men will be willing to attend.

HEALTH PROFESSIONALS

Parents tell us that when their babies are ill or upset, pediatricians and pediatric nurses are very responsive and reassuring. But it is the rare medical practitioner who routinely asks new mothers or fathers about how they are managing. It is even rarer, apparently, to find obstetricians or pediatricians, the most likely health professionals to see parents in the early family-making years, who offer more than a suggestion that the parents "try to relax."

Some parents wind up seeking professional help from a counselor or therapist, almost always for what they feel is an individual problem. Our concern with this approach is that the natural strains of new parenthood may be borne mostly by one of the parents, who sees it as her or his personal problem. While one of the partners may be in need of help to sort out what has triggered his or her distress, individual counseling neglects the fallout of the distress on the couple's relationship.

Peggy sought therapy and found it helped her "get a little clearer about why becoming a mother has been so anxiety-provoking for me," but without Bill there the trouble she and he were having seemed only to get worse. Like all the potential sources of support we have mentioned, individual therapy for only one partner can actually add to the strain that the parents are under *as a couple.* Our hope is that health and mental health professionals will become more aware of the common issues for couples in this major family transition. Since we know that 12.5 percent of the new parents in our study who had no intervention separated or divorced by the time their babies were eighteen months old, the need for help during this crucial period in a marriage cannot be overestimated.

Do friends, family, community services, and health professionals actually help to buffer or protect new parents from life stresses during the transition to parenthood (Nuckolls, Casell, and Kaplan 1972)? Our Important People questionnaire (Curtis-Boles 1979) provided a measure of how often the men and women in our study were in contact with important sources of support, and how satisfying that contact felt. We also obtained a general estimate from a Recent Life Events questionnaire of how much stress each man and woman was contending with based on the sum total of changes in their lives. We presented a long list of potentially stressful events including having a miscarriage, surgery, or major illness; moving to a new home; having problems with alcohol or drugs; losing a close friend or parent; getting promoted; and reentering school.[6] The list included positive and negative life changes on the assumption that both are stressful (Holmes and Rahe 1967).

Given the changes parents were reporting in our interviews and couples groups, we were surprised to find that despite a range of life stress levels among couples who became parents, there was no significant difference between stress in new parents as a group and stress in childless couples. According to this estimate, then, becoming a first-time parent is not accompanied by any more overall life change and stress than being a partner in a comparable childless couple in the first decade of married life.

Does this mean that parents' level of life stress is unimportant in their adaptation during the transition to parenthood? Quite the contrary: New parents who reported more life change (from which we inferred more stress) described lower marital satisfaction at six and eighteen months after their child was born. Furthermore, as their child grew older, parents' social supports became less effective in buffering the impact of life stress on their marriage.

We expected couples with low life stress and high social support to be at an advantage, partners with high life stress and high social support to be doing fairly well, but couples with a great deal of life stress and little support from others to be at risk for serious marital distress (Heming 1985). When their babies were six months old, couples with the most favorable life stress/social support balance were satisfied with their marriage, even if they were contending with many stressful life events besides having a baby.[7] At this point, a kind of Goldilocks principle seems to be operating: when couples' stress level was not too high, not too low, and their level of social support was just right, they were better able to master the expectable stress of becoming parents and keep their marriage on track. But by the time the babies were one and a half years old, partners who reported more stressful life events were less happy with their marriages regardless of the amount of social support they were receiving. Support from others, then, can be especially helpful to couples during the first months of parenthood, but it cannot ultimately prevent the stresses of becoming a family from taking their toll on the marriage.

We have been discussing stressful life events and social support as if they are forces totally outside the couple's control; yet we found that men and women who are more satisfied with their marriage before they have a baby are better able to keep positive ties with people outside the family over the next two years. By contrast, couples who are already in distress as they begin the transition to parenthood may become preoccupied with the baby and their own turmoil, leaving them unwilling or unable to reach out to others.[8] Since support from other important people can make the early strain of transition more manageable, we encourage new parents to line up resources they can count on in the early months, before the cumulative stress of the transition sends them on a downward marital slide.

CHAPTER 7

Legacies from Our Parents

JACKSON: In the family I grew up in, the women always did the household work, regardless. My grandmother never worked. My grandfather worked and brought home the money, so she took care of everything at home. My mother worked, but she still came home and fixed dinner and everything, and then later with my stepmother, it was the same.

Then I marry *this* woman [*laughs affectionately*] and she wants to divide the work at home in half! Well, I say, "This half's buying paper plates!" I can now see that how you deal with your wife and kids is affected by the things that you saw growing up—it sounds obvious now that I've thought about it, but I just didn't realize it before.

TANYA: I grew up in the same kind of family that Jackson did. My mother did it all—looked after me and the kids and my father *and* she had a job too—but I was determined that it wouldn't be like that in our house.

We heard many comments like Jackson's and Tanya's. The couples in our study made it clear that their parents have bequeathed legacies to their children and grandchildren that are powerful and often invisible. In this chapter, we explore how new parents learn about their family legacies. We describe examples of some parents who repeat the nurturing or painful family patterns they grew up with, and others who find ways to break their families' negative cycles.

One major challenge for a couple creating a new family is to figure out how both of their dreams can fit together. How can two people with different experiences in their families of origin create a family in which they can repeat the things each found important and supportive and change the things that hurt them or hampered their development?

Most of the evidence shows that, in general, there is more continuity than discontinuity between the generations: The relationships in the generation we create tend to have more positive outcomes for those of us who felt nurtured by our parents and whose families functioned adequately, and more negative results for those of us who grew up in families with significant rejection, loss, strain, or dysfunction. Nevertheless, there are some compelling exceptions in which individuals and couples with painful early family experiences manage to avoid being bound by the chains of the past, establishing nurturing, effective, and satisfying relationships in their own generation, sometimes by putting the difficult memories into a perspective that allows them to move beyond them. Some manage to accomplish this on their own. Others use the help of friends, religious leaders, or mental health professionals, passing on the benefits through the relationships they create with their partners and their children.

Generational issues are with us always, but at few times are they more salient than when the generational cycle is about to begin again. A first child and grandchild brings the relationships between the parents and their parents into bold relief. There seems to be a reaching out from both generations, especially between mothers and daughters. When the relationships are going well, these close ties can be a great comfort for both generations, although the grandparents' well-meaning attempts at providing help do not always succeed.

For some couples, frequent contact with their parents around the time of the baby's birth is a natural continuation of close and loving relationships. For a few, the older generation's attention is experienced as new and is not easy to manage. When their son, Avi, is six months old, Pauline, thirty-one, and Mel, thirty-three, explain how a new child can provide an opportunity for closeness between generations that have been separated by years of physical and emotional distance:

> PAULINE: My relationship with my parents was very much on hold before Avi was born. I moved away from home about fifteen years ago. We kept in touch, but I didn't spend much time with them. Now they have lots of really strong feelings about Avi, some positive and some negative. It upset my parents a lot that Mel and I chose to not marry. But they came out to see him when he was a month old and then again when he was five months old. They've been here more since he was born than they have in the past ten years.

The visits have been both stressful and intense for Pauline and Mel, but there seem to be a few roses among the thorns:

PAULINE: They were really glad to see the baby and to share in the joy. And that made me very happy. But they are angry, real angry, at us for not getting married. I say it's none of their business, and we certainly don't need that negative atmosphere while we're trying to find our own way with Avi. Mel and I tend to have our worst fights right before they come and right after they leave. I think they are trying to accept the situation. They are very mixed about Mel, but they are accepting me more now.

MEL: My parents also went through a period of being really disappointed and angry that we weren't getting married, but once Avi was born I think they put that aside. My father has really warmed up a lot around the baby. It's hard for me to understand how that changed our relationship, because in some ways he's still the same and in some ways he isn't. He seems warmer when he's with everyone else. With Pauline's parents, I'm not sure where we are. When they left this last time I was shaking my head. I don't feel very close to them at the moment. And when they're here, *we* sure aren't very close to each other, either.

Avi's grandparents' attitudes about their children's lives creep into their relationship with their children and with their grandson. The conflict and distress between the generations spills over into the communication between Pauline and Mel, and into the atmosphere in which Avi first learns about family relationships. While his parents were speaking tensely of these family dynamics, Avi cried vigorously, a common response when a baby picks up on the parents' discomfort.

Pauline and Mel have some recognition of these generational patterns, which bodes well for their eventually being able to deal with their distress as a couple. New parents who do not see the connections between their struggles with their own parents and their distress as a couple are less likely to feel that they are on the same side when they tackle difficult issues in their life together.

A second theme that shows up as Pauline and Mel talk is that the birth of a baby can force some parents and grandparents to grapple once more with issues they have not successfully resolved. The distance between Pauline and her parents did not begin over their disagreement about whether she and Mel should get married so that their grandson would have a "proper" family. Similar disputes about how Pauline was going to live her life played a part in her decision to leave her parents' home at sixteen. Now, with a new baby on the scene, the generations are back in frequent contact. They have an opportunity to put some of the old issues aside and go on with their relationship, though it is possible that the process could get derailed by the unspoken tensions between the generations, tensions that Pauline and Mel talk about endlessly with each other.

As we talk with friends, colleagues, and the parents in our study, we can see how commonly we all make repeated overtures over the years to our children and parents to try to patch up earlier misunderstandings or rifts. One of our findings—something we certainly did not know in our early years of family making—is that all relationships across the generations have set-backs at times, but some of us are lucky enough to make some progress toward mending them.

Occasionally, new parents' attempts to renew closeness with their parents go painfully awry. You may recall Henry from chapter 3, who talked about his and Anna's painful experiences with his unresponsive father. A first-generation Arab-American who had promised his grandfather that he would not marry out of his faith, Henry wound up marrying Anna, an Italian-American. Henry's father refused to see Anna once he learned that she was going to have a baby. By the time their second daughter was born, Henry could tolerate this painful impasse with his father no longer:

> HENRY: Last spring I realized how much I was hurt by the way my father treated me all my life. And I just felt that it was time to let go. I don't want to carry around any more of this pain and anger with me. I've been such an angry young man after all of these years of rejection. Feeling like shit. Not desired. I kept making overtures, taking the baby to see him, and getting shut out. It was just hurting too much. I finally let go and decided I could not see him anymore.

Some grandparents must see their children's moving away or doing things differently as an indication that they no longer care about them or value their way of life. From our conversations with the parents in our study we can say unequivocally that, regardless of the state of their relationships with their parents, adult children not only care about what their parents think and feel but continue to long for their love and approval even when the generational bonds feel strained. Given the many difficult childhood experiences many people have undergone, it is a testimony to the strength of these bonds that so many new parents want to maintain relationships with their parents and create families of their own.

Repeating the Generational Cycle

A widespread belief, supported by a wealth of evidence, is that "good things" and "bad things" cycle through the generations. One of the most negative examples of this tendency can be seen in studies of child abuse, in which parents who abuse their children physically and psychologically tend to have been victims of abuse when they were growing up (Finkelhor, Hotaling, and Yllo 1988; Main and Goldwyn 1984). Patterns replayed down generational lines are not limited to extremes of abuse, of course. Difficult relationships with parents, both past and present, can take their toll on the relationships that couples are trying to create in their new families.

Henry, now the father of two daughters, five and a half and three years old, is explaining that in the same year in which he felt compelled to let go of his father, he and Anna decided that they could not make a go of their marriage:

HENRY: I keep thinking about the fact that my parents also divorced when I was young, and how I vowed that I was going to be so different. And here I wind up in the same boat. I think in some ways, I was a lot like my mother, and Anna was a lot like my father—in the quickness of her mind, her quick wit, her sharp tongue in arguments. I don't think either Anna or my father have ever lost an argument! In the beginning, I held Anna in some awe. There was a kind of comfort too, to have her in my life as a father substitute because I couldn't have him. So, she was kind of disciplinarian for me too but, like my relationship with my father, what I got from my wife had a lot of negative aspects to it. Eventually, it became too much for me.

The legacy of strong admonitions from Henry's grandfather and father to their children and grandchildren has led to painful and severed relationships: between Henry's father and grandfather, between Henry's father and mother, between Henry and his father, and now between Henry and his wife. Despite his determination to stay connected to his father, Henry has not been able to overcome the generational rifts in his family.

Although the generational ties have been hurtful for Henry throughout his lifetime, becoming a parent opened old wounds that had never healed. Feeling deeply attached to his children pushed him to sever his relationship with his father and eventually to end his marriage with Anna, his "substitute father," as he came to see her.

As Dolores, his and Anna's first-born, goes through kindergarten, we hear hints that some of the generational pain may be playing out in Henry's relationships with the younger daughter, Rose. He and Anna are separated, but his daughters are with him almost half the time. Rose is very much like him, he says—so much so that six months ago she rejected him the way he says he rejected her mother. She just didn't want to have anything to do with him, only with her mother. Henry cried in front of Rose and told her why he was hurt. "I think she understood: Since then, she has been sharing with me at such a deeper level—much more than Dolores. We have this intuitive sense of each other. We spend many hours just sitting curled up together, watching out the window of the house, listening to music together. Not talking or doing anything else. That's quite amazing to me."

Henry feels that he has had to pay a price for straying from his grandfather's and his father's directives, and that he has failed by repeating his parents' divorce pattern, which he had vowed to avoid. Although he can articulate the similarities in his father's and Anna's personalities that played a role in his attraction to Anna and his distress with her, he is unable to avoid the negative effects on his marriage. Despite the earlier rifts, Henry has created a very close relationship with both daughters. His thoughtful musings about Rose's difficulty in relating to him illustrate how similarities between parents' and children's personalities can complicate the ways in which the generational patterns play out.

A great deal has recently been written about the mental health of adults whose parents had serious problems with alcohol (Brown 1985), suggesting that alcoholic parents' dysfunction affects their children's development as they are growing up. Our study indicates that there may be long-lasting effects when adult children of alcoholics become parents themselves.

Twenty percent of the parents in our study had childhoods clouded by their fathers' and/or mothers' struggles with alcohol. None reported having current problems themselves with alcohol or drugs, but a few acknowledged that they had had drinking problems in the past. We were frankly surprised at the large number of study participants who had come from alcoholic families, and wondered what special problems they faced as new parents.

What we found was most disturbing: On *every* index of adjustment to parenthood—symptoms of depression, self-esteem, parenting stress, role dissatisfaction, and decline in satisfaction with marriage—men and women whose parents had abused alcohol had significantly greater difficulty (Cowan, Cowan, and Heming 1988). There is no doubt that adult children of alcoholics have a harder time creating a family that satisfies their ideal. Families with serious problems of alcohol use and abuse have been described as placing a premium on keeping negative emotions in check (Steinglass et al. 1987). Family members tend to hold on to secrets, deny any problems, and avoid talking about their inner feelings. This makes life very unpredictable for a child, as the family atmosphere varies markedly depending on whether a parent is sober or intoxicated. Little wonder that when these children become adults creating families of their own, they find it difficult to manage the tension and maintain good feelings in their intimate relationships.

What is even more disturbing about this generational legacy is that by the time their children are preschoolers, these parents describe them as having fewer developmental successes, although our observations show that their children are doing just as well developmentally as the children of the rest of the parents in the study. This suggests that parents who grow up with troubled and ineffective parenting develop unrealistic expectations of what they can expect of their children and, as a result, have difficulty seeing their children's behavior in a positive light.

The plight of these grandchildren of alcoholics did not end in preschool. When they were in kindergarten, we asked their teachers to describe all the children in the classroom (using a checklist of children's behaviors adapted from the work of Earl Schaefer [Schaefer and Hunter 1983]). Without knowing which children were in our study, the teachers more often described the grandchildren of alcoholics as shy or aggressive, and as performing less well in their academic work.

Families with alcohol problems create a legacy that is passed on through successive generations. Even if their children do not abuse alcohol or drugs themselves and are determined to do things differently in their own families, they may find themselves inexorably repeating at least part of a pattern they had vowed to change.

Since we were not able to observe what happened in the parents' families while they were growing up, we do not have firsthand information about how generational cycles recur or get interrupted in these new families. There are hints about how family dynamics recur from one generation to another in a study of four generations by Avshalom Caspi and Glen Elder (1988). The cycle starts with an irritable, unstable child who grows up, marries, and generates tension in the marriage. The husbands and wives in such marriages tend to be less warm and effective parents, and in the next generation their children tend to have behavior problems and to grow up as irritable, unstable individuals. When they become involved as adults in conflictful marriages and have children of their own, the negative cycle begins again.

Despite the aura of Greek tragedy in Caspi and Elder's report, there are two optimistic implications of their formulation. First, they and we have been focusing on the families at the end of the spectrum with problematic legacies. At the other end are adults who grew up with fairly competent, effective, and affectionate parents who recreate this positive atmosphere in their new families. Second, if men and women can break the negative chain at any point—as individuals, in their marriage, or in their relationships with their children—it is likely that they can avoid carrying over such unsatisfying relationships into their new families.

Breaking the Generational Cycle

Most of us have had the experience of having a familiar, hurtful phrase pop out of our mouths in the heat of a struggle with a spouse or child. Can we keep from repeating our painful childhood experiences with our own mates and children? Our results suggest that some men and women manage to come to terms with very painful early experiences in ways that allow them to create new and more adaptive patterns. Some do this difficult work with the help of professional counselors or therapists, and others appear to do it on their own or with their mate. We focus here on continuity and discontinuity across the generations, primarily as the early growing-up years affect present-day couple relationships, with a brief look at how parents' legacies from the past affect their relationships with their children.

CONFLICT IN THE FAMILY OF ORIGIN

Before their memories could become colored by their experiences with their children, we asked the expectant parents in our study about the level of conflict in their families of origin.[1] We grouped the couples into four patterns: (1) both husband and wife described low conflict in their families of origin; (2) both husband and wife described high conflict in their families of origin; (3) his family had high conflict, hers had low conflict; and (4) his family had low conflict, hers had high conflict. The forty-eight couples assessed in pregnancy fell approximately equally into each of the four groups. Did those patterns make a difference to how satisfied couples were with the quality of their marriage during the transition to parenthood?

Couples with the first pattern—low conflict in both partners' families of origin—showed the least drop in marital satisfaction from pregnancy to eighteen months after the birth of their first child. These parents were able to avoid some but not all of the marital tension and conflict that couples tend to experience as they become parents. When both partners came from high-conflict families, they experienced a substantial decline in their satisfaction with marriage over the same period of time. For better or for worse, both groups of couples showed continuity from generation to generation.

What intrigued us was what happened when new parents' families of origin had different levels of conflict. When the husband grew up in a high-conflict family and the wife recalled little conflict in hers, both partners, particularly the wives, became increasingly dissatisfied with their marriage as they became parents. Following Caspi and Elder's formulation, we speculate that when men from high-conflict families experienced the stress of becoming fathers, they expressed more irritability and anger to their wives. Their wives, whose family models left them unprepared to deal with this level of irritability or conflict, reacted with disappointment or distress, which is reflected in their increasing disenchantment with the marriage. In this case, the negative cycle from the husband's family gets replayed, overriding the wife's more benign early experience.

The fourth group of couples managed to avoid repeating the patterns of *her* negative past. When wives from high-conflict families married men from low-conflict families, their slight decline in marital satisfaction during the transition to parenthood was virtually identical to the low-conflict pairs in the first pattern. Our speculation is that the women in these couples may express their irritability or anger during the tense weeks and months of becoming a family, but their husbands do not respond in kind. We know from a number of other in-depth studies of couples that marital satisfaction is affected not so much by the amount of anger either partner expresses but by the spouses' tendency to respond in ways that escalate the irritability, anger, or criticism between them (Gottman and Levenson 1986; Markman and Notarius 1987).

RELATIONSHIPS WITH PARENTS IN THE FAMILY OF ORIGIN

It seems that when partners come from backgrounds with similar levels of conflict, they tend to repeat the patterns they knew in their original families. When they come from different backgrounds, negative cycles are more likely to be repeated if they come through the husband's family line rather than the wife's. We explored these difference patterns by examining in more detail parents' recollections of their early relationships with their parents.

Both John Bowlby in England and Mary Main and her colleagues (Main et al. 1985) in the United States talk about memories of the central relationships in our early family life as providing us with "working models," or pictures of what we expect intimate family relationships to be like. Main has found that when adults describe what are called insecure attachment relationships with their parents, their children are more likely to have insecure attachments to *them* (Main and Goldwyn in press; Main, Kaplan, and Cassidy 1985). We were interested in new parents' models of their early relationships because they may help us understand what we see in the relationships they develop with each other and with their own children.

We used a structured interview created by Mary Main and her colleagues to stimulate parents to think back in some detail to their childhood relationships with their parents.[2]

Interviews and questionnaires can provide only a brief sketch, of course, of what is a very long and complicated process of growing up, becoming adults, and developing intimate relationships, but they help us to explore both continuity and discontinuity between generations.

If parents say, with conviction and supporting detail, that their parents were loving, involved, and comforting to them when they were anxious or upset as children, they can be described as having a model of secure relationships between parents and children. Even if they experienced one or both parents as rejecting, neglectful, or overinvolved, their model would still be described as secure if they talk about both the positive and negative aspects of those relationships in a lucid, free-flowing, coherent manner, giving examples that clearly illustrate their descriptions and not getting lost in intrusive or incoherent thoughts about early difficulties.

Len and Connie originally entered our study as a couple who hadn't yet decided about having children. Connie became pregnant about a year later, and almost four years after that, when little Sam was three and a half, we spoke with both of them about their childhoods. Len provides an example of someone who has managed to gain a perspective on his childhood experiences. He says that he was "a difficult little baby who became a pain in the ass as a kid." His mother was extremely critical, but she spent a great deal of time with her children and Len felt comforted by her when his friends rejected him. His father had a terrible temper. Although he would roughhouse with Len on occasion, he tended to be "either away at work or yelling at home." His parents got along when he was young but their relationship became stormy and they separated for a while later on. Len's childhood memories are mostly about conflict with his parents, but in late adolescence, after his parents got back together, the family drew closer together.

Typical of many men and women who were described as having a secure model of relationships between parents and children, Len's childhood was not ideal. But from his perspective as an adult, he can see that his parents were limited by their own family experiences; he feels that both his mother and his father had been severely deprived as children and that "they were doing the best they could with the resources they were given."

Main and her colleagues are clear that while the traumatic effects of very difficult childhoods may be forever etched in memory, a person can develop a model of relationships that makes it possible to break the links that chain us to the negative patterns of the past. This is dramatized by the fact that two-thirds of the parents in our study who were classified as having secure models of parent-child relationships described very difficult relationships with one or both parents while growing up (Pearson et al. 1991). Several had parents who were physically abusive or mentally ill, or who committed suicide during their childhood. Others experienced their parents' divorce or the death of a parent while they were growing up.

Connie describes a very difficult early family life. An only child, she recalls years of bickering between her alcoholic parents, followed by her father's sudden exit from the family one night when she was ten. She never saw him again. Three years later, she came home from school to find that her mother had committed suicide. Soon after their son, Sam, was born, Connie found herself preoccupied with memories of her parents. When we talked with her about her childhood, she was still struggling to deal with her feelings about these traumatic experiences: "I can't get over the feeling that both my parents abandoned me. When I see how great Len usually is with me and Sam, I get even more upset about what went on while I was growing up." As we do with each parent, we ask Connie why she thought her parents were the way they were. The question stumps her. She is so upset with them for what they did to her, it has not occurred to her to wonder why her parents' lives were in such turmoil.

As individuals with either secure or insecure models of intimate relationships grow up and marry, can their choice of partner affect their sense of security? Using the twenty-seven couples for whom we have complete data on both parents' childhood and their current relationships as couples and as parents, Deborah Cohn helped us explore the possibility that a nurturing marriage can modify the effects of early negative experiences on the parents' relationship as a couple (Cohn et al. 1991).

There are three kinds of pairings that couples can fall into: Both he and she have secure working models of relationships (as did twelve couples in our study); both he and she have insecure working models (five couples); and one parent has a secure working model and the other has an insecure working model (ten couples).

Observing the parents as they work and play together with their three-and-a-half-year-old (see chapter 8), we found that insecure/insecure pairs showed much less cooperation and warmth and expressed much more negative emotion to each other in front of their child than the other two couple pairings. Not surprisingly, in their separate visits, both parents with insecure models were much less warm, engaged, and structuring than other parents in the study.

The secure/secure pairs showed much more positive emotion to each other: They were warm; they talked amiably, and they were cooperative. In their separate visits with their child they were significantly warmer and more effective in helping their children to cope with difficult tasks. Thus, in couples with similarly insecure or secure models of family relationships, continuity prevails across the generations.

Perhaps the most encouraging and provocative finding was that the insecure/secure pairs—in all but two of which it was the wife who had an insecure model of relationships—showed just as much warmth and cooperation with each other during the family visit as the secure/secure pairs did. Furthermore, when women with unresolved feelings about their growing-up years were married to men with a coherent view of even the most difficult early family experiences, the women's parenting was as warm, structuring, and engaged as that of the mothers described as securely attached.*

Something about the quality of the couple relationship appears to be providing a buffer that interrupts the potential carryover of the women's early negative experiences into the relationship with their husbands. And, despite the fact that these mothers had not yet been able to come to terms with their own difficult childhood experiences, the positive relationships with their husbands appeared to be helping them establish nurturant and effective relationships with their children.

In Connie and Len's case, both experienced conflict and difficulty in their families of origin, but they are at different stages of coming to terms with those experiences. The effect of early legacies on their couple relationship now stems not just from the negative experiences themselves but from how each partner has come to understand their effects. Len has not only reestablished a positive relationship with his parents as he moved into adulthood but also come to a more tolerant and understanding view of his mother's and father's earlier relationships with him and with each other. Through his affectionate and understanding relationship with Connie, and his active involvement with their son, Sam, he has helped to make it easier for Connie to avoid replaying the extremely negative relationship she observed during the stormy years of her parents' marriage. Perhaps it is this curative power of the marriage that has enabled Connie and the other women in the insecure/secure couples to establish warm and effective relationships with their children. We will discuss the connection between the quality of the marriage and the quality of the parent-child relationship more in the next chapter.

How do these links between generations operate? Our speculation is that there is a process much like the one we described earlier between husbands who come from families with little conflict and much warmth and their wives who come from families with much conflict and little warmth. The men in these pairs seemed able to de-escalate the conflict between them with

---

*Michael Rutter (1987; Quinton, Rutter, and Liddle 1984) showed this pattern in a well-known study of British families. When mothers who had been reared in institutional homes were able to form positive and satisfying marital relationships, the quality of their parenting did not reflect their own earlier deprivation.

warmth or humor. Since their wives experienced less nurturing in their early relationships, perhaps they found the warmth and responsiveness in their marriages so nurturing that they learned more positive ways of relating by example and worked even harder to maintain the harmony in their marriages.

We are left to wonder whether women with positive early experiences can buffer the effects of their husbands' troubled childhoods on their marriage and life as a family. We did not see enough couples with this pattern to examine what happened to their relationships. Are women with secure models of relationships less willing to marry more troubled men? Are men with insecure models of relationships less willing to commit themselves to women with more nurturant pictures of intimate relationships? The two couples in our study who fit this pattern expressed less warmth to each other during the family visit than did the average couple in the study. It looks as though it is particularly difficult for wives to keep the marriage on an even keel when their husbands have difficult and unresolved relationships with their parents, even if the wives themselves have more positive models. This may be an example of the general phenomenon that men's moods and behavior tend to affect the quality of the marriage more than women's moods and behavior do (Boles 1984). The central issue here may be that men who had difficult childhoods are likely to be either angry or inexpressive. Wives may find either of these extremes more difficult to tolerate in a spouse than husbands do.

From what we have learned about the effects of alcoholism, family conflict, and children's attachment to their parents in the past generation, we draw several general conclusions. There is clearly a tendency for positive or negative experiences from the past to be carried over into the partners' relationship as a couple. The risk of negative carryover is especially strong when both partners bring painful and unresolved family issues to their marriage. These early family difficulties tend to increase the risk that men and women will become more disenchanted with their marriage during the transition to parenthood, which leaves them more irritable and angry and less cooperative with each other and with their children.

What are couples to do when they want to have children of their own but their family histories are bleak? Our findings show that some partners can overcome painful and even traumatic early experiences by creating a more nurturing and satisfying relationship with a spouse. Connie and Len seemed to do well because his view of relationships and his caring of her provided some of the nurturance that she had lacked in her own family. This seemed to lay a foundation for Connie to begin to modify her notion of intimate relationships. Many men and women find this task less formidable with the help of a professional counselor or therapist.

What if neither partner has examined or come to terms with his or her early experiences? We find that many couples tend to work earnestly but silently to create a family environment that will nurture their children. Each attempting to avoid different family traumas, they find to their surprise and disappointment that their plans and goals do not mesh. It seems important for both partners to let each other know about the baggage they feel they are carrying. A collaborative approach may help couples to safeguard the positive legacies and reject the negative legacies from the past as they attempt to build nurturant family relationships with each other and with their children.

CHAPTER 8

Parenting Our Children

BILL: In my house, when I was growing up, any kid who got into danger, like going near a light socket or running out on the road, got a swat on the bottom. I'm not talking about child abuse. I'm talking about a clear warning that some things are not OK to do.

PEGGY: When Bill says that, my heart sinks. Hitting is one of my absolute taboos. In my family, kids got seriously smacked around when my parents got angry. I hope I will never, *ever,* touch Mindy in anger. I'm trying to be patient with Bill, but when I see him swat Mindy, I feel like swatting *him.*

BILL: But you're letting her get away with murder.

PEGGY: I feel like I have to protect her.

BILL: You're protecting her too much. She doesn't know what to do if she can't get her own way. When I picked her up at nursery school last week, I found her standing alone in a corner of the yard both days. The teacher explained that the other kids were starting to avoid her because she wouldn't share the toys or the play equipment.

Legacies from their childhoods have left Bill and Peggy with qualitatively different notions about how to be effective parents. Some couples handle these differences by agreeing to find a middle ground; others, by accepting each other's parenting style with an attitude of "you do it your way and I'll do it mine." But when the marriage is full of conflict, as we have seen in the case of Peggy and Bill, child rearing becomes a prime target for dissension. Strong disagreements between Mindy's parents drive them to take extreme positions with her. Bill is even more determined than he might ordinarily be not to let Mindy "get away" with anything, because he wants to offset what he regards as Peggy's tendency to spoil her. Peggy is more reluctant to set limits than she might normally be, "to make up for Bill's harshness." We don't know whether Mindy is confused by her parents' different strategies or disturbed by their bickering, but we do know that she is having difficulty getting along with the other children at nursery school.

Peggy and Bill illustrate one of our major findings. Everything we have described about parents' transition to parenthood—their ability to make sense of their own childhood experiences, their satisfaction or distress as a couple, their level of stress and support, and their internal conflicts as individuals—seems to come together in their ways of being parents. We see variations on this theme when we talk with Sharon and Daniel. Sharon tells us that she went through a troubled stretch about six months ago when Amy was three. She was depressed, preoccupied with the possibility of returning to work, and feeling guilty that she couldn't seem to pay attention to Amy's needs. Daniel says that he and Sharon kept fighting about how to handle Amy's tantrums when they left her with a baby-sitter. He wanted to be more helpful to Amy when she was upset, "but I got so distressed and frazzled by what was going on with Sharon that I found myself matching Amy yell for yell." The struggles between Amy and her parents are a result of some spillover from Sharon's depression. The tension between Mindy and her parents stems from the fact that Bill and Peggy are reacting to different childhood experiences, which leads to different inclinations about how to handle Mindy. These individual and three-generational issues make parenting especially problematic because they stimulate tension between the parents and give the child conflicting messages about what to expect.

Parenting Styles

In previous chapters we focused on what happened to the parents as they made their journey from couple to family. Here we show that how they cope with their transition to parenthood, and especially with their couple relationship, has short-term and long-term consequences—for the quality of their relationships with their children and, ultimately, for the children's academic and social adjustment at school.* When the transition is difficult for the parents, there tend to be difficulties for the children as well.

*We are not claiming that all of the responsibility for the child's developmental progress can be attributed to the parents' behavior. Many forces, including genetics, the child's temperament, the presence of siblings, and events outside the family, will affect the course of a child's development. What we are focusing on here is the fact that parents' well-being or distress contributes both to their parenting style and to their children's developmental successes and difficulties.

WORKING AND PLAYING WITH PRESCHOOLERS

To get a sense of the relationships between parents and their three-and-a-half-year-olds, we invited each family to our project playroom for three forty-minute visits: one for mother and child, one for father and child, and one for both parents and the child.[1] With the family's consent, we videotaped each visit. In a playful, unstructured part of each visit, we provided a sand tray and a cabinet of miniatures and invited each parent and child to "build a world together in the sand." We also had the parents introduce a number of challenging tasks that would be difficult for children of this age to do: to repeat to their parents a story that we had told the children outside the playroom; to classify shapes or use blocks to match a model we provided; and to make their way through a maze game. The parents were invited to be as involved and helpful as they typically would be at home (Cowan and Cowan 1990; Pratt et al. 1988).

The videotapes of these family visits reveal an amazing variety of reactions between parents and preschoolers. While fiddling nervously with a toy teacup and saucer, Mindy tells her father that she can't remember the story she just heard. He becomes increasingly insistent and tense: "Put that away, Mindy. No play until I find out what the story is. Do it *now!*"—and he takes the teacup away rather forcefully. By contrast, when Willie says, "I forget," his father, Paul, gently leads him: "Was the story about a little kid or a big kid?" "Big." "Boy or girl?" "Girl." "Did she ride an elephant in her pajamas?" "No! A bike."

Members of our staff observed and rated the parents' behavior in the different visits.[2] We use our ratings to summarize two central dimensions of parenting that follow Diana Baumrind's (1979, 1991) scheme for describing parenting style. The first is warmth and responsiveness. Some parents responded warmly to their child's behavior, reacting in a positive way to the child's attempts to get through the maze or to select play materials for the sand world. A few parents reacted to the child in an angry, critical, or threatening tone. A very few were cold and disengaged, and others seemed emotionally removed and preoccupied despite invitations from the child to become involved.

The second major dimension of parenting style has to do with the parents' tendency to provide structure, to set limits, and to encourage the child to try tasks even if they seem difficult. Some parents tended not to help structure the situation even when the child was floundering. Others might say, "I know the puzzle looks confusing, but why don't we start with this part?"

We based our summary descriptions of parents' styles of working and playing with their children on a combination of both the warmth and structuring dimensions: Parents who showed a high degree of warmth, responsiveness, and structure were described as *authoritative*; those at the other end of the continuum, who showed little warmth or structure, were described as *disengaged*; parents who showed little warmth and a lot of anger, structure, and limits were described as *authoritarian*, and those high in warmth but low in structure and limit setting were called *permissive*.

We know from many studies that children of parents with an angry or a cold, demanding, authoritarian parenting style appear to be in the most developmental difficulty, whereas children of parents with a warm but firm authoritative style tend to be more competent both socially and cognitively (Hetherington and Parke 1986; Maccoby and Martin 1983; Mussen, Conger, and Kagan 1984). The children of authoritative parents did better in our study, too; they showed more developmental progress in some laboratory tasks we gave them when they were three and a half, and they had higher achievement scores at the end of their kindergarten year.

We looked more closely to see what else the authoritative parents were doing when they worked or played with their children. Along with our colleague, Michael Pratt (Pratt et al. 1988), we found that parents with an authoritative style supported their children's learning in two ways. First, when their children were confused or having difficulty, authoritative parents modified their help and instruction to meet the children at their level of understanding. Then, once the children grasped the idea of what to do, the parents stepped back and let them proceed on their own.

THE TRANSITION TO PARENTHOOD AND PARENTING STYLE

We found that how parents had managed their lives during the transition to parenthood had a great deal to do with their parenting style when their children were three and a half. Parents with less conflict in their families of origin, greater marital satisfaction during pregnancy, less life stress six months into parenthood, and less depression and marital distress when the children were eighteen months old were more likely to be warm, responsive, structuring, and limit setting with their preschoolers.[3] Conversely, parents who were not feeling good about themselves and their marriage during the transition were more cold, angry, unresponsive, and unable to set limits during the parent-child visits later on (Cowan, Cowan, Schulz, and Heming in press).

We found continuities between how men and women viewed themselves and their lives in pregnancy, how they managed their transitions to parenthood, and the quality of their relationships with their children two to four years later. For couples who began the journey in good shape and who managed to maintain a positive relationship as a couple, these results are reassuring. For couples like Peggy and Bill or Sharon and Daniel, who started their journey in difficulty and experienced additional hardships along the way, individual and marital difficulties tended to spill over into their relationships with their preschoolers.

Because much of the information about the parents in this analysis was obtained after the children were born, one could argue that it is not parents' well-being but children's temperament that affects their parenting style:

When babies are difficult to manage, mothers and fathers have more difficulty making the transition to parenthood and dealing with the children as
preschoolers. We conducted a more stringent test of our idea that the
transition to parenthood provides a context for the development of parent-
child relationships. The information parents provided about themselves during pregnancy, before their children's personalities could have influenced
their parenting behavior, was highly related to the kinds of relationships we
observed between the parents and their children almost four years after they
became a family. Women who were most satisfied with themselves and with
their family division of labor before their babies were born were warmer and
more able to set limits with their preschoolers.[4] A woman's positive feelings
about herself and about the way she and her partner shared the family work
seemed to create a positive climate for her to become a more effective parent.

When we looked for links between a man's life before he became a father
and his parenting style almost four years later, we came up with both
intriguing and puzzling results: Expectant fathers with positive memories of
their parents, higher self-esteem, greater involvement in household tasks,
and lower outside-the-family stress before their babies were born were more
authoritative with their sons four years later, but these qualities of men's lives
did *not* seem to carry over to the tenor of their relationships with daughters.[5]

Why? Our attempts to answer this question led us to two troubling
findings. First, parents, especially fathers, react to boys and girls differently;
girls typically receive less positive treatment. Second, we can trace the origins
of these gender differences in parenting to the fact that couples' marital
difficulties during the transition to parenthood amplify men's tendency to
treat daughters less sympathetically than sons. From our data, it looks like
father-daughter relationships are at risk when the parents' marriage is in
trouble during the early years of becoming a family.

GENDER MAKES A DIFFERENCE

In this age of egalitarian, nonsexist ideology, many parents are trying hard
to defy the old gender stereotypes. Most men and women assured us that the
gender of their child would not make a difference to their style of parenting.
In contrast with past generations, they are more likely to consider buying a
toy truck for a little girl and a doll for a little boy. They are a little less likely
to think that girls need to be protected and boys taught to defend themselves.
Yet our observations of fathers with their three-and-a-half-year-old sons and
daughters showed a familiar theme in studies of parent-child relationships:
Gender makes a difference.

Mothers of sons did not differ as a group from mothers of daughters in
the way they interacted with their preschoolers on any of our parenting style
observations: Some mothers were authoritative, some more disengaged,
some more authoritarian, and some more permissive, but women's parenting
style was not related to the gender of their child. But we observed that fathers
of daughters were a little less authoritative and a lot more authoritarian than

fathers of sons.[6] As a group, fathers of girls were more likely than fathers of boys to react to their children in a colder, more critical manner, to set more limits, and to give them less encouragement to do things their own way. These results are consistent with Jeanne Block's summaries of earlier studies of parents' treatment of boys and girls (Block 1976a, b; 1983).

Our attempt to understand the salience of gender in the relationships between parents and young children led us to see once again the central importance of the parents' marriage and how it changes during their transition from partners to parents. We found one missing piece of the puzzle in our observations of the couple's relationship during the family visit. When the couple worked together cooperatively and responsively, the fathers' separate visits with their daughters went positively too.[7] When we saw conflict and hostility between the parents in front of the child, we were likely to find that the father and daughter were having a difficult time in their separate visit.[8] What startled us about these results was that the state of the marriage did not tend to intrude on the relationship between fathers and sons.

We are concerned about the consequences of the close tie between parents' marital distress and fathers' tendency to react to their preschool girls in a more irritable, cold, angry, authoritarian manner. In a more detailed analysis of the videotaped family visits, Patricia Kerig (1989; Cowan, Cowan, and Kerig in press) looked closely at the parents' specific responses to the children's behavior in our playroom.[9] She found that, overall, girls tended to receive more positive comments from their parents than boys did. Boys got rewarded with positive responses for their independent behavior when they were working at the tasks in our playroom, but girls were more likely to be overridden and negated.

The quality of the parents' marriage plays a crucial role here. Mothers who were more unhappy with their relationships with their husbands tended to be more authoritarian and less authoritative with their children, girls or boys, but *especially when daughters asserted themselves*. The parents who responded most negatively to daughters were fathers who were more distressed in their relationships with their wives. These fathers gave the most negative responses of any parents in the study, no matter what their daughters did. This means that a young daughter whose parents are in conflict is less likely than a son to have even one parent available to be warm and responsive, to be able to structure tasks that are difficult, and to be observant enough to step back when she gets her bearings.

We now have at least a partial answer to why there are such complex patterns in father-son and father-daughter relationships. How a father engages with his preschool-age daughter depends not so much on how he feels about himself and his life, but on how his relationship with his wife turns out in the first few years of raising a family. A father's relationship with his son seems to be tied to how he has been feeling about himself and his life while becoming a parent, quite independent of the atmosphere in his marriage.

A follow-up question is more difficult to answer. Why does a daughter so often become the target of the negative fallout from a conflictful marriage?

We think that this is easier to understand if we look more generally at how the parents' marital quality is related to the tenor of their relationships with their children. Given parents in a marriage with a good deal of unresolved conflict, it seems understandable that some of their frustration will spill over into their relationships with the children. Indeed, the parents in highly conflictful relationships showed colder, more critical, authoritarian parenting styles in three of the four gender combinations: mothers with sons, mothers with daughters, and fathers with daughters. What prevents the spillover from marital to parenting difficulties for fathers of sons?

Although most parents spontaneously mentioned that they would be equally happy to have a son or a daughter, several facts support our hunch that boys are the favored sex for fathers. First, although there were no differences in the self-descriptions of prospective fathers of sons and daughters before their babies were born, two years later, men who had sons used significantly more of the favorable items on the Adjective Check List to describe themselves than men who had daughters.[10] Second, if their first child was a girl, couples were more likely to have a second child by the time the first was eighteen months old.[11] Although there may be many reasons for this phenomenon, it means that many families with first-born girls go through a second transition to parenthood sooner and are subject to more strain than families whose first-born are boys. Third, in the first four years of our study, couples were more likely to separate if their first child was a girl. This is consistent with the results of a much larger study of a national sample by Morgan, Lye, and Condran (1988) and of two in-depth family studies by Jeanne and Jack Block (Block, Block, and Gjerde 1986) and Mavis Hetherington (Hetherington and Anderson 1989).

Joan and Rob are talking with us about this phenomenon just after their son, Chuck, has entered kindergarten. They are describing a very stormy period in their relationship that started when Chuck was about four and lasted almost a year.

> ROB: It was very touch and go for a while. Some of the things we talked about in our couples group were helpful, but after about a year of fighting we found it hard to remember anymore what we could do to make it better. What kept me hanging in there was Chuckie. I know too many men who get divorced and just lose their kids. I wasn't going to let my son go.
>
> JOAN: It's really better now. At the worst times, when I'd almost lost hope, I'd imagine Chuckie growing up without his father there. I know Rob would've been there for him in many ways, but it's not the same . . . especially for a boy.

Mothers and fathers perceive boys as more vulnerable than girls during a separation or divorce: Mothers feel that boys are difficult to rear alone, and a marital split usually deprives sons of having their fathers around full-time. Our hypothesis, then, is that both parents make active efforts not to let marital and other family difficulties erode the quality of the relationship between father and son. Unfortunately, unhappily married men do not generally make the same efforts to safeguard their relationships with their daughters. Fathers tend to treat their young sons fairly well, regardless of how the marriage feels, but their relationships with their daughters are often as troubled as their relationships with their wives.

Our impression is that when the relationship between the parents is tense, a mother and daughter may form a kind of alliance that plays into the father's tendency to see "his women" as a twosome united against him. Bill expressed it directly in a moment of frustration: "I can't deal with either of the women in my family." A mother may be less likely to form this kind of alliance with her son, but even if she does, the father is not as likely to withdraw and leave the parenting of a son to his wife.

We are not suggesting that fathers consciously allow their marital difficulties to erode the relationships with their daughters. As we see it, gender issues become heightened in the natural course of becoming a family. As we have shown, the initial differences between men and women become magnified as they navigate the transition to parenthood. Partners take on more divergent family roles, they report more conflict and disagreement, they feel more distance between them, and a majority become at least somewhat more dissatisfied with their overall relationship. Particularly for couples who have no satisfactory ways of resolving their differences and impasses, this increases the potential for more conflict and criticism between them, which increases the likelihood of children's being exposed to their parents' disagreements. When differences between the parents increased between pregnancy and eighteen months after their child's birth, the parents were more likely to show marital conflict in front of their child when we observed them several years later.[12] The families in which fathers were most negative and ineffective with their three-and-a-half-year-old daughters had a history in which the parents had grown farther apart as they made their transitions to parenthood.

We want to emphasize that our findings are based on group trends and so will not apply in every case. But there is the potential for troubled relationships between parents and children, particularly between fathers and daughters, when the marriage is not going well. Unless parents find ways to buffer their relationships with their children from the effects of their marital unhappiness, it looks like their children will pay a price for the parents' disenchantment, even if, or perhaps especially if, they stay together.

In addition, parents' tendency to praise girls for compliance and to criticize them for asserting themselves may leave girls more vulnerable to depression in adolescence and adulthood (Weissman and Klerman 1977). Depression has been conceptualized by some as a condition of learned helplessness (Seligman 1975) and an inability to take actions in one's own behalf (Beck 1976; Lewinsohn et al. 1981). Our findings suggest that the seeds of girls' conflicts about asserting themselves may actually be sown during their parents' transition to parenthood, when gender issues become heightened because of the parents' distress about unresolved differences between them.

Parents' Well-being and Parenting Style

The gender of the child is an important ingredient of parenting style. How parents fare in other aspects of their lives, often in combination with how their marriage is going, also helps us understand the quality of their relationships with their preschoolers.

As a group, the parents in our study tended to be functioning fairly well, but between 20 percent and 30 percent reported enough symptoms to be at risk for clinical depression during their children's early years (Cowan et al. 1991).[13] Although we expected to observe less effective parenting styles in the parents who were more depressed, we found that parents' depression did not compromise their ability to be warm, responsive, and structuring with their preschoolers unless the marriage was also in difficulty. But parents who were depressed were the ones more likely to have conflictful and hostile interactions as a couple when they were with their child in our playroom (Miller et al. 1991). When there was more conflict between the parents, they were less likely to be authoritative with their child. So, the connections seem to go from depression in one parent, to conflict in the marriage, to less effective parenting. Parents' styles of reacting to their children were related to their feelings of depression when their marriage was also troubled, tense, and conflictful. A warm and cooperative marital relationship appeared to buffer the negative effects of one parent's depression on the relationship with the child (Cowan et al. in press).*

We should not forget the buffering effects of the marriage on parenting that we reported in the last chapter. When wives who had insecure models of parent-child relationships were married to husbands with secure models, the couple seemed to be doing well and both parents were warm, engaged, and structuring with their children. A positive marriage seems to help women break the negative generational cycle and react to their children positively and effectively.

Finally, we know that most women feel powerful conflicts about being home with the children or going back to their work outside the family (Harber 1991). This is another arena in which individual and marital issues play out in the parenting. We found that mothers and fathers who were more satisfied with their work (regardless of how many hours they worked), and more satisfied with the way the two of them resolved issues about child care

---

*In clinical samples of mothers who are seriously depressed (Cutrona and Troutman 1986; Field et al. 1990), researchers do find direct links between parents' depression and parenting style. As Hops, Sherman, and Biglan (1990) point out, however, it is hard to find seriously depressed young mothers with relatively harmonious marriages. It may be that the impact of clinical depression also plays out through tensions in the couple's relationship.

(regardless of their particular child-care arrangements), were more authoritative with their children.[14]

As Peggy and Bill tell us about the strain that is cycling throughout the relationships in their family, we see how this individual-to-marriage-to-parenting connection unfolds. They wind up discussing the issue of being strict or lenient with Mindy almost every morning before Bill leaves for work. Or they fight about whether Peggy should go back to work, whether she can help him solve his business problems, and whether or when they should be planning a second baby. Peggy explains: "We're not making much headway on any of these issues. By the time he closes the door, I'm a wreck. I want to be there for Mindy, but sometimes I'm just too crabby and impatient, especially when she starts getting upset."

Bill is distressed, too, and tries to calm down during the day. He usually feels that he wants to apologize when he gets home, but by then Peggy is often frosty and Mindy sulky. When he feels he can't deal with either of them, he slips into the den to sort out some of the business problems of the day. Peggy and Bill are quite aware that the atmosphere in their relationship is affecting their ability to be responsive to Mindy, but when they are not resolving some of their differences and not feeling taken care of by each other, it is hard for them to be nurturant to their child.

Long-Term Consequences for Children

As we followed each family through their first child's kindergarten year, some of the longer-term effects of the parents' transition to parenthood became evident. The better the parents felt they had managed their transition to parenthood, the better their children were managing their transition from family to school.

Beginning kindergarten is a big step for children and for their parents. Even if they are veterans of day-care centers or nursery schools, children enter the more formal elementary school environment with some apprehension. The school is large, there are children they don't know, and the teacher is a stranger. They don't know where to put their jackets, what the teacher expects, or what the rules are. For most, the challenge will be to make a shift from play and exploration to the more structured academic requirements. To accomplish these serious tasks, they will be asked to sit quietly, to pay attention, and to follow instructions for much of the day.

How did the children in our study adapt to this major transition? Our measures of adaptation focus on children's academic achievement and on their behavior in the classroom. Our information came from two sources: each child's score on the reading recognition and mathematics sections of the Peabody Individual Achievement Test, given by one of our staff members in the summer after kindergarten, and a ninety-one-item checklist that each child's teacher filled out once in late fall and again in late spring of kindergar-

ten year.[15] Because teachers rated each child in the classroom without knowing which children were in our study, we have information about how the
teacher perceived the social and academic adjustment of each child in our
study relative to his or her peers.

Kindergarten children who are described by the teacher as disobedient,
uncooperative, rule-breaking, and prone to fighting we described as *aggressive*. Boys and girls who are shy, prefer solitary activities, and don't make
friends easily we described as *shy and withdrawn*. We say that kindergarteners
who are restless, easily distracted, and unable to concentrate or work quietly
at an activity are having *concentration problems*.

Using a complex statistical equation, we found that a number of measures
combined to predict the child's adaptation to kindergarten: parents with less
conflict in their families of origin; greater marital satisfaction during pregnancy; less life stress six months into parenthood; less depression and marital
distress when the child was eighteen months old; more warmth and cooperation in the couple relationship; and more warmth and structure with the
child at three and a half. We found that how the family was faring during the
pregnancy-to-preschool period was related to the children's ability both to
get along with peers and to accomplish the academic challenges of elementary school (Cowan et al. in press).[16] When families were in difficulty or
distress in many aspects of their lives, their children were described by their
kindergarten teachers as more aggressive or more shy, and more likely to
have problems concentrating in the classroom. These children also had lower
reading and mathematics achievement scores at the end of their kindergarten
year.[17]

It will probably not be surprising to learn that Peggy and Bill's daughter
had a difficult time in kindergarten. Her teacher's description implied that
Mindy had a hot temper, hit other children, and was rarely chosen by others
to play with. She had not yet mastered the rudiments of reading and arithme-
tic that had become the focus of classwork during the second half of the
school year. Unfortunately, Mindy's difficulty became one more thing for her
parents to fight about. Each was still blaming the other for being "too harsh"
or "too soft," still defending his or her own parenting styles based on their
experiences in their original families. Bill's business was still having problems, and Peggy had decided to get a job outside the house instead of helping
Bill with his accounts because things were going so badly between them.

Willie was faring much better than Mindy during his transition to school.
During the early parenthood period, his parents, Beth and Paul, spoke of the
childhood experiences that had left them feeling vulnerable. They seemed to
be using these painful experiences to understand each other's position, to
thrash out their marital differences, and to parent Willie in a style that
combined what was important to each of them. Willie's kindergarten teacher
described him as a delightful, curious, outgoing child who was cooperative
with the other children and doing well in his academic work.

It makes sense that parents' effectiveness at working and playing with
their preschoolers plays a role in how their children acquire their social and
academic skills. What we are learning from our study is that the quality of

the parents' marriage has two important additional contributions to make to children's developmental progress. First, except for fathers of sons, marital conflict tends to spill over into most parent-child relationships in ways that lead maritally distressed parents to be less helpful and supportive of their children's development. Second, conflict between the parents has an even more direct and disruptive effect on the children, suggested by their teachers' descriptions of them as less able to concentrate on their classroom work. While we have known for some time that children tend to have difficulties at school when their parents divorce (Hetherington and Anderson 1989), our study is part of an emerging body of work that illustrates that children whose parents are together but in unhappy or conflictful relationships are also at risk for academic and peer relationship problems as they set out on their school careers.

We end our description of the journey to becoming a family at the beginning of a new transition—a fitting closing, we think, for the saga of modern families, who are always on the move, exploring challenging terrain toward individual and family milestones. The story of how parent-child relationships evolve resembles our accounts of family well-being in every chapter of part II. As men and women cross the great divide from couplehood to parenthood, they tend to get divided from each other. How they feel about themselves, their marriage, their work, their friendships, and their own childhoods is interrelated. The family atmosphere they establish before their children are born tends to be carried over into the early years of child rearing, shaping the tone of the relationships they develop with their children. Ultimately these family relationships become the models that the children draw on as they strike up relationships with other children and tackle the challenges of school.

As clinical psychologists, we are anxious to go beyond describing family dynamics. We can see that children benefit from the strengths their parents bring to the family-making venture and suffer when their parents find the journey perilous. What is both exciting and troubling about our results is that there is some degree of predictability about what will happen five to six years down the road of becoming a family. We have learned that it is possible to identify many of the couples whose marital and parenting relationships are at risk from the state of their relationships during pregnancy and the early family-making years. Our findings make it clear that there is an urgent need for early family interventions so that the parents' distress will not be borne by their children. In part III, we begin by describing a unique intervention for expectant couples. Then we discuss what we have learned from couples with and without the intervention about common pitfalls to effective communication between partners, in the hope that expectant and new parents can learn to help themselves and each other as they make their way along this rugged terrain. Finally, we look back briefly at the journey. We highlight the big issues, describe some warning signals for couples most likely to be at risk for distress, and offer suggestions for couples, health professionals, researchers, and policy makers that might bring more joy and less stress to the family-making process.

PART III

Protecting the Homestead

"*The work being done on your marriage—are you having it done, or are you doing it yourselves?*"

Drawing by Maslin; © 1989
The New Yorker Magazine, Inc.

CHAPTER 9

An Ounce of Prevention: Couples Groups

ANNIE: I don't know what to do. I'm so exhausted from getting up with Carrie two or three times every night for the past week, I can hardly function during the days. Mitch says he's willing to take a turn at least once a night, but he never hears her cry! I'm some mother—I don't even have the energy to smile back when Carrie gurgles.

MITCH: I can hardly believe it when she tells me in the morning that Carrie howled for an hour and a half. I truly don't hear a thing, but Annie doesn't believe me.

ROB: Joan and I had the same fight last week. I haven't been hearing Chuckie either.

JACKSON: And I don't hear Kevin. What is this—new fathers' hearing loss?

MARTIN: It must be genetic. Men aren't wired to hear babies' cries.

This is a conversation from one of our Becoming a Family Project couples groups. Four couples have been meeting weekly and talking with us since the women's seventh month of pregnancy. All have become parents at this point, and the four newborns are asleep either in an infant seat or in a parent's arms. We notice how rare it is for all of the babies to be asleep at once. All eight parents look exhausted.

Versions of this discussion emerged in almost all of our couples groups with new parents. The men are fascinated by their common problem, and the women's reactions range from humor to mild anger to serious distress. As each couple admits to struggling with variations on "new fathers' hearing loss," the tension level in the group lightens. Even though they are weary, both men and women are relieved to find that this is happening to almost everyone else. It seems to mute their consternation and feelings of distress with their partners and allows us to focus on the unexpected impasses between them.

When we ask Annie what happens when she tries to talk to Mitch about how tired she is, she says that he seems sympathetic but she is still the one who gets up at night. She begins to cry as she relates how distant she feels from Mitch. As if she has a direct line to her mother's emotions, little Carrie begins to whimper. Annie becomes distracted trying to soothe her. Without a word, Mitch reaches over to pick her up. "Frankly, I'm stumped," he explains. "If I don't hear Carrie, what am I supposed to do, stay up all night waiting for her to cry? I have to get up first thing to get to work, and I've been doing all the shopping and errands outside the house for weeks, so I'm feeling pretty much at my wits' end too. And when I hear Annie's critical tone . . . well, I just can't talk to her when she's so worked up." At this point Carrie is wailing and Annie moves toward Mitch, signaling that she wants to take Carrie back to her lap.

The rest of us in the room have the vivid impression that Carrie is mirroring her parents' tension and distress. Early on, then, all of the group members get a hint of how parents' emotional states can affect their babies. At the same time, the babies' reactions can keep the parents from taking care of their own needs by completing a conversation that might help them resolve the sticky issues in their relationship.

As we will show, the couples groups we conducted had a marked and profound effect on the parents in the first three years of becoming a family. Although the positive effects did not last forever, they did make a difference in the aspects of parents' lives we have been describing.

What's Out There? Then and Now

Before developing our idea of groups for expectant and new parents in the early 1970s, we scoured the professional literature on pregnancy, new parenthood, and couples therapy, certain that others must have thought of providing services for new parents. We found almost nothing. Since then, we have read of a few interventions for parents whose babies are at risk for difficulty because of the parents' health problems, the baby's prematurity (see Cherniss 1988; Parke and Tinsley 1982; Powell 1987), or retardation (Ramey et al. 1976), but the kinds of groups we developed for ordinary families—in which mental health professionals work with both men and women before their distress warrants longer-term counseling or therapy—simply do not exist.

Long after we had begun, we read about several small pilot studies (Aranoff and Lewis 1979; Colman and Colman 1971; McGuire and Gottlieb 1979; Myers-Walls and Sudsberry 1982) and two major experimental intervention projects in which health professionals worked with expectant parents— expectant mothers in the Washington, D.C., area (Shereshefsky and Yarrow 1973) and expectant couples in London (Clulow 1982). Clulow provides vivid descriptions of how each partner's dynamics play out in the relationship as the couple enters parenthood. By the time these projects were written up and published, however, the services were no longer available because the funding had run out.

Despite extensive documentation of the fact that "social support" is helpful for new parents (e.g., Gottlieb and Pancer 1988; Nuckolls, Cassells, and Kaplan 1972; Wandersman 1987), we have not found any other systematically evaluated groups for couples making the transition to parenthood, in which the leaders are trained to help with a full range of family issues and difficulties: individual, marital, parenting, three-generational, and outside-the-family.

Why We Work with Couples in Groups

Our findings about the central role of marital quality in men's and women's adaptation to parenthood certainly reinforce our strategy of targeting our intervention to couples. While the few existing services for new parents are offered to mothers, fathers' participation is the key to demonstrating that family making is a joint endeavor, not just during pregnancy, labor, and delivery but in the years to come. Men simply have little access to settings in which they can share their experiences about intimate family matters. Given how stressful family life is for so many couples, we feel it is important to help them understand how their increasing differences during this transition may be generating more distance between them.

Why intervene with couples in *groups*? We find that a group setting can provide the kind of ongoing support that contemporary couples often lack if they are creating new families far from their parents and extended families. Groups of people going through similar life experiences help participants "normalize" some of their strain and adjustment difficulties; they discover that other couples are in the same boat and that the strain they are experiencing is expectable at this stage of life (Lieberman 1981). This can strengthen the bond between husbands and wives and undercut their tendency to blame each other for their distress.

Couples rarely have an opportunity to watch and listen as other couples struggle with difficult marital or parenting issues. At best, they get edited versions of another couple's controversy once it has been resolved. In a group with trained leaders, we can provide a learning environment in which men and women can talk about what does and doesn't work and experiment with strategies tailored to their particular situation. Not childbirth preparation and not groups about parenting, our Becoming a Family Project groups are designed to provide couples with a safe environment in which husbands and wives can be encouraged to explore their expectations and realities, their hopes and anxieties, and their successes and disappointments *as they are happening.*

By inviting the babies to become part of the groups, we help parents feel less pulled to stay home with their newborns. Some women say that the groups provided their only contact with other adults in the first month or two of parenthood. Because of the potential isolation and exhaustion these weeks can bring, both parents, but particularly mothers, often feel blue or depressed. Having the babies right there in the groups not only allows the parents to show off their progeny but has the added benefit of allowing the tensions between the parents' and the babies' needs to become visible, as they did in Mitch and Annie's discussion of middle-of-the-night feedings.

We were extremely fortunate to find that the best candidates for staff couples in our longitudinal study were "real-life" couples. Harriet Curtis-Boles and Abner Boles III, and Ellen Garrett and Bill Coysh, married graduate student couples at the time, worked with the two of us for almost four years.[1] Five of the six leaders were clinical psychologists at the pre- or postdoctoral level and the sixth, Ellen, was a businesswoman.

The format for training the group leaders was drawn from our earlier experience with John and Lynne Coie, our collaborators in the pilot study to test our intervention approach (Cowan et al. 1978). At the beginning of the training, all of us completed the study questionnaires that the couples would eventually fill out, as a way to describe our own lives as individuals and as couples. Then, using the semi-structured format we would be using with the couples in the study to talk about our lives as couples, we met weekly as a group over a four-month period.

As we mentioned in the introduction, the twenty-four expectant couples invited to be in one of our couples groups were randomly chosen from all of the expectant couples entering the study. Each was interviewed by a staff couple to acquaint them with the project and with us. Each staff couple conducted two six-month-long groups. Once the groups were under way, we supervised the clinical work in our staff meetings on a weekly and then twice-monthly basis throughout the first and second years of the study. All of us on the staff monitored the process and progress of all six groups.

It is 7:00 P.M. on a Tuesday evening in mid-April, the first meeting of our group. Four couples—Annie and Mitch, Joan and Rob, Tanya and Jackson, and Sandi and Martin—have gathered in the conference room of the Psychology Clinic. The four women are beginning their last trimester of pregnancy. Three of them are still feeling nimble, but Joan says she feels "like a beached whale." We have met each couple in our initial interviews, but they are strangers to one another.

We tell the group members a little about ourselves and ask them what drew them to the project. Because each husband and wife in the group had completed a packet of questionnaires before the first meeting, they have already begun to think about the aspects of family life we will be discussing.

After the introductory session, our evenings usually start with an unstructured "check-in" that gives each person a chance to raise any current concerns and topics for future discussions in the group. A husband or wife faced with an urgent decision about a job or career move is encouraged to sort out the issues involved. The relationship with one man's parents may have become heated around choosing a name for the baby. His wife says she wants him to tell his mother that it is up to them to choose their own baby's name. We try to help both partners figure out what, if anything, they can do to take care of each person's needs.

The second part of each meeting is devoted to a topic that has been selected by us or by the group. During the six months of meeting together, we travel with the couples over our five-domain map of the transition to parenthood, helping them to see how the various territories are connected. In the early meetings, we focus on each of the partners as individuals. Then we move on to talk more about their lives and their dreams about their relationship, their work and family decisions, three-generational issues, and their pressing questions about being parents.

We scheduled the six months of meetings so that couples could spend the first three months *anticipating* how they will manage once they have a baby and the next three exploring their *actual* experience once their babies are born. Over the twenty-four meetings, the couples build a set of shared experiences and ideas.

ANTICIPATION

At first, some husbands seem less comfortable than their wives about volunteering their feelings, questions, or worries, but with the leaders' gentle encouragement the men in every group begin to talk. They describe their experience of the pregnancy, their anxieties about managing the labor and delivery, and especially their pictures about becoming fathers. Group participants soon discover how common it is for men and women to struggle with discrepancies between how they think they are supposed to feel and how they really feel. During late pregnancy, common themes emerge in each of the groups.

Individual Concerns About Pregnancy, Labor, and Delivery   Even though all of the couples in our study attended some kind of childbirth preparation together, both husbands and wives worry about things they cannot raise in such classes. Husbands talk about needing to be strong and protective of their pregnant wives; it would be selfish, they feel, to discuss their own fears and needs. Wives are concerned about what is happening to their bodies and how that makes them feel. Each person in the group gets to hear about his or her mate's worries and about a host of issues that couples do not usually discuss, yet obviously need to discuss. As we encourage this kind of talk, the group members learn from our reactions that we expect men and women to have some of these negative feelings and concerns.

Family Legacies   As we encourage couples to flesh out their pictures of life as a family, they begin to describe their childhood years. Sandi says that her parents are very traditional. Martin's politically radical parents consternate her: "I just assumed that when we got married, the home stuff was my department, but I can never do anything around the house without Martin mixing in. I can't tell whether he's doing it because he wants to or whether he feels he has to because his parents just did everything together." Joan, looking thoughtful, comments: "I'm just beginning to see something. With Rob and me, it's the other way around. He's the one from the family where the women did everything, and my folks were the odd ones who shared. Either way it can lead to things getting mixed up between you." Other couples' stories can help us take a fresh look at our own.

Ideas About Parenting   "Babies should be tended when they are upset so that they will be sure of their parents' love for them." This item from our questionnaire about parenting ideas (Heming, Cowan, and Cowan 1990) usually stimulates heated debate. Some expectant parents focus on the baby's sense of insecurity if left to cry; others are as passionate about not teaching a child to cry for everything he or she needs. Discussing some of these crucial parenting ideas before the baby arrives is one way of preparing for the real dilemmas that every couple will face. When partners discover that they have different notions of how to handle some of these common issues in a setting that is intended to entertain many points of view, there is less chance that they will find themselves startled to be on opposite sides of the debate when the baby is howling in the middle of the night. This initial sharing of expectations about parenting rarely leads to a resolution of partners' differences, but it initiates them into a process of problem solving that can stand them in good stead in the months and years to come.

Work/Family Issues   Every couple faces the problem of how to juggle the pulls between work and family life. Because our group discussions involve a wide range of situations, group members can see that their tension does not stem solely from their inability to fit everything in. We pay attention to each individual's and couple's needs and try to address the forces over which they have little or no control: no paternity leave, career demands, financial worries, and so on.

Marital Conflicts   One evening, Joan and Rob arrive looking tense, faces flushed. Joan looks as if she has been crying. No one comments. The group discussion goes on for a few minutes; then, during a remark about an argument between Sandi and Martin, Joan begins to cry. With our encouragement, she and Rob describe a fight they had on the way to the meeting. They had been at a wedding reception of a friend and were leaving early to be on time for our group. Rob said he wanted to stay. Joan wanted to stay too, but said nothing about that, only insisting that they must leave. We ask a few questions about what had been happening before the fight started. It seems that Joan had asked Rob on the way to the reception whether he had read the childbirth books she had bought. He had brushed off the question, implying that he would get around to it, but he didn't sound as if he was interested in reading them. Joan says she thought, "Uh-oh, he has cold feet about the baby and second thoughts about me, too. And then, when Rob said he didn't want to come to the group tonight, I felt—well, that's really it, he's jumping off the train."

Rob protests: "I don't know where she gets that stuff. I love her. I'm really excited about the baby. But every time I start one of those books, I start getting tight and anxious. I figure it's better if I just let it happen without thinking about it so much." As far as the recent conflict was concerned, he explained: "What I really wanted to do was to stay at that party for a few more minutes and then go off by ourselves. When you blew up, I thought, 'Well, I know what she says about wanting us to be together, but it doesn't sound to me as if she's really interested.' "

This interchange demonstrates how difficult it can be for two people to communicate with each other, especially when one or both of them are apprehensive or tense. One issue tends to spiral into another. Each partner sees the same event differently. Both make quick assumptions about what is going on inside the other without checking them out. Rob doesn't feel right about saying he's anxious, in part to avoid a fight but in part because he doesn't think men ought to feel that way. Joan blows up. Rob backs off. The sad part is that she doesn't let him know that she wants to stay longer too, and he says so little about what is going on inside him that she does not get to find out, until we ask him about it in the group, that he really wanted to be with her alone. By the end of the discussion, Joan and Rob have not resolved the differences that started their fight, but they are working together to figure them out. We can feel the relaxation of the tension between them, and they seem to feel a great deal better about each other.

Joan says she feels self-conscious because she and Rob have taken so much of the group's time. But Sandi says she is relieved to hear them struggle with something that they have not yet resolved: "Martin and I have been having some of the same kind of go-rounds lately, but we haven't had the nerve to bring them here. What we usually tell here is the cleaned-up version. I've learned a lot about how complicated one little spat can be."

AFTER THE BABIES ARRIVE

Soon after the women give birth, the couples bring their infants into the groups. They are eager to describe the details of their labor and delivery. "Old hands" who have been parents for weeks spontaneously bring prepared food and words of wisdom for the newest parents. Men talk animatedly about their ability to handle their wives' long labors and difficult births; they are astounded at the strength the women showed and, to a man, they are amazed at the intensity of their feelings for their newborns. Rob tells Martin, whose baby is due in several days: "You wonder and worry about whether you'll be ready when the time comes, and then you just are. When the doctor told us it would have to be a C-section, Joan and I just got in there and did it. They treated me just like one of the medical team. It was amazing to see that little boy emerge. They asked me to cut the cord! There's been no experience in my life to match it!"

Each of us becomes absorbed in the images of these "birth stories," as the couples come to call them. Throughout the weeks of sharing these experiences, we are continually impressed by how eagerly men, who generally do not find it easy to talk about intimate feelings, are opening up. Slowly, groups of former strangers have come to sound like trusted confidants. After the group meetings end, many participants express their surprise that it was easier to have some of these conversations in a safe setting with people they didn't know well than it is at home or with friends.

In the three months that follow, we return to many of the issues we had discussed before the couples became parents. The earlier discussions have prepared us for talking about how to deal with the stress points in life with a newborn. Some of the partners' joint preparation cushions them from the shock of finding that their fantasy plans do not meet the reality test. We cannot help couples to avoid the stresses of new parenthood, but we can help them to face them, to think about how to deal with them, and to use their strengths to cope more effectively.

Our work in the couples groups sensitizes us to an often ignored aspect of the delicate balance between partners. A father who has been at work all day offers to hold his daughter, to soothe her, to change her. Even though his wife has said that she wants him to become "involved" in caring for the baby, she cannot seem to resist showing him how to hold her when he shows the slightest hesitation at the baby's fussing. "She likes it better if you hold her this way," she encourages. When their daughter cries in the next few moments, he hands her back to his wife, saying to the baby, "Here, sweetie, let's give you back to the 'expert.'" This kind of exchange can leave men feeling like the "second-string" parent and women feeling that they are carrying the whole burden of responding to the baby. Couples can slip into a more traditional division of baby care than either wanted.

Men and women in the group learn to appreciate that each of the issues they explore is related to each of the aspects of life we have been discussing. He wants to be more involved with the baby than his father was with him. She wants a more egalitarian relationship than her parents had, but if he gets to be an expert as a parent *and* in his job outside the family, where will her special contribution lie? The legacies from their families of origin have not given them models to talk about these new concerns easily, and their inability to do so leaves them feeling more distant than they did when they first planned this baby. Each time we venture into new territory, they tie ideas from earlier group discussions to the topic at hand.

> ROB: Last week we were talking about what we wanted to carry over from the families we grew up in, and what we *didn't* want to happen in our families now. Then right now, as we were talking about why I didn't want Joan to go back to work, at first I couldn't figure out why was I so upset. Then I realized I was getting in touch with how much I hated it when my mom wasn't home for me.
>
> JOAN: I'm not sure whether that means it'll be OK with you if I go back, but I'm relieved that at least you're not saying that it's just my problem.

In the last weeks, the groups begin to mirror the couples' lives at home. A father begins talking about how distressed he is that he has had no time alone with his wife since their son's birth, and his wife and baby begin to cry. A mother becomes absorbed in feeding or diapering her daughter, and we all become totally distracted with her, focusing on the baby's whimpers and gurgles and losing our train of thought completely. Even with this lesson before us, partners express surprise at how easily their needs as individuals and couples get sidetracked as they try to cope with the addition of the extraordinary demands of a newborn into their busy lives.

OUR ROLE AS GROUP LEADERS

In the most general sense, we think about our role as leaders as one of encouraging partners to explore the complexity of the exciting yet anxiety-provoking aspects of their journey to parenthood, to talk about the things we had found so difficult to do when we were becoming parents. We help them recognize when unresolved tensions in one aspect of life seem to be spilling over into another aspect.

We do not pretend that we can resolve couples' dilemmas or offer prescriptions to reestablish the balance in their lives. Our task is to slow them down so that they don't simply rush past muddy trails or rocky crevices in hopes of skirting disaster. We know that tension gets stimulated between partners when one is troubled about how the conversation is going, does not let the other know, does not ask a clarifying question, and tries to keep the discussion or debate going. This is a quick route to feeling like adversaries. If partners can learn to explore each person's point of view by amplifying and understanding it, they are much more likely to come out feeling on the same side even if they disagree. If the process feels more equal and productive, the frustration of being at an impasse can sometimes be avoided even if the problem cannot be solved immediately.

When a couple uses the protection of the group to work on a problem they have been unable to resolve by themselves, we encourage both partners to describe their experience of the difficulty. As participants present their individual views, we draw them out, looking for the sources of their different views. Our questions and their answers help to highlight the unique perspectives that no amount of mind reading can unearth.

Few couples have settings in which they can get help in revealing, redefining, and negotiating their problematic differences. The group provides a regular and safe haven in which they are encouraged to explore the major issues and challenges that interfere with their communication. For many couples, the group time is the only time when they talk seriously with each other about anything other than managing tasks and arranging schedules.

SUPPORT OR THERAPY?

When we describe the Becoming a Family groups to professional and lay audiences, we are usually asked whether they are education, support, or therapy groups. We think the groups encompass the best aspects of support groups, consciousness-raising groups, group therapy, and couples therapy.

For fairly well functioning couples, drawing out the participants and working with them when they are stuck helps them to clarify issues, discover some new perspectives on a problem, and expand their repertoire of skills for living as a family. When couples are in serious distress, the discussion in the groups can be both tense and frightening for the members. At times over the years, we have seen a couple through a major crisis. Several months after their babies' births, mothers in two different couples groups had to be hospitalized for serious illnesses. In both cases, frightened, anxious, and sometimes angry fathers were left to care for their infants. We tried to help make sense of these dramatic events for the couple in crisis and for the others in the group as well. Despite their increased feelings of vulnerability, group members rallied, spontaneously offering material and emotional support to the distressed parents and babies.

In one poignant example, Dawn was unexpectedly hospitalized, leaving her husband, Peter, to care for three-month-old Bonnie just as the group meetings were coming to an end. This exceedingly stressful situation was made even more difficult by the fact that Bonnie had not yet learned how to drink from a bottle. Peter came to the next group meeting with the baby, looking exhausted and worried. Bonnie kept wailing frantically, and after several failed attempts to feed her, he felt ready to do the same. Spontaneously, several of the mothers in Peter's group suggested a plan to help until Dawn was well enough to return home. Margaret, one of the mothers in the group who was still breastfeeding her baby, came to the couple's apartment, sent Peter out for a walk, and calmed Bonnie down enough to nurse her. Bonnie soon ate hungrily and fell asleep, quiet for the first time that day. Later in the day, Jenny, another mother from the group, came to visit Peter and Bonnie. Because she had already begun the sensitive task of weaning her baby from breast milk to bottle, Jenny was pretty sure that she would be able to get Bonnie to cooperate with her to drink from a bottle. She worked patiently with Peter and Bonnie until both of them "got the hang of it," as she put it.

The bonds that developed among the members of the group grew very strong as we all weathered Dawn and Peter's crisis.

In both of the groups that experienced severe distress in one of its members, the participants suggested that the group continue meeting a little longer until the distressed couple was on a more even keel. The response was unanimous in each case, and everyone attended faithfully for an extra month beyond our expected ending. We heard recently that two couples in each of these groups have maintained friendships begun more than eleven years ago.

We have become less concerned about deciding whether the groups provide support or therapy. At times, they do both. Because the groups are led by mental health professionals, we can deal directly with new parents' crises and high levels of distress. Could groups without leaders accomplish this task? Of the six groups we conducted for this study, one decided to continue meeting on their own for an additional four months, another for almost a year. In both cases, the couples told us later, they decided to stop meeting regularly when one of the couples began to talk about serious marital difficulties. Without experienced leaders there, they explained, the group did not know how to encourage the safe exploration of one another's marital problems. As Annie told us, "without you, we didn't have what it takes to handle the level of intimacy we had established."

There is one central difference, though, between what goes on in our Becoming a Family Project couples groups and therapy. Couples have not come to us saying that they are in serious distress or that they need to change. We have made it clear that we will help them monitor their own comfort with revealing their thoughts and feelings. Some men and women say less than others, but all say at the end that they have gained something by attending the sessions. At the very least, the comradeship of couples going through a major transition together provides the support and comfort of knowing they are not alone.

Short-Term Effects of the Intervention

Even before interpreting the statistics, there were clear, qualitative signs of the impact the group meetings were having on the parents. In a follow-up interview almost fifteen months after the group ended, Rob said: "Our group got together a couple of weeks ago, and we're planning a reunion on the second anniversary of when the group began. There's something wonderful about all of us knowing each other's kids all their lives. It's like being part of a very special family." Joan added: "Sometimes I feel that it really saved our lives. Our fighting was getting out of control. You probably wouldn't be surprised that we still do it, but we're able to come back to each other when it's over and really work things out."

While we are gratified to know that the couples *say* the groups have been helpful to their adjustment as couples and families, we also want to know whether we can *document* the effects of the intervention: We compared the patterns of the group couples' responses to our questionnaires with those of the couples in our comparison sample before and after having their babies and before and after their group experience. Did couples' patterns of change over the transition to parenthood in each aspect of family life look any different with and without the help of a couples group?

We were amazed and pleased to find that, although we could not see the effects of the intervention on everything we measured, there were statistically significant differences in each aspect of family life between the parents who had participated in a couples group and those who had had no intervention.[2]

SENSE OF SELF AND IDENTITY

The couples groups did not affect men's and women's self-esteem as measured by the difference between descriptions of "Me as I am" and "Me as I'd like to be" on the Adjective Check List. This is consistent with the results of most other studies indicating that self-esteem is a very stable characteristic of adults' personalities (Gough and Heilbrun 1980). We also found no differences in the men's descriptions of themselves on the pie as Parent, Partner, or Worker as a consequence of being in a couples group.

By contrast, the groups did have an impact on women's investment in different aspects of their identity. From pregnancy to six months after birth, mothers with and without a couples group experience similar declines in the size of their Worker/Student identities, but by eighteen months after their first child's birth, mothers who have been in the intervention return to their previous psychological involvement in their Worker or Student self. By contrast, mothers with no intervention have Worker or Student pie pieces that are half the size they were in their pre-baby days. Not only do group mothers come back to their work-related identities earlier, they also show significantly less decline in the Partner/Lover aspect of themselves than mothers without the intervention. It looks as if the group discussions, by encouraging partners to keep a focus on their couple relationship, help the women maintain their identity as wives and partners while they are taking on motherhood and returning to their jobs and careers.

DIVISION OF FAMILY WORK

Group participation has different effects on men's and women's satisfaction with their division of labor in the family. When the babies are six months old, partners' actual division of caring for the baby is no different in the intervention and the nonintervention couples, but fathers who have been in a couples group are *less satisfied* with their involvement in the care of their babies than fathers with no intervention; they want to be doing *more* housework and child care than they actually do. Over the same period, however, their wives are *more satisfied* with the couple's division of labor than wives who were not in one of the groups.

From our discussions in the groups, it is very clear that men want to continue their involvement in outside-the-family work *and* to be significantly involved in caring for their babies. Over the six months of meeting together, as fathers became painfully aware of what it takes to manage a demanding job and the day-to-day care of a household with a baby, their frustration rises. Fathers who are in our intervention groups probably talk more about reconciling these two aspects of their lives than do most men in the first year of new parenthood.

While mothers in the groups feel these work and family pulls too, they are more satisfied than their nonintervention counterparts with the couple's division of labor. Their satisfaction may reflect their appreciation that their husbands are sharing their concern about running the household, raising their child, and keeping their relationship as a couple alive because we talk about these things regularly in the groups. This shared concern may leave the women feeling somewhat less burdened, even if they cannot turn the egalitarian division of labor they envisioned into reality. The group wives' satisfaction may also reflect the fact that they hear other husbands talking about doing less child care than they had expected.

The groups have been over for more than a year by the time the babies are one and a half. At this point, the intervention fathers' satisfaction with who does what has remained stable, whereas fathers without the intervention are becoming significantly *more dissatisfied* with how the family work is divided. Now, fathers from the intervention groups are more satisfied than the comparison fathers with their involvement in caring for the children. Here we see the delicate balance within partners affecting the balance between them. The group women have retained more of their Worker/Student and Partner/Lover identities *and* satisfaction with their division of baby care. This may be helping their husbands reconcile the discrepancies between what they had hoped they could do and what the reality of their lives permits. Some support for this idea comes from our data showing that by the second year of parenthood, husbands and wives from the couples groups are having more similar perceptions of their division of baby care, whereas spouses with no intervention show more discrepant descriptions of theirs.

THE MARRIAGE

Most fathers, in groups and not in groups, reported higher levels of marital conflict and disagreement during the transition to parenthood. An interesting twist here is that the fathers who have been in a couples group say that they have *more* marital conflict about two specific issues: the family division of labor and the quality of time they spend together as a couple. While it is possible that the group discussions contribute to arguments about these aspects of life, it is also possible that partners who have been in a couples group simply talk more about these issues. After the group meetings ended, we asked each couple whether they thought that participating in the study had had any effect on them. Often they replied that they learned they'd do better talking about what is bothering them rather than sweeping it under the rug. As Annie said, "If you don't deal with things directly, they tend to come out anyway. We used to ignore our differences for fear that we'd get into a fight about them. But we're finding that we can handle more conflict than we used to be able to do. We still don't like it very much, but we learned that even when you have a fight, life goes on and nobody dies."

Both husbands and wives from the couples groups report fewer negative changes in their sexual relationship than those without the intervention. The protected setting of the couples groups makes it possible for couples to exchange information about this private aspect of married life. One evening late in her pregnancy, Annie described how she and Mitch were having problems when they tried to make love: "Nothing quite fits together the same way anymore. Last night we were trying to get comfortable, and moving every which way trying not to put too much weight on the baby, and suddenly Mitch fell out of bed!" There was laughter and a few sighs of relief from other group members. We later learned that this was the main topic of conversation for all the couples on their way home.

Sharing personal information was common in every couples group we have led or supervised over the past fifteen years. It clearly relieves tensions for some couples and answers unasked questions for others. The reports of less negative change in the sexual relationships of the intervention couples are consistent with our impression that when group members describe their experiences of these largely unexpected shifts in their sex lives, they feel less worried that something is wrong with them and more hopeful about things getting back to normal. When the leaders who are asking these delicate questions have their own spouses in the room, it appears to give participants the message, "We know that these are intimate matters but we are not embarrassed talking to you about them, if you are comfortable talking with us."

Since moderate but significant increases in overall marital disenchantment are reported by almost every researcher who studies the transition to parenthood, we were especially interested in whether we could show any measurable effects of the intervention on partners' feelings about their marriage. As we described in chapter 5, the marital satisfaction of partners without the intervention declined from pregnancy to six months after birth, and dropped even more sharply between six and eighteen months postpartum. For the intervention group participants too, there was a slight decline from pregnancy to six months after birth, but it was less severe than that of the comparison couples. Then, in contrast to the couples with no intervention, the group couples maintained their level of marital satisfaction over the following year.

Two years after the study began, we learned that ten of the original ninety-six couples had separated or filed for divorce. Four were from the twenty-four originally childless couples; the other six were from the forty-eight couples who had become parents with no intervention. In other words, two years into the study the marriages of 16 percent of the childless couples and 12.5 percent of the couples who had become parents and had no special help had not survived. By contrast, more than a year after the groups ended, *the marriages of all of the couples group participants were still intact.*

Longer-Term Effects of the Intervention

All of the couples who participated in a couples group were still together when the children turned three. It looks as though our work with them as they were becoming parents helped keep their optimism about their relationships alive. Although the numbers are too small to determine the statistical significance of this difference, the trend is certainly an encouraging one. Because there are no other intervention studies of this kind with new parents, we have nothing to go on in terms of how long we can expect this early help for couples to last.

By the time we were ready to begin our follow-up interviews, when the children were three and a half, another couple in the sample of parents with no intervention had separated, bringing the total to 15 percent. (This figure is consistent with the findings of Eiduson in a Southern California sample of new parents [1983], and with the figures from several national samples of families in which it is possible to calculate the age of the children when their parents divorce [Bumpass and Rindfuss 1979; Cherlin 1977; Morgan, Lye, and Condran 1988]). At this point, the first of the intervention couples decided to separate (4 percent). Even so, couples were still more likely to be in intact marriages if they had participated in our intervention before they had their babies—96 percent compared with 85 percent—but there were almost no differences between the two sets of parents on their questionnaire responses.

We confess that we would like to be able to leave our story on a note of optimism, but when we returned to visit the families once again during their children's kindergarten year, the news was discouraging: Six years after the children were born, the divorce rate in families with or without our intervention was up to 20 percent. Five and a half years after the intervention had ended, we could no longer discriminate between the two sets of parents' on any of the measures of parents' sense of self, role arrangements, marital quality, or marital stability—the aspects of life in which the intervention had made a difference earlier. Nor did the parents appear to be significantly different in their interactions with their children. Consistent with this finding, children of intervention parents were doing no better and no worse in their adaptation to kindergarten than the children whose parents had had no intervention.

It is not realistic to expect the effects of a six-month intervention to be evident four or six years later on the parents' relationships as couples, their parenting style, or their children's adaptation to school. By then, couples have been dealing with the effects of having more children, job changes, moves, births, deaths in their extended families, and the strain of working and rearing young children.

How long can intervention effects be expected to last? In a consultation with Enrico Jones, an expert in research on the effects of therapy, we were reminded that very few therapy studies follow clients more than a year after therapy ends, virtually none do two-year follow-ups, and a five-year follow-up is unheard of. While this is not completely reassuring, it gives us some comfort to know that demonstrating intervention effects over a three-year period is something of an achievement.

We can see now that we initiated the Becoming a Family Project with a rather rosy view of preventive interventions. As in the public health disease-prevention model, we hoped we could eliminate, or at least reduce, the incidence of marked distress in fairly well functioning families. It is clear now that the kind of work we have been doing does not *prevent* couples from experiencing the typical changes and strains of new parenthood. Anticipating a particular change and discussing the discrepancies between expectations and reality do not prevent couples from having tense middle-of-the-night discussions after the baby is home, but do make their disagreements, even heated ones, come as less of a shock. Parents also see that other partners have differing opinions on a number of critical issues in their lives.

The groups do not seem to affect basic aspects of men's behavior in their families. In general, fathers in the couples groups do not become appreciably more involved in housework or caring for the baby than fathers without an intervention. But by eighteen months after birth, both men and women who have participated in a couples group are more satisfied with their role arrangements than parents in the comparison subsample, even though group fathers had been less satisfied one year earlier. One possible interpretation of these findings is that the groups function merely as a palliative to help parents feel more satisfied. Another possibility is that experiences in the group affect men's and women's *expectations* about their lives as parents and partners, leaving less discrepancy between what they expected and the reality of their lives (cf. Belsky 1984; Garrett 1983; Parke 1979).

Cognitive theories of stress and emotion (cf. Lazarus 1991) help us to understand what may be happening here. These theories argue that our experience of stress is not determined by specific events, but by whether we interpret these events as likely to cause us physical or psychological harm. In this view, how men and women understand what is happening to them as new parents can affect the way they feel about themselves, each other, and the baby. When group members learn that the shifts they are experiencing are common to this time of life, they are less likely to interpret them as a commentary on their adequacy as individuals or as a couple. They are more likely to be able to engage in collaborative problem solving rather than adversarial sniping. By helping partners take a new perspective on their experiences, mental health professionals can play an essential role in preventing future distress.

We found some support in our interviews for the notion that our intervention was affecting how men and women interpreted their experience. Although partners in both intervention and nonintervention subsamples often recounted difficulties or dilemmas they were experiencing, parents who had been in a couples group appeared to have a more optimistic attitude: "We haven't solved all the 'who does what' issues," Tanya says, "but we're working on them." Parents who had not been in a couples group tended to report changes that seemed to be happening *to* them. One father, for example, said in answer to a question about changes in their relationship, "We're just not spending as much time together as we used to, and when we do, we *find ourselves* bickering a lot." The lower divorce rate among the group participants in their first three years of parenthood suggests that they felt able to do something about the problems in their marriages.

We often hear researchers and clinicians say that it is difficult to get men to consider family issues. A number of men in our study were skeptical about joining the study or about participating in a group. The fact that the interviews and groups were always conducted by a couple seemed to help a great deal. Most of the men became active and responsive participants over the more than six years that we followed them, and no couple ever dropped out of one of our groups. Once in the groups, fathers functioned as ongoing models for one another; as some men became involved in discussion and active caretaking of their newborns, others followed. As they diapered, fed, and soothed their infants, they talked about how to handle their children and keep their marriages vital, defying the stereotype of the uninvolved father. The structure and process of the group reinforced the attitude that, regardless of the inequality of time spent with the baby, fathers and mothers were involved in a joint endeavor to keep their relationships alive as they created new families.

By providing a setting in which both parents can continue to paint their pictures of the kind of life they want to have as a family, the intervention appears to keep some men involved in ongoing talk with their wives about what is and isn't working well. In the second year of parenthood, the men from the couples groups became more satisfied with their own involvement in the care of their children, with their sexual relationships, and with their overall marriages. The work in the group appeared to make it possible for more couples to negotiate work and family balances that left the women feeling more like Workers and Partners in the second year of parenthood.

We mentioned that, in general, men and women tend to become more different from each other as they make the journey from pregnancy to parenthood and this difference seems to contribute to increases in marital conflict and distress. When we compared group couples with the nonintervention couples, we found that partners in the group couples showed significantly less divergence from each other in their roles and perceptions of family life during their transition to parenthood. It seems that our focus on each partner and on the relationship between them interrupts some of the processes that tend to draw husbands and wives apart. This finer balance between the spouses may be contributing to their sustained marital satisfaction and stability during their children's toddler years.

Despite the fact that the groups offer emotional support and that group participants are vocal about the groups' helpfulness, the data from our follow-ups at six months postpartum suggest that participation in a group may actually contribute to some dissatisfaction or distress at first. If our assessment of intervention effects had stopped at that point, we would not have seen any statistically significant differences between couples with and without the intervention. Most of the measurable positive effects appeared eighteen months after birth, more than a year after the groups had disbanded.

As we mentioned in chapter 3, developmental theorists like Erik Erikson (1968), Heinz Werner (1948), and Jean Piaget (1967) propose that conflict, disequilibration, and temporary disorganization are *necessary* for individuals to proceed from one developmental stage to another. The fact that the effects of the intervention were clearer in the second and third years of parenthood than immediately after the intervention suggests that the groups helped parents face the initial strains of the transition, rather than ignore them as unacceptable. By helping men and women slow down to focus on some of the hot spots, we may have temporarily increased the amount of turmoil that couples experienced. But because we also provided a safe setting in which to observe other couples' stress and try new alternatives, the couples may have felt less embarrassed by their own difficulties and stimulated to try some of the strategies we discussed until they experienced some degree of success. We are proposing that some disequilibrium in a protected environment that focuses on successful coping strategies may actually produce the positive effects that we found. The delays we found in the positive effects of the intervention may help explain why intervention studies with a one-time "outcome" measure—often quite soon after an intervention ends—find so few visible effects.

At our three-and-a-half-year follow-up, Joan talked about how grateful she felt for the time she and Rob had in the group to focus on their relationship as a couple. Now that they have had a second baby without a group, she understands even more about the early experiences:

> JOAN: It was so lonely after having Scott, our second. It just wasn't the same and I couldn't figure out why at first. I finally realized that we were not in a group and we didn't have the time to sit down and talk—to each other or to other couples going through it. When the group met weekly, it helped us be more conscious of the issues that we should be talking about and working on. Sometimes it was a real pain, and Rob and I had some tough times then. But I'm not sure some of the problems we had to deal with would have come to our attention except through the groups. And then, after it was over, we continued to work at things for quite a while. But now, with everything happening in our lives, I feel we're getting lost again. There ought to be a group for couples having second kids!

Joan's comments are certainly consistent with our point of view and with our finding that the impact of our intervention declined over time. We feel that we need to extend our version of couples groups, beginning in late pregnancy and continuing with periodic "booster" interventions about every two years. This added assistance would reinforce couple's strengths, encourage them to keep building the skills they need to cope with being parents and partners, and prepare them for the inevitable challenges and crises of this complex and demanding period of family growth.

On the strength of our results showing that parents' ability to cope as individuals, couples, and parents in the preschool period is an excellent predictor of their children's academic and social adaptation to elementary school, we have mounted a new intervention study in which we work with parents during the years surrounding their first child's transition to elementary school. Our Schoolchildren and Their Families Project offers couples several kinds of group and individual consultation. By helping parents work on their confusing or troubling marital and parenting issues, we hope to increase their satisfaction and effectiveness as partners and parents and, in turn, reduce some of the burden that children can carry from their parents' stress and unhappiness. If our work with the couples helps them feel more competent and satisfied as parents and partners, this should free the children to cope more effectively with the academic and social challenges of the early school years. We hope that our work with families undergoing major transitions will encourage other health and mental health professionals to join us in developing these kinds of family-based preventive interventions.

CHAPTER 10

Talk to Me: Hidden Challenges in Couples' Communication

W E CAN IMAGINE A COUPLE who thinks they might be ready to start a family taking a deep breath after reading this book so far and saying to each other, "Okay, here's what we have to do if we're going to make sure that the children we bring into our lives have the right kind of family atmosphere to grow up in. We have to feel good about ourselves and our relationship. We have to work out the 'who does what' problems that we've been skirting. We should try to come to terms with some of what's been troubling us in our relationships with our parents. We need to figure out how we're going to arrange our work lives after the baby comes, where we'll get child care, and whether we can count on friends and family for extra support. And we'd better try to come to some agreements about what we think kids need and how we'll look after those needs. The parenting part might take care of itself if we just make sure that our relationship as a couple is in as good shape as it can be. Now, how do we do that by ourselves?"

This couple is probably concerned because when they try to talk about a disagreement, they typically find themselves becoming tense, angry, and frustrated. The more their tension rises, the less they understand how two people who love each other can be locked in an exchange that feels so terrible. At the height of their argument each would state that the other is the main obstacle to a solution, but inside they both harbor the fear that there is something wrong with them.

Most couples, we have learned, do not know that some conflict and tension are inevitable in any intimate relationship. Nor do they realize that the key to a satisfying marriage is not whether a couple has challenging problems or whether they always resolve them, but *how they talk to each other* about them. In part I, we described couples who coped well with the decision about whether to have a baby. We showed that their effective problem-solving process had positive consequences for their satisfaction with their relationship over the next two years. Videotaping the couples later on as they tried to resolve a difference or disagreement about a "who does what?" issue, Jessica Ball (1984) found that how partners felt about their overall marriage had to do with how they felt about the process of talking about the problem, not with whether the problem was resolved during the discussion. We have a good deal of evidence to show that when spouses' conversations about problems feel productive and satisfying to both of them, it colors the atmosphere of the family in warmer hues by contributing to each partner's sense of well-being and fostering more positive relationships throughout the family.

There are hidden challenges that keep partners from talking with each other in a satisfying way. These challenges exist in all couples and can hinder productive discussion even in the most mundane conversations. Couples are especially prone to stumble over them in the early years of becoming a family because so many decisions that had previously been made by one spouse alone suddenly require complex discussion. "I need to go to the store," a topic that may not even be raised before the baby is born, can require extensive negotiation afterward. Similarly, unless a job change involves a radical move, the decision can be made by one spouse independently in the pre-baby days. But when children are involved, the welfare of the whole family must be taken into account before such a decision can be made.

Spouses' styles of talking to each other are not the sole determinants of how their relationship feels or of how successfully they will adapt to change in each area of family life. However, when one parent is reading the newspaper at the breakfast table while the other is talking to her mother on the telephone, diapering the baby, and having an anxiety attack because she is late for work, we know that she will feel that their communication needs improvement.

The issue for couples is not simply "improving communication skills." The transition to parenthood raises so many issues simultaneously in so many aspects of couples' lives that they find it difficult to prevent the tension from any single topic from spilling over to other areas. Sharon and Daniel illustrate how quickly the spillover can occur if they have no stop mechanism:

SHARON: Last week I asked Daniel to make a call to *one* of the child-care centers. Just one. You would have thought I was asking him to go to the moon and back.

DANIEL: But I had just come home from work. I was tired. You were being totally nasty. I was playing with Amy, looking after her like you asked me to, and you wanted me to call right that second. Besides, you'd just told me that your mom had recommended this place, and you know what I think about *her* judgment.

SHARON: Daniel, this really pisses me off. Grow up for once. I needed some help that day. I really want to get going back to work, and to do that we need to line up some decent child care for Amy. I'm doing most of it and feeling really overwhelmed. You could have been civil about it, even if you couldn't or wouldn't make the call.

DANIEL: You weren't being civil to me then, and you're being downright mean now. And if you're so overwhelmed, how are you going to manage going back to work? Maybe we should wait a while.

If we hadn't proceeded with our interview questions, Sharon and Daniel would have continued to argue, bringing in new issues every few minutes but discussing none of them fully to either partner's satisfaction. Their conversation moved so fast, they did not realize that they had started discussing a child-related issue but moved immediately to Sharon's alleged "nastiness," her vulnerability, her mother's role in their life, Daniel's exhaustion, his civility, and his worry about Sharon going back to work. They were both so preoccupied with their own vulnerability and hurt feelings that they spent their time and energy reacting to the other's attack and defending themselves, getting distracted from trying to find a solution to any of the problems they raised.

We are not intending to say, "If only partners will sit down and talk to each other calmly, everything will be fine." Many of the barriers to effective and satisfying couple communication are deeply ingrained. Especially when partners come to their relationship with legacies of poor communication or angry, hurtful battles, it is difficult to change strategies overnight. Even when they know they must sit down together to face what is bothering them, many couples will have difficulty finding alternatives to the patterns that get them into trouble.

In this chapter we discuss what we have learned from the couples in our study about why communication is so difficult, particularly during their transition to parenthood. In the couples groups, we tried to help parents acquire the skills to spot the hidden challenges that interfere with satisfying communication. This did not necessarily help them avoid discouraging arguments or frosty periods of silence, but it gave both partners a way of thinking about how they might talk with each other in a more collaborative, less adversarial way. It encouraged them to come back together at a calmer time to figure out how they had become adversaries and to try again to work on the problem together.

Let's Talk About Communication

Why is communication between spouses such a problem? And how does the problem get magnified when couples have babies? Let's start with a basic definition. Communication involves an exchange of information. The information can be relatively impersonal and factual ("They're going to build a new freeway outside of town") or relatively personal and emotional ("I'm feeling very depressed today"). Messages sent by a speaker don't really become *communication* until a listener receives them and makes a response ("It's going to take me forever to get to work while they build the freeway"; "I'm sorry you feel depressed").

Communication doesn't rely solely on words. A shrug, a roll of the eyes, an almost imperceptible move toward or away from the other can serve as a commentary on what has been said or on the current state of the relationship. As Gregory Bateson (1972) has observed, "One can't *not* communicate." The husband who fumes silently while his wife describes her harrowing day with the baby is sending a forceful, if not a direct and clear, message about what he is hearing.

Researchers have generally investigated two kinds of couple communication: solving problems and expressing feelings. As we shall see, these two easily become intertwined. Many if not most expressions of anger occur when problem solving has reached an impasse or expressed feelings have not received a sympathetic response. The voluminous body of research and popular writing on marriage contains a wide variety of "explanations" of marital distress (see Jacobson and Gurman 1986). In almost all theories, communication difficulties are treated as deviations from some (usually unspecified) picture of healthy couple functioning. Dan Wile (1981, 1988) questions this premise. His point of view, which we find helpful, is that miscommunication and conflict are natural and inevitable in intimate human relationships and should be taken as signals that something in the relationship needs attention. Marriages become distressed when couples cannot find a way to have the conversations they need to have *after* the inevitable conflicts and frustrations occur.

In their attempts to establish satisfying communication, couples face three hidden challenges whether or not they are parents: striking a balance between individuality and mutuality; understanding that each partner can see things only from his or her own perspective; and dealing with the inevitable differences between the partners in how they talk to each other and regulate their emotions. We say that the challenges are hidden because they influence the tone and content of conversations in ways that couples rarely see. When partners become parents, they face a fourth hidden challenge: keeping discussions about the child from getting mixed up in their own individual and mutual conflicts. Unaware, for example, that a disagreement about whether to give in to their child's demands reflects unresolved tension about whether one spouse will give in to the other, couples often find that their conversations are taking strange turns and that they are feeling surprisingly upset.

Because daily decision making is now so urgent and necessary, these hidden challenges in couples' communication make it more likely that new parents will lose their balance in their struggle to reestablish their equilibrium.

BALANCING INDIVIDUALITY AND MUTUALITY: ME, YOU, AND US

Each of us is a separate individual who needs some degree of connectedness to feel secure in the world. The overarching issue for couples is the challenge of balancing these needs for individuality and mutuality. How can I develop in my own way, follow my own path, without becoming separated and isolated from my partner? How can we share our lives, enrich our sense of connection, and still be the kind of person each of us wants and needs to be? When maintaining connectedness and intimacy seems to demand that we give up something essential to ourselves, trying to pursue our own hopes and dreams can result in more conflict and less intimacy in our marriage.

Couples may have been struggling with this dilemma for months or years, but the need to resolve it feels urgent after the birth of a first child. Compromises that worked well before the child arrived must often be renegotiated. Both partners' energy is limited. Investment in their personal development feels like it comes at the expense of family relationships. Involvement in family relationships seems to leave fewer resources for creating time and opportunities to develop as an individual.

Mark is a twenty-six-year-old law student, and Ingrid, also twenty-six, sells computer software. Mark has been a part-time rock musician while in law school, playing gigs three or four nights a week. They tell us that he has cut back his time with the group to once a week, which he sees as a big sacrifice. But he feels he doesn't get any credit for it. Ingrid knows that music is important to him, but feels that she and Jason need him at home now. Before Jason was born, Ingrid worked hard at her job and didn't mind the evenings that Mark was out with the band. They gave her a chance to read, relax, or have dinner with her friends. They planned to have Jason and they love him, but his presence raises a dilemma that Ingrid and Mark did not have to think about before. In this conversation Mark is concerned with meeting his own needs, while Ingrid is focused on maintaining and enhancing relationships in the family. Given their different agendas, conflict between the two of them is virtually inevitable.

Each time they discuss this issue, the conversation gets more heated and a resolution seems farther away. Ingrid calls Mark selfish. Mark calls Ingrid possessive. Each is focused on the negative qualities of the other, unaware that both are struggling with a universal dilemma: The two sets of needs are both legitimate but difficult to satisfy simultaneously, especially when a baby has just been added to the mix.

We think that individuality and mutuality are both necessary for healthy relationships. The amount of individuality or mutuality in a relationship does not define how well that relationship functions. Rather than embracing either one, each couple must find the *balance* between the two orientations that creates an atmosphere conducive to the development of the individuals and the relationship. What does this balance look like in a couple? Wile (1988) describes the optimal situation as one in which individuals who differ with each other share the same platform, from which they are willing to have discussions about their relationship not only when things are going well but also, and especially, when things are not going well. Jessica Ball (1984) found that when partners feel that they are "on the same side of the net" even when they disagree, they feel better about the resolution of discussions of specific problems and better about their overall marriage.

Who are the parents most likely to achieve such a balance? Our impression is that they combine three important qualities. First, both partners seem to have a firm sense of themselves as individuals; they feel separate from their parents, from each other, and from their children, and yet they are connected with all of them. Second, the partners seem to be able to tolerate their own ambivalence so that they can understand both sides of an issue or problem. They do not feel that they have to fight to change their partner's outlook on life, though they are willing to fight to change their partner's mind on a given issue. Third, they have a *process* for discussing issues; they don't avoid conflict and they don't prolong fruitless stalemates. We asked Beth and Paul about how they dealt with a conflict or disagreement between them in the past year. They looked at each other and laughed:

PAUL: Is it safe to discuss?

BETH: I think so, but you never know what's left over. It was important for me to take the kids in my class to an out-of-state drama festival. They'd won the regionals here, and it was a very big deal for them—and for me. But it was going to be a week long, and Willie was barely weaned. Because of how the festival runs, I just couldn't take him with me. Looking back on it now, I'm not sure why it was so important, but it was—absolutely. And it was just the wrong time for Paul, because he was coming up for his qualifying exams.

PAUL: You're being kind. Time wasn't really the issue. I just wasn't ready to look after Willie on my own for a week.

BETH: But you started by giving me all sorts of reasons why it was a bad idea for *me* and for *Willie* if I went.

PAUL: Well, that was just the first two weeks of our negotiations.

BETH: We had one really bad fight. And then—I have to give you credit for this—you came to me and you said, "I know this is important to you, and I don't understand why. But it's important to me that you get to do what really matters to you. So let's work out some way to do it." And once the pressure was off, you started to talk about your own concerns about looking after Willie, which I could understand, so I phoned my mom and asked her if she could come and stay here while I was away. She gave me a bit of a hard time about going, but she had to admit that if Willie wasn't going to be with his mother, being with his grandmother was almost as good.

Many couples might have begun as Beth and Paul did, on opposite sides of the fence because their individual needs at the moment are colliding, but after two weeks of unresolved tension, they might have either escalated the fight into a full-fledged battle or backed off in hurt silence. Together, Beth and Paul were able to find the resources to keep coming back to the problem until each of their needs could be recognized and addressed.

Are we simply saying that couples who balance individuality and mutuality come to the transition to parenthood in good shape? No. Some of the couples in our study who did not start off that way managed to get clearer about these issues by struggling with them together. In a few cases, it took the help of a therapist. And some of the couples in our intervention groups, with guidance from the leaders and examples from other couples, became more able to integrate these two important aspects of family life over time. What we are saying is that when the dilemma of reconciling individual and mutual goals can be discussed directly, couples like Beth and Paul can shift from a debate about whether she should go on the trip to a more collaborative discussion about how both partners can get their legitimate needs met.

WE ARE STUCK WITH OUR OWN UNIQUE PERSPECTIVES

A second existential dilemma at the heart of our efforts to communicate can never be completely resolved. Each of us, as independent beings, can never know for certain what is going on in the mind and heart of another person. Two individuals, even if they have a high level of social skill and empathy, cannot be sure that they understand fully what is meant by what someone says or does. When Sharon tells Daniel that he is ignoring the fact that Amy needs a lot of attention, she is really thinking about how often her own parents left her alone when she was growing up. When Daniel says that he is giving Amy more than enough attention, he is thinking of his overprotective parents, who rarely left him on his own. Sharon and Daniel tend to distort each other's comments because each sees the world through different lenses, colored in this case by their experiences in earlier relationships. Neither partner really knows what the other means by "a lot of" or "enough" attention, and neither one asks a clarifying question.

More often than not, we assume that we know what others mean—they mean what *we* would mean if we used the same words or actions. We may not realize that there is a difference in interpretation until an argument erupts. ("I didn't know that you meant *two hours*. I consider *fifteen minutes* of Amy's crying a long time.") Because partners often give words different interpretations, it might be useful to assume that communication between spouses, like negotiations between countries at the United Nations, can benefit from the help of a translator.

Two problems described by marital researchers and couples therapists—
"mind reading" and "negative attributions"—can be traced to the fact that
we can never completely transcend our own perspective. Both seem to increase during couples' transition to parenthood.

Mind Reading   In our naïve assumption that we know what our partner
is thinking and feeling, we act as if we can read his or her mind. In intimate
relationships we frequently *can* guess what our spouse is thinking or feeling.
Each partner develops a kind of shorthand understanding of what his or her
spouse needs, what pleases, and what angers. The problem is that some mind
reading is, inevitably, off base and can lead to unexpected and inappropriate
behavior.

We have described Peggy and Bill's stormy relationship, after a pregnancy
in which Peggy was vulnerable and in discomfort. Eighteen months after
giving birth, she has not officially gone back to work, but she is directly
involved in taking care of Bill's business accounts. The day after one of their
fights, they tell us, Bill stops to buy flowers for Peggy. On the way home he
remembers that the last time he bought flowers, Peggy was suspicious that
he was covering something up. On the way home, he wonders, "Why can't
she trust me? Here I am, working hard, being a faithful husband, trying to do
something nice, and when I get home she's just going to jump on me. She
doesn't appreciate me for what I am. I wanted this to be a nice evening, and
she's going to ruin it with her nagging." He opens the door, thrusts the
flowers angrily at Peggy, and marches off to the den. Like many of us, Bill has
indulged in mind reading: He gets angry at what he thinks Peggy is thinking
and feeling before he has checked out his assumptions.

Bill is not the only mind reader in the family. Both he and Peggy assume
that they know what is in each other's minds and hearts, especially when it
comes to discussing their interactions with Mindy. The following day, still
smarting from the aftermath of their fight and Bill's strange behavior, Peggy
explained, she saw the following scene: "There's Bill, locked in his office next
to our back bedroom, and Mindy bangs on the door, shouting 'Daddy,
Daddy,' and Bill doesn't respond. Mindy bangs louder, and Bill gets furious,
because he thinks Mindy is trying to manipulate him. I see it so differently.
Mindy was missing her dad and wanting to talk to him. I think Bill was just
trying to get back at me, because of the fight the other night." Bill's interpretation? "No, no, no. *I* was trying to teach Mindy that she just can't barge in
whenever she wants. I don't think this is really about Mindy. You're just trying
to make me feel guilty."

New parents are vulnerable and uncertain. They often assume that there
is a right way to do things with their children, if only they could know what
it is. They see their partner doing something that surprises, displeases, or
even frightens them. Given rushed schedules and high tension, they may read
their partner's mind in an attempt to understand what is going on—and
easily come up with an interpretation that leads to misunderstandings and
hurt feelings.

Negative Attribution   A human tendency, described by "attribution theorists" in social psychology (Kelley et al. 1983), is to ask ourselves why people do what they do. We tend to explain *other people's* troubling behavior as reflecting their personality or motives, while we tend to explain *our own* troubling behavior as due to positive motivation or to circumstances beyond our control (Baucom, Sayers, and Duhe 1989).

When Peggy sees Bill do something that she wouldn't do, she attempts to figure it out in her own terms. Initially, she can't understand why Bill would ignore Mindy's cries. She would never shut Mindy out of a room, unless, perhaps, she was so upset with Bill that she did it in retaliation. She is making an assumption about Bill's motivation. Bill, on the other hand, sees himself as involved in fulfilling his role as a father and teaching his daughter not to intrude when he is working. Since the intensity of Peggy's feelings leads him to question his own strategy with Mindy, he accuses Peggy of trying to make him feel guilty.

The issue here is not only that Peggy and Bill are mind reading. Each is also attributing negative motivations to the other's behavior. And nothing we know of gets spouses angrier than being accused of harboring negative motivations—even if, or especially if, the accusation hits home. In the process of trying to understand what is happening to them, Peggy and Bill are focusing on what Wile (1988) calls "character flaws" in their partner and not on their own behavior. Partners tend to feel righteous about their own actions and skeptical about the actions of the other. The attribution problem usually cuts both ways and escalates the level of marital conflict.

Barbara Epperson's study (Epperson, Cowan, and Cowan 1991), based on data from our Becoming a Family Project, shows that negative attributions made by husbands and wives may have important implications for predicting the fate of their marriage. Surprisingly, partners' level of satisfaction with marriage when they entered our study did not predict who would later divorce. The best predictor was the number of negative adjectives (aggressive, fussy, nervous, sarcastic) one partner chose from the Adjective Check List to describe the other. That is, marital dissolution was predicted not by the kind of marriage couples believed they were in, but by the kind of partners they believed they were married to. The connection between partners' negative attributions and marital dissolution was stronger for couples who became parents than it was for the nonparent couples in our study.

Partners in transition to parenthood are especially prone to forget that other people have different points of view. As they gain confidence interpreting their infant's cries, smiles, and body movements, they begin to assume that they know what he or she feels and needs. When partners talk to each other, they make the same assumption. They may be wrong about both their baby and their partner, but only the partner can fight back verbally. As the stress of this life transition mounts, it becomes increasingly difficult for each partner to tell the difference between "this is what I'm hearing" and "this is what he/she is saying." Conflicts between partners multiply in the resulting confusion.

DIFFERENCES BETWEEN PARTNERS ARE INEVITABLE

Given the fact that husbands and wives are trapped in their own perspectives, that they have different personalities and different legacies from the past, it should come as no surprise to find that they are likely to perceive, remember, and react to the same events quite differently and to have different styles of talking to each other and expressing their feelings. The dilemma contributing to communication difficulties is this: Part of what attracts us to a partner is the way that person is different from us. But as the relationship unfolds, those intriguing differences grow larger and increasingly problematic.

It really doesn't matter what kinds of questions we ask couples—simple factual ones about their incomes or whether they experienced any job changes in the last six months, or questions that call for complex evaluations of emotion-laden issues—husbands and wives often have different perceptions of reality.

Memories Particularly vexing differences occur in partners' recollections of past conversations. Alice and Andy, one of the Yes-No couples who were still struggling late in the pregnancy with the decision about having a child, recalled their first conversation about the pregnancy:

ALICE: The first time I told you I was pregnant, you swallowed hard, but you said that you'd support me all the way.

ANDY: Alice, I never said anything like that.

ALICE: You did too, Andy. We were at dinner, remember? In that little restaurant with the pink tablecloths.

ANDY: I remember the restaurant, but. . . .

This conversation went on for quite some time, both partners becoming increasingly insistent that their memory of the event was the correct one. But in the absence of a videotaped record of their life together, there is no way for couples to arrive at the "truth" of who said or did what five minutes, five days, or five months later.

It is not only the past that provokes disagreements between partners about the perception of events. Is the house picked up? Yes, according to one partner; no, according to the other. Is the baby dressed warmly enough? Maybe/Maybe not. Is your mother intruding on our lives? Yes/No. Is your work demanding too much of your time and energy? I don't think so/ Definitely.

How We Talk The sociolinguist Deborah Tannen, in her recent best-seller, *You Just Don't Understand* (1990), claims that men and women speak different languages and approach conversations in different ways. Men talk to exchange information ("report talk"), and women talk to extend intimacy ("rapport talk"). Men try to maintain a one-up position, rarely revealing their vulnerabilities. Women try to increase symmetry, revealing their vulnerabilities as a way of keeping the relationship even. Men value their autonomy; they don't like to ask for directions or to be told what to do. Women search for connectedness; asking for help and checking what others want helps to enrich their relationships.

In Jessica Ball's (1984) study of husband-wife differences in communication style, twenty-seven of the Becoming a Family couples were invited to discuss a "who does what?" issue in front of a videotape camera. She then invited each partner separately to watch the tape and comment on the interaction. She found that wives raised problems more often, talked more in the first few minutes of the discussion, and were generally perceived by both partners as having more influence over the way the discussion went as a whole. These findings might lead to the interpretation that women have more conversational control, at least in the initial phases of talks about problems. When they watched and commented on the videotape, however, the women tended to say that they saw themselves as being in an entirely supplicatory position throughout these talks. As one woman explained: "It *looks* like I'm running the whole show here, but all the while I'm going on and on, I'm waiting on edge with suspense. What if he doesn't want to work on this with me? I'll feel totally crushed and helpless."

Fifty-nine percent of the men and 81 percent of the women elaborated their perceptions that, regardless of the wife's activity level or the floor time she occupied, the husband typically had veto power over the discussion as a whole: He controlled whether there would be a dialogue at all and under what terms and circumstances it would occur, as well as having final say over the outcome. In our study, men were described as exerting their control largely through either nonresponse or angry outbursts.

This gender difference in communication style leads to many conversational impasses. When problems are raised, as we've seen mostly by women, their partners tend to jump into the problem-solving mode with quick solutions. Men's well-intentioned responses often backfire for several reasons. First, husbands' solutions are often presented prematurely, before their wives feel that they have been understood. Second, when a husband offers a quick solution, he sends a message that conveys: "Oh, this problem is easy to solve; here's what you do," as if his wife can't see the obvious. The couple's conversation often shifts abruptly to a debate on the merits of "his" proposal to solve "her" problem. This restricts the possibility of exploring a number of alternatives and choosing the best available one. In our group meetings we often asked couples to "have a discussion, not make a decision" until both partners had completed exploring the problem. Given this framework, men were able to hold back on their initial tendency to make proposals because they knew that the decision phase was built into the process.

Regulating Feelings   Recent research by the psychologists John Gottman, Robert Levenson, and others supports and extends the notion that men and women deal with problem-solving discussions in different ways (Gottman and Levenson 1989; Markman and Notarius 1987). Using videotape of couples discussing a "hot issue," these psychologists have found that women take the initiative and that men tend not to raise issues that will lead to conflict. When conflict does arise, husbands tend to become more rational and avoidant as their wives become more emotional and engaged. In marriages that are already in trouble, this combination of mismatched styles leads to an escalation of the conflict by wives and withdrawal by husbands (Gottman and Levenson 1989).

Women's tendency in conflictful exchanges, it has been observed, is to become more expressive, while men's is to "stonewall" (Levenson and Gottman 1985). Under what he perceives as attack in conversation, a man tends to talk less, to make his face impassive and his body unexpressive, and to offer fewer head nods and less eye contact to his partner. In the face of this reaction, the woman becomes more directly expressive and more upset about the interaction. In happily married couples, men tend to engage in the discussion without withdrawing to this extent, but in distressed marriages, if husbands' attempts to withdraw are followed by wives' pursuit of them, the men respond to the women's anger or sadness with their own anger, or contempt. The wives, in turn, then become even more angry. This escalating pattern is typical of spouses whose marriages are distressed now, and it also predicts decline in marital satisfaction over the next few years (Gottman and Krokoff 1989).

We believe that the tendency for women to raise potentially explosive issues for the couple is amplified after a baby arrives. Mothers are primarily responsible for either looking after the child during the day or making the necessary child-care arrangements. When the couple comes together at the end of the day, the child-related problems are most likely to be brought up by the wives. Husbands sometimes feel that if their wives did not raise problems about the child, there wouldn't *be* any. As the messengers, wives are often the targets of their husbands' anger for being the bearers of bad news.

In the research just mentioned, partners discussing "hot" marital issues were hooked up to equipment that measured their level of physiological arousal—heart rate, pulse, blood flow, and so on. When the conversation heated up, women tried to keep it going and men, as just explained, shut down (Gottman and Levenson 1989; Markman and Notarius 1987). But, in contrast to their impassive exteriors, men became highly aroused during the conflict, a physiological arousal that lasted much longer than that of their wives. Men's stonewalling, it seems, may be an attempt to avoid the uncomfortable consequences of the physiological disruption. Not only did the women's physiological arousal during the argument not reach as high a level as their partners' but, once women expressed their feelings, their physiological responses shifted more quickly back to normal.

What these studies point out is that, although it looks to women as though their husbands are unfeeling or uncaring during important discussions, they may in fact be feeling a great deal. Unfortunately, men's self-protective maneuvers, combined with women's active pursuit of upsetting issues, can have debilitating effects on the relationship between them.

How Differences Create Communication Pitfalls   The researchers whose work we have been describing make very broad generalizations about differences between men and women. In our view, the essential importance of their work is not that women are always ready to engage in conflict and men always to stonewall. In some couples, the reverse pattern can be found at least some of the time. What is central, we believe, is that differences between partners in their styles of communicating and regulating their emotions present particularly powerful obstacles to satisfying couple communication. Partners begin a conversation, find that they disagree, and are drawn even farther apart by the clash in their characteristic ways of attempting to resolve the problem.

The picture we get from Gottman and Levenson's research is that as a husband and wife talk with each other, sending words and nonverbal signals back and forth, each is focused on three channels of information: the words, the tone, and the feelings or reactions. First, they attend to the meaning of the words, trying to interpret from their own perspective what their partner is literally saying. As we have seen, this in itself can be a difficult task. Second, they are paying attention to tone of the message: Is it hostile, loving, complaining, complimentary? If one partner's tone turns negative, it gets harder for the other to track the content of what is being said. *But they continue the conversation anyway.* In the meantime, a third channel, the physiological system, is bouncing around, sending messages of arousal—excitement, tension, anxiety—into an already complex exchange. One partner may need to damp things down just when the other is letting feelings out at full tilt.

All of this monitoring makes it hard to have a relaxed conversation. When the marriage is not going well, the differences between husbands' and wives' strategies are exaggerated, making an unsatisfying exchange more likely. When a baby comes along and the initial differences between husbands and wives are magnified, there may be more exaggerated discrepancies in their communication styles. In an atmosphere heated up by frequent marital conflict or cooled down by withdrawal in hopes of avoiding a fight, partners are less likely to talk to each other about their deep and private feelings. While this strategy may reduce fighting temporarily, it also tends to reduce the feeling of intimacy. One or both partners may conclude that they are not entitled to feel the way they do, even if the feeling is not expressed.

Looking back at Mindy's birth, Peggy and Bill described just such a situation. Bill was supposed to be the "coach," the strong one, when Peggy was in labor. He was terrified but tried not to let it show. As Peggy instructed and requested him to do various things, he became more and more closed and sarcastic. She got more and more angry. It wasn't until Mindy was nearly six months old that they talked about it. Peggy asked Bill why he didn't tell her what he was going through, and he said, "As the labor got more intense, I kept feeling more and more frightened and that's just not what was supposed to be happening. It was just the worst time to say anything like that to you."

Pauline and Mel described an argument they have very frequently. Every time Pauline's parents come to visit, she is reduced to tears. Her mother criticizes how Pauline and Mel handle Avi, how the house looks, their neighborhood, and on and on. Mel shrugs it off, but Pauline takes it to heart. "I want her to tell her mother either to shut up or to stay away," he told us. But Pauline said that she could never do that: "It would just tear her away from us and her grandson, just when we're reconnecting after all these years. Besides, she has so little in life. She did the best she could with me and my sister. It would be ungrateful and immature of me to get angry with her now."

The problems go deeper than the simple facts that Bill does not want to admit his fear and Pauline feels she cannot tell her mother what she thinks: One spouse does not feel *entitled* to express the negative but very human feelings he or she is experiencing. Keeping quiet rarely works. Negative feelings tend to pop out indirectly, increasing the distance between the two people in the relationship and decreasing the probability of dealing constructively with the problems that led to the feelings in the first place.

The early months of parenthood provide fertile soil for "unentitlement." Parents have many notions of how they're supposed to feel. Friends, neighbors, and family smile at the baby and tell new parents how proud and happy they must feel. But sometimes new parents are overwhelmed and frightened. Can they admit it to themselves? Can they tell each other? Trying to "protect" their partners from worry, they often deprive them of emotional support. What a relief it usually is when a husband admits that he is having a hard time of it, and his wife says, "I thought it was only me." Or when a wife admits that she doesn't always know what to do when the baby keeps crying, and her husband is relieved that he is not the only one at a loss.

When emotional regulation is out of balance in a marriage, the partners may not be able to tell whether they are being heard, especially if one partner stonewalls. Much of the force and repetition in a couple's arguments may come from partners feeling they have not been heard, or have not gotten their point across, so they make the point again, louder and more forcefully (Wile 1988). Wile advises couples who are saying things for the second or third time at ever-increasing decibel levels to take this as a signal that their communication process is not working. Rather than continuing the escalation, it is time to back up and check out whether the messages are getting through.

With these examples of heated exchange and conflict between spouses, it would be easy to get the impression that new parents argue all the time. Most don't. What's more, after the heat of an argument, most hesitate to return to the issues that upset them. Each partner fears that bringing it up again will just mean they will fight again, and hopes that if they don't talk about the problem, it will go away. These fears have some validity. Returning to unresolved issues does sometimes start up the unpleasant cycle again. Not rocking the boat becomes an even more urgent goal when a family is already sailing on choppy seas. New parents have little uninterrupted time for each other, and little surplus energy. "Why ask for trouble?" they might think, and we certainly understand their reluctance to get back into a conflict. But unless they reopen contentious issues during a period of calm, they will not be able to create ways of recovering from fights or profiting from them so that the next time they will not be as devastating.

BRINGING THE CHILD INTO THE STRUGGLE

Many of the examples we have given in this chapter show that discussions about the child figured largely in the communication problems of the couples in our study. How could it be otherwise? Differences between partners' points of view, communication styles, and ways of regulating emotion are inevitable. Even when their fundamental values are fairly similar, parents' reactions to the child are bound to highlight some areas of difference between them. We find that differences between husbands and wives about their children generate much more heat than most other topics of conversation or argument. The parent role occupies a central part of their identity. Many, but not all, parents believe that how the child "turns out" is ultimately a reflection on them. This places high stakes on the resolution of even minor disagreements.

We are concerned in this section with the subtle ways in which children become enmeshed in conflicts between their parents that are not really of the children's making. There is an inherent possibility that parents might "triangulate" the child into their overt or hidden conflicts, a notion that has several connotations, all of them negative (see, for example, Bowen 1978). In one meaning, the parents cannot distinguish between what they each want and need for themselves and what they believe the child needs. Their differences of opinion or arguments about the child are difficult to resolve because they are not really talking about what they think they are talking about.

For example, Tanya says that Kevin needs to be cuddled more, and Jackson says that Kevin needs room to breathe. Tanya may want more cuddling for Kevin, but she may also need more cuddling for herself. She doesn't feel entitled to ask for it, but it remains a salient issue for her and she raises it at every opportunity. Jackson probably feels the need for some freedom for himself. Not feeling entitled to ask for it, instead he ardently defends his son's need for breathing space.

A second way couples triangulate their child into their relationship is by fighting about the child as a way of avoiding their own issues. Peggy and Bill have used this mode a great deal, arguing about Mindy and how each one should treat her while avoiding some of the more difficult problems in their communication with each other.

A third variety of triangulation looks different from the first two, but serves the same function. Some parents become almost totally involved in their children's lives, neglecting the issues in their relationships as couples. Based on the results of the development of the children in our study, these devoted parents might do better to redirect some of their energies. Focusing on the marriage to the detriment of the child would, of course, be just as bad.

We are guided here by the findings we have already made clear: When parents feel satisfied about themselves and their relationship as a couple, their relationships with their children seem to be more effective, and their children wind up better equipped to handle the challenges of their lives inside and outside the family.

Communication and Family Breakdown

We have shown what a challenge it is for men and women to communicate effectively and how the arrival of a child seems to make miscommunication and conflict more probable. Alice and Andy are one of almost 20 percent of the couples who were not able to maintain their marriages through the child's transition to elementary school. While they spoke positively about their relationship when we first met them, they continued to be in pain over their serious altercation about the unintended pregnancy. Here is a case where the individual needs of both partners clearly clashed with their mutual goals, but because they loved each other, Alice and Andy tried to patch over their differences and went ahead and had the baby. Over time, they forgot that each of them must be experiencing the transition to parenthood differently. Their relationships with Jessica were genuinely warm and adoring, but when they were in difficulty about issues in the couple relationship, Andy became angry again and this created a good deal of tension between them. As more time passed and other life stresses confronted them, Andy began to feel that Alice was not the person he thought he knew.

Given their large age difference, and very different experiences of growing up, it is not surprising that each had different perceptions and feelings about what it would mean to become a parent. Although they appeared to have been successful in calming the conflict that had erupted when Alice told Andy she was pregnant, the events that followed suggested that they never truly came to terms with their different experiences of the decision making.

About three months after Jessica was born, Andy began to have serious difficulty in controlling his anger with Alice. The earlier wounds that they had covered over began to fester. Each felt that their hard-won agreements in pregnancy had been violated, but they did not feel safe enough to talk to each other directly about their disappointment or their fear. Rather than confront their distress or ask for help, they decided that a move across the country to a less hectic setting might reduce some of the pressure they were feeling.

Over the next several years, they vacillated between periods of optimism and serious distress. They had pulled themselves away from the support of their friends, and it took a long time for both of them to find work they found rewarding. When their relationship was not going well, each of them felt somehow unmoored. Their best times seemed to revolve around Jessica, but that did not help them to work out the unresolved issues in their relationship to either one's satisfaction. Looking back, they felt that it all began to unravel soon after the move, when Alice became ill and her mother died within a month's time. As Alice withdrew from Andy to tend to her emotional and physical wounds, he felt abandoned again, as he must have felt when she insisted on having a child so early in their relationship.

By the time Alice pulled herself together, this time with some professional help, she and Andy had decided that they needed to separate. Both of them were distressed about splitting up their family and tried on more than one occasion to reconsider the plan, at least for Jessica's sake. But the magic had gone out of their marriage. Around the time of Jessica's fourth birthday, they separated for good.

For her part, Jessica appears to be doing quite well. Andy and Alice have maintained their devotion to her, arranging shared custody and visitation. At our kindergarten assessment, Jessica seemed shy, a little withdrawn, but able to use fantasy play to express her feelings when her mother was nearby. When she is in familiar territory she seems to cope well with the demands of other adults, and from her teacher's point of view, she is making a relatively good adjustment to both the academic and social demands of kindergarten. Because both of her parents have continued to communicate with her warmly and responsively, while building a reliable structure for her life with each of them, she will probably be able to concentrate enough to meet the challenges of school fairly well. Much later on, when it comes to working out the most painful parts of her intimate adult relationships, she may experience some difficulties (Wallerstein and Blakeslee 1989).

Communication and Family Adaptation

Our chronicle of the hidden challenges to effective and satisfying couple communication can be used to tell a more optimistic story. It is not a story without conflict, miscommunication, or withdrawal to neutral corners. The couples who come through the transition to parenthood on their feet are those who have been able to treat their problems in connecting with each other not as a failure or a deliberate attempt at sabotage by their partners but as a signal that something is not working. They have found ways to return to rocky territory, joining forces to figure out how they lost their way. They manage, then, to feel on the same side even while they are in the process of resolving their differences.

These couples are not saints or Pollyannas. They fight when they have something to fight about. Occasionally, when they try to understand a blow-up, the process goes awry and the fight starts again. But they have taken some risks to develop ways of thinking and discussing what happens when they talk to each other. They recognize the problem of balancing their individual and mutual needs with the needs of their children. They know that their unique perspectives will at times contribute to their misunderstandings.

And they have developed the ability to tolerate their different styles of dealing with emotionally loaded issues.

In these couples, it is not always the wife who raises the difficult issues. The husbands try to overcome their distaste for trouble or conflict, and attempt to engage rather than withdraw when something needs to be dealt with. Both partners work to avoid escalating angry or hurtful exchanges. Some of the time, they are able to express their negative feelings and to tolerate some distress in the other. They try to listen and to let each other know they are being heard. When they get upset about something their spouse is doing, they consider whether that raises an issue *they* should be dealing with before they try to get their spouse to do things differently. Perhaps most important of all, they are willing to rock the boat by stopping escalating arguments between them or by coming back to discussions that became hurtful or unproductive, in order to figure out what went wrong. Finally, the couples who communicate effectively are able to avoid triangulating their children into their marriage. They can disagree about child-rearing issues and argue vociferously, but these disagreements do not become substitutes for attending to their own relationship.

Let us assure you that we do not know any couples who can do all this all the time. But those who can express their views and feelings, and do not feel as though their negative feelings are going to escalate out of control, feel more energetic and optimistic about themselves and their relationship.

CHAPTER 11

Who Is at Risk and What Can Be Done?

SINCE THE BEGINNING OF OUR PILOT STUDY eighteen years ago, we have followed more than 100 couples through their transition to first-time parenthood. The experience has been both inspiring and sobering. We feel great admiration for these new pioneers, making their journey to parenthood in a world that was transformed while they were growing up. Not always knowing which way to turn, they have managed to show great determination, fortitude, and optimism—and surprisingly good humor.

We also come away with great concern about the burdens contemporary parents and children are shouldering. Our results show that the natural processes of becoming a family place women, men, and their relationships as couples at risk for increased disenchantment and strain. When parents are in distress during the children's preschool years, the children are at risk for academic and social difficulties as they begin their academic careers. Let us be clear: "At risk" does not mean that depression, marital distress, ineffective parenting, difficulty with peers, or academic problems are inevitable. Some individuals and families in the most adverse circumstances show surprising resilience. What we mean is that a majority of couples becoming new parents can expect to encounter increasing strain and distress in their intimate relationships during the family-making years.

In our attempts to understand this troubling phenomenon, we made some unexpected discoveries. Despite the fact that medical checkups are offered from the beginning of pregnancy and childbirth preparation classes are available during the last trimester, couples begin to be at risk even earlier—as soon as they start considering whether and when to start their family. Medical and childbirth services help partners focus on the physical aspects of pregnancy, labor, and delivery, but they miss the subtle and complex psychological changes that begin to affect the couple long before their baby is born.

We had underestimated the salience of the differences between men and women in this family-making period. We found that during the process of becoming parents, men and women experience qualitatively different psychological changes. They describe different shifts in the parent aspect of their identities and make different arrangements for their work inside and outside the family. These differences are accompanied by more disagreement and arguing as a couple, a feeling of more distance between them and less satisfaction with their overall marriage. Hoping to feel closer by creating a family together, partners get discouraged when the process of moving from partners to parents pushes them farther apart.

We should have been prepared for the fact that the most problematic issue for men and women in the early family years is who cares for the children. Neither the traditional male/female division nor the new egalitarian sharing arrangements stand out as ideal: Modern couples get penalized either way. When one parent brings home the bacon while the other stays home to look after the child, both can feel underappreciated and strapped economically, which burdens the marriage and the children. When both parents work outside the family, they tend to feel better about themselves and about their contributions to the family economy, but parents and children are breathless, often missing the opportunity for intimate moments. Although each of these alternatives has costs and benefits, we find that when men are more involved in the care of their children, they feel better about themselves, their wives feel better about themselves, and they both feel better about their marriage. Even more important than who actually does what is how the arrangements are negotiated and how both partners feel about the outcome. This makes it clear that each couple must find the balance that works for them.

We certainly knew from our own lives that having a baby can reawaken issues from one's childhood, but we found that the power of these legacies catches most parents off guard. We did not fully appreciate the magic that babies provide to link the generations of a family. The birth of a baby gives new parents an opportunity to reconnect with their parents and grandparents. A baby can give one partner a chance to teach the other about caring relationships between parents and children. It looks as if a warm, collaborative couple relationship can help some partners with inadequate parenting to break the generational cycle of dysfunctional relationships. Nevertheless, there is disquieting evidence that unless men and women are able to come to terms with the difficulties of their growing-up years, or to marry a spouse who has, their family patterns tend to be replayed across the generations.

Although we expected anxieties and conflicts about support or stress from work, child care, and friendships to spill over into both the marriage and the parent-child relationships, the pervasiveness of parents' struggles around these issues was a surprise. It has been eye-opening for us to see the paradox inherent in a country that professes to care so much about the development of its children and the preservation of the family unit offering virtually no resources to deal with these issues.

We are convinced that most new parents are doing the best they can against tremendous odds. Some of their tensions are generated by their attempts to follow strong but conflicting societal prescriptions. On one hand, we are surrounded by powerful messages about individualism: Each of us should make every effort to develop as fully as we can. There is some degree of governmental and educational support for acting on this message, and hard work toward self-fulfillment, individual achievement, and advancement pays off. On the other hand, our society sends us messages about the importance of enhancing the quality and sanctity of family life—to maintain the family as a "haven in a heartless world." But with no support from government or business and little support from medical and mental health services, which focus on individuals, couples who share this priority are on their own.

What the couples in our studies have shown us is that keeping a marriage viable while creating a family requires a delicate balance—within each partner, between the spouses, and between family and work. Each man and woman comes to the family-making enterprise with a particular set of strengths and vulnerabilities in the central aspects of their lives. As they become parents, each aspect of life requires rethinking and readjustment—a tall order, as we have seen. The combination of strengths and vulnerabilities that each couple brings to the transition affects the ease or difficulty of their journey from couple to family.

Who Is at Risk?

The changes associated with parenthood take place within a context of consistency and predictability. Individuals and couples who are doing well in pregnancy will probably continue to do well after the baby arrives; those in difficulty in the early phases of the transition tend to be struggling later on, with each other and with their children. Distress before the baby is born in any of the arenas of family life we studied should serve as a warning that there may be trouble ahead—for the marriage and possibly for the children's development.

How parents feel about themselves plays an important role in their experience of early parenthood. If they are disappointed with themselves before they have a baby—depressed or with low self-esteem—partners are likely to feel disappointed in their early years as parents. We have illustrated how parents' negative feelings about themselves foreshadow more symptoms of depression and higher levels of parenting stress, as well as greater conflict as a couple and with their children during the preschool period four years later.

Many aspects of the parents' marriage can put them at risk in the early parenthood years. The atmosphere of their journey to becoming a family is affected by the partners' approach to deciding whether to have a baby. Spouses who describe their general decision-making process as unproductive and unsatisfying are more likely to make their decision to become a family without working through one or both partners' hesitation or ambivalence. As we have seen, the greatest risk for the stability of the couple's marriage was going ahead with a pregnancy over the continuing objection of a husband who did not feel ready to become a parent: All of the couples faced with this agonizing dilemma had divorced by the time their first child entered kindergarten.

During pregnancy, other aspects of a couple's relationship serve as early warning signals: partners' negative views of each other; distress about the division of family labor; discontent with their arrangements for the care of their child; pessimism about their ability to make family decisions that meet both spouses' needs; dissatisfaction with how the overall marriage feels. All of these signals predicted expectant mothers' and fathers' later difficulties in managing their relationship as a couple.

As we have noted, men and women whose own childhoods were clouded with painful experiences—absent, rejecting, abusive, or alcoholic parents—tended to have more difficulty with each other and with their children. Although the stresses of pregnancy and the first few months of parenthood inevitably lessen, couples who begin their journey from partners to parents contending with a great deal of additional life stress from relationships, illness, or problems at work were more likely to be grappling with more strain later on.

We found that risks for couples pose risks for their children. Strain within the marriage during the transition to parenthood was reflected in parents' responsiveness or tension two years later, as they worked and played with their three-and-a-half-year-olds. Parents who were in the most unhappy marriages treated their sons and daughters in a cold, critical, more authoritarian manner. Here again, gender differences took center stage. Fathers who were unhappy with their wives reacted most harshly to their preschool daughters. We are especially concerned about the risk for girls' development when their parents, particularly their fathers, are distressed about the marriage. Children whose parents were unhappily married during pregnancy and the preschool period had more difficulty adjusting to elementary school two years later.

We all "know" that communication is central to couple relationships. What has become clear to us in the course of our study is the variety of ways in which ordinary problems in communication between partners can be exaggerated in the turmoil that follows the birth of a baby. If we think about parents' communication skills and impasses as laying the foundation for children to learn about solving problems, the links between the state of the parents' lives in pregnancy and the children's adjustment to kindergarten almost six years later become more understandable.

We have shown that hard times in the life of a family with young children do not come out of the blue. The transition to parenthood seems to act as an amplifier, tuning couples in to the resources they have, and turning up the volume on their existing difficulties in managing their lives and family relationships. We were able to predict with some accuracy how couples would fare as parents of young children, based on the interview and questionnaire information they gave us during the pregnancy. This means that we have the tools to identify potential distress and to help couples prevent at least some of this distress before it begins to tear their families apart.

Implications of Our Results

FOR COUPLES

We have noted that outside of couples counseling or therapy, there are currently no systematically evaluated services that offer expectant couples a protective setting in which they can begin to take stock of what works well and what doesn't before they become parents. Based on what we have learned both from the couples in our group intervention and from those who did well without the help of a couples group, we have compiled a list of things that expectant couples and new parents can do on their own to reduce the expected strain and enjoy more of the positive side of becoming a family. Although some of these ideas may sound very simple and obvious, we have found that many partners *think* of them without actually trying them. We believe it is never too late to give them a chance.

Share expectations. Many husbands and wives who are expecting a baby neglect to share their notions of the ideal family. They seem to assume that once they have decided to have a baby, their ideal family picture will take shape spontaneously. Others are understandably reluctant to talk about their hopes and anxieties because they are afraid that disagreement or conflict might result from finding they differ on important issues.

Much will depend on the nature and disposition of the child and on the parents' own reactions once the baby finally arrives, but it is our impression that men and women who can talk to each other about what they hope will happen, and what they are concerned might happen, begin their lives as parents feeling better prepared to deal with both the positive and the negative realities.

Give yourselves regular "checkups." Many couples who were *not* in the intervention groups in our study told us that filling out our questionnaires independently and then talking about their responses together had a powerful impact on their transition to parenthood. Some called our questionnaires and interviews their "checkups" because they offered an opportunity to take stock of how they were doing and to think about where they might make some adjustments before their disenchantment got the better of them.

Some of the questions that we describe throughout the book may be a starting point for couples to talk about how they feel they are doing in the major parts of their life together. These checkups should never begin in the middle of a fight, however; they require quiet, uninterrupted time when both partners feel free to explore their reactions.

Make time to talk with each other. New parents have very few opportunities for quiet time together. Most will be unable to spend an idyllic weekend away by themselves and many will not be able to afford to go out to lunch or dinner, with the new expenses of hospital bills, baby equipment, and child care. We suggest that partners try to make a regular time each week to go for a walk, to talk with no interruptions—to touch base with each other.

Many husbands and wives say that the day gets away from them. By the time everything is cleaned up at night, they are too exhausted for intimate conversation. It sounds terribly artificial, but making an appointment or a date can be useful—even if the laundry or dinner dishes have to wait or if the "date" must be rescheduled because of a crying baby or their own fatigue. Parents say that just knowing that they will have a time to be together can make a difference and get them through a strenuous week.

Negotiate an agenda. Spouses sometimes have a hard time agreeing on whether a particular issue is a problem. She feels overloaded with family work and wants to talk about his doing more. His evaluation of the situation is that she is wasting some of her efforts, and he has a plan for how she can be more efficient with her time or more effective as a parent. Besides, he feels that they are not getting out enough and wants to discuss that, whereas she knows that she will have difficulty finding a sitter she can feel comfortable with and fears that he will not understand her point of view. It is easy to see how either partner might want to skip such discussions.

Our general rule for ourselves and other couples is this: If one partner feels that something is a problem, at least for the moment it is a problem. And, because one partner's problem can raise a difficulty for the other, we recommend discussing only one problem at a time, however difficult it may feel to limit the discussion, with an explicit agreement that other difficulties will be addressed at the next opportunity. If they can trust that both of their issues will be addressed in time, they are less likely to sabotage today's discussion.

Adopt an experimental attitude. There are two important principles involved in this single point. First, life changes rapidly with a growing infant. "Solutions" that worked well for some weeks or months can suddenly seem totally ineffective. This is not a sign that the original plan was inappropriate or that one partner has not kept up his or her end of the bargain, but rather that something has shifted. An attitude that says, in effect, "let's try this and see if it works," can be helpful—whether it be a variation on the baby's feeding schedule, a new way of responding to her crying, or a plan for talking to the baby-sitter.

Couples find it useful to adopt this kind of experimental attitude toward problems in their relationship, too. When things go wrong or tempers run hot, many of us are quick to blame our partner for our distress. The idea of taking a fight as information that something is wrong in the relationship is quite helpful (Wile 1988). The trick is not to worry that you are having a struggle, or to avoid a fight; every couple has both trivial and important issues to work out. It helps to take a step back and shift from a "What are you doing wrong?" position to a "What's going on in our lives that this is happening now?" attitude. The recovery from these kinds of conversations after fights have erupted can be both healing and productive.

Don't ignore sex and intimacy. Women's physical changes and the couple's exhaustion typically lead to a decline in the frequency of sex both in pregnancy and after the baby arrives. The absence of sex can feel like a longtime drought. We have read advice columns that support the "if you're even partially ready, go for it" attitude. It seems to us that there is a territory between total deprivation and a return to the old pattern of more frequent and satisfying lovemaking. If partners are able to discuss it at all, and some find sex an awkward and difficult topic at this time, they can recognize that there are opportunities for nonsexual intimacy: touching, hugging, cuddling. This is often what is being missed most. Sometimes, the discovery that your partner is missing the intimacy, too, results in increased feelings of closeness.

Line up support in the early stages. Our finding that support from other people is helpful in alleviating parents' stress in the early months as a family suggests that couples should consider arranging for people or services who can provide support and relief when the going gets rough. This is difficult to do at the height of the transition, when most of the parents' attention is focused on how to juggle everything they used to do *and* take care of the new baby.

Talk with a friend or co-worker. As we described in chapter 9, participating in an ongoing group with the help of trained mental health professionals and other couples becoming parents can buffer men's and women's dissatisfaction and keep their marital disenchantment from getting out of hand, at least for the first few years. Although these kinds of groups are not available at this time, the kind of sharing of experiences and information that our groups provided might come from special friends or co-workers who are willing to talk about their experiences of being partners and parents. While we believe that working with mental health professionals increases the odds of making headway on difficult relationship issues, some new parents find that there are people with whom they can broach some of their questions and concerns.

For partners who are experiencing a fair amount of strain or impasse—about deciding to have children, about resolving conflict or differences in their relationship, or about how to handle confusing dilemmas with their children or parents—help is available in the mental health community. If you do not know where to begin to find competent help, start with your medical doctor, your child's pediatrician, your rabbi or minister, or a trusted friend or co-worker. You may be surprised to find that people you know are knowledgeable about helpers in your own or a neighboring community.

Often a local college or university will offer counseling or therapy in a clinic, and your local Mental Health Association will usually be able to direct you to help in your area.

Find the delicate balance. Understandably, the primary item on the agenda of most expectant and new parents is making things right for the baby. Yet what parents do directly for and with their children is only part of what it takes to create healthy children and family relationships. How parents feel about themselves, each other, their parents, their work, and their friendships all plays a part in creating a family environment that promotes or interferes with the children's ability to cope with new tasks and form satisfying relationships.

We certainly do not advocate the "me-generation" stereotype of parents ignoring their children's needs in order to pursue their own happiness, but many of the couples we spoke to appeared to be at the other extreme, ignoring opportunities to satisfy their own basic relationship needs "for the sake of the children." Especially when both parents work, they may hesitate to take the time to nurture their relationship as a couple because they are away from their children so many hours a week and want to spend all their nonworking hours with them. Although it clearly takes ingenuity and juggling, we believe that the children will ultimately do best in their development when their mothers and fathers find ways to balance their own needs with those of their children.

This is by no means an exhaustive list. It is meant to convey that the modern journey to parenthood, exciting and fulfilling as it is, is beset with many roadblocks. We are finding that even couples who do not ordinarily need the services of mental health professionals experience stress in the early years of family life. If this applies to you or someone you know, take heart. Most men and women need to muster all the strength and skills they have to make this journey. Almost all parents say that the lessons they learn along the way are well worth the effort. They are learning not to give up their dreams but to redefine them based on today's realities.

FOR CHILD AND FAMILY RESEARCHERS

In the past decade we have seen the beginning of a rapprochement between family researchers who study children's development and investigators interested in families with at least one member in psychological or physical distress. Studies of parent-child relationships no longer look only at mothers and children. Fathers have "become" important in psychological studies of children's development.

Even so, it is time to think about fathers' active role in the family not as "mothers' helpers" but as full-fledged parents with independent needs, agendas, and points of view. In two-parent families, even when the parents are divorced, it will never be possible to understand how one parent affects the child's development without knowing something about what the other parent is doing. Almost two decades ago, Barclay Martin (1975) pointed out that even when both parents are included in the same study, researchers rarely look at their combined impact on the child. Sadly, this situation has not changed appreciably since then.

The time is ripe for an even more systemic look at the way in which family functioning affects children's development. As we have shown throughout this book, the quality of the parents' marriage is an essential ingredient of the tone and quality of life in the family. We have seen that how mothers, fathers, and children cope with their early family transitions depends in large part on how the couple is managing their relationship. It seems that the parents' marriage can magnify the difficulties in each of the family domains when it is in trouble as well as acting as a buffer, protecting couples from additional strain when it is going well.

For a very long time, psychologists have been studying the development and adaptation of *individuals*. Our study and several other recent investigations (Hinde and Stevenson-Hinde 1988) remind us that most growth and development, of children and grownups, occurs in *relationships*. Our research methods, assessment tools, and concepts are still very bound to the perspective of the individual. We must continue to search for both methodological and theoretical breakthroughs to do justice to the complexity of understanding what makes relationships work.

FOR HEALTH PROFESSIONALS

Our results also contain a message for obstetricians, pediatricians, and family medicine practitioners and their patients. As we have pointed out, the focus of medical care for pregnant women is almost entirely on the physical health of the mother and fetus. Later, as pediatricians and family doctors take over the family's care, the focus of care shifts to the child's physical health. We are concerned about the fact that fathers must make their own adjustments to pregnancy and parenthood. When fathers adapt poorly, particularly when the quality of their relationships with their wives is unhappy or stormy, the well-being of the entire family is affected.

We often lament that, in addition to the rest of their burdens of work and family, mothers end up in charge of the family's health. Instead of casually allowing men to come along on their wives' visits to the obstetrician or their child's appointments to the pediatrician, health care professionals might consider offering fathers a formal invitation to accompany their wives and children or to visit on their own. We have noticed that a few medical practitioners in our area (Northern California) have begun to hold some regular evening office hours to make it possible for men with nine-to-five work schedules to take part in their family's health care. Only if we make it possible for men to become involved are they likely to ask questions, discuss their concerns, and gather their own information.

As part of an effort at screening and prevention, medical doctors could think of each visit as an opportunity for a *family* checkup. We are not suggesting a total revamping of the health delivery system, but one or two questions about how the family is doing at regular visits. Medical doctors are probably in the best positions to help pinpoint family difficulties before they reach that critical stage when problems become very difficult to treat.

Finally, even if doctors do not pose these family-oriented questions, patients can raise their own questions or concerns. If doctors seem reluctant to broach these psychological family issues, they can at least be helpful in suggesting other resources.

FOR MENTAL HEALTH PROFESSIONALS

We hope that the results of our study will be useful to counselors and therapists. In reading the psychotherapy literature, we have been struck by the number of case histories in which it is mentioned in an aside that the patient has recently become a parent; the discussion of the patient's "problem" proceeds, and the issue never seems to be referred to again. Even if the adult's adaptation to parenthood is not the focus of the therapy, the therapist might pay attention to whether the focal issues could have been exacerbated by the natural stress and vulnerability that accompanies this major adult transition.

It is our hope that therapists working with mothers, fathers, couples, children, or families will be able to use the information here to reassure their patients that even if it is unwelcome, some stress in the family-making years may be normal and expectable. Our experience in working with couples in groups is that this kind of information can help parents put their distress in perspective, and buffer their feelings of helplessness or depression about being in over their heads or alone in their distress.

Finally, we hope to stimulate some mental health professionals to consider more active, preventive work with new families. We believe that the transition to parenthood is an optimal time to provide services for couples who are planning to have a baby. If there were more preventive services for couples like the one we have described here, men and women would get the idea that family making is a challenge for any couple and that there are things partners can do to be better prepared. In talking with other professionals in the United States, Canada, England, and Scotland, we have received very enthusiastic comments about the kind of groups we created, but with the exception of several colleagues who have told us they are pilot-testing similar interventions,* we are not aware of anyone attempting to develop similar groups to help couples with their marital and parenting dilemmas. We would be glad to talk with other professionals interested in trying this kind of intervention.

FOR FAMILY POLICY

We are sadly aware that the millions of parents who are rearing their children in poverty and countless others who are mentally ill constitute a vast under-

*Ed Bader, Toronto; Kuno Beller, Munich; Alan Bennett, London; and Howard Markman, Denver (personal communication, 1991).

served population at risk of repeating dysfunctional cycles in the next generations. At the same time, we have become alarmed by the millions of average
families with poor to barely adequate financial and emotional resources who
are creating families under unnecessarily stressful conditions. They too are
underserved.

We believe that the results of our longitudinal research and intervention
study document the costly consequences of disenchantment and distress in
the early family years for each parent, their marriage, and their children's
emotional, social, and academic development. Governments have an obligation to provide both mental health and prevention services to reduce the
present level of family distress and promote the well-being of their citizens.
There is much to be done with limited resources. Services for partners
becoming parents will be expensive, but we are convinced that providing *no*
services will be more costly in the long run—to all of us.

Parental leave policies and more flexible work schedules for mothers and
fathers are essential to parents' ability to start their families on sound footing.
If parents and children in dual-worker families are to flourish, decent, affordable child care is a necessity. There is no single prescription for the best
balance of work and family for the optimal development of young children.
The policies that politicians propose must allow for a great range of diversity
in families, so that parents are supported in choosing the arrangements that
make sense *for them*.

Specific policies have the potential to improve the quality of family life,
but a fundamental change in outlook will be necessary before most of them
can be enacted. The overarching concern of government and business with
fostering the development of the individual is contributing to the burdens of
parents and children. The philosophy, psychology, and economics of the
American dream are personified by the Horatio Alger myth, not by a real
commitment to building satisfying relationships in families and communities. The irony is that failure to provide real incentives for strengthening
family relationships may be contributing to our children's inability to develop either the motivation or the skills needed to survive in our complex
world.

A Final Word

We have been moved by our journey—our personal one and the one we took
with the generous couples who allowed us into their lives. Like us, all of them
would make the journey to parenthood if they had to decide again. Our own
children have enriched our lives immeasurably. Each one has played an
extraordinary role in our development and our understanding of what it
means to be partners and parents.

We have emphasized the most difficult parts of becoming a family because the conspiracy of silence that surrounds this period leaves couples

feeling that they are the only ones having a hard time. While we believe that difficulties and challenges are necessary for the growth of parents and children, we urge that more attention be given to those who need some assistance along the way. Our warnings are intended as weather advisories—not to advise couples to stay home, but to set out with the necessary gear to withstand the storms. We hope that parents, researchers, and health and mental health professionals will feel better equipped to understand the becoming a family journey so that couples can come closer to building the homestead of their dreams.

NOTES

CHAPTER 2   TO BE OR NOT TO BE A PARENT

1. The coding scheme was created by Jessica Ball who, with Frank Jaffe, rated the responses. The ratings revealed that husbands and wives showed substantial agreement in their problem-solving accounts ($r = .65$).

2. Although men do not have a monopoly on ambivalence about or opposition to parenthood, we were not likely to encounter women who still had a *strong* negative reaction to becoming a parent in the third trimester of pregnancy. Warren Miller's study (1978) shows that as the pregnancy progresses, women shift increasingly toward wanting the baby, regardless of whether conception was intended. In our study, men's ambivalence during pregnancy about becoming a parent was one of the strongest predictors of their own and their wives' later symptoms of depression, parenting stress, and marital dissatisfaction (Heming 1985, 1987).

CHAPTER 4   WHAT'S HAPPENING TO ME?

1. We use a standardized questionnaire created for our research called The Pie (Cowan and Cowan 1990a) with circles 4 inches in diameter.

2. Analyses of change from pregnancy until eighteen months after birth are based on data from forty-seven couples who became parents (twenty-three couples who participated in groups and twenty-four couples who filled out questionnaires both before and after the birth of their babies) and fifteen couples who remained

married and childless over the same period of time. Because they did not provide before-baby information, the twenty-four couples who filled out questionnaires only after the birth of their child were not included in the results reported in this chapter.

3. At six months postpartum, the correlation between the Parent piece of the pie and self-esteem for men was $r = .21$; $p < .05$) and for women $r = -.25$; $p < .05$). The discrepancy between partners in the size of the Parent piece of the pie and its relation to decline in marital satisfaction was determined by two multiple regression equations, one for men and one for women. As a predictor of eighteen-month postpartum marital satisfaction, we first partialed out prebirth marital satisfaction scores on step 1 of the equation. Then we entered a measure of between-partner difference in size of the Parent piece at six months after the child's birth. This measure accounts for a significant 17 percent of the decline in men's marital satisfaction during the transition to parenthood (F change = 12.3; df = 2/45; $p < .001$) and 11 percent of the decline in women's marital satisfaction during the same period (F change = 9.30; df = 2/45; $p < .001$).

4. There are thirty-two personality trait subscales on the Adjective Check List including adjustment, autonomy, aggression, counseling readiness, dominance, nurturance, need for achievement, masculinity, and femininity. There are fewer statistically significant changes over time on these scales than we would expect to occur by chance (only in two of thirty-two scales, one for men and one for women).

5.

| | Correlations Between Pie Pieces in Pregnancy and | | | |
| | 6 months after birth | | 18 months after birth | |
Pregnancy	*Men*	*Women*	*Men*	*Women*
Partner	.46*	—	.41*	.36*
Worker	.51*	.58*	.47*	.61**
Leisure	.33*	.49*	.42*	.56**

*$p < .01$
**$p < .001$

CHAPTER 5   WHAT'S HAPPENING TO US?

1. In the pregnancy version of the section on caring for the baby, there were twelve questions. In subsequent follow-ups the number of items was increased to capture some of the new tasks associated with the care of toddlers, preschoolers, and school-aged children.

2. Item correlations between spouses' ratings on household and child-care tasks averaged between .72 and .85 over all assessment periods. Item correlations between spouses' ratings of decision making were lower, averaging .35 to .42, probably because the range of ratings on these items was quite restricted.

3. Ratings of the father's involvement and satisfaction with his involvement were correlated with well-being in four domains:
   Individual: self-esteem (Adjective Check List [Gough and Heilbrun 1980]) and symptoms of depression (CES-D [Radloff 1977]);
   Couple: marital satisfaction (Short Marital Adjustment Test [Locke and Wallace 1959]) and family cohesion (high warmth, high expressiveness, and low conflict—Family Environment Scale [Moos 1974]);

Parent-child: parenting stress (Parenting Stress Index [Abidin 1983]); and *Outside the Family:* life stress (Recent Life Events [Horowitz et al. 1977]) and social support (Important People [Curtis-Boles 1979]). Our index of the balance between stress and support gives the highest scores to people with low life stress and high social support.

4.

When Fathers Participate More in Child-Care Tasks

Measure of Well-being	Pregnancy		6 months after birth		18 months after birth	
	Fathers	Mothers	Fathers	Mothers	Fathers	Mothers
Self-esteem			.26*	.27*		
Parenting stress			−.27*	−.20*	−.27*	−.29*
Depression					−.29*	−.27*
Marital satisfaction		.26*	.30**	.32**		.33*
Family cohesion	.33*	.32**	.23*	.26*		.22*
Positive balance between social support and life stress			.24*	.34**		

*p < .05
**p < .01

5. The connection between fathers' involvement and change in marital satisfaction was assessed in two multiple regression equations, one for fathers and one for mothers. As a predictor of eighteen-month postpartum marital satisfaction, we first partialed out prebirth marital satisfaction scores on step 1 of the equation. Then we entered a measure of fathers' involvement at six months after birth (either fathers' ratings or mothers' ratings). We find that fathers' daily involvement with the child-care tasks, as they perceive it, accounts for a statistically significant 6 percent of the increase in his marital satisfaction from pregnancy to eighteen months postpartum (F change = 3.80; df = 2/45; p < .05). His involvement as *she* perceives it accounts for 12 percent of the variance in her marital satisfaction change over the same period (F change = 9.66; df = 2/45; p < .003).

6. "Who does what" issues take second place as a subject of marital arguments when children are three and a half, yielding to conflictual issues about the marriage. They reemerge as the top contender for creating conflict by the time children are in kindergarten.

7. The range of conflict and disagreement change is from a 1.5-point-per-item average reduction in conflict to a 3.7-point-per-item increase on this 7-point scale.

8. There are more psychometrically elegant measures of marital satisfaction, but as Gottman (1979) points out, they are all highly correlated with one another and the Locke-Wallace has the advantage of brevity.

9. In our study, as in many others, the spouses' scores show correlations of about .60.

10. The multiple correlation was R = .64 for men's marital satisfaction and .61 for women's.

11. To test this idea statistically, we constructed a difference index, giving higher scores to couples in which he and she had greater differences between their scores on our key measures. The index included differences between husbands' and wives' reports of the state of things in each of the family domains: the size of the Parent piece of the pie chart; their satisfaction with who does what; the positive changes in their sexual relationship; their ideas about parenting; their description of their families of origin; and their balance of life stress and social support.

CHAPTER 6   BEYOND THE DOORSTEP: NEW PROBLEMS, NEW SOLUTIONS

1. In a multiple regression equation predicting mothers' symptoms of depression on the Center for the Epidemiological Study of Depression scale (Radloff 1977), we entered women's self-esteem scores in pregnancy on the first step. Their self-esteem accounts for about 9 percent of the variance in their depression scores two years later. On a second step, we entered women's work status (full-time home, part-time work, full-time work). Mothers' work status accounted for an additional 10 percent of the variance in their depression scores, over and above their earlier self-esteem (adjusted R-squared = .18).

2. Six months after giving birth, wives' employment is correlated with husbands' involvement in household tasks ($r = .22; p < .03$) and child care ($r = .51; p < .001$). Eighteen months after having a baby, wives' employment is no longer correlated with husbands' involvement in household tasks, but the more she works, the more child care he does ($r = .42; p < .01$).

3. Disagreement in their "How I would like it to be" ratings of bringing in family income on our Who Does What? questionnaire.

4. The more "other care" for the child, the smaller the Mother piece of the pie (six months: $r = -.32$; $df = 31$; $p < .08$; eighteen months: $r = -.44$; $df = 31$; $p < .004$).

5. The questionnaire is called Important People (Curtis-Boles 1979). We do not instruct people about whether they can or should put their spouse on the list. Some do, some do not. New parents' important people usually include current friends, co-workers, childhood friends, sisters, brothers, mothers, fathers, aunts, uncles, and a few important acquaintances. Each person named is given a score that combines frequency of contact multiplied by the parent's satisfaction with that relationship. Our index of positive social support is calculated by adding the scores for all four people to make one index.

6. Our Recent Life Events questionnaire is adapted slightly from Horowitz et al. (1969). Life change items are weighted based on estimates by mental health professionals of the stress-inducing qualities of those events, with more recent events given higher weighting.

7. Multiple regression equations indicate that the life stress/social support balance accounts for a significant proportion of the variance in men's and women's marital satisfaction, over and above their level of life stress or social support. The balance index adds a significant 9 to 12 percent of the variance in marital satisfaction for both parents (increase in R-squared) at six and eighteen months after birth.

8. The correlation between marital satisfaction in pregnancy and positive social support at eighteen months after birth was $r = .35$ ($p < .01$) for women and $r = .27$ ($p < .05$) for men.

CHAPTER 7   LEGACIES FROM OUR PARENTS

1. Conflict in the parents' childhood families was assessed by their descriptions of their families of origin on the conflict subscale of the Family Environment Scale (Moos 1974).

Conflict Pattern in the Family of Origin	Decline in Marital Satisfaction (average number of points)	
	Men	Women
Both partners recall low conflict	6	7
Both partners recall high conflict	17	13
His family had high conflict; hers had low	15	21
Her family had high conflict; his had low	9	9

2. The Adult Attachment Interview (George, Kaplan, and Main 1984) stimulates parents to think back in some detail to their childhood relationships with their parents. Men and women are asked to think of five adjectives that would describe their relationships with their mothers and their fathers. They are asked what their parents did when the children were hurt, and how they as children handled their own feelings of rejection, of feeling threatened, and of separations or losses of important people while they were growing up. Have their relationships with their parents changed in any major way between their childhood and now? Why do they think their parents behaved as they did? How do they think those past experiences affect their lives now?

CHAPTER 8   PARENTING OUR CHILDREN

1. Because a number of the original seventy-two families with children moved out of state, we were able to visit with only fifty-two (72 percent) when the children were three and a half. We have whole family observations on only forty-six because six of the families were divorced by then.
2. The male-female staff team in charge of the parent-child visits rated a number of qualities of the parents' behavior: pleasure/displeasure, coldness/warmth, responsiveness, interactiveness, confidence in the parental role, anger, respect for the child's autonomy, limit setting, maturity demands, structure, creativity, activity level, respect for the child's autonomy, and clarity of communication.

   The ratings are grouped into five categories or factors (for details, see Pratt et al. 1988) and the factors are combined into two summary scores. Parents with high scores on the *authoritative* index show pleasure, warmth, and responsiveness and are very highly engaged with the child during the visit. They also structure the tasks to help the child, express very little anger, and convey their expectation that the child will *try* most of the tasks. By contrast, parents with low scores on these qualities—little pleasure and responsiveness, and little structure and encouragement to try the tasks—appear to be fairly uninvolved or disengaged. They do not react to their child very much either positively or negatively.

   The same summary ratings can be regrouped to reflect *authoritarian* parenting style. Parents with high scores on this index show little pleasure, warmth, or responsiveness, and a fair amount of anger, limit setting, and expectations that the child do the tasks. Parents with low scores on the authoritarian index show warmth and responsiveness but do almost no structuring or limit setting; they can be described as permissive. They are generally warm and allow the children to do what they wish.

Baumrind describes authoritative, authoritarian, permissive, and disengaged styles as types. Here we treat them as bipolar continua: authoritative-disengaged and authoritarian-permissive.

3. The data presented here are derived from a latent variable path model (Cowan et al. in press). Latent variables are statistical combinations of two or more variables assumed to measure the same construct. We constructed latent variables in pregnancy, and six and eighteen months after birth, to predict parenting warmth and structure when the child was three and a half. Each latent variable contained measures from both husbands and wives. In pregnancy we assessed couples' marital satisfaction (Locke and Wallace 1959) and conflict in the family of origin (Family Environment Scale, Moos 1974). At six months postpartum we combined his and her life stress events (Horowitz et al. 1977). At eighteen months postpartum we included a measure of his and her symptoms of depression (Center for Epidemiological Studies in Depression Scale, Radloff 1977) and also measured their marital satisfaction again.

When children were three and a half, we assessed both parents' observed warmth and responsiveness to the child (mothers and fathers in separate visits) and their observed structure and limit setting with the child (mothers and fathers in separate visits). The measures from the transition to parenthood (pregnancy to eighteen months after birth) combine to predict 53 percent of the variance in parents' structuring and 28 percent of the variance in parents' warmth to the child. If we add to the equation the observed interaction between parents in the whole family visits when the child is three and a half, the combined variables account for almost 70 percent of the variance in parents' warmth during the separate parent-child visits.

4. Women's self-esteem (Adjective Check List) and satisfaction with division of family labor (Who Does What?) in pregnancy were correlated with authoritative parenting style (boys and girls combined): Self-esteem ($r = .52$; $df = 42$; $p < .001$); satisfaction with division of family labor ($r = .51$; $df = 42$; $p < .001$).

5. More authoritative fathers of three-and-a-half-year-old sons, previously assessed in pregnancy, showed more positive memories of their parents on the Family Relationships Questionnaire (Cowan and Cowan 1983; $r = .39$; $df = 19$; $p < .05$); higher self-esteem ($r = .44$; $df = 19$; $p < .05$); greater satisfaction with the division of family labor ($r = .42$; $df = 19$; $p < .05$) and lower outside-the-family life stress scores on the Recent Life Events scale (Horowitz et al. 1977; $r = -.43$; $df = 19$; $p < .05$).

6. Fathers of girls were observed to be marginally less authoritative ($t = 1.50$; $df = 45$; $p < .07$) and significantly more authoritarian ($t = 2.26$; $df = 45$; $p < .01$) than fathers of boys.

7. We combined our ratings of the parents' style of interacting as a couple during the whole family visit into two summary scores. The first describes positive interaction and the second captures conflictful interaction between the parents in front of the child. Couples high on the positive interaction index showed more warmth, responsiveness, and pleasure between them than couples with low scores. Couples with high scores on conflictful interaction showed more disagreement,

anger, and competitiveness and less cooperation with each other during the family visit.

8. When the couple was rated as higher in conflict in the family visit, fathers were more authoritarian (cold, critical, structuring, limit setting) with their daughters in the separate father-child visit ($r = .60$; df $= 21$; $p < .001$).

9. Unlike most studies that report correlations between average levels of parents' and children's responses across a whole observation period, Kerig's (1989) provides a microanalysis of how each parent responds when the child shows a specific behavior, providing even stronger evidence of the links between parents' and children's behavior.

10. Boys were coded 0; girls were coded 1. Correlation between sex of child and favorable items for fathers describing themselves on the Adjective Check List: $r = -.32$; df $= 44$; $p < .05$.

11. Correlations between having a girl and having a second child before the first was eighteen months old: $r = .25$; df $= 44$; $p < .05$.

12. Increasing discrepancies between the size of his and her Parent piece of the pie ($r = .34$; $p < .01$) and his and her satisfaction with their division of labor ($r = .57$; $p < .001$) from pregnancy to eighteen months after birth predicted greater conflict between parents (observed) when the child was three and a half.

13. Symptoms of depression were measured by the Center for Epidemiological Studies in Depression Scale (Radloff 1977) and by the Hopkins Symptom Checklist (Derogatis, Lipman, and Covi 1973).

14. Satisfaction with work involvement was measured by the discrepancy between the size of the Worker piece of parents' actual and ideal pie. Parents who were more satisfied with their psychological involvement with work outside the family were more authoritative with their children (fathers: $r = .47$ df $= 45$; $p < .001$; mothers: $r = .30$; df $= 45$; $p < .05$). Parents more satisfied with their process of resolving child-care issues (Leventhal-Belfer 1990) were more authoritative (fathers: $r = .28$; df $= 45$; $p < .05$; mothers: $r = .52$; df $= 45$; $p < .001$).

15. Our Child Adaptive Behavior Inventory is a modification of Schaefer and Hunter's inventory (1983). We added items concerning peer relationships and behavior problems.

16. Because our statistical analyses could not include well-being in each domain at each time period, we were forced to be selective. Except for the assessments of marital functioning in pregnancy and eighteen months and three and a half years after birth, we chose measures from one additional aspect of family life at each time period.

    We selected pairs of measures of family functioning from each aspect of family life—one for mothers and one for fathers. We began with both parents' remembered conflict in their families of origin and low marital satisfaction in pregnancy. We added information about parents' life stress six months after birth, and their symptoms of depression and low marital satisfaction when their child was eighteen months old. This is the same information that helped us predict the level of conflict between the partners in the family visit and low levels of warmth and structure in the separate playroom visits for the parents and their child (see p. 153).

17. The combined family model from pregnancy to preschool accounts for 60 percent of the variance in kindergarten teachers' ratings of children's aggression, 42 percent of the variance in teachers' ratings of concentration problems in the classroom, and 47 percent of the variance in children's academic achievement

(reading and math scores) on the Peabody Individual Achievement Test. (For details, see Cowan et al. in press.)

CHAPTER 9   AN OUNCE OF PREVENTION: COUPLES GROUPS

1. While there are some clear advantages to having married couples as leaders, we have trained graduate student male-female teams to lead groups for couples with young children (Chavez et al. 1988). For our new intervention study with parents of children making the transition to school, we have recruited eight mental health professionals, two couples in which the partners are married to each other, and two others in which the co-leaders are not related.
2. Mean differences and statistical tests of the intervention effects can be found in Cowan et al. (1985). Additional details concerning intervention effects are in Cowan and Cowan (1987b) and C. Cowan (1988).

REFERENCES

Abidin, R. (1983). *Parenting stress index manual.* Charlottesville, VA: Pediatric Psychology Press.

Alexander, K. L., & Entwisle, D. (1988). Achievement in the first 2 years of school: Patterns and processes. *Monographs of the Society for Research in Child Development, 53* (2, Serial No. 218).

Aranoff, J. L., & Lewis, S. (1979). An innovative group experience for couples expecting their first child. *American Journal of Family Therapy, 7,* 51–55.

Ball, F. L. J. (1984). *Understanding and satisfaction in marital problem solving: A hermeneutic inquiry.* Unpublished doctoral dissertation, University of California, Berkeley.

Barnett, R. C., & Baruch, G. K. (1988). Correlates of fathers' participation in family work. In P. Bronstein & C. P. Cowan (Eds.), *Fatherhood today: Men's changing role in the family* (pp. 66–78). New York: Wiley.

Baruch, G. K., Barnett, R. C., & Rivers, C. (1983). *Lifeprints: New patterns of love and work for today's women.* New York: McGraw-Hill.

Bateson, G. (1972). *Steps to an ecology of mind.* New York: Ballantine Books.

Bateson, G., Jackson, D. D., Haley, J., & Weakland, J. (1956). Towards a theory of schizophrenia. *Behavioral Science, 1,* 251–264.

Baucom, D. H., Sayers, S. L., & Duhe, A. (1989). Attributional style and attributional patterns among married couples. *Journal of Personality and Social Psychology, 56,* 596–607.

Baum, F., & Cope, D. R. (1980). Some characteristics of intentionally childless wives in Britain. *Journal of Biosocial Science, 12,* 287–299.

Baumrind, D. (1979). The development of instrumental competence through socialization. In A. D. Pick (Ed.), *Minnesota symposia on child psychology* (Vol. 7).
Minneapolis: University of Minnesota Press.

Baumrind, D. (1991). Effective parenting during the early adolescent transition. In
P. A. Cowan & E. M. Hetherington (Eds.), *Family transitions: Advances in family
research* (Vol. 2, pp. 111–164). Hillsdale, NJ: Lawrence Erlbaum Associates.

Beck, A. (1976). *Cognitive therapy and the emotional disorders.* New York: International Universities Press.

Bellah, R. N., Madsen, R., Sullivan, W. M., Swidler, A., & Tipton, S. M. (1985). *Habits
of the heart: Individualism and commitment in American life.* Berkeley, CA: University
of California Press.

Belsky, J. (1984). The determinants of parenting: A process model. *Child
Development, 55,* 83–96.

Belsky, J. (1988). The "effects" of infant daycare reconsidered. *Early Childhood Research Quarterly, 3,* 235–272.

Belsky, J. (1990). Parental and nonparental child care and children's socioemotional
development: A decade in review. *Journal of Marriage and the Family, 52,* 885–903.

Belsky, J., Lang, M., & Rovine, M. (1985). Stability and change across the
transition to parenthood: A second study. *Journal of Personality and Social Psychology, 50,* 517–522.

Belsky, J., & Rovine, M. (1988). Nonmaternal care in the first year of life
and the security of infant-parent attachment. *Child Development, 59,* 157–167.

Belsky, J., & Rovine, M. (1990). Patterns of marital change across the transition to
parenthood. *Journal of Marriage and the Family, 52,* 109–123.

Belsky, J., & Steinberg, L. (1978). The effects of day care: A critical review. *Child Development, 49,* 929–949.

Belsky, J., Steinberg, L., & Walker, A. (1982). The ecology of day care. In M. E. Lamb
(Ed.), *Nontraditional families* (pp. 71–116). Hillsdale, NJ: Lawrence Erlbaum
Associates.

Belsky, J., Ward, H., & Rovine, M. (1986). Prenatal expectations, post-natal
experiences and the transition to parenthood. In R. Ashmore & D. Brodzinsky
(Eds.), *Perspectives on the family.* Hillsdale, NJ: Lawrence Erlbaum Associates.

Benedek, T. (1959). Parenthood as a developmental phase. *Journal of the American
Psychoanalytic Association, 7,* 389–417.

Benedek, T. (1970). Parenthood during the life cycle. In E. J. Anthony & T. Benedek
(Eds.), *Parenthood: Its psychology and psychopathology.* Boston: Little, Brown.

Bernard, J. (1972). *The future of marriage.* New York: World.

Bittman, S., & Zalk, S. R. (1978). *Expectant fathers.* New York: Hawthorne.

Block, J. H. (1976a). Debatable conclusions about sex differences. *Contemporary
Psychology, 21,* 517–522.

Block, J. H. (1976b). Issues, problems, and pitfalls in assessing sex differences: A
critical review of *The psychology of sex differences. Merrill-Palmer Quarterly, 222,*
283–308.

Block, J. H. (1983). Differential premises arising from differential socialization of the
sexes: Some conjectures. *Child Development, 54,* 1335–1354.

Block, J. H. (1984). *Sex role identity and ego development.* San Francisco, CA:
Jossey-Bass.

Block, J. H., & Block, J (1980). The role of ego-control and ego-resiliency in the
organization of behavior. In W. A. Collins (Ed.), *Minnesota symposia on child
psychology* (Vol. 13). Hillsdale, NJ: Lawrence Erlbaum Associates.

Block, J. H., Block, J., & Gjerde, P. F. (1986). The personality of children prior to divorce: A prospective study. *Child Development, 57,* 827–840.

Block, J. H., Block, J., & Morrison, A. (1981). Parental agreement-disagreement on child-rearing orientations and gender-related personality correlates in children. *Child Development, 52,* 965–974.

Boles, A. (1984). *Predictors and correlates of marital satisfaction during the transition to parenthood.* Unpublished doctoral dissertation, University of California, Berkeley.

Bombardieri, M. (1981). *The baby decision: How to make the most important choice of your life.* New York: Rawson Associates.

Bowen, M. (1978). *Family therapy in clinical practice.* New York: Jason Aronson.

Bowlby, J. (1969–80). *Attachment and loss* (Vols. 1–3). London: Hogarth Press.

Bozett, F. W. (1988). Gay fatherhood. In P. Bronstein & C. P. Cowan (Eds.), *Fatherhood today: Men's changing role in the family* (pp. 214–235). New York: Wiley.

Bradburn, I., & Kaplan, J. (in press). Continuity and change in the transition to parenthood: A tale of two families. In P. A. Cowan, D. Field, D. Hansen, A. Skolnick, & G. E. Swanson (Eds.), *Family, self, and society: Toward a new agenda for family research.* Hillsdale, NJ: Lawrence Erlbaum Associates.

Brodzinsky, D. (1987). Adjustment to adoption: A psychosocial perspective. *Clinical Psychology Review, 7,* 25–47.

Bronfenbrenner, U. (1979). *The ecology of human development.* Cambridge, MA: Harvard University Press.

Bronfenbrenner, U., & Crouter, A. (1982). Work and family through time and space. In S. Kamerman & C. Hayes (Eds.), *Families that work: Children in a changing world.* Washington, DC: National Academy Press.

Brown, S. (1985). *Treating the alcoholic: A developmental model of recovery.* New York: Wiley.

Bumpass, L., & Rindfuss, R. R. (1979). Children's experience of marital disruption. *American Journal of Sociology, 85,* 49–65.

Caspi, A., & Elder, G. H., Jr. (1988). Emergent family patterns: The intergenerational construction of problem behavior and relationships. In R. A. Hinde & J. Stevenson-Hinde (Eds.), *Relationships within families: Mutual influences* (pp. 218–240). Oxford: Clarendon Press.

Catalyst (1988). Workplace policies: New options for fathers. In P. Bronstein & C. P. Cowan (Eds.), *Fatherhood today: Men's changing role in the family* (pp. 323–340). New York: Wiley.

Chavez, D., Corkery, L., Epperson, B., Gordon, D., Kline, M., McHale, J., Soulé, C., Sullivan, C., Weinberg, G., Cowan, C. P., & Cowan, P. A. (1988, April). Parents and partners: A preventive intervention for parents of preschoolers. Workshop sponsored by Prevention Section of American Orthopsychiatric Association, San Francisco.

Cherlin, A. (1977). The effect of children on marital dissolution. *Demography, 14,* 264–272.

Cherniss, D. S. (1988). Stability and growth in parent-support services: A national study of peer support for parents of preterm and high-risk infants. In C. F. Z. Boukydis (Ed.), *Research on support for parents in the postnatal period.* Norwood, NJ: Ablex.

Chodorow, N. J. (1978). *The reproduction of mothering.* Berkeley, CA: University of California Press.

Clarke-Stewart, A. (1989). Infant day care: Maligned or malignant? *American Psychologist, 44,* 266–273.

Clulow, C. F. (1982). *To have and to hold: Marriage, the first baby and preparing couples for parenthood.* Aberdeen: Aberdeen University Press.

Cohn, D. A., Cowan, P. A., Cowan, C. P., & Pearson, J. (1991). Mothers' and fathers' working models of childhood attachment relationships, parenting styles, and child behavior. Unpublished manuscript.

Cohn, D. A., Silver, D., Cowan, P. A., Cowan, C. P., & Pearson, J. (1991, April). Working models of attachment and marital relationships. Paper presented in a symposium chaired by D. Cohn on Working Models of Attachment and Couple Relationships at the meetings of the Society for Research in Child Development, Seattle, WA.

Colman, A. D., & Colman, L. L. (1971). *Pregnancy: The psychological experience.* New York: Herder & Herder.

Cowan, C. P. (1988). Working with men becoming fathers: The impact of a couples group intervention. In P. Bronstein & C. P. Cowan (Eds.), *Fatherhood today: Men's changing role in the family* (pp. 276–298). New York: Wiley.

Cowan, C. P., & Cowan, P. A. (1983). *Family relationships questionnaire.* Becoming a Family Project, University of California, Berkeley.

Cowan, C. P., & Cowan, P. A. (1987a). Men's involvement in parenthood: Identifying the antecedents and understanding the barriers. In P. Berman & F. Pedersen (Eds.), *Men's transitions to parenthood: Longitudinal studies of early family experience* (pp. 145–174). Hillsdale, NJ: Erlbaum.

Cowan, C. P., & Cowan, P. A. (1987b). A preventive intervention for couples becoming parents. In C. F. Z. Boukydis (Ed.), *Research on support for parents and infants in the postnatal period* (pp. 225–251). Norwood, NJ: Ablex.

Cowan, C. P., & Cowan, P. A. (1988). Who does what when partners become parents: Implications for men, women, and marriage. *Marriage & Family Review, 13,* 105–132.

Cowan, C. P., & Cowan, P. A. (1990a). The Pie. In J. Touliatos, B. F. Perlmutter, & M. A. Straus (Eds.), *Handbook of family measurement techniques* (pp. 278–279). Newbury Park: Sage.

Cowan, C. P., & Cowan, P. A. (1990b). Who Does What? In J. Touliatos, B. F. Perlmutter, & M. A. Straus (Eds.), *Handbook of family measurement techniques* (pp. 447–448). Newbury Park: Sage.

Cowan, C. P., Cowan, P. A., Coie, L., & Coie, J. D. (1978). Becoming a family: The impact of a first child's birth on the couple's relationship. In W. B. Miller and L. F. Newman (Eds.), *The first child and family formation* (pp. 296–324). Chapel Hill, NC: Carolina Population Center.

Cowan, C. P., Cowan, P. A., & Heming, G. (1988, November). Adult children of alcoholics: What happens when they form new families? Paper presented to the National Council on Family Relations, Philadelphia, PA.

Cowan, C. P., Cowan, P. A., Heming, G., Garrett, E., Coysh, W. S., Curtis-Boles, H., & Boles, A. J. (1985). Transitions to parenthood: His, hers, and theirs. *Journal of Family Issues, 6,* 451–481.

Cowan, C. P., Cowan, P. A., Heming, G., & Miller, N. B. (1991). Becoming a family: Marriage, parenting, and child development. In P. A. Cowan & E. M. Hetherington (Eds.), *Family transitions: Advances in family research* (Vol. 2, pp. 79–109). Hillsdale, NJ: Lawrence Erlbaum Associates.

Cowan, P. A. (1988a). Becoming a father: A time of change, an opportunity for development. In P. Bronstein & C. P. Cowan (Eds.), *Fatherhood today: Men's changing role in the family* (pp. 13–35). New York: Wiley.

Cowan, P. A. (1988b). Developmental psychopathology: A nine-cell map of the territory. In E. Nannis & P. A. Cowan (Eds.), *Developmental psychopathology and its treatment: New directions for child development* (Number 39, pp. 5–30). San Francisco: Jossey-Bass.

Cowan, P. A., & Cowan, C. P. (1988). Changes in marriage during the transition to parenthood: Must we blame the baby? In G. Y. Michaels & W. A. Goldberg (Eds.), *The transition to parenthood: Current theory and research* (pp. 114–154). Cambridge: Cambridge University Press.

Cowan, P. A., & Cowan, C. P. (1990). Becoming a family: Research and intervention. In I. E. Sigel and G. H. Brody (Eds.), *Methods of family research: Biographies of research projects I: Normal families*. Hillsdale, NJ: Lawrence Erlbaum Associates.

Cowan, P. A., Cowan, C. P., & Kerig, P. (in press). Mothers, fathers, sons, and daughters: Gender differences in family formation and parenting style. In P. A. Cowan, D. Field, D. Hansen, A. Skolnick, & G. E. Swanson (Eds.), *Family, self, and society: Toward a new agenda for family research*. Hillsdale, NJ: Lawrence Erlbaum Associates.

Cowan, P. A., Cowan, C. P., Schulz, M., & Heming, G. (in press). Prebirth to preschool family factors predicting children's adaptation to kindergarten. In R. Parke & S. Kellam (Eds.), *Exploring family relationships with other social contexts: Advances in family research* (Vol. 4). Hillsdale, NJ: Lawrence Erlbaum Associates.

Cowan, P. A., & Hetherington, E. M. (Eds.). (1991). *Family transitions: Advances in family research* (Vol. 2). Hillsdale, NJ: Lawrence Erlbaum Associates.

Coysh, W. S. (1983). *Factors influencing men's roles in caring for their children and the effects of father involvement*. Unpublished doctoral dissertation, University of California, Berkeley.

Crnic, K. A., Greenberg, M. T., Ragozin, A. S., Robinson, N. M., & Basham, R. B. (1983). Effects of stress and social support on mothers and premature and full-term infants. *Child Development, 54,* 209–217.

Crockenberg, S. B. (1981). Infant irritability, mother responsiveness, and social support influences on the security of infant-mother attachment. *Child Development, 52,* 857–865.

Curtis, J. L. (1955). A psychiatric study of 55 expectant fathers. *U.S. Armed Forces Medical Journal, 6,* 937–950.

Curtis-Boles, H. (1979). Important people. Becoming a Family Project, University of California, Berkeley.

Cutrona, C. E., & Troutman, B. R. (1986). Social support, infant temperament, and parenting self-efficacy: A mediational model of postpartum depression. *Child Development, 57,* 1507–1518.

Daniels, P., & Weingarten, K. (1982). *Sooner or later: The timing of parenthood in adult lives*. New York: W. W. Norton.

Daniels, P., & Weingarten, K. (1988). The fatherhood click: The timing of parenting in men's lives. In P. Bronstein & C. P. Cowan (Eds.). *Fatherhood today: Men's changing role in the family* (pp. 36–52). New York: Wiley.

Derogatis, L. R., Lipman, R. S., & Covi, L. (1973). SCL-90: An outpatient psychiatric rating scale. Preliminary report. *Psychopharmacology Bulletin, 9,* 1–25.

Dura, J., & Kiecolt-Glazer, J. K. (1991). Family transitions, stress, and health. In P. A. Cowan & E. M. Hetherington (Eds.), *Family transitions: Advances in family research* (Vol. 2, pp. 59–78). Hillsdale, NJ: Lawrence Erlbaum Associates.

Ehrensaft, D. (1987). *Parenting together: Men and women sharing the care of their children*. New York: Free Press.

Eiduson, B. T. (1983). Conflict and stress in non-traditional families: Impact on children. *American Journal of Orthopsychiatry, 53* (3), 426–435.

Epperson, B., Cowan, C. P., & Cowan, P. A. (1991). Predictors of divorce: A small-sample prospective study. Unpublished manuscript.

Erikson, E. (1950). *Childhood and society*. New York: W. W. Norton.

Erikson, E. (1959). Identity and the life cycle. *Psychological Issues, 1,* 1–171.

Erikson, E. (1968). *Identity, youth and crisis*. New York: W. W. Norton.

Fawcett, J. T. (1988). The value of children and the transition to parenthood. In R. Palkovitz & M. B. Sussman (Eds.), *Transitions to parenthood* (pp. 11–34). New York: Haworth Press.

Feldman, S. S., & Nash, S. C. (1984). The transition from expectancy to parenthood: Impact of the firstborn child on men and women. *Sex Roles, 11,* 84–96.

Field, T., Healy, B., Goldstein, S., & Guthertz, M. (1990). Behavior-state matching and synchrony in mother-infant interactions of nondepressed versus depressed dyads. *Developmental Psychology, 26,* 7–14.

Finkelhor, D., with Hotaling, G., & Yllo, K. (1988). *Stopping family violence: Research priorities for the coming decade*. Beverly Hills, CA: Sage.

Framo, J. L. (1981). The intergration of marital therapy with sessions with family of origin. In A. S. Gurman and D. P. Kniskern (Eds.), *Handbook of family therapy*. New York: Bruner/Mazel.

Freud, A. (1965). *Normality and pathology in childhood*. New York: International Universities Press.

Friedan, B. (1963). *The feminine mystique*. New York: Dell.

Garrett, E. T. (1983, August). Women's experiences of early parenthood: Expectation vs. reality. Paper presented at the American Psychological Association Meetings, Anaheim, CA.

George, C., Kaplan, N., & Main, M. (1984). *Attachment interview for adults*. Unpublished manuscript. University of California, Berkeley.

Gilligan, C. (1982). *In a different voice: Psychological theory and women's development*. Cambridge, MA.: Harvard University Press.

Glick, P. C., & Lin, S. (1986). Recent changes in divorce and remarriage. *Journal of Marriage and the Family, 48,* 737–747.

Goldberg, W. A., Michaels, G. Y., & Lamb, M. (1985). Husbands' and wives' adjustment to pregnancy and first parenthood. *Journal of Family Issues, 6,* 483–504.

Gottlieb, B.H., & Pancer, S. M. (1988). Social networks and the transition to parenthood. In G. Y. Michaels & W. A. Goldberg (Eds.), *The transition to parenthood: Current theory and research* (pp. 235–269). Cambridge: Cambridge University Press.

Gottman, J. M. (1979). *Marital interaction: Experimental investigations*. New York: Academic Press.

Gottman, J. M., & Krokoff, L. J. (1989). Marital interaction and satisfaction: A longitudinal view. *Journal of Consulting and Clinical Psychology, 57,* 47–52.

Gottman, J. M., & Levenson, R. M. (1986). Assessing the role of emotion in marriage. *Behavioral Assessment, 8,* 31–48.

Gottman, J. M., & Levenson, R. W. (1989). The social psychophysiology of marriage. In P. Noller & M. A. Fitzpatrick (Eds.), *Perspectives on marital interaction*. San Diego, CA: College Hill Press.

Gough, H. G., Fioravanti, M., & Lazzari, R. (1982). Some implications of self versus ideal congruence on the revised adjective check list. *Journal of Consulting Psychology, 44,* 1214–1220.

Gough, H. G., & Heilbrun, A. B., Jr. (1965, 1980). *The adjective check list manual.* Palo Alto, CA: Consulting Psychologists Press.

Greenberger, E., & Goldberg, W. A. (1989). Work, parenting, and the socialization of children. *Developmental Psychology, 25,* 22–35.

Grossman, F., Eichler, L., & Winickoff, S. (1980). *Pregnancy, birth, and parenthood.* San Francisco: Jossey-Bass.

Haley, J. (1976). *Problem-solving therapy.* San Francisco: Jossey-Bass.

Hanson, S. M. H. (1988). Divorced fathers with custody. In P. Bronstein & C. P. Cowan (Eds.), *Fatherhood today: Men's changing role in the family* (pp. 166–194). New York: Wiley.

Harber, K. (1991). *To work or not to work: The impact on new mothers.* Unpublished doctoral dissertation. Center for Psychological Studies, Albany, CA.

Heinicke, C. M., Diskin, S. D., Ramsay-Klee, D. M., & Oates, D. S. (1986). Pre- and postbirth antecedents of 2-year-old attention, capacity for relationships and verbal expressiveness. *Developmental Psychology, 22,* 777–787.

Heming, G. (1985). *Predicting adaptation in the transition to parenthood.* Unpublished doctoral dissertation, University of California, Berkeley.

Heming, G. (1987, April). Predicting adaptation during the transition to parenthood. Paper presented to the Society for Research in Child Development, Baltimore, MD.

Heming, G., Cowan, P. A., & Cowan, C. P. (1990). Ideas about parenting. In J. Touliatos, B. F. Perlmutter, & M. A. Straus (Eds.), *Handbook of family measurement techniques* (pp. 362–363). Newbury Park, CA: Sage Publications.

Hetherington, E. M., Cox, E. M., & Cox, R. (1982). Effects of divorce on parents and children. In M. E. Lamb (Ed.), *Nontraditional families.* Hillsdale, NJ: Lawrence Erlbaum Associates.

Hetherington, E. M., & Parke, R. D. (1986). *Child psychology: A contemporary viewpoint.* (3rd ed.). New York: McGraw-Hill.

Hinde, R. A., & Stevenson-Hinde, J. (1988). *Relationships within families: Mutual influences.* Oxford: Clarendon Press.

Hobbs, D., & Cole, S. (1977). Transition to parenthood: A decade replication. *Journal of Marriage and the Family, 38,* 723–731.

Hochschild, A. (1989). *The second shift: Working parents and the revolution at home.* New York: Viking Penguin.

Hoffman, L. (1989). Effects of maternal employment in the two-parent family. *American Psychologist, 44,* 283–292.

Hoffman, L., & Hoffman, M. (1973). The value of children to parents. In J. T. Fawcett (Ed.), *Psychological perspectives on population* (pp. 106–151). New York: Basic Books.

Hoffman, L. W., & Nye, F. I. (1974). *Working mothers.* San Francisco, CA: Jossey-Bass.

Holmes, T. H., & Rahe, R. H. (1967). The social adjustment rating scale. *Journal of Psychosomatic Research, 11,* 213–218.

Hops, H., Sherman, L., & Biglan, A. (1990). Maternal depression, marital discord, and children's behavior: A developmental perspective. In G. R. Patterson (Ed.), *Advances in family research: Depression and aggression: Two facets of family interactions* (Vol. 1). Hillsdale, NJ: Lawrence Erlbaum Associates.

Horowitz, M., Schaefer, C., Hiroto, D., Wilner, N., & Levin, B. (1977). Life event questionnaire for measuring presumptive stress. *Psychosomatic Medicine, 39,* 413–431.

Jacobson, N. S., & Gurman, A. S. (1986). *Clinical handbook of marital therapy.* New York: Guilford.

Janis, I. (1958). *Psychological stress: Psychoanalytic and behavioral studies of surgical patients.* New York: Wiley.

Kelley, H. H., Berscheid, E., Christensen, A., Harvey, J. H., Huston, T. L., Levinger, G., McClintock, E., & Peplau, L. A. (1983). *Close relationships.* New York: W. H. Freeman.

Kerig, P. K. (1989). *The engendered family: The influence of marital satisfaction on gender differences in parent-child interaction.* Unpublished doctoral dissertation. University of California, Berkeley.

Kumar, R., & Robson, K. M. (1984). A prospective study of emotional disorders in childbearing women. *British Journal of Psychiatry, 144,* 35–47.

LaRossa, R., & LaRossa, M. M. (1981). *Transition to parenthood: How infants change families.* Beverly Hills: Sage.

Lazarus, R. L. (1991). *Emotion and adaptation.* Oxford: Oxford University Press.

Lazarus, R. L., & Folkman, S. (1984). *Stress, appraisal, and coping.* New York: Springer.

Leifer, M. (1980). *Psychological effects of motherhood: A study of first pregnancy.* New York: Praeger.

LeMasters, E. E. (1957). Parenthood as crisis. *Marriage and Family Living, 19,* 352–355.

Levant, R. F. (1988). Education for fatherhood. In P. Bronstein & C. P. Cowan (Eds.), *Fatherhood today: Men's changing role in the family* (pp. 253–275). New York: Wiley.

Leventhal-Belfer, L. J. (1990). *Child care, parents, and partners: A new perspective.* Unpublished doctoral dissertation, University of California, Berkeley.

Leventhal-Belfer, L. J., Cowan, P. A., & Cowan, C. P. (in press). Child care as a couples' issue: The links between parents' satisfaction with child care decisions, partners' satisfaction, and adaptation to parenthood. *American Journal of Orthopsychiatry.*

Levenson, R. W., & Gottman, J. M. (1985). Physiological and affective predictors of change in relationship satisfaction. *Journal of Personality and Social Psychology, 49,* 85–94.

Lewinsohn, P. H., Steinmetz, J. L., Larsen, D. W., & Franklin, J. (1981). Depression-related cognitions: Antecedents or consequences? *Journal of Abnormal Psychology, 90,* 213–219.

Lewis, J. M., Owen, M. T., & Cox, M. J. (1988). The transition to parenthood: III. Incorporation of the child into the family. *Family Process, 27,* 411–421.

Lewis, R. A., & Spanier, G. B. (1979). Theorizing about the quality and stability of marriage. In W. R. Burr, R. Hill, F. I. Nye, & I. L. Reiss (Eds.), *Contemporary theories about the family* (Vol. 1, pp. 269–294). New York: Free Press.

Lieberman, M. A. (1981). The effects of social support in response to stress. In L. Goldberger & S. Breznitz (Eds.), *Handbook of stress* (pp. 764–781). New York: Free Press.

Locke, H., & Wallace, K. (1959). Short marital adjustment and prediction tests: Their reliability and validity. *Marriage and Family Living, 21,* 251–255.

Loewen, J. W. (1988). Visitation fatherhood. In P. Bronstein & C. P. Cowan (Eds.), *Fatherhood today: Men's changing role in the family* (pp. 195–213). New York: Wiley.

Lowe, L. (1991). *Transition to grandmotherhood*. Unpublished doctoral dissertation, Center for Psychological Studies, Albany, CA.

Lowinsky, N. R. (1990). Mother of mothers: The power of the grandmother in the female psyche. In C. Zweig (Ed.), *To be a woman: The birth of the conscious feminine* (pp. 86–97). Los Angeles: J. P. Tarcher.

Lowinsky, N. R. (1992). *Stories from the motherline: Reclaiming the mother-daughter bond, finding our feminine souls*. Los Angeles: J. P. Tarcher.

Maccoby, E. E., & Martin, J. A. (1983). Socialization in the context of the family: Parent-child interaction. In E. M. Hetherington (Ed.), P. H. Mussen (Series Ed.), *Handbook of child psychology: Vol. 4. Socialization, personality and social development* (4th ed., pp. 1–101). New York: Wiley.

McGuire, J. C., & Gottlieb, B. (1979). Social support groups among new parents: An experimental study in primary prevention. *Journal of Clinical Child Psychology, 8,* 111–116.

McHale, S. M., & Huston, T. L. (1985). The effect of the transition to parenthood on the marriage relationship. *Journal of Family Issues, 6,* 409–433.

Main, M., & Goldwyn, R. (1984). Predicting rejection of her infant from mother's representation of her own experience: Implications for the abused-abusing intergenerational cycle. *Child Abuse and Neglect, 8,* 203–217.

Main, M., & Goldwyn, R. (in press). Adult attachment classification system. In M. Main (Ed.), *A typology of human attachment organization: Assessed in discourse, drawings and interviews*. New York: Cambridge University Press.

Main, M., Kaplan, N., & Cassidy, J. (1985). Security in infancy, childhood, and adulthood: A move to the level of representation. In I. Bretherton & E. Waters (Eds.), *Growing points of attachment theory and research. Monographs of the Society for Research in Child Development, 50* (Serial No. 209, pp. 66–106).

Martin, B. (1975). Parent-child relations. In F. D. Horowitz (Ed.), *Review of child development research* (Vol. 4, pp. 463–540). Chicago: University of Chicago Press.

Markman, H. J., & Kadushin, F. S. (1986). Preventive effects of Lamaze training for first-time parents: A short-term longitudinal study. *Journal of Consulting and Clinical Psychology, 54,* 872–874.

Markman H., & Notarius C. (1987). Coding marital and family interaction. In T. Jacob (Ed.), *Family interaction and psychopathology* (pp. 329–390). New York: Plenum.

Menning, B. (1977). *Infertility: A guide for childless couples*. Englewood Cliffs, NJ: Prentice-Hall.

Michaels, G. Y. (1988). Motivational factors in the decision and timing of pregnancy. In G. Y. Michaels & W. A. Goldberg (Eds.), *The transition to parenthood: Current theory and research* (pp. 23–61). Cambridge: Cambridge University Press.

Miller, N. B., Cowan, P. A., Cowan, C. P., Hetherington, E. M., & Clingempeel, G. (1991, August). Externalizing in preschoolers and early adolescents: A cross-study replication of a family model. Paper presented to the American Sociological Association, Cincinnati, OH.

Miller, W. (1978). The intendedness and wantedness of the first child. In W. Miller and L. Newman (Eds.), *The first child and family formation* (pp. 209–243). Chapel Hill, NC: Carolina Population Center.

Minuchin, S., & Fishman, H. C. (1981). *Family therapy techniques*. Cambridge, MA: Harvard University Press.

Moorehouse, M. (in press). Work and family dynamics. In P. A. Cowan, D. Field, D.

Hansen, A. Skolnick, & G. E. Swanson (Eds.), *Family, self, and society: Toward a new agenda for family research*. Hillsdale, NJ: Lawrence Erlbaum Associates.

Moos, R. H. (1974). *Family Environment Scale*. Palo Alto, CA: Consulting Psychologists Press.

Morgan, S. P., Lye, D. N., & Condran, G. A. (1988). Sons, daughters, and the risk of marital disruption. *American Journal of Sociology, 94,* 110–129.

Mussen, P. H., Conger, J. P., & Kagan, J. (1984). *Child development and personality* (6th ed.). New York: Harper & Row.

Myers-Walls, J. A., & Sudsberry, R. L. (1982). Parent education during the transition into parenthood. In N. Stinnett, J. DeFrain, K. King, H. Lingren, G. Rowe, S. van Zandt, & R. Williams (Eds.), *Family strengths: Positive models for family life* (pp. 49–65). Lincoln: University of Nebraska Press.

Nathanson, S. (1989). *Soul crisis: One woman's journey through abortion to renewal*. New York: New American Library.

Nott, P. N., Franklin, M., Armitage, C., & Gelder, M. G. (1976). Hormonal changes and mood in the puerperium. *British Journal of Psychiatry, 128,* 379–383.

Nuckolls, K. B., Cassell, J., & Kaplan, B. H. (1972). Psychosocial assets, life crisis, and the prognosis of pregnancy. *American Journal of Epidemiology, 95,* 431–441.

Oakley, A. (1980). *Women confined*. Oxford: Martin Robertson.

Oakley, A. (1986). *From here to maternity*. New York: Viking Penguin.

O'Donnel, J. P., & VanTuinen, M. V. (1979). Behavior problems of preschool children: Dimensions and congenital correlates. *Journal of Abnormal Child Psychology, 7,* 61–75.

O'Hara, M. W. (1986). Social support, life events, and depression during pregnancy and the puerperim. *Archives of General Psychiatry, 43,* 569–573.

Olson, L. (1983). *Costs of children*. Lexington, MA: D. C. Heath.

Osofsky, H. (1982). Expectant and new fatherhood as a developmental crisis. *Bulletin of the Menninger Clinic, 46,* 209–230.

Osofsky, J. D., & Osofsky, H. J. (1984). Psychological and developmental perspectives on expectant and new parenthood. In R. D. Parke (Ed.), *Review of child development research: Vol. 7. The family* (pp. 372–397). Chicago: University of Chicago Press.

Parens, H. (1975). Parenthood as a developmental phase. *Journal of the American Psychoanalytic Association, 23,* 154–165.

Parke, R. D. (1979). Perspectives on father-infant interaction. In J. Osofsky (Ed.), *Handbook of infant development* (pp. 549–590). New York: Wiley.

Parke, R. D., & Tinsley, B. (1982). The early environment of the at-risk infant: Expanding the social context. In D. D. Bricker (Ed.), *Intervention with at-risk and handicapped infants*. Baltimore: University Park Press.

Parkes, C. M. (1971). Psycho-social transitions: A field for study. *Social Science and Medicine 5,* 101–115.

Parlee, M. B. (1973). The premenstrual syndrome. *Psychological Bulletin, 83,* 454–465.

Parsons, T., & Bales, R. F. (1955). *Family, socialization, and interaction process*. Glencoe, IL: Free Press.

Patterson, G. (Ed.). (1990). *Depression and aggression: Two facets of family interactions: Advances in family research* (Vol. 1). Hillsdale, NJ: Lawrence Erlbaum Associates.

Pearson, J. L., Cohn, D. A., Cowan, P. A., & Cowan, C. P. (1991). Adults' working models of attachment: Self-defined resiliency and adult adjustment. Unpublished manuscript.

Phillips, D. A., & Howes, C. (1987). Indicators of quality in child care: Review of research. In D. A. Phillips (Ed.), *Quality in child care: What does research tell us?* (pp. 1–20). Research Monograph of the National Association for the Education of Young Children.

Piaget, J. (1967). *Six psychological studies* (D. Elkind, Ed.). New York: Random House.

Pleck, J. (1985). *Working wives/working husbands.* Beverly Hills, CA: Sage.

Powell, D. R. (1987). A neighborhood approach to parent support groups. *Journal of Community Psychology, 15,* 51–62.

Pratt, M., Kerig, P., Cowan, P. A., & Cowan, C. P. (1988). Mothers and fathers teaching three-year-olds: Authoritative parenting and adult scaffolding of young children's learning. *Developmental Psychology, 24,* 832–839.

Pratt, M., Kerig, P., Cowan, P. A., & Cowan, C. P. (in press). Family worlds: Couple satisfaction, parenting style, and mothers' and fathers' speech to young children, *Merrill-Palmer Quarterly.*

Pruett, K. D. (1986). *The nurturing father.* New York: Warner.

Quindlen, A. (May 21, 1991). Speech to National Press Club. National Public Radio.

Quinton, D., Rutter, M., & Liddle, C. (1984). Institutional rearing, parenting difficulties, and marital support. *Psychological Medicine, 14,* 107–124.

Radin, N. (1988). Primary caregiving fathers of long duration. In P. Bronstein & C. P. Cowan (Eds.), *Fatherhood today: Men's changing role in the family* (pp. 127–143). New York: Wiley.

Radloff, L. (1977). Sex differences in depression: The effects of occupation and marital status. *Sex Roles, 1,* 249–265.

Ramey, C. T., Collier, A. M., Sparling, J. J., Loda, F. A., Campbell, F. A., Ingram, D. L., & Finkelstein, N. W. (1976). The Carolina Abecedarian Project: A longitudinal and multidisciplinary approach to the prevention of developmental retardation. In T. Tjossem (Ed.), *Intervention strategies for high-risk infants and young children* (pp. 629–665). Baltimore, MD: University Park Press.

Rapoport, R., Rapoport, R., & Strelitz, Z. (1977). *Mothers, fathers, and society: Towards new alliances.* New York: Basic Books.

Robinson, J. (1977). *Changes in American's use of time: 1975–1976—A progress report.* Cleveland, Ohio: Communications Research Center, Cleveland State University.

Russell, G. (1983). *The changing role of fathers?* St. Lucia: University of Queensland Press.

Rutter, M. (1987). Psychosocial resilience and protective mechanisms. *American Journal of Orthopsychiatry, 57,* 316–331.

Scarr, S. (1984). *Mother care, other care.* New York: Basic Books.

Schaefer, E. S., & Hunter, W. M. (1983, April). Mother-infant interaction and maternal psychosocial predictors of kindergarten adaptation. Paper presented to the Society for Research in Child Development, Detroit, MI.

Schulz, M. (1991, April). Linkages among both parents' work roles, parenting style, and children's adjustment to school. Paper presented at the meetings of the Society for Research in Child Development, Seattle, WA.

Schwebel, A. I., Fine, M., & Moreland, J. R. (1988). Clinical work with divorced and widowed fathers: The adjusting family model. In P. Bronstein & C. P. Cowan (Eds.), *Fatherhood today: Men's changing role in the family* (pp. 299–322). New York: Wiley.

Seligman, M. E. P. (1975). *Helplessness: On depression, development, and death.* San Francisco: W. H. Freeman.

Shapiro, C. H. (1982). The impact of infertility in the marital relationship. *Social Casework, 63,* 387–393.

Shereshefsky, P., & Yarrow, L. J. (Eds.). (1973). *Psychological aspects of a first pregnancy and early postnatal adaptation.* New York: Raven Press.

Sheehy, G. (1976). *Passages: Predictable crises in adult life.* New York: E. P. Dutton.

Skolnick, A. (1991). *Embattled paradise: The American family in an age of uncertainty.* New York: Basic Books.

Snarey, J., Son, L., Kuehne, V., Hauser, S., & Vaillant, G. (1987). The role of parenting in men's psychosocial development: A longitudinal study of early adulthood infertility and midlife generativity. *Developmental Psychology, 23,* 593–603.

Stafford, R., Backman, E., & Dibona, P. (1977). The division of labor among cohabiting and married couples. *Journal of Marriage and the Family, 39,* 43–57.

Steinberg, L., & Belsky, J. (1991). *Infancy, childhood, and adolescence: Development in context.* New York: McGraw-Hill.

Steinglass, P., with Bennett, L. A., Wolin, S. J., & Reiss, D. (1987). *The alcoholic family.* New York: Basic Books.

Szinovacz, M. E. (1977). Role allocation, family structure and female employment. *Journal of Marriage and the Family, 39,* 781–791.

Tannen, D. (1990). *You just don't understand: Women and men in conversation.* New York: William Morrow.

Teachman, J. D., Polonko, K. A., & Scanzoni, J. (1987). Demography of the family. In M. B. Sussman & S. K. Steinmetz (Eds.), *Handbook of marriage and the family* (pp. 3–36). New York: Plenum.

Tinsley, B. J., & Parke, R. D. (1988). The role of grandfathers in the context of the family. In P. Bronstein & C. P. Cowan (Eds.), *Fatherhood today: Men's changing role in the family* (pp. 236–252). New York: Wiley.

Towne, R. D., & Afterman, J. (1955). Psychoses in males related to parenthood. *Bulletin of the Menninger Clinic, 19,* 19.

Trethowan, W. H., & Conlan, M. F. (1965). The couvade syndrome. *British Journal of Psychiatry, 111,* 57–66.

Wainwright, W. H. (1966). Fatherhood as a precipitant of mental illness. *American Journal of Psychiatry, 123,* 40–44.

Wallerstein, J., & Blakeslee, S. (1989). *Second chances: Men, women, and children a decade after divorce.* New York: Ticknor & Fields.

Wandersman, L. P. (1987). Parent-infant support groups: Matching programs to needs and strengths of families. In C. F. Z. Boukydis (Ed.), *Research on support for parents in the postnatal period.* Norwood, NJ: Ablex.

Weissman, M. M., & Klerman, G. L. (1977). Sex differences and the epidemiology of depression. *Archives of General Psychiatry, 34,* 98–112.

Weitzman, L. J. (1985). *The divorce revolution: The unexpected social and economic consequences for women and children in America.* New York: Free Press.

Wenner, N. K., Cohen, M. B., Weigert, E. V., Kvarnes, R. G., Ohaneson, E. M., & Fearing, J. M. (1969). Emotional problems in pregnancy. *Psychiatry, 32,* 389–410.

Werner, H. (1948). *The comparative psychology of mental development.* New York: Follett.

Whelan, E. M. (1975). *A baby? . . . maybe: A guide to making the most fateful decision of your life.* New York: Bobbs-Merrill.

Wile, D. (1981). *Couples therapy: A nontraditional approach.* New York: Wiley.

Wile, D. (1988). *After the honeymoon: How conflict can improve your relationship.* New York: Wiley.

Zajicek, E. (1981). The experience of being pregnant. In S. Wolkind and E. Zajicek

(Eds.), *Pregnancy: A psychological and social study* (pp. 31–56). London: Academic Press/New York: Grune & Stratton.

Zaslow, M., Pedersen, F., Kramer, E., Cain, R., Suwalsky, J., & Fivel, M. I. (1981, April). Depressed mood in new fathers: Interview and behavioral correlates. Paper presented at the Society for Research in Child Development, Boston, MA.

Zilboorg, G. (1931). Depressive reactions related to parenthood. *American Journal of Psychiatry, 87,* 927–962.

INDEX

Abortion, 23

Acceptance-of-Fate couples, 33, 39–41; marital satisfaction of, 46–47, 111; pregnancy and, 48

Adjective Check List, 81, 84–85, 88, 156, 176, 192

Adoption, 12

Affairs, extramarital, 56n

Age: of couples in study, 7; self-esteem with parenthood and, 85–88

Aggression, of children, 160

Alcoholism, 142–43, 146

Alice and Andy (case study), 24, 43–45, 47, 56, 79, 193, 199–200

Ambivalent couples, 34, 39n, 41–42; marital satisfaction of, 46–47, 111; pregnancy and, 48, 49, 59–60

Anna and Henry (case study), 66, 68, 140–42

Annie and Mitch (case study), 165, 166, 168–69, 178

Antonucci, Toni, 88

Anxiety: concerning childbirth, 71; of expectant fathers, 55–58; importance of discussing, 62–63, 69, 206; of pregnant women, 54–55

Ariel and Harry (case study), 40

Attachment: insecure, 145–48; secure, 145–48

Attribution theory, 192

Authoritarian parenting style, 153–56

Authoritative parenting style, 152–55, 158

Baby sitters, 131

Ball, Jessica, 185, 189, 194

Bateson, Gregory, 187

Baumrind, Diana, 152

Becoming a Family Project, x–xi, 7–12, 29–30, 89, 202–13; at-risk couples in, 204–6; couple relationship and development of children, 10–12, 209–10; couples groups, 165–83; couples in, 7–10, 168; implications of results, 206–12;

Becoming a Family Project (*continued*)
Phase I, 10–11; Phase II, 10–12; staff couples in, 9*n*, 168. *See also* Case studies

Bedtime routines, 79

Belsky, Jay, 4, 8, 110, 112, 126

Bernard, Jessie, 92

Beth and Paul (case study), 37–38, 49, 51–52, 55, 56, 62, 63, 110, 130, 152, 160, 189–90

Birth control, 22; in Acceptance-of-Fate couples, 40; hazards of, 23; new forms of, 23

Birthrate, 23–24

Blaming behavior, 110, 160, 167

Block, Jack, 156

Block, Jeanne, 155, 156

Boles, Abner, III, 9*n*, 168

Bowlby, John, 145

Brazelton, Barry, 127

Breastfeeding, 103–4, 106, 174–75

Breast infections, 106

Bronfenbrenner, Urie, 5

Canada, 27

Career issues: attitudes and practices in workplace, 123; balance of family life with work life, 115, 116, 123–24; child care as, 104, 126–29, 158–59; for father after birth of child, 77–79, 104, 117–23; identity as parent, 82, 86–88; impact of working women on children, 124–25; for mother after birth of child, 77–79, 116–22, 124–25; of new parents, 77–79, 117–22; parenthood decision and, 35; parents' work patterns, 122–25; pregnancy and, 55–56, 60, 63, 67–68, 122–23; self-esteem of parents, 86–88; women's work history and well-being during pregnancy, 122–23; work/family arrangements and, 117–22

Case studies: age of couples in, 7; Alice and Andy, 24, 43–45, 47, 56, 79, 193, 199–200; Anna and Henry, 66, 68, 140–42; Annie and Mitch, 165, 166, 168–69, 178; Ariel and Harry, 40; Beth and Paul, 37–38, 49, 51–52, 55, 56, 62, 63, 110, 130, 152, 160, 189–90; Celie and Ray, 104,

113; Cindy and James, 28, 64, 66, 120–21; Connie and Len, 145–48; Dawn and Peter, 174–75; Evelyn and Marty, 35–36; Gail and Michael, 117–19, 122–23, 128–29; Helen and Al, 55–56, 63; Ingrid and Mark, 188; Joan and Rob, 31, 32, 41–42, 61, 64–65, 80, 106–7, 156, 165, 168–71, 173, 175, 182–83; Josie and Doug, 55, 76, 78, 79, 93–94, 103; Karen and Seth, 38, 39; Marian and Bruce, 87–88; Natalie and Victor, 16–22, 26–27, 76–77, 95–97, 102, 104, 121–22, 129; Pauline and Mel, 138–39, 196–97; Peggy and Bill, 33, 49, 51, 53, 55, 57–61, 80–81, 105–6, 112–13, 133–35, 150–52, 159, 160, 191, 192, 196, 198; Sandi and Martin, 107, 168–71; Shannon and John, 24–25, 36–37, 98, 103, 114–15, 132; Sharon and Daniel, 15–16, 23, 62–63, 77–79, 91–92, 106, 119, 120, 151, 185–86, 190; Sheila and Bart, 40–41; Sonia and Eduardo, 49–50, 55, 59, 69; Stephanie and Art, 82–83, 108, 115–16, 131; subjects of, 7–12; Tanya and Jackson, 71, 86–87, 97–100, 102, 130, 137, 165, 168–69, 181, 198; Valerie and Tom, 43; Yu-Mei and Steve, 42, 45

Caspi, Avshalom, 143, 144

Celie and Ray (case study), 104, 113

Center for Epidemiological Study of Depression Scale (CES-D), 8

Cesarean section delivery, 71, 76, 106, 172

Child abuse, 140

Childbirth, 171–72; anxiety of, 54–58, 71; breastfeeding after, 103–4, 106, 174–75; career issues of parents following, 77–79, 104, 116–25; cesarean section delivery, 71, 76, 106, 172; preparing for, 69–71; timing of, 23. *See also* Pregnancy

Childbirth preparation classes, 3–4, 54, 70–71, 111–12, 169

Child care, 104, 115, 116, 125–31; choice to use, 126–29; conflict about, 20–21, 158–59; development of children and, 126; division of labor in, 20–22, 26–27, 97–99, 101–3, 111–12; financial arrangements and, 31–32, 119, 124, 127; gender stereotypes in, 130–31, 172–73; men as primary caretakers, 100–101; prevalence of use of, 125–26; as problem for couples, 203; shortage of, 125–26; types of, 129–31. *See also* Family roles; Work/family arrangements

Chodorow, Nancy, 128

Choices. *See* Decision-making process

Cindy and James (case study), 28, 64, 66, 120–21

Cognitive development: child care outside home and, 126; work by mothers outside home and, 125

Cohn, Deborah, 146

Coie, John, 4, 168

Coie, Lynne, 4, 168

Communication, 2, 3, 184–201, 205–6; by Ambivalent couples, 42; in decision-making process, 36; defined, 187; differences between partners and, 193–97; difficulty of, within couples, 171; discussion of child and, 187, 198–99; emotional intimacy of new parents, 105–6; of expectations and anxiety, 62–63, 69, 206; family adaptation and, 200–201; family breakdown and, 199–200; gender and style of, 193–94; hidden challenges of, 187–97; importance of, in couples, 21–22; individuality vs. mutuality and, 188–90; making time for, 207; marital satisfaction and, 46–47, 195–97; memories and, 193; mind reading and, 191; negative attribution and, 192; one-sided perspectives and, 190–92; outside couple relationship, 3; regulating feeling in, 194–97; sexuality during pregnancy and, 59–61; shifts in, 18–19; triangulation of child in, 198–99. *See also* Decision-making process

Conflict: about child care, 20–21, 158–59; about family roles, 107–8, 128–29; of Ambivalent couples, 34, 41–42; around career issues vs. child care, 158–59; between dependency and individuality, 28–29, 63–64, 68; exploration of marital, 170–71; in family of origin, 64–67, 143–44; of family values, 27–28; gender stereotypes in handling, 195–97; impact on children, 161; increased choices and, 23–24; individuality and, 28–29, 63–64, 68; intergenerational patterns during pregnancy, 64–67, 143–44; intimacy and, 185, 187; isolation and, 24–25; parenthood as source of, 35–36, 107–10, 120, 196–99; parenting style and, 150–51, 154–58, 161; problem-solving effectiveness and, 46–47; social policy and, 26–27; triangulation of children in, 198–99; unshared expectations during pregnancy and, 61–63, 206; women's roles and, 25–26, 118–20; over work/family arrangements, 25–26, 118–20; of Yes-No couples, 34, 42–45

Connie and Len (case study), 145–48

Counseling, 134–35, 208–9

Couples groups, 9, 9n, 165–83, 206, 208–9; anticipation of parenthood and, 169–71; group leader role in, 173–74; longer-term effects of, 179–83; realities of parenthood and, 171–73; reasons for intervention with, 167–75; resources available for parents, 166–67; short-term effects of, 175–79; as support vs. therapy, 174–75

Couples in study. *See* Case studies

Couvade syndrome, 52

Cox, Martha, 5

Coysh, Bill, 9n, 168

Crisis: characteristics of, 6–7; couples groups and, 174–75; dealing with, 69

Curtis-Boles, Harriet, 9n, 168

Dawn and Peter (case study), 174–75

Day care. *See* Child care

Death, 115

Decision-making process, 31–47, 185, 205; Acceptance-of-Fate couples and, 33, 39–41, 46–47; Ambivalent couples and, 34, 39n, 41–42, 46–47; costs of having children, 31–32, 127; family making and, 32–34; as family role, 97; marital satisfaction and, 46–47, 97; Planners and, 33, 34–39; psychological aspects of having children, 32; Yes-No couples and, 34, 39n, 42–45. *See also* Problem-solving process

Dependency issues: parenting style and, 155, 157–58; during pregnancy, 63–64, 68

Depression, 205; child-care arrangements and, 131; of mothers, 29, 95, 122–23; of

Depression *(continued)*
  new fathers, 102; parenting style and, 158, 158n; prediction of, 89; return to work by mother and, 122–23; scale for measuring, 8; vulnerability of girls to, 157–58
Disengaged parenting style, 152–53
Division of labor. *See* Family roles
Divorce and separation: decision to have children and, 32; in family of origin, 141–42, 145, 146; formation of family and, 2–3; gender differences in relationships with children and, 156–57; hormone changes and, 54; impact of couples groups on, 178–79; impact on children, 161; infertility and, 39; negative attribution and, 192; of new parents, 107–10; of nonparents, 84, 109; of parents vs. nonparents, 109; rate of, x; repeating generational cycles and, 141–42, 145, 146; by Yes-No couples, 43–45, 47. *See also* Marital satisfaction
Doctors, as part of support system, 134–35, 210–11
Doering, Susan, 51
Due date surprises, 38–39
Dura, Jason, 54
Dysfunctional families: alcoholism in, 142–43, 146; child abuse in, 140; parenting decision and, 43–45. *See also* Family of origin

Egalitarian system, 93–95, 97, 104; child care and, 20–22, 26–27; decline in marital satisfaction with children and, 110–13; in family decision making, 97; of nonparents, 96; as unfulfilled promise, 100. *See also* Family roles
Eighteen-month-postpartum period: family roles in, 96, 98–99, 101–2; marital satisfaction in, 106, 110
Elder, Glen, 143, 144
Emotional intimacy. *See* Intimacy
England, 27
Entwisle, Doris, 51
Episiotomy, 106, 112
Epperson, Barbara, 192

Erikson, Erik, 69, 182
Evelyn and Marty (case study), 35–36
Expectant couples, 43–45; ambivalence in, 34, 41–42, 46–47; anxiety of, 54–58, 71; before and after childbirth, 9–10; childbirth preparation classes for, 3–4, 54, 70–71, 111–12, 169; child care division of labor and, 97–98; conflict in family of origin, 64–67, 143–44; in couples groups, 9, 9n, 165–83; marital satisfaction of, 8, 46–47, 108; resources available for, 166–67; therapy groups for, 4, 9, 9n, 165–83; transition to parenthood and, 153–54; unplanned pregnancy and, 33, 39–41. *See also* Couples groups; Fathers; Mothers; Pregnancy
Expectations: about parenting, 170; for child care division of labor, 97–98, 111–12; couples groups and, 180; of family roles after childbirth, 97–98, 111–12; importance of sharing, 61–63, 206; unshared, during pregnancy, 61–63
Extended family relationships, 137–49; alcoholism and, 142–43, 146; breaking the generational cycle in, 143–48; child abuse and, 140; child-care support and, 121–22, 133; conflict and, 64–67, 139–40, 143–44; egalitarian roles and, 104; impact of birth of child on, 138–39; during pregnancy, 64–67; repairing misunderstandings and rifts in, 139–40; repeating generational cycle in, 140–43; shifts of roles in, 5, 19; as support system, 121–22, 133. *See also* Family of origin
Extramarital affairs, 56n

Family life, domains of, 16–22, 44–45; extended family relationships, 5, 19, 137–49; identity, 5, 16–17, 75–90; marital satisfaction, 5, 17–19, 91–113; parenting style and first child, 5, 20–22, 150–61; stress outside the family, 5, 19–20, 205
Family of origin: alcoholism in, 142–43, 146; birth of baby and, 138, 203–4; child abuse in, 140; child care by father and,

103–4; choice to use child care and, 128–29; conflict in, 64–67, 139–40, 143–44; couples groups in exploring, 170, 172–73; difficulty of parenting decision and, 43–45; divorce and separation in, 141–42, 145, 146; family roles and, 95, 104; pregnancy and memories of childhood, 65, 69; relationship with parents in, 144–48; repairing misunderstandings and rifts in, 139–40; as support system, 121–22, 133. *See also* Extended family relationships

Family policy, 104, 131; lack of, 27, 204, 211–12

Family Research Consortium, 5

Family roles, 92–104; child care and, 20–22, 26–27, 97–99, 101–3, 111–12, 128–31; conflict around, 107–8, 128–29; egalitarian approach to, 93–95, 97; family decisions in, 97; father's involvement in, 26, 92–104; his and her view of division of labor in, 99–100; household and family tasks, 93–97; impact of couples groups on, 176–77, 179–81; lack of equity in, 93–95; marital satisfaction and, 92–104, 176–77; of nonparents, 97, 100; sharing of, 62–63; shifts in, 17–19, 80–84, 89, 105–7; transition to parenthood and, 157; Who Does What? questionnaire, 95–100, 194. *See also* Child care; Decision-making process; Egalitarian system; Fathers; Mothers; Parenthood; Work/family arrangements

Family size, 23–24

Fathers: active role of, 209–10; anxiety of expectant, 52, 55–58; career issues and birth of child, 77–79, 104, 117–22, 123; in choice of child-care arrangements, 100–101, 130–31; depression of, 102; family roles of, 26, 93–95, 100–101; impact of couples groups on, 180, 181; involvement of, in family roles, 92–104; juggling work and family, 123–24; parenting style and gender of child, 154–58, 161; participation in pregnancy process, 210; paternity leave, 104, 123; postpartum stress of, 28, 29–30n, 102; return to work after childbirth, 116–17; self-esteem with parenthood and, 85–88;

support groups for, 134. *See also* Gender stereotypes; Marital satisfaction; Men; Parenthood

Feldman, Shirley, 4

Financial arrangements, 119, 124; child care and, 127; costs of having children, 31–32

First trimester of pregnancy, 51, 59

Flexible work schedules, 27, 212

Friends, as social supports, 132–33, 208–9

Gail and Michael (case study), 117–19, 122–23, 128–29

Garrett, Ellen, 9n, 168

Geijer, Gustav, 92

Gender stereotypes: about mothers' work, 116–17; for child care, 130–31, 172–73; in communication style, 193–94; conflict and, 195–97; parenting style of father and, 154–58, 161. *See also* Men; Women

Gottman, John, 194–96

Gough, Harrison, 85

Grandparents: alcoholism of, 142–43, 146; birth of grandchildren and, 138, 203–4; child care by, 121–22, 133; egalitarian family roles and, 104; role shifts and, 5, 19. *See also* Extended family relationships; Family of origin

Grossman, Frances, 4

Harber, Karen, 120

Health professionals, as part of support system, 134–35, 210–11

Heilbrun, Alfred, 85

Heinicke, Christoph, 4

Helen and Al (case study), 55–56, 63

Heming, Gertrude, 4, 89

Hetherington, Mavis, 5, 156

Hochschild, Arlie, 26, 94–95, 100, 125

Hoffman, Lois, 37

Hoffman, Martin, 37

Hormonal changes: physical symptoms of

Hormonal changes *(continued)*
  pregnancy and, 51–52; psychological
  symptoms of pregnancy and, 53–55
Huston, Ted, 5

Identity, 75–90; as career issue, 82, 86–88;
  changes in, with parenthood, 80–83;
  connection between well-being and, 83–
  84; dependency issues during pregnancy, 63–64, 68; impact of couples
  groups on, 176, 179; shifts in, 5, 16–17,
  83–84, 106–7. *See also* Individuality;
  Self-esteem
Illness, 115
Important People questionnaire, 135–36
Independence. *See* Individuality
Individual counseling, 134–35, 208–9
Individuality, 28–29, 204; balancing mutuality with, 188–90; dependency issues
  during pregnancy, 63–64, 68; one-sided
  perspective and, 190–92
Infertility, 38–39
Ingrid and Mark (case study), 188
Inner life. *See* Identity; Self-esteem
Insecure attachment relationships, 145–48
Institute of Human Development (University of California at Berkeley), 11–12
Intimacy: balancing individuality and
  mutuality in, 188–90; conflict and, 185,
  187; family roles and, 105–6, 129;
  friendships and, 132–33, 208–9; insecure attachment relationships and, 145–
  48; making time for, 207; one-sided perspective and, 190–92; during pregnancy,
  56, 58–61; secure attachment relationships and, 145–48
Isolation: of new mothers, 20; as stress of
  parenthood, 22, 24–25

Janis, Irving, 55*n*
Jealousy, of grandparents, 19
Joan and Rob (case study), 31, 32, 41–42,
  61, 64–65, 80, 106–7, 156, 165, 168–71,
  173, 175, 182–83
Jones, Enrico, 180

Josie and Doug (case study), 55, 76, 78, 79,
  93–94, 103

Karen and Seth (case study), 38, 39
Kerig, Patricia, 155
Kiecolt-Glazer, Janice, 54
Kindergarten period, 11–12, 159–61, 179,
  200

Labor, division of. *See* Family roles
Leach, Penelope, 127
LeMasters, Edward E., 6–7, 29
Levenson, Robert, 194–96
Leventhal-Belfer, Laurie, 127
Life Events questionnaire, 135
Locke-Wallace Brief Marital Adjustment
  Test, 8
Loneliness, of new mothers, 20
Lowinsky, Naomi, 66, 129

Main, Mary, 145, 146
Marian and Bruce (case study), 87–88
Marital dance, 103–4
Marital satisfaction, 6, 91–113; of Acceptance-of-Fate couples, 46–47, 111; of
  Ambivalent couples, 46–47, 111; communication styles and, 46–47, 195–97;
  conflict in family of origin and, 144; decision-making process and, 46–47, 111;
  depression and, 122–23, 158; development of children and, 10–12, 209–10; of
  expectant couples, 8, 46–47, 108; exploring conflicts and, 170–71; family
  roles and, 92–104, 176–77; impact of
  couples groups on, 176–79; impact of
  parental depression on children, 158;
  impact on parenting style, 205; Locke-
  Wallace Brief Marital Adjustment Test,
  8; of new parents, 135–36; of nonparents, 46–47, 109–110; parenting style
  and, 154–58, 161; reasons for decline in,
  110–13; transition to parenthood and,
  135–36, 153–54, 177–79; work/family

arrangements and, 117–22. *See also* Communication; Divorce and separation; Family roles; Fathers; Mothers

Martin, Barclay, 210

Maternity leave, 104, 119, 120, 123

McHale, Susan, 5

Memories, in communication process, 193

Men: communication style of, 193–94; conflict in family of origin and, 144; discomfort with child care, 103; at eighteen-month-postpartum period, 77–79, 81–82, 87–88; expectations during pregnancy and, 65, 69; family roles of, 26, 93–95, 100–101; identity as parents, 80–81; mood changes during pregnancy, 55–58; networks of friends of, 132; participation in childbirth process, 71; physical changes during pregnancy and, 52; as primary caretakers, 100–101; at six-month-postpartum point, 77, 101, 102; Who Does What? questionnaire and, 95–100, 194. *See also* Fathers; Gender stereotypes

Mental health professionals, 134–35, 208–9, 211

Mikus, Karen, 88

Miller, Warren, 40

Mind reading, 191

Miscarriage, 54

Mood changes: of men during pregnancy, 55–58; of women during pregnancy, 53–55

Morning sickness, 51

Motherline, 66, 129

Mothers: attitudes toward choice to use child care, 127–29; depression of, 29, 95, 122–23; impact of working, on children, 124–25; involvement of, in family roles, 92–104; isolation of, 20; number of working, 117; maternity leave, 104, 119, 120, 123; parenting style and gender of child, 154–58, 161; postpartum stress of, 28, 29–30n; return to work after childbirth, 116–17; role in finding child-care arrangements, 130–31; second shift for working, 26, 94–95, 100, 125; self-esteem with parenthood and, 85–88; support groups for, 134; work/family arrangements, 117–22; work history of,

and well-being during pregnancy, 122–23. *See also* Marital satisfaction; Pregnancy; Women

Moving, as source of stress, 2, 22, 24–25, 116, 199–200

Mutuality: balancing individuality with, 188–90; dependency issues during pregnancy, 63–64, 68. *See also* Intimacy

Natalie and Victor (case study), 16–22, 26–27, 76–77, 95–97, 102, 104, 121–22, 129

National Institute of Mental Health, 5

Negative attribution, 192

Nonparents, 10; ambivalence in, 41; egalitarian family roles of, 96; family decisions and, 97; identity shifts and, 83–84; marital satisfaction of, 46–47, 109–10; as Planners, 35–36; satisfaction with family roles, 100; as Yes-No couples, 43

Nott, P. N., 53

Oakley, Ann, 70

Open relationships, 56n

Osofsky, Howard, 5

Osofsky, Joy, 4–5

Parental leave, 27, 104, 119, 120, 123, 212

Parent-child relationship: family of origin issues and, 137–49; gender differences regarding marital separation, 156–57; relationship between parents and, 11

Parenthood: alcoholism in family of origin and, 142–43, 146; ambivalence regarding, 34, 41–42, 46–47; anticipation of, with couples group, 169–71; conflict and, 35–36, 107–10; as crisis, 6–7; dealing with conflict in early stage of, 196–99; dealing with realities of, 171–73; difficulty of, 22–30; difficulty of preparing for, 43–45, 75–76; honeymoon period in, 76–77; identity changes with, 75–90; increased choices and, 22–24; in-

Parenthood (*continued*)
creased emotional burden with, 28–29;
isolation in, 20, 22, 24–25; need for new
role models and, 27–28; psychological
changes and, 79–90; realities of, and
couples groups, 171–73; reasons for
seeking, 36–38, 40; single parents, 12;
social policy and, 26–27, 104; teenage
parents, 8. *See also* Decision-making
process; Family roles; Fathers; Marital
satisfaction; Mothers
Parenting style, 20–22, 150–61; authoritarian, 153–56; authoritative, 153–55, 158;
conflict and, 150–51, 154–58, 161; dependency issues and, 155, 157–58; depression and, 158; dimensions of, 152–
53; exploring attitudes toward, 170;
gender of child and, 154–58, 161; impact of couples groups on, 179–80;
long-term consequences for children,
159–61; permissive, 153, 154; transition
to parenthood and, 153–54; well-being
of parents and, 158–59; working and
playing with preschoolers, 152–58. *See
also* Fathers; Mothers
Parke, Ross, 5
Parkes, C. Murray, 17
Parlee, Mary Brown, 53
Passages (Sheehy), 117
Paternity leave, 104, 123
Pauline and Mel (case study), 138–39,
196–97
Peabody Individual Achievement Test, 159
Peggy and Bill (case study), 33, 49, 51, 53,
55, 57–61, 80–81, 105–6, 112–13, 133–
35, 150–52, 159, 160, 191, 192, 196, 198
Permissive parenting style, 153, 154
Personality traits, 85, 88–90
Physicians, as part of support system, 134–
35, 210–11
Piaget, Jean, 182
Planners, 33, 34–39, 114–15; due date sur-
prises, 38–39; expectant couples, 33,
34–39; infertility, 38–39; marital satis-
faction of, 46–47, 111; nonparents, 35–
36; pregnancy and, 48, 49–50; problem-
solving effectiveness of, 46–47
Pratt, Michael, 153
Pregnancy, 48–71; Acceptance-of-Fate

couples and, 48; Ambivalent couples
and, 48, 49, 59–60; anxiety concerning,
54–58, 71; career issues and, 55–56, 60,
63, 67–68, 122–23; childbirth preparation classes, 3–4, 54, 70–71, 111–12,
169; *couvade* syndrome, 52; decision-
making process of couple and, 32; dependency issues during, 63–64, 68; due
date surprises, 38–39; family of origin
issues and, 65, 69; first trimester, 51, 59;
individual concerns about, 169–70; infertility, 38–39; intergenerational shifts
and, 64–67; intimacy during, 56, 58–61;
as medical condition, 49, 50, 70; mood
changes during, 53–58; as opportunity
for development, 68–69; physical
changes after, 106–7; physical changes
during, 51–52, 58–59, 203; planned, 36–
38, 48–50; preparing for birth and, 69–
71; psychological changes during, 52–
64, 203; relationships outside family
and, 67–68; second trimester, 54, 59;
sexuality during, 56, 56*n*, 58–61; third
trimester, 51, 54, 59, 96, 97; transition to
parenthood during, 135–36, 153–54;
unplanned, 33, 39–41; unshared expectations and, 61–63; work history of
mother and, 122–23. *See also* Childbirth;
Decision-making   process;   Fathers;
Mothers; Parenthood
Preschool period, xi, 11–12; kindergarten,
11–12, 159–61, 179, 200; parenting
style and, 152–58
Problem-solving process: experimental attitude in, 207–8; gender differences in,
194; handling feelings in, 194–97; marital satisfaction and, 46–47; Planners and,
46–47. *See also* Decision-making process

Quality of marriage. *See* Marital satisfaction

Reproduction of Mothering, The (Chodorow), 128
Role models: lack of male nurturers as, 103;
need for new family, 27–28

Roles. *See* Family roles

Rutter, Michael, 147*n*

Sandi and Martin (case study), 107, 168–71

Scarr, Sandra, 126

Schaefer, Earl, 142

Schoolchildren and Their Families Project, 183

Second shift, for working mothers, 26, 94–95, 100, 125

Second Shift, The (Hochschild), 94–95, 100

Second trimester of pregnancy, 54, 59

Secure attachment relationships, 145–48

Self-development, 28–29; pregnancy as opportunity for, 68–69

Self-employed women, 123

Self-esteem, 204–5; changes in, with parenthood, 81, 84–88; depression and eighteen-month-postpartum period, 122–23; father's involvement in family tasks and, 100–104; identity as parent and, 81, 84–88; impact of couples groups on, 176, 179; stability of, 88–90. *See also* Identity; Individuality

Self-fulfillment, 28–29

Sense of self. *See* Identity; Self-esteem

Separation, marital. *See* Divorce and separation

Sexuality: impact of couples groups on, 178; importance of, 208; parenthood and, 87–88; during pregnancy, 56, 56*n*, 58–61; shifts in family roles and, 106–7

Shannon and John (case study), 24–25, 36–37, 98, 103, 114–15, 132

Sharon and Daniel (case study), 15–16, 23, 62–63, 77–79, 91–92, 106, 119, 120, 151, 185–86, 190

Sheehy, Gail, 117

Sheila and Bart (case study), 40–41

Shyness, of children, 160

Single parenthood, 12

Six-month-postpartum period: family roles in, 96, 98; father's involvement in child care, 77, 101, 102; impact of couples groups and, 182; need for support in, 135–36; wife's satisfaction with marriage

in, 106; work/family arrangements in, 117, 118

Social development: child care outside home and, 126; work by mothers outside home and, 125

Social policy, 26–27, 104, 131, 204, 211–12

Social support, 131–36, 167; couples groups, 9, 9*n*, 165–83, 206, 208–9; extended family, 121–22, 133; friends, 132–33, 208–9; health professionals, 134–135, 208–11; mothers' and fathers' support groups, 134; moving and loss of, 2, 22, 24–25, 116, 199–200; planning to obtain, 208; stress and, 115

Sonia and Eduardo (case study), 49–50, 55, 59, 69

Spencer Foundation, xvii

Spillover effects, 5–6, 21, 153, 156, 161, 173

Spock, Benjamin, 127

Stephanie and Art (case study), 82–83, 108, 115–16, 131

Stereotypes, gender. *See* Gender stereotypes

Stress, 5, 19–20, 205; anticipation of, 55*n*; cognitive theories of, 180; decline in marital satisfaction and, 111; father's involvement in child care and, 101–3; hormone changes and, 54; isolation in parenthood, 22, 24–25; of new parents, 28, 29–30*n*, 135–36; support systems and, 115; of work/family arrangements, 117–18, 123–24

Student, mother as, 120–21

Suicide, 146

Support groups, 134. *See also* Couples groups

Sweden, 27

Tannen, Deborah, 193–94

Tanya and Jackson (case study), 71, 86–87, 97–100, 102, 130, 137, 165, 168–69, 181, 198

Teenage parents, 8

Third trimester of pregnancy, 51, 54, 59, 96, 97

Tinsley, Barbara, 5
Triangulation, 198–99

Unplanned pregnancy, 33, 39–41; Ambivalent couples and, 34, 41–42

Valerie and Tom (case study), 43
Values, conflict of family, 27–28

Werner, Heinz, 182
White, Burton, 127
Who Does What? questionnaire, 95–100, 194
Wile, Dan, 187
Withdrawal, of children, 160
Women: career prospects and motherhood, 35; communication style of, 193–94; conflict in family of origin and, 144; at eighteen-month-postpartum period, 77–79, 81–82, 87–88; family roles of, 25–26, 35, 93–95, 118–20; identity as parents, 80–82; mood changes during pregnancy, 53–55; physical changes during pregnancy and, 51–52, 58–59, 203; position of, in society, 92–93; return to work after childbirth, 77, 78, 116–17; at six-month-postpartum point, 77; Who Does What? questionnaire and, 95–100, 194; in work force, 93. *See also* Childbirth; Gender stereotypes; Mothers; Parenthood; Pregnancy
Work/family arrangements, 117–22; balance in, 115, 116, 123–24; exploring attitudes toward, 170; financial, 119, 124; mother as student, 120–21; mother at home, but unhappy, 117–19; mother planned to work, but changed mind, 119–21; mother works and likes it, 121–22. *See also* Family roles
Work force, women in, 25–27

Yes-No couples, 34, 39n, 42–45: marital satisfaction of, 46–47, 111; pregnancy and, 48
You Just Don't Understand (Tannen), 193–94
Yu-Mei and Steve (case study), 42, 45

Zajicek, Eva, 51

ANN RADCLIFFE

The ROMANCE *of the* FOREST

THE NOVELS OF ANN RADCLIFFE

The Castles of Athlin and Dunbayne (1789)

A Sicilian Romance (1790)

The Romance of the Forest (1791)

The Mysteries of Udolpho (1794)

The Italian (1797)

Gaston de Blondeville (1826)

ANN RADCLIFFE

The ROMANCE
of the FOREST

A Gothic Novel

Edited by Sandra K. Williams

IDLE SPIDER BOOKS
Sacramento, California

The Romance of the Forest: A Gothic Novel (Reader's Edition)
by Ann Radcliffe

Edited by Sandra K. Williams

Notes, map, and editorial changes
copyright © 2013 Sandra K. Williams

The Romance of the Forest was first published in 1791

This edition published in 2013 by
Idle Spider Books
www.idlespiderbooks.com

Design and typesetting by
Williams Writing, Editing & Design
Text set in Weiss BT

Idle Spider Books™ and the spider colophon are
trademarks of Williams Writing, Editing, & Design
www.williamswriting.com

ISBN 978-0-9797290-4-1

EDITOR'S NOTE

This edition has been copyedited to current American practice in respect to punctuation. Spelling has been standardized throughout using the author's preferred spelling when it could be determined. In some places words and phrases have been reordered—and in a very few cases altered or removed—to improve ease of comprehension. The interspersed poems have been eliminated. However, no scenes, no events, and no descriptions have been removed: the work stands as Ann Radcliffe wrote it, polished for today's readers.

If you need an exact reproduction of the original text or extensive footnotes, you may prefer one of the many other editions that are available. This is the *reader's* edition, intended for whiling away a solitary evening, when of course those hollow sighings and those shapes flitting past your curtains are merely the sounds and shadows of nearby branches twisting in the wind . . .

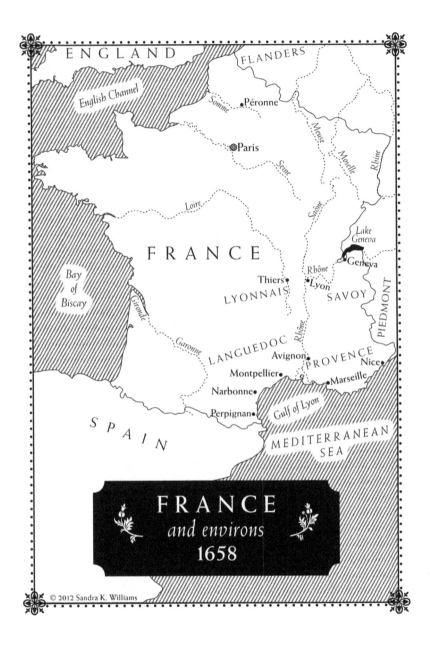

FRANCE
and environs
1658

© 2012 Sandra K. Williams

Ere the bat hath flown

His cloister'd flight, ere to black Hecate's summons

The shard-born beetle with his drowsy hums

Hath rung night's yawning peal, there shall be done

A deed of dreadful note.

—Shakespeare, *Macbeth*

CHAPTER 1

And I another,
So weary with disasters, tugg'd with fortune,
That I would set my life on any chance,
To mend it, or be rid on't.

Shakespeare, *King John*

When once sordid interest seizes on the heart, it freezes up the source of every warm and liberal feeling; it is an enemy alike to virtue and to taste—this it perverts, and that it annihilates. The time may come, my friend, when death shall dissolve the sinews of avarice, and justice be permitted to resume her rights."

Such were the words of the advocate Nemours to Pierre de la Motte, as the latter stepped at midnight into the carriage which was to bear him far from Paris, from his creditors and the persecution of the laws. La Motte thanked him for this last instance of his kindness, the assistance he had given him in escape; and when the carriage drove away uttered a sad adieu! The gloom of the hour, and the peculiar emergency of his circumstances, sank him in silent reverie.

As Madame de la Motte leaned from the coach window and gave a last look to the walls of Paris—Paris, the scene of her former happiness, and the residence of many dear friends—the fortitude which had till now supported her yielded to the force of grief. "Farewell all!" sighed she. "This last look and we are separated forever!"

Tears followed her words, and, sinking back, she resigned herself to the stillness of sorrow. The recollection of former times pressed heavily upon her heart; a few months before she was surrounded by friends, fortune, and consequence; now she was deprived of all, a miserable exile from her native place, without home, without comfort—almost without hope. It was not the least of her afflictions that she had been obliged to quit Paris without bidding adieu to her only son, who was now on duty with his regiment in Germany. Such had been the precipitancy of this removal that, had she even known where he was stationed, she had no time to inform him of it, or of the alteration in his father's circumstances.

Pierre de la Motte was a gentleman, descended from an ancient house of France. He was a man whose passions often overcame his reason and, for a time, silenced his conscience; but though the image of virtue which Nature had impressed upon his heart was sometimes obscured by the passing influence of vice, it was never wholly obliterated. With strength of mind sufficient to have withstood temptation, he would have been a good man; as it was, he was always a weak, and sometimes a vicious, member of society. Yet his mind was active and his imagination vivid, which, cooperating with the force of passion, often dazzled his judgement and subdued principle. Thus he was a man, infirm in purpose and visionary in virtue: in a word, his conduct was suggested by feeling, rather than principle; and his virtue, such as it was, could not stand the pressure of occasion.

Early in life he had married Constance Valentia, a beautiful and elegant woman, attached to her family and beloved by them. Her birth was equal, her fortune superior to his; and their nuptials had been celebrated under the auspices of an approving and flattering world. Her heart was devoted to La Motte, and for some time she found in him an affectionate husband; but, allured by the gaieties of Paris, he was soon devoted to its luxuries, and in a few years his fortune and affection were equally lost in dissipation. A false pride had still operated against his interest, and withheld him from honourable retreat while it was yet in his power; the habits which he had acquired enchained him to the scene of his former pleasure, and thus he had continued an expensive style of life till the means of prolonging it were exhausted. He at length awoke from this lethargy of security, but it was only to plunge into new error, and to attempt schemes for the reparation of his fortune which served to sink him deeper in destruction. The consequence of a transaction in which he thus engaged now drove him, with the small wreck of his property, into dangerous and ignominious exile.

It was his design to pass into one of the southern provinces and there seek, near the borders of the kingdom, an asylum in some obscure village. His family consisted of his wife, and two faithful domestics, the man Peter and the woman Annette, who followed the fortunes of their master.

The night was dark and tempestuous. About three leagues from Paris, after driving for some time over a wild heath where many ways crossed, the servant Peter, who now acted as postillion, stopped and acquainted La Motte with his perplexity. The sudden stopping of the carriage roused the latter from his reverie, and filled the whole party with the terror of pursuit; he was unable to supply the necessary direction, and the extreme darkness made it dangerous to proceed without one. During this period of distress, a light was perceived at some distance, and after much doubt and hesitation La Motte, in the hope of obtaining assistance, alighted and advanced toward it; he proceeded slowly, from the fear of unknown pits. The light issued from the window of a small and ancient house which stood alone on the heath, at the distance of half a mile.

Having reached the door, he stopped for some moments, listening in apprehensive anxiety—no sound was heard but that of the wind, which swept in hollow gusts over the waste. At length he ventured to knock, and after waiting some time, during which he indistinctly heard several voices in conversation, someone within inquired what he wanted. La Motte answered that he was a traveler who had lost his way, and desired to be directed to the nearest town.

"That," said the person, "is seven miles off, and the road bad enough, even if you could see it. If you only want a bed, you may have it here, and had better stay."

The "pitiless pelting"[1] of the storm, which at this time beat with increasing fury upon La Motte, inclined him to give up the attempt of proceeding farther till daylight; but desirous of seeing the person with whom he conversed before he ventured to expose his family by calling up the carriage, he asked to be admitted. The door was now opened by a tall figure with a light, who invited La Motte to enter. He followed the man through a passage into a room almost unfurnished, in one corner of which a bed was spread upon the floor. The forlorn and desolate aspect of this apartment made La Motte shrink involuntarily, and he was turning to go out when the man suddenly pushed him back, and he heard the door locked upon him. His heart failed, yet he made a desperate though vain effort to force the door, and called loudly for release. No answer was returned; but he distinguished the voices of men in the room above, and not doubting but their intention was to rob and murder him, his agitation at first overcame his reason. By the light of some almost-expiring embers, he perceived a window, but the hope which this discovery revived was quickly lost when he found the aperture guarded by strong iron bars. Such preparation for security surprised him, and confirmed his worst apprehensions. Alone, unarmed, beyond the chance of assistance—he saw himself in the power of people, whose trade was apparently rapine!—murder their means! After revolving every possibility of escape, he endeavoured to await the event with fortitude; but La Motte could boast of no such virtue.

---

1. Poor naked wretches, whereso'er you are, / That bide the pelting of this pitiless storm, / How shall your houseless heads and unfed sides, / Your loop'd and window'd raggedness, defend you / From seasons such as these?—Shakespeare, *King Lear.*

The voices had ceased, and all remained still for a quarter of an hour when, between the pauses of the wind, he thought he distinguished the sobs and moaning of a female. He listened attentively and became confirmed in his conjecture; it was too evidently the accent of distress. The remains of his courage forsook him, and a terrible surmise darted with the rapidity of lightning cross his brain. It was probable that his carriage had been discovered by the people of the house, who, with a design of plunder, had secured his servant and brought hither Madame de la Motte. He was the more inclined to believe this by the stillness which had for sometime reigned in the house, previous to the sounds he now heard. Or it was possible that the inhabitants were not robbers, but persons to whom he had been betrayed by his friend or servant, and who were appointed to deliver him into the hands of justice. Yet he hardly dared to doubt the integrity of his friend, who had been entrusted with the secret of his flight and the plan of his route, and had procured him the carriage in which he had escaped. "Such depravity," exclaimed La Motte, "cannot surely exist in human nature, much less in the heart of Nemours!"

This ejaculation was interrupted by a noise in the passage leading to the room: it approached—the door was unlocked—and the man who had admitted La Motte into the house entered leading, or rather forcibly dragging along, a beautiful girl who appeared to be about eighteen. Her features were bathed in tears, and she seemed to suffer the utmost distress.

The man fastened the lock and put the key in his pocket. He then advanced to La Motte, who had before observed other persons in the passage, and pointed a pistol at his breast. "You are wholly in our power," said he. "No assistance can reach you. If you wish to save your life, swear that you will convey this girl where I may never see her more; or rather consent to take her with you, for your oath I would not believe, and I can take care you shall not find me again.—Answer quickly, you have no time to lose."

He now seized the trembling hand of the girl, who shrank aghast with terror, and hurried her toward La Motte, whom surprise still kept silent. She sank at his feet and, with supplicating eyes that streamed with tears, implored him to have pity on her. Notwithstanding his present agitation, he found it impossible to contemplate the beauty and distress of the object before him with indifference. Her youth, her apparent innocence—the artless energy of her manner forcibly assailed his heart, and he was going to speak when the ruffian, who mistook the silence of astonishment for that of hesitation, prevented him.

"I have a horse ready to take you from hence," said he, "and I will direct you over the heath. If you return within an hour, you die. After then, you are at liberty to come here when you please."

La Motte without answering raised the lovely girl from the floor, and was so much relieved from his own apprehensions that he had leisure to attempt dissipating hers.

"Let us be gone," said the ruffian, "and have no more of this nonsense; you may think yourself well off it's no worse. I'll go and get the horse ready."

The last words roused La Motte and perplexed him with new fears; he dreaded to discover[2] his carriage, lest its appearance might tempt the banditti[3] to plunder; and to depart on horseback with this man might produce a consequence yet more to be dreaded. Madame de la Motte, wearied with apprehension, would probably send to the house for her husband. All the former danger would be incurred, with the additional evil of his being separated from his family, and the chance of being detected by the emissaries of justice in endeavouring to recover them. As these reflections passed over his mind in tumultuous rapidity, a noise was again heard in the passage, an uproar and scuffle ensued, and in the same moment he could distinguish the voice of his servant, who had been sent by Madame de la Motte in search of him. Being now determined to disclose what could not long be concealed, he exclaimed

2. Expose; display.
3. Bandits.

aloud that a horse was unnecessary, that he had a carriage at some distance which would convey them from the heath, the man who was seized being his servant.

The ruffian, speaking through the door, bid him be patient awhile and he should hear more from him. La Motte now turned his eyes upon his unfortunate companion, who, pale and exhausted, leaned for support against the wall. Her features, which were delicately beautiful, had gained from distress an expression of captivating sweetness: she had

> An eye
> As when the blue sky trembles thro' a cloud
> Of purest white.[4]

A habit of grey camlet[5] with short flashed sleeves showed but did not adorn her figure; it was thrown open at the bosom, upon which part of her hair had fallen in disorder, while the light veil hastily thrown on had in her confusion been suffered to fall back. Every moment of further observation heightened the surprise of La Motte, and interested him more warmly in her favour. Such elegance and apparent refinement, contrasted with the desolation of the house and the savage manners of its inhabitants, seemed to him like a romance of imagination rather than an occurrence of real life. He endeavoured to comfort her, and his sense of compassion was too sincere to be misunderstood.

Her terror gradually subsided into gratitude and grief. "Ah, sir," said she, "Heaven has sent you to my relief, and will surely reward you for your protection. I have no friend in the world, if I do not find one in you."

La Motte was assuring her of his kindness when he was interrupted by the entrance of the ruffian, and he desired to be conducted to his family.

"All in good time," replied the ruffian. "I have taken care of one of them, and will of you, please St. Peter; so be comforted."

---

4. James Thomson, *The Tragedy of Sophonisba.*
5. An expensive fabric imported from the Orient.

These comfortable words renewed the terror of La Motte, who now earnestly begged to know if his family were safe.

"O! as for that matter they are safe enough, and you will be with them presently; but don't stand parleying here all night. Do you choose to go or stay? You know the conditions." He called in some companions, and they now bound the eyes of La Motte and of the young lady, whom terror had hitherto kept silent, and then placing them on two horses, a man mounted behind each, they immediately galloped off.

They had proceeded in this way near half an hour when La Motte entreated to know whither he was going. "You will know that by and by," said the ruffian, "so be at peace." Finding interrogatories useless, La Motte resumed silence till the horses stopped. His conductor then hallooed, and was answered by voices at some distance. In a few moments the sound of carriage wheels was heard and, presently after, the words of a man directing Peter which way to drive. As the carriage approached, La Motte called and, to his inexpressible joy, was answered by his wife.

"You are now beyond the borders of the heath, and may go which way you will," said the ruffian. "If you return within an hour, you will be welcomed by a brace of bullets."

This was a very unnecessary caution to La Motte, whom they now released. The young stranger sighed deeply as she entered the carriage; and the ruffian, having bestowed upon the servant Peter some directions and more threats, waited to see him drive off. They did not wait long.

La Motte immediately gave a short relation of what had passed at the house, including an account of the manner in which the young stranger, whom they now knew as Adeline, had been introduced to him. During this narrative, her deep convulsive sighs frequently drew the attention of Madame de la Motte, whose compassion became gradually interested on her behalf, and who now endeavoured to tranquillize her spirits. The unhappy girl answered her kindness in artless and simple expressions, and then relapsed into tears and silence. Madame forbore for the present to ask any questions that might lead to a discovery of her connections, or seem to require an explanation of the late adventure, which now furnishing her with a new subject of reflection, the sense of her own misfortunes pressed less heavily upon her mind. The distress of La Motte was even for a while suspended; he ruminated on the late scene, and it appeared like a vision, or one of those improbable fictions that sometimes are exhibited in a romance: he could reduce it to no principles of probability, or render it comprehensible by any endeavour to analyse it. The present charge, and the chance of future trouble brought upon him by this adventure, occasioned some dissatisfaction; but the beauty and seeming innocence of Adeline united with the pleadings of humanity in her favour, and he determined to protect her.

The tumult of emotions which had passed in the bosom of Adeline began now to subside; terror was softened into anxiety, and despair into grief. The sympathy so evident in the manners of her companions, particularly in those of Madame de la Motte, soothed her heart and encouraged her to hope for better days.

Dismally and silently the night passed on, for the minds of the travelers were too much occupied by their several sufferings to admit of conversation. The dawn so anxiously watched for at length appeared, and introduced the strangers more fully to each other. Adeline derived comfort from the looks of Madame de la Motte, who gazed frequently and attentively at her. For her part, Madame de la Motte thought she had seldom seen a countenance so interesting, or a form so striking. The languor[6] of sorrow threw a melancholy grace upon Adeline's features that appealed immediately to the heart; and there was a penetrating sweetness in her blue eyes which indicated an intelligent and amiable mind.

La Motte now looked anxiously from the coach window, that he might judge of their situation and observe whether he was followed. The obscurity of the dawn confined his views, but no person appeared. The sun at length tinted the eastern

6. Weakness, inertia.

clouds and the tops of the highest hills, and soon after burst in full splendour on the scene. The terrors of La Motte began to subside, and the griefs of Adeline to soften. They entered upon a lane confined by high banks and overarched by trees, on whose branches appeared the first green buds of spring glittering with dews. The fresh breeze of the morning animated the spirits of Adeline, whose mind was delicately sensible to the beauties of nature. As she viewed the flowery luxuriance of the turf and the tender green of the trees, or caught, between the opening banks, a glimpse of the varied landscape, rich with wood and fading into blue and distant mountains, her heart expanded in momentary joy. With Adeline the charms of external nature were heightened by those of novelty: she had seldom seen the grandeur of an extensive prospect, or the magnificence of a wide horizon—and not often the picturesque beauties of more confined scenery. Her mind had not lost by long oppression that elastic energy which resists calamity; else, however susceptible might have been her original taste, the beauties of nature would no longer have charmed her thus easily even to temporary repose.

The road at length wound down the side of a hill, and La Motte, again looking anxiously from the window, saw before him an open champaign[7] country, through which the road, wholly unsheltered from observation, extended almost in a direct line. The danger of these circumstances alarmed him, for his flight might without difficulty be traced for many leagues from the hills he was now descending. Of the first peasant that passed, he inquired for a road among the hills, but heard of none. La Motte now sank into his former terrors. Madame, notwithstanding her own apprehensions, endeavoured to reassure him, but finding her efforts ineffectual, she also retired to the contemplation of her misfortunes. Often, as they went on, did La Motte look back upon the country they had passed, and often did imagination suggest to him the sounds of distant pursuits.

7. Level open country.

The travelers stopped to breakfast in a village where the road was obscured by woods, and La Motte's spirits again revived. Adeline appeared more tranquil than she had yet been, and La Motte now asked for an explanation of the scene he had witnessed on the preceding night. The inquiry renewed all her distress, and with tears she entreated for the present to be spared on the subject. La Motte pressed it no further, but he observed that for the greater part of the day she seemed to remember it in melancholy and dejection. They now traveled among the hills and were therefore in less danger of observation; but La Motte avoided the great towns, and stopped in obscure ones no longer than to refresh the horses. About two hours after noon, the road wound into a deep valley watered by a rivulet and overhung with wood. La Motte called to Peter, and ordered him to drive to a thickly embowered[8] spot that appeared on the left. Here he alighted with his family, and Peter having spread the provisions on the turf, they seated themselves and partook of a repast which in other circumstances would have been thought delicious. Adeline endeavoured to smile, but the languor of grief was now heightened by indisposition. The violent agitation of mind and fatigue of body which she had suffered for the last twenty-four hours had overpowered her strength, and when La Motte led her back to the carriage, her whole frame trembled with illness. But she uttered no complaint, and having long observed the dejection of her companions, she made a feeble effort to enliven them.

They continued to travel throughout the day without any accident or interruption, and about three hours after sunset arrived at Monville, a small town where La Motte determined to pass the night. Repose was, indeed, necessary to the whole party, whose pale and haggard looks, as they alighted from the carriage, were but too obvious to pass unobserved by the people of the inn. As soon as beds could be prepared, Adeline withdrew to her chamber, accompanied by Madame de la Motte, whose concern for the fair stranger made her exert

8. Sheltered or enclosed.

every effort to soothe and console her. Adeline wept in silence, and taking the hand of Madame, pressed it to her bosom. These were not merely tears of grief—they were mingled with those which flow from the grateful heart when unexpectedly it meets with sympathy. Madame de la Motte understood them. After some momentary silence, she renewed her assurances of kindness, and entreated Adeline to confide in her friendship; but she carefully avoided any mention of the subject which had before so much affected her. Adeline at length found words to express her sense of this goodness, which she did in a manner so natural and sincere that Madame, finding herself much affected, took leave of her for the night.

In the morning, La Motte rose at an early hour, impatient to be gone. Everything was prepared for his departure, and the breakfast had been waiting some time, but Adeline did not appear. Madame de la Motte went to her chamber, and found her sunk in a disturbed slumber. Her breathing was short and irregular—she frequently started, or sighed, and sometimes she muttered an incoherent sentence. While Madame gazed with concern upon her languid countenance, she awoke and, looking up, gave her hand to Madame de la Motte, who found it burning with fever. She had passed a restless night; as she now attempted to rise, her head, which beat with intense pain, grew giddy, her strength failed, and she sank back.

Madame was much alarmed, being at once convinced that it was impossible she could travel, and that a delay might prove fatal to her husband. She went to inform him of the truth, and his distress may be more easily imagined than described. He saw all the inconvenience and danger of delay, yet he could not so far divest himself of humanity as to abandon Adeline to the care, or rather to the neglect, of strangers. He sent immediately for a physician, who pronounced her to be in a high fever and said a removal in her present state must be fatal. La Motte now determined to wait the event, and endeavoured to calm the transports of terror which at times assailed him. In the meanwhile, he took such precautions as his situation admitted of, passing the greater part of the day out of the village, in a spot from whence he had a view of the road for some distance; yet to be exposed to destruction by the illness of a girl whom he did not know, and who had actually been forced upon him, was a misfortune to which La Motte had not philosophy enough to submit with composure.

Adeline's fever continued to increase during the whole day, and at night, when the physician took his leave, he told La Motte the event would very soon be decided. La Motte received this intelligence with real concern. The beauty and innocence of Adeline had overcome the disadvantageous circumstances under which she had been introduced to him, and he now gave less consideration to the inconvenience she might hereafter occasion him than to the hope of her recovery.

Madame de la Motte watched over her with tender anxiety, and observed with admiration her patient sweetness and mild resignation. Adeline amply repaid her, though she thought she could not. "Young as I am," she would say, "and deserted by those upon whom I have a claim for protection, I can remember no connection to make me regret life so much, as that I hoped to form with you. If I live, my conduct will best express my sense of your goodness; words are but feeble testimonies."

The sweetness of her manners so much attracted Madame de la Motte that she watched the crisis of her disorder with a solicitude which precluded every other interest. Adeline passed a very disturbed night, and when the physician appeared in the morning, he gave orders that she should be indulged with whatever she liked, and answered the inquiries of La Motte with a frankness that left him nothing to hope.

In the meantime, his patient, after drinking profusely of some mild liquids, fell asleep, in which she continued for several hours, and so profound was her repose that her breath alone gave sign of existence. She awoke free from fever, and with no other disorder than weakness, which in a few days she overcame so well as to be able to set out with La Motte for B———, a village off the great road, which he thought it prudent to quit. There they passed the following night, and early the next morning commenced their journey upon a wild and woody tract of country. They stopped about noon at a solitary village, where they took refreshments and obtained directions for passing the vast forest of Fontanville, upon the borders of which they now were. La Motte wished at first to take a guide, but he apprehended more evil from the discovery he might make of his route than he hoped for benefit from assistance in the wilds of this uncultivated tract.

La Motte now designed to pass on to Lyon, where he could either seek concealment in its neighbourhood, or embark on the Rhône for Geneva, should the emergency of his circumstances hereafter require him to leave France. It was about twelve o'clock at noon, and he was desirous to hasten forward, that he might pass the forest of Fontanville and reach the town on its opposite borders before nightfall. Having deposited a fresh stock of provisions in the carriage and received such directions as were necessary concerning the roads, they again set forward, and in a short time entered the forest. It was now the latter end of April, and the weather was remarkably temperate and fine. The balmy freshness of the air, which breathed the first pure essence of vegetation, and the gentle warmth of the sun, whose beams vivified every hue of nature and opened every floweret of spring, revived Adeline, and inspired her with life and health. As she inhaled the breeze, her strength seemed to return, and as her eyes wandered through the romantic glades that opened into the forest, her heart was gladdened with complacent delight. When from these objects she turned her regard upon Monsieur and Madame de la Motte, to whose tender attentions she owed her life and in whose looks she now read esteem and kindness, her bosom glowed with sweet affections, and she experienced a force of gratitude which might be called sublime.

For the remainder of the day they continued to travel without seeing a hut or meeting a human being. It was now near sunset, and the prospect being closed on all sides by the forest, La Motte began to have apprehensions that his servant had mistaken the way. The road, if a road it could be called which afforded only a slight track upon the grass, was sometimes overrun by luxuriant vegetation, and sometimes obscured by the deep shades,[9] and Peter at length stopped, uncertain of the way. La Motte, who dreaded being benighted in a scene so wild and solitary as this forest, and whose apprehensions of banditti were very sanguine, ordered him to proceed at any rate, and if he found no track, to endeavour to gain a more open part of the forest. With these orders, Peter again set forward, but having proceeded some way and his views being still confined by woody glades and forest walks, he began to despair of extricating himself, and stopped for further orders. The sun was now set, but as La Motte looked anxiously from the window, he observed upon the vivid glow of the western horizon some dark towers rising from among the trees at a little distance, and ordered Peter to drive toward them. "If they belong to a monastery," said he, "we may probably gain admittance for the night."

The carriage drove along under the shade of "melancholy boughs,"[10] through which the evening twilight, which yet coloured the air, diffused a solemnity that vibrated in thrilling sensations upon the hearts of the travelers. Expectation kept them silent. The present scene recalled to Adeline a remembrance of the late terrific circumstances, and her mind responded but too easily to the apprehension of new misfortunes. La Motte alighted at the foot of a green knoll which, the trees again opening to light, permitted a nearer, though imperfect, view of the edifice.

9. Shadows that gather as the sun sets.
10. But whate'er you are / That in this desert inaccessible, / Under the shade of melancholy boughs, / Lose and neglect the creeping hours of time.—Shakespeare, *As You Like It.*

[15]

CHAPTER 2

How these antique towers
And vacant courts chill the suspended soul,
Till expectation wears the cast of fear;
And fear, half ready to become devotion,
Mumbles a kind of mental orison,
It knows not wherefore:
What a kind of being is circumstance!

Horace Walpole, *The Mysterious Mother*

He approached, and perceived the Gothic remains of an abbey: it stood on a kind of rude lawn, overshadowed by high and spreading trees, which seemed coeval with the building, and diffused a romantic gloom around. The greater part of the pile appeared to be sinking into ruins, and that which had withstood the ravages of time showed the remaining features of the fabric[11] more awful in decay. The lofty battlements, thickly enwreathed with ivy, were half demolished, and become the residence of birds of prey. Huge fragments of the eastern tower, which was almost demolished, lay scattered amid the high grass that waved slowly in the breeze.

11. Structure or building.

The thistle shook there its lonely head; the moss whistled
to the wind.[12]

A Gothic gate, richly ornamented with fretwork, which
opened into the main body of the edifice, but which was now
obstructed with brushwood, remained entire. Above the vast
and magnificent portal of this gate arose a window of the
same order, whose pointed arches still exhibited fragments of
stained glass, once the pride of monkish devotion. La Motte,
thinking it possible it might yet shelter some human being,
advanced to the gate and lifted a massy[13] knocker. The hollow
sounds rang through the emptiness of the place. After waiting
a few minutes, he forced back the gate, which was heavy with
iron work and creaked harshly on its hinges.

He entered what appeared to have been the chapel of the
abbey, where the hymn of devotion had once been raised and
the tear of penitence had once been shed—sounds which
could now only be recalled by imagination, tears of penitence
which had been long since fixed in fate. La Motte paused a moment, for he felt a sensation of sublimity rising into terror—a
suspension of mingled astonishment and awe! He surveyed the
vastness of the place, and as he contemplated its ruins, fancy
bore him back to past ages. "And these walls," said he, "where
once superstition lurked and austerity anticipated an earthly
purgatory, now tremble over the mortal remains of the beings
who reared them!"

The deepening gloom now reminded La Motte that he had
no time to lose, but curiosity prompted him to explore farther,
and he obeyed the impulse. As he walked over the broken
pavement, the sound of his steps ran in echoes through the
place, and seemed like the mysterious accents of the dead,
reproving the sacrilegious mortal who thus dared to disturb
their precincts.

From this chapel he passed into the nave of the great church,

12. James Macpherson, *The Poems of Ossian*.
13. Massive.

of which one window, more perfect than the rest, opened upon a long vista of the forest, through which was seen the rich colouring of evening, melting by imperceptible gradations into the solemn grey of upper air. Dark hills, whose outline appeared distinct upon the vivid glow of the horizon, closed the perspective. Several of the pillars which had once supported the roof remained the proud effigies of sinking greatness, and seemed to nod at every murmur of the blast over the fragments of those that had fallen a little before them.

La Motte sighed. The comparison between himself and the gradation of decay which these columns exhibited was but too obvious and affecting. "A few years," said he, "and I shall become like the mortals on whose relics I now gaze, and like them too, I may be the subject of meditation to a succeeding generation, which shall totter but a little while over the object they contemplate, e'er they also sink into the dust."

Retiring from this scene, he walked through the cloisters till a door which communicated with the lofty part of the building attracted his curiosity. He opened this and perceived, across the foot of the staircase, another door; but now, partly checked by fear and partly by the recollection of the surprise his family might feel in his absence, he returned with hasty steps to his carriage, having wasted some of the precious moments of twilight, and gained no information.

Some slight answer to Madame de la Motte's inquiries, and a general direction to Peter to drive carefully on and look for a road, was all that his anxiety would permit him to utter. The night shade fell thick around, which, deepened by the gloom of the forest, soon rendered it dangerous to proceed. Peter stopped, but La Motte, persisting in his first determination, ordered him to go on. Peter ventured to remonstrate, Madame de la Motte entreated, but La Motte reproved—commanded, and at length repented; for the hind wheel rising upon the stump of an old tree which the darkness had prevented Peter from observing, the carriage was in an instant overturned.

The party, as may be supposed, were much terrified, but no one was materially hurt, and having disengaged themselves from their perilous situation, La Motte and Peter endeavoured to raise the carriage. The extent of this misfortune was now discovered, for they perceived that the wheel was broke. Their distress was reasonably great, for not only was the coach disabled from proceeding, but it could not even afford a shelter from the cold dews of the night, it being impossible to preserve it in an upright situation.

After a few moment's silence, La Motte proposed that they should return to the ruins which they had just quitted, which lay at a very short distance, and pass the night in the most habitable part of them; that when morning dawned, Peter should take one of the coach horses and endeavour to find a road and a town, from whence assistance could be procured for repairing the carriage. This proposal was opposed by Madame de la Motte, who shuddered at the idea of passing so many hours of darkness in a place so forlorn as the monastery. Terrors which she neither endeavoured to examine nor combat overcame her, and she told La Motte she had rather remain exposed to the unwholesome dews of night than encounter the desolation of the ruins. La Motte had at first felt an equal reluctance to return to this spot, but having subdued his own feelings, he resolved not to yield to those of his wife.

The horses being now disengaged from the carriage, the party moved toward the edifice. As they proceeded, Peter struck a light, and they entered the ruins by the flame of sticks, which he had collected. The partial gleams thrown across the fabric seemed to make its desolation more solemn, while the obscurity of the greater part of the pile heightened its sublimity and led fancy on to scenes of horror.

Adeline, who had hitherto remained in silence, now uttered an exclamation of mingled admiration and fear. A kind of pleasing dread thrilled her bosom and filled all her soul. Tears started into her eyes; she wished, yet feared, to go on; she hung upon the arm of La Motte, and looked at him with a sort of hesitating interrogation.

He opened the door of the great hall, and they entered; its extent was lost in gloom.

"Let us stay here," said Madame de la Motte, "I will go no farther."

La Motte pointed to the broken roof, and was proceeding when he was interrupted by an uncommon noise which passed along the hall. They were all silent—it was the silence of terror.

Madame de la Motte spoke first. "Let us quit this spot," said she. "Any evil is preferable to the feeling which now oppresses me. Let us retire instantly."

The stillness had for some time remained undisturbed, and La Motte, ashamed of the fear he had involuntarily betrayed, now thought it necessary to affect a boldness which he did not feel. He, therefore, opposed ridicule to the terror of Madame, and insisted upon proceeding. Thus compelled to acquiesce, she traversed the hall with trembling steps. They came to a narrow passage, and Peter's sticks being nearly exhausted, they awaited here while he went in search of more.

The almost-expiring light flashed faintly upon the walls of the passage, showing the recess more horrible. Across the hall, the greater part of which was concealed in shadow, the feeble ray spread a tremulous gleam, exhibiting the chasm in the roof, while many nameless objects were seen imperfectly through the dusk. Adeline with a smile inquired of La Motte if he believed in spirits. The question was ill-timed, for the present scene impressed its terrors upon La Motte, and in spite of endeavour, he felt a superstitious dread stealing upon him. He was now, perhaps, standing over the ashes of the dead. If spirits were ever permitted to revisit the earth, this seemed the hour and the place most suitable for their appearance.

La Motte remaining silent, Adeline said, "Were I inclined to superstition——"

She was interrupted by a return of the noise which had been lately heard. It sounded down the passage at whose entrance they stood, and sank gradually away. Every heart palpitated, and they remained listening in silence. A new subject of apprehension seized La Motte: the noise might proceed from banditti, and he hesitated whether it would be safe to proceed. Peter now came with the light. Madame refused to enter the passage. La Motte was not much inclined to it, but Peter, in whom curiosity was more prevalent than fear, readily offered his services. La Motte, after some hesitation, suffered him to go while he awaited at the entrance the result of the inquiry. The extent of the passage soon concealed Peter from view, and the echoes of his footsteps were lost in a sound which rushed along the avenue, and became fainter and fainter till it sank into silence. La Motte now called aloud to Peter, but no answer was returned; at length they heard the sound of a distant footstep, and Peter soon after appeared, breathless and pale with fear.

When he came within hearing of La Motte, he called out, "An[14] it please your honour, I've done for them, I believe, but I've had a hard bout. I thought I was fighting with the devil."

"What are you speaking of?" said La Motte.

"They were nothing but owls and rooks after all," continued Peter, "but the light brought them all about my ears, and they made such a confounded clapping with their wings that at first I thought I had been beset with a legion of devils. But I have drove them all out, master, and you have nothing to fear now."

The latter part of the sentence, intimating a suspicion of his courage, La Motte could have dispensed with, and to retrieve in some degree his reputation, he made a point of proceeding through the passage. They now moved on with alacrity, for, as Peter said, they had "nothing to fear."

The passage led into a large area, on one side of which, over a range of cloisters, appeared the west tower and a lofty part of the edifice; the other side was open to the woods. La Motte led the way to a door of the tower, which he now perceived was the same he had formerly entered; but he found some difficulty in advancing, for the area was overgrown with brambles and nettles, and the light which Peter carried afforded only an uncertain gleam. When he unclosed the door, the dismal aspect of the place revived the apprehensions of Madame de la Motte, and extorted from Adeline an inquiry whither they

14. If.

were going. Peter held up the light to show the narrow staircase that wound round the tower; but La Motte, observing a second door, drew back the rusty bolts and entered a spacious apartment which, from its style and condition, was evidently of a much later date than the other part of the structure. Though desolate and forlorn, it was very little impaired by time; the walls were damp but not decayed, and the glass was yet firm in the windows.

They passed on to a suite of apartments resembling the first they had seen, and expressed their surprise at the incongruous appearance of this part of the edifice with the mouldering walls they had left behind. These apartments conducted them to a winding passage that received light and air through narrow cavities placed high in the wall, and was at length closed by a door barred with iron. After with some difficulty opening it, they entered a vaulted room. La Motte surveyed it with a scrutinizing eye, and endeavoured to conjecture for what purpose it had been guarded by a door of such strength; but he saw little within to assist his curiosity. The room appeared to have been built in modern times upon a Gothic plan. Adeline approached a large window that formed a kind of recess raised by one step over the level of the floor; she observed to La Motte that the whole floor was inlaid with mosaic work; which drew from him a remark that the style of this apartment was not strictly Gothic. He passed on to a door which appeared on the opposite side of the apartment, and unlocking it, found himself in the great hall by which he had entered the fabric.

He now perceived what the gloom had before concealed, a spiral staircase which led to a gallery above; and which, from its present condition, seemed to have been built with the more modern part of the fabric, though this also affected the Gothic mode of architecture: La Motte had little doubt that these stairs led to apartments corresponding with those he had passed below, and hesitated whether to explore them; but the entreaties of Madame, who was much fatigued, prevailed with him to defer all further examination. After some deliberation regarding in which of the rooms they should pass the night, they determined to return to that which opened from the tower.

A fire was kindled on a hearth, which it is probable had not for many years before afforded the warmth of hospitality. Peter and Annette having spread the provision he had brought from the coach, La Motte and his family, encircled round the fire, partook of a repast which hunger and fatigue made delicious. Apprehension gradually gave way to confidence, for they now found themselves in something like a human habitation, and they had leisure to laugh at their late terrors; but as the blast[15] shook the doors, Adeline often started, and threw a fearful glance around. They continued to laugh and talk cheerfully for a time; yet their merriment was transient,[16] if not affected; for a sense of their peculiar and distressed circumstances pressed upon their recollection, and sank each individual into languor and pensive silence. Adeline felt the forlornness of her condition with energy; she reflected upon the past with astonishment, and anticipated the future with fear. She found herself wholly dependent upon strangers, with no other claim than what distress demands from the common sympathy of kindred beings; sighs swelled her heart, and the frequent tear started to her eye; but she checked it, ere it betrayed on her cheek the sorrow which she thought it would be ungrateful to reveal.

La Motte broke this meditative silence by directing the fire to be renewed for the night, and the door to be secured: this seemed a necessary precaution, even in this solitude, and was effected by means of large stones piled against it, for other fastening there was none. It had frequently occurred to La Motte that this apparently forsaken edifice might be a place of refuge to banditti. Here was solitude to conceal them, and a wild and extensive forest to assist their schemes of rapine, and to perplex with its labyrinths those who might be bold enough to attempt pursuit. These apprehensions, however, he hid within his own bosom, saving his companions from a

15. A forceful gust of wind.
16. Of brief duration.

share of the uneasiness they occasioned. Peter was ordered to watch at the door, and having given the fire a rousing stir, our desolate party drew round it, and sought in sleep a short oblivion of care.

The night passed on without disturbance. Adeline slept, but uneasy dreams fleeted[17] before her fancy, and she awoke at an early hour. The recollection of her sorrows arose upon her mind, and yielding to their pressure, her tears flowed silently and fast. That she might indulge them without restraint, she went to a window that looked upon an open part of the forest; all was gloom and silence; she stood for some time viewing the shadowy scene.

The first tender tints of morning now appeared on the verge of the horizon, stealing upon the darkness—so pure, so fine, so ætherial! it seemed as if heaven was opening to the view. The dark mists were seen to roll off to the west as the tints of light grew stronger, deepening the obscurity of that part of the hemisphere, and involving the features of the country below; meanwhile, in the east, the hues became more vivid, darting a trembling lustre far around, till a ruddy glow which fired all that part of the heavens announced the rising sun. At first, a small line of inconceivable splendour emerged on the horizon, where, quickly expanding, the sun appeared in all its glory, unveiling the whole face of nature, vivifying every colour of the landscape, and sprinkling the dewy earth with glittering light. The low and gentle responses of birds awakened by the morning ray now broke the silence of the hour, their soft warbling rising by degrees till they swelled the chorus of universal gladness. Adeline's heart swelled too with gratitude and adoration. The scene before her soothed her mind, and exalted her thoughts to the great Author of Nature; she uttered an involuntary prayer: "Father of good, who made this glorious scene! I resign myself to thy hands: thou wilt support me under my present sorrows, and protect me from future evil."

Thus confiding in the benevolence of God, she wiped the

17. Drifted, flowed.

tears from her eyes while the sweet union of conscience and reflection rewarded her trust, and her mind, losing the feelings which had lately oppressed it, became tranquil and composed. La Motte awoke soon after, and Peter prepared to set out on his expedition. As he mounted his horse, he said, "An it please you, master, I think we had as good look no farther for an habitation till better times turn up, for nobody will think of looking for us here. When one sees the place by daylight, it's none so bad but what a little patching up would make it comfortable enough."

La Motte made no reply, but he thought of Peter's words. During the intervals of the night when anxiety had kept him waking, the same idea had occurred to him; concealment was his only security, and this place afforded it. The desolation of the spot was repulsive to his wishes, but he had only a choice of evils—a forest with liberty was not a bad home for one who had too much reason to expect a prison. As he walked through the apartments and examined their condition more attentively, he perceived they might easily be made habitable; and now surveying them under the cheerfulness of morning, his design strengthened; and he mused upon the means of accomplishing it, which nothing seemed so much to obstruct as the apparent difficulty of procuring food.

He communicated his thoughts to Madame de la Motte, who felt repugnance to the scheme. La Motte, however, seldom consulted his wife till he had determined how to act; and he had already resolved to be guided in this affair by the report of Peter. If he could discover a town in the neighbourhood of the forest where provisions and other necessaries could be procured, he would seek no farther for a place of rest.

In the meantime, he spent the anxious interval of Peter's absence in examining the ruin and walking over the environs;[18] they were sweetly romantic, and the luxuriant woods with which they abounded seemed to sequester this spot from the rest of the world. Frequently a natural vista would yield

18. Surroundings.

a view of the country terminated by hills which, retiring in distance, faded into the blue horizon. A stream, various and musical in its course, wound at the foot of the lawn on which stood the abbey; here it silently glided beneath the shades, feeding the flowers that bloomed on its banks, and diffusing dewy freshness around; there it spread in broad expanse today, reflecting the sylvan scene, and the wild deer that tasted its waves. La Motte observed everywhere a profusion of game; the pheasants scarcely flew from his approach, and the deer gazed mildly at him as he passed. They were strangers to man!

On his return to the abbey, La Motte ascended the stairs that led to the tower. About halfway up, a door appeared in the wall; it yielded without resistance to his hand, but a sudden noise within, accompanied by a cloud of dust, made him step back and close the door. After waiting a few minutes, he again opened it, and perceived a large room of the more modern building. The remains of tapestry hung in tatters upon the walls, which were become the residence of birds of prey, whose sudden flight on the opening of the door had brought down a quantity of dust and occasioned the noise. The windows were shattered, and almost without glass; but he was surprised to observe some remains of furniture: chairs, whose fashion and condition bore the date of their antiquity, a broken table, and an iron grate almost consumed by rust.

On the opposite side of the room was a door, which led to another apartment proportioned like the first but hung with arras[19] somewhat less tattered. In one corner stood a small bedstead, and a few shattered chairs were placed round the walls. La Motte gazed with a mixture of wonder and curiosity. "'Tis strange," said he, "that these rooms, and these alone, should bear the marks of inhabitation. Perhaps some wretched wanderer like myself may have here sought refuge from a persecuting world, and here perhaps laid down the load of existence; perhaps, too, I have followed his footsteps but to mingle my dust with his!"

19. A tapestry wall hanging.

He turned suddenly, and was about to quit the room when he perceived a small door near the bed; it opened into a closet[20] which was lighted by one small window, and was in the same condition as the apartments he had passed, except that it was destitute even of the remains of furniture. As he walked over the floor, he thought he felt one part of it shake beneath his steps and, examining, found a trapdoor. Curiosity prompted him to explore further, and with some difficulty he opened it. It disclosed a staircase which terminated in darkness. La Motte descended a few steps, but was unwilling to trust the abyss; and after wondering for what purpose it was so secretly constructed, he closed the trap, and quitted this suite of apartments.

The stairs in the tower above were so much decayed that he did not attempt to ascend them. He returned to the hall, and by the spiral staircase which he had observed the evening before reached the gallery, and found another suite of apartments entirely unfurnished, very much like those below.

He renewed with Madame de la Motte his former conversation respecting the abbey, and she exerted all her endeavours to dissuade him from his purpose, acknowledging the solitary security of the spot, but pleading that other places might be found equally well adapted for concealment and more for comfort. This La Motte doubted: besides, the forest abounded with game, which would at once afford him amusement and food, a circumstance, considering his small stock of money, by no means to be overlooked. He had suffered his mind to dwell so much upon the scheme that it was become a favourite one. Adeline listened in silent anxiety to the discourse, and waited the issue of Peter's report.

The morning passed, but Peter did not return. Our solitary party took their dinner of the provision they had fortunately brought with them, and afterward they walked forth into the woods. Adeline, who never suffered any good to pass unnoticed because it came attended with evil, forgot for a while the

20. A small room for privacy.

desolation of the abbey in the beauty of the adjacent scenery. The pleasantness of the shades soothed her heart, and the varied features of the landscape amused her fancy; she almost thought she could be contented to live here. Already she began to feel an interest in the concerns of her companions, and for Madame de la Motte she felt more; it was the warm emotion of gratitude and affection.

The afternoon wore away, and they returned to the abbey. Peter was still absent, and his absence now began to excite surprise and apprehension. The approach of darkness also threw a gloom upon the hopes of the wanderers: another night must be passed under the same forlorn circumstances as the preceding one; and what was still worse, with a very scanty stock of provisions. The fortitude of Madame de la Motte now entirely forsook her, and she wept bitterly. Adeline's heart was as mournful as Madame's, but she rallied her drooping spirits, and gave the first instance of her kindness by endeavouring to revive those of her friend.

La Motte was restless and uneasy, and leaving the abbey, he walked alone the way which Peter had taken. He had not gone far when he perceived him between the trees, leading his horse. "What news, Peter?" hallooed La Motte. Peter came on, panting for breath, and said not a word, till La Motte repeated the question in a tone of somewhat more authority.

"Ah, bless you, master!" said he, when he had taken breath to answer. "I am glad to see you. I thought I should never have got back again; I've met with a world of misfortunes."

"Well, you may relate them hereafter; let me hear whether you have discovered—"

"Discovered!" interrupted Peter. "Yes, I am discovered with a vengeance! If your honour will look at my arms, you'll see how I am discovered."

"Discoloured! I suppose you mean," said La Motte. "But how came you in this condition?"

"Why, I'll tell you how it was, sir; your honour knows I learned a smack of boxing of that Englishman that used to come with his master to our house."

"Well, well—tell me where you have been."

"I scarcely know myself, master; I've been where I got a sound drubbing, but then it was in your business, and so I don't mind. But if ever I meet with that rascal again—!"

"You seem to like your first drubbing so well that you want another, and unless you speak more to the purpose, you shall soon have one."

Peter was now frightened into method, and endeavoured to proceed. "When I left the old abbey," said he, "I followed the way you directed, and turning to the right of that grove of trees yonder, I looked this way and that to see if I could see a house, or a cottage, or even a man, but not a soul of them was to be seen, and so I jogged on, near the value of a league, I warrant, and then I came to a track. Oh! oh! says I, we have you now; this will do—paths can't be made without feet. However, I was out in my reckoning, for the devil a bit of a soul could I see, and after following the track this way and that way for the third of a league, I lost it, and had to find out another."

"Is it impossible for you to speak to the point?" said La Motte. "Omit these foolish particulars, and tell whether you have succeeded."

"Well, then, master, to be short, for that's the nearest way after all, I wandered a long while at random, I did not know where, all through a forest like this, and I took special care to note how the trees stood, that I might find my way back. At last I came to another path, and was sure I should find something now, though I had found nothing before, for I could not be mistaken twice; so, peeping between the trees, I spied a cottage, and I gave my horse a lash that sounded through the forest, and I was at the door in a minute. They told me there was a town about half a league off, and bade me follow the track and it would bring me there; so it did, and my horse, I believe, smelt the corn in the manger by the rate he went at. I inquired for a wheelwright, and was told there was but one in the place, and he could not be found. I waited and waited, for I knew it was in vain to think of returning without doing my business. The man at last came home from the country, and I told him how long I had waited; for, says I, I knew it was in vain to return without my business."

"Do be less tedious," said La Motte, "if it is in thy nature."

"It is in my nature," answered Peter, "and if it was more in my nature, your honour should have it all. Would you think it, sir, the fellow had the impudence to ask a louis d'or[21] for mending the coach wheel! I believe in my conscience he saw I was in a hurry and could not do without him. A louis d'or! says I, my master shall give no such price, he sha'n't be imposed upon by no such rascal as you. Whereupon the fellow looked glum, and gave me a douse o' the chops.[22] With this, I up with my fist and gave him another, and should have beat him presently, if another man had not come in, and then I was obliged to give up."

"And so you are returned as wise as you went?"

"Why, master, I hope I have too much spirit to submit to a rascal, or let you submit to one either. Besides, I have bought some nails to try if I can't mend the wheel myself—I had always a hand at carpentry."

"Well, I commend your zeal in my cause, but on this occasion it was rather ill-timed. And what have you got in that basket?"

"Why, master, I bethought me that we could not get away from this place till the carriage was ready to draw us, and in the meantime, says I, nobody can live without victuals, so I'll e'en lay out the little money I have and take a basket with me."

"That's the only wise thing you have done yet, and this, indeed, redeems your blunders."

"Why now, master, it does my heart good to hear you speak; I knew I was doing for the best all the while, but I've had a hard job to find my way back; and here's another piece of ill luck, for the horse has got a thorn in his foot."

21. A French gold coin.
22. Douse o' the chops: a blow in the jaw or mouth.

La Motte made inquiries concerning the town, and found it was capable of supplying him with provision, and what little furniture was necessary to render the abbey habitable. This intelligence almost settled his plans, and he ordered Peter to return on the following morning and make inquiries concerning the abbey. If the answers were favourable to his wishes, he commissioned him to buy a cart and load it with some furniture, and some materials necessary for repairing the modern apartments.

Peter stared. "What, does your honour mean to live here?"

"Why, suppose I do?"

"Why then your honour has made a wise determination, according to my hint; for your honour knows I said—"

"Well, Peter, it is not necessary to repeat what you said; perhaps I had determined on the subject before."

"Egad, master, you're in the right, and I'm glad of it, for I believe we shall not quickly be disturbed here, except by the rooks and owls. Yes, yes—I warrant I'll make it a place fit for a king; and as for the town, one may get anything, I'm sure of that, though they think no more about this place than they do about India or England, or any of those places."

They now reached the abbey, where Peter was received with great joy; but the hopes of his mistress and Adeline were repressed when they learned that he returned without having executed his commission and heard his account of the town. La Motte's orders to Peter were heard with almost equal concern by Madame and Adeline; but the latter concealed her uneasiness, and used all her efforts to overcome that of her friend. The sweetness of her behaviour and the air of satisfaction she assumed sensibly affected Madame, and discovered to her a source of comfort which she had hitherto overlooked. The affectionate attentions of her young friend promised to console her for the want of other society, and her conversation to enliven the hours which might otherwise be passed in painful regret.

The observations and general behaviour of Adeline already

bespoke a good understanding and an amiable heart, but she had yet more—she had genius.[23] She was now in her nineteenth year; her figure of the middling size, and turned to the most exquisite proportion; her hair was dark auburn, her eyes blue, and whether they sparkled with intelligence, or melted with tenderness, they were equally attractive. Her form had the airy lightness of a nymph, and when she smiled, her countenance might have been drawn for the younger sister of Hebe.[24] The captivations of her beauty were heightened by the grace and simplicity of her manners, and confirmed by the intrinsic value of a heart

> That might be shrin'd in crystal,
> And have all its movements scann'd.[25]

The servant Annette now kindled the fire for the night; Peter's basket was opened, and supper prepared. Madame de la Motte was still pensive and silent.

"There is scarcely any condition so bad," said Adeline, "but we may one time or other wish we had not quitted it. Honest Peter, when he was bewildered in the forest, or had two enemies to encounter instead of one, confesses he wished himself at the abbey. And I am certain there is no situation so destitute but comfort may be extracted from it. The blaze of this fire shines yet more cheerfully from the contrasted dreariness of the place; and this plentiful repast is made yet more delicious from the temporary want we have suffered. Let us enjoy the good and forget the evil."

"You speak, my dear," replied Madame de la Motte, "like one whose spirits have not been often depressed by misfortune"— Adeline sighed—"and whose hopes are, therefore, vigorous."

"Long suffering," said La Motte, "has subdued in our minds that elastic energy which repels the pressure of evil and dances to the bound of joy. But I speak in rhapsody, though only from

23. Intellectual power.
24. The Greek goddess of youth.
25. Thomas Moore, *Alciphron*.

the remembrance of such a time. I once, like you, Adeline, could extract comfort from most situations."

"And may now, my dear sir," said Adeline. "Still believe it possible, and you will find it is so."

"The illusion is gone—I can no longer deceive myself."

"Pardon me, sir, if I say it is now only you deceive yourself, by suffering the cloud of sorrow to tinge every object you look upon."

"It may be so," said La Motte, "but let us leave the subject."

After supper, the doors were secured, as before, for the night, and the wanderers resigned themselves to repose.

On the following morning, Peter again set out for the little town of Auboine, and the hours of his absence were again spent by Madame de la Motte and Adeline in much anxiety and some hope, for the intelligence he might bring concerning the abbey might yet release them from the plans of La Motte. Toward the close of day he was descried coming slowly on; and the cart which accompanied him too certainly confirmed their fears. He brought materials for repairing the place, and some furniture.

Of the abbey he gave an account, of which the following is the substance: It belonged, together with a large part of the adjacent forest, to a nobleman, who now resided with his family on a remote estate. He inherited it, in right of his wife, from his father-in-law, who had caused the more modern apartments to be erected, and had resided in them some part of every year for the purpose of shooting and hunting. It was reported that some person was, soon after the property came to the present possessor, brought secretly to the abbey and confined in these apartments; who or what he was had never been conjectured, and what became of him nobody knew. The report died gradually away, and many persons entirely disbelieved the whole of it. But however this affair might be, certain it was, the present owner had visited the abbey only two summers since his succeeding to it; and the furniture, after some time, was removed.

This circumstance had at first excited surprise, and various reports arose in consequence, but it was difficult to know what ought to be believed. Among the rest, it was said that strange appearances had been observed at the abbey, and uncommon noises heard; and though this report had been ridiculed by sensible persons as the idle superstition of ignorance, it had fastened so strongly upon the minds of the common people that for the last seventeen years none of the peasantry had ventured to approach the spot. The abbey was now, therefore, abandoned to decay.

La Motte ruminated upon this account. At first it called up unpleasant ideas, but they were soon dismissed, and considerations more interesting to his welfare took place: he congratulated himself that he had now found a spot where he was not likely to be either discovered or disturbed; yet it could not escape him that there was a strange coincidence between one part of Peter's narrative, and the condition of the chambers that opened from the tower above stairs. The remains of furniture, of which the other apartments were void—the solitary bed—the number and connection of the rooms, were circumstances that united to confirm his opinion. This, however, he concealed in his own breast, for he already perceived that Peter's account had not assisted in reconciling his family to the necessity of dwelling at the abbey.

But they had only to submit in silence, and whatever disagreeable apprehension might intrude upon them, they now appeared willing to suppress the expression of it. Peter, indeed, was exempt from any evil of this kind; he knew no fear, and his mind was now wholly occupied with his approaching business. Madame de la Motte, with a placid kind of despair, endeavoured to reconcile herself to that which no effort of understanding could teach her to avoid, and which an indulgence in lamentation could only make more intolerable. Indeed, though a sense of the immediate inconveniences to be endured at the abbey had made her oppose the scheme of living there, she did not really know how their situation could be improved by removal. Yet her thoughts often wandered toward Paris, and reflected the retrospect of past times with the images of weeping friends left, perhaps, forever. The affectionate endearments of her only son, whom, from the danger of his situation and the obscurity of hers, she might reasonably fear never to see again, arose upon her memory and overcame her fortitude. "Why—why was I reserved for this hour?" she would say, "and what will be my years to come?"

Adeline had no retrospect of past delight to give emphasis to present calamity—no weeping friends—no dear regretted objects to point the edge of sorrow, and throw a sickly hue upon her future prospects. She knew not yet the pangs of disappointed hope, or the acuter sting of self-accusation; she had no misery but what patience could assuage or fortitude overcome.

At the dawn of the following day Peter arose to his labour. He proceeded with alacrity, and in a few days, two of the lower apartments were so much altered for the better that La Motte began to exult, and his family to perceive that their situation would not be so miserable as they had imagined. The furniture Peter had already brought was disposed in these rooms, one of which was the vaulted apartment. Madame de la Motte furnished this as a sitting room, preferring it for its large Gothic window that descended almost to the floor, admitting a prospect of the lawn and the picturesque scenery of the surrounding woods.

Peter having returned to Auboine for a further supply, all the lower apartments were in a few weeks not only habitable but comfortable. These, however, being insufficient for the accommodation of the family, a room above stairs was prepared for Adeline: it was the chamber that opened immediately from the tower, and she preferred it to those beyond because it was less distant from the family, and the windows fronting an avenue of the forest afforded a more extensive prospect. The tapestry that was decayed and hung loosely from the walls was now nailed up and made to look less desolate; and though the room had still a solemn aspect from its spaciousness and the narrowness of the windows, it was not uncomfortable.

The first night that Adeline retired hither, she slept little.

The solitary air of the place affected her spirits, the more so, perhaps, because she had with friendly consideration endeavoured to support them in the presence of Madame de la Motte. She remembered the narrative of Peter, several circumstances of which had impressed her imagination in spite of her reason, and she found it difficult wholly to subdue apprehension. At one time, terror so strongly seized her mind that she had even opened the door with an intention of calling Madame de la Motte; but listening for a moment on the stairs of the tower, everything seemed still. At length, she heard the voice of La Motte speaking cheerfully, and the absurdity of her fears struck her forcibly; she blushed that she had for a moment submitted to them, and returned to her chamber wondering at herself.

CHAPTER 3

Are not these woods
More free from peril than the envious court?
Here feel we not the penalty of Adam,
The season's difference, as the icy fang
And churlish chiding of the winter's wind.

Shakespeare, *As You Like It*

L a Motte arranged his little plan of living. His mornings were usually spent in shooting or fishing, and the dinner thus provided by his industry he relished with a keener appetite than had ever attended him at the luxurious tables of Paris. The afternoons he passed with his family; sometimes he would select a book from the few he had brought with him, and endeavour to fix his attention to the words his lips repeated, but his mind suffered little abstraction from its own cares, and the sentiment he pronounced left no trace behind it. Sometimes he conversed, but oftener sat in gloomy silence, musing upon the past or anticipating the future.

At these moments Adeline, with a sweetness almost irresistible, endeavoured to enliven his spirits and to withdraw him from himself. Seldom she succeeded, but when she did the grateful looks of Madame de la Motte and the benevolent feelings of her own bosom realized the cheerfulness she had at first only assumed. Adeline's mind had the happy art, or perhaps it were more just to say the happy nature, of accommodating itself to her situation. Her present condition, though forlorn, was not devoid of comfort, and this comfort was confirmed by her virtues. So much she won upon the affections of her protectors that Madame de la Motte loved her as her child, and La Motte himself, though a man little susceptible of tenderness, could not be insensible to her solicitudes. Whenever he relaxed from the sullenness of misery, it was at the influence of Adeline.

Peter brought a weekly supply of provisions from Auboine, and on those occasions always quitted the town by a route contrary to that leading to the abbey. Several weeks having passed without molestation, La Motte dismissed all apprehension of pursuit, and at length became tolerably reconciled to the complexion of his circumstances. As habit and effort strengthened the fortitude of Madame de la Motte, the features of misfortune appeared to soften. The forest, which at first seemed to her a frightful solitude, had lost its terrific aspect; and that edifice, whose half-demolished walls and gloomy desolation had struck her mind with the force of melancholy and dismay, was now beheld as a domestic asylum and a safe refuge from the storms of power.

She was a sensible and highly accomplished woman, and it became her chief delight to form the rising graces of Adeline, who had, as has been already shown, a sweetness of disposition which made her quick to repay instruction with improvement, and indulgence with love. Never was Adeline so pleased as when she anticipated Madame's wishes, and never so diligent as when she was employed in Madame's business. The little affairs of the household she overlooked and managed with such admirable exactness that Madame de la Motte had neither anxiety nor care concerning them. And Adeline formed for herself in this barren situation many amusements that occasionally banished the remembrance of her misfortunes. La Motte's books were her chief consolation. With one of these she would frequently ramble into the forest, where the river winding through a glade diffused coolness, and with its murmuring accents invited repose; there she would seat herself and, resigned to the illusions of the page, pass many hours in oblivion of sorrow.

Madame de la Motte had frequently expressed curiosity concerning the events of Adeline's life, and by what circumstances she had been thrown into a situation so perilous and mysterious as that in which La Motte had found her. Adeline had given a brief account of the manner in which she had been brought thither, but had always with tears entreated to be spared for that time from a particular relation of her history. Her spirits were not then equal to retrospection, but now that they were soothed by quiet and strengthened by confidence, she one day gave Madame de la Motte the following narration.

ᕙ༺ᐛ༻ᕗ

I am the only child, said Adeline, of Louis de St. Pierre, a chevalier[26] of reputable family, but of small fortune, who for many years resided at Paris. Of my mother I have a faint remembrance; I lost her when I was only seven years old, and this was my first misfortune. At her death, my father gave up housekeeping, boarded me in a convent, and quitted Paris. Thus was I, at this early period of my life, abandoned to strangers. My father came sometimes to Paris; he then visited me, and I well remember the grief I used to feel when he bade me farewell. On these occasions, which wrung my heart with grief, he appeared unmoved, so that I often thought he had little tenderness for me. But he was my father, and the only person to whom I could look up for protection and love.

In this convent I continued till I was twelve years old. A thousand times I had entreated my father to take me home, but at first motives of prudence, and afterward of avarice, prevented him. I was now removed from this convent, and placed in another, where I learned my father intended I should take the veil. I will not attempt to express my surprise and grief

26. Knight.

on this occasion. Too long I had been immured in the walls of a cloister, and too much had I seen of the sullen misery of its votaries, not to feel horror and disgust at the prospect of being added to their number.

The lady abbess was a woman of rigid decorum and severe devotion, exact in the observance of every detail of form, and she never forgave an offence against ceremony. It was her method, when she wanted to make converts to her order, to denounce and terrify rather than to persuade and allure. Hers were the arts of cunning practised upon fear, not those of sophistication upon reason. She employed numberless stratagems to gain me to her purpose, and they all wore the complexion of her character. But in the life to which she would have devoted me, I saw too many forms of real terror to be overcome by the influence of her ideal host, and was resolute in rejecting the veil. Here I passed several years of miserable resistance against cruelty and superstition. My father I seldom saw; when I did, I entreated him to alter my destination, but he objected that his fortune was insufficient to support me in the world, and at length denounced vengeance on my head if I persisted in disobedience.

You, my dear Madame, can form little idea of the wretchedness of my situation, condemned to perpetual imprisonment, and imprisonment of the most dreadful kind, or to the vengeance of a father from whom I had no appeal. My resolution relaxed—for some time I paused upon the choice of evils—but at length the horrors of the monastic life rose so fully to my view that fortitude gave way before them. Excluded from the cheerful intercourse of society—from the pleasant view of nature—almost from the light of day—condemned to silence—rigid formality—abstinence and penance—condemned to forgo the delights of a world which imagination painted in the gayest and most alluring colours, and whose hues were, perhaps, not the less captivating because they were only ideal—such was the state to which I was destined. Again my resolution was invigorated: my father's cruelty subdued tenderness, and roused indignation. "Since he can forget," said

I, "the affection of a parent, and condemn his child without remorse to wretchedness and despair, the bond of filial and parental duty no longer subsists between us—he has himself dissolved it, and I will yet struggle for liberty and life."

Finding me unmoved by menace, the lady abbess had now recourse to more subtle measures. She condescended to smile, and even to flatter; but hers was the distorted smile of cunning, not the gracious emblem of kindness; it provoked disgust, instead of inspiring affection. She painted the character of a vestal[27] in the most beautiful tints of art—its holy innocence—its mild dignity—its sublime devotion. I sighed as she spoke. This she regarded as a favourable symptom, and proceeded on her picture with more animation. She described the serenity of a monastic life—its security from the seductive charms, restless passions, and sorrowful vicissitudes of the world—the rapturous delights of religion, and the sweet reciprocal affection of the sisterhood.

So highly she finished the piece, that the lurking lines of cunning would, to an inexperienced eye, have escaped detection. Mine was too sorrowfully informed. Too often had I witnessed the secret tear and bursting sigh of vain regret, the sullen pinings of discontent, and the mute anguish of despair. My silence and my manner assured her of my incredulity, and it was with difficulty that she preserved a decent composure.

My father, as may be imagined, was highly incensed at my perseverance, which he called obstinacy, but, what will not be so easily believed, he soon after relented and appointed a day to take me from the convent. O! judge of my feelings when I received this intelligence. The joy it occasioned awakened all my gratitude; I forgot the former cruelty of my father, and that the present indulgence was less the effect of his kindness than of my resolution. I wept that I could not indulge his every wish.

What days of blissful expectation were those that preceded my departure! The world, from which I had been hitherto secluded—the world, in which my fancy had been so often

27. A chaste woman; a nun.

delighted to roam—whose paths were strewn with fadeless roses—whose every scene smiled in beauty and invited to delight—where all the people were good, and all the good happy—Ah! then that world was bursting upon my view. Let me catch the rapturous remembrance before it vanish! It is like the passing lights of autumn, that gleam for a moment on a hill, and then leave it to darkness. I counted the days and hours that withheld me from this fairyland. It was in the convent only that people were deceitful and cruel; it was there only that misery dwelt. I was quitting it all! How I pitied the poor nuns that were to be left behind. I would have given half that world I prized so much, had it been mine, to have taken them out with me.

The long-wished-for day at last arrived. My father came, and for a moment my joy was lost in the sorrow of bidding farewell to my poor companions, for whom I had never felt such warmth of kindness as at this instant. I was soon beyond the gates of the convent. I looked around me, and viewed the vast vault of heaven no longer bounded by monastic walls, and the green earth extended in hill and dale to the round verge of the horizon! My heart danced with delight, tears swelled in my eyes, and for some moments I was unable to speak. My thoughts rose to Heaven in sentiments of gratitude to the Giver of all good!

At length, I returned to my father. "Dear sir," said I, "how I thank you for my deliverance, and how I wish I could do everything to oblige you."

"Return, then, to your convent," said he, in a harsh accent.

I shuddered; his look and manner jarred the tone of my feelings; they struck discord upon my heart, which had before responded only to harmony. The ardour of joy was in a moment repressed, and every object around me was saddened with the gloom of disappointment. It was not that I suspected my father would take me back to the convent, but that his feelings seemed so very dissonant to the joy and gratitude which I had but a moment before felt and expressed to him.

"Pardon, Madame, a relation of these trivial circumstances; the strong vicissitudes of feeling which they impressed upon my heart make me think them important, when they are, perhaps, only disgusting."

"No, my dear," said Madame de la Motte, "they are interesting to me; they illustrate little traits of character, which I love to observe. You are worthy of all my regard, and from this moment I give my tenderest pity to your misfortunes, and my affection to your goodness."

These words melted the heart of Adeline; she kissed the hand which Madame held out, and remained a few minutes silent. At length she said, "May I deserve this goodness! and may I ever be thankful to God, who, in giving me such a friend, has raised me to comfort and hope!"

My father's house was situated a few leagues on the other side of Paris, and on our way to it, we passed through that city. What a novel scene! Where were now the solemn faces, the demure manners I had been accustomed to see in the convent? Every countenance was here animated, either by business or pleasure; every step was airy, and every smile was gay. All the people appeared like friends; they looked and smiled at me; I smiled again, and wished to have told them how pleased I was. *How delightful*, thought I, *to live surrounded by friends!*

What crowded streets! What magnificent hotels! What splendid equipages! I scarcely observed that the streets were narrow, or the way dangerous. What bustle, what tumult, what delight! I could never be sufficiently thankful that I was removed from the convent. Again, I was going to express my gratitude to my father, but his looks forbade me, and I was silent. I am too diffuse; even the faint forms which memory reflects of passed delight are grateful to the heart. The shadow of pleasure is still gazed upon with a melancholy enjoyment, though the substance is fled beyond our reach.

Having quitted Paris, which I left with many sighs, and gazed upon till the towers of every church dissolved in distance from my view, we entered upon a gloomy and unfrequented road. It was evening when we reached a wild heath; I looked round in search of a human dwelling, but could find none; and not a human being was to be seen. I experienced something of what I used to feel in the convent; my heart had not been so sad since I left it. Of my father, who still sat in silence, I inquired if we were near home; he answered in the affirmative. Night came on, however, before we reached the place of our destination; it was a lone house on the waste; but I need not describe it to you, Madame. When the carriage stopped, two men appeared at the door and assisted us to alight; so gloomy were their countenances, and so few their words, I almost fancied myself again in the convent. Certain it is, I had not seen such melancholy faces since I quitted it. *Is this a part of the world I have so fondly contemplated?* thought I.

The interior appearance of the house was desolate and mean; I was surprised that my father had chosen such a place for his habitation, and also that no woman was to be seen; but I knew that inquiry would only produce a reproof, and was therefore silent. At supper, the two men I had before seen sat down with us; they said little, but seemed to observe me much. I was confused and displeased, which my father noticing, he frowned at them with a look which convinced me he meant more than I comprehended. When the cloth was drawn, my father took my hand and conducted me to the door of my chamber; having sat down the candle and wished me good night, he left me to my own solitary thoughts.

How different were they from those I had indulged a few hours before! Then expectation, hope, delight, danced before me; now melancholy and disappointment chilled the ardour of my mind, and discoloured my future prospect. The appearance of everything around conduced[28] to depress me. On the floor lay a small bed without curtains or hangings; two old chairs and a table were all the remaining furniture in the room. I went to the window, with an intention of looking out upon the surrounding scene, and found it was grated. I was shocked at this circumstance, and comparing it with the lonely situation and the strange appearance of the house, together with the countenances and behaviour of the men who had supped with us, I was lost in a labyrinth of conjecture.

At length I lay down to sleep, but the anxiety of my mind prevented repose; gloomy unpleasing images flitted before my fancy, and I fell into a sort of waking dream: I thought that I was in a lonely forest with my father; his looks were severe, and his gestures menacing: he upbraided me for leaving the convent, and while he spoke drew from his pocket a mirror, which he held before my face; I looked in it and saw—my blood now thrills as I repeat it—I saw myself wounded, and bleeding profusely. Then I thought myself in the house again; and suddenly heard these words, in accents so distinct, that for some time after I awoke, I could scarcely believe them ideal,[29] "Depart this house, destruction hovers here."

I was awakened by a footstep on the stairs; it was my father retiring to his chamber; the lateness of the hour surprised me, for it was past midnight.

On the following morning, the party of the preceding evening assembled at breakfast, and were as gloomy and silent as before. The table was spread by a boy of my father's, but the cook and the housemaid, whatever they might be, were invisible.

The next morning I was surprised, on attempting to leave my chamber, to find the door locked; I waited a considerable time before I ventured to call; when I did, no answer was

28. Lead to a result; contributed.
29. Existing in imagination only.

returned; I then went to the window and called more loudly, but my own voice was still the only sound I heard. Near an hour I passed in a state of surprise and terror not to be described. At length, I heard a person coming upstairs, and I renewed the call; I was answered that my father had that morning set off for Paris, whence he would return in a few days; in the meanwhile he had ordered me to be confined in my chamber. On my expressing surprise and apprehension at this circumstance, I was assured I had nothing to fear, and that I should live as well as if I were at liberty.

The latter part of this speech seemed to contain an odd kind of comfort; I made little reply, but submitted to necessity. Once more I was abandoned to sorrowful reflection; what a day was the one I now passed! alone, and agitated with grief and apprehension. I endeavoured to conjecture the cause of this harsh treatment, and at length concluded it was designed by my father as a punishment for my former disobedience. But why abandon me to the power of strangers, to men whose countenances bore the stamp of villainy so strongly as to impress even my inexperienced mind with terror! Surmise involved me only deeper in perplexity, yet I found it impossible to forbear pursuing the subject; and the day was divided between lamentation and conjecture. Night at length came, and such a night! Darkness brought new terrors: I looked round the chamber for some means of fastening my door on the inside, but could perceive none; at last I contrived to place the back of a chair in an oblique direction, so as to render it secure.

I had scarcely done this, and lay down upon my bed in my clothes, not to sleep, but to watch, when I heard a rap at the door of the house, which was opened and shut so quickly that the person who had knocked seemed only to deliver a letter or message. Soon after, I heard voices at intervals in a room below stairs, sometimes speaking very low, and sometimes rising, all together, as if in dispute. Something more excusable than curiosity made me endeavour to distinguish what was said, but in vain; now and then a word or two reached me, and once I heard my name repeated, but no more.

Thus passed the hours till midnight, when all became still. I had lain for some time in a state between fear and hope when I heard the lock of my door gently moved backward and forward; I started up, and listened; for a moment it was still, then the noise returned, and I heard a whispering without; my spirits died away, but I was yet sensible. Presently an effort was made at the door, as if to force it; I shrieked aloud, and immediately heard the voices of the men I had seen at my father's table: they called loudly for the door to be opened, and on my returning no answer, uttered dreadful execrations. I had just strength sufficient to move to the window, in the desperate hope of escaping thence, but my feeble efforts could not even shake the bars. O! how can I recollect these moments of horror, and be sufficiently thankful that I am now in safety and comfort!

They remained some time at the door, then they quitted it, and went downstairs. How my heart revived at every step of their departure; I fell upon my knees, thanked God that he had preserved me this time, and implored his further protection. I was rising from this short prayer when suddenly I heard a noise in a different part of the room, and on looking round, I perceived the door of a small closet open, and two men enter the chamber.

They seized me, and I sank senseless in their arms; how long I remained in this condition I know not, but on reviving, I perceived myself again alone, and heard several voices from below stairs. I had presence of mind to run to the door of the closet, my only chance of escape; but it was locked! I then recollected it was possible that the ruffians might have forgot to turn the key of the chamber door, which was held by the chair; but here, also, I was disappointed. I clasped my hands in an agony of despair, and stood for some time immoveable.

A violent noise from below roused me, and soon after I heard people ascending the stairs: I now gave myself up for lost. The steps approached, the door of the closet was again unlocked. I stood calmly, and again saw the men enter the chamber. I neither spoke, nor resisted: the faculties of my soul were wrought up beyond the power of feeling, as a violent blow on the body stuns for a while the sense of pain. They led me downstairs; the door of a room below was thrown open, and I beheld a stranger. It was then that my senses returned; I shrieked and resisted, but was forced along. It is unnecessary to say that this stranger was Monsieur La Motte, or to add that I shall forever bless him as my deliverer.

Adeline ceased to speak; Madame de la Motte remained silent. There were some circumstances in Adeline's narrative which raised all her curiosity. She asked if Adeline believed her father to be a party in this mysterious affair. Adeline, though it was impossible to doubt that he had been principally and materially concerned in some part of it, thought, or said she thought, he was innocent of any intention against her life.

"Yet what motive," said Madame de la Motte, "could there be for a degree of cruelty so apparently unprofitable?"

Here the inquiry ended; and Adeline confessed she had pursued it till her mind shrank from all further research.

Madame de la Motte now expressed without reserve the sympathy which such uncommon misfortune excited, and this expression of it strengthened the tie of mutual friendship. Adeline felt her spirits relieved by the disclosure she had made to Madame de la Motte; and the latter acknowledged the value of the confidence by an increase of affectionate attentions.

CHAPTER 4

My way of life
Is fall'n into the sere, the yellow leaf.

Shakespeare, *Macbeth*

Full oft, unknowing and unknown,
He wore his endless noons alone,
Amid th' autumnal wood:
Oft was he wont in hasty fit,
Abrupt the social board to quit.

Thomas Warton, "The Suicide"

La Motte had now passed above a month in this seclusion; and his wife had the pleasure to see him recover
tranquillity and even cheerfulness. In this pleasure Adeline warmly participated, and she might justly have congratulated herself as one cause of his restoration; her cheerfulness
and delicate attention had effected what Madame de la Motte's
greater anxiety had failed to accomplish. La Motte did not
seem regardless of her amiable disposition, and sometimes
thanked her in a manner more earnest than was usual with
him. She, in her turn, considered him as her only protector,
and now felt toward him the affection of a daughter.

The time she had spent in this peaceful retirement had
softened the remembrance of past events and restored her

mind to its natural tone. When memory brought back to her view her former short and romantic expectations of happiness, though she gave a sigh to the rapturous illusion, she less lamented the disappointment than rejoiced in her present security and comfort.

But the satisfaction which La Motte's cheerfulness diffused around him was of short continuance; he became suddenly gloomy and reserved; the society of his family was no longer grateful to him; and he would spend whole hours in the most secluded parts of the forest, devoted to melancholy and secret grief. He did not, as formerly, indulge the humour of his sadness without restraint in the presence of others; he now evidently endeavoured to conceal it, and affected a cheerfulness that was too artificial to escape detection.

His servant Peter, either impelled by curiosity or kindness, sometimes followed him, unseen, into the forest. He observed him frequently retire to one particular spot in a remote part, which having gained, he always disappeared before Peter, who was obliged to follow at a distance, could exactly notice where. All his endeavours, now prompted by wonder and invigorated by disappointment, were unsuccessful, and he was at length compelled to endure the tortures of unsatisfied curiosity.

This change in the manners and habits of her husband was too conspicuous to pass unobserved by Madame de la Motte, who endeavoured, by all the stratagems which affection could suggest or female invention supply, to win him to her confidence. He seemed insensible to the influence of the first, and withstood the wiles of the latter. Finding all her efforts insufficient to dissipate the glooms which overhung his mind or to penetrate their secret cause, she desisted from further attempt, and endeavoured to submit to this mysterious distress.

Week after week elapsed, and the same unknown cause sealed the lips and corroded the heart of La Motte. The place of his visitation in the forest had not been traced. Peter had frequently examined round the spot where his master disappeared but had never discovered any recess which could be supposed to conceal him. The astonishment of the servant was at length raised to an insupportable degree, and he communicated to his mistress the subject of it.

The emotion which this information excited she disguised from Peter, and reproved him for the means he had taken to gratify his curiosity. But she revolved this circumstance in her thoughts, and comparing it with the late alteration in his temper, her uneasiness was renewed and her perplexity considerably increased. After much consideration, being unable to assign any other motive for his conduct, she began to attribute it to the influence of illicit passion; and her heart, which now outran her judgement, confirmed the supposition and roused all the torturing pangs of jealousy.

Comparatively speaking, she had never known affliction till now: she had abandoned her dearest friends and connections—had relinquished the gaieties, the luxuries, and almost the necessaries of life—fled with her family into exile, an exile the most dreary and comfortless, experiencing the evils of reality, and those of apprehension, united; all these she had patiently endured, supported by the affection of him for whose sake she suffered. Though that affection, indeed, had for some time appeared to be abated, she had borne its decrease with fortitude, but the last stroke of calamity, hitherto withheld, now came with irresistible force—the love, of which she lamented the loss, she now believed was transferred to another.

The operation of strong passion confuses the powers of reason and warps them to its own particular direction. Her usual degree of judgement, unopposed by the influence of her heart, would probably have pointed out to Madame de la Motte some circumstances upon the subject of her distress equivocal, if not contradictory, to her suspicions. No such circumstances appeared to her, and she did not long hesitate to decide that Adeline was the object of her husband's attachment. Her beauty out of the question, who else, indeed, could it be in a spot thus secluded from the world?

The same cause destroyed, almost at the same moment, her only remaining comfort; and when she wept that she could no longer look for happiness in the affection of La Motte, she wept also that she could no longer seek solace in the friendship of Adeline. She had too great an esteem for her to doubt at first the integrity of her conduct, but in spite of reason, her heart no longer expanded to her with its usual warmth of kindness. She shrank from her confidence; and as the secret broodings of jealousy cherished her suspicions, she became less kind to her, even in manner.

Adeline, observing the change, at first attributed it to accident, and afterward to a temporary displeasure arising from some little inadvertency in her conduct. She, therefore, increased her assiduities; but perceiving, contrary to all expectation, that her efforts to please failed of their usual consequence and that the reserve of Madame's manner rather increased than abated, she became seriously uneasy, and resolved to seek an explanation. This Madame de la Motte as sedulously avoided, and was for some time able to prevent. Adeline, however, too much interested in the event to yield to delicate scruples, pressed the subject so closely that Madame, at first agitated and confused, at length invented some idle excuse, and laughed off the affair.

She now saw the necessity of subduing all appearance of reserve toward Adeline, and though her art could not conquer the prejudices of passion, it taught her to assume, with tolerable success, the aspect of kindness. Adeline was deceived, and was again at peace. Indeed, confidence in the sincerity and goodness of others was her weakness. But the pangs of stifled jealousy struck deeper to the heart of Madame de la Motte, and she resolved, at all events, to obtain some certainty upon the subject of her suspicions.

She now condescended to a meanness which she had before despised, and ordered Peter to watch the steps of his master in order to discover, if possible, the place of his visitation! So much did passion win upon her judgement, by time and indulgence, that she sometimes ventured even to doubt the integrity of Adeline, and afterward proceeded to believe it possible that the object of La Motte's rambles might be an assignation with her. What suggested this conjecture was that Adeline frequently took long walks alone in the forest, and sometimes was absent from the abbey for many hours. This circumstance, which Madame de la Motte had at first attributed to Adeline's fondness for the picturesque beauties of nature, now operated forcibly upon her imagination, and she could view it in no other light than as affording an opportunity for secret conversation with her husband.

Peter obeyed the orders of his mistress with alacrity, for they were warmly seconded by his own curiosity. All his endeavours were, however, fruitless; he never dared to follow La Motte near enough to observe the place of his last retreat. Her impatience thus heightened by delay and her passion stimulated by difficulty, Madame de la Motte now resolved to apply to her husband for an explanation of his conduct.

After some consideration concerning the manner most likely to succeed with him, she went to La Motte, but when she entered the room where he sat, she fell at his feet, forgetting all her concerted address, and was for some moments lost in tears.

Surprised at her attitude and distress, he inquired the occasion of it, and was answered that it was caused by his own conduct. "My conduct! What part of it, pray?" inquired he.

"Your reserve, your secret sorrow, and frequent absence from the abbey."

"Is it then so wonderful that a man who has lost almost everything should sometimes lament his misfortunes? or so criminal to attempt concealing his grief that he must be blamed for it by those whom he would save from the pain of sharing it?"

Having uttered these words, he quitted the room, leaving Madame de la Motte lost in surprise, but somewhat relieved from the pressure of her former suspicions. Still, however, she pursued Adeline with an eye of scrutiny, and the mask of kindness would sometimes fall off and discover the features of distrust. Adeline, without exactly knowing why, felt less at ease and less happy in her presence than formerly; her spirits drooped, and she would often, when alone, weep at the forlornness of her condition. Formerly, her remembrance of past sufferings was lost in the friendship of Madame de la

Motte; now, though her behaviour was too guarded to betray any striking instance of unkindness, there was something in her manner which chilled the hopes of Adeline, unable as she was to analyse it. But a circumstance which soon occurred suspended for a while the jealousy of Madame de la Motte, and roused her husband from his state of gloomy stupefaction.

Peter, having been one day to Auboine for the weekly supply of provisions, returned with intelligence that awakened in La Motte new apprehension and anxiety.

"Oh, sir! I've heard something that has astonished me, as well it may," cried Peter, "and so it will you, when you come to know it. As I was standing in the blacksmith's shop, while the smith was driving a nail into the horse's shoe—by the bye, the horse lost it in an odd way, I'll tell you, sir, how it was—"

"Nay, prithee leave it till another time, and go on with your story."

"Why then, sir, as I was standing in the blacksmith's shop, comes in a man with a pipe in his mouth, and a large pouch of tobacco in his hand—"

"Well, what has the pipe to do with the story?"

"Nay, sir, you put me out; I can't go on unless you let me tell it my own way. As I was saying—with a pipe in his mouth—I think I was there, your honour!"

"Yes, yes."

"He sets himself down on the bench and, taking the pipe from his mouth, says to the blacksmith, 'Neighbour, do you know anybody of the name of La Motte hereabouts?' Bless your honour, I turned all of a cold sweat in a minute!—Is not your honour well, shall I fetch you anything?"

"No—but be short in your narrative."

"'La Motte! La Motte!' said the blacksmith, 'I think I've heard the name.' 'Have you?' said I. 'You're cunning then, for there's no such person hereabouts, to my knowledge.'"

"Fool!—why did you say that?"

"Because I did not want them to know your honour was here, and if I had not managed very cleverly, they would have found me out. 'There is no such person hereabouts, to my knowledge,' says I. 'Indeed!' says the blacksmith, 'you know more of the neighbourhood than I do then.' 'Aye,' says the man with the pipe, 'that's very true. How came you to know so much of the neighbourhood? I came here twenty-six years ago, come next St. Michael, and you know more than I do. How came you to know so much?'

"With that he put his pipe in his mouth, and gave a whiff full in my face. Lord! your honour, I trembled from head to foot. 'Nay, as for that matter,' says I, 'I don't know more than other people, but I'm sure I never heard of such a man as that.' 'Pray,' says the blacksmith, staring me full in the face, 'an't you the man that was inquiring sometime since about St. Clair's abbey?' 'Well, what of that?' says I. 'What does that prove?' 'Why, they say somebody lives in the abbey now,' said the man, turning to the other, 'and, for aught I know, it may be this same La Motte.' 'Aye, or for aught I know either,' says the man with the pipe, getting up from the bench, 'and you know more of this than you'll own. I'll lay my life on't, this Monsieur La Motte lives at the abbey.' 'Aye,' says I, 'you are out there, for he does not live at the abbey now.'"

"Confound your folly!" cried La Motte, "but be quick—how did the matter end?"

"'My master does not live there now,' said I. 'Oh! oh!' said the man with the pipe. 'He is your master, then? And pray how long has he left the abbey—and where does he live now?' 'Hold,' said I, 'not so fast—I know when to speak and when to hold my tongue—but who has been inquiring for him?'

"'What! he expected somebody to inquire for him?' says the man. 'No,' says I, 'he did not, but if he did, what does that prove?—that argues nothing.' With that, he looked at the blacksmith, and they went out of the shop together, leaving my horse's shoe undone. But I never minded that, for the moment they were gone, I mounted and rode away as fast as I could. But in my fright, your honour, I forgot to take the roundabout way, and so came straight home."

La Motte, extremely shocked at Peter's intelligence, made no other reply than by cursing his folly, and immediately went in search of Madame, who was walking with Adeline on the banks of the river. La Motte was too much agitated to soften his information by preface. "We are discovered!" said he, "the king's officers have been inquiring for me at Auboine, and Peter has blundered upon my ruin." He then informed her of what Peter had related, and bade her prepare to quit the abbey.

"But whither can we fly?" said Madame de la Motte, scarcely able to support herself.

"Anywhere!" said he. "To stay here is certain destruction. We must take refuge in Switzerland, I think. If any part of France would have concealed me, surely it had been this!"

"Alas, how are we persecuted!" rejoined Madame. "This spot is scarcely made comfortable before we are obliged to leave it, and go we know not whither."

"I wish we may not yet know whither," replied La Motte, "that is the least evil that threatens us. Let us escape a prison, and I care not whither we go. But return to the abbey immediately, and pack up what moveables you can."

A flood of tears came to the relief of Madame de la Motte, and she hung upon Adeline's arm, silent and trembling. Adeline, though she had no comfort to bestow, endeavoured to command her feelings and appear composed.

"Come," said La Motte, "we waste time; let us lament hereafter, but at present prepare for flight. Exert a little of that fortitude which is so necessary for our preservation. Adeline does not weep, yet her state is as wretched as your own, for I know not how long I shall be able to protect her."

Notwithstanding her terror, this reproof touched the pride of Madame de la Motte, who dried her tears but disdained to reply, and looked at Adeline with a strong expression of displeasure. As they moved silently toward the abbey, Adeline asked La Motte if he was sure they were the king's officers who inquired for him.

"I cannot doubt it," he replied. "Who else could possibly inquire for me? Besides, the behaviour of the man who mentioned my name puts the matter beyond a question."

"Perhaps not," said Madame de la Motte. "Let us wait till morning ere we set off. We may then find it will be unnecessary to go."

"We may, indeed; the king's officers would probably by that time have told us as much." La Motte went to give orders to Peter.

"Set off in an hour," said Peter. "Lord bless you, master! Only consider the coach wheel; it would take me a day at least to mend it, for your honour knows I never mended one in my life."

This was a circumstance which La Motte had entirely overlooked. When they settled at the abbey, Peter had at first been too busy in repairing the apartments to remember the carriage, and afterward, believing it would not quickly be wanted, he had neglected to do it. La Motte's temper now entirely forsook him, and with many execrations he ordered Peter to go to work immediately. But on searching for the materials formerly bought, they were nowhere to be found, and Peter at length remembered, though he was prudent enough to conceal this circumstance, that he had used the nails in repairing the abbey.

It was now, therefore, impossible to quit the forest that night, and La Motte had only to consider the most probable plan of concealment should the officers of justice visit the ruin before the morning; a circumstance which the thoughtlessness of Peter in returning from Auboine by the straightway made not unlikely.

At first, indeed, it occurred to him that, though his family could not be removed, he might himself take one of the horses and escape from the forest before night. But he thought there would still be some danger of detection in the towns through which he must pass, and he could not well bear the idea of leaving his family unprotected without knowing when he could return to them, or whither he could direct them to follow him. La Motte was not a man of very vigorous resolution, and he was, perhaps, rather more willing to suffer in company than alone.

After much consideration, he recollected the trapdoor of

the closet belonging to the chambers above. It was invisible to the eye and, whatever might be its direction, it would securely shelter him, at least, from discovery. Having deliberated further upon the subject, he determined to explore the recess to which the stairs led, and thought it possible that for a short time his whole family might be concealed within it. There was little time between the suggestion of the plan and the execution of his purpose, for darkness was spreading around, and in every murmur of the wind he thought he heard the voices of his enemies.

He called for a light and ascended alone to the chamber. When he came to the closet, it was some time before he could find the trapdoor, so exactly did it correspond with the boards of the floor. At length, he found and raised it. The chill damps of long confined air rushed from the aperture, and he stood for a moment to let them pass ere he descended. As he stood looking down the abyss, he recollected the report which Peter had brought concerning the abbey, and it gave him an uneasy sensation. But this soon yielded to more pressing interests.

The stairs were steep, and in many places trembled beneath his weight. Having continued to descend for some time, his feet touched the ground, and he found himself in a narrow passage; but as he turned to pursue it, the damp vapours curled round him and extinguished the light. He called aloud for Peter but could make nobody hear, and after some time, he endeavoured to find his way up the stairs. In this, with difficulty, he succeeded and, passing the chambers with cautious steps, descended the tower.

The security which the place he had just quitted seemed to promise was of too much importance to be slightly rejected, and he determined immediately to make another experiment with the light. Having now fixed it in a lanthorn, he descended a second time to the passage. The current of vapours occasioned by the opening of the trapdoor was abated, and the fresh air thence admitted had began to circulate. La Motte passed on unmolested.

The passage was of considerable length, and led him to a door which was fastened. He placed the lanthorn at some distance to avoid the current of air, and applied his strength to the door. It shook under his hands but did not yield. Upon examining it more closely, he perceived the wood round the lock was decayed, probably by the damps, and this encouraged him to proceed. After some time it gave way to his effort, and he found himself in a square stone room.

He stood for some time to survey it. The walls, which were dripping with unwholesome dews, were entirely bare and afforded not even a window. A small iron grate alone admitted the air. At the further end, near a low recess, was another door. La Motte went toward it and, as he passed, looked into the recess. Upon the ground within it stood a large chest, which he went forward to examine. Lifting the lid, he saw the remains of a human skeleton. Horror struck upon his heart, and he involuntarily stepped back. During a pause of some moments, his first emotions subsided. That thrilling curiosity which objects of terror often excite in the human mind impelled him to take a second view of this dismal spectacle.

La Motte stood motionless as he gazed; the object before him seemed to confirm the report that some person had formerly been murdered in the abbey. At length he closed the chest. He advanced to the second door, which also was fastened, but the key was in the lock. He turned it with difficulty, and then found the door was held by two strong bolts. Having undrawn these, it disclosed a flight of steps, which he descended. They terminated in a chain of low vaults, or rather cells, that, from the manner of their construction and present condition, seemed to have been coeval with the most ancient parts of the abbey. La Motte, in his then-depressed state of mind, thought them the burial places of the monks, who formerly inhabited the pile above; but they were more calculated for places of penance for the living than of rest for the dead.

Having reached the extremity of these cells, the way was again closed by a door. La Motte now hesitated whether he should attempt to proceed any farther. The present spot seemed to afford the security he sought. Here he might pass the night unmolested by apprehension of discovery, and it was most probable that if the officers arrived in the night and found the abbey vacated, they would quit it before morning, or at least before he could have any occasion to emerge from concealment. These considerations restored his mind to a state of greater composure. His only immediate care was to bring his family as soon as possible to this place of security, lest the officers should come unawares upon them; and while he stood thus musing, he blamed himself for delay.

But an irresistible desire of knowing to what this door led arrested his steps, and he turned to open it. The door, however, was fastened, and as he attempted to force it, he suddenly thought he heard a noise above. It now occurred to him that the officers might already have arrived, and he quitted the cells with precipitation, intending to listen at the trapdoor.

There, thought he, *I may wait in security, and perhaps hear something of what passes. My family will not be known, or, at least, not hurt, and their uneasiness on my account, they must learn to endure.*

These were the arguments of La Motte, in which, it must be owned, selfish prudence was more conspicuous than tender anxiety for his wife. He had by this time reached the bottom of the stairs when, on looking up, he perceived the trapdoor was left open, and ascending in haste to close it, he heard footsteps advancing through the chambers above. Before he could descend entirely out of sight, he again looked up and perceived through the aperture the face of a man looking down upon him.

"Master," cried Peter.

La Motte was somewhat relieved at the sound of his voice, though angry that he had occasioned him so much terror. "What brings you here, and what is the matter below?"

"Nothing, sir, nothing's the matter, only my mistress sent me to see after your honour."

"There's nobody there then," said La Motte, "setting his foot upon the step."

"Yes, sir, there is my mistress and Mademoiselle Adeline and—"

"Well," said La Motte briskly, "go your ways, I am coming."

He informed Madame de la Motte where he had been and of his intention of secreting himself, and deliberated upon the means of convincing the officers, should they arrive, that he had quitted the abbey. For this purpose, he ordered all the moveable furniture to be conveyed to the cells below. La Motte himself assisted in this business, and every hand was employed for dispatch. In a very short time, the habitable part of the fabric was left almost as desolate as he had found it. He then bade Peter take the horses to a distance from the abbey, and turn them loose. After further consideration, he thought it might contribute to mislead them if he placed in some conspicuous part of the fabric an inscription signifying his condition, and mentioning the date of his departure from the abbey. Over the door of the tower, which led to the habitable part of the structure, he therefore cut the following lines.

"O ye! whom misfortune may lead to this spot,
Learn that there are others as miserable as yourselves."
P——— L—— M———, a wretched exile, sought within these walls a refuge from persecution, on the 27th of April 1658, and quitted them on the 12th of July in the same year, in search of a more convenient asylum.

After engraving these words with a knife, the small stock of provisions remaining from the week's supply (for Peter, in his fright, had returned unloaded from his last journey) was put into a basket, and La Motte having assembled his family, they all ascended the stairs of the tower and passed through the chambers to the closet. Peter went first with a light, and with some difficulty found the trapdoor. Madame de la Motte shuddered as she surveyed the gloomy abyss; but they were all silent.

La Motte now took the light and led the way; Madame followed, and then Adeline, followed by the servant Annette.

[61]

"These old monks loved good wine, as well as other people," said Peter, who brought up the rear. "I warrant your honour, now, this was their cellar; I smell the casks already."

"Peace," said La Motte, "reserve your jokes for a proper occasion."

"There is no harm in loving good wine, as your honour knows."

"Have done with this buffoonery," said La Motte, in a tone more authoritative, "and go first." Peter obeyed.

They came to the vaulted room. The dismal spectacle he had seen here deterred La Motte from passing the night in this chamber; and the furniture had, by his own order, been conveyed to the cells below. He was anxious that his family should not perceive the skeleton, an object which would probably excite a degree of horror not to be overcome during their stay. La Motte now passed the chest in haste; and Madame de la Motte and Adeline were too much engrossed by their own thoughts to give minute attention to external circumstances.

When they reached the cells, Madame de la Motte wept at the necessity which condemned her to a spot so dismal. "Alas," said she, "are we, indeed, thus reduced! The apartments above, formerly appeared to me a deplorable habitation; but they are a palace compared to these."

"True, my dear," said La Motte, "and let the remembrance of what you once thought them soothe your discontent now; these cells are also a palace, compared to the Bicêtre or the Bastille[30] and to the terrors of further punishment which would accompany them. Let the apprehension of the greater evil teach you to endure the less; I am contented if we find here the refuge I seek."

Madame de la Motte was silent, and Adeline, forgetting her late unkindness, endeavoured as much as she could to console her; while her heart was sinking with the misfortunes which she could not but anticipate, she appeared composed and even cheerful. She attended Madame de la Motte with the

30. Bicêtre, a notorious prison, military hospital, and insane asylum located south of Paris; Bastille, a fortress in Paris used as a royal prison.

most watchful solicitude, and felt so thankful that La Motte was now secreted within this recess that she almost lost her perception of its glooms and inconveniences.

This she artlessly expressed to him, who could not be insensible to the tenderness it discovered. Madame de la Motte was also sensible of it, and it renewed a painful sensation. The effusions of gratitude she mistook for those of tenderness.

La Motte returned frequently to the trapdoor to listen if anybody was in the abbey, but no sound disturbed the stillness of night. At length they sat down to supper; the repast was a melancholy one.

"If the officers do not come hither tonight," said Madame de la Motte, sighing, "suppose, my dear, Peter returns to Auboine tomorrow. He may there learn something more of this affair, or at least he might procure a carriage to convey us hence."

"To be sure he might," said La Motte peevishly, "and people to attend it also. Peter would be an excellent person to show the officers the way to the abbey, and to inform them of what they might else be in doubt about, my concealment here."

"How cruel is this irony!" replied Madame de la Motte. "I proposed only what I thought would be for our mutual good; my judgement was, perhaps, wrong, but my intention was certainly right." Tears swelled into her eyes as she spoke these words. Adeline wished to relieve her; but delicacy kept her silent.

La Motte observed the effect of his speech, and something like remorse touched his heart. He approached and took her hand. "You must allow for the perturbation of my mind," said he. "I did not mean to afflict you thus. The idea of sending Peter to Auboine, where he has already done so much harm by his blunders, teased me, and I could not let it pass unnoticed. No, my dear, our only chance of safety is to remain where we are while our provisions last. If the officers do not come here tonight, they probably will tomorrow, or perhaps the next day. When they have searched the abbey without finding me, they will depart; we may then emerge from this recess, and take measures for removing to a distant country."

Madame de la Motte acknowledged the justice of his words, and her mind being relieved by the little apology he had made, she became tolerably cheerful. Supper being ended, La Motte stationed the faithful though simple Peter at the foot of the steps that ascended to the closet; there to keep watch during the night. Having done this, he returned to the lower cells, where he had left his little family. The beds were spread, and having mournfully bade each other good night, they lay down, and implored rest.

Adeline's thoughts were too busy to suffer her to repose, and when she believed her companions were sunk in slumbers, she indulged the sorrow which reflection brought. She also looked forward to the future with the most mournful apprehension. *Should La Motte be seized, what is to become of me? I would then be a wanderer in the wide world, without friends to protect or money to support me; the prospect is gloomy—is terrible!* She surveyed it and shuddered! The distresses, too, of Monsieur and Madame de la Motte, whom she loved with the most lively affection, formed no inconsiderable part of hers.

Sometimes she looked back to her father; but in him she only saw an enemy, from whom she must fly. This remembrance heightened her sorrow, yet it was not the recollection of the suffering he had occasioned her by which she was so much afflicted as by the sense of his unkindness; she wept bitterly. At length, with that artless piety which innocence only knows, she addressed the Supreme Being, and resigned herself to his care. Her mind then gradually became peaceful and reassured, and soon after she sank to repose.

CHAPTER 5

A Surprise—An Adventure—A Mystery

The night passed without any alarm; Peter had remained upon his post, and heard nothing that prevented his sleeping. La Motte heard him, long before he saw him, most musically snoring; though it must be owned there was more of the bass than of any other part of the gamut in his performance. He was soon roused by the bravura of La Motte, whose notes sounded discord to his ears, and destroyed the torpor of his tranquillity.

"God bless you, master, what's the matter?" cried Peter, waking. "Are they come?"

"Yes, for aught you care, they might be come. Did I place you here to sleep, sirrah?"

"Bless you, master," returned Peter, "sleep is the only comfort to be had here; I'm sure I would not deny it to a dog in such a place as this."

La Motte sternly questioned him concerning any noise he might have heard in the night, and Peter full as solemnly protested he had heard none; an assertion which was strictly true, for he had enjoyed the comfort of being asleep the whole time.

La Motte ascended to the trapdoor and listened attentively. No sounds were heard, and as he ventured to lift it, the full light of the sun burst upon his sight, the morning being now far advanced; he walked softly along the chambers, and looked

[65]

through a window; no person was to be seen. Encouraged by this apparent security, he ventured down the stairs of the tower, and entered the first apartment. He was proceeding toward the second when, suddenly recollecting himself, he first peeped through the crevice of the door which stood half open. He looked, and distinctly saw a person whose back was toward him sitting near the window, upon which his arm rested.

The discovery so much shocked him that for a moment he lost all presence of mind, and was utterly unable to move from the spot. The person arose, and turned his head. La Motte now recovered himself, and quitting the apartment as quickly, and at the same time as silently, as possible, ascended to the closet. He raised the trapdoor and descended, but before he closed it heard the footsteps of a person entering the outer chamber. Bolts or other fastening to the trap there was none; and his security depended solely upon the exact correspondence of the boards. The outer door of the stone room had no means of defence, and the fastenings of the inner one were on the wrong side to afford security, even till some means of escape could be found.

When he reached this room, he paused, and heard distinctly persons walking in the closet above. While he was listening, he heard a voice call him by name, and instantly fled to the cells below, expecting every moment to hear the trap lifted and the footsteps of pursuit; but he was fled beyond the reach of hearing either. Having thrown himself on the ground at the farthest extremity of the vaults, he lay for some time breathless with agitation. Madame de la Motte and Adeline, in the utmost terror, inquired what had happened. It was some time before he could speak; when he did, it was almost unnecessary, for the distant noises which sounded from above informed his family of a part of the truth.

The sounds did not seem to approach, but Madame de la Motte, unable to command her terror, shrieked aloud; this redoubled the distress of La Motte.

"You have already destroyed me," cried he. "That shriek

has informed them where I am." He traversed the cells with clasped hands and quick steps.

Adeline stood pale and still as death, supporting Madame de la Motte, whom with difficulty she prevented from fainting.

"O! Dupras! Dupras! you are already avenged!" said he in a voice that seemed to burst from his heart; there was a pause of silence. "But why should I deceive myself with a hope of escaping? Why do I wait here for their coming? Let me rather end these torturing pangs by throwing myself into their hands at once."

As he spoke, he moved toward the door, but the distress of Madame de la Motte arrested his steps. "Stay," said she, "for my sake, stay; do not leave me thus, nor throw yourself voluntarily into destruction!"

"Surely, sir," said Adeline, "you are too precipitate; this despair is useless, as it is ill-founded. We hear no person approaching; if the officers had discovered the trapdoor, they would certainly have been here before now."

The words of Adeline stilled the tumult of his mind: the agitation of terror subsided, and reason beamed a feeble ray upon his hopes. He listened attentively, and perceiving that all was silent, advanced with caution to the stone room; and thence to the foot of the stairs that led to the trapdoor. It was closed; no sound was heard above.

He watched a long time, and the silence continuing, his hopes strengthened. At length, he began to believe that the officers had quitted the abbey; the day, however, was spent in anxious watchfulness. He did not dare to unclose the trapdoor; and he frequently thought he heard distant noises. It was evident, however, that the secret of the closet had escaped discovery; and on this circumstance he justly founded his security. The following night was passed, like the day, in trembling hope and incessant watching.

But the necessities of hunger now threatened them. The provisions, which had been distributed with the nicest economy, were nearly exhausted, and the most deplorable consequences might be expected from their remaining longer in concealment. Thus circumstanced, La Motte deliberated upon the most prudent method of proceeding. There appeared no other alternative than to send Peter to Auboine, the only town from which he could return within the time prescribed by their necessities. There was game, indeed, in the forest; but Peter could neither handle a gun nor use a fishing rod to any advantage.

It was, therefore, agreed he should go to Auboine for a supply of provisions, and at the same time bring materials for mending the coach wheel, that they might have some ready conveyance from the forest. La Motte forbade Peter to ask any questions concerning the people who had inquired for him or take any methods for discovering whether they had quitted the country, lest his blunders should again betray him. He ordered him to be entirely silent as to these subjects, and to finish his business, and to leave the place with all possible dispatch.

A difficulty yet remained to be overcome: Who should first venture abroad into the abbey to learn whether it was vacated by the officers of justice? La Motte considered that if he was again seen, he should be effectually betrayed; a circumstance which would not be so certain if one of his family was observed, for they were all unknown to the officers. It was necessary, however, that the person he sent should have courage enough to go through with the inquiry, and wit enough to conduct it with caution. Peter, perhaps, had the first, but was certainly destitute of the last. Annette had neither. La Motte looked at his wife, and asked her if, for his sake, she dared to venture. Her heart shrank from the proposal, yet she was unwilling to refuse or appear indifferent upon a point so essential to the safety of her husband.

Adeline observed in her countenance the agitation of her mind, and surmounting the fears which had hitherto kept her silent, she offered herself to go. "They will be less likely to offend me," said she, "than a man."

Shame would not suffer La Motte to accept her offer; and

Madame, touched by the magnanimity of her conduct, felt a momentary renewal of all her former kindness.

Adeline pressed her proposal so warmly, and seemed so much in earnest, that La Motte began to hesitate. "You, sir," said she, "once preserved me from the most imminent danger, and your kindness has since protected me. Do not refuse me the satisfaction of deserving your goodness by a grateful return of it. Let me go into the abbey, and if by so doing, I should preserve you from evil, I shall be sufficiently rewarded for what little danger I may incur, for my pleasure will be at least equal to yours."

Madame de la Motte could scarcely refrain from tears as Adeline spoke; and La Motte, sighing deeply, said, "Well, be it so; go, Adeline, and from this moment consider me as your debtor."

Adeline stayed not to reply, but taking a light, quitted the cells.

La Motte followed to raise the trapdoor, and cautioned her to look, if possible, into every apartment before she entered it. "If you should be seen," said he, "you must account for your appearance so as not to discover me. Your own presence of mind may assist you, I cannot. God bless you!"

When she was gone, Madame de la Motte's admiration of her conduct began to yield to other emotions. Distrust gradually undermined kindness, and jealousy raised suspicions. *It must be a sentiment more powerful than gratitude*, thought she, *that could teach Adeline to subdue her fears. What but Love could influence her to a conduct so generous!* Madame de la Motte, when she found it impossible to account for Adeline's conduct without alleging some interested motives for it, however her suspicions might agree with the practice of the world, had surely forgotten how much she once admired the purity and disinterestedness of her young friend.

Adeline, meanwhile, ascended to the chambers. The cheerful beams of the sun played once more upon her sight, and reanimated her spirits; she walked lightly through the apartments, nor stopped till she came to the stairs of the tower. Here she stood for some time, but no sounds met her ear save the sighing of the wind among the trees, and at length she descended. She passed the apartments below without seeing any person; and the little furniture that remained seemed to stand exactly as she had left it. She now ventured to look out from the tower. The only animate objects that appeared were the deer, quietly grazing under the shade of the woods. Her favourite little fawn distinguished Adeline, and came bounding toward her with strong marks of joy. She was somewhat alarmed lest the animal, being observed, should betray her, and walked swiftly away through the cloisters.

She opened the door that led to the great hall of the abbey, but the passage was so gloomy and dark that she feared to enter it, and started back. It was necessary, however, that she should examine further, particularly on the opposite side of the ruin, of which she had hitherto had no view. But her fears returned when she recollected how far it would lead her from her only place of refuge, and how difficult it would be to retreat. She hesitated what to do; but when she recollected her obligations to La Motte and considered this as perhaps her only opportunity of doing him a service, she determined to proceed.

As these thoughts passed rapidly over her mind, she raised her innocent looks to heaven, and breathed a silent prayer. With trembling steps she proceeded over fragments of the ruin, looking anxiously around, and often starting as the breeze rustled among the trees, mistaking it for the whisperings of men. She came to the lawn which fronted the fabric, but no person was to be seen, and her spirits revived. The great door of the hall she now endeavoured to open, but suddenly remembering that it was fastened by La Motte's orders, she proceeded to the north end of the abbey and, having surveyed the prospect around as far as the thick foliage of the trees would permit without perceiving any person, she turned her steps to the tower from which she had issued.

Adeline was now light of heart, and returned with impatience to inform La Motte of his security. In the cloisters she was again met by her little favourite, and stopped for a moment to caress it. The fawn seemed sensible to the sound of her voice, and discovered new joy; but while she spoke it suddenly started from her hand, and looking up, she perceived the door of the passage leading to the great hall open, and a man in the habit of a soldier issue forth.

With the swiftness of an arrow she fled along the cloisters, nor once ventured to look back; but a voice called to her to stop, and she heard steps advancing quick in pursuit. Before she could reach the tower, her breath failed her, and she leaned against a pillar of the ruin, pale and exhausted. The man came up, and gazing at her with a strong expression of surprise and curiosity, he assumed a gentle manner, assured her she had nothing to fear, and inquired if she belonged to La Motte. Observing that she still looked terrified and remained silent, he repeated his assurances and his question.

"I know that he is concealed within these ruins," said the stranger. "The occasion of his concealment I also know; but it is of the utmost importance I should see him, and he will then be convinced he has nothing to fear from me."

Adeline trembled so excessively that it was with difficulty she could support herself; she hesitated, and knew not what to reply. Her manner seemed to confirm the suspicions of the stranger, and her consciousness of this increased her embarrassment: he took advantage of it to press her further. Adeline, at length, replied, "La Motte had some time since resided at the abbey."

"And does still, madam," said the stranger. "Lead me to where he may be found—I must see him, and—"

"Never, sir," replied Adeline, "and I solemnly assure you, it will be in vain to search for him."

"That I must try," resumed he, "since you, madam, will not assist me. I have already followed him to some chambers above, where I suddenly lost him: thereabouts he must be concealed, and it's plain, therefore, they afford some secret passage."

Without waiting Adeline's reply, he sprang to the door of the tower. She now thought it would betray a consciousness of the truth of his conjecture to follow him, and resolved to remain below. But upon further consideration, it occurred to her that he might steal silently into the closet, and possibly surprise La Motte at the door of the trap. She therefore hastened after him, that her voice might prevent the danger she apprehended. He was already in the second chamber when she overtook him; she immediately began to speak aloud.

This room he searched with the most scrupulous care, but finding no private door or other outlet, he proceeded to the closet: then it was, that it required all her fortitude to conceal her agitation.

He continued the search. "Within these chambers, I know he is concealed," said he, "though hitherto I have not been able to discover how. It was hither I followed a man whom I believe to be him, and he could not escape without a passage; I shall not quit the place till I have found it."

He examined the walls and the boards, but without discovering the division of the floor, which, indeed, so exactly corresponded that La Motte himself had not perceived it by the eye, but by the trembling of the floor beneath his feet. "Here is some mystery," said the stranger, "which I cannot comprehend, and perhaps never shall."

He was turning to quit the closet when—who can paint the distress of Adeline upon seeing the trapdoor gently raised!— La Motte himself appeared.

"Hah!" cried the stranger, advancing eagerly to him. La Motte sprang forward, and they were locked in each other's arms.

The astonishment of Adeline for a moment surpassed even her former distress; but a remembrance darted across her mind which explained the present scene, and before La Motte could exclaim "My son!" she knew the stranger as such. Peter, who stood at the foot of the stairs and heard what passed above, flew to acquaint his mistress with the joyful discovery, and in a few moments, she was folded in the embrace of her son, Louis. This spot, so lately the mansion of despair, seemed metamorphosed into the palace of pleasure, and the walls echoed only to the accents of joy and congratulation.

The joy of Peter on this occasion was beyond expression: he acted a perfect pantomime—he capered about—clasped his hands—ran to his young master—shook him by the hand, in spite of the frowns of La Motte; ran everywhere, without knowing for what, and gave no rational answer to anything that was said to him.

After their first emotions were subsided, La Motte, as if suddenly recollecting himself, resumed his wonted solemnity. "I am to blame," said he, "thus to give way to joy, when I am still, perhaps, surrounded by danger. Let us secure a retreat while it is yet in our power," continued he, "in a few hours the king's officers may search for me again."

Louis comprehended his father's words, and immediately relieved his apprehensions by the following relation.

۶ֶ؇ꝏ؇۶

A letter from Monsieur Nemours containing an account of your flight from Paris reached me at Péronne,[31] where I was then upon duty with my regiment. He mentioned that you was gone toward the south of France, but as he had not since heard from you, he was ignorant of the place of your refuge. It was about this time that I was dispatched into Flanders,[32] and being unable to obtain further intelligence of you, I passed some weeks of very painful solicitude. At the conclusion of the campaign, I obtained leave of absence, and immediately set out for Paris, hoping to learn from Nemours where you had found an asylum.

Of this, however, he was equally ignorant with myself. He informed me that you had once before written to him from D———, upon your second day's journey from Paris, under an assumed name, as had been agreed upon; and that you then said the fear of discovery would prevent your hazarding another letter. He, therefore, remained ignorant of your

31. A town in northern France near the border of Belgium.
32. Present-day Belgium.

abode, but said he had no doubt you had continued your journey to the southward. Upon this slender information I quitted Paris in search of you, and proceeded immediately to V———, where my inquiries concerning your farther progress were successful as far as M———. There they told me you had stayed some time, on account of the illness of a young lady; a circumstance which perplexed me much, as I could not imagine what young lady would accompany you. I proceeded, however, to L———, but there all traces of you seemed to be lost. As I sat musing at the window of the inn, I observed some scribbling on the glass, and the curiosity of idleness prompted me to read it. I thought I knew the characters, and the lines I read confirmed my conjecture, for I remembered to have heard you often repeat them.

Here I renewed my inquiries concerning your route, and at length I made the people of the inn recollect you, and traced you as far as Auboine. There I again lost you, till upon my return from a fruitless inquiry in the neighbourhood, the landlord of the little inn where I lodged told me he believed he had heard news of you, and immediately recounted what had happened at a blacksmith's shop a few hours before.

His description of Peter was so exact that I had not a doubt it was you who inhabited the abbey; and as I knew your necessity for concealment, Peter's denial did not shake my confidence. The next morning, with the assistance of my landlord, I found my way hither, and having searched every visible part of the fabric, I began to credit Peter's assertion; your appearance, however, destroyed this fear by proving that the place was still inhabited, for you disappeared so instantaneously that I was not certain it was you whom I had seen. I continued seeking you till near the close of day, and till then scarcely quitted the chambers whence you had disappeared. I called on you repeatedly, believing that my voice might convince you of your mistake. At length, I retired to pass the night at a cottage near the border of the forest.

I came early this morning to renew my inquiries, and hoped

that, believing yourself safe, you would emerge from concealment. But how I was disappointed to find the abbey as silent
and solitary as I had left it the preceding evening! I was returning once more from the great hall when the voice of this
young lady caught my ear, and effected the discovery I had
so anxiously sought.

This little narrative entirely dissipated the late apprehensions of
La Motte, but he now dreaded that the inquiries of his son and
his own obvious desire of concealment might excite a curiosity
amongst the people of Auboine, and lead to a discovery of his
true circumstances. However, for the present he determined
to dismiss all painful thoughts, and endeavour to enjoy the
comfort which the presence of his son had brought him. The
furniture was removed to a more habitable part of the abbey,
and the cells were again abandoned to their own glooms.

The arrival of her son seemed to have animated Madame
de la Motte with new life, and all her afflictions were, for the
present, absorbed in joy. She often gazed silently on him with
a mother's fondness, and her partiality heightened every improvement which time had wrought in his person and manner.
He was now in his twenty-third year; his person was manly
and his air military; his manners were unaffected and graceful,
rather than dignified; and though his features were irregular,
they composed a countenance which, having seen it once, you
would seek again.

She made eager inquiries after the friends she had left at
Paris, and learned that within the few months of her absence
some had died and others quitted the place. La Motte also
learned that a very strenuous search for him had been prosecuted at Paris. Though this intelligence was only what he had
before expected, it shocked him so much that he now declared
it would be expedient to remove to a distant country. Louis
did not scruple to say that he thought he would be as safe at

the abbey as at any other place, and repeated what Nemours had said, that the king's officers had been unable to trace any part of his route from Paris.

"Besides," resumed Louis, "this abbey is protected by a supernatural power, and none of the country people dare approach it."

"Please you, my young master," said Peter, who was waiting in the room, "we were frightened enough the first night we came here, and I, myself, God forgive me! thought the place was inhabited by devils, but they were only owls, and such like, after all."

"Your opinion was not asked," said La Motte. "Learn to be silent."

Peter was abashed. When he had quitted the room, La Motte asked his son with seeming carelessness, "What were the reports circulated by the country people?"

"O! sir," replied Louis, "I cannot recollect half of them. I remember, however, they said that many years ago a person— but nobody had ever seen him, so we may judge how far the report ought to be credited—a person was privately brought to this abbey, and confined in some part of it, and that there were strong reasons to believe he came unfairly to his end."

La Motte sighed.

"They further said," continued Louis, "that the spectre of the deceased had ever since watched nightly among the ruins. And to make the story more wonderful, for the marvellous is the delight of the vulgar, they added that there was a certain part of the ruin from whence no person that had dared to explore it had ever returned. Thus people who have few objects of real interest to engage their thoughts conjure up for themselves imaginary ones."

La Motte sat musing. "And what were the reasons," said he, at length awaking from his reverie, "they pretended to assign for believing the person confined here was murdered?"

"They did not use a term so positive as that," replied Louis.

"True," said La Motte, recollecting himself, "they only said he came unfairly to his end."

"That is a nice distinction," said Adeline.

"Why, I could not well comprehend what these reasons were," resumed Louis. "The people indeed say that the person who was brought here was never known to depart, but I do not find it certain that he ever arrived; that there was strange privacy and mystery observed while he was here; and that the abbey has never since been inhabited by its owner. There seems, however, to be nothing in all this that deserves to be remembered."

La Motte raised his head as if to reply, when the entrance of Madame turned the discourse upon a new subject, and it was not resumed that day.

Peter was now dispatched for provisions, while La Motte and Louis retired to consider how far it was safe for them to continue at the abbey. La Motte, notwithstanding the assurances lately given him, could not but think that Peter's blunders and his son's inquiries might lead to a discovery of his residence. He revolved this in his mind for some time, but at length a thought struck him, that the latter of these circumstances might considerably contribute to his security.

"If you," said he to Louis, "return to the inn at Auboine, from whence you were directed here, and without seeming to intend giving intelligence, do give the landlord an account of your having found the abbey uninhabited, and then add that you had discovered the residence of the person you sought in some distant town, it would suppress any reports that may at present exist, and prevent the belief of any in future. And if, after all this, you can trust yourself for presence of mind and command of countenance so far as to describe some dreadful apparition, I think these circumstances, together with the distance of the abbey and the intricacies of the forest, could entitle me to consider this place as my castle."

Louis agreed to all that his father had proposed, and on the following day executed his commission with such success that the tranquillity of the abbey may be then said to have been entirely restored.

Thus ended this adventure, the only one that had occurred

to disturb the family during their residence in the forest. Adeline, removed from the apprehension of those evils with which the late situation of La Motte had threatened her and from the depression which her interest in his occasioned her, now experienced a more than usual complacency of mind. She thought too that she observed in Madame de la Motte a renewal of her former kindness, and this circumstance awakened all her gratitude and imparted to her a pleasure as lively as it was innocent. The satisfaction with which the presence of her son inspired Madame de la Motte, Adeline mistook for kindness to herself, and she exerted her whole attention in an endeavour to become worthy of it.

But the joy which his unexpected arrival had given to La Motte quickly began to evaporate, and the gloom of despondency again settled on his countenance. He returned frequently to his haunt in the forest; the same mysterious sadness tinctured his manner and revived the anxiety of Madame de la Motte, who was resolved to acquaint her son with this subject of distress and solicit his assistance to penetrate its source.

Her jealousy of Adeline, however, she could not communicate, though it again tormented her and taught her to misconstrue with wonderful ingenuity every look and word of La Motte, and often to mistake the artless expressions of Adeline's gratitude and regard for those of warmer tenderness. Adeline had formerly accustomed herself to long walks in the forest, and the design Madame had formed of watching her steps had been frustrated by the late circumstances, and was now entirely overcome by her sense of its difficulty and danger. To employ Peter in the affair would be to acquaint him with her fears, and to follow her herself would most probably betray her scheme by making Adeline aware of her jealousy. Being thus restrained by pride and delicacy, she was obliged to endure the pangs of uncertainty concerning the greatest part of her suspicions.

To Louis, however, she related the mysterious change in his father's temper. He listened to her account with very earnest attention, and the surprise and concern impressed upon his countenance spoke how much his heart was interested. He was, however, involved in equal perplexity with herself upon this subject, and readily undertook to observe the motions of La Motte, believing his interference likely to be of equal service both to his father and his mother. He saw in some degree the suspicions of his mother, but as he thought she wished to disguise her feelings, he suffered her to believe that she succeeded.

He now inquired concerning Adeline, and listened with great apparent interest to her little history, of which his mother gave a brief relation. So much pity did he express for her condition, and so much indignation at the unnatural conduct of her father, that the apprehensions which Madame de la Motte began to form of his having discovered her jealousy yielded to those of a different kind. She perceived that the beauty of Adeline had already fascinated his imagination, and she feared that her amiable manners would soon impress his heart. Had her first fondness for Adeline continued, she would still have looked with displeasure upon their attachment as an obstacle to the promotion and the fortune she hoped to see one day enjoyed by her son. On these she rested all her future hopes of prosperity, and regarded the matrimonial alliance which he might form as the only means of extricating his family from their present difficulties. She therefore touched lightly upon Adeline's merit, joined coolly with Louis in compassionating her misfortunes, and with her censure of the father's conduct mixed an implied suspicion of that of Adeline's. The means she employed to repress the passions of her son had a contrary effect. The indifference which she repressed toward Adeline increased his pity for her destitute condition, and the tenderness with which she affected to judge the father heightened his honest indignation at his character.

As he quitted Madame de la Motte, he saw his father cross the lawn and enter the deep shade of the forest on the left. He judged this to be a good opportunity of commencing his plan and, quitting the abbey, slowly followed at a distance. La Motte continued to walk straight forward, and seemed so deeply wrapt in thought that he looked neither to the right or left, and scarcely lifted his head from the ground. Louis had followed him near half a mile when he saw him suddenly strike into an avenue of the forest which took a different direction from the way he had hitherto gone. He quickened his steps that he might not lose sight of him but, having reached the avenue, found the trees so thickly interwoven that La Motte was already hid from his view.

He continued, however, to pursue the way before him. It conducted him through the most gloomy part of the forest he had yet seen, till at length it terminated in an obscure recess overarched with high trees, whose interwoven branches secluded the direct rays of the sun and admitted only a sort of solemn twilight. Louis looked around in search of La Motte, but he was nowhere to be seen. While he stood surveying the place and considering what further should be done, he observed through the gloom an object at some distance, but the deep shadow that fell around prevented his distinguishing what it was.

In advancing, he perceived the ruins of a small building, which from the traces that remained appeared to have been a tomb. As he gazed upon it, he thought, *Here are probably deposited the ashes of some ancient monk, once an inhabitant of the abbey; perhaps of the founder who, after having spent a life of abstinence and prayer, sought in heaven the reward of his forbearance upon earth. Peace be to his soul! but did he think a life of mere negative virtue deserved an eternal reward? Mistaken man! Reason, had you trusted to its dictates, would have informed you that the active virtues, the adherence to the golden rule, "Do as you would be done unto," could alone deserve the favour of a Deity whose glory is benevolence.*

He remained with his eyes fixed upon the spot, and presently saw a figure arise under the arch of the sepulchre. It started, as if on perceiving him, and immediately disappeared. Louis, though unused to fear, felt at that moment an uneasy sensation, but almost immediately it struck him that this was La Motte himself. He advanced to the ruin and called him. No answer was returned, and he repeated the call, but all was yet still as the grave. He then went up to the archway and endeavoured to examine the place where he had disappeared, but the shadowy obscurity rendered the attempt fruitless. He observed, however, an entrance to the ruin a little to the right, and had advanced some steps down a kind of dark passage when, recollecting that this place might be the haunt of banditti, his danger alarmed him, and he retreated with precipitation.

He walked toward the abbey by the way he came, and finding no person followed him and believing himself again in safety, his former surmise returned, and he thought it was La Motte he had seen. He mused upon this strange possibility, and endeavoured to assign a reason for so mysterious a conduct, but in vain. Notwithstanding this, his belief of it strengthened, and he entered the abbey under as full a conviction as the circumstances would admit of, that it was his father who had appeared in the sepulchre. On entering what was now used as a parlour, he was much surprised to find him quietly seated there with Madame de la Motte and Adeline, and conversing as if he had been returned some time.

He took the first opportunity of acquainting his mother with his late adventure, and of inquiring how long La Motte had been returned before him; when learning that it was near half an hour, his surprise increased, and he knew not what to conclude.

Meanwhile, a perception of the growing partiality of Louis cooperated with the canker of suspicion to destroy in Madame de la Motte that affection which pity and esteem had formerly excited for Adeline. Her unkindness was now too obvious to escape the notice of her to whom it was directed, and being noticed, it occasioned an anguish which Adeline found it very difficult to endure. With the warmth and candour of youth, she sought an explanation of this change of behaviour and an opportunity of exculpating herself from any intention of provoking it. But this Madame de la Motte artfully evaded, while at the same time she threw out hints that involved Adeline in deeper perplexity, and served to make her present affliction more intolerable.

I have lost that affection, she would think, *which was my all. It was my only comfort—yet I have lost it—and this without even knowing my offence. But I am thankful I have not merited unkindness, and though she has abandoned me, I shall always love her.*

Thus distressed, she would frequently leave the parlour and, retiring to her chamber, yield to a despondency which she had never known till now.

One morning, being unable to sleep, she arose at a very early hour. The faint light of day now trembled through the clouds and, gradually spreading from the horizon, announced the rising sun. Every feature of the landscape was slowly unveiled, moist with the dews of night, and brightening with the dawn, till at length the sun appeared and shed the full flood of day. The beauty of the hour invited her to walk, and she went forth into the forest to taste the sweets of morning. The carols of new-waked birds saluted her as she passed, and the fresh gale came scented with the breath of flowers, whose tints glowed more vivid through the dewdrops that hung on the leaves.

She wandered on without noticing the distance and, following the windings of the river, came to a dewy glade, whose woods, sweeping down to the very edge of the water, formed a scene so sweetly romantic that she seated herself at the foot of a tree to contemplate its beauty. These images insensibly soothed her sorrow and inspired her with that soft and pleasing melancholy so dear to the feeling mind. For some time she sat lost in a reverie, while the flowers that grew on the banks beside her seemed to smile in new life, and drew from her a comparison with her own condition. She mused and sighed, and then, in a voice whose charming melody was modulated by the tenderness of her heart, she sang a pensive air.

A distant echo lengthened out her tones, and she sat listening to the soft response, till repeating the last stanza of the song, she was answered by a voice almost as tender, and less distant. She looked round in surprise, and saw a young man in hunter's dress leaning against a tree and gazing on her with that deep attention which marks an enraptured mind.

A thousand apprehensions shot athwart her busy thought,

and she now first remembered her distance from the abbey. She rose in haste to be gone when the stranger respectfully advanced; but observing her timid looks and retiring steps, he paused. She pursued her way toward the abbey, and though many reasons made her anxious to know whether she was followed, delicacy forbade her to look back.

When she reached the abbey, finding the family was not yet assembled to breakfast, she retired to her chamber, where her whole thoughts were employed in conjectures concerning the stranger; believing that she was interested on this point no further than as it concerned the safety of La Motte, she indulged without scruple the remembrance of that dignified air and manner which so much distinguished the youth she had seen. After revolving the circumstance more deeply, she believed it impossible that a person of his appearance should be engaged in a stratagem to betray a fellow creature; and though she was destitute of a single circumstance that might assist her surmises of who he was or what was his business in an unfrequented forest, she rejected, unconsciously, every suspicion injurious to his character. Upon further deliberation, therefore, she resolved not to mention this little circumstance to La Motte, well knowing that though his danger might be imaginary, his apprehensions would be real, and would renew all the sufferings and perplexity from which he was but just released. She resolved, however, to refrain for some time walking in the forest.

When she came down to breakfast, she observed Madame de la Motte to be more than usually reserved. La Motte entered the room soon after her, and made some trifling observations on the weather; and having endeavoured to support an effort at cheerfulness, sank into his usual melancholy. Adeline watched the countenance of Madame with anxiety; and when there appeared in it a gleam of kindness, it was as sunshine to her soul; but Madame very seldom suffered Adeline thus to flatter herself. Her conversation was restrained, and often pointed at something more than could be understood. The entrance of Louis was a very seasonable relief to Adeline, who almost feared to trust her voice with a sentence, lest its trembling accents should betray her uneasiness.

"This charming morning drew you early from your chamber," said Louis, addressing Adeline.

"You had, no doubt, a pleasant companion too," said Madame de la Motte. "A solitary walk is seldom agreeable."

"I was alone, madam," replied Adeline.

"Indeed! your own thoughts must be highly pleasing then."

"Alas!" returned Adeline, a tear, in spite of her efforts, starting to her eye, "there are now few subjects of pleasure left for them."

"That is very surprising," pursued Madame de la Motte.

"Is it indeed surprising, madam, for those who have lost their last friend to be unhappy?"

Madame de la Motte's conscience acknowledged the rebuke, and she blushed. "Well," resumed she after a short pause, and looking earnestly at La Motte, "that is not your situation, Adeline."

Adeline, whose innocence protected her from suspicion, did not regard this circumstance but, smiling through her tears, said she rejoiced to hear her say so.

During this conversation, La Motte had remained absorbed in his own thoughts; and Louis, unable to guess at what it pointed, looked alternately at his mother and Adeline for an explanation. The latter he regarded with an expression so full of tender compassion that it revealed at once to Madame de la Motte the sentiments of his soul; and she immediately replied to the last words of Adeline with a very serious air: "A friend is only estimable when our conduct deserves one; the friendship that survives the merit of its object is a disgrace, instead of an honour, to both parties."

The manner and emphasis with which she delivered these words again alarmed Adeline, who mildly said, "I hope I should never deserve such censure."

Madame was silent; but Adeline was so much shocked by what had already passed that tears sprang from her eyes, and she hid her face with her handkerchief.

Louis now rose with some emotion. La Motte, roused from his reverie, inquired what was the matter; but before he could receive an answer, he seemed to have forgot that he had asked the question.

"Adeline may give you her own account," said Madame de la Motte.

"I have not deserved this," said Adeline, rising, "but since my presence is displeasing, I will retire."

She was moving toward the door when Louis, who was pacing the room in apparent agitation, gently took her hand, saying, "Here is some unhappy mistake," and would have led her to the seat.

But her spirits were too much depressed to endure longer restraint. Withdrawing her hand, "Suffer me to go," said she. "If there is any mistake, I am unable to explain it." Saying this, she quitted the room.

Louis's eyes followed her to the door. "Surely, madam," said he, turning to his mother, "you are to blame. My life on it, she deserves your warmest tenderness."

"You are very eloquent in her cause, sir," said Madame. "May I presume to ask what has interested you thus in her favour?"

"Her own amiable manners," rejoined Louis, "which no one can observe without esteeming them."

"But you may presume too much on your own observations; it is possible these amiable manners may deceive you."

"Your pardon, madam; I may without presumption affirm they cannot deceive me."

"You have, no doubt, good reasons for this assertion, and I perceive, by your admiration of this artless innocent, she has succeeded in her design of entrapping your heart."

"Without designing it, she has won my admiration, which would not have been the case had she been capable of the conduct you mention."

Madame de la Motte was going to reply but was prevented by her husband, who, again roused from his reverie, inquired into the cause of dispute. "Away with this ridiculous behaviour," said he, in a voice of displeasure. "Adeline has omitted some household duty, I suppose, and an offence so heinous deserves severe punishment, no doubt. But let me be no more disturbed with your petty quarrels; if you must be tyrannical, madam, indulge your humour in private."

Saying this, he abruptly quitted the room, and Louis immediately followed. Madame was left to her own unpleasant reflections. Her ill-humour proceeded from the usual cause. She had heard of Adeline's walk, and La Motte having gone forth into the forest at an early hour, her imagination, heated by the broodings of jealousy, suggested that they had appointed a meeting. This was confirmed to her by the entrance of Adeline, quickly followed by La Motte; and her perceptions thus jaundiced by passion, neither the presence of her son nor her usual attention to good manners had been able to restrain her emotions. The behaviour of Adeline in the late scene she considered as a refined piece of art, and the indifference of La Motte as affected. So true is it, that

> Trifles light as air
> Are to the jealous confirmations strong
> As proofs of holy writ.[33]

And so ingenious was she "to wrench the true cause the false way."[34]

Adeline had retired to her chamber to weep. When her first agitations were subsided, she took an ample view of her conduct, and perceiving nothing of which she could accuse herself, she became more satisfied, deriving her best comfort from the integrity of her intentions. In the moment of accusation, innocence may sometimes be oppressed with the punishment due only to guilt; but reflection dissolves the illusion of terror and brings to the aching bosom the consolations of virtue.

When La Motte quitted the room, he had gone into the

---

33. Shakespeare, *Othello.*
34. Shakespeare, *Henry IV.*

forest, which Louis observed. He followed and joined him with an intention of touching upon the subject of his melancholy.

"It is a fine morning, sir," said Louis, "if you will give me leave, I will walk with you."

La Motte, though dissatisfied, did not object; and after they had proceeded some way, he changed the course of his walk, striking into a path contrary to that which Louis had observed him take on the foregoing day.

Louis remarked that the avenue they had quitted was "more shady, and therefore more pleasant." La Motte seemed to not notice this remark. "It leads to a singular spot," continued he, "which I discovered yesterday."

La Motte raised his head; Louis proceeded to describe the tomb, and the adventure he had met with.

During this relation, La Motte regarded him with attention, while his own countenance suffered various changes. "You were very daring," said La Motte, "to examine that place, particularly when you ventured down the passage. I would advise you to be more cautious how you penetrate the depths of this forest. I myself have not ventured beyond a certain boundary, and am, therefore, uninformed what inhabitants it may harbour. Your account has alarmed me," continued he, "for if banditti are in the neighbourhood, I am not safe from their depredations: 'tis true, I have but little to lose, except my life."

"And the lives of your family," rejoined Louis.

"Of course," said La Motte.

"It would be well to have more certainty upon that head," rejoined Louis. "I am considering how we may obtain it."

"'Tis useless to consider that," said La Motte. "The inquiry itself brings danger with it; your life would, perhaps, be paid for the indulgence of your curiosity; our only chance of safety is by endeavouring to remain undiscovered. Let us move toward the abbey."

Louis knew not what to think, but said no more upon the subject. La Motte soon after relapsed into a fit of musing; and his son now took occasion to lament that depression of spirits which he had lately observed in him.

"Rather lament the cause of it," said La Motte with a sigh.

"That I do, most sincerely, whatever it may be. May I venture to inquire, sir, what is this cause?"

"Are, then, my misfortunes so little known to you," rejoined La Motte, "as to make that question necessary? Am I not driven from my home, from my friends, and almost from my country? And shall it be asked why I am afflicted?"

Louis felt the justice of this reproof, and was a moment silent. "That you are afflicted, sir, does not excite my surprise," resumed he. "It would, indeed, be strange, were you not."

"What then does excite your surprise?"

"The air of cheerfulness you wore when I first came hither."

"You lately lamented that I was afflicted," said La Motte, "and now seem not very well pleased that I once was cheerful. What is the meaning of this?"

"You much mistake me," said his son, "nothing could give me so much satisfaction as to see that cheerfulness renewed. The same cause of sorrow existed at that time, yet you was then cheerful."

"That I was then cheerful," said La Motte, "you might, without flattery, have attributed to yourself; your presence revived me, and I was relieved at the same time from a load of apprehensions."

"Why, as the same cause exists, are you not still cheerful?"

"And why do you not recollect that it is your father you thus speak to?"

"I do, sir, and nothing but anxiety for my father could have urged me thus far; it is with inexpressible concern I perceive you have some secret cause of uneasiness. Reveal it, sir, to those who claim a share in all your affliction, and suffer them, by participation, to soften its severity."

Louis looked up, and observed the countenance of his father, pale as death; his lips trembled while he spoke. "Your penetration, however you may rely upon it, has in the present instance deceived you. I have no subject of distress but what you are already acquainted with, and I desire this conversation may never be renewed."

"If it is your desire, of course, I obey," said Louis, "but, pardon me, sir, if—"

"I will not pardon you, sir," interrupted La Motte, "let the discourse end here." Saying this, he quickened his steps, and Louis, not daring to pursue the matter, walked quietly on till he reached the abbey.

Adeline passed the greatest part of the day alone in her chamber, where, having examined her conduct, she endeavoured to fortify her heart against the unmerited displeasure of Madame de la Motte. This was a task more difficult than that of self-acquittance. She loved her, and had relied on her friendship, which, notwithstanding the conduct of Madame, still appeared valuable to her. It was true, she had not deserved to lose it, but Madame was so averse to explanation that there was little probability of recovering it, however ill-founded might be the cause of her dislike. At length, she reasoned, or rather, perhaps, persuaded herself into tolerable composure; for to resign a real good with contentment is less an effort of reason than of temper.

For many hours she busied herself upon a piece of work which she had undertaken for Madame de la Motte; and this she did without the least intention of conciliating her favour, but because she felt there was something in thus repaying unkindness which was suitable to her own temper, her sentiments, and her pride. Self-love may be the center round which the human affections move, for whatever motive conduces to self-gratification may be resolved into self-love; yet some of these affections are in their nature so refined that though we cannot deny their origin, they almost deserve the name of virtue. Of this species was that of Adeline.

In this employment and in reading Adeline passed as much of the day as possible. From books, indeed, she had constantly derived her chief information and amusement. Those belonging to La Motte were few but well chosen, and Adeline could find pleasure in reading them more than once. When her mind was discomposed by the behaviour of Madame de la Motte, or by a retrospection of her early misfortunes, a book was the opiate that lulled it to repose. La Motte had several of the best English poets, a language which Adeline had learned in the convent; their beauties, therefore, she was capable of tasting, and they often inspired her with enthusiastic delight.

At the decline of day, she quitted her chamber to enjoy the sweet evening hour but strayed no farther than an avenue near the abbey, which fronted the west. She read a little, but, finding it impossible any longer to abstract her attention from the scene around, she closed the book and yielded to the sweet complacent melancholy which the hour inspired. The air was still, the sun, sinking below the distant hill, spread a purple glow over the landscape, and touched the forest glades with softer light. A dewy freshness was diffused upon the air. As the sun descended, the dusk came silently on, and the scene assumed a solemn grandeur.

On her return to the abbey she was joined by Louis, who after some conversation said, "I am much grieved by the scene to which I was witness this morning, and have longed for an opportunity of telling you so. My mother's behaviour is too mysterious to be accounted for, but it is not difficult to perceive she labours under some mistake. What I have to request is that whenever I can be of service to you, you will command me."

Adeline thanked him for this friendly offer, which she felt more sensibly than she chose to express. "I am unconscious," said she, "of any offence that may have deserved Madame de la Motte's displeasure, and am, therefore, totally unable to account for it. I have repeatedly sought an explanation, which she has as anxiously avoided; it is better, therefore, to press the subject no further. At the same time, sir, suffer me to assure you, I have a just sense of your goodness."

Louis sighed, and was silent. "I wish you would permit me," resumed he, "to speak with my mother upon this subject. I am sure I could convince her of her error."

"By no means," replied Adeline. "Madame de la Motte's displeasure has given me inexpressible concern; but to compel her to an explanation would only increase this displeasure, instead of removing it. Let me beg of you not to attempt it."

"I submit to your judgement," said Louis, "but for once it is with reluctance. I should esteem myself most happy if I could be of service to you."

He spoke this with an accent so tender that Adeline, for the first time, perceived the sentiments of his heart. A mind more fraught with vanity than hers would have taught her long ago to regard the attentions of Louis as the result of something more than well-bred gallantry. She did not appear to notice his last words, but remained silent, and involuntarily quickened her pace. Louis said no more but seemed sunk in thought, and this silence remained uninterrupted till they entered the abbey.

CHAPTER 6

Hence, horrible shadow!
Unreal mockery, hence!

Shakespeare, *Macbeth*

Near a month elapsed without any remarkable occurrence: the melancholy of La Motte suffered little abatement; and the behaviour of Madame to Adeline, though somewhat softened, was still far from kind. Louis, by numberless little attentions, testified his growing affection for Adeline, who continued to treat them as passing civilities.

It happened one stormy night, as they were preparing for rest, that they were alarmed by a trampling of horses near the abbey. The sound of several voices succeeded, and a loud knocking at the great gate of the hall soon after confirmed the alarm. La Motte had little doubt that the officers of justice had discovered his retreat, and the perturbation of fear almost confounded his senses; however, he ordered the lights to be extinguished and a profound silence to be observed, unwilling to neglect even the slightest possibility of security. There was a chance, he thought, that the persons might suppose the place uninhabited, and believe they had mistaken the object of their search. His orders were scarcely obeyed when the knocking was renewed, and with increased violence. La Motte now repaired to a small grated window in the portal of the gate, that he might observe the number and appearance of the strangers.

The darkness of the night baffled his purpose; he could only perceive a group of men on horseback, but listening attentively, he distinguished a part of their discourse. Several of the men contended that they had mistaken the place, till a person, who from his authoritative voice appeared to be their leader, affirmed that the lights had issued from this spot, and he was positive there were persons within. Having said this, he again knocked loudly at the gate, and was answered only by hollow echoes. La Motte's heart trembled at the sound, and he was unable to move.

After waiting some time, the strangers seemed as if in consultation, but their discourse was conducted in such a low tone of voice that La Motte was unable to distinguish its purport. They withdrew from the gate as if to depart, but he presently thought he heard them amongst the trees on the other side of the fabric, and soon became convinced they had not left the abbey. A few minutes held La Motte in a state of torturing suspense; he quitted the grate, where Louis now stationed himself, for that part of the edifice which overlooked the spot where he supposed them to be waiting.

The storm was now loud, and the hollow blasts which rushed among the trees prevented his distinguishing any other sound. Once, in the pauses of the wind, he thought he heard distinct voices; but he was not long left to conjecture, for the renewed knocking at the gate again appalled him; and regardless of the terrors of Madame de la Motte and Adeline, he ran to try his last chance of concealment, by means of the trapdoor.

Soon after, the violence of the assailants seeming to increase with every gust of the tempest, the gate, which was old and decayed, burst from its hinges, and admitted them to the hall. At the moment of their entrance, a scream from Madame de la Motte, who stood at the door of an adjoining apartment, confirmed the suspicions of the principal stranger, who continued to advance as fast as the darkness would permit him.

Adeline had fainted and Madame de la Motte was calling loudly for assistance when Peter entered with lights, and discovered the hall filled with men, and his young mistress senseless upon the floor. A chevalier now advanced and, soliciting pardon of Madame for the rudeness of his conduct, was attempting an apology when perceiving Adeline, he hastened to raise her from the ground. But Louis, who now returned, caught her in his arms, and desired the stranger not to interfere.

The person to whom he spoke this wore the star of one of the first orders in France, and had an air of dignity which declared him to be of superior rank. He appeared to be about forty, but perhaps the spirit and fire of his countenance made the impression of time upon his features less perceptible. His softened aspect and insinuating manners while, regardless of himself, he seemed attentive only to the condition of Adeline, gradually dissipated the apprehensions of Madame de la Motte, and subdued the sudden resentment of Louis. Upon Adeline, who was yet insensible, he gazed with an eager admiration which seemed to absorb all the faculties of his mind. She was, indeed, an object not to be contemplated with indifference.

Her beauty, touched with the languid delicacy of illness, gained from sentiment what it lost in bloom. The negligence of her dress, loosened for the purpose of freer respiration, discovered those glowing charms that her auburn tresses, which fell in profusion over her bosom, shaded but could not conceal.

There now entered another stranger, a young chevalier who, having spoken hastily to the elder, joined the general group that surrounded Adeline. He was of a person in which elegance was happily blended with strength, and had a countenance animated, but not haughty; noble, yet expressive of peculiar sweetness. What rendered it at present more interesting was the compassion he seemed to feel for Adeline, who now revived and saw him, the first object that met her eyes, bending over her in silent anxiety.

On perceiving him, a blush of quick surprise passed over her cheek, for she knew him to be the stranger she had seen in the forest. Her countenance instantly changed to the paleness of terror when she observed the room crowded with people. Louis now supported her into another apartment, where the two chevaliers, who followed her, again apologised for the alarm they had occasioned.

The elder, turning to Madame de la Motte, said, "You are, no doubt, madam, ignorant that I am the proprietor of this abbey."

She started.

"Be not alarmed, madam, you are safe and welcome. This ruinous spot has been long abandoned by me, and if it has afforded you a shelter I am happy."

Madame de la Motte expressed her gratitude for this condescension, and Louis declared his sense of the politeness of the Marquis de Montalt, for that was the name of the noble stranger.

"My chief residence," said the marquis, "is in a distant province, but I have a château near the borders of the forest, and in returning from an excursion, I have been benighted and lost my way. A light which gleamed through the trees attracted me hither, and such was the darkness without that I did not know it proceeded from the abbey till I came to the door."

The noble deportment of the strangers, the splendour of their apparel, and, above all, this speech dissipated every remaining doubt of Madame's, and she was giving orders for refreshments to be set before them when La Motte, who had listened and was now convinced he had nothing to fear, entered the apartment.

He advanced toward the marquis with a complacent air, but as he would have spoke, the words of welcome faltered on his lips, his limbs trembled, and a ghastly paleness overspread his countenance. The marquis was little less agitated and, in the first moment of surprise, put his hand upon his sword, but recollecting himself, he withdrew it, and endeavoured to obtain a command of features. A pause of agonizing silence ensued. La Motte made some motion toward the door, but his agitated frame refused to support him, and he sank into a chair, silent and exhausted. The horror of his countenance, together with his whole behaviour, excited the utmost surprise in Madame, whose eyes inquired of the marquis more than he thought proper to answer. His looks increased, instead of explaining, the mystery, and expressed a mixture of emotions which she could not analyse. Meanwhile, she endeavoured to soothe and revive her husband, but he repressed her efforts and, averting his face, covered it with his hands.

The marquis, seeming to recover his presence of mind, was stepping to the door of the hall where his people were assembled when La Motte, starting from his seat with a frantic air, called on him to return. The marquis looked back and stopped, still hesitating whether to proceed; the supplications of Adeline, who was now returned, added to those of La Motte, determined him, and he sat down.

"I request of you, my lord," said La Motte, "that we may converse for a few moments by ourselves."

"The request is bold, and the indulgence, perhaps, dangerous," said the marquis. "It is more also than I will grant. You can have nothing to say with which your family are not acquainted—speak your purpose and be brief."

La Motte's complexion varied with every sentence of this speech. "Impossible, my lord," said he. "My lips shall close forever ere they pronounce before another human being the words reserved for you alone. I entreat—I supplicate of you a few moments' private discourse." As he pronounced these words, tears swelled into his eyes, and the marquis, softened by his distress, consented, though with evident emotion and reluctance, to his request.

La Motte took a light and led the marquis to a small room in a remote part of the edifice, where they remained near an hour. Madame, alarmed by the length of their absence, went in quest of them. As she drew near, a curiosity, in such circumstances perhaps not unjustifiable, prompted her to listen.

La Motte just then exclaimed, "The frenzy of despair!" Some words followed, delivered in a low tone which she could not understand. "I have suffered more than I can express," continued he. "The same image has pursued me in my midnight dream, and in my daily wanderings. There is no punishment, short of death, which I would not have endured to regain the state of mind with which I entered this forest. I again address myself to your compassion."

A loud gust of wind that burst along the passage where Madame de la Motte stood overpowered his voice and that of the marquis, who spoke in reply, but she soon after distinguished these words: "Tomorrow, my lord, if you return to these ruins, I will lead you to the spot."

"That is scarcely necessary, and may be dangerous," said the marquis.

"From you, my lord, I can excuse these doubts," resumed La Motte, "but I will swear whatever you shall propose. Yes," continued he, "whatever may be the consequence, I will swear to submit to your decree!"

The rising tempest again drowned the sound of their voices, and Madame de la Motte vainly endeavoured to hear those words, upon which probably hung the explanation of this mysterious conduct. They now moved toward the door, and she retreated with precipitation to the apartment where she had left Adeline with Louis and the young chevalier.

Hither the marquis and La Motte soon followed, the first haughty and cool, the latter somewhat more composed than before, though the impression of horror was not yet faded from his countenance. The marquis passed on to the hall where his retinue awaited. The storm was not yet subsided, but he seemed impatient to be gone, and ordered his people to be in readiness. La Motte observed a sullen silence, frequently pacing the room with hasty steps, and sometimes lost in reverie. Meanwhile, the marquis, seating himself by Adeline, directed to her his whole attention, except when sudden fits of absence came over his mind and suspended him in silence. At these times the young chevalier addressed Adeline, who, with diffidence and some agitation, shrank from the observance of both.

The marquis had been near two hours at the abbey, and the tempest still continuing, Madame de la Motte offered him a bed. A look from her husband made her tremble for the consequence. Her offer was, however, politely declined, the marquis being evidently as impatient to be gone as his tenant appeared distressed by his presence. He often returned to the hall, and from the gates raised a look of impatience to the clouds. Nothing was to be seen through the darkness of night—nothing heard but the howlings of the storm.

The morning dawned before he departed. As he was preparing to leave the abbey, La Motte again drew him aside, and held him for a few moments in close conversation. His impassioned gestures, which Madame de la Motte observed from a remote part of the room, added to her curiosity a degree of wild apprehension derived from the obscurity of the subject. Her endeavour to distinguish the corresponding words was baffled by the low voice in which they were uttered.

The marquis and his retinue at length departed, and La Motte, having himself fastened the gates, silently and dejectedly withdrew to his chamber. The moment they were alone, Madame seized the opportunity of entreating her husband to explain the scene she had witnessed.

"Ask me no questions," said La Motte sternly, "for I will answer none. I have already forbade your speaking to me on this subject."

"What subject?" said his wife.

La Motte seemed to recollect himself. "No matter—I was mistaken—I thought you had repeated these questions before."

"Ah!" said Madame de la Motte, "it is then as I suspected: your former melancholy and the distress of this night have the same cause."

"And why should you either suspect or inquire? Am I always to be persecuted with conjectures?"

"Pardon me, I meant not to persecute you; but my anxiety for your welfare will not suffer me to rest under this dreadful uncertainty. Let me claim the privilege of a wife, and share the affliction which oppresses you. Deny me not."

La Motte interrupted her. "Whatever may be the cause of the emotions which you have witnessed, I swear that I will not now reveal it. A time may come when I shall no longer judge concealment necessary; till then be silent, and desist from importunity; above all, forbear to remark to anyone what you may have seen uncommon in me. Bury your surmise in your own bosom, as you would avoid my curse and my destruction." The determined air with which he spoke this, while his countenance was overspread with a livid hue, made his wife shudder; and she forbore all reply.

Madame de la Motte retired to bed, but not to rest. She ruminated on the past occurrence; and her surprise and curiosity concerning the words and behaviour of her husband were but more strongly stimulated by reflection. One truth, however, appeared; she could not doubt but the mysterious conduct of La Motte, which had for so many months oppressed her with anxiety, and the late scene with the marquis originated from the same cause. This belief, which seemed to prove how unjustly she had suspected Adeline, brought with it a pang of self-accusation. She looked forward with impatience to the morrow, which would lead the marquis again to the abbey. Wearied nature at length resumed its rights, and yielded a short oblivion of care.

At a late hour the next day, the family assembled to breakfast. Each individual of the party appeared silent and abstracted, but very different was the aspect of their features, and still more the complexion of their thoughts. La Motte seemed agitated by impatient fear, yet the sullenness of despair overspread his countenance. A certain wildness in his eye at times expressed the sudden start of horror, and again his features would sink into the gloom of despondency.

Madame de la Motte seemed harassed with anxiety; she watched every turn of her husband's countenance, and impatiently waited the arrival of the marquis. Louis was composed and thoughtful. Adeline seemed to feel her full share of uneasiness. She had observed the behaviour of La Motte the preceding night with much surprise, and the happy confidence she had hitherto reposed in him was shaken. She feared also lest the exigency of his circumstances should precipitate him again into the world, and that he would be either unable or unwilling to afford her a shelter beneath his roof.

During breakfast, La Motte frequently rose to the window, from whence he cast many an anxious look. His wife understood too well the cause of his impatience, and endeavoured to repress her own. In these intervals, Louis attempted by whispers to obtain some information from his father, but La Motte always returned to the table, where the presence of Adeline prevented further discourse.

After breakfast, as he walked upon the lawn, Louis would have joined him, but La Motte peremptorily declared he intended to be alone, and soon after, the marquis having not yet arrived, proceeded to a greater distance from the abbey.

Adeline retired into their usual working room with Madame de la Motte, who affected an air of cheerfulness, and even of kindness. Feeling the necessity of offering some reason for the striking agitation of La Motte and of preventing the surprise which the unexpected appearance of the marquis would occasion Adeline, if she was left to connect it with his behaviour of the preceding night, she mentioned that the marquis and La Motte had long been known to each other, and that this unexpected meeting, after an absence of many years and under circumstances so altered and humiliating on the part of the latter, had occasioned him much painful emotion. This had been heightened by a consciousness that the marquis had formerly misinterpreted some circumstances in his conduct toward him which had caused a suspension of their intimacy.

This account did not bring conviction to the mind of Adeline, for it seemed inadequate to the degree of emotion the marquis and La Motte had mutually betrayed. Her surprise was excited and her curiosity awakened by the words which were meant to delude them both. But she forbore to express her thoughts.

Madame, proceeding with her plan, said, "The marquis is now expected, and I hope whatever differences remain will be perfectly adjusted."

Adeline blushed, and endeavouring to reply, her lips faltered. Conscious of this agitation, and of the observance of Madame de la Motte, her confusion increased, and her endeavours to suppress served only to heighten it. Still she tried to renew the discourse, and still she found it impossible to collect her thoughts. Shocked lest Madame should apprehend the sentiment which had till this moment been concealed almost from herself, her colour fled, she fixed her eyes on the ground, and for some time found it difficult to respire. Madame de la Motte inquired if she was ill, and Adeline, glad of the excuse, withdrew to the indulgence of her own thoughts, which were now wholly engrossed by the expectation of seeing again the young chevalier who had accompanied the marquis.

As she looked from her room, she saw at a distance the marquis on horseback with several attendants, and she hastened to apprise Madame de la Motte of his approach. In a short time, he arrived at the gates, and Madame and Louis went out to receive him, La Motte being not yet returned. He entered the hall, followed by the young chevalier, and accosting Madame with a sort of stately politeness, inquired for La Motte, whom Louis now went to seek.

The marquis remained for a few minutes silent, and then asked of Madame de la Motte, "How does your fair daughter do?"

Madame understood it was Adeline he meant and answered his inquiry. She slightly[35] said that Adeline was not related to them, and upon some indication of the marquis's wish, sent for her.

Adeline entered the room with a modest blush and a timid air which seemed to engage all his attention. His compliments she received with a sweet grace, but when the younger chevalier approached the warmth of his manner rendered hers involuntarily more reserved, and she scarcely dared to raise her eyes from the ground, lest they should encounter his.

La Motte now entered and apologised for his absence, which

35. With marked indifference.

the marquis noticed only by a slight inclination of his head, by his looks expressing at the same time both distrust and pride. They immediately quitted the abbey together, and the marquis beckoned his attendants to follow at a distance. La Motte forbade his son to accompany him, but Louis observed he took the way into the thickest part of the forest. He was lost in a chaos of conjecture concerning this affair, but curiosity and anxiety for his father induced him to follow at some distance.

In the meantime, the young stranger, whom the marquis addressed by the name of Theodore, remained at the abbey with Madame de la Motte and Adeline. The former, with all her address, could scarcely conceal her agitation during this interval. She moved involuntarily to the door whenever she heard a footstep, and several times she went to the hall door in order to look into the forest, but as often returned, checked by disappointment. No person appeared.

Theodore seemed to address as much of his attention to Adeline as politeness would allow him to withdraw from Madame de la Motte. His manners so gentle, yet dignified, insensibly subdued her timidity and banished her reserve. Her conversation no longer suffered a painful constraint, but gradually disclosed the beauties of her mind and seemed to produce a mutual confidence. A similarity of sentiment soon appeared, and Theodore, by the impatient pleasure which animated his countenance, seemed frequently to anticipate the thought of Adeline.

To them the absence of the marquis was short, though long to Madame de la Motte, whose countenance brightened when she heard the trampling of horses at the gate. The marquis appeared but for a moment, and passed on with La Motte to a private room, where they remained for some time in conference, immediately after which he departed. With an expression of tender regret Theodore took leave of Adeline, who with La Motte and Madame attended them to the gates, and often as he went looked back upon the abbey, till the intervening branches entirely excluded it from his view.

The transient glow of pleasure diffused over the cheek of

Adeline disappeared with the young stranger, and she sighed as she turned into the hall. The image of Theodore pursued her to her chamber; she recollected with exactness every particular of his late conversation—his sentiments so congenial with her own—his manners so engaging—his countenance so animated—so ingenuous and so noble, in which manly dignity was blended with the sweetness of benevolence—these, and every other grace, she recollected, and a soft melancholy stole upon her heart. *I shall see him no more,* thought she. A sigh that followed told her more of her heart than she wished to know. She blushed, and sighed again, and then suddenly recollecting herself, she endeavoured to divert her thoughts to a different subject. La Motte's connection with the marquis for some time engaged her attention, but unable to develop the mystery that attended it, she sought a refuge from her own reflections in the more pleasing ones to be derived from books.

During this time, Louis, shocked and surprised at the extreme distress which his father had manifested upon the first appearance of the marquis, addressed him upon the subject. He had no doubt that the marquis was intimately concerned in the event which made it necessary for La Motte to leave Paris, and he spoke his thoughts without disguise, lamenting at the same time the unlucky chance which had brought him to seek refuge in a place, of all others, the least capable of affording it—the estate of his enemy. La Motte did not contradict this opinion of his son's, and joined in lamenting the evil fate which had conducted him thither.

The term of Louis's absence from his regiment was now nearly expired, and he took occasion to express his sorrow that he must soon be obliged to leave his father in circumstances so dangerous as the present. "I should leave you, sir, with less pain," continued he, "was I sure I knew the full extent of your misfortunes. At present I am left to conjecture evils which perhaps do not exist. Relieve me, sir, from this state of painful uncertainty, and suffer me to prove myself worthy of your confidence."

"I have already answered you on this subject," said La Motte, "and forbade you to renew it. I am now obliged to tell you, I care not how soon you depart, if I am to be subjected to these inquiries." La Motte walked abruptly away, and left his son to doubt and concern.

The arrival of the marquis had dissipated the jealous fears of Madame de la Motte, and she awoke to a sense of her cruelty toward Adeline. When she considered her orphan state—the uniform affection which had appeared in her behaviour—the mildness and patience with which she had borne her injurious treatment, she was shocked, and took an early opportunity of renewing her former kindness. But she could not explain this seeming inconsistency of conduct without betraying her late suspicions, which she now blushed to remember, nor could she apologise for her former behaviour without giving this explanation. She contented herself, therefore, with expressing in her manner the regard which was thus revived. Adeline was at first surprised, but she felt too much pleasure at the change to be scrupulous in inquiring its cause.

But notwithstanding the satisfaction which Adeline received from the revival of Madame de la Motte's kindness, her thoughts frequently recurred to the peculiar and forlorn circumstances of her condition. She could not help feeling less confidence than she had formerly done in the friendship of Madame de la Motte, whose character now appeared less amiable than her imagination had represented it, and seemed strongly tinctured with caprice. Her thoughts often dwelt upon the strange introduction of the marquis at the abbey, and on the mutual emotions and apparent dislike of La Motte and himself; and under these circumstances, it equally excited her surprise that La Motte should choose, and that the marquis should permit him, to remain in his territory.

Her mind returned the oftener to this subject, perhaps, because it was connected with Theodore; but it returned unconscious of the idea which attracted it. She attributed the interest she felt in the affair to her anxiety for the welfare of La Motte, and for her own future destination, which was now so deeply involved in his. Sometimes, indeed, she caught herself busy in conjecture as to the degree of relationship in which Theodore stood to the marquis, but she immediately checked her thoughts, and severely blamed herself for having suffered them to stray to an object which she perceived was too dangerous to her peace.

CHAPTER 7

Present fears
Are less than horrible imaginings.

Shakespeare, *Macbeth*

Afew days after the occurrence related in the preceding chapter, as Adeline was alone in her chamber she was roused from a reverie by a trampling of horses near the gate, and on looking from the casement, she saw the Marquis de Montalt enter the abbey. This circumstance surprised her, and an emotion whose cause she did not trouble herself to inquire for made her instantly retreat from the window. The same cause, however, led her thither again as hastily, but the object of her search did not appear, and she was in no haste to retire.

As she stood musing and disappointed, the marquis came out with La Motte and, immediately looking up, saw Adeline and bowed. She returned his compliment respectfully, and withdrew from the window, vexed at having been seen there. They went into the forest, but the marquis's attendants did not, as before, follow them thither. When they returned, which was not till after a considerable time, the marquis immediately mounted his horse and rode away.

For the remainder of the day, La Motte appeared gloomy

and silent, and was frequently lost in thought. Adeline observed him with particular attention and concern; she perceived that he was always more melancholy after an interview with the marquis, and was now surprised to hear that the latter had appointed to dine the next day at the abbey.

When La Motte mentioned this, he added some high eulogiums[36] on the character of the marquis, and particularly praised his generosity and nobleness of soul. At this instant, Adeline recollected the anecdotes she had formerly heard concerning the abbey, and they threw a shadow over the brightness of that excellence which La Motte now celebrated. The account, however, did not appear to deserve much credit, a part of it having been already proved false, as far as a negative will admit of demonstration; for it had been reported that the abbey was haunted, and no supernatural appearance had ever been observed by the present inhabitants.

Adeline, however, ventured to inquire whether it was the present marquis of whom those injurious reports had been raised.

La Motte answered her with a smile of ridicule. "Stories of ghosts and hobgoblins have always been admired and cherished by the vulgar," said he. "I am inclined to rely upon my own experience at least as much as upon the accounts of these peasants. If you have seen anything to corroborate these accounts, pray inform me of it, that I may establish my faith."

"You mistake me, sir," said she, "it was not concerning supernatural agency that I would inquire. I alluded to a different part of the report, which hinted that some person had been confined here by order of the marquis, who was said to have died unfairly. This was alleged as a reason for the marquis's having abandoned the abbey."

"All the mere coinage of idleness," said La Motte, "a romantic tale to excite wonder. To see the marquis is alone sufficient to refute this; and if we credit half the number of those stories

36. Eulogy; high praise.

that spring from the same source, we prove ourselves little superior to the simpletons who invent them. Your good sense, Adeline, I think, will teach you the merit of disbelief."

Adeline blushed and was silent; but La Motte's defence of the marquis appeared much warmer and more diffuse than was consistent with his own disposition, or required by the occasion. His former conversation with Louis occurred to her, and she was the more surprised at what passed at present.

She looked forward to the morrow with a mixture of pain and pleasure, the expectation of seeing again the young chevalier occupying her thoughts, and agitating them with a various emotion; now she feared his presence, and now she doubted whether he would come. At length she observed this, and blushed to find how much he engaged her attention. The morrow arrived—the marquis came—but he came alone; and the sunshine of Adeline's mind was clouded, though she was able to wear her usual air of cheerfulness. The marquis was polite, affable, and attentive; to manners the most easy and elegant was added the last refinement of polished life. His conversation was lively, amusing, sometimes even witty; and discovered great knowledge of the world, or what is often mistaken for it: an acquaintance with the higher circles and with the topics of the day.

Here La Motte was also qualified to converse with him, and they entered into a discussion of the characters and manners of the age with great spirit, and some humour. Madame de la Motte had not seen her husband so cheerful since they left Paris, and sometimes she could almost fancy she was there. Adeline listened till the cheerfulness, which she had at first only assumed, became real. The address of the marquis was so insinuating and affable that her reserve insensibly gave way before it, and her natural vivacity resumed its long-lost empire.

At parting, the marquis told La Motte he rejoiced at having found so agreeable a neighbour. La Motte bowed. "I shall sometimes visit you," continued the marquis, "and I lament that I cannot at present invite Madame de la Motte and her fair friend to my château, but it is undergoing some repairs, which make it but an uncomfortable residence."

The vivacity of La Motte disappeared with his guest, and he soon relapsed into fits of silence and abstraction.

"The marquis is a very agreeable man," said Madame de la Motte.

"Very agreeable," replied he.

"And seems to have an excellent heart," she resumed.

"An excellent one," said La Motte.

"You seem discomposed, my dear; what has disturbed you?"

"Not in the least—I was only thinking, that with such agreeable talents, and such an excellent heart, it was a pity the marquis should—"

"What? my dear," said Madame with impatience.

"That the marquis should—should suffer this abbey to fall into ruins," replied La Motte.

"Is that all!" said Madame with disappointment.

"That is all, upon my honour," said La Motte, and left the room.

Adeline's spirits, no longer supported by the animated conversation of the marquis, sank into languor, and when he departed, she walked pensively into the forest. She followed a little romantic path that wound along the margin of the stream and was overhung with deep shades. The tranquillity of the scene, which autumn now touched with its sweetest tints, softened her mind to a tender kind of melancholy, and she suffered a tear which, she knew not wherefore, had stolen into her eye, to tremble there unchecked. She came to a little lonely recess formed by high trees; the wind sighed mournfully among the branches, and as it waved their lofty heads scattered their leaves to the ground. She seated herself on a bank beneath, and indulged the melancholy reflections that pressed on her mind.

"O! could I dive into futurity and behold the events which await me!" said she. "I should, perhaps, by constant contemplation, be enabled to meet them with fortitude. An orphan in this wide world—thrown upon the friendship of strangers for comfort, and upon their bounty for the very means of existence, what but evil have I to expect! Alas, my father! how could you thus abandon your child—how leave her to the storms of life—to sink, perhaps, beneath them? Alas, I have no friend!"

She was interrupted by a rustling among the fallen leaves; she turned her head, and perceiving the marquis's young friend, arose to depart.

"Pardon this intrusion," said he, "your voice attracted me hither, and your words detained me. My offence, however, brings with it its own punishment, having learned your sorrows—how can I help feeling them myself? would that my sympathy, or my suffering, could rescue you from them!" He hesitated. "Would that I could deserve the title of your friend, and be thought worthy of it by yourself!"

The confusion of Adeline's thoughts could scarcely permit her to reply; she trembled and gently withdrew her hand, which he had taken while he spoke. "You have, perhaps, heard, sir, more than is true; I am, indeed, not happy, but a moment of dejection has made me unjust, and I am less unfortunate than I have represented. When I said I had no friend, I was ungrateful to the kindness of Monsieur and Madame de la Motte, who have been more than friends—have been as parents to me."

"If so, I honour them," cried Theodore with warmth, "and if I did not feel it to be presumption, I would ask why you are unhappy? But—" He paused.

Adeline, raising her eyes, saw him gazing upon her with intense and eager anxiety, and her looks were again fixed upon the ground.

"I have pained you," said Theodore, "by an improper request. Can you forgive me, and also when I add that it was an interest in your welfare which urged my inquiry?"

"Forgiveness, sir, it is unnecessary to ask. I am certainly obliged by the compassion you express. But the evening is cold; if you please, we will walk toward the abbey."

As they moved on, Theodore was for some time silent. At

length, he said, "It was but lately that I solicited your pardon, and I shall now, perhaps, have need of it again; but you will do me the justice to believe that I have a strong and, indeed, a pressing reason to inquire how nearly you are related to Monsieur La Motte."

"We are not at all related," said Adeline, "but the service he has done me I can never repay, and I hope my gratitude will teach me never to forget it."

"Indeed!" said Theodore, surprised, "and may I ask how long you have known him?"

"Rather, sir, let me ask why these questions should be necessary?"

"You are just," said he, with an air of self-condemnation. "My conduct has deserved this reproof; I should have been more explicit." He looked as if his mind was labouring with something which he was unwilling to express. "But you know not how delicately I am circumstanced," continued he, "yet I will aver that my questions are prompted by the tenderest interest in your happiness—and even by my fears for your safety."

Adeline started.

"I fear you are deceived," said he. "I fear there's danger near you."

Adeline stopped and, looking earnestly at him, begged he would explain himself. She suspected that some mischief threatened La Motte; and Theodore continuing silent, she repeated her request.

"If La Motte is concerned in this danger," said she, "let me entreat you to acquaint him with it immediately. He has but too many misfortunes to apprehend."

"Excellent Adeline!" cried Theodore, "that heart must be adamant that would injure you. How shall I hint what I fear is too true, and how forbear to warn you of your danger without—"

He was interrupted by a step among the trees, and presently after saw La Motte cross into the path they were in. Adeline felt confused at being thus seen with the chevalier, and was hastening to join La Motte, but Theodore detained her, and entreated a moment's attention.

[111]

"There is now no time to explain myself," said he, "yet what I would say is of the utmost consequence to yourself. Promise, therefore, to meet me in some part of the forest at about this time tomorrow evening; you will then, I hope, be convinced that my conduct is directed neither by common circumstances, nor by common regard."

Adeline shuddered at the idea of making an appointment; she hesitated, and at length entreated Theodore not to delay till tomorrow an explanation which appeared to be so important, but to follow La Motte and inform him of his danger immediately.

"It is not with La Motte I would speak," replied Theodore. "I know of no danger that threatens him—but he approaches, be quick, lovely Adeline, and promise to meet me."

"I do promise," said Adeline, with a faltering voice. "I will come to the spot where you found me this evening, an hour earlier tomorrow." Saying this, she withdrew her trembling hand, which Theodore had pressed to his lips in token of acknowledgement, and he immediately disappeared.

La Motte now approached Adeline, who, fearing that he had seen Theodore, was in some confusion.

"Whither is Louis gone so fast?" said La Motte.

She rejoiced to find his mistake, and suffered him to remain in it. They walked pensively toward the abbey, where Adeline, too much occupied by her own thoughts to bear company, retired to her chamber. She ruminated upon the words of Theodore, and the more she considered them, the more she was perplexed. Sometimes she blamed herself for having made an appointment, doubting whether he had not solicited it for the purpose of pleading a passion; and now delicacy checked this thought, and made her vexed that she had presumed upon having inspired one. She recollected the serious earnestness of his voice and manner when he entreated her to meet him; and as they convinced her of the importance of the subject, she shuddered at a danger which she could not comprehend, looking forward to the morrow with anxious impatience.

Sometimes too a remembrance of the tender interest he

had expressed for her welfare, and of his correspondent[37] look and air, would steal across her memory, awakening a pleasing emotion and a latent hope that she was not indifferent to him. From reflections like these she was roused by a summons to supper. The repast was a melancholy one, it being the last evening of Louis's stay at the abbey. Adeline, who esteemed him, regretted his departure, while his eyes were often bent on her with a look which seemed to express that he was about to leave the object of his affection. She endeavoured by her cheerfulness to reanimate the whole party, and especially Madame de la Motte, who frequently shed tears.

"We shall soon meet again," said Adeline, "in happier circumstances, I trust."

La Motte sighed.

The countenance of Louis brightened at her words. "Do you wish it?" said he, with peculiar emphasis.

"Most certainly I do," she replied. "Can you doubt my regard for my best friends?"

"I cannot doubt anything that is good of you," said he.

"You forget you have left Paris," said La Motte to his son, while a faint smile crossed his face. "Such a compliment would there be in character with the place—in these solitary woods it is quite outré."

"The language of admiration is not always that of compliment, sir," said Louis.

Adeline, willing to change the discourse, asked to what part of France he was going. He replied that his regiment was now at Péronne, and he should go immediately thither. After some mention of indifferent subjects, the family withdrew for the night to their several chambers.

The approaching departure of her son occupied the thoughts of Madame de la Motte, and she appeared at breakfast with eyes swollen with weeping. The pale countenance of Louis seemed to indicate that he had rested no better than his mother. When breakfast was over, Adeline retired for a while, that

37. Corresponding, matching.

she might not interrupt, by her presence, their last conversation. As she walked on the lawn before the abbey, she returned in thought to the occurrence of yesterday evening, and her impatience for the appointed interview increased.

She was soon joined by Louis. "It was unkind of you to leave us," said he, "in the last moments of my stay. Could I hope that you would sometimes remember me when I am far away, I should depart with less sorrow." He then expressed his concern at leaving her, and though he had hitherto armed himself with resolution to forbear a direct avowal of an attachment which must be fruitless, his heart now yielded to the force of passion, and he told what Adeline every moment feared to hear.

"This declaration," said Adeline, endeavouring to overcome the agitation it excited, "gives me inexpressible concern."

"O, say not so!" interrupted Louis, "but give me some slender hope to support me in the miseries of absence. Say that you do not hate me—Say—"

"That I do most readily say," replied Adeline in a tremulous voice, "if it will give you pleasure to be assured of my esteem and friendship—receive this assurance: as the son of my best benefactors, you are entitled to—"

"Name not benefits," said Louis, "your merits outrun them all, and suffer me to hope for a sentiment less cool than that of friendship, as well as to believe that I do not owe your approbation of me to the actions of others. I have long borne my passion in silence, because I foresaw the difficulties that would attend it, nay, I have even dared to endeavour to overcome it; I have dared to believe it possible, forgive the supposition, that I could forget you—and—"

"You distress me," interrupted Adeline. "This is a conversation which I ought not to hear. I am above disguise, and therefore assure you that, though your virtues will always command my esteem, you have nothing to hope from my love. Were it even otherwise, our circumstances would effectually decide for us. If you are really my friend, you will rejoice that I am spared this struggle between affection and prudence. Let me hope also that time will teach you to reduce love within the limits of friendship."

"Never!" cried Louis vehemently. "Were this possible, my passion would be unworthy of its object." While he spoke, Adeline's favourite fawn came bounding toward her. This circumstance affected Louis even to tears. "This little animal," said he, after a short pause, "first conducted me to you: it was witness to that happy moment when I first saw you, surrounded by attractions too powerful for my heart; that moment is now fresh in my memory, and the creature comes even to witness this sad one of my departure." Grief interrupted his utterance.

When he recovered his voice, he said, "Adeline! when you look upon your little favourite and caress it, remember the unhappy Louis, who will then be far—far from you. Do not deny me the poor consolation of believing this!"

"I shall not require such a monitor to remind me of you," said Adeline with a smile. "Your excellent parents and your own merits have sufficient claim upon my remembrance. Could I see your natural good sense resume its influence over passion, my satisfaction would equal my esteem for you."

"Do not hope it," said Louis, "nor will I wish it—for passion here is virtue." As he spoke, he saw La Motte turn round an angle of the abbey. "The moments are precious," said he, "I am interrupted. O! Adeline, farewell! and say that you will sometimes think of me."

"Farewell," said Adeline, who was affected by his distress. "Farewell! and peace attend you. I will think of you with the affection of a sister."

He sighed deeply, and pressed her hand. La Motte, winding round another projection of the ruin, again appeared; Adeline left them together and withdrew to her chamber, oppressed by the scene. Louis's passion and her esteem were too sincere not to inspire her with a strong degree of pity for his unhappy attachment. She remained in her chamber till he had quitted the abbey, unwilling to subject him or herself to the pain of a formal parting.

As evening and the hour of appointment drew nigh, Adeline's impatience increased; yet when the time arrived, her resolution failed, and she faltered from her purpose. There was something on her part of indelicacy and dissimulation in an appointed interview that shocked her. She recollected the tenderness of Theodore's manner, and several little circumstances which seemed to indicate that his heart was not unconcerned in the event. Again she was inclined to doubt whether he had not obtained her consent to this meeting upon some groundless suspicion; and she almost determined not to go. Yet it was possible Theodore's assertion might be sincere, and her danger real; the chance of this made her delicate scruples appear ridiculous; she wondered that she had for a moment suffered them to weigh against so serious an interest, and blaming herself for the delay they had occasioned, hastened to the place of appointment.

The little path which led to this spot was silent and solitary, and when she reached the recess, Theodore had not arrived. A transient pride made her unwilling he should find that she was more punctual to his appointment than himself; and she turned from the recess into a track which wound among the trees to the right. Having walked some way without seeing any person or hearing a footstep, she returned; but he was not come, and she again left the place. A second time she came back, and Theodore was still absent. Recollecting the time at which she had quitted the abbey, she grew uneasy, and calculated that the hour appointed was now much exceeded. She was offended and perplexed; but she seated herself on the turf, and was resolved to wait the event. After remaining there till the fall of twilight in fruitless expectation, her pride became more alarmed; she feared that he had discovered something of the partiality he had inspired, and believing that he now treated her with purposed neglect, she quitted the place with disgust and self-accusation.

When these emotions subsided, and reason resumed its influence, she blushed for what she termed this childish effervescence of self-love. She recollected, as if for the first time, these words of Theodore: "I fear you are deceived, and that some danger is near you." Her judgement now acquitted the offender, and she saw only the friend. The import of these words, whose truth she no longer doubted, again alarmed her. Why did he trouble himself to come from the château on purpose to hint her danger, if he did not wish to preserve her? And if he wished to preserve her, what but necessity could have withheld him from the appointment?

These reflections decided her at once. She resolved to repair on the following day at the same hour to the recess, whither the interest which she believed him to take in her fate would no doubt conduct him in the hope of meeting her. That some evil hovered over her she could not disbelieve, but what it might be, she was unable to guess. Monsieur and Madame de la Motte were her friends, and who else, removed beyond the reach of her father as she now thought herself, could injure her? But why did Theodore say she was deceived? She found it impossible to extricate herself from the labyrinth of conjecture, but endeavoured to command her anxiety till the following evening. In the meantime she engaged herself in efforts to amuse Madame de la Motte, who required some relief after the departure of her son.

Thus oppressed by her own cares and interested by those of Madame de la Motte, Adeline retired to rest. She soon lost her recollection, but it was only to fall into harassed slumbers, such as but too often haunt the couch of the unhappy. At length her perturbed fancy suggested the following dream.

She thought she was in a large old chamber belonging to the abbey, more ancient and desolate than any she had yet seen. It was strongly barricaded, yet no person appeared. While she stood musing and surveying the apartment, she heard a low voice call her, and looking toward the place whence it came, she perceived by the dim light of a lamp a figure stretched on a bed that lay on the floor. The voice called again, and approaching the bed, she distinctly saw the features of a man who appeared to be dying. A ghastly paleness overspread his countenance, yet there was an expression of mildness and dignity in it which strongly interested her.

While she looked on him, his features changed and seemed convulsed in the agonies of death. The spectacle shocked her, and she started back, but he suddenly stretched forth his hand and, seizing hers, grasped it with violence. She struggled in terror to disengage herself, and again looking on his face, saw a man who appeared to be about thirty, with the same features, but in full health, and of a most benign countenance. He smiled tenderly upon her and moved his lips as if to speak, when the floor of the chamber suddenly opened and he sank from her view. The effort she made to save herself from following awoke her.

This dream had so strongly impressed her fancy that it was some time before she could overcome the terror it occasioned, or even be perfectly convinced she was in her own apartment. At length, however, she composed herself to sleep; again she fell into a dream.

She thought she was bewildered in some winding passages of the abbey; that it was almost dark, and that she wandered about a considerable time without being able to find a door. Suddenly she heard a bell toll from above, and soon after a confusion of distant voices. She redoubled her efforts to extricate herself. Presently all was still, and at length, wearied with the search, she sat down on a step that crossed the passage. She had not been long here when she saw a light glimmer at a distance on the walls, but a turn in the passage, which was very long, prevented her seeing its source. It continued to glimmer faintly for some time and then grew stronger, when she saw a man enter the passage. He was habited in a long black cloak like those usually worn by attendants at funerals, and bearing a torch. He called to her to follow him, and led her through a long passage to the foot of a staircase. Here she feared to proceed, and was running back when the man suddenly turned to pursue her, and with the terror which this occasioned, she awoke.

Shocked by these visions, and more so by their seeming connection, which now struck her, she endeavoured to continue awake, lest their terrific images should again haunt her mind; after some time, however, her harassed spirits again sank into slumber, though not to repose.

She now thought herself in a large old gallery, and saw at one end of it a chamber door standing a little open and within a light. She went toward it, and perceived the man she had before seen standing at the door and beckoning her toward him. With the inconsistency so common in dreams she no longer endeavoured to avoid him, but advancing, followed him into a suite of very ancient apartments hung with black and lighted up as if for a funeral. Still he led her on, till she found herself in the same chamber she remembered to have seen in her former dream. A coffin, covered with a pall, stood at the farther end of the room; some lights surrounded it, and several persons who appeared to be in great distress.

Suddenly, she thought these persons were all gone, and that she was left alone; that she went up to the coffin, and while she gazed upon it, she heard a voice speak, as if from within, but she saw nobody. The man she had before seen soon after stood by the coffin, and lifting the pall, she saw beneath it a dead person, whom she thought to be the dying chevalier she had seen in her former dream: his features were sunk in death, but they were yet serene. While she looked at him, a stream of blood gushed from his side and descended to the floor, the whole chamber overflowing. At the same time some words were uttered in the voice she heard before, but the horror of the scene so entirely overcame her that she started and awoke.

When she had recovered her recollection, she raised herself in the bed to be convinced it was a dream she had witnessed, and the agitation of her spirits was so great that she feared to be alone, and almost determined to call Annette. The features of the deceased person and the chamber where he lay were strongly impressed upon her memory, and she still thought she heard the voice and saw the countenance which her dream represented. The longer she considered these dreams, the more she was surprised: they were so very terrible, returned so often, and seemed to be so connected with each other that she could scarcely think them accidental; yet why they should be supernatural, she could not tell. She slept no more that night.

CHAPTER 8

When these prodigies
Do so conjointly meet, let not men say
"These are their reasons; they are natural"
For I believe they are portentous things.

Shakespeare, *Julius Caesar*

When Adeline appeared at breakfast, her harassed
and languid countenance struck Madame de la
Motte, who inquired if she was ill; Adeline, forcing
a smile upon her features, said she had not rested well, for she
had had very disturbed dreams; she was about to describe
them, but a strong and involuntary impulse prevented her. At
the same time, La Motte ridiculed her concern so unmercifully
that she was almost ashamed to have mentioned it, and tried
to overcome the remembrance of its cause.

After breakfast, she endeavoured to employ her thoughts by
conversing with Madame de la Motte; but they were really engaged by the incidents of the last two days, the circumstance
of her dreams, and her conjectures concerning the information
to be communicated to her by Theodore. They had thus sat for
some time when a sound of voices arose from the great gate
of the abbey; and on going to the casement, Adeline saw the
marquis and his attendants on the lawn below. The portal of

the abbey concealed several people from her view, and among these it was possible might be Theodore, who had not yet appeared; she continued to look for him with great anxiety, till the marquis entered the hall with La Motte and some other persons, soon after which Madame went to receive him, and Adeline retired to her own apartment.

A message from La Motte, however, soon called her to join the party, where she vainly hoped to find Theodore. The marquis arose as she approached, and having paid her some general compliments, the conversation took a very lively turn. Adeline, finding it impossible to counterfeit cheerfulness while her heart was sinking with anxiety and disappointment, took little part in it: Theodore was not once named. She would have asked concerning him, had it been possible to inquire with propriety; but she was obliged to content herself with hoping, first, that he would arrive before dinner, and then before the departure of the marquis.

Thus the day passed in expectation and disappointment. The evening was now approaching, and she was condemned to remain in the presence of the marquis, apparently listening to a conversation which in truth she scarcely heard, while the opportunity that would decide her fate was, perhaps, escaping. She was suddenly relieved from this state of torture, and thrown into one, if possible, still more distressing.

The marquis inquired for Louis, and being informed of his departure, mentioned that Theodore Peyrou had that morning set out for his regiment in a distant province. He lamented the loss he should sustain by his absence, and expressed some very flattering praise of his talents. The shock of this intelligence overpowered the long-agitated spirits of Adeline; the blood forsook her cheeks, and a sudden faintness came over her, from which she recovered only to a consciousness of having discovered her emotion, and the danger of relapsing into a second fit.

She retired to her chamber, where, being once more alone, her oppressed heart found relief from tears, in which she freely indulged. Ideas crowded so fast upon her mind that it was long ere she could arrange them so as to produce anything like reasoning. She endeavoured to account for the abrupt departure of Theodore. *Is it possible,* thought she, *that he should take an interest in my welfare, and yet leave me exposed to the full force of a danger which he himself foresaw? Or am I to believe that he has trifled with my simplicity for an idle frolic, and has now left me to the wondering apprehension he has raised? Impossible! a countenance so noble, and a manner so amiable, could never disguise a heart capable of forming so despicable a design. No!—whatever is reserved for me, let me not relinquish the pleasure of believing that he is worthy of my esteem.*

She was awakened from thoughts like these by a peal of distant thunder, and now perceived that the gloominess of evening was deepened by the coming storm; it rolled onward, and soon after the lightning began to flash along the chamber. Adeline was superior to the affectation of fear, and was not apt to be terrified; but she now felt it unpleasant to be alone, and hoping that the marquis might have left the abbey, she went down to the sitting room; but the threatening aspect of the heavens had hitherto detained him, and now the evening tempest made him rejoice that he had not quitted a shelter. The storm continued, and night came on. La Motte pressed his guest to take a bed at the abbey, and he at length consented; a circumstance which threw Madame de la Motte into some perplexity as to the accommodation to be afforded him; after some time, she arranged the affair to her satisfaction; resigning her own apartment to the marquis, and that of Louis to two of his superior attendants; Adeline, it was further settled, should give up her room to Monsieur and Madame de la Motte, and remove to an inner chamber, where a small bed, usually occupied by Annette, was placed for her.

At supper, the marquis was less gay than usual; he frequently addressed Adeline, who still appeared pale and languid, and his look and manner seemed to express the tender interest which her indisposition had excited. Adeline, as usual, made an effort to forget her anxiety and appear happy; but the veil of assumed cheerfulness was too thin to conceal the features of sorrow, and her feeble smiles only added a peculiar softness to her air.

[123]

The marquis conversed with her on a variety of subjects, and displayed an elegant mind. The observations of Adeline, which when called upon she gave with reluctant modesty in words at once simple and forceful, seemed to excite his admiration, which he sometimes betrayed by an inadvertent expression.

Adeline retired early to her room, which adjoined on one side Madame de la Motte's, and on the other the closet formerly mentioned. It was spacious and lofty, and what little furniture it contained was falling to decay; but perhaps the present tone of her spirits might contribute more than these circumstances to give that air of melancholy which seemed to reign in it. She was unwilling to go to bed, lest the dreams that had lately pursued her should return; and determined to sit up till she found herself oppressed by sleep, when it was probable her rest would be profound. She placed the light on a small table and, taking a book, continued to read for above an hour, till her mind refused any longer to abstract itself from its own cares, and she sat for some time leaning pensively on her arm.

The wind was high, and as it whistled through the desolate apartment and shook the feeble doors, she often started, and sometimes even thought she heard sighs between the pauses of the gust; but she checked these illusions, which the hour of the night and her own melancholy imagination conspired to raise. As she sat musing, her eyes fixed on the opposite wall, she perceived the arras with which the room was hung wave backward and forward; she continued to observe it for some minutes, and then rose to examine it further. It was moved by the wind, and she blushed at the momentary fear it had excited; but she observed that the tapestry was more strongly agitated in one particular place than elsewhere, and a noise that seemed something more than that of the wind issued thence. The old bedstead which La Motte had found in this apartment had been removed to accommodate Adeline, and it was behind the place where this had stood that the wind seemed to rush with particular force. Curiosity prompted her to examine still further; she felt about the tapestry, and perceiving the wall behind shake under her hand, she lifted the arras and discovered a small door, whose loosened hinges admitted the wind and occasioned the noise she had heard.

The door was held only by a bolt, having undrawn which and brought the light, she descended by a few steps into another chamber: she instantly remembered her dreams. The chamber was not much like that in which she had seen the dying chevalier and afterward the bier, but it gave her a confused remembrance of one through which she had passed. Holding up the light to examine it more fully, she was convinced by its structure that it was part of the ancient foundation. A shattered casement, placed high from the floor, seemed to be the only opening to admit light. She observed a door on the opposite side of the apartment, and after some moments of hesitation gained courage and determined to pursue the inquiry. *A mystery seems to hang over these chambers*, thought she, *which it is, perhaps, my lot to develop; I will, at least, see to what that door leads.*

She stepped forward, and having unclosed it, proceeded with faltering steps along a suite of apartments resembling the first in style and condition, and terminating in one exactly like that where her dream had represented the dying person; the remembrance struck so forcibly upon her imagination that she was in danger of fainting; looking round the room, she almost expected to see the phantom of her dream.

Unable to quit the place, she sat down on some old lumber to recover herself, while her spirits were nearly overcome by a superstitious dread such as she had never felt before. She wondered to what part of the abbey these chambers belonged, and that they had so long escaped detection. The casements were all too high to afford any information from without. When she was sufficiently composed to consider the direction of the rooms and the situation of the abbey, there appeared not a doubt that they formed an interior part of the original building.

As these reflections passed over her mind, a sudden gleam of moonlight fell upon some object without the casement. Being now sufficiently composed to wish to pursue the inquiry and believing this object might afford her some means of learning the situation of these rooms, she combated her remaining terrors and, in order to distinguish it more clearly, removed the light to an outer chamber; but before she could return, a heavy cloud was driven over the face of the moon, and all without was perfectly dark. She stood for some moments waiting a returning gleam, but the obscurity continued. As she went softly back for the light, her foot stumbled over something on the floor, and while she stooped to examine it, the moon again shone, so that she could distinguish through the casement the eastern towers of the abbey. This discovery confirmed her former conjectures concerning the interior situation of these apartments. The obscurity of the place prevented her discovering what it was that had impeded her steps, but having brought the light forward, she perceived on the floor an old dagger. With a trembling hand she took it up, and upon a closer view perceived that it was spotted and stained with rust.

Shocked and surprised, she looked round the room for some object that might confirm or destroy the dreadful suspicion which now rushed upon her mind; but she saw only a great chair with broken arms that stood in one corner of the room, and a table in a condition equally shattered, except that in another part lay a confused heap of things which appeared to be old lumber. She went up to it, and perceived a broken bedstead with some decayed remnants of furniture covered with dust and cobwebs, and which seemed, indeed, as if they had not been moved for many years. Desirous, however, of examining further, she attempted to raise what appeared to have been part of the bedstead, but it slipped from her hand and, rolling to the floor, brought with it some of the remaining lumber. Adeline started aside and saved herself, and when the noise it made had ceased, she was about to leave the chamber when she heard a small rustling sound and saw something falling gently among the lumber.

It was a small roll of paper tied with a string and covered with dust. Adeline took it up, and on opening it perceived handwriting. She attempted to read it, but the part of the manuscript she looked at was so much obliterated that she found this difficult, though what few words were legible impressed her with curiosity and terror, and induced her to return with it immediately to her chamber.

Having reached her own room, she fastened the private door, and let the arras fall over it as before. It was now midnight. The stillness of the hour, interrupted only at intervals by the hollow sighings of the blast, heightened the solemnity of Adeline's feelings. She wished she was not alone, and before she proceeded to look into the manuscript, listened whether Madame de la Motte was not in her chamber: not the least sound was heard, and she gently opened the door. The profound silence within almost convinced her that no person was there, but willing to be further satisfied, she brought the light and found the room empty. The lateness of the hour made her wonder that Madame de la Motte was not in her chamber, and she proceeded to the top of the tower stairs to hearken if any person was stirring.

She heard the sound of voices from below, and amongst the rest, that of La Motte speaking in his usual tone. Being now satisfied that all was well, she turned toward her room, when she heard the marquis pronounce her name with very unusual emphasis. She paused.

"I adore her," pursued he, "and by heaven—"

He was interrupted by La Motte. "My lord, remember your promise."

"I do," replied the marquis, "and I will abide by it. But we trifle. Tomorrow I will declare myself, and I shall then know both what to hope and how to act."

Adeline trembled so excessively that she could scarcely support herself. She wished to return to her chamber, yet she was too much interested in the words she had heard not to be anxious to have them more fully explained. There was an interval of silence, after which they conversed in a lower tone. Adeline remembered the hints of Theodore and determined, if possible, to be relieved from the terrible suspense she now suffered. She stole softly down a few steps, that she might catch the accents of the speakers, but they were so low that she could only now and then distinguish a few words.

"Her father, say you?" said the marquis.

"Yes, my lord, her father. I am well informed of what I say."

Adeline shuddered at the mention of her father, a new terror seized her, and with increasing eagerness she endeavoured to distinguish their words, but for some time found this to be impossible.

"Here is no time to be lost," said the marquis, "tomorrow then."

She heard La Motte rise, and believing it was to leave the room, she hurried up the steps and, having reached her chamber, sank almost lifeless in a chair.

It was her father only of whom she thought. She doubted not that he had pursued and discovered her retreat, and though this conduct appeared very inconsistent with his former behaviour in abandoning her to strangers, her fears suggested that it would terminate in some new cruelty. She did not hesitate to pronounce this the danger of which Theodore had warned her; but it was impossible to surmise how he had gained his knowledge of it, or how he had become sufficiently acquainted with her story except through La Motte, her apparent friend and protector, whom she was thus, though unwillingly, led to suspect of treachery. Why, indeed, should La Motte conceal from her only his knowledge of her father's intention, unless he designed to deliver her into his hands? Yet it was long ere she could bring herself to believe this conclusion possible. To discover depravity in those whom we have loved is one of the most exquisite tortures to a virtuous mind, and the conviction is often rejected before it is finally admitted.

The words of Theodore, which told her he was fearful she was deceived, confirmed this most painful apprehension of La Motte, with another yet more distressing, that Madame de la Motte was also united against her. This thought for a moment subdued terror and left her only grief; she wept bitterly. *Is this human nature?* cried she. *Am I doomed to find everybody deceitful?* An unexpected discovery of vice in those whom we have admired inclines us to extend our censure of the individual to the species; we henceforth contemn[38] appearances, and too hastily conclude that no person is to be trusted.

Adeline determined to throw herself at the feet of La Motte on the following morning, and implore his pity and protection. Her mind was now too much agitated by her own interests to permit her to examine the manuscripts, and she sat musing in her chair till she heard the steps of Madame de la Motte when she retired to bed. La Motte soon after came up to his chamber, and Adeline, the mild, persecuted Adeline, who had now passed two days of torturing anxiety, and one night of terrific visions, endeavoured to compose her mind to sleep. In the present state of her spirits, she quickly caught alarm, and she had scarcely fallen into a slumber when she was roused by a loud and uncommon noise. She listened, and thought the sound came from the apartments below, but in a few minutes there was a hasty knocking at the door of La Motte's chamber.

La Motte, who had just fallen asleep, was not easily to be roused, but the knocking increased with such violence that Adeline, extremely terrified, arose and went to the door that opened from her chamber into his with a design to call him. She was stopped by the voice of the marquis, which she now clearly distinguished at the door. He called to La Motte to rise immediately, and Madame de la Motte endeavoured at the same time to rouse her husband, who at length awoke in much alarm, and soon after joining the marquis, they went downstairs together. Adeline now dressed herself, as well as her trembling hands would permit, and went into the adjoining chamber, where she found Madame de la Motte extremely surprised and terrified.

The marquis, in the meantime, with great agitation told La Motte that he recollected having appointed some persons to meet him upon business of importance early in the morning, and it was therefore necessary for him to set off for his château immediately. As he said this and desired that his servants might

38. View with contempt.

be called, La Motte could not help observing the ashy paleness of his countenance, or expressing some apprehension that his lordship was ill. The marquis assured him he was perfectly well, but desired that he might set out immediately. Peter was now ordered to call the other servants, and the marquis, having refused to take any refreshment, bade La Motte a hasty adieu, and as soon as his people were ready left the abbey.

La Motte returned to his chamber, musing on the abrupt departure of his guest, whose emotion appeared much too strong to proceed from the cause assigned. He appeased the anxiety of Madame de la Motte, and at the same time excited her surprise, by acquainting her with the occasion of the late disturbance. Adeline, who had retired from the chamber on the approach of La Motte, looked out from her window on hearing the trampling of horses. It was the marquis and his people, who just then passed at a little distance. Unable to distinguish who the persons were, she was alarmed at observing such a party about the abbey at that hour, and calling to inform La Motte of the circumstance, was made acquainted with what had passed.

At length she retired to her bed, and her slumbers were this night undisturbed by dreams.

When she arose in the morning, she observed La Motte walking alone in the avenue below, and she hastened to seize the opportunity which now offered of pleading her cause. She approached him with faltering steps, while the paleness and timidity of her countenance discovered the disorder of her mind. Her first words, without entering upon any explanation, implored his compassion. La Motte stopped and, looking earnestly in her face, inquired whether any part of his conduct toward her merited the suspicion which her request implied. Adeline for a moment blushed that she had doubted his integrity, but the words she had overheard returned to her memory.

"Your behaviour, sir," said she, "I acknowledge to have been kind and generous, beyond what I had a right to expect, but—"

And she paused. She knew not how to mention what she blushed to believe. La Motte continued to gaze on her in silent expectation, and at length desired her to proceed and explain her meaning. She entreated that he would protect her from her father.

La Motte looked surprised and confused. "Your father!" said he.

"Yes, sir," replied Adeline, and continued her endeavours to interest his pity. "I am not ignorant that he has discovered my retreat. I have everything to dread from a parent who has treated me with such cruelty as you was witness of, and I again implore that you will save me from his hands."

La Motte stood fixed in thought. "What reason have you to suppose, or rather, how have you learned that your father pursues you?"

The question confused Adeline, who blushed to acknowledge that she had overheard his discourse, and disdained to invent or utter a falsity; at length she confessed the truth. The countenance of La Motte instantly changed to a savage fierceness, and sharply rebuking her for a conduct to which she had been rather tempted by chance than prompted by design, he inquired what she had overheard that could so much alarm her. She faithfully repeated the substance of the incoherent sentences that had met her ear.

While she spoke, he regarded her with a fixed attention. "And was this all you heard? Is it from these few words that you draw such a positive conclusion? Examine them, and you will find they do not justify it."

She now perceived what the fervor of her fears had not permitted her to observe before, that the words, unconnectedly as she heard them, imported little, and that her imagination had filled up the void in the sentences so as to suggest the evil apprehended. Notwithstanding this, her fears were little abated.

"Your apprehensions are, doubtless, now removed," resumed La Motte, "but to give you a proof of the sincerity which you have ventured to question, I will tell you they were just. You seem alarmed, and with reason. Your father has discovered your residence, and has already demanded you. It is true that from a motive of compassion I have refused to resign you, but I have neither authority to withhold nor means to defend you. When he comes to enforce his demand, you will perceive this. Prepare yourself, therefore, for the evil which you see is inevitable."

Adeline for some time could speak only by her tears. At length, with a fortitude which despair had roused, she said, "I resign myself to the will of Heaven!"

La Motte gazed on her in silence, and a strong emotion appeared in his countenance. He forbore, however, to renew the discourse, and withdrew to the abbey, leaving Adeline in the avenue, absorbed in grief.

A summons to breakfast hastened her to the parlour, where she passed the morning in conversation with Madame de la Motte, to whom she told all her apprehensions and expressed all her sorrow. Pity and superficial consolation was all that Madame de la Motte could offer, though apparently much affected by Adeline's discourse. Thus the hours passed heavily away, while the anxiety of Adeline continued to increase, and the moment of her fate seemed fast approaching. Dinner was scarcely over when Adeline was surprised to see the marquis arrive. He entered the room with his usual ease and, apologising for the disturbance he had occasioned on the preceding night, repeated what he had before told La Motte.

The remembrance of the conversation she had overheard at first gave Adeline some confusion, and withdrew her mind from a sense of the evils to be apprehended from her father. The marquis, who was as usual attentive to Adeline, seemed affected by her apparent indisposition, and expressed much concern for that dejection of spirits which, notwithstanding every effort, her manner betrayed. When Madame de la Motte withdrew, Adeline would have followed her, but the marquis entreated a few moment's attention, and led her back to her seat. La Motte immediately disappeared.

Adeline knew too well what would be the purport of the marquis's discourse, and his words soon increased the confusion which her fears had occasioned. While he was declaring the ardour of his passion in such terms as but too often make vehemence pass for sincerity, Adeline, to whom this declaration if honourable was distressing, and if dishonourable was shocking, interrupted him and thanked him for the offer of a distinction which, with a modest but determined air, she said she must refuse. She rose to withdraw.

"Stay, too lovely Adeline!" said he, "and if compassion for my sufferings will not interest you in my favour, allow a consideration of your own dangers to do so. Monsieur La Motte has informed me of your misfortunes and of the evil that now threatens you; accept from me the protection which he cannot afford."

Adeline continued to move toward the door, when the marquis threw himself at her feet and, seizing her hand, impressed it with kisses. She struggled to disengage herself.

"Hear me, charming Adeline! hear me," cried the marquis. "I exist but for you. Listen to my entreaties and my fortune shall be yours. Do not drive me to despair by ill-judged rigour, or because—"

"My lord," interrupted Adeline, with an air of ineffable dignity, and still affecting to believe his proposal honourable, "I am sensible of the generosity of your conduct, and also flattered by the distinction you offer me. I will, therefore, say something more than is necessary to a bare expression of the denial which I must continue to give. I cannot bestow my heart. You cannot obtain more than my esteem, to which, indeed, nothing can so much contribute as a forbearance from any similar offers in future."

She again attempted to go, but the marquis prevented her and, after some hesitation, again urged his suit, though in terms that would no longer allow her to misunderstand him. Tears swelled into her eyes, but she endeavoured to check them and, with a look in which grief and indignation seemed to struggle for preeminence, she said, "My lord, this is unworthy of reply, let me pass."

For a moment, he was awed by the dignity of her manner, and he threw himself at her feet to implore forgiveness. But she waved her hand in silence and hurried from the room.

When she reached her chamber, she locked the door and, sinking into a chair, yielded to the sorrow that pressed at her heart. And it was not the least of her sorrow to suspect that La Motte was unworthy of her confidence; for it was almost impossible that he could be ignorant of the real designs of the marquis. Madame de la Motte, she believed, was imposed upon by a specious pretence of honourable attachment; and thus was she spared the pang which a doubt of her integrity would have added.

She threw a trembling glance upon the prospect around her. On one side was her father, whose cruelty had already been too plainly manifested; and on the other, the marquis pursuing her with insult and vicious passion. She resolved to acquaint Madame de la Motte with the purport of the late conversation, and in the hope of her protection and sympathy, she wiped away her tears and was leaving the room just as Madame de la Motte entered it. While Adeline related what had passed, her friend wept and appeared to suffer great agitation. She endeavoured to comfort her, and promised to use her influence in persuading La Motte to prohibit the addresses of the marquis.

"You know, my dear," added Madame, "that our present circumstances oblige us to preserve terms with the marquis, and you will, therefore, suffer as little resentment to appear in your manner toward him as possible; conduct yourself with your usual ease in his presence, and I doubt not this affair will pass over without subjecting you to further solicitation."

"Ah, madam!" said Adeline, "how hard is the task you assign me! I entreat you that I may never more be subjected to the humiliation of being in his presence; that whenever he visits the abbey, I may be suffered to remain in my chamber."

"This," said Madame de la Motte, "I would most readily consent to, would our situation permit it. But you well know our asylum in this abbey depends upon the goodwill of the marquis, which we must not wantonly lose; and surely such a conduct as you propose would endanger this. Let us use milder measures, and we shall preserve his friendship without subjecting you to any serious evil. Appear with your usual complacence; the task is not so difficult as you imagine."

Adeline sighed. "I obey you, madam," said she, "it is my duty to do so; but I may be pardoned for saying—it is with extreme reluctance."

Madame de la Motte promised to go immediately to her husband, and Adeline departed, though not convinced of her safety, yet somewhat more at ease.

She soon after saw the marquis depart, and as there now appeared to be no obstacle to the return of Madame de la Motte, she expected her with extreme impatience. After thus waiting near an hour in her chamber, she was at length summoned to the parlour, and there found Monsieur La Motte alone.

He arose upon her entrance, and for some minutes paced the room in silence. He then seated himself, and addressed her: "What you have mentioned to Madame de la Motte," said he, "would give me much concern, did I consider the behaviour of the marquis in a light so serious as she does. I know that young ladies are apt to misconstrue the unmeaning gallantry of fashionable manners, and you, Adeline, can never be too cautious in distinguishing between a levity of this kind, and a more serious address."

Adeline was surprised and offended that La Motte should think so lightly both of her understanding and disposition as his speech implied. "Is it possible, sir," said she, "that you have been apprised of the marquis's conduct?"

"It is very possible, and very certain," replied La Motte with some asperity, "and very possible, also, that I may see this affair with a judgement less discoloured by prejudice than you do. But, however, I shall not dispute this point. I shall only request that, since you are acquainted with the emergency of my circumstances, you will conform to them and not, by an ill-timed resentment, expose me to the enmity of the marquis. He is now my friend, and it is necessary to my safety that he should continue such; but if I suffer any part of my family to treat him with rudeness, I must expect to see him my enemy. You may surely treat him with complaisance."

[135]

Adeline thought the term rudeness a harsh one, as La Motte applied it, but she forbore from any expression of displeasure. "I could have wished, sir," said she, "for the privilege of retiring whenever the marquis appeared, but since you believe this conduct would affect your interest, I ought to submit."

"This prudence and goodwill delight me," said La Motte, "and since you wish to serve me, know that you cannot more effectually do it than by treating the marquis as a friend."

The word friend, as it stood connected with the marquis, sounded dissonantly to Adeline's ear; she hesitated and looked at La Motte. "As your friend, sir," said she; "I will endeavour to—" Treat him as mine, she would have said, but she found it impossible to finish the sentence. She entreated his protection from the power of her father.

"What protection I can afford is yours," said La Motte, "but you know how destitute I am both of the right and the means of resisting him, and also how much I require protection myself. Since he has discovered your retreat, he is probably not ignorant of the circumstances which detain me here, and if I oppose him, he may betray me to the officers of the law as the surest method of obtaining possession of you. We are encompassed with dangers," continued La Motte. "Would I could see any method of extricating ourselves!"

"Quit this abbey," said Adeline, "and seek an asylum in Switzerland or Germany; you will then be freed from further obligation to the marquis and from the persecution you dread. Pardon me for thus offering advice which is certainly, in some degree, prompted by a sense of my own safety, but which at the same time seems to afford the only means of ensuring yours."

"Your plan is reasonable," said La Motte, "had I money to execute it. As it is, I must be contented to remain here, as little known as possible, and defending myself by making those who know me my friends. Chiefly I must endeavour to preserve the favour of the marquis. He may do much, should your father even pursue desperate measures. But why do I talk thus? Your father may ere this have commenced these measures, and the effects of his vengeance may now be hanging over my head. My regard for you, Adeline, has exposed me to this; had I resigned you to his will, I should have remained secure."

Adeline was so much affected by this instance of La Motte's kindness, which she could not doubt, that she was unable to express her sense of it. When she could speak, she uttered her gratitude in the most lively terms.

"Are you sincere in these expressions?" said La Motte.

"Is it possible I can be less than sincere?" replied Adeline, weeping at the idea of ingratitude.

"Sentiments are easily pronounced," said La Motte, "though they may have no connection with the heart; I believe them to be sincere so far only as they influence our actions."

"What mean you, sir?" said Adeline with surprise.

"I mean to inquire whether, if an opportunity should ever offer of thus proving your gratitude, you would adhere to your sentiments?"

"Name one that I shall refuse," said Adeline with energy.

"If, for instance, the marquis should hereafter avow a serious passion for you and offer you his hand, would no petty resentment, no lurking prepossession for some more happy lover, prompt you to refuse it?"

Adeline blushed and fixed her eyes on the ground. "You have, indeed, sir, named the only means I should reject of evincing my sincerity. The marquis I can never love nor, to speak sincerely, ever esteem. I confess the peace of one's whole life is too much to sacrifice even to gratitude."

La Motte looked displeased. "'Tis as I thought," said he, "these delicate sentiments make a fine appearance in speech, and render the person who utters them infinitely amiable; but bring them to the test of action, and they dissolve into air, leaving only the wreck of vanity behind."

This unjust sarcasm brought tears to her eyes. "Since your safety, sir, depends upon my conduct," said she, "resign me to my father. I am willing to return to him, since my stay here must involve you in new misfortune. Let me not prove myself unworthy of the protection I have hitherto experienced by preferring my own welfare to yours. When I am gone, you will have no reason to apprehend the marquis's displeasure, which you may probably incur if I stay here, for I feel it impossible that I could even consent to receive his addresses, however honourable were his views."

La Motte seemed hurt and alarmed. "This must not be," said he. "Let us not harass ourselves by stating possible evils, and then to avoid them fly to those which are certain. No, Adeline, though you are ready to sacrifice yourself to my safety, I will not suffer you to do so. I will not yield you to your father but upon compulsion. Be satisfied, therefore, upon this point. The only return I ask is a civil deportment toward the marquis."

"I will endeavour to obey you, sir," said Adeline.

Madame de la Motte now entered the room, and this conversation ceased. Adeline passed the evening in melancholy thoughts, and retired as soon as possible to her chamber, eager to seek in sleep a refuge from sorrow.

CHAPTER 9

Full many a melancholy night
He watch'd the slow return of light;
And sought the powers of sleep,
To spread a momentary calm
O'er his sad couch, and in the balm
Of bland oblivion's dews his burning eyes
    to steep.

Thomas Warton, "The Suicide"

The manuscript found by Adeline the preceding night had several times occurred to her recollection in the course of the day, but she had then been either too much interested by the events of the moment or too apprehensive of interruption to attempt a perusal of it. She now took it from the drawer in which it had been deposited and, intending only to look cursorily over the few first pages, sat down with it by her bedside.

She opened it with an eagerness of inquiry which the discoloured and almost obliterated ink but slowly gratified. The first words on the page were entirely lost, but those that appeared to commence the narrative were as follows:

O! ye, whoever ye are, whom chance, or misfortune, may hereafter conduct to this spot—to ye I speak—to ye reveal the story of my wrongs, and ask ye to avenge them. Vain hope! yet it imparts some comfort to believe it possible that what I now write may one day meet the eye of a fellow creature; that the words which tell my sufferings may one day draw pity from the feeling heart.

Yet stay your tears—your pity now is useless: long since have the pangs of misery ceased; the voice of complaining is passed away. It is weakness to wish for compassion which cannot be felt till I shall sink in the repose of death, and taste, I hope, the happiness of eternity!

Know then, that on the night of the 12th of October in the year 1642, on the road to Caux, at the very spot where a column is erected to the memory of the immortal Henry, I was arrested by four ruffians who, after disabling my servant, bore me through wilds and woods to this abbey. Their demeanour was not that of common banditti, and I soon perceived they were employed by a superior power to perpetrate some dreadful purpose. Entreaties and bribes were vainly offered them to discover their employer and abandon their design: they would not reveal even the least circumstance of their intentions.

But when, after a long journey, they arrived at this edifice, their base employer was at once revealed, and his horrid scheme but too well understood. What a moment was that! All the thunders of Heaven seemed launched at this defenceless head! O fortitude! nerve my heart to—

Adeline's light was now expiring in the socket, and the paleness of the ink baffled her efforts to discriminate the letters. It was impossible to procure a light from below without discovering that she was yet up, a circumstance which would excite surprise and lead to explanations such as she did not wish to enter upon. Thus compelled to suspend the inquiry which so many attendant circumstances had rendered awfully interesting, she retired to her humble bed.

What she had read of the manuscript awakened a dreadful interest in the fate of the writer, and called up terrific images to her mind. *In these apartments!* thought she, and she shuddered and closed her eyes. At length, she heard Madame de la Motte enter her chamber, and the phantoms of fear, beginning to dissipate, left her to repose.

In the morning she was awakened by Madame de la Motte, and found to her disappointment that she had slept so much beyond her usual time as to be unable to renew the perusal of the manuscript. La Motte appeared uncommonly gloomy, and Madame wore an air of melancholy which Adeline attributed to the concern she felt for her. Breakfast was scarcely over when the sound of horses' feet announced the arrival of a stranger, and Adeline, from the oriel recess of the hall, saw the marquis alight. She retreated with precipitation and, forgetting the request of La Motte, was hastening to her chamber, but the marquis was already in the hall, and seeing her leaving it, turned to La Motte with a look of inquiry. La Motte called her back, and by a frown too intelligent reminded her of her promise. She summoned all her spirits to her aid but advanced, notwithstanding, in visible emotion, while the marquis addressed her as usual, the same easy gaiety playing upon his countenance and directing his manner.

Adeline was surprised and shocked at this careless confidence, which, however, by awakening her pride, communicated to her an air of dignity that abashed him. He spoke with hesitation, and frequently appeared abstracted from the subject of discourse. At length arising, he begged Adeline would favour him with a few moments' conversation. Monsieur and Madame de la Motte were now leaving the room when Adeline, turning to the marquis, told him she would not hear any conversation except in the presence of her friends. But she said it in vain, for they were gone; and La Motte, as he withdrew, expressed by his looks how much an attempt to follow would displease him.

She sat for some time in silence, and trembling expectation.

"I am sensible," said the marquis at length, "that the conduct to which the ardour of my passion lately betrayed me has injured me in your opinion, and that you will not easily restore me to your esteem; but I trust the offer which I now make you, both of my title and fortune, will sufficiently prove the sincerity of my attachment, and atone for the transgression which love only prompted."

After this specimen of commonplace verbosity, which the marquis seemed to consider as a prelude to triumph, he attempted to impress a kiss upon the hand of Adeline, who, withdrawing it hastily, said, "You are already, my lord, acquainted with my sentiments upon this subject, and it is almost unnecessary for me now to repeat that I cannot accept the honour you offer me."

"Explain yourself, lovely Adeline! I am ignorant that till now I ever made you this offer."

"Most true, sir," said Adeline, "and you do well to remind me of this since, after having heard your former proposal, I cannot listen for a moment to any other." She rose to quit the room.

"Stay, madam," said the marquis, with a look in which offended pride struggled to conceal itself. "Do not suffer an extravagant resentment to operate against your true interests; recollect the dangers that surround you, and consider the value of an offer which may afford you at least an honourable asylum."

"My misfortunes, my lord, whatever they are, I have never obtruded upon you; you will, therefore, excuse my observing that your present mention of them conveys a much greater appearance of insult than compassion."

The marquis, though with evident confusion, was going to reply; but Adeline would not be detained, and retired to her chamber. Destitute as she was, her heart revolted from the proposal of the marquis, and she determined never to accept it. To her dislike of his general disposition and the aversion excited by his late offer was added, indeed, the influence of a prior attachment, and of a remembrance which she found it impossible to erase from her heart.

The marquis stayed to dine, and in consideration of La Motte, Adeline appeared at table, where the former gazed upon her with such frequent and silent earnestness that her distress became insupportable, and when the cloth was drawn, she instantly retired. Madame de la Motte soon followed, and it was not till evening that she had an opportunity of returning to the manuscript. When Monsieur and Madame de la Motte were in their chamber and all was still, she drew forth the narrative and, trimming her lamp, sat down to read as follows:

The ruffians unbound me from my horse, and led me through the hall up the spiral staircase of the abbey. Resistance was useless, but I looked around in the hope of seeing some person less obdurate than the men who brought me hither; someone who might be sensible to pity and capable, at least, of civil treatment. I looked in vain; no person appeared, and this circumstance confirmed my worst apprehensions. The secrecy of the business foretold a horrible conclusion. Having passed some chambers, they stopped in one hung with old tapestry. I inquired why we did not go on, and was told I should soon know.

At that moment, I expected to see the instrument of death uplifted, and silently recommended myself to God. But death was not then designed for me; they raised the arras, and discovered a door, which they then opened. Seizing my arms, they led me through a suite of dismal chambers beyond. Having reached the farthest of these, they again stopped. The horrid gloom of the place seemed congenial to murder, and inspired deadly thoughts. Again I looked round for the instrument of destruction, and again I was respited. I supplicated to know what was designed me; it was now unnecessary to ask who was the author of the design. They were silent to my question, but at length told me this chamber was my prison. Having said this, and set down a jug of water, they left the room, and I heard the door barred upon me.

O sound of despair! O moment of unutterable anguish! The pang of death itself is, surely, not superior to that I then suffered. Shut out from day, from friends, from life— for such I must foretell it—in the prime of my years, in the height of my transgressions, and left to imagine horrors more terrible than any, perhaps, which certainty could give—I sink beneath the—

Here several pages of the manuscript were decayed with damp and totally illegible. With much difficulty Adeline made out the following lines:

Three days have now passed in solitude and silence; the horrors of death are ever before my eyes, let me endeavour to prepare for the dreadful change! When I awake in the morning I think I shall not live to see another night, and when night returns, that I must never more unclose my eyes on morning. Why am I brought hither—why confined thus rigorously—but for death! Yet what action of my life has deserved this at the hand of a fellow creature?—Of —

O my children! O friends far distant! I shall never see you more—never more receive the parting look of kind-ness—never bestow a parting blessing!—Ye know not my wretched state—alas! ye cannot know it by human means. Ye believe me happy, or ye would fly to my relief. I know that what I now write cannot avail me, yet there is comfort in pouring forth my griefs; and I bless that man, less sav-age than his fellows, who has supplied me these means of recording them. Alas! he knows full well that from this in-dulgence he has nothing to fear. My pen can call no friends to succour me, nor reveal my danger ere it is too late. O! ye, who may hereafter read what I now write, give a tear to my sufferings: I have wept often for the distresses of my fellow creatures!

Adeline paused. Here the wretched writer appealed directly to her heart; he spoke in the energy of truth, and by a strong illusion of fancy, it seemed as if his past sufferings were at this moment present. She was for some time unable to proceed, and sat in musing sorrow. *In these very apartments*, thought she, *this poor sufferer was confined—here he—* Adeline started, and thought she heard a sound, but the stillness of night was undisturbed. *In these very chambers, these lines were written—these lines, from which he then derived a comfort in believing they would hereafter be read by some pitying eye: this time is now come. Your miseries, O injured being! are lamented, where they were endured. Here, where you suffered, I weep for your sufferings!*

Her imagination was now strongly impressed, and to her distempered senses the suggestions of a bewildered mind appeared with the force of reality. Again she started and listened, and thought she heard "Here" distinctly repeated by a whisper immediately behind her. The terror of the thought, however, was but momentary, she knew it could not be; convinced that her fancy had deceived her, she took up the manuscript and again began to read.

For what am I reserved! Why this delay? If I am to die— why not quickly? Three weeks have I now passed within these walls, during which time no look of pity has softened my afflictions; no voice, save my own, has met my ear. The countenances of the ruffians who attend me are stern and inflexible, and their silence is obstinate. This stillness is dreadful! O! ye, who have known what it is to live in the depths of solitude, who have passed your dreary days without one sound to cheer you; ye, and ye only, can tell what now I feel; and ye may know how much I would endure to hear the accents of a human voice.

O dire extremity! O state of living death! What dreadful stillness! All around me is dead; and do I really exist, or am I but a statue? Is this a vision? Are these things real? Alas, I am bewildered!—this deathlike and perpetual silence— this dismal chamber—the dread of further sufferings have disturbed my fancy. O for some friendly breast to lay my weary head on! some cordial accents to revive my soul!

I write by stealth. He who furnished me with the means, I fear, has suffered for some symptoms of pity he may have discovered for me. I have not seen him for several days: perhaps he is inclined to help me, and for that reason is forbid to come. O that hope! but how vain. Never more must I quit these walls while life remains. Another day is gone, and yet I live; at this time tomorrow night my sufferings may be sealed in death. I will continue my journal nightly, till the hand that writes shall be stopped by death: when the journal ceases, the reader will know I am no more. Perhaps, these are the last lines I shall ever write

Adeline paused, while her tears fell fast. *Unhappy man! and was there no pitying soul to save thee! Great God! thy ways are wonderful!* While she sat musing, her fancy, which now wandered in the regions of terror, gradually subdued reason. There was a glass before her upon the table, and she feared to raise her looks toward it, lest some other face than her own should meet her eyes: other dreadful ideas and strange images of fantastic thought now crossed her mind.

A hollow sigh seemed to pass near her. *Holy Virgin, protect me!* cried she, and threw a fearful glance round the room. *This is surely something more than fancy.* Her fears so far overcame her that she was several times upon the point of calling up part of the family, but unwillingness to disturb them, and a dread of ridicule, withheld her. She was also afraid to move and almost to breathe. As she listened to the wind that murmured at the casements of her lonely chamber, she again thought she heard a sigh. Her imagination refused any longer the control of reason. When she turned her eyes, a figure, whose exact form she could not distinguish, appeared to pass along an obscure part of the chamber. A dreadful chillness came over her, and she sat fixed in her chair. At length a deep sigh somewhat relieved her oppressed spirits, and her senses seemed to return.

All remaining quiet, after some time she began to question whether her fancy had not deceived her, and she so far conquered her terror as to desist from calling Madame de la Motte. Her mind was, however, so much disturbed that she did not venture to trust herself that night again with the manuscript; but, having spent some time in prayer, and in endeavouring to compose her spirits, she retired to bed.

When she awoke in the morning, the cheerful sunbeams

played upon the casements and dispelled the illusions of darkness. Her mind, soothed and invigorated by sleep, rejected the mystic and turbulent promptings of imagination. She arose refreshed and thankful; but upon going down to breakfast, this transient gleam of peace fled upon the appearance of the marquis, whose frequent visits at the abbey, after what had passed, not only displeased but alarmed her. She saw that he was determined to persevere in addressing her, and the boldness and insensibility of this conduct, while it excited her indignation, increased her disgust. In pity to La Motte, she endeavoured to conceal these emotions, though she now thought that he required too much from her complaisance, and began seriously to consider how she might avoid the necessity of continuing it. The marquis behaved to her with the most respectful attention; but Adeline was silent and reserved, and seized the first opportunity of withdrawing.

As she passed up the spiral staircase, Peter entered the hall below, and seeing Adeline, he stopped and looked earnestly at her. She did not observe him, but he called her softly, and she then saw him make a signal as if he had something to communicate. In the next instant La Motte opened the door of the vaulted room, and Peter hastily disappeared. She proceeded to her chamber, ruminating upon this signal, and the cautious manner in which Peter had given it.

But her thoughts soon returned to their wonted subjects. Three days were now passed, and she heard no intelligence of her father; she began to hope that he had relented from the violent measures hinted at by La Motte, and that he meant to pursue a milder plan. But when she considered his character, this appeared improbable, and she relapsed into her former fears. Her residence at the abbey was now become painful, from the perseverance of the marquis and the conduct which La Motte obliged her to adopt; yet she could not think without dread of quitting it to return to her father.

The image of Theodore often intruded upon her busy thoughts, and brought with it a pang which his strange departure occasioned. She had a confused notion that his fate was somehow connected with her own; and her struggles to prevent the remembrance of him served only to show how much her heart was his.

To divert her thoughts from these subjects and gratify the curiosity so strongly excited on the preceding night, she now took up the manuscript but was hindered from opening it by the entrance of Madame de la Motte, who came to tell her the marquis was gone. They passed their morning together in work and general conversation, La Motte not appearing till dinner, when he said little, and Adeline less. She asked him, however, if he had heard from her father.

"I have not heard from him," said La Motte, "but there is good reason, as I am informed by the marquis, to believe he is not far off."

Adeline was shocked, yet she was able to reply with becoming firmness. "I have already, sir, involved you too much in my distress, and now see that resistance will destroy you without serving me; I am, therefore, contented to return to my father, and thus spare you further calamity."

"This is a rash determination," replied La Motte, "and if you pursue it, I fear you will severely repent. I speak to you as a friend, Adeline, and desire you will endeavour to listen to me without prejudice. The marquis, I find, has offered you his hand. I know not which circumstance most excites my surprise, that a man of his rank and consequence should solicit a marriage with a person without fortune or ostensible connections, or that a person so circumstanced should even for a moment reject the advantages thus offered her. You weep, Adeline; let me hope that you are convinced of the absurdity of this conduct, and will no longer trifle with your good fortune. The kindness I have shown you must convince you of my regard, and that I have no motive for offering you this advice but your advantage. It is necessary, however, to say that, should your father not insist upon your removal, I know not how long my circumstances may enable me to afford even the humble pittance you receive here. Still you are silent."

The anguish which this speech excited suppressed her utterance, and she continued to weep. At length she said, "Suffer me, sir, to go back to my father. I should, indeed, make an ill return for the kindness you mention, could I wish to stay after what you now tell me; and to accept the marquis I feel to be impossible." The remembrance of Theodore arose to her mind, and she wept aloud.

La Motte sat for some time musing. "Strange infatuation," said he. "Is it possible that you can persist in this heroism of romance, and prefer a father so inhuman as yours to the Marquis de Montalt! A destiny so full of danger to a life of splendour and delight!"

"Pardon me," said Adeline, "a marriage with the marquis would be splendid, but never happy. His character excites my aversion, and I entreat, sir, that he may no more be mentioned."

CHAPTER 10

Nor are those empty-hearted, whose low sound
Reverbs no hollowness.

Shakespeare, *King Lear*

The conversation related in the last chapter was interrupted by the entrance of Peter, who as he left the room looked significantly at Adeline and almost beckoned. She was anxious to know what he meant, and soon after went into the hall, where she found him loitering. The moment he saw her, he made a sign of silence and beckoned her into the recess.

"Well, Peter, what is it you would say?" said Adeline.

"Hush, mam'selle; for heaven's sake speak lower; if we should be overheard, we are all blown up."

Adeline begged him to explain what he meant.

"Yes, mam'selle, that is what I have wanted all day long. I have watched and watched for an opportunity, and looked and looked, till I was afraid my master himself would see me, but all would not do; you would not understand."

Adeline entreated he would be quick.

"Yes, mam'selle, but I'm so afraid we shall be seen; but I would do much to serve such a good young lady, for I could not bear to think of what threatened you without telling you of it."

"For God's sake," said Adeline, "speak quickly, or we shall be interrupted."

"Well, then; but you must first promise by the Holy Virgin never to say it was I that told you. My master would—"

"I do, I do!" said Adeline.

"Well, then—on Monday evening as I—hark! did not I hear a step? do, mam'selle, just step this way to the cloisters. I would not for the world we should be seen. I'll go out at the hall door and you can go through the passage. I would not for the world we should be seen."

Adeline was much alarmed by Peter's words, and hurried to the cloisters.

He quickly appeared and, looking cautiously round, resumed his discourse. "As I was saying, mam'selle, Monday night, when the marquis slept here, you know he sat up very late, and I can guess, perhaps, the reason of that. Strange things came out, but it is not my business to tell all I think."

"Pray do speak to the purpose," said Adeline impatiently, "what is this danger which you say threatens me? Be quick, or we shall be observed."

"Danger enough, mam'selle," replied Peter, "if you knew all, and when you do, what will it signify, for you can't help yourself. But that's neither here nor there; I was resolved to tell you, though I may repent it."

"Or rather you are resolved not to tell me," said Adeline, "for you have made no progress toward it. But what do you mean? You was speaking of the marquis."

"Hush, mam'selle, not so loud. The marquis, as I said, sat up very late and my master sat up with him. One of his men went to bed in the oak room, and the other stayed to undress his lord. So as we were sitting together—Lord have mercy! it made my hair stand on end! I tremble yet. So as we were sitting together—but as sure as I live, yonder is my master; I caught a glimpse of him between the trees. If he sees me it is all over with us. I'll tell you another time."

So saying, he hurried into the abbey, leaving Adeline in a state of alarm, curiosity, and vexation. She walked out into the forest, ruminating upon Peter's words and endeavouring to guess to what they alluded; there Madame de la Motte joined her, and they conversed on various topics till they reached the abbey.

Adeline watched in vain through that day for an opportunity of speaking with Peter. While he waited at supper, she occasionally observed his countenance with great anxiety, hoping it might afford her some degree of intelligence on the subject of her fears. When she retired, Madame de la Motte accompanied her to her chamber, and continued to converse with her for a considerable time, so that she had no means of obtaining an interview with Peter.

Madame de la Motte appeared to labour under some great affliction, and when Adeline, noticing this, entreated to know the cause of her dejection, tears started into her eyes, and she abruptly left the room.

This behaviour of Madame de la Motte concurred with Peter's discourse to alarm Adeline, who sat pensively upon her bed, given up to reflection, till she was roused by the sound of a clock which stood in the room below, and which now struck twelve. She was preparing for rest when she recollected the manuscript and was unable to conclude the night without reading it. The first words she could distinguish were the following:

Again I return to this poor consolation—again I have been permitted to see another day. It is now midnight! My solitary lamp burns beside me; the time is awful, but to me the silence of noon is as the silence of midnight: a deeper gloom is all in which they differ. The still, unvarying hours are numbered only by my sufferings! Great God! when shall I be released!

But whence this strange confinement? I have never injured him. If death is designed me, why this delay; and for what but death am I brought hither? This abbey—alas!

Here the manuscript was again illegible, and for several pages Adeline could only make out disjointed sentences.

O bitter draught! when, when shall I have rest! O my friends! will none of ye fly to aid me; will none of ye avenge my sufferings? Ah! when it is too late—when I am gone forever, ye will endeavour to avenge them.

Once more is night returned to me. Another day has passed in solitude and misery. I have climbed to the casement, thinking the view of nature would refresh my soul, and somewhat enable me to support these afflictions. Alas! even this small comfort is denied me, the windows open toward other parts of this abbey, and admit only a portion of that day which I must never more fully behold. Last night! last night! O scene of horror!

Adeline shuddered. She feared to read the coming sentence, yet curiosity prompted her to proceed. Still she paused; an unaccountable dread came over her. *Some horrid deed has been done here,* thought she; *the reports of the peasants are true. Murder has been committed.* The idea thrilled her with horror. She recollected the dagger which had impeded her steps in the secret chamber, and this circumstance served to confirm her most terrible conjectures. She wished to examine it, but it lay in one of these chambers, and she feared to go in quest of it.

"Wretched, wretched victim!" she exclaimed, "could no friend rescue thee from destruction! O that I had been near! yet what could I have done to save thee? Alas! nothing. I forget that even now, perhaps, I am like thee abandoned to dangers from which I have no friend to succour me. Too surely I guess the author of thy miseries!"

She stopped, and thought she heard a sigh, as on the preceding night, pass along the chamber. Her blood was chilled, and she sat motionless. The lonely situation of her room, remote from the rest of the family, who were almost beyond call—for she was now in her old apartment, from which Madame de la Motte had removed—struck so forcibly upon her imagination that she with difficulty preserved herself from fainting. She sat for a considerable time, but all was still. When she was somewhat recovered, her first design was to alarm the family;

but further reflection again withheld her. She endeavoured to compose her spirits, and addressed a short prayer to that Being who had hitherto protected her in every danger. While she was thus employed, her mind gradually became elevated and reassured; a sublime complacency filled her heart, and she sat down once more to pursue the narrative.

Several lines that immediately followed were obliterated.

He told me I should not be permitted to live long, not more than three days, and bade me choose whether I would die by poison or the sword. O the agonies of that moment! Great God! thou seest my sufferings! I often viewed, with a momentary hope of escaping, the high grated windows of my prison—all things within the compass of possibility I was resolved to try, and with an eager desperation I climbed toward the casements, but my foot slipped, and falling back to the floor, I was stunned by the blow.

On recovering, the first sounds I heard were the steps of a person entering my prison. A recollection of the past returned, and deplorable was my condition. I shuddered at what was to come. The same man approached; he looked at me at first with pity, but his countenance soon recovered its natural ferocity. Yet he did not then come to execute the purposes of his employer: I am reserved to another day—Great God, thy will be done!

Adeline could not go on. All the circumstances that seemed to corroborate the fate of this unhappy man crowded upon her mind. The reports concerning the abbey—the dreams, which had forerun her discovery of the private apartments—the singular manner in which she had found the manuscript, and the apparition which she now believed she had really seen. She blamed herself for having not yet mentioned the discovery of the manuscript and chambers to La Motte, and resolved to delay the disclosure no longer than the following morning. The immediate cares that had occupied her mind, and a fear of losing the manuscript before she had read it, had hitherto kept her silent.

Such a combination of circumstances she believed could only be produced by some supernatural power operating for the retribution of the guilty. These reflections filled her mind with a degree of awe which the loneliness of the large old chamber in which she sat, and the hour of the night, soon heightened into terror. She had never been superstitious, but circumstances so uncommon had hitherto conspired in this affair that she could not believe them accidental. Her imagination, wrought upon by these reflections, again became sensible to every impression; she feared to look round, lest she should again see some dreadful phantom, and she almost fancied she heard voices swell in the storm which now shook the fabric.

Still she tried to command her feelings so as to avoid disturbing the family, but they became so painful that even the dread of La Motte's ridicule had hardly power to prevent her quitting the chamber. Her mind was now in such a state that she found it impossible to pursue the story in the manuscript, though to avoid the tortures of suspense she had attempted it. She laid it down again, and tried to argue herself into composure. *What have I to fear?* thought she. *I am at least innocent, and I shall not be punished for the crime of another.*

The violent gust of wind that now rushed through the whole suite of apartments so forcibly shook the door that led from her late bedchamber to the private rooms that Adeline, unable to remain longer in doubt, ran to see from whence the noise issued. The arras which concealed the door was violently agitated, and she stood for a moment observing it in indescribable terror, till believing it was swayed by the wind, she made a sudden effort to overcome her feelings, and was stooping to raise it. At that instant, she thought she heard a voice. She stopped and listened, but everything was still; yet apprehension so far overcame her that she had no power either to examine or to leave the chambers.

In a few moments the voice returned; she was now convinced she had not been deceived, for, though low, she heard it distinctly, and was almost sure it repeated her own name. So much was her fancy affected that she even thought it was the same voice she had heard in her dreams. This conviction entirely subdued the small remains of her courage, and sinking into a chair, she lost all recollection.

How long she remained in this state she knew not, but when she recovered, she exerted all her strength and reached the winding staircase, where she called aloud. No one heard her, and she hastened, as fast as her feebleness would permit, to the chamber of Madame de la Motte. She tapped gently at the door, and was answered by Madame, who was alarmed at being awakened at so unusual an hour, and believed that some danger threatened her husband. When she understood that it was Adeline, and that she was unwell, she quickly came to her relief. The terror that was yet visible in Adeline's countenance excited her inquiries, and the occasion of it was explained to her.

Madame was so much discomposed by the relation that she called La Motte from his bed, who, more angry at being disturbed than interested in the agitation he witnessed, reproved Adeline for suffering her fancies to overcome her reason. She now mentioned the discovery she had made of the inner chambers and the manuscript, circumstances which roused the attention of La Motte so much that he desired to see the manuscript and resolved to go immediately to the apartments described by Adeline.

Madame de la Motte endeavoured to dissuade him from his purpose; but La Motte, with whom opposition had always an effect contrary to the one designed, and who wished to throw further ridicule upon the terrors of Adeline, persisted in his intention. He called to Peter to attend with a light, and insisted that Madame de la Motte and Adeline should accompany him. Madame de la Motte desired to be excused, and Adeline at first declared she could not go; but he would be obeyed.

They ascended the tower, and entered the first chambers together, for each of the party was reluctant to be the last; in the second chamber all was quiet and in order. Adeline presented the manuscript and pointed to the arras which concealed the door. La Motte lifted the arras and opened the door, but Madame de la Motte and Adeline entreated to go no farther—again he called to them to follow. All was quiet in the first chamber; he expressed his surprise that the room should so long have remained undiscovered, and was proceeding to the second, but suddenly stopped.

"We will defer our examination till tomorrow," said he. "The damps of these apartments are unwholesome at any time, but they strike one more sensibly at night. I am chilled. Peter, remember to throw open the windows early in the morning, that the air may circulate."

"Lord bless your honour," said Peter, "don't you see I can't reach them? Besides, I don't believe they are made to open; see what strong iron bars there are; the room looks, for all the world, like a prison; I suppose this is the place the people meant when they said nobody that had been in ever came out."

La Motte, who during this speech had been looking attentively at the high windows, which at first he had certainly not observed closely, now interrupted the eloquence of Peter, and bade him carry the light before them. They all willingly quitted these chambers and returned to the room below, where a fire was lighted, and the party remained together for some time.

La Motte, for reasons best known to himself, attempted to ridicule the discovery and fears of Adeline, till she, with a seriousness that checked him, entreated he would desist. He was silent, and soon after Adeline, encouraged by the return of daylight, ventured to her chamber and for some hours experienced the blessing of undisturbed repose.

On the following day, Adeline's first care was to obtain an interview with Peter, whom she had some hopes of seeing as she went downstairs; he, however, did not appear, and she proceeded to the sitting room, where she found La Motte, apparently much disturbed. Adeline asked him if he had looked at the manuscript.

"I have run my eye over it," said he, "but it is so much obscured by time that it can scarcely be deciphered. It appears to exhibit a strange romantic story; and I do not wonder that, after you had suffered its terrors to impress your imagination, you fancied you saw spectres and heard wondrous noises."

Adeline thought La Motte did not choose to be convinced, and she therefore forbore reply. During breakfast, she often looked with anxious inquiry at Peter, who waited, and from his countenance was still more assured that he had something of importance to communicate. In the hope of some conversation with him, she left the room as soon as possible, and repaired to her favourite avenue, where she had not long remained when he appeared.

"God bless you! mam'selle," said he, "I'm sorry I frighted you so last night."

"Frighted me," said Adeline, "how was you concerned in that?"

He then informed her that when he thought Monsieur and Madame de la Motte were asleep, he had stole to her chamber door with an intention of giving her the sequel of what he had begun in the morning; that he had called several times as loudly as he dared, but receiving no answer, he believed she was asleep or did not choose to speak with him, and he had therefore left the door. This account of the voice she had heard relieved Adeline's spirits; she was even surprised that she did not know it till, remembering the perturbation of her mind for some time preceding, this surprise disappeared.

She entreated Peter to be brief in explaining the danger with which she was threatened. "If you'll let me go on my own way, mam'selle, you'll soon know it; but if you hurry me and ask me questions, here and there, out of their places, I don't know what I am saying."

"Be it so," said Adeline, "only remember that we may be observed."

"Yes, mam'selle, I'm as much afraid of that as you are, for I believe I should be almost as ill off; however, that is neither here nor there, but I'm sure if you stay in this old abbey another night, it will be worse for you; for, as I said before, I know all about it."

"What mean you, Peter?"

"Why, about this scheme that's going on."

"What, then, is my father—?"

"Your father," interrupted Peter, "Lord bless you, that is all fudge to frighten you; your father, nor nobody else, has ever sent after you; I dare say, he knows no more of you than the pope does—not he."

Adeline looked displeased. "You trifle," said she. "If you have anything to tell, say it quickly; I am in haste."

"Bless you, young lady, I meant no harm, I hope you're not angry; but I'm sure you can't deny that your father is cruel. But, as I was saying, the Marquis de Montalt likes you, and he and my master"—Peter looked round—"have been laying their heads together about you."

Adeline turned pale—she comprehended a part of the truth, and eagerly entreated him to proceed.

"They have been laying their heads together about you. This is what Jacques, the marquis's man, tells me: Says he, 'Peter, you little know what is going on—I could tell all if I chose it, but it is not for those who are trusted to tell again. I warrant now your master is close enough with you.' Upon which I was piqued, and resolved to make him believe I could be trusted as well as he. 'Perhaps not,' says I, 'perhaps I know as much as you, though I do not choose to brag on't,' and I winked. 'Do you so?' says he, 'then you are closer than I thought for. She is a fine girl,' says he, meaning you, mam'selle, 'but she is nothing but a poor foundling after all—so it does not much signify.' I had a mind to know further what he meant—so I did not knock him down. By seeming to know as much as he, I at last made him discover all, and he told me—but you look pale, mam'selle, are you ill?"

"No," said Adeline, in a tremulous accent, and scarcely able to support herself, "pray proceed."

"And he told me that the marquis had been courting you

a good while, but you would not listen to him, and had even pretended he would marry you, and all would not do. 'As for marriage,' says I, 'I suppose she knows the marchioness is alive; and I'm sure she is not one for his turn upon other terms.'"

"The marchioness is really living then!" said Adeline.

"O yes, mam'selle! we all know that, and I thought you had known it too. 'We shall see that,' replies Jacques, 'at least, I believe that our master will outwit her.' I stared; I could not help it. 'Aye,' says he, 'you know your master has agreed to give her up to my lord.'"

"Good God! what will become of me?" exclaimed Adeline.

"Aye, mam'selle, I am sorry for you; but hear me out. When Jacques said this, I quite forgot myself. 'I'll never believe it,' said I; 'I'll never believe my master would be guilty of such a base action; he'll not give her up, or I'm no Christian.' 'Oh!' said Jacques, 'for that matter, I thought you'd known all, else I should not have said a word about it. However, you may soon satisfy yourself by going to the parlour door, as I have done; they're in consultation about it now, I dare say.'"

"You need not repeat any more of this conversation," said Adeline, "but tell me the result of what you heard from the parlour."

"Why, mam'selle, when he said this, I took him at his word and went to the door where, sure enough, I heard my master and the marquis talking about you. They said a great deal which I could make nothing of, but at last I heard the marquis say, 'You know the terms; on these terms only will I consent to bury the past in ob—ob—oblivion'—that was the word. Monsieur La Motte then told the marquis, if he would return to the abbey upon such a night, meaning this very night, mam'selle, everything should be prepared according to his wishes. 'Adeline shall then be yours, my lord,' said he. 'You are already acquainted with her chamber.'"

At these words, Adeline clasped her hands and raised her eyes to Heaven in silent despair.

Peter went on. "When I heard this, I could not doubt what Jacques had said. 'Well,' said he, 'what do you think of it now?'

'Why, that my master's a rascal,' says I. 'It's well you don't think mine one too,' says he. 'Why, as for that matter,' says I—"

Adeline, interrupting him, inquired if he had heard anything further.

"Just then," said Peter, "we heard Madame de la Motte come out from another room, and so we made haste back to the kitchen."

"She was not present at this conversation then?" said Adeline.

"No, mam'selle, but my master has told her of it, I warrant."

Adeline was almost as much shocked by this apparent perfidy of Madame de la Motte as by a knowledge of the destruction that threatened her. After musing a few moments in extreme agitation, she said, "Peter, you have a good heart, and feel a just indignation at your master's treachery—will you assist me to escape?"

"Ah, mam'selle!" said he, "how can I assist you? Besides, where can we go? I have no friends about here, no more than yourself."

"O!" replied Adeline, in extreme emotion, "we fly from enemies; strangers may prove friends; assist me but to escape from this forest, and you will claim my eternal gratitude; I have no fears beyond it."

"Why, as for this forest," replied Peter, "I am weary of it myself though, when we first came, I thought it would be fine living here; at least, I thought it was very different from any life I had ever lived before. But these ghosts that haunt the abbey, I am no more a coward than other men, but I don't like them; and then there is so many strange reports abroad; and my master—I thought I could have served him to the end of the world, but now I care not how soon I leave him, for his behaviour to you, mam'selle."

"You consent, then, to assist me in escaping?" said Adeline with eagerness.

"Why as to that, mam'selle, I would willingly if I knew where to go. To be sure, I have a sister lives in Savoy, but that is a great way off; and I have saved a little money out of my wages, but that won't carry us such a long journey."

"Regard not that," said Adeline, "if I was once beyond this forest, I would then endeavour to take care of myself, and repay you for your kindness."

"O! as for that, madam——"

"Well, well, Peter, let us consider how we may escape. This night, say you, this night—the marquis is to return?"

"Yes, mam'selle, tonight, about dark. I have just thought of a scheme: My master's horses are grazing in the forest, we may take one of them, and send it back from the first stage. But how shall we avoid being seen? Besides, if we go off in the daylight, he will soon pursue and overtake us; and if you stay till night, the marquis will be come, and then there is no chance. If they miss us both at the same time too, they'll guess how it is, and set off directly. Could not you contrive to go first and wait for me till the hurly-burly's over? Then, while they're searching in the place underground for you, I can slip away, and we should be out of their reach before they thought of pursuing us."

Adeline agreed to the truth of all this, and was somewhat surprised at Peter's sagacity. She inquired if he knew of any-place in the neighbourhood of the abbey where she could remain concealed till he came with a horse.

"Why yes, madam, there is a place, now I think of it, where you may be safe enough, for nobody goes near; but they say it's haunted, and perhaps you would not like to go there."

Adeline, remembering the last night, was somewhat startled at this intelligence; but a sense of her present danger pressed again upon her mind, and overcame every other apprehension. "Where is this place?" said she. "If it will conceal me, I shall not hesitate to go."

"It is an old tomb that stands in the thickest part of the forest about a quarter of a mile off the nearest way, and almost a mile the other. When my master used to hide himself so much in the forest, I have followed him somewhere thereabouts, but I did not find out the tomb till t'other day. However, that's neither here nor there; if you dare venture to it, mam'selle, I'll show you the nearest way." So saying, he pointed to a winding path on the right.

Adeline, having looked round without perceiving any person near, directed Peter to lead her to the tomb; they pursued the path till, turning into a gloomy romantic part of the forest almost impervious to the rays of the sun, they came to the spot whither Louis had formerly traced his father.

The stillness and solemnity of the scene struck awe upon the heart of Adeline, who paused and surveyed it for some time in silence. At length, Peter led her into the interior part of the ruin, to which they descended by several steps.

"Some old abbot," said he, "was formerly buried here, as the marquis's people say; and it's like enough that he belonged to the abbey yonder. But I don't see why he should take it in his head to walk; he was not murdered, surely?"

"I hope not," said Adeline.

"That's more than can be said for all that lies buried at the abbey, though, and—"

Adeline interrupted him. "Hark! Surely I hear a noise," said she. "Heaven protect us from discovery!"

They listened, but all was still, and they went on. Peter opened a low door, and they entered upon a dark passage, frequently obstructed by loose fragments of stone, and along which they moved with caution.

"Whither are we going?" said Adeline.

"I scarcely know myself," said Peter, "for I never was so far before; but the place seems quiet enough." Something obstructed his way; it was a door, which yielded to his hand, and discovered a kind of cell, obscurely seen by the twilight admitted through a grate above. A partial gleam shot athwart the place, leaving the greatest part of it in shadow.

Adeline sighed as she surveyed it. "This is a frightful spot," said she, "but if it will afford me a shelter, it is a palace. Remember, Peter, that my peace and honour depend upon your faithfulness; be both discreet and resolute. In the dusk of the evening I can pass from the abbey with least danger of being observed, and in this cell I will wait your arrival. As soon as Monsieur and Madame de la Motte are engaged in searching the vaults, you will bring here a horse; three knocks upon the tomb shall inform me of your arrival. For Heaven's sake be cautious, and be punctual."

"I will, mam'selle, let come what may."

They reascended to the forest, and Adeline, fearful of observation, directed Peter to return first to the abbey, and invent some excuse for his absence if he had been missed. When she was again alone, she yielded to a flood of tears, and indulged the excess of her distress. She saw herself without friends, without relations, destitute, forlorn, and abandoned to the worst of evils. Betrayed by the very persons to whose comfort she had so long administered, whom she had loved as her protectors and revered as her parents! These reflections touched her heart with the most afflicting sensations, and the sense of her immediate danger was for a while absorbed in the grief occasioned by a discovery of such guilt in others.

At length she roused all her fortitude and, turning toward the abbey, endeavoured to await with patience the hour of evening, and to sustain an appearance of composure in the presence of Monsieur and Madame de la Motte. For the present she wished to avoid seeing either of them, doubting her ability to disguise her emotions; having reached the abbey, she therefore passed on to her chamber. Here she endeavoured to direct her attention to indifferent subjects, but in vain; the danger of her situation and the severe disappointment she had received in the character of those whom she had so much esteemed and even loved, pressed hard upon her thoughts. To a generous mind few circumstances are more afflicting than a discovery of perfidy in those whom we have trusted, even though it may fail of any absolute inconvenience to ourselves. The behaviour of Madame de la Motte in thus, by concealment, conspiring to her destruction, particularly shocked her.

How has my imagination deceived me! thought she. *What a picture did it draw of the goodness of the world! And must I then believe that everybody is cruel and deceitful? No—let me still be deceived, and still suffer, rather than be condemned to a state of such wretched suspicion.* She now endeavoured to extenuate the conduct of Madame de la Motte by attributing it to a fear of her husband. *She dare not oppose his will, else she would warn me of my danger, and assist me to escape from it. No—I will never believe her capable of conspiring my ruin. Terror alone keeps her silent.*

Adeline was somewhat comforted by this thought. The benevolence of her heart taught her, in this instance, to sophisticate.[39] She perceived not that, by ascribing the conduct of Madame de la Motte to terror, she only softened the degree of her guilt, imputing it to a motive less depraved but not less selfish. She remained in her chamber till summoned to dinner, when, drying her tears, she descended with faltering steps and a palpitating heart to the parlour. When she saw La Motte, in spite of all her efforts she trembled and grew pale; she could not behold, even with apparent indifference, the man who she knew had destined her to destruction. He observed her emotion and inquired if she was ill; she saw the danger to which her agitation exposed her. Fearful lest La Motte should suspect its true cause, she rallied all her spirits and, with a look of complacency, answered she was well.

During dinner she preserved a degree of composure that effectually concealed the varied anguish of her heart. When she looked at La Motte, terror and indignation were her predominant feelings. But when she regarded Madame de la Motte, it was otherwise; gratitude for her former tenderness had long been confirmed into affection, and her heart now swelled with the bitterness of grief and disappointment. Madame de la Motte appeared depressed, and said little. La Motte seemed anxious to prevent thought by assuming a fictitious and unnatural gaiety; he laughed and talked, and threw off frequent bumpers[40] of wine: it was the mirth of desperation. Madame became alarmed and would have restrained him, but he persisted in his libations to Bacchus till reflection seemed to be almost overcome.

39. To alter deceptively.
40. Glasses filled to the brim.

Madame de la Motte, fearful that in the carelessness of the present moment he might betray himself, withdrew with Adeline to another room. Adeline recollected the happy hours she once passed with her, when confidence banished reserve, and sympathy and esteem dictated the sentiments of friendship. Now those hours were gone forever; she could no longer unbosom her griefs to Madame de la Motte, no longer even esteem her. Yet, notwithstanding all the danger to which she was exposed by the criminal silence of the latter, she could not converse with her, consciously for the last time, without feeling a degree of sorrow which wisdom may call weakness, but to which benevolence will allow a softer name.

Madame de la Motte, in her conversation, appeared to labour under an almost equal oppression with Adeline; her thoughts were abstracted from the subject of discourse, and there were long and frequent intervals of silence. Adeline more than once caught her gazing with a look of tenderness upon her, and saw her eyes fill with tears. By this circumstance she was so much affected that she was several times upon the point of throwing herself at her feet, and imploring her pity and protection. Cooler reflection showed her the extravagance and danger of this conduct: she suppressed her emotions, but they at length compelled her to withdraw from the presence of Madame de la Motte.

CHAPTER 11

Thou, to whom the world unknown
With all its shadowy shapes is shown;
Who seest appall'd th' unreal scene,
While fancy lifts the veil between:
Ah, Fear! ah, frantic Fear!
I see, I see thee near.
I know thy hurry'd step, thy haggard eye!
Like thee I start, like thee disorder'd fly!

William Collins, "Ode to Fear"

Adeline anxiously watched from her chamber window the sun set behind the distant hills, and the time of her departure draw nigh. It set with uncommon splendour and threw a fiery gleam athwart the woods and upon some scattered fragments of the ruins, which she could not gaze upon with indifference. *Never again, probably, shall I see the sun sink below those hills,* thought she, *or illumine this scene! Where shall I be when next it sets—where this time tomorrow? Sunk, perhaps, in misery!* She wept to the thought. *A few hours, and the marquis will arrive—a few hours, and this abbey will be a scene of confusion and tumult: every eye will be in search of me, every recess will be explored.* These reflections inspired her with new terror, and increased her impatience to be gone.

Twilight gradually came on, and she now thought it sufficiently dark to venture forth; but before she went, she kneeled down and addressed herself to Heaven. She implored support and protection, and committed herself to the care of the God of mercies. Having done this, she quitted her chamber, and passed with cautious steps down the winding staircase. No person appeared, and she proceeded through the door of the tower into the forest. She looked around; the gloom of the evening obscured every object.

With a trembling heart she sought the path pointed out by Peter, which led to the tomb; having found it, she passed along forlorn and terrified. Often did she start as the breeze shook the light leaves of the trees, or as the bat flitted by, gamboling in the twilight; and often, as she looked back toward the abbey, she thought she distinguished, amid the deepening gloom, the figures of men. Having proceeded some way, she suddenly heard the feet of horses, and soon after a sound of voices, among which she distinguished that of the marquis: they seemed to come from the quarter she was approaching, and evidently advanced. Terror for some minutes arrested her steps; she stood in a state of dreadful hesitation: to proceed was to run into the hands of the marquis; to return was to fall into the power of La Motte.

After remaining for some time uncertain whither to fly, the sounds suddenly took a different direction, and wheeled toward the abbey. Adeline had a short cessation of terror. She now understood that the marquis had passed this spot only on his way to the abbey, and she hastened to secrete herself in the ruin. At length, after much difficulty, she reached it, the deep shades almost concealing it from her search. She paused at the entrance, awed by the solemnity that reigned within, and the utter darkness of the place; at length she determined to watch without till Peter should arrive. *If any person approaches,* thought she, *I can hear them before they can see me, and I can then secrete myself in the cell.*

She leaned against a fragment of the tomb in trembling expectation, and as she listened, no sound broke the silence of the hour. The state of her mind can only be imagined by considering that upon the present time turned the crisis of her fate. *They have now,* thought she, *discovered my flight; even now they are seeking me in every part of the abbey. I hear their dreadful voices call me; I see their eager looks.* The power of imagination almost overcame her. While she yet looked around, she saw lights moving at a distance; sometimes they glimmered between the trees, and sometimes they totally disappeared.

They seemed to be in a direction with the abbey; and she now remembered that in the morning she had seen a part of the fabric through an opening in the forest. She had, therefore, no doubt that the lights she saw proceeded from people in search of her, who not finding her at the abbey, she feared, might direct their steps toward the tomb. Her place of refuge now seemed too near her enemies to be safe, and she would have fled to a more distant part of the forest, but recollected that Peter would not know where to find her.

While these thoughts passed over her mind, she heard distant voices in the wind, and was hastening to conceal herself in the cell when she observed the lights suddenly disappear. All was soon after hushed in silence and darkness, yet she endeavoured to find the way to the cell. She remembered the situation of the outer door and of the passage, and having passed these she unclosed the door of the cell. Within, it was utterly dark. She trembled violently but entered; and having felt about the walls, at length she seated herself on a projection of stone.

She here again addressed herself to Heaven, and endeavoured to reanimate her spirits till Peter should arrive. Above half an hour elapsed in this gloomy recess, and no sound foretold his approach. Her spirits sank; she feared some part of their plan was discovered or interrupted, and that he was detained by La Motte. This conviction operated sometimes so strongly upon her fears as to urge her to quit the cell alone, and seek in flight her only chance of escape.

While this design was fluctuating in her mind, she distinguished through the grate above a clattering of hoofs. The noise approached, and at length stopped at the tomb. In the succeeding moment she heard three strokes of a whip; her heart beat, and for some moments her agitation was such that she made no effort to quit the cell. The strokes were repeated; she now roused her spirits and, stepping forward, ascended to the forest. She called, "Peter!" for the deep gloom would not permit her to distinguish either man or horse. She was quickly answered, "Hush! mam'selle, our voices will betray us."

They mounted and rode off as fast as the darkness would permit. Adeline's heart revived at every step they took. She inquired what had passed at the abbey, and how he had contrived to get away.

"Speak softly, mam'selle; you'll know all by and by, but I can't tell you now."

He had scarcely spoke ere they saw lights move along at a distance; and coming now to a more open part of the forest, he set off on a full gallop, and continued the pace till the horse could hold it no longer. They looked back; no lights appearing, Adeline's terror subsided. She inquired again what had passed at the abbey when her flight was discovered.

"You may speak without fear of being heard," said she. "We are gone beyond their reach, I hope."

"Why, mam'selle," said he, "you had not been gone long before the marquis arrived, and Monsieur de la Motte then found out you was fled. Upon this a great rout[41] there was, and he talked a great deal with the marquis."

"Speak louder," said Adeline, "I cannot hear you."

"I will, mam'selle."

"Oh! heavens!" interrupted Adeline. "What voice is this? It is not Peter's. For God's sake, tell me who you are and whither I am going?"

"You'll know that soon enough, young lady," answered the stranger, for it was indeed not Peter. "I am taking you where my master ordered."

Adeline, not doubting he was the marquis's servant, attempted to leap to the ground, but the man, dismounting, bound her to the horse. One feeble ray of hope at length

41. Wild confusion.

beamed upon her mind: she endeavoured to soften the man to pity and pleaded with all the genuine eloquence of distress; but he understood his interest too well to yield even for a moment to the compassion which, in spite of himself, her artless supplication inspired.

She now resigned herself to despair, and in passive silence submitted to her fate. They continued thus to travel, till a storm of rain, accompanied by thunder and lightning, drove them to the covert[42] of a thick grove. The man believed this a safe situation, and Adeline was now too careless of life to attempt convincing him of his error. The storm was violent and long, but as soon as it abated they set off on full gallop, and having continued to travel for about two hours, they came to the borders of the forest, and soon after to a high lonely wall, which Adeline could just distinguish by the moonlight which now streamed through the parting clouds.

Here they stopped; the man dismounted, and having opened a small door in the wall, he unbound Adeline, who shrieked, though involuntarily and in vain, as he took her from the horse. The door opened upon a narrow passage dimly lighted by a lamp which hung at the farther end. He led her on; they came to another door; it opened and disclosed a magnificent saloon, splendidly illuminated, and fitted up in the most airy and elegant taste.

The walls were painted in fresco, representing scenes from Ovid, and hung above with silk drawn up in festoons and richly fringed. The sofas were of a silk to suit the hangings. From the centre of the ceiling, which exhibited a scene depicting the Armida of Tasso,[43] descended a silver lamp of Etruscan form; it diffused a blaze of light that, reflected from large pier glasses, completely illuminated the saloon. Busts of Horace, Ovid, Anacreon, Tibullus, and Petronius Arbiter[44] adorned

42. Shelter.
43. In Torquato Tasso's epic poem *Gerusalemme liberata*, Armida is a sorceress who tries to seduce the Crusader Rinaldo.
44. Horace, Ovid, and Tibullus, Roman poets; Anacreon, Greek poet; Petronius, Roman writer.

the recesses, and stands of flowers placed in Etruscan vases breathed the most delicious perfume. In the middle of the apartment stood a small table spread with a collation of fruits, ices, and liquors. No person appeared. The whole seemed the works of enchantment, and rather resembled the palace of a fairy than anything of human conformation.

Adeline was astonished, and inquired where she was, but the man refused to answer her questions and, having desired her to take some refreshment, left her. She walked to the windows, from which a gleam of moonlight discovered to her an extensive garden where groves and lawns, and water glittering in the moonbeams, composed a scenery of varied and romantic beauty. *What can this mean!* thought she. *Is this a charm to lure me to destruction?* She endeavoured, with a hope of escaping, to open the windows, but they were all fastened; she next attempted several doors, and found them also secured.

Perceiving all chance of escape was removed, she remained for some time given up to sorrow and reflection, but was at length drawn from her reverie by the notes of soft music breathing such dulcet and entrancing sounds as suspended grief, and waked the soul to tenderness and pensive pleasure. Adeline listened in surprise, and insensibly became soothed and interested; a tender melancholy stole upon her heart, and subdued every harsher feeling; but the moment the strain ceased, the enchantment dissolved, and she returned to a sense of her situation.

Again the music sounded—"music such as charmeth sleep"[45] —and again she gradually yielded to its sweet magic. A female voice, accompanied by a lute, a hautboy,[46] and a few other instruments, now gradually swelled into a tone so exquisite as raised attention into ecstasy. It sank by degrees, and touched a few simple notes with pathetic softness, when the measure was suddenly changed to a gay and airy melody.

The music ceased, but the sound still vibrated on her

45. Shakespeare, *A Midsummer Night's Dream.*
46. Oboe.

imagination, and she was sunk in the pleasing languor they had inspired when the door opened, and the Marquis de Montalt appeared. He approached the sofa where Adeline sat, and addressed her, but she heard not his voice—she had fainted. He endeavoured to recover her, and at length succeeded; but when she unclosed her eyes and again beheld him, she relapsed into a state of insensibility, and having in vain tried various methods to restore her, he was obliged to call assistance. Two young women entered, and when she began to revive, he left them to prepare her for his reappearance. When Adeline perceived that the marquis was gone and that she was in the care of women, her spirits gradually returned; she looked at her attendants and was surprised to see so much elegance and beauty.

Some endeavour she made to interest their pity, but they seemed wholly insensible to her distress, and began to talk of the marquis in terms of the highest admiration. They assured her it would be her own fault if she was not happy, and advised her to appear so in his presence. It was with the utmost difficulty that Adeline forbore to express the disdain which was rising to her lips, and that she listened to their discourse in silence. But she saw the inconvenience and fruitlessness of opposition, and she commanded her feelings.

They were thus proceeding in their praises of the marquis when he himself appeared, and upon his waving his hand, they immediately quitted the apartment. Adeline beheld him with a kind of mute despair while he approached and took her hand, which she hastily withdrew; turning from him with a look of unutterable distress, she burst into tears. He was for some time silent, and appeared softened by her anguish. But again approaching and addressing her in a gentle voice, he entreated her pardon for the step which despair and, as he called it, love had prompted. She was too much absorbed in grief to reply, till he solicited a return of his love, when her sorrow yielded to indignation and she reproached him with his conduct. He pleaded that he had long loved and sought her upon honourable terms, and his offer of those terms he began to repeat,

[173]

but raising his eyes toward Adeline, he saw in her looks the contempt which he was conscious he deserved.

For a moment he was confused, and seemed to understand both that his plan was discovered and his person despised; but soon resuming his usual command of feature, he again pressed his suit and solicited her love. A little reflection showed Adeline the danger of exasperating his pride by an avowal of the contempt which his pretended offer of marriage excited; and she thought it not improper, upon an occasion in which the honour and peace of her life was concerned, to yield somewhat to the policy of dissimulation. She saw that her only chance of escaping his designs depended upon delaying them, and she now wished him to believe her ignorant that the marchioness was living, and that his offers were delusive.

He observed her pause and, in the eagerness to turn her hesitation to his advantage, renewed his proposal with increased vehemence. "Tomorrow shall unite us, lovely Adeline; tomorrow you shall consent to become the Marchioness de Montalt. You will then return my love and—"

"You must first deserve my esteem, my lord."

"I will—I do deserve it. Are you not now in my power, and do I not forbear to take advantage of your situation? Do I not make you the most honourable proposals?"

Adeline shuddered. "If you wish I should esteem you, my lord, endeavour, if possible, to make me forget by what means I came into your power; if your views are indeed honourable, prove them so by releasing me from my confinement."

"Can you then wish, lovely Adeline, to fly from him who adores you?" replied the marquis, with a studied air of tenderness. "Why will you exact so severe a proof of my disinterestedness, a disinterestedness which is not consistent with love? No, charming Adeline, let me at least have the pleasure of beholding you, till the bonds of the church shall remove every obstacle to my love. Tomorrow—"

Adeline saw the danger to which she was now exposed, and interrupted him. "Deserve my esteem, sir, and then you will obtain it. As a first step toward which, liberate me from a confinement that obliges me to look on you only with terror and aversion. How can I believe your professions of love while you show that you have no interest in my happiness?"

Thus did Adeline, to whom the arts and the practice of dissimulation were hitherto equally unknown, condescend to make use of them in disguising her indignation and contempt. But though these arts were adopted only for the purpose of self-preservation, she used them with reluctance, and almost with abhorrence; for her mind was habitually impregnated with the love of virtue in thought, word, and action, and while her end in using them was certainly good, she scarcely thought that end could justify the means.

The marquis persisted in his sophistry. "Can you doubt the reality of that love which, to obtain you, has urged me to risk your displeasure? But have I not consulted your happiness, even in the very conduct which you condemn? I have removed you from a solitary and desolate ruin to a gay and splendid villa, where every luxury is at your command, and where every person shall be obedient to your wishes."

"My first wish is to go hence," said Adeline. "I entreat, I conjure you, my lord, no longer to detain me. I am a friendless and wretched orphan, exposed to many evils and, I fear, abandoned to misfortune. I do not wish to be rude, but allow me to say that no misery can exceed that I shall feel in remaining here, or indeed, in being anywhere pursued by the offers you make me!" Adeline had now forgot her policy; tears prevented her from proceeding, and she turned away her face to hide her emotion.

"By Heaven! Adeline, you do me wrong," said the marquis, rising from his seat and seizing her hand. "I love, I adore you; yet you doubt my passion, and are insensible to my vows. Every pleasure possible to be enjoyed within these walls you shall partake, but beyond them you shall not go."

She disengaged her hand and in silent anguish walked to a distant part of the saloon; deep sighs burst from her heart, and almost fainting, she leaned on a window frame for support.

The marquis followed her. "Why thus obstinately persist

in refusing to be happy?" said he. "Recollect the proposal I have made you, and accept it while it is yet in your power. Tomorrow a priest shall join our hands. Surely, being in my power as you are, it must be your interest to consent to this?"

Adeline could answer only by tears; she despaired of softening his heart to pity, and feared to exasperate his pride by disdain. He now led her, and she suffered him, to a seat near the banquet, at which he pressed her to partake of a variety of confectionaries, particularly of some liquors, of which he himself drank freely; Adeline accepted only of a peach.

And now the marquis, who interpreted her silence into a secret compliance with his proposal, resumed all his gaiety and spirit, while the long and ardent regards he bestowed on Adeline overcame her with confusion and indignation. In the midst of the banquet, soft music again sounded the most tender and impassioned airs; but its effect on Adeline was now lost, her mind being too much embarrassed and distressed by the presence of the marquis to admit even the soothings of harmony. A song was now heard, written with that sort of impotent art by which some voluptuous poets believe they can at once conceal and recommend the principles of vice. Adeline received it with contempt and displeasure, and the marquis, perceiving its effect, presently made a sign for another composition which, adding the force of poetry to the charms of music, might withdraw her mind from the present scene, and enchant it in sweet delirium.

When the voice ceased, a mournful strain played with exquisite expression sounded from a distant horn; sometimes the notes floated on the air in soft undulations—now they swelled into full and sweeping melody, and now died faintly into silence; when again they rose and trembled in sounds so sweetly tender as drew tears from Adeline and exclamations of rapture from the marquis, he threw his arm round her and would have pressed her toward him, but she liberated herself from his embrace, and with a look on which was impressed the firm dignity of virtue yet touched with sorrow, she awed him to forbearance. Conscious of a superiority which he was ashamed to acknowledge, and endeavouring to despise the influence which he could not resist, he stood for a moment the slave of virtue, though the votary[47] of vice. Soon, however, he recovered his confidence and began to plead his love; Adeline, no longer animated by the spirit she had lately shown, and sinking beneath the languor and fatigue which the various and violent agitations of her mind produced, entreated he would leave her to repose.

The paleness of her countenance and the tremulous tone of her voice were too expressive to be misunderstood; and the marquis, bidding her remember tomorrow, with some hesitation withdrew. The moment she was alone, she yielded to the bursting anguish of her heart and was so absorbed in grief that it was some time before she perceived she was in the presence of the young women who had lately attended her, and who had entered the saloon soon after the marquis quitted it; they came to conduct her to her chamber. She followed them for some time in silence till, prompted by desperation, she again endeavoured to awaken their compassion; but again the praises of the marquis were repeated, and perceiving that all attempts to interest them in her favour were in vain, she dismissed them.

She secured the door through which they had departed, and then, in the languid hope of discovering some means of escape, she surveyed her chamber. The airy elegance with which it was fitted up, and the luxurious accommodations with which it abounded, seemed designed to fascinate the imagination and to seduce the heart. The hangings were of straw-coloured silk adorned with a variety of landscapes and historical paintings, the subjects of which partook of the voluptuous character of the owner; the chimneypiece, of Parian marble,[48] was ornamented with several reposing figures from the antique. The bed was of silk the colour of the hangings, richly fringed with purple and silver, and the head made in the form of a canopy. The steps, which were placed near the

47. Enthusiast.
48. Marble quarried from the Greek island Páros.

bed to assist in ascending it, were supported by cupids, apparently of solid silver. China vases filled with perfume stood in several of the recesses, upon stands of the same structure as the toilet, which was magnificent, and ornamented with a variety of trinkets.

Adeline threw a transient look upon these various objects, and proceeded to examine the windows, which descended to the floor and opened into balconies toward the garden she had seen from the saloon. They were now fastened, and her efforts to move them were ineffectual; at length she gave up the attempt. A door next attracted her notice, which she found was not fastened; it opened upon a dressing closet, to which she descended by a few steps. Two windows appeared, and she hastened toward them; one refused to yield, but her heart beat with sudden joy when the other opened to her touch.

In the transport of the moment, she forgot that its distance from the ground might yet deny the escape she meditated. She returned to lock the door of the closet to prevent a surprise, which, however, was unnecessary, that of the bedroom being already secured. She now looked out from the window; the garden lay before her, and she perceived that the window, which descended to the floor, was so near the ground that she might jump from it with ease. Almost in the moment she perceived this, she sprang forward and alighted safely in an extensive garden, resembling more an English pleasure ground than a series of French parterres.[49]

Thence she had little doubt of escaping, either by some broken fence or low part of the wall; she tripped lightly along, for hope played round her heart. The clouds of the late storm were now dispersed, and the moonlight, which slept on the lawns and spangled the flowerets yet heavy with raindrops, afforded her a distinct view of the surrounding scenery. She followed the direction of the high wall that adjoined the château till it was concealed from her sight by a thick wilderness so entangled with boughs and obscured by darkness that she

49. Ornamental gardens with paths.

feared to enter, and turned aside into a walk on the right; it conducted her to the margin of a lake overhung with lofty trees.

The moonbeams danced upon the waters that with gentle undulation played along the shore, a scene of tranquil beauty which would have soothed a heart less agitated than was that of Adeline; she sighed as she transiently surveyed it, and passed hastily on in search of the garden wall, from which she had now strayed a considerable way. After wandering for some time through alleys and over lawns without meeting with anything like a boundary to the grounds, she again found herself at the lake, and now traversed its border with the footsteps of despair. Tears rolled down her cheeks. The scene around her exhibited only images of peace and delight; every object seemed to repose; not a breath waved the foliage, not a sound stole through the air: it was in her bosom only that tumult and distress prevailed. She still pursued the windings of the shore, till an opening in the woods conducted her up a gentle ascent; the path now wound along the side of a hill, where the gloom was so deep that it was with some difficulty she found her way. Suddenly, however, the avenue opened to a lofty grove, and she perceived a light issue from a recess at some distance.

She paused, and her first impulse was to retreat, but listening and hearing no sound, a faint hope beamed upon her mind, that the person to whom the light belonged might be won to favour her escape. She advanced with trembling and cautious steps toward the recess, that she might secretly observe the person before she ventured to enter it. Her emotion increased as she approached, and having reached the bower, she beheld through an open window the marquis reclining on a sofa, near which stood a table covered with fruit and wine. He was alone, and his countenance was flushed with drinking.

While she gazed, fixed to the spot by terror, he looked up toward the casement; the light gleamed full upon her face, but she stayed not to learn whether he had observed her, for, with the swiftness of sound, she left the place and ran, without knowing whether she was pursued. Having gone a considerable way, fatigue at length compelled her to stop, and she threw herself upon the turf, almost fainting with fear and languor. She knew if the marquis detected her in an attempt to escape, he would probably burst the bounds which he had hitherto prescribed to himself, and that she had the most dreadful evils to expect. The palpitations of terror were so strong that she could with difficulty breathe.

She watched and listened in trembling expectation, but no form met her eye, no sound her ear; in this state she remained a considerable time. She wept, and the tears she shed relieved her oppressed heart. *O my father! why did you abandon your child? If you knew the dangers to which you have exposed her, you would surely pity and relieve her. Alas! shall I never find a friend; am I destined still to trust and be deceived? Peter too, could he be treacherous?* She wept again, and then returned to a sense of her present danger, and to a consideration of the means of escaping it—but no means appeared.

To her imagination the grounds were boundless; she had wandered from lawn to lawn, and from grove to grove, without perceiving any termination to the place; the garden wall she could not find, but she resolved neither to return to the château, nor to relinquish her search. As she was rising to depart, she perceived a shadow move along at some distance; she stood still to observe it. It slowly advanced and then disappeared, but presently she saw a person emerge from the gloom and approach the spot where she stood. She had no doubt that the marquis had observed her, and she ran with all possible speed to the shade of some woods on the left. Footsteps pursued her, and she heard her name repeated, while she in vain endeavoured to quicken her pace.

Suddenly the sound of pursuit turned, and sank away in a different direction. She paused to take breath; she looked around and no person appeared. She now proceeded slowly along the avenue, and had almost reached its termination when she saw the same figure emerge from the woods and dart across the avenue; it instantly pursued her and approached.

A voice called her, but she was gone beyond its reach, for she had sunk senseless upon the ground. It was long before she revived; when she did, she found herself in the arms of a stranger, and made an effort to disengage herself.

"Fear nothing, lovely Adeline," said he, "fear nothing: you are in the arms of a friend who will encounter any hazard for your sake; who will protect you with his life." He pressed her gently to his heart. "Have you then forgot me?"

She looked earnestly at him, and was now convinced that it was Theodore who spoke. Joy was her first emotion; but recollecting his former abrupt departure at a time so critical to her safety, and that he was the friend of the marquis, a thousand mingled sensations struggled in her breast, and overwhelmed her with mistrust, apprehension, and disappointment.

Theodore raised her from the ground, and while he yet supported her, he said, "Let us immediately fly from this place. A carriage waits to receive us; it shall go wherever you direct, and convey you to your friends."

This last sentence touched her heart. "Alas, I have no friends!" said she, "nor do I know whither to go."

Theodore gently pressed her hand between his, and in a voice of the softest compassion said, "My friends then shall be yours; suffer me to lead you to them. But I am in agony while you remain in this place; let us hasten to quit it."

Adeline was going to reply when voices were heard among the trees, and Theodore, supporting her with his arm, hurried her along the avenue; they continued their flight till Adeline, panting for breath, could go no farther.

Having paused awhile and heard no footsteps in pursuit, they renewed their course. Theodore knew that they were now not far from the garden wall; but he was also aware that in the intermediate space several paths wound from remote parts of the grounds into the walk he was to pass, from whence the marquis's people might issue and intercept him. He, however, concealed his apprehensions from Adeline, and endeavoured to soothe and support her spirits.

At length they reached the wall, and Theodore was leading her toward a low part of it, near which stood the carriage,
when again they heard voices in the air. Adeline's spirits and
strength were nearly exhausted, but she made a last effort
to proceed, and she now saw at some distance the ladder by
which Theodore had descended to the garden.

"Exert yourself yet a little longer," said he, "and you will be
in safety."

He held the ladder while she ascended; the top of the wall
was broad and level, and Adeline, having reached it, remained
there till Theodore followed and drew the ladder to the other
side.

When they had descended, the carriage appeared in waiting, but without the driver. Theodore feared to call, lest his
voice should betray him. He therefore put Adeline into the
carriage, and went himself in search of the postillion, whom he
found asleep under a tree at some distance; having awakened
him, they returned to the vehicle, which soon drove furiously
away. Adeline did not yet dare to believe herself safe, but after
proceeding a considerable time without interruption, joy burst
upon her heart, and she thanked her deliverer in terms of the
warmest gratitude. The sympathy expressed in the tone of his
voice and manner proved that his happiness, on this occasion,
almost equalled her own.

As reflection gradually stole upon her mind, anxiety superseded joy; in the tumult of the late moments she thought only
of escape, but the circumstances of her present situation now
appeared to her, and she became silent and pensive. She had
no friends to whom she could fly, and was going she knew not
whither with a young chevalier almost a stranger to her. She
remembered how often she had been deceived and betrayed
where she trusted most, and her spirits sank. She remembered
also the former attention which Theodore had shown her, and
dreaded lest his conduct might be prompted by a selfish passion. She saw this to be possible, but she disdained to believe
it probable, and felt that nothing could give her greater pain
than to doubt the integrity of Theodore.

He interrupted her reverie, by recurring[50] to her late situation at the abbey. "You would be much surprised," said he, "and, I fear, offended that I did not attend my appointment at the abbey after the alarming hints I had given you in our last interview. That circumstance has perhaps injured me in your esteem, if indeed I was ever so happy as to possess it, but my designs were overruled by those of the Marquis de Montalt; and I think I may venture to assert that my distress upon this occasion was, at least, equal to your apprehensions."

Adeline said, "I was much alarmed by the hints you had given me, and by your failing to afford further information concerning the subject of my danger; and—"

She checked the sentence that hung upon her lips, for she perceived that she was unwarily betraying the interest he held in her heart. There were a few moments of silence, and neither party seemed perfectly at ease.

Theodore, at length, renewed the conversation. "Suffer me to acquaint you," said he, "with the circumstances that withheld me from the interview I solicited; I am anxious to exculpate myself." Without waiting her reply, he proceeded to inform her that the marquis had by some inexplicable means learned or suspected the subject of their last conversation and, perceiving his designs were in danger of being counteracted, had taken effectual means to prevent her obtaining further intelligence of them. Adeline immediately recollected that Theodore and herself had been seen in the forest by La Motte, who had no doubt suspected their growing intimacy, and had taken care to inform the marquis how likely he was to find a rival in his friend.

Theodore continued his tale, as follows.

On the day following that on which I last saw you, the marquis, who is my colonel, commanded me to prepare to attend

50. Going back in thought or speech.

my regiment, and appointed the following morning for my journey. This sudden order gave me some surprise, but I was not long in doubt concerning the motive for it. A servant of the marquis, who had been long attached to me, entered my room soon after I had left his lord. Expressing concern at my abrupt departure, he dropped some hints respecting it which excited my surprise. I inquired further, and was confirmed in the suspicions I had for some time entertained of the marquis's designs upon you.

Jacques further informed me that our late interview had been noticed and communicated to the marquis. His information had been obtained from a fellow servant, and it alarmed me so much that I engaged him to send me intelligence from time to time concerning the proceedings of the marquis. I now looked forward to the evening, which would bring me again to your presence with increased impatience, but the ingenuity of the marquis effectually counteracted my endeavours and wishes; he had made an engagement to pass the day at the villa of a nobleman some leagues distant, and notwithstanding all the excuses I could offer, I was obliged to attend him. Thus compelled to obey, I passed a day of more agitation and anxiety than I had ever before experienced. It was midnight before we returned to the marquis's château. I arose early in the morning to commence my journey, and resolved to seek an interview with you before I left the province.

When I entered the breakfast room, I was much surprised to find there already the marquis, who, commending the beauty of the morning, declared his intention of accompanying me as far as Chineau. Thus unexpectedly deprived of my last hope, my countenance, I believe, expressed what I felt, for the scrutinizing eye of the marquis instantly changed from seeming carelessness to displeasure. The distance from Chineau to the abbey was at least twelve leagues; yet I had once some intention of returning from thence when the marquis should leave me, till I recollected the very remote chance there would even then be of seeing you alone, and also that if I was observed by La Motte, it would awaken all his suspicions, and caution him against any future plan I might see it expedient to attempt. I therefore proceeded to join my regiment.

Jacques sent me frequent accounts of the operations of the marquis, but his manner of relating them was so very confused that they only served to perplex and distress me. His last letter, however, alarmed me so much that my residence in quarters became intolerable; and as I found it impossible to obtain leave of absence, I secretly left the regiment and concealed myself in a cottage about a mile from the château, that I might obtain the earliest intelligence of the marquis's plans. Jacques brought me daily information, and at last an account of the horrible plot which was laid for the following night.

I saw little probability of warning you of your danger. If I ventured near the abbey, La Motte might discover me and frustrate every attempt on my part to save you; yet I determined to encounter this risk for the chance of seeing you, and toward evening I was preparing to set out for the forest when Jacques arrived and informed me that you was to be brought to the château. My plan was thus rendered less difficult. I learned also that the marquis, by means of those refinements in luxury with which he is but too well acquainted, designed, now that his apprehension of losing you was no more, to seduce you to his wishes and impose upon you by a fictitious marriage. Having obtained information concerning the situation of the room allotted you, I ordered a chaise to be in waiting, and with a design of scaling your window and conducting you thence, I entered the garden at midnight.

Theodore having ceased to speak, Adeline said, "I know not how words can express my sense of the obligations I owe you, or my gratitude for your generosity."

"Ah! call it not generosity," he replied, "it was love." He paused.

Adeline was silent.

After some moments of expressive emotion, he resumed,

"But pardon this abrupt declaration; yet why do I call it abrupt, since my actions have already disclosed what my lips have never, till this instant, ventured to acknowledge." He paused again.

Adeline was still silent.

"Yet do me the justice to believe that I am sensible of the impropriety of pleading my love at present, and have been surprised into this confession. I promise also to forbear from a renewal of the subject till you are placed in a situation where you may freely accept or refuse the sincere regards I offer you. If I could, however, now be certain that I possess your esteem, it would relieve me from much anxiety."

Adeline felt surprised that he should doubt her esteem for him after the signal[51] and generous service he had rendered her, but she was not yet acquainted with the timidity of love. "Do you then," said she, in a tremulous voice, believe me ungrateful? It is impossible I can consider your friendly interference in my behalf without esteeming you."

Theodore immediately took her hand and pressed it to his lips in silence. They were both too much agitated to converse, and continued to travel for some miles without exchanging a word.

51. Notable.

CHAPTER 12

And *Hope* enchanted smil'd, and wav'd her
    golden hair;
And longer had she sung—but with a frown,
Revenge impatient rose.

    William Collins, "Ode to the Passions"

The dawn of morning now trembled through the clouds when the travelers stopped at a small town to change horses. Theodore entreated Adeline to alight and take some refreshment, and to this she at length consented. But the people of the inn were not yet up, and it was some time before the knocking and roaring of the postillion could rouse them.

Having taken some slight refreshment, Theodore and Adeline returned to the carriage. The only subject upon which Theodore could have spoke with interest, delicacy forbade him at this time to notice; and after pointing out some beautiful scenery on the road and making other efforts to support a conversation, he relapsed into silence. His mind, though still anxious, was now relieved from the apprehension that had long oppressed it. When he first saw Adeline, her loveliness made a deep impression on his heart; there was a sentiment in her beauty which his mind immediately acknowledged, and the effect of which her manners and conversation had afterward confirmed. Her charms appeared to him like those so finely described since by an English poet:

> So soft, so delicate, so sweet she came,
> Youth's damask glow just dawning on her cheek.[52]

A knowledge of her destitute condition, and of the dangers with which she was environed,[53] had awakened in his heart the tenderest touch of pity, and assisted the change of admiration into love. The distress he suffered when compelled to leave her exposed to these dangers, without being able to warn her of them, can only be imagined. During his residence with his regiment, his mind was the constant prey of terrors which he saw no means of combating but by returning to the neighbourhood of the abbey, where he might obtain early intelligence of the marquis's schemes and be ready to give his assistance to Adeline.

Leave of absence he could not request without betraying his design where most he dreaded it should be known, and at length, with a generous rashness which, though it defied law, was impelled by virtue, he secretly quitted his regiment. The progress of the marquis's plan he had observed with trembling anxiety, till the night that was to decide the fate of Adeline and himself roused all his mind to action, and involved him in a tumult of hope and fear—horror and expectation.

Never, till the present hour, had he ventured to believe she was in safety. Now the distance they had gained from the château, without perceiving any pursuit, increased his best hopes. It was impossible he could sit by the side of his beloved Adeline and receive assurances of her gratitude and esteem without venturing to hope for her love. He congratulated himself as her preserver, and anticipated scenes of happiness when she should be under the protection of his family. The clouds of misery and apprehension disappeared from his mind, and left it to the sunshine of joy. When a shadow of fear would

52. Attributed to Oliver Goldsmith.
53. Surrounded.

sometimes return, or when he recollected with compunction the circumstances under which he had left his regiment, stationed as it was upon the frontiers and in a time of war, he looked at Adeline, and her countenance with instantaneous magic beamed peace upon his heart.

But Adeline had a subject of anxiety from which Theodore was exempt; the prospect of her future days was involved in darkness and uncertainty. Again she was going to claim the bounty of strangers—again going to encounter the uncertainty of their kindness; exposed to the hardships of dependence, or to the difficulty of earning a precarious livelihood. These anticipations obscured the joy occasioned by her escape, and by the affection which the conduct and avowal of Theodore had exhibited. The delicacy of his behaviour, in forbearing to take advantage of her present situation to plead his love, increased her esteem and flattered her pride.

Adeline was lost in meditation upon subjects like these when the postillion stopped the carriage and, pointing to part of a road which wound down the side of a hill they had passed, said there were several horsemen in pursuit! Theodore immediately ordered him to proceed with all possible speed, and to strike out of the great road into the first obscure way that offered. The postillion cracked his whip in the air, and set off as if he were flying for life. In the meanwhile Theodore endeavoured to reanimate Adeline, who was sinking with terror, and who now thought if she could only escape from the marquis, she could defy the future.

Presently they struck into a bye[54] lane screened and overshadowed by thick trees; Theodore again looked from the window, but the closing boughs prevented his seeing far enough to determine whether the pursuit continued. For his sake Adeline endeavoured to disguise her emotions.

"This lane," said Theodore, "will certainly lead to a town or village, and then we have nothing to apprehend; for, though my single arm could not defend you against the number of

54. Off the main route.

our pursuers, I have no doubt of being able to interest some of the inhabitants in our behalf."

Adeline appeared to be comforted by the hope this reflection suggested, and Theodore again looked back, but the windings of the road closed his view, and the rattling of the wheels overcame every other sound. At length he called to the postillion to stop, and having listened attentively without perceiving any sound of horses, he began to hope they were now in safety.

"Do you know where this road leads?" said he.

The postillion answered that he did not, but he saw some houses through the trees at a distance, and believed it led to them. This was most welcome intelligence to Theodore, who looked forward and perceived the houses. The postillion set off.

"Fear nothing, my adored Adeline," said he, "you are now safe; I will part with you but with life."

Adeline sighed, not for herself only, but for the danger to which Theodore might be exposed.

They had continued to travel in this manner for near half an hour when they arrived at a small village, and soon after stopped at an inn, the best the place afforded. As Theodore lifted Adeline from the chaise, he again entreated her to dismiss her apprehensions, and spoke with a tenderness to which she could reply only by a smile that ill concealed her anxiety. After ordering refreshments, he went out to speak with the landlord, but had scarcely left the room when Adeline observed a party of horsemen enter the inn yard, and she had no doubt these were the persons from whom they fled. The faces of two of them only were turned toward her, but she thought the figure of one of the others not unlike that of the marquis.

Her heart was chilled, and for some moments the powers of reason forsook her. Her first design was to seek concealment; but while she considered the means one of the horsemen looked up to the window near which she stood, and after his speaking to his companions, they entered the inn. To quit the room without being observed was impossible; to remain there, alone and unprotected as she was, would almost be equally dangerous. She paced the room in an agony of terror, often secretly calling on Theodore, and often wondering he did not return. These were moments of indescribable suffering.

A loud and tumultuous sound of voices now arose from a distant part of the house, and she soon distinguished the words of the disputants. "I arrest you in the king's name," said one; "and bid you, at your peril, attempt to go from hence, except under a guard."

The next minute Adeline heard the voice of Theodore in reply. "I do not mean to dispute the king's orders," said he, "and I give you my word of honour not to go without you. But first unhand me, that I may return to that room; I have a friend there whom I wish to speak with."

To this proposal they at first objected, considering it merely as an excuse to obtain an opportunity of escaping; but after much altercation and entreaty, his request was granted. He sprang forward toward the room where Adeline remained, and while a sergeant and corporal followed him to the door, the two soldiers went out into the yard of the inn to watch the windows of the apartment.

With an eager hand he unclosed the door, but Adeline hastened not to meet him, for she had fainted almost at the beginning of the dispute. Theodore called loudly for assistance, and the mistress of the inn soon appeared with her stock of remedies, which were administered in vain to Adeline, who remained insensible, and by breathing alone gave signs of her existence. The distress of Theodore was in the meantime heightened by the appearance of the officers, who, laughing at the discovery of his pretended friend, declared they could wait no longer. Saying this, they would have forced him from the inanimate form of Adeline, over whom he hung in unutterable anguish, when fiercely turning upon them, he drew his sword, and swore no power on earth should force him away before the lady recovered.

The men, enraged by the action and the determined air of Theodore, exclaimed, "Do you oppose the king's orders?" and advanced to seize him, but he presented the point of his sword, and bid them at their peril approach. One of them immediately drew; Theodore kept his guard, but did not advance.

"I demand only to wait here till the lady recovers," said he. "You understand the alternative."

The man, already exasperated by the opposition of Theodore, regarded the latter part of his speech as a threat and became determined not to give up the point; he pressed forward, and while his comrade called the men from the yard, Theodore wounded him slightly in the shoulder, and received himself the stroke of a sabre on his head.

The blood gushed furiously from the wound; Theodore, staggering to a chair, sank into it just as the remainder of the party entered the room, and Adeline unclosed her eyes to see him ghastly pale, and covered with blood. She uttered an involuntary scream, and exclaiming, "They have murdered him," nearly relapsed.

At the sound of her voice he raised his head and, smiling, held out his hand to her. "I am not much hurt," said he faintly, "and shall soon be better, if indeed you are recovered."

She hastened toward him, and gave her hand. "Is nobody gone for a surgeon?" said she, with a look of agony.

"Do not be alarmed," said Theodore. "I am not so ill as you imagine."

The room was now crowded with people whom the report of the affray had brought together; among these was a man who acted as physician, apothecary, and surgeon to the village, and who now stepped forward to the assistance of Theodore.

Having examined the wound, he declined giving his opinion, but ordered the patient to be immediately put to bed, to which the officers objected, alleging that it was their duty to carry him to the regiment.

"That cannot be done without great danger to his life," replied the doctor, "and—"

"Oh! his life," said the sergeant, "we have nothing to do with that, we must do our duty."

Adeline, who had hitherto stood in trembling anxiety, could now no longer be silent. "Since the surgeon," said she, "has declared it his opinion that this gentleman cannot be removed in his present condition without endangering his life, you will remember that if he dies, yours will probably answer it."

"Yes," rejoined the surgeon, who was unwilling to relinquish his patient, "I declare before these witnesses that he cannot be removed with safety. You will do well, therefore, to consider the consequences. He has received a very dangerous wound, which requires the most careful treatment, and the event is even then doubtful; but if he travels, a fever may ensue, and the wound will then be mortal."

Theodore heard this sentence with composure, but Adeline could with difficulty conceal the anguish of her heart. She roused all her fortitude to suppress the tears that struggled in her eyes; and though she wished to interest the humanity or to awaken the fears of the men on behalf of their unfortunate prisoner, she dared not to trust her voice with utterance.

From this internal struggle she was relieved by the compassion of the people who filled the room. They, becoming clamorous in the cause of Theodore, declared the officers would be guilty of murder if they removed him.

"Why he must die at any rate," said the sergeant, "for quitting his post, and drawing upon me in the execution of the king's orders."

A faint sickness seized the heart of Adeline, and she leaned for support against Theodore's chair, whose concern for himself was for a while suspended in his anxiety for her. He supported her with his arm and, forcing a smile, said in a low voice which she only could hear, "This is a misrepresentation; I doubt not, when the affair is inquired into, it will be settled without any serious consequences."

Adeline knew these words were uttered only to console her, and therefore did not give much credit to them, though Theodore continued to give her similar assurances of his safety.

Meanwhile the mob, whose compassion for him had been gradually excited by the obduracy of the officer, were now roused to pity and indignation by the seeming certainty of his punishment and the unfeeling manner in which it had been denounced.[55] In a short time they became so much enraged that, partly from a dread of further consequences, and partly from the shame which their charges of cruelty occasioned, the sergeant consented that Theodore should be put to bed till his commanding officer might direct what was to be done. Adeline's joy at this circumstance overcame for a moment the sense of her misfortunes, and of her situation.

She waited in an adjoining room the sentence of the surgeon, who was now engaged in examining the wound; and though the accident would in any other circumstances have severely afflicted her, she now lamented it the more because she considered herself as the cause of it, and because the misfortune, by illustrating more fully the affection of her lover, drew him closer to her heart, and seemed therefore to sharpen the poignancy of her affliction. The dreadful assertion that Theodore, should he recover, would be punished with death, she scarcely dared to consider, but endeavoured to believe that it was no more than a cruel exaggeration of his antagonist.

Upon the whole, Theodore's present danger, together with the attendant circumstances, awakened all her tenderness and discovered to her the true state of her affections. The graceful form, the noble, intelligent countenance, and the engaging manners which she had at first admired in Theodore became afterward more interesting by that strength of thought and elegance of sentiment exhibited in his conversation. His conduct since her escape had excited her warmest gratitude, and the danger which he had now encountered on her behalf called forth her tenderness and heightened it into love. The veil was removed from her heart, and she saw, for the first time, its genuine emotions.

The surgeon at length came out of Theodore's chamber into the room where Adeline was waiting to speak with him. She inquired concerning the state of his wound.

"You are a relation of the gentleman's, I presume, madam; his sister, perhaps."

55. Proclaimed.

The question vexed and embarrassed her, and without answering it, she repeated her inquiry.

"Perhaps, madam, you are more nearly related," pursued the surgeon, seeming also to disregard her question, "perhaps you are his wife." Adeline blushed, and was about to reply, but he continued his speech. "The interest you take in his welfare is, at least, very flattering, and I would almost consent to exchange conditions with him, were I sure of receiving such tender compassion from so charming a lady." Saying this, he bowed to the ground.

Adeline, assuming a very reserved air, said, "Now, sir, that you have concluded your compliment, you will, perhaps, attend to my question: I have inquired how you left your patient."

"That, madam, is perhaps a question very difficult to be resolved; and it is likewise a very disagreeable office to pronounce ill news—I fear he will die." The surgeon opened his snuffbox and presented it to Adeline.

"Die!" she exclaimed in a faint voice. "Die!"

"Do not be alarmed, madam," resumed the surgeon, observing her grow pale, "do not be alarmed. It is possible that the wound may not have reached the—," he stammered. "In that case the—," stammering again, "is not affected; and if so, the interior membranes of the brain are not touched. In this case the wound may, perhaps, escape inflammation, and the patient may possibly recover. But if, on the other hand—"

"I beseech you, sir, to speak intelligibly," interrupted Adeline, "and not to trifle with my anxiety. Do you really believe him in danger?"

"In danger, madam," exclaimed the surgeon, "in danger! yes, certainly, in very great danger." Saying this, he walked away with an air of chagrin and displeasure.

Adeline remained for some moments in the room, in an excess of sorrow which she found it impossible to restrain, and then drying her tears and endeavouring to compose her countenance, she went to inquire for the mistress of the inn, to whom she sent a waiter. After expecting her in vain for some time, she rang the bell, and sent another message somewhat more pressing. Still the hostess did not appear, and Adeline at length went herself downstairs, where she found her surrounded by a number of people, relating with a loud voice and various gesticulations the particulars of the late accident.

Perceiving Adeline, she called out, "Oh! here is mademoiselle herself," and the eyes of the assembly were immediately turned upon her. Adeline, whom the crowd prevented from approaching the hostess, now beckoned her and was going to withdraw, but the landlady, eager in the pursuit of her story, disregarded the signal. In vain did Adeline endeavour to catch her eye; it glanced everywhere but upon her, who was unwilling to attract the further notice of the crowd by calling out.

"It is a great pity, to be sure, that he should be shot," said the landlady, "he's such a handsome man; but they say he certainly will if he recovers. Poor gentleman! he will very likely not suffer though, for the doctor says he will never go out of this house alive."

Adeline now spoke to a man who stood near, and desiring he would tell the hostess she wished to speak with her, left the place.

In about ten minutes the landlady appeared. "Alas! mademoiselle," said she, "your brother is in a sad condition; they fear he won't get over it."

Adeline inquired whether there was any other medical person in the town than the surgeon whom she had seen.

"Lord, madam, this is a rare healthy place; we have little need of medicine people here; such an accident never happened in it before. The doctor has been here ten years, but there's very bad encouragement for his trade, and I believe he's poor enough himself. One of the sort's quite enough for us."

Adeline interrupted her to ask some questions concerning Theodore, whom the hostess had attended to his chamber. She inquired how he had borne the dressing of the wound, and whether he appeared to be easier after the operation; questions to which the hostess gave no very satisfactory answers. She now inquired whether there was any surgeon in the neighbourhood of the town, and was told there was not.

The distress visible in Adeline's countenance seemed to excite the compassion of the landlady, who now endeavoured to console her in the best manner she was able. She advised her to send for her friends, and offered to procure a messenger. Adeline sighed and said it was unnecessary.

"I don't know, mam'selle, what you may think necessary," continued the hostess, "but I know I should think it very hard to die in a strange place with no relations near me, and I dare say the poor gentleman thinks so himself; and besides, who is to pay for his funeral if he dies?"

Adeline begged she would be silent, and desiring that every proper attention might be given, she promised her a reward for her trouble, and requested pen and ink immediately.

"Ay, to be sure, mam'selle, that is the proper way; why your friends would never forgive you if you did not acquaint them; I know it by myself. And as for taking care of him, he shall have everything the house affords, and I warrant there is never a better inn in the province, though the town is none of the biggest."

Adeline was obliged to repeat her request for pen and ink before the loquacious hostess would quit the room.

The thought of sending for Theodore's friends had, in the tumult of the late scenes, never occurred to her, and she was now somewhat consoled by the prospect of comfort which it opened for him. When the pen and ink were brought, she wrote the following note to Theodore.

"In your present condition, you have need of every comfort that can be procured you, and surely there is no cordial more valuable in illness than the presence of a friend. Suffer me, therefore, to acquaint your family with your situation; it will be a satisfaction to me and, I doubt not, a consolation to you."

In a short time after she had sent the note, she received a message from Theodore, entreating most respectfully but earnestly to see her for a few minutes. She immediately went to his chamber, and found her worst apprehensions confirmed by the languor expressed in his countenance, while the shock she received, together with her struggle to disguise her emotions, almost overcame her.

"I thank you for this goodness," said he, extending his hand, which she received, and sitting down by the bed she burst into a flood of tears. When her agitation had somewhat subsided and she removed her handkerchief from her eyes, she again looked on Theodore, a smile of the tenderest love expressed his sense of the interest she took in his welfare and administered a temporary relief to her heart.

"Forgive this weakness," said she. "My spirits have of late been so variously agitated—"

Theodore interrupted her. "These tears are most flattering to my heart. But, for my sake, endeavour to support yourself. I doubt not I shall soon be better; the surgeon—"

"I do not like him," said Adeline, "but tell me how you find yourself?"

He assured her that he was now much easier than he had yet been, and mentioning her kind note, he led to the subject on account of which he had solicited to see her. "My family," said he, "reside at a great distance from hence, and I well know their affection is such that, were they informed of my situation, no consideration, however reasonable, could prevent their coming to my assistance; but before they can arrive, their presence will probably be unnecessary."

Adeline looked earnestly at him.

"I should probably be well," pursued he, smiling, "before a letter could reach them; it would therefore occasion them unnecessary pain and, moreover, a fruitless journey. For your sake, Adeline, I could wish they were here, but a few days will more fully show the consequences of my wound. Let us wait at least till then, and be directed by circumstances."

Adeline forbore to press the subject further, and turned to one more immediately interesting. "I much wish," said she, "that you had a more able surgeon; you know the geography of the province better than I do; are we in the neighbourhood of any town likely to afford you other advice?"

"I believe not," said he, "and this is an affair of little consequence, for my wound is so inconsiderable that a very moderate share of skill may suffice to cure it. But why, my beloved

Adeline, do you give way to this anxiety? Why suffer yourself to be disturbed by this tendency to forebode the worst? I am willing, perhaps presumptuously so, to attribute it to your kindness, and suffer me to assure you that, while it excites my gratitude, it increases my tenderest esteem. O Adeline! since you wish my speedy recovery, let me see you composed; while I believe you to be unhappy I cannot be well."

She assured him she would endeavour to be at least tranquil, and fearing the conversation if prolonged would be prejudicial to him, she left him to repose.

As she turned out of the gallery, she met the hostess, upon whom certain words of Adeline had operated as a talisman, transforming neglect and impertinence into officious civility. She came to inquire whether the gentleman above stairs had everything that he liked, for she was sure it was her endeavour that he should. "I have got him a nurse, mam'selle, to attend him, and I dare say she will do very well, but I will look to that, for I shall not mind helping him myself sometimes. Poor gentleman! how patiently he bears it! One would not think now that he believes he is going to die; yet the doctor told him so himself, or at least as good."

Adeline was extremely shocked at this imprudent conduct of the surgeon, and after ordering a slight dinner dismissed the landlady.

Toward evening the surgeon again made his appearance. After having passed some time with his patient, he returned to the parlour, according to the desire of Adeline, to inform her of his patient's condition.

He answered Adeline's inquiries with great solemnity. "It is impossible to determine positively at present, madam, but I have reason to adhere to the opinion I gave you this morning. I am not apt, indeed, to form opinions upon uncertain grounds. I will give you a singular instance of this: It is not above a fortnight since I was sent for to a patient at some leagues' distance. I was from home when the messenger arrived, and the case being urgent, before I could reach the patient another physician was consulted, who had ordered such medicines as he thought proper, and the patient had been apparently relieved by them. His friends were congratulating themselves upon his improvement and had agreed in opinion with the physician that there was no danger in his case, when I arrived. 'Depend upon it,' said I, 'you are mistaken; these medicines cannot have relieved him; the patient is in the utmost danger.' The patient groaned, but my brother physician persisted in affirming that the remedies he had prescribed would not only be certain but speedy, some good effect having been already produced by them. Upon this I lost all patience, and adhering to my opinion that these effects were fallacious and the case desperate, I assured the patient himself that his life was in the utmost danger. I am not one of those, madam, who deceive their patients to the last moment; but you shall hear the conclusion.

"My brother physician was, I suppose, enraged by the firmness of my opposition, for he assumed a most angry look, which did not in the least affect me, and turning to the patient, desired he would decide upon which of our opinions to rely, for he must decline acting with me. The patient did me the honour," pursued the surgeon with a smile of complacency, smoothing his ruffles, "to think more highly of me than perhaps I deserved, for he immediately dismissed my opponent. 'I could not have believed,' said he, as the physician left the room, 'I could not have believed that a man who has been so many years in the profession could be so wholly ignorant of it.'

"'I could not have believed it either,' said I. 'I am astonished that he was not aware of my danger,' resumed the patient. 'I am astonished likewise,' replied I. I was resolved to do what I could for the patient, for he was a man of understanding, as you perceive, and I had a regard for him. I therefore altered the prescriptions, and myself administered the medicines, but all would not do; my opinion was verified, and he died even before the next morning."

Adeline, who had been compelled to listen to this long story, sighed at the conclusion of it.

"I don't wonder that you are affected, madam," said the surgeon, "the instance I have related is certainly a very affecting one. It distressed me so much that it was some time before I could think, or even speak, concerning it. But you must allow, madam," continued he, lowering his voice and bowing with a look of self-congratulation, "that this was a striking instance of the infallibility of my judgement."

Adeline shuddered at the infallibility of his judgement, and made no reply.

"It was a shocking thing for the poor man," resumed the surgeon.

"It was, indeed, very shocking," said Adeline.

"It affected me a good deal when it happened," continued he.

"Undoubtedly, sir," said Adeline.

"But time wears away the most painful impressions."

"I think you mentioned it was about a fortnight since this happened."

"Somewhere thereabouts," replied the surgeon, without seeming to understand the observation.

"And will you permit me, sir, to ask the name of the physician who so ignorantly opposed you?"

"Certainly, madam; it is Lafance."

"He lives in the obscurity he deserves, no doubt," said Adeline.

"Why no, madam, he lives in a town of some note, at about the distance of four leagues from hence, and affords one instance, among many others, that the public opinion is generally erroneous. You will hardly believe it, but I assure you it is a fact that this man comes into a great deal of practice, while I am suffered to remain here, neglected and, indeed, very little known."

During his narrative, Adeline had been considering by what means she could discover the name of the physician, for the instance that had been produced to prove his ignorance and the infallibility of his opponent had completely settled her opinion concerning them both. She now, more than ever, wished to deliver Theodore from the hands of the surgeon and was musing on the possibility when he, with so much self-security, developed the means.

She asked him a few more questions concerning the state of Theodore's wound, and was told it was much as it had been, but that some degree of fever had come on.

"But I have ordered a fire to be made in the room," continued the surgeon, "and some additional blankets to be laid on the bed; these, I doubt not, will have a proper effect. In the meantime, they must be careful to keep from him every kind of liquid, except some cordial draughts which I shall send. He will naturally ask for drink, but it must, on no account, be given to him."

"You do not approve, then, of the method, which I have somewhere heard of," said Adeline, "of attending to nature in these cases."

"Nature, madam!" pursued he, "Nature is the most improper guide in the world. I always adopt a method directly contrary to what she would suggest; for what can be the use of Art, if she is only to follow Nature? This was my first opinion on setting out in life, and I have ever since strictly adhered to it. From what I have said, madam, you may perhaps perceive that my opinions may be depended on; what they once are they always are, for my mind is not of that frivolous kind to be affected by circumstances."

Adeline was fatigued by this discourse, and impatient to impart to Theodore her discovery of a physician, but the surgeon seemed by no means disposed to leave her, and was expatiating upon various topics with new instances of his surprising sagacity, when the waiter brought a message that some person desired to see him. He was, however, engaged upon too agreeable a topic to be easily prevailed upon to quit it, and it was not till after a second message was brought that he made his bow to Adeline and left the room. The moment he was gone she sent a note to Theodore, entreating his permission to call in the assistance of the physician.

The conceited manners of the surgeon had by this time given Theodore a very unfavourable opinion of his talents, and the last prescription had so fully confirmed it, that he now readily consented to have other advice. Adeline immediately inquired for a messenger, but recollecting that the residence of the physician was still a secret, she applied to the hostess, who being really ignorant of it or pretending to be so, gave her no information. What further inquiries she made were equally ineffectual, and she passed some hours in extreme distress, while the disorder of Theodore rather increased than abated.

When supper appeared, she asked the boy who waited if he knew a physician of the name of Lafance, in the neighbourhood.

"Not in the neighbourhood, madam, but I know Doctor Lafance of Chancy, for I come from the town."

Adeline inquired further, and received very satisfactory answers. But the town was at some leagues' distance, and the delay this circumstance must occasion again alarmed her; she however ordered a messenger to be immediately dispatched, and having sent again to inquire concerning Theodore, retired to her chamber for the night.

The continued fatigue she had suffered for the last fourteen hours overcame anxiety, and her harassed spirits sank to repose. She slept till late in the morning, and was then awakened by the landlady, who came to inform her that Theodore was much worse and to inquire what should be done.

Adeline, finding that the physician was not arrived, immediately arose and hastened to inquire further concerning Theodore. The hostess informed her that he had passed a very disturbed night; that he had complained of being very hot, and desired that the fire in his room might be extinguished; but that the nurse knew her duty too well to obey him, and had strictly followed the doctor's orders. She added that he had taken the cordial draughts regularly but had, notwithstanding, continued to grow worse, and at last became light-headed. In the meantime, the boy who had been sent for the physician was still absent.

"And no wonder," continued the hostess. "Why, only consider, it's eight leagues off, and the lad had to find the road, bad as it is, in the dark. But indeed, mam'selle, you might as well have trusted our doctor, for we never want anybody else, not we in the town here; and if I might speak my mind, Jacques had better have been sent off for the young gentleman's friends than for this strange doctor that nobody knows."

After asking some further questions concerning Theodore, the answers to which rather increased than diminished her alarm, Adeline endeavoured to compose her spirits, and await in patience the arrival of the physician. She was now more sensible than ever of the forlornness of her own condition and of the danger of Theodore's, and earnestly wished that his friends could be informed of his situation; a wish which could not be gratified, for Theodore, who alone could acquaint her with their place of residence, was deprived of recollection.

When the surgeon returned and perceived the situation of his patient, he expressed no surprise; but having asked some questions and given a few general directions, he went down to Adeline. After paying her his usual compliments, he suddenly assumed an air of importance. "I am sorry, madam," said he, "that it is my office to communicate disagreeable intelligence, but I wish you to be prepared for the event which, I fear, is approaching."

Adeline comprehended his meaning, and though she had hitherto given little faith to his judgement, she could not hear him hint at the immediate danger of Theodore without yielding to the influence of fear. She entreated him to acquaint her with all he apprehended.

He then proceeded to say that Theodore was, as he had foreseen, much worse this morning than he had been the preceding night; and the disorder having now affected his head, there was every reason to fear it would prove fatal in a few hours. "The worst consequences may ensue," continued he. "If the wound becomes inflamed, there will be very little chance of his recovery."

Adeline listened to this sentence with a dreadful calmness, and gave no utterance to grief, either by words or tears.

"The gentleman, I suppose, madam, has friends, and the sooner you inform them of his condition the better. If they reside at any distance, it is indeed too late; but there are other necessary—you are ill, madam."

Adeline made an effort to speak, but in vain, and the surgeon now called loudly for a glass of water; she drank it, and a deep sigh that she uttered seemed somewhat to relieve her oppressed heart; tears succeeded. In the meantime, the surgeon, perceiving she was better though not well enough to listen to his conversation, took his leave, and promised to return in an hour.

The physician she had sent for was not yet arrived, and Adeline awaited his appearance with a mixture of fear and anxious hope. About noon he came, and having been informed of the accident by which the fever was produced and of the treatment which the surgeon had given it, he ascended to Theodore's chamber.

In a quarter of an hour he returned to the room where Adeline expected him. "The gentleman is still delirious," said he, "but I have ordered him a composing draught."

"Is there any hope, sir?" inquired Adeline.

"Yes, madam, certainly there is hope; the case at present is somewhat doubtful, but a few hours may enable me to judge with more certainty. In the meantime, I have directed that he shall be kept quiet, and be allowed to drink freely of some diluting liquids."

He had scarcely, at Adeline's request, recommended a surgeon instead of the one at present employed, when the latter gentleman entered the room and, perceiving the physician, threw a glance of mingled surprise and anger at Adeline, who retired with him to another apartment, where she dismissed him with a politeness which he did not deign to return, and which he certainly did not deserve.

Early the following morning the surgeon arrived, but either the medicines or the crisis of the disorder had thrown Theodore into a deep sleep, in which he remained for several hours. The physician now gave Adeline reason to hope for a favourable issue, and every precaution was taken to prevent his being disturbed. He awoke perfectly sensible and free from fever, and his first words inquired for Adeline, who soon learned that he was out of danger.

In a few days he was sufficiently recovered to be removed from his chamber to a room adjoining, where Adeline met him with a joy which she found it impossible to repress; and the observance of this lighted up his countenance with pleasure. Indeed Adeline, sensible to the attachment he had so nobly testified, and softened by the danger he had encountered, no longer attempted to disguise the tenderness of her esteem, and was at length brought to confess the interest his first appearance had impressed upon her heart.

After an hour of affecting conversation, in which the happiness of a young and mutual attachment occupied all their minds and excluded every idea not in unison with delight, they returned to a sense of their present embarrassments. Adeline recollected that Theodore was arrested for disobedience of orders and deserting his post; and Theodore, that he must shortly be torn away from Adeline, who would be left exposed to all the evils from which he had so lately rescued her. This thought overwhelmed his heart with anguish; and after a long pause he ventured to propose what his wishes had often suggested, a marriage with Adeline before he departed from the village. This solution was the only means of preventing, perhaps, an eternal separation, and though he saw the many dangerous inconveniences to which she would be exposed by a marriage with a man circumstanced like himself, yet these appeared so unequal to those she would otherwise be left to encounter alone that his reason could no longer scruple to adopt what his affection had suggested.

Adeline was for some time too much agitated to reply; and though she had little to oppose to the arguments and pleadings of Theodore, though she had no friends to control, and no contrariety of interests to perplex her, she could not bring herself to consent thus hastily to a marriage with a man of whom she had little knowledge, and to whose family and connections she had no sort of introduction. At length, she entreated he would drop the subject, and the conversation for the remainder of the day was more general yet still interesting.

That similarity of taste and opinion which had at first attracted them was every moment now more fully disclosed. Their discourse was enriched by elegant literature, and endeared by mutual regard. Adeline had enjoyed few opportunities of reading, but the books to which she had access, operating upon a mind eager for knowledge and upon a taste peculiarly sensible of the beautiful and the elegant, had impressed all their excellencies upon her understanding. Theodore had received from nature many of the qualities of genius, and from education all that it could bestow; to these were added a noble independency of spirit, a feeling heart, and manners which partook of a happy mixture of dignity and sweetness.

In the evening, an officer—one of the officers who, upon the representation of the sergeant, was sent by the persons employed to prosecute military criminals—arrived at the village. Entering the apartment of Theodore, from which Adeline immediately withdrew, the officer informed him, with an air of infinite importance, that he should set out on the following day for headquarters. Theodore answered that he was not able to bear the journey, and referred him to his physician.

The officer replied that he should take no such trouble, it being certain that the physician might be instructed what to say, and that he should begin his journey on the morrow. "Here has been delay enough already," said he, "and you will have sufficient business on your hands when you reach headquarters; for the sergeant, whom you have severely wounded, intends to appear against you; and this, with the offence you have committed by deserting your post—"

Theodore's eyes flashed fire. "Deserting!" said he, rising from his seat and darting a look of menace at his accuser. "Who dares brand me with the name of deserter?" But instantly recollecting how much his conduct had appeared to justify the accusation, he endeavoured to stifle his emotions, and with a firm voice and composed manner said that when he reached headquarters, he should be ready to answer whatever might be brought against him, but that till then he should be silent.

The boldness of the officer was repressed by the spirit and

dignity with which Theodore spoke these words, and muttering a reply that was scarcely audible, he left the room.

Theodore sat musing on the danger of his situation; he knew that he had much to apprehend from the peculiar circumstances attending his abrupt departure from his regiment, it having been stationed in a garrison town upon the Spanish frontiers, where the discipline was very severe; and from the power of his colonel, the Marquis de Montalt, whom pride and disappointment would now rouse to vengeance, and probably render indefatigable in the accomplishment of his destruction. But his thoughts soon fled from his own danger to that of Adeline, and in the consideration of this, all his fortitude forsook him. He could not support the idea of leaving her exposed to the evils he foreboded, nor indeed of a separation so sudden as that which now threatened him; and when she again entered the room, he renewed his solicitations for a speedy marriage, with all the arguments that tenderness and ingenuity could suggest.

Adeline, when she learned that he was to depart on the morrow, felt as if bereaved of her last comfort. All the horrors of his situation arose to her mind, and she turned from him in unutterable anguish. Considering her silence as a favourable presage, he repeated his entreaties that she would consent to be his, and thus give him a surety that their separation should not be eternal.

Adeline sighed deeply at these words. "And who can know that our separation will not be eternal," said she, "even if I could consent to the marriage you propose? But while you hear my determination, forbear to accuse me of indifference, for indifference toward you would indeed be a crime, after the services you have rendered me."

"And is a cold sentiment of gratitude all that I must expect from you?" said Theodore. "I know that you are going to distress me with a proof of your indifference, which you mistake for the suggestions of prudence; and that I shall be compelled to look without reluctance upon the evils that may shortly await me. Ah, Adeline! if you mean to reject this, perhaps the last proposal which I can ever make to you, cease, at least, to deceive yourself with an idea that you love me; that delirium is fading even from my mind."

"Can you then so soon forget our conversation of this morning?" replied Adeline, "and can you think so lightly of me as to believe I would profess a regard which I do not feel? If, indeed, you can believe this, I shall do well to forget that I ever made such an acknowledgement, and you, that you heard it."

"Forgive me, Adeline, forgive the doubts and inconsistencies I have betrayed: let the anxieties of love and the emergency of my circumstances plead for me."

Adeline, smiling faintly through her tears, held out her hand, which he seized and pressed to his lips.

"Yet do not drive me to despair by a rejection of my suit," continued Theodore. "Think what I must suffer to leave you here destitute of friends and protection."

"I am thinking how I may avoid a situation so deplorable," said Adeline. "They say there is a convent which receives boarders within a few miles, and thither I wish to go."

"A convent!" rejoined Theodore. "Would you go to a convent? Do you know the persecutions you would be liable to, and that if the marquis should discover you, there is little probability the superior would resist his authority, or at least his bribes?"

"All this I have considered," said Adeline, "and am prepared to encounter it rather than enter into an engagement which at this time can be productive only of misery to us both."

"Ah, Adeline! could you think thus, if you truly loved? I see myself about to be separated, and that, perhaps, forever, from the object of my tenderest affections—and I cannot but express all the anguish I feel—I cannot forbear to repeat every argument that may afford even the slightest possibility of altering your determination. But you, Adeline, you look with complacency upon a circumstance which tortures me with despair."

Adeline, who had long strove to support her spirits in his presence while she adhered to a resolution which reason suggested, but which the pleadings of her heart powerfully opposed, was unable longer to command her distress, and burst into tears.

Theodore was in the same moment convinced of his error, and shocked at the grief he had occasioned. He drew his chair toward her, and taking her hand, again entreated her pardon, and endeavoured in the tenderest accents to soothe and comfort her.

"What a wretch was I to cause you this distress by questioning that regard with which I can no longer doubt you honour me! Forgive me, Adeline; say but you forgive me, and whatever may be the pain of this separation, I will no longer oppose it."

"You have given me some pain," said Adeline, "but you have not offended me."

She then mentioned some further particulars concerning the convent. Theodore endeavoured to conceal the distress which the approaching separation occasioned him, and to consult with her on these plans with composure. His judgement by degrees prevailed over his passions, and he now perceived that the plan she suggested would afford her best chance of security. He considered, what in the first agitation of his mind had escaped him, that he might be condemned upon the charges brought against him, and that his death, should they have been married, would not only deprive her of her protector, but leave her more immediately exposed to the designs of the marquis, who would doubtless attend his trial.

Astonished that he had not noticed this before, and shocked at the unwariness by which he might have betrayed her into so dangerous a situation, he became at once reconciled to the idea of leaving her in a convent. He could have wished to place her in the asylum of his own family, but the circumstances under which she must be introduced were so awkward and painful, and, above all, the distance at which they resided would render a journey so highly dangerous for her, that he forbore to propose it. He entreated only that she would allow him to write to her; but recollecting that his letters might be a means of betraying the place of her residence to the marquis, he checked himself.

"I must deny myself even this melancholy pleasure," said he, "lest my letters should discover your abode; yet how shall I be able to endure the impatience and uncertainty to which prudence condemns me! If you are in danger, I shall be ignorant of it; though, indeed, did I know it," said he with a look of despair, "I could not fly to save you. O exquisite misery! 'Tis now only I perceive all the horrors of confinement—'tis now only that I understand all the value of liberty!"

His utterance was interrupted by the violent agitation of his mind; he rose from his chair, and walked with quick paces about the room. Adeline sat, overcome by the description which Theodore had given of his approaching situation, and by the consideration that she might remain in the most terrible suspense concerning his fate. She saw him in a prison—pale—emaciated—in chains—she saw all the vengeance of the marquis descending upon him, and this for his noble exertions in her cause. Theodore, alarmed by the placid despair expressed in her countenance, threw himself into a chair by hers and, taking her hand, attempted to speak comfort to her, but the words faltered on his lips, and he could only bathe her hand with tears.

This mournful silence was interrupted by the arrival of a carriage at the inn. Arising, Theodore went to the window that opened into the yard. The darkness of the night prevented his distinguishing the objects without, but a light now brought from the house showed him a carriage and four attended by several servants. Presently he saw a gentleman wrapped up in a roquelaure[56] alight and enter the inn, and in the next moment he heard the voice of the marquis.

He had flown to support Adeline, who was sinking with terror, when the door opened and the marquis, followed by the officers and several servants, entered. Fury flashed from his

56. A knee-length cloak.

eyes as they glanced upon Theodore, who hung over Adeline with a look of fearful solicitude.

"Seize that traitor," said he, turning to the officers. "Why have you suffered him to remain here so long?"

"I am no traitor," said Theodore, with a firm voice and the dignity of conscious worth, "but a defender of innocence, of one whom the treacherous Marquis de Montalt would destroy."

"Obey your orders," said the marquis to the officers.

Adeline shrieked, held faster by Theodore's arm, and entreated the men not to part them.

"Force only can effect it," said Theodore, as he looked round for some instrument of defence, but he could see none, and in the same moment they surrounded and seized him.

"Dread everything from my vengeance," said the marquis to Theodore, as he caught the hand of Adeline, who had lost all power of resistance and was scarcely sensible of what passed. "Dread everything from my vengeance; you know you have deserved it."

"I defy your vengeance," cried Theodore, "and dread only the pangs of conscience, which your power cannot inflict upon me, though your vices condemn you to its tortures."

"Take him instantly from the room, and see that he is strongly fettered," said the marquis. "He shall soon know what a criminal who adds insolence to guilt may suffer."

Theodore was now forced out of the room, exclaiming, "O Adeline! farewell!"

Adeline, whose torpid senses were roused by his voice and his last looks, fell at the feet of the marquis and with tears of agony implored compassion for Theodore, but her pleadings for his rival served only to irritate the pride and exasperate the hatred of the marquis. He denounced vengeance on his head, and imprecations too dreadful for the spirits of Adeline, whom he compelled to rise; and then, endeavouring to stifle the emotions of rage which the presence of Theodore had excited, he began to address her with his usual expressions of admiration.

The wretched Adeline, who still continued to plead for her

unhappy lover, was at length alarmed by the returning rage which the countenance of the marquis expressed. Exerting all her remaining strength, she sprang from his grasp toward the door of the room. He seized her hand before she could reach it and, regardless of her shrieks, brought her back to her chair. He was going to speak when voices were heard in the passage, and immediately the landlord and his wife, whom Adeline's cries had alarmed, entered the apartment. The marquis, turning furiously to them, demanded what they wanted; but not waiting for their answer, he bade them attend him, and as they were quitting the room, she heard the door locked upon her.

Adeline now ran to the windows, which were unfastened and opened into the inn yard. All was dark and silent. She called aloud for help, but no person appeared; and the windows were so high that it was impossible to escape unassisted. She walked about the room in an agony of terror and distress, now stopping to listen and fancying she heard voices disputing below, and now quickening her steps as suspense increased the agitation of her mind.

She had continued in this state for near half an hour when she suddenly heard a violent noise in the lower part of the house, which increased till all was uproar and confusion. People passed quickly through the passages, and doors were frequently opened and shut. She called, but received no answer. It immediately occurred to her that Theodore, having heard her screams, had attempted to come to her assistance, and that the bustle had been occasioned by the opposition of the officers. Knowing their fierceness and cruelty, she was seized with dreadful apprehensions for the life of Theodore.

A confused uproar of voices now sounded from below, and the screams of women convinced her there was fighting; she even thought she heard the clashing of swords. The image of Theodore dying by the hands of the marquis now rose to her imagination, and the terrors of suspense became almost insupportable. She made a desperate effort to force the door and again called for help, but her trembling hands were powerless, and every person in the house seemed to be too much engaged even to hear her. A loud shriek now pierced her ears, and amidst the tumult that followed, she clearly distinguished deep groans. This confirmation of her fears deprived her of all her remaining spirits, and growing faint, she sank almost lifeless into a chair near the door. The uproar gradually subsided till all was still, but nobody returned to her. Soon after she heard voices in the yard, but she had no power to walk across the room even to ask the questions she wished, yet feared, to have answered.

About a quarter of an hour elapsed when the door was unlocked, and the hostess appeared with a countenance as pale as death.

"For God's sake," said Adeline, "tell me what has happened? Is he wounded? Is he killed?"

"He is not dead, mam'selle, but—"

"He is dying then?—tell me where he is—let me go."

"Stop, mam'selle," cried the hostess, "you are to stay here, I only want the hartshorn out of that cupboard there."

Adeline tried to escape by the door, but the hostess, pushing her aside, locked it, and went downstairs.

Adeline's distress now entirely overcame her, and she sat motionless and scarcely conscious that she existed till roused by a sound of footsteps near the door, which was again opened. Three men, whom she knew to be the marquis's servants, entered. She had sufficient recollection to repeat the questions she had asked the landlady, but they answered only that a chaise was waiting for her at the door and she must come with them. Still she urged her questions.

"Tell me if he lives," cried she.

"Yes, mam'selle, he is alive, but he is terribly wounded, and the surgeon is just come to him."

As they spoke they hurried her along the passage, and without noticing her entreaties and supplications to know whither she was going, they had reached the foot of the stairs, when her cries brought several people to the door. To these the hostess related that the lady was the wife of a gentleman just arrived, who had overtaken her in her flight with a gallant; an account which the marquis's servants corroborated.

"'Tis the gentleman who has just fought the duel," added the hostess, "and it was on her account."

Adeline, partly disdaining to take any notice of this artful story, and partly from her desire to know the particulars of what had happened, contented herself with repeating her inquiries; to which one of the spectators at last replied that the gentleman was desperately wounded. The marquis's people would now have hurried her into the chaise, but she sank lifeless in their arms, and her condition so interested the humanity of the spectators that, notwithstanding their belief of what had been said, they opposed the effort made to carry her, senseless as she was, into the carriage.

She was at length taken into a room and, by proper applications, restored to her senses. There she so earnestly besought an explanation of what had happened that the hostess acquainted her with some particulars of the late rencounter.[57]

"When the gentleman that was ill heard your screams, madam," said she, "he became quite outrageous, as they tell me, and nothing could pacify him. The marquis, for they say he is a marquis, but you know best, was then in the room with my husband and I, and when he heard the uproar, he went down to see what was the matter; and when he came into the room where the captain was, he found him struggling with the sergeant. Then the captain was more outrageous than ever; and notwithstanding he had one leg chained, and no sword, he contrived to get the sergeant's cutlass out of the scabbard, and immediately flew at the marquis, and wounded him desperately; upon which he was secured."

"It is the marquis then who is wounded," said Adeline. "The other gentleman is not hurt?"

"No, not he," replied the hostess, "but he will smart for it by and by, for the marquis swears he will do for him."

57. Hostile meeting.

Adeline, for a moment, forgot all her misfortunes and all her danger in thankfulness for the immediate escape of Theodore; and she was proceeding to make some further inquiries concerning him when the marquis's servants entered the room and declared they could wait no longer. Adeline, now awakened to a sense of the evils with which she was threatened, endeavoured to win the pity of the hostess, who, however, was, or affected to be, convinced of the truth of the marquis's story, and therefore insensible to all she could urge. Again she addressed his servants, but in vain; they would neither suffer her to remain longer at the inn or inform her whither she was going. In the presence of several persons already prejudiced by the injurious assertions of the hostess, Adeline was hurried into the chaise, and her conductors mounting their horses, the whole party was very soon beyond the village.

Thus ended Adeline's share of an adventure begun with a prospect, not only of security, but of happiness; an adventure which had attached her more closely to Theodore, and shown him to be more worthy of her love; but which, at the same time, had distressed her by new disappointment, produced the imprisonment of her generous and now-adored lover, and delivered both himself and her into the power of a rival irritated by delay, contempt, and opposition.

CHAPTER 13

Nor sea, nor shade, nor shield, nor rock, nor cave,
Nor silent deserts, nor the sullen grave,
What flame-ey'd Fury means to smite, can save.

Francis Quarles, "Emblem XII"

The surgeon of the place, having examined the marquis's wound, gave him an immediate opinion upon
it, and ordered that he should be put to bed. But the
marquis, ill as he was, had scarcely any other apprehension
than that of losing Adeline, and declared he should be able to
begin his journey in a few hours. With this intention, he had
begun to give orders for keeping horses in readiness, when
the surgeon persisting most seriously, and even passionately,
to exclaim that his life would be the sacrifice of his rashness,
he was carried to a bedchamber, where his valet alone was
permitted to attend him.

This man, the convenient confidant of all his intrigues, had
been the chief instrument in assisting his designs concerning
Adeline, and was indeed the very person who had brought
her to the marquis's villa on the borders of the forest. To him
the marquis gave his further directions concerning her; and
foreseeing the inconvenience as well as the danger of detaining
her at the inn, he had ordered him, with several other servants,
to carry her away immediately in a hired carriage. The valet

having gone to execute his orders, the marquis was left to his own reflections, and to the violence of contending passions.

The reproaches and continued opposition of Theodore, the favoured lover of Adeline, exasperated his pride and roused all his malice. He could not for a moment consider this opposition, which was in some respects successful, without feeling an excess of indignation and inveteracy,[58] such as the prospect of a speedy revenge could alone enable him to support.

When he had discovered Adeline's escape from the villa, his surprise at first equalled his disappointment; after exhausting the paroxysms of his rage upon his domestics, he dispatched them all different ways in pursuit of her, going himself to the abbey in the faint hope that, destitute as she was of other succour, she might have fled thither. La Motte, however, being as much surprised as himself and as ignorant of the route which Adeline had taken, the marquis returned to the villa, impatient of intelligence, and found some of his servants arrived without any news of Adeline, and those who came afterward were as successless as the first.

A few days after, a letter from the lieutenant colonel of the regiment informed him that Theodore had quitted his company and had been for some time absent, nobody knew where. This information confirming a suspicion which had frequently occurred to him, that Theodore had been by some means or other instrumental in the escape of Adeline, all his other passions became for a time subservient to his revenge, and he gave orders for the immediate pursuit and apprehension of Theodore. But Theodore, in the meantime, had been overtaken and secured.

It was in consequence of having formerly observed the growing partiality between him and Adeline, and of intelligence received from La Motte, who had noticed their interview in the forest, that the marquis had resolved to remove a rival so dangerous to his love, and so likely to be informed of his designs. He had therefore told Theodore, in a manner

58. Tenacity.

as plausible as he could, that it would be necessary for him to join the regiment; a notice which affected him only as it related to Adeline, and which seemed the less extraordinary as he had already been at the villa a much longer time than was usual with the officers invited by the marquis. Theodore, indeed, very well knew the character of the marquis, and had accepted his invitation rather from an unwillingness to show any disrespect to his colonel by a refusal than from a sanguine expectation of pleasure.

From the men who had apprehended Theodore, the marquis received the information which had enabled him to pursue and recover Adeline; but though he had now effected this, he was internally a prey to the corrosive effects of disappointed passion and exasperated pride. The anguish of his wound was almost forgotten in that of his mind, and every pang he felt seemed to increase his thirst of revenge, and to recoil with new torture upon his heart. While he was in this state, he heard the voice of the innocent Adeline imploring protection; but her cries excited in him neither pity or remorse. When soon after the carriage drove away, and he was certain both that she was secured and that Theodore was wretched, he seemed to feel some cessation of mental pain.

Theodore, indeed, did suffer all that a virtuous mind labouring under oppression so severe could feel; but he was at least free from those inveterate and malignant passions which tore the bosom of the marquis, and which inflict upon the possessor a punishment more severe than any they can prompt him to imagine for another. What indignation he might feel toward the marquis was at this time secondary to his anxiety for Adeline. His captivity was painful, as it prevented his seeking a just and honourable revenge; but it was dreadful, as it withheld him from attempting the rescue of her whom he loved more than life.

When he heard the wheels of the carriage that contained her drive off, he felt an agony of despair which almost overcame his reason. Even the stern hearts of the soldiers who attended him were not wholly insensible to his wretchedness, and by venturing to blame the conduct of the marquis, they endeavoured to console their prisoner. The physician, who was just arrived, entered the room during this paroxysm of his distress, and both feeling and expressing much concern at his condition, inquired with strong surprise why he had been thus precipitately removed to a room so very unfit for his reception.

Theodore explained to him the reason of this, of the distress he suffered, and of the chains by which he was disgraced; and perceiving the physician listened to him with attention and compassion, he became desirous of acquainting him with some further particulars, for which purpose he desired the soldiers to leave the room. The men, complying with his request, stationed themselves on the outside of the door.

He then related all the particulars of the late transaction, and of his connection with the marquis. The physician attended to his narrative with deep concern, and his countenance frequently expressed strong agitation. When Theodore concluded, he remained for some time silent and lost in thought; at length, awaking from his reverie, he said, "I fear your situation is desperate. The character of the marquis is too well-known to suffer him either to be loved or respected; from such a man you have nothing to hope, for he has scarcely anything to fear. I wish it was in my power to serve you, but I see no possibility of it."

"Alas!" said Theodore, "my situation is indeed desperate, and—for that suffering angel—" Deep sobs interrupted his voice, and the violence of his agitation would not allow him to proceed.

The physician could only express the sympathy he felt for his distress, and entreat him to be more calm, when a servant entered the room from the marquis, who desired to see the physician immediately. After some time, he said he would attend the marquis, and having endeavoured to attain a degree of composure which he found it difficult to assume, he wrung the hand of Theodore and quitted the room, promising to return before he left the house.

He found the marquis much agitated both in body and

mind, and rather more apprehensive for the consequences of the wound than he had expected. His anxiety for Theodore now suggested a plan, by the execution of which he hoped he might be able to serve him. Having felt his patient's pulse and asked some questions, he assumed a very serious look.

The marquis, who watched every turn of his countenance, desired he would, without hesitation, speak his opinion.

"I am sorry to alarm you, my lord, but here is some reason for apprehension: how long is it since you received the wound?"

"Good God! there is danger then!" cried the marquis, adding some bitter execrations against Theodore.

"There certainly is danger," replied the physician. "A few hours may enable me to determine its degree."

"A few hours, sir!" interrupted the marquis, "a few hours!"

The physician entreated him to be more calm.

"Confusion!" cried the marquis. "A man in health may, with great composure, entreat a dying man to be calm. Theodore will be broke upon the wheel for it, however."

"You mistake me, sir," said the physician. "If I believed you a dying man, or, indeed, very near death, I should not have spoken as I did. But it is of consequence I should know how long the wound has been inflicted."

The marquis's terror now began to subside, and he gave a circumstantial account of the affray[59] with Theodore, representing that he had been basely used in an affair where his own conduct had been perfectly just and humane. The physician heard this relation with great coolness and without making any comment upon it. When it concluded he told the marquis he would prescribe a medicine which he wished him to take immediately.

The marquis, again alarmed by the gravity of his manner, entreated he would declare most seriously whether he thought him in immediate danger. The physician hesitated, and the anxiety of the marquis increased. "It is of consequence," said he, "that I should know my exact situation."

59. Brawl.

The physician then said that if he had any worldly affairs to settle, it would be as well to attend to them, for that it was impossible to say what might be the event.

He then turned the discourse and said he had just been with the young officer under arrest, who, he hoped, would not be removed at present, as such a procedure must endanger his life. The marquis uttered a dreadful oath and, cursing Theodore for having brought him to his present condition, said he should depart with the guard that very night. Against the cruelty of this sentence, the physician ventured to expostulate. Endeavouring to awaken the marquis to a sense of humanity, he pleaded earnestly for Theodore. But these entreaties and arguments seemed, by displaying to the marquis a part of his own character, to rouse his resentment and rekindle all the violence of his passions.

The physician at length withdrew in despondency, after promising, at the marquis's request, not to leave the inn. He had hoped to obtain some advantages both for Adeline and Theodore by aggravating his danger; but the plan had quite a contrary effect, for the apprehension of death, so dreadful to the guilty mind of the marquis, instead of awakening penitence increased his desire of vengeance against the man who had brought him to such a situation. He determined to have Adeline conveyed where Theodore, should he by any accident escape, could never obtain her; and thus to secure to himself at least some means of revenge. He knew, however, that when Theodore was once safely conveyed to his regiment, his destruction was certain, for should he even be acquitted of the intention of deserting, he would be condemned for having assaulted his superior officer.

The physician returned to the room where Theodore was confined. The violence of his distress was now subsided into a stern despair more dreadful than the vehemence which had lately possessed him. The guard having left the room in compliance with his request, the physician repeated to him some part of his conversation with the marquis. Theodore, after expressing his thanks, said he had nothing more to hope. For himself he felt little; it was for his family and for Adeline he suffered. He inquired what route she had taken and, though he had no prospect of deriving advantage from the information, desired the physician to assist him in obtaining it; but the landlord and his wife either were, or affected to be, ignorant of the matter, and it was in vain to apply to any other person.

The sergeant now entered with orders from the marquis for the immediate departure of Theodore, who heard the message with composure, though the physician could not help expressing his indignation at this precipitate removal and his dread of the consequences that might attend it. Theodore had scarcely time to declare his gratitude for the kindness of this valuable friend before the soldiers entered the room to conduct him to the carriage in waiting.

As he bade him farewell, Theodore slipped his purse into his hand, and turning abruptly away, told the soldiers to lead on; but the physician stopped him, and refused the present with such serious warmth that he was compelled to resume[60] it. He wrung the hand of his new friend and, being unable to speak, hurried away. The whole party immediately set off, and the unhappy Theodore was left to the remembrance of his past hopes and sufferings, his anxiety for the fate of Adeline, the contemplation of his present wretchedness, and the apprehension of what might be reserved for him in future. For himself, indeed, he saw nothing but destruction, and was only relieved from total despair by a feeble hope that she, whom he loved better than himself, might one time enjoy that happiness of which he did not venture to look for a participation.

60. Take again.

CHAPTER 14

If the midnight bell
Did with his iron tongue and brazen mouth
Sound on into the drowsy race of night;
If this same were a churchyard where we stand,
And thou possessed with a thousand wrongs;
Or if that surly spirit, melancholy,
Had bak'd thy blood and made it heavy-thick;

. . . .

Then, in despite of brooded watchful day,
I would into thy bosom pour my thoughts.

. . . .

Have you the heart? When your head did but ache,
I knit my handkerchief about your brows—

. . . .

And with my hand at midnight held your head;
And, like the watchful minutes to the hour,
Still and anon cheer'd up the heavy time.

Shakespeare, *King John*

Meanwhile the persecuted Adeline continued to travel all night with little interruption. Her mind suffered such a tumult of grief, regret, despair, and terror that she could not be said to think. The marquis's valet, who had placed himself in the chaise with her, at first seemed inclined to talk, but her inattention soon silenced him, and he left her to the indulgence of her own misery.

They seemed to travel through obscure lanes and byways, along which the carriage drove as furiously as the darkness would permit. When the dawn appeared, she perceived herself on the borders of a forest, and renewed her entreaties to know whither she was going. The man replied that he had no orders to tell, but she would soon see. Adeline, who had hitherto supposed they were carrying her to the villa, now began to doubt it; and as every place appeared less terrible to her imagination than that, her despair began to abate, and she thought only of the devoted Theodore, whom she knew to be the victim of malice and revenge.

They now entered upon the forest, and it occurred to her that she was going to the abbey; for though she had no remembrance of the scenery through which she passed, it was not the less probable that this was the forest of Fontanville, whose boundaries were much too extensive to have come within the circle of her former walks. This conjecture revived a terror, little inferior to that occasioned by the idea of going to the villa, for at the abbey she would be equally in the power of the marquis and also in that of her cruel enemy, La Motte. Her mind revolted at the picture her fancy drew, and as the carriage moved under the shades, she threw from the window a look of eager inquiry for some object which might confirm or destroy her present surmise; she did not long look before an opening in the forest showed her the distant towers of the abbey. "I am, indeed, lost then!" said she, bursting into tears.

They were soon at the foot of the lawn, and Peter was running to open the gate at which the carriage stopped. When he saw Adeline, he looked surprised and made an effort to speak, but the chaise now drove up to the abbey, where, at the door of the hall, La Motte himself appeared. As he advanced to take her from the carriage, an universal trembling seized her; it was with the utmost difficulty she supported herself, and for some moments she neither observed his countenance nor heard his voice. He offered his arm to assist her into the abbey, which she at first refused, but having tottered a few paces, she was obliged to accept. They then entered the vaulted room, where she sank into a chair, a flood of tears coming to her relief. La Motte did not interrupt the silence, which continued for some time, but paced the room in seeming agitation. When Adeline was sufficiently recovered to notice external objects, she observed his countenance, and there read the tumult of his soul, while he was struggling to assume a firmness which his better feelings opposed.

La Motte now took her hand and would have led her from the room, but she stopped and with a kind of desperate courage made an effort to engage him to pity and to save her.

He interrupted her. "It is not in my power," said he, in a voice of emotion. "I am not master of myself or my conduct; inquire no further—it is sufficient for you to know that I pity you; more I cannot do."

He gave her no time to reply but, taking her hand, led her to the stairs of the tower, and from thence to the chamber she had formerly occupied. "Here you must remain for the present," said he, "in a confinement, which is, perhaps, almost as involuntary on my part as it can be on yours. I am willing to render it as easy as possible, and have therefore ordered some books to be brought you."

Adeline made an effort to speak, but he hurried from the room, seemingly ashamed of the part he had undertaken, and unwilling to trust himself with her tears. She heard the door of the chamber locked, and then, looking toward the windows, perceived they were secured: the door that led to the other apartments was also fastened. Such preparation for security shocked her, and hopeless as she had long believed herself, she now perceived her mind sink deeper in despair. When the tears she shed had somewhat relieved her, and her thoughts could turn from the subjects of her immediate concern, she was thankful for the total seclusion allotted her, since it would spare her the pain she must feel in the presence of Monsieur and Madame de la Motte, and allow the unrestrained indulgence of her own sorrow and reflection; reflection which, however distressing, was preferable to the agony inflicted on the mind when, agitated by care and fear, it is obliged to assume an appearance of tranquillity.

In about a quarter of an hour, her chamber door was unlocked, and Annette appeared with refreshments and books. She expressed satisfaction at seeing Adeline again but seemed fearful of speaking, knowing probably that it was contrary to the orders of La Motte, who, she said, was waiting at the bottom of the stairs. When Annette was gone, Adeline took some refreshment, which was indeed necessary, for she had tasted nothing since she left the inn.

She was pleased, but not surprised, that Madame de la Motte did not appear. She, it was evident, shunned her from a consciousness of her own ungenerous conduct, a consciousness which offered some presumption that she was still not wholly unfriendly to her. She reflected upon the words of La Motte, "I am not master of myself, or my conduct," and though they afforded her no hope, she derived some comfort, poor as it was, from the belief that he pitied her. After some time spent in miserable reflection and various conjectures, her long-agitated spirits seemed to demand repose, and she lay down to sleep.

Adeline slept quietly for several hours, and awoke with a mind refreshed and tranquillized. To prolong this temporary peace and to prevent, therefore, the intrusion of her own thoughts, she examined the books La Motte had sent her. Among these she found some that in happier times had elevated her mind and interested her heart; although their effect was now weakened, they were still able to soften for a time the sense of her misfortunes.

But this Lethean[61] medicine to a wounded mind was but a temporary blessing; the entrance of La Motte dissolved the illusions of the page and awakened her to a sense of her own situation. He came with food and, having placed it on the table, left the room without speaking. Again she endeavoured to

61. Of the river Lethe, whose water inspires forgetfulness.

read, but his appearance had broken the enchantment—bitter reflection returned to her mind, and brought with it the image of Theodore—of Theodore lost to her forever!

La Motte, meanwhile, experienced all the terrors that could be inflicted by a conscience not wholly hardened to guilt. He had been led on by passion to dissipation—and from dissipation to vice; but having once touched the borders of infamy, the progressive steps followed each other fast, and he now saw himself the pander[62] of a villain, and the betrayer of an innocent girl whom every plea of justice and humanity called upon him to protect. He contemplated his picture—he shrank from it, but he could change its deformity only by an effort too nobly daring for a mind already diminished by vice. He viewed the dangerous labyrinth into which he was led, and perceived, as if for the first time, the progression of his guilt; from this labyrinth he weakly imagined further guilt could alone extricate him. Instead of employing his mind upon the means of saving Adeline from destruction and himself from being instrumental to it, he endeavoured only to lull the pangs of conscience and to persuade himself into a belief that he must proceed in the course he had begun. He knew himself to be in the power of the marquis, and he dreaded that power more than the sure, though distant, punishment that awaits upon guilt. The honour of Adeline and the quiet of his own conscience he consented to barter for a few years of existence.

He was ignorant of the present illness of the marquis, or he would have perceived that there was a chance of escaping the threatened punishment at a price less enormous than infamy, and he would, perhaps, have endeavoured to save Adeline and himself by flight. But the marquis, foreseeing the possibility of this, had ordered his servants carefully to conceal the circumstance which detained him, and to acquaint La Motte that he should be at the abbey in a few days, at the same time directing his valet to await him there. Adeline, as he expected, had neither inclination nor opportunity to mention it, and thus

62. Pimp.

La Motte remained ignorant of the circumstance which might have preserved him from further guilt and Adeline from misery.

Most unwillingly had La Motte made his wife acquainted with the action which had made him absolutely dependent upon the will of the marquis, but the perturbation of his mind partly betrayed him: frequently in his sleep he muttered incoherent sentences, and frequently would start from his slumber and call in passionate exclamation upon Adeline. These instances of a disturbed mind had alarmed and terrified Madame de la Motte, who watched while he slept and soon gathered from his words a confused idea of the marquis's designs.

She hinted her suspicions to La Motte, who reproved her for having entertained them, but his manner increased instead of repressing her fears for Adeline; fears which the conduct of the marquis soon confirmed. On the night that he slept at the abbey, it had occurred to her that whatever scheme was in agitation would now most probably be discussed, and anxiety for Adeline made her stoop to a meanness which, in other circumstances, would have been despicable. She quitted her room and, concealing herself in an apartment adjoining that in which she had left the marquis and her husband, listened to their discourse. It turned upon the subject she had expected, and disclosed to her the full extent of their designs. Terrified for Adeline, and shocked at the guilty weakness of La Motte, she was for some time incapable of thinking, or determining how to proceed. She knew her husband to be under great obligation to the marquis, whose territory thus afforded him a shelter from the world, and that it was in the power of the former to betray him into the hands of his enemies. She believed also that the marquis would do this if provoked, yet she thought upon such an occasion La Motte might find some way of appeasing the marquis without subjecting himself to dishonour. After some further reflection, her mind became more composed, and she returned to her chamber, where La Motte soon followed. Her spirits, however, were not now in a state to encounter either his displeasure or his opposition, which she had too much reason to expect whenever she should mention the subject of her concern, and she therefore resolved not to notice it till the morrow.

On the morrow, she told La Motte all he had uttered in his dreams, and mentioned other circumstances which convinced him it was in vain any longer to deny the truth of her apprehensions. His wife then represented to him how possible it was to avoid the infamy into which he was about to plunge by quitting the territories of the marquis, and pleaded so warmly for Adeline that La Motte, in sullen silence, appeared to meditate upon the plan. His thoughts were, however, very differently engaged. He was conscious of having deserved from the marquis a dreadful punishment, and knew that if he exasperated him by refusing to acquiesce with his wishes, he had little to expect from flight, for the eye of justice and revenge would pursue him with indefatigable research.

La Motte meditated how to break this to his wife, for he perceived that there was no other method of counteracting her virtuous compassion for Adeline and the dangerous consequences to be expected from it than by opposing it with terror for his safety, and this could be done only by showing her the full extent of the evils that must attend the resentment of the marquis. Vice had not yet so entirely darkened his conscience, but that the blush of shame stained his cheek, and his tongue faltered when he would have told his guilt.

At length, finding it impossible to mention particulars, he told her that, on account of an affair which no entreaties should ever induce him to explain, his life was in the power of the marquis. "You see the alternative," said he. "Take your choice of evils, and, if you can, tell Adeline of her danger and sacrifice my life to save her from a situation which many would be ambitious to obtain."

Madame de la Motte, condemned to the horrible alternative of permitting the seduction of innocence or of dooming her husband to destruction, suffered a distraction of thought which defied all control. Perceiving, however, that an opposition to the designs of the marquis would ruin La Motte and avail Adeline little, she determined to yield and endure in silence.

At the time when Adeline was planning her escape from the abbey, the significant looks of Peter had led La Motte to suspect the truth and to observe them more closely. He had seen them separate in the hall in apparent confusion, and had afterward observed them conversing together in the cloisters. Circumstances so unusual left him not a doubt that Adeline had discovered her danger and was concerting[63] with Peter some means of escape. Affecting, therefore, to be informed of the whole affair, he charged Peter with treachery toward himself, and threatened him with the vengeance of the marquis if he did not disclose all he knew. The menace intimidated Peter, and supposing that all chance of assisting Adeline was gone, he made a circumstantial confession and promised to forbear acquainting Adeline with the discovery of the scheme. In this promise he was seconded by inclination, for he feared to meet the displeasure which Adeline, believing he had betrayed her, might express.

On the evening of the day on which Adeline's intended escape was discovered, the marquis designed to come to the abbey, and it had been agreed that he should then take Adeline to his villa. La Motte had immediately perceived the advantage of permitting Adeline, in the belief of being undiscovered, to repair to the tomb. It would prevent much disturbance and opposition, and spare himself the pain he must feel in her presence when she should know that he had betrayed her. A servant of the marquis might go at the appointed hour to the tomb and, wrapt in the disguise of night, take her quietly thence in the character of Peter. Thus, without resistance, she would be carried to the villa, nor discover her mistake till it was too late to prevent its consequence.

When the marquis did arrive, La Motte, who was not so much intoxicated by the wine he had drank as to forget his

63. Planning.

prudence, informed him of what had happened and what he had planned, and the marquis approving it, his servant was made acquainted with the signal, which afterward betrayed Adeline to his power.

A deep consciousness of the unworthy neutrality she had observed in Adeline's concerns made Madame de la Motte anxiously avoid seeing her now that she was again in the abbey. Adeline understood this conduct, and she rejoiced that she was spared the anguish of meeting as an enemy her whom she had once considered as a friend. Several days now passed in solitude, in miserable retrospection, and in dreadful expectation. The perilous situation of Theodore was almost the constant subject of her thoughts. Often did she breathe an agonizing wish for his safety, and often look round the sphere of possibility in search of hope; but hope had almost left the horizon of her prospect, and when it did appear, it sprang only from the death of the marquis, whose vengeance threatened most certain destruction.

The marquis, meanwhile, lay at the inn at Caux, in a state of very doubtful recovery. The physician and surgeon, neither of whom he would dismiss nor suffer to leave the village, proceeded upon contrary principles, and the good effect of what the one prescribed was frequently counteracted by the injudicious treatment of the other. Humanity alone prevailed on the physician to continue his attendance. The malady of the marquis was also heightened by the impatience of his temper, the terrors of death, and the irritation of his passions. One moment he believed himself dying, another he could scarcely be prevented from attempting to follow Adeline to the abbey. So various were the fluctuations of his mind, and so rapid the schemes that succeeded each other, that his passions were in a continual state of conflict. The physician attempted to persuade him that his recovery greatly depended upon tranquillity, and to prevail upon him to attempt at least some command of his feelings, but he was soon silenced, in hopeless disgust, by the impatient answers of the marquis.

At length the servant who had carried off Adeline returned,

and the marquis, having ordered him into his chamber, asked so many questions in a breath that the man knew not which to answer. At length he pulled a folded paper from his pocket, which he said had been dropped in the chaise by Mademoiselle Adeline, and as he thought his lordship would like to see it, he had taken care of it. The marquis stretched forth his hand with eagerness and received a note addressed to Theodore. On perceiving the superscription, the agitation of jealous rage for a moment overcame him, and he held it in his hand unable to open it.

He, however, broke the seal, and found it to be a note of inquiry written by Adeline to Theodore during his illness, which from some accident she had been prevented from sending him. The tender solicitude it expressed for his recovery stung the soul of the marquis, and drew from him a comparison of her feelings on the illness of his rival and that of himself.

"She could be solicitous for his recovery," said he, "but for mine, she only dreads it."

As if willing to prolong the pain this little billet had excited, he then read it again. Again he cursed his fate and execrated his rival, giving himself up, as usual, to the transports of his passion. He was going to throw it from him when his eyes caught the seal, and he looked earnestly at it. His anger seemed now to have subsided; he deposited the note carefully in his pocketbook, and was for some time lost in thought.

After many days of hopes and fears, the strength of his constitution overcame his illness, and he was well enough to write several letters, one of which he immediately sent off to prepare La Motte for his reception. The same policy, which had prompted him to conceal his illness from La Motte, now urged him to say what he knew would not happen, that he should reach the abbey on the day after his servant. He repeated this injunction, that Adeline should be strictly guarded, and renewed his promises of reward for the future services of La Motte.

La Motte, to whom each succeeding day had brought new surprise and perplexity concerning the absence of the marquis, received this notice with uneasiness, for he had begun to hope that the marquis had altered his intentions concerning Adeline, being either engaged in some new adventure, or obliged to visit his estates in some distant province; he would have been willing thus to have got rid of an affair which was to reflect so much dishonour on himself.

This hope was now vanished, and he directed Madame to prepare for the reception of the marquis. Adeline passed these days in a state of suspense, which was now cheered by hope, and now darkened by despair. This delay, so much exceeding her expectation, seemed to prove that the illness of the marquis was dangerous; and when she looked forward to the consequences of his recovery, she could not be sorry that it was so. So odious was the idea of him to her mind that she would not suffer her lips to pronounce his name, nor make the inquiry of Annette which was of such consequence to her peace.

It was about a week after the receipt of the marquis's letter that Adeline one day saw from her window a party of horsemen enter the avenue, and knew them to be the marquis and his attendants. She retired from the window in a state of mind not to be described and, sinking into a chair, was for some time scarcely conscious of the objects around her. When she had recovered from the first terror which his appearance excited, she again tottered to the window; the party was not in sight, but she heard the trampling of horses and knew that the marquis had wound round to the great gate of the abbey. She addressed herself to Heaven for support and protection, and, her mind being now somewhat composed, sat down to wait the event.

La Motte received the marquis with expressions of surprise at his long absence, and the latter, merely saying he had been detained by illness, proceeded to inquire for Adeline. He was told she was in her chamber, from whence she might be summoned if he wished to see her. The marquis hesitated, and at length excused himself, but desired she might be strictly watched.

"Perhaps, my lord," said La Motte, smiling. "Adeline's obstinacy has been too powerful for your passion; you seem less interested concerning her than formerly."

"O! by no means," replied the marquis, "she interests me, if possible, more than ever; so much, indeed, that I cannot have her too closely guarded; and I therefore beg, La Motte, that you will suffer nobody to attend her but when you can observe them yourself. Is the room where she is confined sufficiently secure?"

La Motte assured him it was, but at the same time expressed his wish that she was removed to the villa. "If by any means," said he, "she should contrive to escape, I know what I must expect from your displeasure; and this reflection keeps my mind in continual anxiety."

"This removal cannot be at present," said the marquis. "She is safer here, and you do wrong to disturb yourself with any apprehension of her escape, if her chamber is really so secure as you represent it."

"I can have no motive for deceiving you, my lord, in this point."

"I do not suspect you of any," said the marquis. "Guard her carefully, and trust me, she will not escape. I can rely upon my valet, and if you wish it, he shall remain here."

La Motte thought there could be no occasion for him, and it was agreed that the man should go home.

The marquis, after remaining about half an hour in conversation with La Motte, left the abbey, and Adeline saw him depart with a mixture of surprise and thankfulness that almost overcame her. She had waited in momentary expectation of being summoned to appear, and had been endeavouring to arm herself with resolution to support his presence. She had listened to every voice that sounded from below, and at every step that crossed the passage, her heart had palpitated with dread, lest it should be La Motte coming to lead her to the marquis. This state of suffering had been prolonged almost beyond her power of enduring it when she heard voices under her window and, rising, saw the marquis ride away. After giving way to the joy and thankfulness that swelled her heart, she endeavoured to account for this circumstance, which, considering what had passed, was certainly very strange. It appeared, indeed, wholly inexplicable, and after much fruitless inquiry, she quitted the subject, endeavouring to persuade herself that it could only portend good.

The time of La Motte's usual visitation now drew near, and Adeline expected it in the trembling hope of hearing that the marquis had ceased his persecution; but he was, as usual, sullen and silent, and it was not till he was about to quit the room that Adeline had the courage to inquire when the marquis was expected again.

La Motte, opening the door to depart, replied, "On the following day."

Adeline, whom fear and delicacy embarrassed, saw she could obtain no intelligence of Theodore but by a direct question; she looked earnestly, as if to speak, and he stopped, but she blushed and was still silent, till upon his again attempting to leave the room, she faintly called him back.

"I would ask," said she, "after that unfortunate chevalier who has incurred the resentment of the marquis by endeavouring to serve me. Has the marquis mentioned him?"

"He has," replied La Motte, "and your indifference toward the marquis is now fully explained."

"Since I must feel resentment toward those who injure me," said Adeline, "I may surely be allowed to be grateful toward those who serve me. Had the marquis deserved my esteem, he would have possessed it."

"Well, well," said La Motte, "this young hero who, it seems, has been brave enough to lift his arm against his colonel is taken care of, and I doubt not will soon be sensible of the value of his quixotism."

Indignation, grief, and fear struggled in the bosom of Adeline; she disdained to give La Motte an opportunity of again pronouncing the name of Theodore, yet the uncertainty under which she laboured urged her to inquire whether the marquis had heard of him since he left Caux.

"Yes," said La Motte, "he has been safely carried to his regiment, where he is confined till the marquis can attend to appear against him."

Adeline had neither power nor inclination to inquire further, and La Motte quitting the chamber, she was left to the misery he had renewed. Though this information contained no new circumstance of misfortune—for she now heard confirmed what she had always expected—a weight of new sorrow seemed to fall upon her heart, and she perceived that she had unconsciously cherished a latent hope of Theodore's escape before he reached the place of his destination. All hope was now, however, gone; he was suffering the miseries of a prison, and the tortures of apprehension both for his own life and her safety. She pictured to herself the dark damp dungeon where he lay, loaded with chains and pale with sickness and grief; she heard him, in a voice that thrilled her heart, call upon her name, and raise his eyes to Heaven in silent supplication. She saw the anguish of his countenance, the tears that fell slowly on his cheek, and remembering at the same time the generous conduct that had brought him to this abyss of misery, and that it was for her sake he suffered, grief resolved itself into despair, her tears ceased to flow, and she sank silently into a state of dreadful torpor.

On the morrow the marquis arrived, and departed as before. Several days then elapsed, and he did not appear till one evening, as La Motte and his wife were in their usual sitting room, he entered, and conversed for some time upon general subjects, from which, however, he by degrees fell into a reverie.

After a pause of silence, he rose and drew La Motte to the window. "I would speak with you alone," said he, "if you are at leisure; if not, another time will do."

La Motte, assuring him he was perfectly so, would have conducted him to another room, but the marquis proposed a walk in the forest.

They went out together, and when they had reached a solitary glade, where the spreading branches of the beech and oak deepened the shades of twilight and threw a solemn obscurity around, the marquis turned to La Motte and addressed him: "Your condition, La Motte, is unhappy; this abbey is a melancholy residence for a man like you fond of society, and like you also qualified to adorn it."

La Motte bowed.

"I wish it was in my power to restore you to the world," continued the marquis. "Perhaps, if I knew the particulars of the affair which has driven you from it, I might perceive that my interest could effectually serve you. I think I have heard you hint it was an affair of honour."

La Motte was silent.

"I mean not to distress you, however; nor is it common curiosity that prompts this inquiry, but a sincere desire to befriend you. You have already informed me of some particulars of your misfortunes. I think the liberality of your temper led you into expenses which you afterward endeavoured to retrieve by gaming."

"Yes, my lord," said La Motte, "'tis true that I dissipated the greater part of an affluent fortune in luxurious indulgences, and that I afterward took unworthy means to recover it; but I wish to be spared upon this subject. I would, if possible, lose the remembrance of a transaction which must forever stain my character, and the rigorous effect of which, I fear, it is not in your power, my lord, to soften."

"You may be mistaken on this point," replied the marquis. "My interest at court is by no means inconsiderable. Fear not from me any severity of censure; I am not at all inclined to judge harshly of the faults of others. I well know how to allow for the emergency of circumstances, and, I think, La Motte, you have hitherto found me your friend."

"I have, my lord."

"And when you recollect that I have forgiven a certain transaction of late date—"

"It is true, my lord; and allow me to say, I have a just sense of your generosity. The transaction you allude to is by far the worst of my life, and what I have to relate cannot, therefore, lower me in your opinion. When I had dissipated the greatest part of my property in habits of voluptuous pleasure, I had recourse to gaming to supply the means of continuing them. A run of good luck, for some time, enabled me to do this, and encouraging my most sanguine expectations, I continued in the same career of success.

"Soon after this a sudden turn of fortune destroyed my hopes, and reduced me to the most desperate extremity. In one night my money was lowered to the sum of two hundred louis. These I resolved to stake also, and with them my life; for it was my resolution not to survive their loss. Never shall I forget the horrors of that moment on which hung my fate, nor the deadly anguish that seized my heart when my last stake was gone. I stood for some time in a state of stupefaction till, roused to a sense of my misfortune, my passion made me pour forth execrations on my more fortunate rivals, and act all the frenzy of despair.

"During this paroxysm of madness, a gentleman who had been a silent observer of all that passed approached me. 'You are unfortunate, sir,' said he.

"'I need not be informed of that, sir,' I replied.

"'You have, perhaps, been ill used,' resumed he.

"'Yes, sir, I am ruined, and therefore it may be said I am ill used.'

"'Do you know the people you have played with?'

"'No, but I have met them in the first circles.'

"'Then I am probably mistaken,' said he, and walked away. His last words roused me, and raised a hope that my money had not been fairly lost. Wishing for further information, I went in search of the gentleman, but he had left the rooms. I, however, stifled my transports, returned to the table where I had lost my money, placed myself behind the chair of one of the persons who had won it, and closely watched the game. For some time I saw nothing that could confirm my suspicions, but was at length convinced they were just.

"When the game was ended I called one of my adversaries out of the room, and telling him what I had observed, threatened instantly to expose him if he did not restore my property. The man was, for some time, as positive as myself; and, assuming the bully, threatened me with chastisement for my scandalous assertions. I was not, however, in a state of mind to be frightened, and his manner served only to exasperate my temper, already sufficiently inflamed by misfortune. After retorting[64] his threats, I was about to return to the apartment we had left and expose what had passed when, with an insidious smile and a softened voice, he begged I would favour him with a few moments' attention, and allow him to speak with the gentleman his partner. To the latter part of his request I hesitated, but in the meantime, the gentleman himself entered the room. His partner related to him in few words what had passed between us, and the terror that appeared in his countenance sufficiently declared his consciousness of guilt.

"They then drew aside and remained a few minutes in conversation together, after which they approached me with an offer, as they phrased it, of a compromise. I declared, however, against anything of this kind, and swore nothing less than the whole sum I had lost should content me.

"'Is it not possible, monsieur, that you may be offered something as advantageous as the whole?'

"I did not understand their meaning, but, after they had continued for some time to give distant hints of the same sort, they proceeded to explain. Perceiving their characters wholly in my power, they wished to secure my interest to their party, and therefore, informing me that they belonged to an association of persons who lived upon the folly and inexperience of others, they offered me a share in their concern. My fortunes were desperate, and the proposal now made me would not only produce an immediate supply, but enable me to return to those scenes of dissipated pleasure to which passion had at first, and long habit afterward, attached me. I closed with the offer, and thus sank from dissipation into infamy."

La Motte paused, as if the recollection of these times filled him with remorse.

64. Returning.

The marquis understood his feelings. "You judge too rigorously of yourself," said he. "There are few persons, let their appearance of honesty be what it may, who in such circumstances would have acted better than you have done. Had I been in your situation, I know not how I might have acted. That rigid virtue which shall condemn you may dignify itself with the appellation of wisdom, but I wish not to possess it; let it still reside where it generally is to be found, in the cold bosoms of those who, wanting feeling to be men, dignify themselves with the title of philosophers. But pray proceed."

"Our success was for some time unlimited, for we held the wheel of fortune, and trusted not to her caprice. Thoughtless and voluptuous by nature, my expenses fully kept pace with my income. An unlucky discovery of the practices of our party was at length made by a young nobleman, which obliged us to act for some time with the utmost circumspection. It would be tedious to relate the particulars which made us at length so suspected that the distant civility and cold reserve of our acquaintance rendered the frequenting of public assemblies both painful and unprofitable. We turned our thoughts to other modes of obtaining money, and a swindling transaction in which I engaged, to a very large amount, soon compelled me to leave Paris. You know the rest, my lord."

La Motte was now silent, and the marquis continued for some time musing. "You perceive, my lord," at length resumed La Motte, "you perceive that my case is hopeless."

"It is bad, indeed, but not entirely hopeless. From my soul I pity you. Yet, if you should return to the world, and incur the danger of prosecution, I think my interest with the minister might save you from any severe punishment. You seem, however, to have lost your relish for society, and perhaps do not wish to return to it."

"Oh! my lord, can you doubt this? But I am overcome with the excess of your goodness; would to Heaven it were in my power to prove the gratitude it inspires."

"Talk not of goodness," said the marquis. "I will not pretend that my desire of serving you is unalloyed by any degree of self-interest. I will not affect to be more than man, and, trust me, those who do are less. It is in your power to testify your gratitude, and bind me to your interest forever." He paused.

"Name but the means," cried La Motte, "name but the means, and if they are within the compass of possibility they shall be executed."

The marquis was still silent.

"Do you doubt my sincerity, my lord, that you are yet silent? Do you fear to repose a confidence in the man whom you have already loaded with obligation? who lives by your mercy, and almost by your means."

The marquis looked earnestly at him, but did not speak.

"I have not deserved this of you, my lord; speak, I entreat you."

"There are certain prejudices attached to the human mind," said the marquis in a slow and solemn voice, "which it requires all our wisdom to keep from interfering with our happiness; certain set notions, acquired in infancy, and cherished involuntarily by age, which grow up and assume a gloss so plausible that few minds, in what is called a civilized country, can afterward overcome them. Truth is often perverted by education. While the refined Europeans boast a standard of honour and a sublimity of virtue which often leads them from pleasure to misery, and from nature to error, the simple, uninformed American follows the impulse of his heart, and obeys the inspiration of wisdom."

The marquis paused, and La Motte continued to listen in eager expectation.

"Nature, uncontaminated by false refinement," resumed the marquis, "everywhere acts alike in the great occurrences of life. The Indian discovers his friend to be perfidious, and he kills him; the wild Asiatic does the same; the Turk, when ambition fires or revenge provokes, gratifies his passion at the expense of life, and does not call it murder. Even the polished Italian, distracted by jealousy or tempted by a strong circumstance of advantage, draws his stiletto, and accomplishes his purpose. It is the first proof of a superior mind to liberate itself from prejudices of country, or of education. You are silent, La Motte; are you not of my opinion?"

"I am attending, my lord, to your reasoning."

"There are, I repeat it," said the marquis, "people of minds so weak as to shrink from acts they have been accustomed to hold wrong, however advantageous. They never suffer themselves to be guided by circumstances, but fix for life upon a certain standard, from which they will, on no account, depart. Self-preservation is the great law of nature; when a reptile hurts us, or an animal of prey threatens us, we think no further but endeavour to annihilate it. When my life, or what may be essential to my life, requires the sacrifice of another, or even if some passion, wholly unconquerable, requires it, I should be a madman to hesitate. La Motte, I think I may confide in you—there are ways of doing certain things—you understand me. There are times, and circumstances, and opportunities—you comprehend my meaning."

"Explain yourself, my lord."

"Kind services that—in short there are services, which excite all our gratitude, and which we can never think repaid. It is in your power to place me in such a situation."

"Indeed! My lord, name the means."

"I have already named them. This abbey well suits the purpose; it is shut up from the eye of observation; any transaction may be concealed within its walls; the hour of midnight may witness the deed, and the morn shall not dawn to disclose it; these woods tell no tales. Ah! La Motte, am I right in trusting this business with you; may I believe you are desirous of serving me, and of preserving yourself?" The marquis paused, and looked steadfastly at La Motte, whose countenance was almost concealed by the gloom of evening.

"My lord, you may trust me in anything; explain yourself more fully."

"What security will you give me for your faithfulness?"

"My life, my lord; is it not already in your power?"

The marquis hesitated, and then said, "Tomorrow, about this time, I shall return to the abbey, and will then explain my meaning if, indeed, you shall not already have understood it. You, in the meantime, will consider your own powers of resolution, and be prepared either to adopt the purpose I shall suggest, or to declare you will not."

La Motte made some confused reply.

"Farewell till tomorrow," said the marquis, "remember that freedom and affluence are now before you." He moved toward the abbey and, mounting his horse, rode off with his attendants.

La Motte walked slowly home, musing on the late conversation.

CHAPTER 15

Danger, whose limbs of giant mould
What mortal eye can fix'd behold?
Who stalks his round, an hideous form,
Howling amidst the midnight storm,

. . . .

And with him thousand phantoms join'd,
Who prompt to deeds accurs'd the mind;

. . . .

On whom that rav'ning brood of Fate,
Who lap the blood of Sorrow, wait;
Who, Fear! this ghastly train can see,
And look not madly wild like thee!

William Collins, "Ode to Fear"

The marquis was punctual to the hour. La Motte received him at the gate, but he declined entering, and said he preferred a walk in the forest. Thither, therefore, La Motte attended him.

After some general conversation, the marquis said, "Well, have you considered what I said, and are you prepared to decide?"

"I have, my lord, and will quickly decide when you shall further explain yourself. Till then I can form no resolution."

The marquis appeared dissatisfied, and was a moment silent.

"Is it then possible," he at length resumed, "that you do not understand? This ignorance is surely affected. La Motte, I expect sincerity. Tell me, therefore, is it necessary I should say more?"

"It is, my lord," said La Motte immediately. "If you fear to confide in me freely, how can I fully accomplish your purpose?"

"Before I proceed further," said the marquis, "let me administer some oath which shall bind you to secrecy. But this is scarcely necessary; for, could I even doubt your word of honour, the remembrance of a certain transaction would point out to you the necessity of being as silent yourself as you must wish me to be."

There was now a pause of silence, during which both the marquis and La Motte betrayed some confusion.

"I think, La Motte," said he, "I have given you sufficient proof that I can be grateful; the services you have already rendered me with respect to Adeline have not been unrewarded."

"True, my lord, I am ever willing to acknowledge this, and am sorry it has not been in my power to serve you more effectually. Your further views respecting her I am ready to assist."

"I thank you. Adeline—" The marquis hesitated.

"Adeline," rejoined La Motte, eager to anticipate his wishes, "has beauty worthy of your pursuit. She has inspired a passion of which she ought to be proud, and at any rate, she shall soon be yours. Her charms are worthy of—"

"Yes, yes," interrupted the marquis, "but—" He paused.

"But they have given you too much trouble in the pursuit," said La Motte, "and to be sure, my lord, it must be confessed they have; but this trouble is all over—you may now consider her as your own."

"I would do so," said the marquis, fixing an eye of earnest regard upon La Motte. "I would do so."

"Name your hour, my lord; you shall not be interrupted. Beauty such as Adeline's—"

"Watch her closely," interrupted the marquis, "and on no account suffer her to leave her apartment. Where is she now?"

"Confined in her chamber."

"Very well. But I am impatient."

"Name your time, my lord—tomorrow night."

"Tomorrow night," said the marquis, "tomorrow night. Do you understand me now?"

"Yes, my lord, this night, if you wish it so. But had you not better dismiss your servants, and remain yourself in the forest. You know the door that opens upon the woods from the west tower. Come thither about twelve—I will be there to conduct you to her chamber. Remember, then, my lord, that tonight—"

"Adeline dies!" interrupted the marquis, in a low voice scarcely human. "Do you understand me now?"

La Motte shrunk aghast. "My lord!"

"La Motte!" said the marquis.

There was a silence of several minutes, in which La Motte endeavoured to recover himself. "Let me ask, my lord, the meaning of this?" said he, when he had breath to speak. "Why should you wish the death of Adeline—of Adeline whom so lately you loved?"

"Make no inquiries for my motive," said the marquis, "but it is as certain as that I live that she you name must die. This is sufficient."

The surprise of La Motte equalled his horror.

"The means are various," resumed the marquis. "I could have wished that no blood might be spilt; and there are drugs sure and speedy in their effect, but they cannot be soon or safely procured. I also wish it over—it must be done quickly—this night."

"This night, my lord!"

"Aye, this night, La Motte; if it is to be, why not soon? Have you no convenient drug at hand?"

"None, my lord."

"I feared to trust a third person, or I should have been provided," said the marquis. "As it is, take this poniard;[65] use it as occasion offers, but be resolute."

La Motte received the poniard with a trembling hand, and

_____

65. A slim dagger.

continued to gaze upon it for some time, scarcely knowing what he did.

"Put it up," said the marquis, "and endeavour to recollect yourself."

La Motte obeyed, but continued to muse in silence. He saw himself entangled in the web which his own crimes had woven. Being in the power of the marquis, he knew he must either consent to the commission of a deed, the enormity[66] of which, depraved as he was, he shrank from in horror, or sacrifice fortune, freedom, probably life itself, to the refusal. He had been led on by slow gradations from folly to vice till he now saw before him an abyss of guilt which startled even the conscience that so long had slumbered. The means of retreating were desperate—to proceed was equally so.

When he considered the innocence and the helplessness of Adeline, her orphan state, her former affectionate conduct, and her confidence in his protection, his heart melted with compassion for the distress he had already occasioned her, and shrank in terror from the deed he was urged to commit. But when, on the other hand, he contemplated the destruction that threatened him from the vengeance of the marquis, and then considered the advantages that were offered him of favour, freedom, and probably fortune, terror and temptation contributed to overcome the pleadings of humanity, and silence the voice of conscience. In this state of tumultuous uncertainty he continued for some time silent, until the voice of the marquis roused him to a conviction of the necessity of at least appearing to acquiesce in his designs.

"Do you hesitate?" said the marquis.

"No, my lord, my resolution is fixed—I will obey you. But methinks it would be better to avoid bloodshed. Strange secrets have been revealed by—"

"Aye, but how avoid it?" interrupted the marquis. "Poison I will not venture to procure. I have given you one sure instru-

66. Great wickedness.

ment of death. You also may find it dangerous to inquire for a drug."

La Motte perceived that he could not purchase poison without incurring a discovery much greater than that he wished to avoid. "You are right, my lord, and I will follow your orders implicitly."

The marquis now proceeded, in broken sentences, to give further directions concerning this dreadful scheme. "In her sleep," said he, "at midnight; the family will then be at rest."

Afterward they planned a story which was to account for her disappearance, and by which it was to seem that she had sought an escape in consequence of her aversion to the addresses of the marquis. The doors of her chamber and of the west tower were to be left open to corroborate this account, and many other circumstances were to be contrived to confirm the suspicion. They further consulted how the marquis was to be informed of the event; and it was agreed that he should come as usual to the abbey on the following day.

"Tonight, then," said the marquis. "I may rely upon your resolution."

"You may, my lord."

"Farewell, then. When we meet again—"

"When we meet again," said La Motte, "it will be done."

He followed the marquis to the abbey, and having seen him mount his horse and wished him a good night, he retired to his chamber, where he shut himself up.

Adeline, meanwhile, in the solitude of her prison, gave way to the despair which her condition inspired. She tried to arrange her thoughts, and to argue herself into some degree of resignation; but reflection, by representing the past, and reason, by anticipating the future, brought before her mind the full picture of her misfortunes, and she sank in despondency. Of Theodore, who by a conduct so noble had testified his attachment and involved himself in ruin, she thought with a degree of anguish infinitely superior to any she had felt upon any other occasion.

That the very exertions which had deserved all her gratitude, and awakened all her tenderness, should be the cause of his destruction was a circumstance so much beyond the ordinary bounds of misery that her fortitude sank at once before it. The idea of Theodore suffering—Theodore dying—was forever present in her imagination and, frequently excluding the sense of her own danger, made her conscious only of his. Sometimes the hope he had given her of being able to vindicate his conduct, or at least to obtain a pardon, would return; but it was like the faint beam of an April morn, transient and cheerless. She knew that the marquis, stung with jealousy and exasperated to revenge, would pursue him with unrelenting malice.

Against such an enemy, what could Theodore oppose? Conscious rectitude would not avail him to ward off the blow which disappointed passion and powerful pride directed. Her distress was considerably heightened by reflecting that no intelligence of him could reach her at the abbey, and that she must remain she knew not how long in the most dreadful suspense concerning his fate. From the abbey she saw no possibility of escaping. She was a prisoner in a chamber enclosed at every avenue: she had no opportunity of conversing with any person who could afford her even a chance of relief, and she saw herself condemned to await in passive silence the impending destiny, infinitely more dreadful to her imagination than death itself.

Thus circumstanced, she yielded to the pressure of her misfortunes, and would sit for hours motionless and given up to thought. "Theodore!" she would frequently exclaim, "you cannot hear my voice, you cannot fly to help me, yourself a prisoner and in chains." The picture was too horrid. The swelling anguish of her heart would subdue her utterance—tears bathed her cheeks—and she became insensible to everything but the misery of Theodore.

On this evening her mind had been remarkably tranquil; and as with a still and melancholy pleasure she watched from her window the setting sun, the fading splendour of the western horizon, and the gradual approach of twilight, her thoughts bore her back to the time when, in happier circumstances, she had watched the same appearances. She recollected also the evening of her temporary escape from the abbey, when from this same window she had viewed the declining sun—how anxiously she had awaited the fall of twilight—how much she had endeavoured to anticipate the events of her future life—with what trembling fear she had descended from the tower and ventured into the forest. These reflections produced others that filled her heart with anguish and her eyes with tears.

While she was lost in her melancholy reverie she saw the marquis mount his horse and depart from the gates. The sight of him revived, in all its force, a sense of the misery he inflicted on her beloved Theodore, and a consciousness of the evils which more immediately threatened herself. She withdrew from the window in an agony of tears. After a considerable time, her frame was quite exhausted, and she retired early to rest.

La Motte remained in his chamber till supper obliged him to descend. At table his wild and haggard countenance, which, in spite of all his endeavours, betrayed the disorder of his mind, and his long and frequent fits of abstraction surprised as well as alarmed Madame de la Motte. When Peter left the room she tenderly inquired what had disturbed him, and he with a distorted smile tried to be gay, but the effort was beyond his art and he quickly relapsed into silence. When Madame de la Motte spoke he strove to conceal the absence of his thoughts, but he answered so entirely from the purpose that his abstraction became still more apparent. Observing this, Madame de la Motte appeared to take no notice of his present temper; and they continued to sit in uninterrupted silence till the hour of rest, when they retired to their chamber.

La Motte lay in a state of disturbed watchfulness for some time, and his frequent starts awoke Madame, who, however, being pacified by some trifling excuse, soon went to sleep again. This agitation continued till near midnight when, recollecting that the time was now passing in idle reflection which ought to be devoted to action, he stole silently from his bed, wrapped himself in his nightgown, and, taking the lamp which burned nightly in his chamber, passed up the spiral staircase. As he went he frequently looked back and often started and listened to the hollow sighings of the blast.

His hand shook so violently when he attempted to unlock the door of Adeline's chamber that he was obliged to set the lamp on the ground and apply both his hands. The noise he made with the key induced him to suppose he must have awakened her; but when he opened the door and perceived the stillness that reigned within, he was convinced she was asleep. When he approached the bed he heard her gently breathe, and soon after sigh—and he stopped; but silence returning, he again advanced, and then heard her sing in her sleep. As he listened he distinguished some notes of a melancholy little air which, in her happier days, she had often sung to him. The low and mournful accent in which she now uttered them expressed too well the tone of her mind.

La Motte now stepped hastily toward the bed, when, breathing a deep sigh, she was again silent. He undrew the curtain, and saw her lying in a profound sleep, her cheek, wet with tears, resting upon her arm. He stood a moment looking at her; and as he viewed her innocent and lovely countenance, pale in grief, the light of the lamp shone strong upon her eyes, awaking her.

Perceiving a man, she uttered a scream. Her recollection returning, she knew him to be La Motte, and it instantly recurring to her that the marquis was at hand, she raised herself in bed, and implored pity and protection. La Motte stood looking eagerly at her, but without replying.

The wildness of his looks and the gloomy silence he preserved increased her alarm, and with tears of terror she renewed her supplication. "You once saved me from destruction," cried she. "O save me now! Have pity upon me—I have no protector but you."

"What is it you fear?" said La Motte in a tone scarcely articulate.

"O save me—save me from the marquis!"

"Rise then," said he, "and dress yourself quickly—I shall be back again in a few minutes." He lighted a candle that stood on the table, and left the chamber.

Adeline immediately arose and endeavoured to dress, but her thoughts were so bewildered that she scarcely knew what she did, and her whole frame was so violently agitated that it was with the utmost difficulty she preserved herself from fainting. She threw her clothes hastily on, and then sat down to await the return of La Motte. A considerable time elapsed, yet he did not appear, and having in vain endeavoured to compose her spirits, the pain of suspense at length became so insupportable that she opened the door of her chamber and went to the top of the staircase to listen. She thought she heard voices below, but considering that if the marquis was there her appearance could only increase her danger, she checked the step she had almost involuntarily taken to descend. Still she listened, and still thought she distinguished voices. Soon after she heard a door shut, and then footsteps, and she hastened back to her chamber.

Near a quarter of an hour elapsed and La Motte did not appear. Again she thought she heard a murmur of voices below, and also passing steps, and at length, her anxiety not suffering her to remain in her room, she moved through the passage that communicated with the spiral staircase; but all was now still. In a few moments, however, a light flashed across the hall, and La Motte appeared at the door of the vaulted room. He looked up and, seeing Adeline in the gallery, beckoned her to descend.

She hesitated and looked toward her chamber, but La Motte now approached the stairs. With faltering steps, she went to meet him. "I fear the marquis may see me," said she, whispering. "Where is he?"

La Motte took her hand and led her on, assuring her she had nothing to fear from the marquis. The wildness of his looks, however, and the trembling of his hand seemed to contradict this assurance, and she inquired whither he was leading her.

"To the forest," said La Motte, "that you may escape from the abbey—a horse waits for you without. I can save you by no other means."

New terror seized her. She could scarcely believe that La Motte, who had hitherto conspired with the marquis and had so closely confined her, should now himself undertake her escape, and she at this moment felt a dreadful presentiment, which it was impossible to account for, that he was leading her out to murder her in the forest. Again shrinking back, she supplicated his mercy. He assured her he meant only to protect her, and desired she would not waste time.

There was something in his manner that spoke sincerity, and she suffered him to conduct her to a side door that opened into the forest, where she could just distinguish through the gloom a man on horseback. This brought to her remembrance the night in which she had quitted the tomb, when trusting the person who appeared she had been carried to the marquis's villa. La Motte called, and was answered by Peter, whose voice somewhat reassured Adeline.

He then told her that the marquis would return to the abbey on the following morning, and that this could be her only opportunity of escaping his designs; that she might rely upon La Motte's word that Peter had orders to carry her wherever she chose. But as he knew the marquis would be indefatigable in search of her, he advised her by all means to leave the kingdom, which she might do with Peter, who was a native of Savoy, and would convey her to the house of his sister. There she might remain till La Motte himself, who did not now think it would be safe to continue much longer in France, should join her. He entreated her, whatever might happen, never to mention the events which had passed at the abbey.

"To save you, Adeline, I have risked my life; do not increase my danger and your own by any unnecessary discoveries. We may never meet again, but I hope you will be happy; and remember, when you think of me, that I am not quite so bad as I have been tempted to be."

Having said this, he gave her some money, which he told

her would be necessary to defray the expenses of her journey. Adeline could no longer doubt his sincerity, and her transports of joy and gratitude would scarcely permit her to thank him. She wished to have bid Madame de la Motte farewell, and indeed earnestly requested it; but he again told her she had no time to lose, and having wrapped her in a large cloak, he lifted her upon the horse. She bade him adieu with tears of gratitude, and Peter set off as fast as the darkness would permit.

When they had gone some way, he said, "I am glad with all my heart, mam'selle, to see you again. Who would have thought, after all, that my master himself would have bid me take you away! Well, to be sure, strange things come to pass, but I hope we shall have better luck this time."

Adeline, not choosing to reproach him with the treachery of which she feared he had been formerly guilty, thanked him for his good wishes, and said she hoped they should be more fortunate; but Peter, in his usual strain of eloquence, proceeded to undeceive her in this point, and to acquaint her with every circumstance which his memory, and it was naturally a strong one, could furnish.

Peter expressed such an artless interest in her welfare, and such a concern for her disappointment, that she could no longer doubt his faithfulness; and this conviction not only strengthened her confidence in the present undertaking but made her listen to his conversation with kindness and pleasure.

"I should never have stayed at the abbey till this time," said he, "if I could have got away, but my master frighted me so about the marquis, and I had not money enough to carry me into my own country, so that I was forced to stay. It's well we have got some solid louis d'ors now, for I question, mam'selle, whether the people on the road would have taken those trinkets you formerly talked of for money."

"Possibly not," said Adeline. "I am thankful to Monsieur La Motte that we have more certain means of procuring conveniences. What route shall you take when we leave the forest, Peter?"

Peter mentioned very correctly a great part of the road to

Lyon. "And then," said he, "we can easily get to Savoy, and that will be nothing. My sister—God bless her!—I hope is living; I have not seen her many a year; but if she is not, all the people will be glad to see me, and you will easily get a lodging, mam'selle, and everything you want."

Adeline resolved to go with him to Savoy. La Motte, who knew the character and designs of the marquis, had advised her to leave the kingdom and had told her what her fears would have suggested, that the marquis would be indefatigable in search of her. His motive for this advice must be a desire of serving her; why else, when she was already in his power, should he remove her to another place, and even furnish her with money for the expenses of a journey?

At Leloncourt, where Peter said he was well-known, she would be most likely to meet with protection and comfort, even should his sister be dead; and its distance and solitary situation were circumstances that pleased her. These reflections would have pointed out to her the prudence of proceeding to Savoy, had she been less destitute of resources in France; in her present situation they proved it to be necessary.

She inquired further concerning the route they were to take, and whether Peter was sufficiently acquainted with the road.

"When once I get to Thiers, I know it well enough," said Peter, "for I have gone it many a time in my younger days, and anybody will tell us the way there."

They traveled for several hours in darkness and silence, and it was not till they emerged from the forest that Adeline saw the morning light streak the eastern clouds. The sight cheered and revived her; and as she traveled silently along, her mind revolved the events of the past night and meditated plans for the future. The present kindness of La Motte appeared so very different from his former conduct that it astonished and perplexed her, and she could only account for it by attributing it to one of those sudden impulses of humanity which sometimes operate even upon the most depraved hearts.

But when she recollected his former words—"that he was not master of himself"—she could scarcely believe that mere pity could induce him to break the bonds which had hitherto so strongly held him, and then, considering the altered conduct of the marquis, she was inclined to think that she owed her liberty to some change in his sentiments toward her; yet the advice La Motte had given her to quit the kingdom, and the money with which he had supplied her for that purpose, seemed to contradict this opinion, and involved her again in doubt.

Peter now got directions to Thiers, which place they reached without any accident, and there stopped to refresh themselves. As soon as Peter thought the horse sufficiently rested, they again set forward, and from the rich plains of the Lyonnais[67] Adeline for the first time caught a view of the distant alps, whose majestic heads, seeming to prop the vault of heaven, filled her mind with sublime emotions.

In a few hours they reached the vale in which stands the city of Lyon, whose beautiful environs, studded with villas and rich with cultivation, withdrew Adeline from the melancholy contemplation of her own circumstances, and her more painful anxiety for Theodore.

When they reached that busy city, her first care was to inquire concerning the passage of the Rhône; but she forbore to make these inquiries of the people of the inn, considering that if the marquis should trace her thither they might enable him to pursue her route. She, therefore, sent Peter to the quays to hire a boat, while she herself took a slight repast, it being her intention to embark immediately. Peter presently returned, having engaged a boat and men to take them up the Rhône to the nearest part of Savoy, from whence they were to proceed by land to the village of Leloncourt.

Having taken some refreshment, she ordered him to conduct her to the vessel. A new and striking scene presented itself to Adeline, who looked with surprise upon the river gay with vessels and the quay crowded with busy faces, and felt the contrast which the cheerful objects around bore to herself—to

67. A former province of France.

her an orphan, desolate, helpless, and flying from persecution and her country. She spoke with the master of the boat, and having sent Peter back to the inn for the horse—La Motte's gift to Peter in lieu of some arrears of wages—they embarked.

As they slowly passed up the Rhône, whose steep banks, crowned with mountains, exhibited the most various, wild, and romantic scenery, Adeline sat in pensive reverie. The novelty of the scene through which she floated, now frowning with savage grandeur, and now smiling in fertility and gay with towns and villages, soothed her mind, and her sorrow gradually softened into a gentle and not unpleasing melancholy. She had seated herself at the head of the boat, where she watched its sides cleave the swift stream and listened to the dashing of the waters.

The boat, slowly opposing the current, passed along for some hours, and at length the veil of evening was stretched over the landscape. The weather was fine, and Adeline, regardless of the dews that now fell, remained in the open air observing the objects darken round her, the gay tints of the horizon fade away, and the stars gradually appear, trembling upon the lucid mirror of the waters. The scene was now sunk in deep shadow, and the silence of the hour was broken only by the measured dashing of the oars, and now and then by the voice of Peter speaking to the boatmen. Adeline sat lost in thought; the forlornness of her circumstances came heightened to her imagination.

She saw herself surrounded by the darkness and stillness of night, in a strange place far distant from any friends, going she scarcely knew whither under the guidance of strangers, and pursued perhaps by an inveterate[68] enemy. She pictured to herself the rage of the marquis now that he had discovered her flight, and though she knew it very unlikely he should follow her by water, for which reason she had chosen that manner of traveling, she trembled at the portrait her fancy drew. Her thoughts then wandered to the plan she should adopt after

68. Confirmed.

reaching Savoy; and much as her experience had prejudiced her against the manners of a convent, she saw no place more likely to afford her a proper asylum. At length she retired to the little cabin for a few hours' repose.

When Adeline left the abbey, La Motte had remained for some time at the gate, listening to the steps of the horse that carried her till the sound was lost in distance; he then turned into the hall with a lightness of heart to which he had long been a stranger. The satisfaction of having thus preserved her, as he hoped, from the designs of the marquis overcame for a while all sense of the danger in which this step must involve him. But when he returned entirely to his own situation, the terrors of the marquis's resentment struck their full force upon his mind, and he considered how he might best escape it.

It was now past midnight—the marquis was expected early on the following day; and in this interval it at first appeared probable to him that he might quit the forest. There was only one horse; but he considered whether it would be best to set off immediately for Auboine, where a carriage might be procured to convey his family and his moveables from the abbey, or quietly to await the arrival of the marquis, and endeavour to impose upon him by a forged story of Adeline's escape.

The time which must elapse before a carriage could reach the abbey would leave him scarcely sufficient time to escape from the forest; what money he had remaining from the marquis's bounty would not carry him far, and when it was expended he must probably be at a loss for subsistence, should he not before then be detected. By remaining at the abbey it would appear that he was unconscious of deserving the marquis's resentment, and though he could not expect to impress a belief upon him that his orders had been executed, he might make it appear that Peter only had been accessory to the escape of Adeline; an account which would seem the more probable from Peter's having been formerly detected in a similar scheme. He believed also that if the marquis should threaten to deliver him into the hands of justice, he might save himself by a menace of disclosing the crime he had commissioned him to perpetrate.

Thus arguing, La Motte resolved to remain at the abbey and await the event of the marquis's disappointment.

When the marquis did arrive and was informed of Adeline's flight, the strong workings of his soul which appeared on his countenance for a while alarmed and terrified La Motte. He cursed himself and her in terms of such coarseness and vehemence as La Motte was astonished to hear from a man whose manners were generally amiable, whatever might be the violence and criminality of his passions. To invent and express these terms seemed to give him not only relief, but delight; yet he appeared more shocked at the circumstance of her escape than exasperated at the carelessness of La Motte, and recollecting at length that he wasted time, he left the abbey and dispatched several of his servants in pursuit of her.

When he was gone, La Motte, believing his story had succeeded, returned to the pleasure of considering that he had done his duty, and to the hope that Adeline was now beyond the reach of pursuit. This calm was of short continuance. In a few hours the marquis returned, accompanied by the officers of justice. The affrighted La Motte, perceiving him approach, endeavoured to conceal himself but was seized and carried to the marquis, who drew him aside.

"I am not to be imposed upon," said he, "by such a superficial story as you have invented. You know your life is in my hands: tell me instantly where you have secreted Adeline, or I will charge you with the crime you have committed against me; but upon your disclosing the place of her concealment, I will dismiss the officers and, if you wish it, assist you to leave the kingdom. You have no time to hesitate, and may know that I will not be trifled with."

La Motte attempted to appease the marquis, and affirmed that Adeline was really fled he knew not whither. "You will remember, my lord, that your character is also in my power, and that if you proceed to extremities, you will compel me to reveal in the face of day that you would have made me a murderer."

"And who will believe you?" said the marquis. "The crimes that banished you from society will be no testimony of your veracity, and that with which I now charge you will bring with it a sufficient presumption that your accusation is malicious. Officers, do your duty."

They entered the room and seized La Motte, whom terror now deprived of all power of resistance, could resistance have availed him, and in the perturbation of his mind he informed the marquis that Adeline had taken the road to Lyon. This discovery, however, was made too late to serve himself; the marquis seized the advantage it offered, but the charge had been given, and with the anguish of knowing that he had exposed Adeline to danger without benefiting himself, La Motte submitted in silence to his fate. Scarcely allowing him time to collect what little effects might easily be carried with him, the officers conveyed him from the abbey; but the marquis, in consideration of the extreme distress of Madame de la Motte, directed one of his servants to procure a carriage from Auboine that she might follow her husband.

The marquis, in the meantime, now acquainted with the route Adeline had taken, sent forward his faithful valet to trace her to her place of concealment, and return immediately with intelligence to the villa.

Abandoned to despair, La Motte and his wife quitted the forest of Fontanville, which had for so many months afforded them an asylum, and embarked once more upon the tumultuous world where justice would meet La Motte in the form of destruction. They had entered the forest as a refuge, rendered necessary by the former crimes of La Motte, and for some time found in it the security they sought; but other offenses, for even in that sequestered spot there happened to be temptation, soon succeeded, and his life, already sufficiently marked by the punishment of vice, now afforded him another instance of this great truth, "That where guilt is, there peace cannot enter."[69]

69. Source not found.

CHAPTER 16

Hail, awful scenes, that calm the troubled breast,
And woo the weary to profound repose!

James Beattie, *The Minstrel*

Adeline and Peter proceeded on their voyage without any accident, and landed in Savoy, where Peter placed her upon the horse, and himself walked beside her. When he came within sight of his native mountains, his extravagant joy burst forth into frequent exclamations, and he would often ask Adeline if she had ever seen such hills in France.

"No, no," said he, "the hills there are very well for French hills, but they are not to be named on the same day with ours."

Adeline, lost in admiration of the astonishing and tremendous scenery around her, assented very warmly to the truth of Peter's assertion, which encouraged him to expatiate[70] more largely upon the advantages of his country; its disadvantages he totally forgot, and though he gave away his last sous to the children of the peasantry that run barefooted by the side of the horse, he spoke of nothing but the happiness and content of the inhabitants.

His native village, indeed, was an exception to the general character of the country, and to the usual effects of an

70. Speak at length.

arbitrary government; it was flourishing, healthy, and happy, and these advantages it chiefly owed to the activity and attention of the benevolent clergyman whose cure[71] it was.

Adeline, who now began to feel the effects of long anxiety and fatigue, much wished to arrive at the end of her journey, and inquired impatiently of Peter concerning it. Her spirits thus weakened, the gloomy grandeur of the scenes which had so lately awakened emotions of delightful sublimity now awed her into terror; she trembled at the sound of the torrents rolling among the clefts[72] and thundering in the vale below, and shrank from the view of the precipices which sometimes overhung the road, and at others appeared beneath it. Fatigued as she was, she frequently dismounted to climb on foot the steep flinty road, which she feared to travel on horseback.

The day was closing when they drew near a small village at the foot of the Savoy Alps, and the sun in all its evening splendour, now sinking behind their summits, threw a farewell gleam athwart the landscape, so soft and glowing as drew from Adeline, languid as she was, an exclamation of rapture.

The romantic situation of the village next attracted her notice. It stood at the foot of several stupendous mountains, which at some little distance formed a chain round a lake, and the woods that swept from their summits almost embosomed the village. The lake, unruffled by the lightest air, reflected the vermeil[73] tints of the horizon with the sublime scenery on its borders, darkening every instant with the falling twilight.

When Peter perceived the village, he burst into a shout of joy. "Thank God," said he, "we are near home; there is my dear native place. It looks just as it did twenty years ago; and there are the same old trees growing round our cottage yonder, and the huge rock that rises above it. My poor father died there, mam'selle. Pray Heaven my sister be alive; it is a long while since I saw her."

71. Pastoral charge.
72. Fissures.
73. Vivid reddish orange.

Adeline listened with a melancholy pleasure to these artless expressions of Peter, who in retracing the scenes of his former days seemed to live them over again.

As they approached the village, he continued to point out various objects of his remembrance. "And there too is the good pastor's château; look, mam'selle, that white house, with the smoke curling, that stands on the edge of the lake yonder. I wonder whether he is alive yet. He was not old when I left the place, and as much beloved as ever man was; but death spares nobody!"

They had by this time reached the village, which was extremely neat, though it did not promise much accommodation. Peter had hardly advanced ten steps before he was accosted by some of his old acquaintance, who shook hands, and seemed not to know how to part with him. He inquired for his sister, and was told she was alive and well. As they passed on, so many of his old friends flocked round him that Adeline became quite weary of the delay. Many whom he had left in the vigour of life were now tottering under the infirmities of age, while their sons and daughters, whom he had known only in the playfulness of infancy, were grown from his remembrance, and in the pride of youth. At length they approached the cottage and were met by his sister, who, having heard of his arrival, came and welcomed him with unfeigned joy.

On seeing Adeline, she seemed surprised but assisted her to alight and, conducting her into a small but neat cottage, received her with a warmth of ready kindness which would have graced a better situation. Adeline desired to speak with her alone, for the room was now crowded with Peter's friends, and then acquainting her with such particulars of her circumstances as it was necessary to communicate, desired to know if she could be accommodated with lodging in the cottage.

"Yes, mam'selle," said the good woman, "such as it is, you are heartily welcome. I am only sorry it is not better. But you seem ill, mam'selle; what shall I get you?"

Adeline, who had been long struggling with fatigue and indisposition, now yielded to their pressure. She said she was, indeed, ill; but hoped that rest would restore her, and desired a bed might be immediately prepared. The good woman went out to obey her, and soon returning, showed her to a little cabin, where she retired to a bed whose cleanliness was its only recommendation.

But, notwithstanding her fatigue, she could not sleep, and her mind, in spite of all her efforts, returned to the scenes that were past or presented gloomy and imperfect visions of the future.

The difference between her own condition and that of other persons educated as she had been struck her forcibly, and she wept. *They,* thought she, *have friends and relations, all striving to save them not only from what may hurt but what may displease them; watching not only for their present safety, but for their future advantage, and preventing them even from injuring themselves. But during my whole life I have never known a friend; have been in general surrounded by enemies, and very seldom exempt from some circumstance either of danger or calamity. Yet surely I am not born to be forever wretched; the time will come when—* She began to think she might one time be happy, but recollecting the desperate situation of Theodore, she thought, *No, I can never hope even for peace!*

Early the following morning the good woman of the house came to inquire how she had rested, and found she had slept little, and was much worse than on the preceding night. The uneasiness of her mind contributed to heighten the feverish symptoms that attended her, and in the course of the day her disorder began to assume a serious aspect. She observed its progress with composure, resigning herself to the will of God, and feeling little to regret in life. Her kind hostess did everything in her power to relieve her, and as there was neither physician nor apothecary in the village, nature was deprived of none of her advantages. Notwithstanding this, the disorder rapidly increased, and on the third day from its first attack she became delirious; after which she sank into a state of stupefaction.

How long she remained in this deplorable condition she knew not; but on recovering her senses she found herself in an apartment very different from any she remembered. It was spacious and almost beautiful, the bed and everything around being in one style of elegant simplicity. For some minutes she lay in a trance of surprise, endeavouring to recollect her scattered ideas of the past, and almost fearing to move, lest the pleasing vision should vanish from her eyes.

At length she ventured to raise herself, when she presently heard a soft voice speaking near her, and the bed curtain on one side was gently undrawn by a beautiful girl. As she leaned forward over the bed and with a smile of mingled tenderness and joy inquired of her patient how she did, Adeline gazed in silent admiration upon the most interesting female countenance she had ever seen, in which the expression of sweetness, united with lively sense and refinement, was chastened by simplicity.

Adeline at length recollected herself sufficiently to thank her kind inquirer, and begged to know to whom she was obliged and where she was.

The lovely girl pressed her hand. "'Tis we who are obliged," said she. "Oh! how I rejoice to find that you have recovered your recollection."

She said no more, but flew to the door of the apartment and disappeared. In a few minutes she returned with an elderly lady who, approaching the bed with an air of tender interest, asked concerning the state of Adeline, to which the latter replied as well as the agitation of her spirits would permit, and repeated her desire of knowing to whom she was so greatly obliged.

"You shall know that hereafter," said the lady. "At present be assured that you are with those who will think their care much overpaid by your recovery; submit, therefore, to everything that may conduce to it, and consent to be kept as quiet as possible."

Adeline gratefully smiled, and bowed her head in silent assent. The lady now quitted the room for a medicine; having given which to Adeline, the curtain was closed, and she was left to repose. But her thoughts were too busy to suffer her to profit by the opportunity. She contemplated the past and viewed the present, and when she compared them, the contrast struck her with astonishment. The whole appeared like one of those sudden transitions so frequent in dreams, in which we pass from grief and despair, we know not how, to comfort and delight.

Yet she looked forward to the future with a trembling anxiety that threatened to retard her recovery, and which, when she remembered the words of her generous benefactress, she endeavoured to suppress. Had she better known the disposition of the persons in whose house she now was, her anxiety, as far as it regarded herself must in a great measure have been done away; for La Luc, its owner, was one of those rare characters to whom misfortune seldom looks in vain, and whose native goodness, confirmed by principle, is uniform and unassuming in its acts. The following little picture of his domestic life, his family and his manners, will more fully illustrate his character. It was drawn from the life, and its exactness will, it is hoped, compensate for its length.

The Family of La Luc

But half mankind, like Handel's fool, destroy,
Through rage and ignorance, the strain of joy;
Irregularly wild their passions roll
Through Nature's finest instrument, the soul:
While men of sense, with Handel's happier skill,
Correct the taste, and harmonize the will;
Teach their affections, like his notes, to flow,
Nor rais'd too high, nor ever sunk too low;
Till ev'ry virtue, measur'd and refin'd,
As fits the concert of the master-mind,
Melts in its kindred sounds, and pours along
Th' according music of the moral song.

James Cawthorn, "Life Unhappy"

In the village of Leloncourt, celebrated for its picturesque situation at the foot of the Savoy Alps, lived Arnaud La Luc, a clergyman, descended from an ancient family of France, whose decayed fortunes occasioned them to seek a retreat in Switzerland in an age when the violence of civil commotion seldom spared the conquered. He was minister of the village, and equally loved for the piety and benevolence of the Christian as respected for the dignity and elevation of the philosopher. His was the philosophy of nature, directed by common sense. He despised the jargon of the modern schools and the brilliant absurdities of systems which have dazzled without enlightening, and guided without convincing, their disciples.

His mind was penetrating; his views extensive; and his systems, like his religion, were simple, rational, and sublime. The people of his parish looked up to him as to a father; for while his precepts directed their minds, his example touched their hearts.

In early youth La Luc lost a wife whom he tenderly loved. This event threw a tincture of soft and interesting melancholy over his character, which remained when time had mellowed the remembrance that occasioned it. Philosophy had strengthened, not hardened, his heart; it enabled him to resist the pressure of affliction, rather than to overcome it.

Calamity taught him to feel with peculiar sympathy the distresses of others. His income from the parish was small, and what remained from the divided and reduced estates of his ancestors did not much increase it; but though he could not always relieve the necessities of the indigent, his tender pity and holy conversation seldom failed in administering consolation to the mental sufferer. On these occasions the sweet and exquisite emotions of his heart have often induced him to say that could the voluptuary[74] be once sensible of these feelings, he would never after forego "the luxury of doing good."

"Ignorance of true pleasure," he would say, "more frequently than temptation to that which is false, leads to vice."

La Luc had one son and a daughter, who were too young when their mother died to lament their loss. He loved them with peculiar tenderness, as the children of her whom he never

74. Person whose primary interest is sensory pleasure.

ceased to deplore;[75] and it was for some time his sole amusement to observe the gradual unfolding of their infant minds, and to bend them to virtue. His was the deep and silent sorrow of the heart; his complaints he never obtruded upon others, and very seldom did he even mention his wife. His grief was too sacred for the eye of the vulgar. Often he retired to the deep solitude of the mountains, and amid their solemn and tremendous scenery would brood over the remembrance of times past, and resign himself to the luxury of grief. On his return from these little excursions he was always more placid and contented. A sweet tranquillity, which arose almost to happiness, was diffused over his mind, and his manners were more than usually benevolent. As he gazed on his children, and fondly kissed them, a tear would sometimes steal into his eye, but it was a tear of tender regret, unmingled with the darker qualities of sorrow, and was most precious to his heart.

On the death of his wife he received into his house a maiden sister, a sensible, worthy woman, who was deeply interested in the happiness of her brother. Her affectionate attention and judicious conduct anticipated the effect of time in softening the poignancy of his distress, and her unremitted care of his children, while it proved the goodness of her own heart, attracted her more closely to his.

It was with inexpressible pleasure that he traced in the infant features of Clara the resemblance of her mother. The same gentleness of manner and the same sweetness of disposition soon displayed themselves, and as she grew up her actions frequently reminded him so strongly of his lost wife as to fix him in reveries which absorbed all his soul.

Engaged in the duties of his parish, the education of his children, and in philosophic research, his years passed in tranquillity. The tender melancholy with which affliction had tinctured his mind was, by long indulgence, become dear to him, and he would not have relinquished it for the brightest dream of airy happiness. When any passing incident disturbed him,

75. Feel grief for.

he retired for consolation to the idea of her he so faithfully loved, and yielding to a gentle, and what the world would call a romantic, sadness, gradually reassumed his composure. This was the secret luxury to which he withdrew from temporary disappointment—the solitary enjoyment which dissipated the cloud of care, and blunted the sting of vexation—which elevated his mind above this world, and opened to his view the sublimity of another.

The spot he now inhabited, the surrounding scenery, the romantic beauties of the neighbouring walks, were dear to La Luc, for they had once been loved by Clara; they had been the scenes of her tenderness, and of his happiness.

His château stood on the border of a small lake that was almost environed by mountains of stupendous height, which, shooting into a variety of grotesque forms, composed a scenery singularly solemn and sublime. Dark woods intermingled with bold projections of rock, sometimes barren, and sometimes covered with the purple bloom of wildflowers, impended[76] over the lake, and were seen in the clear mirror of its waters. The wild and alpine heights which rose above were either crowned with perpetual snows, or exhibited tremendous crags and masses of solid rock, whose appearance was continually changing as the rays of light were variously reflected on their surface, and whose summits were often wrapt in impenetrable mists. Some cottages and hamlets, scattered on the margin of the lake or seated in picturesque points of view on the rocks above, were the only objects that reminded the beholder of humanity.

On the side of the lake, nearly opposite to the château, the mountains receded, and a long chain of alps was seen stretching in perspective. Their innumerable tints and shades, some veiled in blue mists, some tinged with rich purple, and others glittering in partial light, gave luxurious and magical colouring to the scene.

The château was not large, but it was convenient,[77] and was

76. Hanging suspended or hovering threateningly.
77. Comfortable.

characterized by an air of elegant simplicity and good order. The entrance was a small hall which, opening by a glass door into the garden, afforded a view of the lake with the magnificent scenery exhibited on its borders. On the left of the hall was La Luc's study, where he usually passed his mornings, and adjoining was a small room fitted up with chemical apparatus, astronomical instruments, and other implements of science. On the right was the family parlour, and behind it a room which belonged exclusively to his sister, Madame La Luc. Here were deposited various medicines and botanical distillations, together with the apparatus for preparing them. From this room the whole village was liberally supplied with physical comfort; for it was the pride of Madame to believe herself skilful in relieving the disorders of her neighbours.

Behind the château rose a tuft of pines, and in front a gentle declivity[78] covered with verdure and flowers extended to the lake, whose waters flowed even with the grass, and gave freshness to the acacias that waved over its surface. Flowering shrubs, intermingled with mountain ash, cypress, and evergreen oak, marked the boundary of the garden.

At the return of spring it was his daughter Clara's care to direct the young shoots of the plants, to nurse the budding flowers, and to shelter them with the luxuriant branches of the shrubs from the cold blasts that descended from the mountains. In summer she usually rose with the sun, and visited her favourite flowers while the dew yet hung glittering on their leaves. The freshness of early day, with the glowing colouring which then touched the scenery, gave a pure and exquisite delight to her innocent heart. Born amid scenes of grandeur and sublimity, she had quickly imbibed a taste for their charms, which taste was heightened by the influence of a warm imagination. To view the sun rising above the alps, tingeing their snowy heads with light, and suddenly darting its rays over the whole face of nature—to see the fiery splendour of the clouds reflected in the lake below, and the roseate tints first steal upon

78. Descending slope.

the rocks above—were among the earliest pleasures of which Clara was susceptible. From being delighted with the observance of nature, she grew pleased with seeing it finely imitated, and soon displayed a taste for poetry and painting. When she was about sixteen she often selected from her father's library those of the Italian poets most celebrated for picturesque beauty, and would spend the first hours of morning in reading them under the shade of the acacias that bordered the lake. Here too she would often attempt rude sketches of the surrounding scenery, and at length by repeated efforts, assisted by some instruction from her brother, she succeeded so well as to produce twelve drawings in crayon which were judged worthy of decorating the parlour of the château.

Young La Luc played the flute, and she listened to him with exquisite delight, particularly when he stood on the margin of the lake under her beloved acacias. Her voice was sweet and flexible, though not strong, and she soon learned to modulate it to the instrument. She knew nothing of the intricacies of execution; her airs were simple, and her style equally so, but she soon gave them a touching expression, inspired by the sensibility of her heart, which seldom left those of her hearers unaffected.

It was the happiness of La Luc to see his children happy, and in one of his excursions to Geneva, whither he went to visit some relations of his late wife, he bought Clara a lute. She received it with more gratitude than she could express; and having learned one air, she hastened to her favourite acacias, and played it again and again till she forgot everything besides. Her little domestic duties, her books, her drawing, even the hour which her father dedicated to her improvement, when she met her brother in the library and with him partook of knowledge, even this hour passed unheeded by. La Luc suffered it to pass. Madame was displeased that her niece neglected her domestic duties, and wished to reprove her, but La Luc begged she would be silent. "Let experience teach her her error," said he. "Precept seldom brings conviction to young minds."

Madame objected that experience was a slow teacher.

"It is a sure one," replied La Luc, "and is not infrequently the quickest of all teachers. When it cannot lead us into serious evil, it is well to trust to it."

The second day with Clara passed as the first, and the third as the second. She could now play several tunes; she came to her father and repeated what she had learnt.

At supper the cream was not dressed, and there was no fruit on the table. La Luc inquired the reason; Clara recollected it, and blushed. She observed that her brother was absent, but nothing was said. Toward the conclusion of the repast he appeared; his countenance expressed unusual satisfaction, but he seated himself in silence. Clara inquired what had detained him from supper, and learnt that he had been to a sick family in the neighbourhood with the weekly allowance which her father gave them. La Luc had entrusted the care of this family to his daughter, and it was her duty to have carried them their little allowance on the preceding day, but she had forgot everything but music.

"How did you find the woman?" said La Luc to his son.

"Worse, sir," he replied, "for her medicines had not been regularly given, and the children had had little or no food today."

Clara was shocked. *No food today!* said she to herself, *and I have been playing all day on my lute, under the acacias by the lake!*

Her father did not seem to observe her emotion, but turned to his son.

"I left her better," said the latter. "The medicines I carried eased her pain, and I had the pleasure to see her children make a joyful supper."

Clara, perhaps for the first time in her life, envied him his pleasure; her heart was full, and she sat silent. *No food today!* thought she.

She retired pensively to her chamber. The sweet serenity with which she usually went to rest was vanished, for she could no longer reflect on the past day with satisfaction.

What a pity, thought she, *that what is so pleasing should be the cause of so much pain! This lute is my delight, and my torment!* This reflection occasioned her much internal debate; but before she could come to any resolution upon the point in question, she fell asleep.

She awoke very early the next morning, and impatiently watched the progress of the dawn. The sun at length appearing, she arose and, determined to make all the atonement in her power for her former neglect, hastened to the cottage. Here she remained a considerable time, and when she returned to the château her countenance had recovered all its usual serenity. She resolved, however, not to touch her lute that day.

Till the hour of breakfast she busied herself in binding up the flowers and pruning the shoots that were too luxuriant, and she at length found herself, she scarcely knew how, beneath her beloved acacias by the side of the lake. *Ah!* thought she, with a sigh, *how sweetly would the song I learned yesterday sound now over the waters!* But she remembered her determination, and checked the step she was involuntarily taking toward the château.

She attended her father in the library at the usual hour, and learned, from his discourse with her brother on what had been read the two preceding days, that she had lost much entertaining knowledge. She requested her father would inform her to what this conversation alluded, but he calmly replied that she had preferred another amusement at the time when the subject was discussed, and must therefore content herself with ignorance.

"You would reap the rewards of study from the amusements of idleness," said he. "Learn to be reasonable—do not expect to unite inconsistencies."

Clara felt the justness of this rebuke, and remembered her lute. "What mischief has it occasioned!" sighed she. "Yes, I am determined not to touch it at all this day. I will prove that I am able to control my inclinations when I see it is necessary so to do." Thus resolving, she applied herself to study with more than usual assiduity.

She adhered to her resolution, and toward the close of day went into the garden to amuse herself. The evening was still and uncommonly beautiful. Nothing was heard but the faint shivering of the leaves, which returned but at intervals, making silence more solemn, and the distant murmurs of the torrents that rolled among the cliffs. As she stood by the lake, and watched the sun slowly sinking below the alps, whose summits were tinged with gold and purple; as she saw the last rays of light gleam upon the waters whose surface was not curled by the lightest air, she sighed. *Oh! how enchanting would be the sound of my lute at this moment, on this spot, and when everything is so still around me!*

The temptation was too powerful for the resolution of Clara; she ran to the château, returned with the instrument to her dear acacias, and beneath their shade continued to play till the surrounding objects faded in darkness from her sight. But the moon arose and, shedding a trembling lustre on the lake, made the scene more captivating than ever.

It was impossible to quit so delightful a spot; Clara repeated her favourite airs again and again. The beauty of the hour awakened all her genius; she never played with such expression before, and she listened with increasing rapture to the tones as they languished over the waters and died away on the distant air. She was perfectly enchanted. *No! nothing was ever so delightful as to play on the lute beneath her acacias, on the margin of the lake, by moonlight!*

When she returned to the château, supper was over. La Luc had observed Clara, and would not suffer her to be interrupted.

When the enthusiasm of the hour was past, she recollected that she had broken her resolution, and the reflection gave her pain. "I prided myself on controlling my inclinations," said she aloud to herself, "and I have weakly yielded to their direction. But what evil have I incurred by indulging them this evening? I have neglected no duty, for I had none to perform. Of what then have I to accuse myself? It would have been absurd to have kept my resolution, and denied myself a pleasure when there appeared no reason for this self-denial."

She paused, not quite satisfied with this reasoning. Suddenly resuming her enquiry, she said, "But how am I certain that I should have resisted my inclinations if there had been a reason for opposing them? If the poor family whom I neglected yesterday had been unsupplied today, I fear I should again have forgotten them while I played on my lute on the banks of the lake."

She then recollected all that her father had at different times said on the subject of self-command, and she felt some pain.

"No," said she, "if I do not consider that to preserve a resolution which I have once solemnly formed is a sufficient reason to control my inclinations, I fear no other motive would long restrain me. I seriously determined not to touch my lute this whole day, and I have broken my resolution. Tomorrow perhaps I may be tempted to neglect some duty, for I have discovered that I cannot rely on my own prudence. Since I cannot conquer temptation, I will fly from it."

On the following morning she brought her lute to La Luc, and begged he would receive it again, and at least keep it till she had taught her inclinations to submit to control.

The heart of La Luc swelled as she spoke. "No, Clara," said he, "it is unnecessary that I should receive your lute; the sacrifice you would make proves you worthy of my confidence. Take back the instrument; since you have sufficient resolution to resign it when it leads you from duty, I doubt not that you will be able to control its influence now that it is restored to you."

Clara felt a degree of pleasure and pride at these words, such as she had never before experienced; but she thought that to deserve the commendation they bestowed, it was necessary to complete the sacrifice she had begun. In the virtuous enthusiasm of the moment the delights of music were forgotten in those of aspiring to well-earned praise, and when she refused the lute thus offered, she was conscious only of exquisite sensations. "Dear sir," said she, tears of pleasure swelling in her eyes, "allow me to deserve the praises you bestow, and then I shall indeed be happy."

La Luc thought she had never resembled her mother so much as at this instant, and tenderly kissing her, he for some moments wept in silence. When he was able to speak, he said, "You do already deserve my praises, and I restore your lute as a reward for the conduct which excites them." This scene called back recollections too tender for the heart of La Luc, and giving Clara the instrument, he abruptly quitted the room.

La Luc's son, a youth of much promise, was designed by his father for the church, and had received from him an excellent education. However, it was thought necessary he should finish at an university. That of Geneva was fixed upon by La Luc. His scheme had been to make his son not a scholar only; he was ambitious that he should also be enviable as a man. From early infancy he had accustomed him to hardihood and endurance, and as he advanced in youth, he encouraged him in manly exercises, and acquainted him with the useful arts as well as with abstract science.

He was high-spirited and ardent in his temper, but his heart was generous and affectionate. He looked forward to Geneva, and to the new world it would disclose, with the sanguine expectations of youth; and in the delight of these expectations was absorbed the regret he would otherwise have felt at a separation from his family.

A brother of the late Madame La Luc, who was by birth an English woman, resided at Geneva with his family. To have been related to his wife was a sufficient claim upon the heart of La Luc, and he had, therefore, always kept up an intercourse with Mr. Audley, though the difference in their characters and manner of thinking would never permit this association to advance into friendship. La Luc now wrote to him, signifying an intention of sending his son to Geneva, and recommending him to his care; to this letter Mr. Audley returned a friendly answer. When a short time after an acquaintance of La Luc's was called to Geneva, he determined that his son should accompany him. The separation was painful to La Luc, and almost insupportable to Clara. Madame was grieved, and took care that he should have a sufficient quantity of medicines put up in his traveling trunk; she was also at some pains to point out their virtues and the different complaints for which they were requisite, but she was careful to deliver her lecture during the absence of her brother.

La Luc, with his daughter, accompanied his son on horseback to the next town, which was about eight miles from Leloncourt, and there again enforcing all the advice he had formerly given him respecting his conduct and pursuits, and again yielding to the tender weakness of the father, he bade him farewell. Clara wept, and felt more sorrow at this parting than the occasion could justify; but this was almost the first time she had known grief, and she artlessly yielded to its influence.

La Luc and Clara traveled pensively back, and the day was closing when they came within view of the lake, and soon after of the château. Never had it appeared gloomy till now; but now Clara wandered forlornly through every deserted apartment where she had been accustomed to see her brother, and recollected a thousand little circumstances which, had he been present, she would have thought immaterial, but on which imagination now stamped a value. The garden, the scenes around, all wore a melancholy aspect, and it was long ere they resumed their natural character and Clara recovered her vivacity.

Near four years had elapsed since this separation when one evening, as Madame La Luc and her niece were sitting at work together in the parlour, a good woman in the neighbourhood desired to be admitted. She came to ask for some medicines, and the advice of Madame La Luc.

"Here is a sad accident happened at our house, Madame," said she. "I am sure my heart aches for the poor young creature."

Madame La Luc desired she would explain herself, and the woman proceeded to say that her brother Peter, whom she had not seen for so many years, was arrived, and had brought a young lady to her cottage, who she verily believed was dying. She described her disorder, and acquainted Madame with what particulars of her mournful story Peter had related, failing not to exaggerate such as her compassion for the unhappy stranger and her love of the marvellous prompted.

The account appeared a very extraordinary one to Madame;

but pity for the forlorn condition of the young sufferer induced her to inquire further into the affair.

"Do let me go to her, madam," said Clara, who had been listening with ready compassion to the poor woman's narrative. "Do suffer me to go—she must want comforts, and I wish much to see how she is."

Madame asked some further questions concerning her disorder, and then, taking off her spectacles, she rose from her chair and said she would go herself. Clara desired to accompany her. They put on their hats and followed the good woman to the cottage, where, in a very small, close room, on a miserable bed, lay Adeline, pale, emaciated, and unconscious of all around her.

Madame turned to the woman, and asked how long she had been in this way, while Clara went up to the bed, and taking the almost lifeless hand that lay on the quilt, looked anxiously in her face. "She observes nothing," said she, "poor creature! I wish she was at the château; she would be better accommodated, and I could nurse her there."

The woman told Madame La Luc that the young lady had lain in that state for several hours.

Madame examined her pulse, and shook her head. "This room is very close," said she.

"Very close indeed," cried Clara eagerly. "Surely she would be better at the château, if she could be moved."

"We will see about that," said her aunt. "In the meantime let me speak to Peter; it is some years since I saw him."

She went to the outer room, followed by Clara, and the woman ran out of the cottage to look for him. When she was gone, Clara said, "This is a miserable habitation for the poor stranger; she will never be well here. Do, madam, let her be carried to our house; I am sure my father would wish it. Besides, there is something in her features, even inanimate as they now are, that prejudices me in her favour."

"Shall I never persuade you to give up that romantic notion of judging people by their faces?" said her aunt. "What sort of a face she has is of very little consequence—her condition is lamentable, and I am desirous of altering it; but I wish first to ask Peter a few questions concerning her."

"Thank you, my dear aunt," said Clara; "she will be removed then."

Madame La Luc was going to reply; but Peter now entered and, expressing great joy at seeing her again, inquired how Monsieur La Luc and Clara did. Clara immediately welcomed honest Peter to his native place, and he returned her salutation with many expressions of surprise at finding her so much grown. "Though I have so often dandled you in my arms, mam'selle, I should never have known you again. Young twigs shoot fast, as they say."

Madame La Luc now inquired into the particulars of Adeline's story, and heard as much as Peter knew of it, being only that his late master found her in a very distressed situation, and that he had himself brought her from the abbey to save her from a French marquis. The simplicity of Peter's manner would not suffer her to question his veracity, though some of the circumstances he related excited all her surprise, and awakened all her pity.

Tears frequently stood in Clara's eyes during the course of his narrative, and when he concluded, she said, "Dear madam, I am sure when my father learns the history of this unhappy young woman he will not refuse to be a parent to her, and I will be her sister."

"She deserves it all," said Peter, "for she is very good indeed." He then proceeded in a strain of praise which was very unusual with him.

"I will go home and consult with my brother about her," said Madame La Luc, rising. "She certainly ought to be removed to a more airy room. The château is so near that I think she may be carried thither without much risk."

"Heaven bless you! madam," cried Peter, rubbing his hands, "for your goodness to my poor young lady."

La Luc had just returned from his evening walk when they reached the château. Madame told him where she had been, and related the history of Adeline and her present condition.

"By all means have her removed hither," said La Luc, whose eyes bore testimony to the tenderness of his heart. "She can be better attended to here than in Susan's cottage." "I knew you would say so, my dear father," said Clara. "I will go and order the green bed to be prepared for her." "Be patient, niece," said Madame La Luc. "There is no occasion for such haste; some things are to be considered first—but you are young and romantic."

La Luc smiled.

"The evening is now closed," resumed Madame. "It will, therefore, be dangerous to remove her before morning. Early tomorrow a room shall be got ready, and she shall be brought here; in the meantime I will go and make up a medicine, which I hope may be of service to her."

Clara reluctantly assented to this delay, and Madame La Luc retired to her closet.

On the following morning Adeline, wrapped in blankets, and sheltered as much as possible from the air, was brought to the château, where the good La Luc desired she might have every attention paid her, and where Clara watched over her with unceasing anxiety and tenderness. She remained in a state of torpor during the greater part of the day, but toward evening she breathed more freely; and Clara, who still watched by her bed, had at length the pleasure of perceiving that her senses were restored. It was at this moment that she found herself in the situation from which we have digressed to give this account of the venerable La Luc and his family. The reader will find that his virtues and his friendship to Adeline deserved this notice.

CHAPTER 17

Still Fancy, to herself unkind,
Awakes to grief the soften'd mind,
And points the bleeding friend.

William Collins, "Ode to a Lady"

Adeline, assisted by a fine constitution, and the kind attentions of her new friends, was in a little more than a week so much recovered as to leave her chamber. She was introduced to La Luc, whom she met with tears of gratitude, and thanked for his goodness in a manner so warm, yet so artless, as interested him still more in her favour. During the progress of her recovery, the sweetness of her behaviour had entirely won the heart of Clara, and greatly interested that of her aunt, whose reports of Adeline, together with the praises bestowed by Clara, had excited both esteem and curiosity in the breast of La Luc; and he now met her with an expression of benignity which spoke peace and comfort to her heart.

She had acquainted Madame La Luc with such particulars of her story as Peter, either through ignorance or inattention, had not communicated, suppressing only, through a false delicacy perhaps, an acknowledgement of her attachment to Theodore. These circumstances were repeated to La Luc, who, ever sensible to the sufferings of others, was particularly interested by the singular misfortunes of Adeline.

Near a fortnight had elapsed since her removal to the château, when one morning La Luc desired to speak with her alone. She followed him into his study, and then in a manner the most delicate he told her that, as he found she was so unfortunate in her father, he desired she would henceforth consider him as her parent, and his house as her home.

"You and Clara shall be equally my daughters," continued he. "I am rich in having such children."

The strong emotions of surprise and gratitude for some time kept Adeline silent.

"Do not thank me," said La Luc. "I know all you would say, and I know also that I am but doing my duty. I thank God that my duty and my pleasures are generally in unison."

Adeline wiped away the tears which his goodness had excited, and was going to speak; but La Luc pressed her hand and, turning away to conceal his emotion, walked out of the room.

Adeline was now considered as a part of the family, and in the parental kindness of La Luc, the sisterly affection of Clara, and the steady and uniform regard of Madame, she would have been happy as she was thankful, had not unceasing anxiety for the fate of Theodore, of whom in this solitude she was less likely than ever to hear, corroded her heart and embittered every moment of reflection. Even when sleep obliterated for a while the memory of the past, his image frequently arose to her fancy, accompanied by all the exaggerations of terror. She saw him in chains and struggling in the grasp of ruffians, or saw him led, amidst the dreadful preparations for execution, into the field; she saw the agony of his look, and heard him repeat her name in frantic accents, till the horrors of the scene overcame her, and she awoke.

A similarity of taste and character attached her to Clara, yet the misery that preyed upon her heart was of a nature too delicate to be spoken of, and she never mentioned Theodore even to her friend. Her illness had yet left her weak and languid, and the perpetual anxiety of her mind contributed to prolong this state. She endeavoured, by strong and almost continual efforts, to abstract her thoughts from their mournful subject, and was often successful. She found a melancholy pleasure in listening to the soft tones of Clara's lute, and would often soothe her mind by attempting to repeat the airs she heard. La Luc had an excellent library, and the instruction it offered at once gratified her love of knowledge, and withdrew her mind from painful recollections. His conversation too afforded her another refuge from misery.

But her chief amusement was to wander among the sublime scenery of the adjacent country, sometimes with Clara, though often with no other companion than a book. There were indeed times when the conversation of her friend imposed a painful restraint, and when given up to reflection, she would ramble alone through scenes whose solitary grandeur assisted and soothed the melancholy of her heart. Here she would retrace all the conduct of her beloved Theodore, and endeavour to recollect his exact countenance, his air, and his manner. Now she would weep at the remembrance, and then suddenly considering that he had perhaps already suffered an ignominious death for her sake, even in consequence of the very action which had proved his love, a dreadful despair would seize her and, arresting her tears, would threaten to bear down every barrier that fortitude and reason could oppose.

Fearing longer to trust her own thoughts, she would hurry home and by a desperate effort try to lose the remembrance of the past in the conversation of La Luc. Her melancholy, when he observed it, La Luc attributed to a sense of the cruel treatment she had received from her father, a circumstance which, by exciting his compassion, endeared her more strongly to his heart; while that love of rational conversation, which in her calmer hours so frequently appeared, opened to him a new source of amusement in the cultivation of a mind eager for knowledge and susceptible of all the energies of genius.

The gentleness of her manners, partaking so much of that pensive character which marked La Luc's, was soothing to his heart, and tinctured his behaviour with a degree of tenderness that imparted comfort to her, and gradually won her entire confidence and affection. She saw with extreme concern the declining state of his health, and united her efforts with those of the family to amuse and revive him.

The pleasing society of which she partook and the quietness of the country at length restored her mind to a state of tolerable composure. She was now acquainted with all the wild walks of the neighbouring mountains and never tired of viewing their astonishing scenery. She often indulged herself in traversing alone their unfrequented paths, where now and then a peasant from a neighbouring village was all that interrupted the profound solitude. She generally took with her a book so that if she perceived her thoughts inclined to fix on the one object of her grief, she might force them to a subject less dangerous to her peace. She had become a tolerable proficient in English while at the convent where she received her education, and the instruction of La Luc, who was well acquainted with the language, now served to perfect her. He was partial to the English; he admired their character and the constitution of their laws, and his library contained a collection of their best authors, particularly of their philosophers and poets. Adeline found that no species of writing had power so effectually to withdraw her mind from the contemplation of its own misery as the higher kinds of poetry, and in these her taste soon taught her to distinguish the superiority of the English from that of the French. The genius of the language, more perhaps than the genius of the people, if indeed the distinction may be allowed, occasioned this.

She frequently took a volume of Shakespeare or Milton and, having gained some wild eminence, would seat herself beneath the pines, whose low murmurs soothed her heart and conspired with the visions of the poet to lull her to forgetfulness of grief.

One evening when Clara was engaged at home, Adeline wandered alone to a favourite spot among the rocks that bordered the lake. It was an eminence which commanded an entire view of the lake and of the stupendous mountains that environed it. A few ragged thorns grew from the precipice beneath, which descended perpendicularly to the water's edge; and above rose a thick wood of larch, pine, and fir, intermingled with some chestnut and mountain ash. The evening was fine, and the air so still that it scarcely waved the light leaves of the trees around, or rimpled[79] the broad expanse of the waters below. Adeline gazed on the scene with a kind of still rapture, and watched the sun sinking amid a crimson glow which tinted the bosom of the lake and the snowy heads of the distant alps. The delight which the scenery inspired, of a kind which "soothes every gust of passion into peace,"[80] was now heightened by the tones of a French horn, and looking on the lake, she perceived at some distance a pleasure boat. As it was a spectacle rather uncommon in this solitude, she concluded the boat contained a party of foreigners come to view the wonderful scenery of the country, or perhaps of Genevois,[81] who chose to amuse themselves on a lake as grand, though much less extensive, than their own; and the latter conjecture was probably just.

As she listened to the mellow and enchanting tones of the horn, which gradually sank away in distance, the scene appeared more lovely than before. La Luc, observing how much Adeline was charmed with the features of the country and desirous of amusing her melancholy, which, notwithstanding her efforts, was often too apparent, wished to show her other scenes than those to which her walks were circumscribed. He proposed a party on horseback to take a nearer view of the glaciers; to attempt their ascent was a difficulty and fatigue to which neither La Luc, in his present state of health, nor Adeline, were equal. She had not been accustomed to ride single, and the mountainous road they were to pass made the experiment rather dangerous; but she concealed her fears, and they were not sufficient to make her wish to forego an enjoyment such as was now offered her.

79. Wrinkled, rippled.
80. James Thomson, *The Seasons*.
81. Natives of Geneva.

The following day was fixed for this excursion. La Luc and his party arose at an early hour, and having taken a slight breakfast, they set out toward the Glacier of Montanvert,[82] which lay at a few leagues' distance. Peter carried a small basket of provisions; and it was their plan to dine on some pleasant spot in the open air.

It is unnecessary to describe the high enthusiasm of Adeline, the more complacent pleasure of La Luc, and the transports of Clara as the scenes of this romantic country shifted to their eyes. Now frowning in dark and gloomy grandeur, it exhibited only tremendous rocks, and cataracts rolling from the heights into some deep and narrow valley, along which their united waters roared and foamed, and burst away to regions inaccessible to mortal foot, and now the scene arose less fiercely wild as "the pomp of groves and garniture of fields"[83] were intermingled with the ruder features of nature, and while the snow froze on the summit of the mountain, the vine blushed at its foot.

Engaged in interesting conversation and by the admiration which the country excited, they traveled on till noon, when they looked round for a pleasant spot where they might rest and take refreshment. At some little distance they perceived the ruins of a fabric which had once been a castle; it stood almost on a point of rock that overhung a deep valley; and its broken turrets rising from among the woods that embosomed it heightened the picturesque beauty of the object.

The edifice invited curiosity, and the shades, repose; La Luc and his party advanced. They seated themselves on the grass under the shade of some high trees near the ruins. An opening in the woods afforded a view of the distant alps; the deep silence of solitude reigned. For some time they were lost in meditation. Adeline felt a sweet complacency, such as she had long been a stranger to. Looking at La Luc, she perceived a tear stealing down his cheek, while the elevation of his mind

82. Now known as the Mer de Glace.
83. James Beattie, *The Minstrel.*

was strongly expressed on his countenance. He turned on Clara his eyes, which were now filled with tenderness, and made an effort to recover himself.

"The stillness and total seclusion of this scene," said Adeline, "the stupendous mountains, the gloomy grandeur of these woods, together with that monument of faded glory on which the hand of time is so emphatically impressed, diffuse a sacred enthusiasm over the mind and awaken sensations truly sublime."

La Luc was going to speak, but Peter came forward and desired to know whether he had not better open the wallet,[84] as he fancied his honour and the young ladies must be main[85] hungry, jogging on so far up hill and down before dinner. They acknowledged the truth of honest Peter's suspicion, and accepted his hint.

Refreshments were spread on the grass, and having seated themselves under the canopy of waving woods surrounded by the sweets of wild flowers, they inhaled the pure breeze of the alps, which might be called spirit of air, and partook of a repast which these circumstances rendered delicious.

When they arose to depart, Clara said, "I am unwilling to quit this charming spot. How delightful would it be to pass one's life beneath these shades with the friends who are dear to one!"

La Luc smiled at the romantic simplicity of the idea, but Adeline sighed deeply at the image of felicity, and of Theodore, which it recalled, and turned away to conceal her tears.

They now mounted their horses, and soon after arrived at the foot of Montanvert. The emotions of Adeline, as she contemplated in various points of view the astonishing objects around her, surpassed all expression; and the feelings of the whole party were too strong to admit of conversation. The profound stillness which reigned in these regions of solitude inspired awe, and heightened the sublimity of the scenery to an exquisite degree.

84. Bag for carrying items while traveling.
85. Very great in degree, considerable.

"It seems," said Adeline, "as if we were walking over the ruins of the world, and were the only persons who had survived the wreck. I can scarcely persuade myself that we are not left alone on the globe."

"The view of these objects," said La Luc, "lift the soul to their Great Author, and we contemplate with a feeling almost too vast for humanity the sublimity of his nature in the grandeur of his works." La Luc raised his eyes, filled with tears, to heaven, and was for some moments lost in silent adoration.

They quitted these scenes with extreme reluctance; but the hour of the day, and the appearance of the clouds, which seemed gathering for a storm, made them hasten their departure. Could she have been sheltered from its fury, Adeline almost wished to have witnessed the tremendous effect of a thunderstorm in these regions.

They returned to Leloncourt by a different route, and the shade of the overhanging precipices was deepened by the gloom of the atmosphere. It was evening when they came within view of the lake, which the travelers rejoiced to see, for the storm so long threatened was now fast approaching; the thunder murmured among the alps; and the dark vapours that rolled heavily along their sides heightened their dreadful sublimity. La Luc would have quickened his pace, but the road winding down the steep mountainside made caution necessary. The darkening air and the lightnings that now flashed along the horizon terrified Clara, but she withheld the expression of her fear in consideration of her father. A peal of thunder, which seemed to shake the earth to its foundations and was reverberated in tremendous echoes from the cliffs, burst over their heads. Clara's horse took fright at the sound, and setting off, hurried her with amazing velocity down the mountain toward the lake which washed its foot. The agony of La Luc, who viewed her progress in the horrible expectation of seeing her dashed down the precipice that bordered the road, is not to be described.

Clara kept her seat, but terror had almost deprived her of sense. Her efforts to preserve herself were mechanical, for she scarcely knew what she did. The horse carried her safely almost to the foot of the mountain, but was making toward the lake when a gentleman who traveled along the road caught the bridle as the animal endeavoured to pass. The sudden stopping of the horse threw Clara to the ground, and impatient of restraint, the animal burst from the hand of the stranger, and plunged into the lake.[86] The violence of the fall deprived Clara of recollection; but while the stranger endeavoured to support her, his servant ran to fetch water.

She soon recovered and, unclosing her eyes, found herself in the arms of a chevalier, who appeared to support her with difficulty. The compassion expressed in his countenance while he inquired how she did revived her spirits, and she was endeavouring to thank him for his kindness when La Luc and Adeline came up. The terror impressed on her father's features was perceived by Clara, languid as she was. She tried to raise herself, and said with a faint smile, which betrayed instead of disguising her sufferings, "Dear sir, I am not hurt." Her pale countenance and the blood that trickled down her cheek contradicted her words. But La Luc, to whom terror had suggested the utmost possible evil, now rejoiced to hear her speak; he recalled some presence of mind, and while Adeline applied her salts, he chafed her temples.

When she revived she told him how much she was obliged to the stranger. La Luc endeavoured to express his gratitude; but the former, interrupting him, begged he might be spared the pain of receiving thanks for having followed only an impulse of common humanity.

They were now not far from Leloncourt; but the evening was almost shut in, and the thunder murmured deeply among the hills. La Luc was distressed how to convey Clara home.

In endeavouring to raise her from the ground, the stranger betrayed such evident symptoms of pain that La Luc inquired

---

86. While no further mention of the horse is made, one may be assured that the creature, suffering no serious injury, swam to shore and was safely retrieved.

concerning it. The sudden jerk which the horse had given the arm of the chevalier in escaping from his hold had violently sprained his shoulder and rendered his arm almost useless. The pain was exquisite, and La Luc, whose fears for his daughter were now subsiding, was shocked at the circumstance, and pressed the stranger to accompany him to the village, where relief might be obtained. He accepted the invitation, and Clara, being at length placed on a horse led by her father, was conducted to the château.

When Madame, who had been looking out for La Luc some time, perceived the cavalcade approaching, she was alarmed and her apprehensions were confirmed when she saw the situation of her niece. Clara was carried into the house, and La Luc would have sent for a surgeon, but there was none within several leagues of the village; neither were there any of the physical profession within the same distance.

Clara was assisted to her chamber by Adeline, and Madame La Luc undertook to examine the wounds. The result restored peace to the family; for though she was much bruised, she had escaped material injury; a slight contusion on the forehead had occasioned the bloodshed which at first alarmed La Luc. Madame undertook to restore her niece in a few days with the assistance of a balsam[87] composed by herself, on the virtues of which she descanted[88] with great eloquence, till La Luc interrupted her by reminding her of the condition of her patient. Madame, having bathed Clara's bruises and given her a cordial of incomparable efficacy, left her, and Adeline watched in the chamber of her friend till she retired to her own for the night.

La Luc, whose spirits had suffered much perturbation, was now tranquillized by the report his sister made of Clara. He introduced the stranger and, having mentioned the accident he had met with, desired that he might have immediate assistance. Madame hastened to her closet, and it is perhaps difficult to determine whether she felt most concern for the

87. Healing ointment, balm.
88. Commented.

sufferings of her guest or pleasure at the opportunity thus offered of displaying her physical skill. However this might be, she quitted the room with great alacrity, and very quickly returned with a vial containing her inestimable balsam, and having given the necessary directions for the application of it, she left the stranger to the care of his servant.

La Luc insisted that the chevalier, Monsieur Verneuil, should not leave the château that night, and he very readily submitted to be detained. His manners during the evening were as frank and engaging as the hospitality and gratitude of La Luc were sincere, and they soon entered into interesting conversation. Monsieur Verneuil conversed like a man who had seen much, and thought more, and if he discovered any prejudice in his opinions, it was evidently the prejudice of a mind which, seeing objects through the medium of its own goodness, tinges them with the hue of its predominant quality. La Luc was much pleased, for in his retired situation he had not often an opportunity of receiving the pleasure which results from a communion of intelligent minds. He found that Monsieur Verneuil had traveled. La Luc having asked some questions relative to England, they fell into discourse concerning the national characters of the French and English.

"If it is the privilege of wisdom," said Monsieur Verneuil, "to look beyond happiness, I own I had rather be without it. When we observe the English laws, writings, and conversation, and at the same time mark their countenances, manners, and the frequency of suicide among them, we are apt to believe that wisdom and happiness are incompatible. If, on the other hand, we turn to their neighbours, the French, and see their wretched policy, their sparkling but sophistical discourse, their frivolous occupations, and withal their gay animated air, we shall be compelled to acknowledge that happiness and folly too often dwell together."

"It is the end of wisdom," said La Luc, "to attain happiness, and I can hardly dignify that conduct or course of thinking which tends to misery with the name of wisdom. By this rule, perhaps, the folly, as we term it, of the French deserves, since its effect is happiness, to be called wisdom. That airy thought-lessness, which seems alike to contemn reflection and anticipation, produces all the effect of it without reducing its subjects to the mortification of philosophy. But in truth wisdom is an exertion of mind to subdue folly; and as the happiness of the French is less the consequence of mind than of constitution, it deserves not the honours of wisdom."

Discoursing on the variety of opinions that are daily formed on the same conduct, La Luc observed how much that which is commonly called opinion is the result of passion and temper.

"True," said Monsieur Verneuil, "there is a tone of thought, as there is a key note in music, that leads all its weaker affections. Thus where the powers of judging may be equal, the disposition to judge is different, and the actions of men are at least but too often arraigned by whim and caprice, by partial vanity and the humour of the moment."

Here La Luc took occasion to reprobate[89] the conduct of those writers, who, by showing the dark side only of human nature, and by dwelling on the evils only which are incident to humanity, have sought to degrade man in his own eyes, and to make him discontented with life.

"What should we say of a painter," continued La Luc, "who collected in his piece objects of a black hue only, who presented you with a black man, a black horse, a black dog, and tells you that his is a picture of nature, and that nature is black? 'Tis true, you would reply, the objects you exhibit do exist in nature, but they form a very small part of her works. You say that nature is black, and, to prove it, you have collected on your canvas all the animals of this hue that exist. But you have forgot to paint the green earth, the blue sky, the white man, and objects of all those various hues with which creation abounds, and of which black is a very inconsiderable part."

The countenance of Monsieur Verneuil lightened with peculiar animation during the discourse of La Luc. "To think well of his nature," said he, "is necessary to the dignity and

89. Condemn as unworthy.

the happiness of man. There is a decent pride which becomes every mind, and is congenial to virtue. That consciousness of innate dignity, which shows him the glory of his nature, will be his best protection from the meanness of vice. Where this consciousness is wanting," continued Monsieur Verneuil, "there can be no sense of moral honour, and consequently none of the higher principles of action. What can be expected of him who says it is his nature to be mean and selfish? Or who can doubt that he who thinks thus, thinks from the experience of his own heart, from the tendency of his own inclinations? Let it always be remembered, that he who would persuade men to be good, ought to show them that they are great."

"You speak," said La Luc, "with the honest enthusiasm of a virtuous mind, and in obeying the impulse of your heart, you utter the truths of philosophy; and, trust me, a bad heart and a truly philosophic head has never yet been united in the same individual. Vicious inclinations not only corrupt the heart but the understanding, and thus lead to false reasoning. Virtue only is on the side of truth."

La Luc and his guest, mutually pleased with each other, entered upon the discussion of subjects so interesting to them both that it was late before they parted for the night.

CHAPTER 18

'Twas such a scene as gave a kind relief
To memory, in sweetly pensive grief.

    Joseph Trapp, "Virgil's Tomb"

Mine be the breezy hill that skirts the down,
Where a green grassy turf is all I crave,
With here and there a violet bestrewn,

. . . .

And many an evening sun shine sweetly on my
    grave.

    James Beattie, *The Minstrel*

Repose had so much restored Clara that, when Adeline, anxious to know how she did, went early in the morning to her chamber, she found her already risen and ready to attend the family at breakfast. Monsieur Verneuil appeared also, but his looks betrayed a want of rest, and indeed he had suffered during the night a degree of anguish from his arm which it was an effort of some resolution to endure in silence. It was now swelled and somewhat inflamed, and this might in some degree be attributed to the effect of Madame La Luc's balsam, whose restorative qualities had for once failed. The whole family sympathised with his sufferings, and Madame, at the request of Monsieur Verneuil, abandoned her balsam and substituted an emollient[90] fomentation.[91]

From an application of this he, in a short time, found an abatement of the pain, and returned to the breakfast table with greater composure. The happiness which La Luc felt at seeing his daughter in safety was very apparent, but the warmth of his gratitude toward her preserver he found it difficult to express. Clara spoke the genuine emotions of her heart with artless but modest energy, and testified sincere concern for the sufferings which she had occasioned Monsieur Verneuil.

The pleasure received from the company of his guest, and the consideration of the essential services he had rendered him, cooperated with the natural hospitality of La Luc, and he pressed Monsieur Verneuil to remain some time at the château. "I can never repay the services you have done me," said La Luc, "yet I seek to increase my obligations to you by requesting you will prolong your visit, and thus allow me an opportunity of cultivating your acquaintance."

Monsieur Verneuil, who at the time he met La Luc was traveling from Geneva to a distant part of Savoy merely for the purpose of viewing the country, being now delighted with his host and with everything around him, willingly accepted the invitation. In this circumstance prudence concurred with inclination, for in his present situation to have pursued his journey on horseback would have been dangerous, if not impracticable.

The morning was spent in conversation, in which Monsieur Verneuil displayed a mind enriched with taste, enlightened by science, and enlarged by observation. The situation of the château and the features of the surrounding scenery charmed him, and in the evening he found himself able to walk with La Luc and explore the beauties of this romantic region. As they passed through the village, the salutations of the peasants, in whom love and respect were equally blended, and their eager inquiries after Clara bore testimony to the character of La Luc,

90. Soothing.
91. Hot moist substance.

while his countenance expressed a serene satisfaction arising from the consciousness of deserving and possessing their love.

"I live surrounded by my children," said he, turning to Monsieur Verneuil, who had noticed their eagerness, "for such I consider my parishioners. In discharging the duties of my office, I am repaid not only by my own conscience, but by their gratitude. There is a luxury in observing their simple and honest love which I would not exchange for anything the world calls blessings."

"Yet the world, sir, would call the pleasures of which you speak romantic," said Monsieur Verneuil, "for to be sensible of this pure and exquisite delight requires a heart untainted with the vicious pleasures of society—pleasures that deaden its finest feelings and poison the source of its truest enjoyments."

They pursued their way along the borders of the lake, sometimes under the shade of hanging woods, and sometimes over hillocks of turf, where the scene opened in all its wild magnificence. Monsieur Verneuil often stopped in raptures to observe and point out the singular beauties it exhibited, while La Luc, pleased with the delight his friend expressed, surveyed with more than usual satisfaction the objects which had so often charmed him before. But there was a tender melancholy in the tone of his voice and his countenance, which arose from the recollection of having often traced those scenes and partook of the pleasure they inspired with her who had long since bade them an eternal farewell.

They presently quitted the lake and, winding up a steep ascent between the woods, came after an hour's walk to a green summit which appeared, among the savage rocks that environed it, like the blossom on the thorn. It was a spot formed for solitary delight, inspiring that soothing tenderness so dear to the feeling mind, and which calls back to memory the images of passed regret, softened by distance and endeared by frequent recollection. Wild shrubs grew from the crevices of the rocks beneath, and the high trees of pine and cedar that waved above afforded a melancholy and romantic shade. The silence of the scene was interrupted only by the breeze as it rolled over the woods, and by the solitary notes of the birds that inhabited the cliffs.

From this point the eye commanded an entire view of those majestic and sublime alps whose aspect fills the soul with emotions of indescribable awe, and seems to lift it to a nobler nature. The village and the château of La Luc appeared in the bosom of the mountains, a peaceful retreat from the storms that gathered on their tops. All the faculties of Monsieur Verneuil were absorbed in admiration, and he was for some time quite silent; at length, bursting into a rhapsody, he turned and would have addressed La Luc, when he perceived him at a distance leaning against a rustic urn over which dropped, in beautiful luxuriance a weeping willow.

As he approached, La Luc quitted his position and advanced to meet him, while Monsieur Verneuil inquired upon what occasion the urn had been erected. La Luc, unable to answer, pointed to it and walked silently away. Monsieur Verneuil, approaching the urn, read the following inscription:

To the memory of Clara La Luc: This urn is erected on
the spot which she loved, in testimony of the affection of a
husband.

Monsieur Verneuil now comprehended the whole and, feeling for his friend, was hurt that he had noticed this monument of his grief. He rejoined La Luc, who was standing on the point of the eminence contemplating the landscape below with an air more placid, and touched with the sweetness of piety and resignation. He perceived that Monsieur Verneuil was somewhat disconcerted, and he sought to remove his uneasiness.

"You will consider it," said he, "as a mark of my esteem that I have brought you to this spot. It is never profaned by the presence of the unfeeling. They would deride the faithfulness of an attachment which has so long survived its object, and which, in their own breasts, would quickly have been lost amidst the dissipation of general society. I have cherished in my heart the remembrance of a woman whose virtues claimed all my love: I have cherished it as a treasure to which I could withdraw from temporary cares and vexations in the certainty of finding a soothing, though melancholy, comfort."

La Luc paused. Monsieur Verneuil expressed the sympathy he felt, but he knew the sacredness of sorrow, and soon relapsed into silence.

"One of the brightest hopes of a future state," resumed La Luc, "is that we shall meet again those whom we have loved upon earth. And perhaps our happiness may be permitted to consist very much in the society of our friends, purified from the frailties of mortality, with the finer affections more sweetly attuned, and with the faculties of mind infinitely more elevated and enlarged. We shall then be enabled to comprehend subjects which are too vast for human conception; to comprehend, perhaps, the sublimity of that Deity who first called us into being. These views of futurity, my friend, elevate us above the evils of this world, and seem to communicate to us a portion of the nature we contemplate. Call them not the illusions of a visionary brain: I trust in their reality. Of this I am certain, that whether they are illusions or not, a faith in them ought to be cherished for the comfort it brings to the heart, and reverenced for the dignity it imparts to the mind. Such feelings make a happy and an important part of our belief in a future existence: they give energy to virtue, and stability to principle."

"This," said Monsieur Verneuil, "is what I have often felt, and what every ingenuous mind must acknowledge."

La Luc and Monsieur Verneuil continued in conversation till the sun had left the scene. The mountains, darkened by twilight, assumed a sublimer aspect, while the tops of some of the highest alps were yet illumined by the sun's rays, and formed a striking contrast to the shadowy obscurity of the world below. As they descended through the woods and traversed the margin of the lake, the stillness and solemnity of the hour diffused a pensive sweetness over their minds, and sank them into silence.

They found supper spread, as was usual, in the hall, whose

[299]

windows opened upon a garden, where the flowers might be said to yield their fragrance in gratitude to the refreshing dews. The windows were embowered with eglantine and other sweet shrubs, which hung in wild luxuriance around, and formed a beautiful and simple decoration. Clara and Adeline loved to pass the evenings in this hall, where they had acquired the first rudiments of astronomy, and from which they had a wide view of the heavens. La Luc pointed out to them the planets and the fixed stars, explained their laws, and from thence taking occasion to mingle moral with scientific instruction, would often ascend toward that great first cause, whose nature soars beyond the grasp of human comprehension.

"No study," he would sometimes say, "so much enlarges the mind, or impresses it with so sublime an idea of the Deity, as that of astronomy. When the imagination launches into the regions of space, and contemplates the innumerable worlds which are scattered through it, we are lost in astonishment and awe. This globe appears as a mass of atoms in the immensity of the universe, and man a mere insect. Yet how wonderful! that man, whose frame is so diminutive in the scale of being, should have powers which spurn the narrow boundaries of time and place, soar beyond the sphere of his existence, penetrate the secret laws of nature, and calculate their progressive effects. O! how expressively does this prove the spirituality of our Being! Let the materialist consider it, and blush that he has ever doubted."

In this hall the whole family now met at supper, and during the remainder of the evening the conversation turned upon general subjects, in which Clara joined in modest and judicious remark. La Luc had taught her to familiarize her mind to reasoning, and had accustomed her to deliver her sentiments freely: she spoke them with a simplicity extremely engaging, and which convinced her hearers that the love of knowledge, not the vanity of talking, induced her to converse. Monsieur Verneuil evidently endeavoured to draw forth her sentiments, and Clara, interested by the subjects he introduced, a stranger to affectation, and pleased with the opinions he expressed, answered them with frankness and animation. They retired mutually pleased with each other.

Monsieur Verneuil was about six and thirty; his figure manly, his countenance frank and engaging. A quick penetrating eye, whose fire was softened by benevolence, disclosed the chief traits of his character; he was quick to discern, but generous to excuse, the follies of mankind; and while no one more sensibly felt an injury, none more readily accepted the concession of an enemy.

He was by birth a Frenchman. A fortune lately devolved to him had enabled him to execute the plan, which his active and inquisitive mind had suggested, of viewing the most remarkable parts of the continent. He was peculiarly susceptible of the beautiful and sublime in nature. To such a taste Switzerland and the adjacent country was, of all others, the most interesting; and he found the scenery it exhibited infinitely surpassing all that his glowing imagination had painted; he saw with the eye of a painter, and felt with the rapture of a poet.

In the habitation of La Luc he met with the hospitality, the frankness, and the simplicity so characteristic of the country; in his venerable host he saw the strength of philosophy united with the finest tenderness of humanity—a philosophy which taught him to correct his feelings, not to annihilate them; in Clara, the bloom of beauty, with the most perfect simplicity of heart; and in Adeline all the charms of elegance and grace, with a genius deserving of the highest culture. In this family picture the goodness of Madame La Luc was not unperceived or forgotten. The cheerfulness and harmony that reigned within the château was delightful; but the philanthropy which, flowing from the heart of the pastor, was diffused though the whole village and united the inhabitants in the sweet and firm bonds of social compact was divine. The beauty of its situation conspired with these circumstances to make Leloncourt seem almost a Paradise.

Monsieur Verneuil sighed that he must so soon quit it. "I ought to seek no farther," said he, "for here wisdom and happiness dwell together."

The admiration was reciprocal; La Luc and his family found themselves much interested in Monsieur Verneuil, and looked forward with regret to the time of his departure. So warmly they pressed him to prolong his visit, and so powerfully his own inclinations seconded theirs, that he accepted the invitation. La Luc omitted no circumstance which might contribute to the amusement of his guest, who had in a few days recovered the use of his arm, so they made several excursions among the mountains. Adeline and Clara, whom the care of Madame had restored to her usual health, were generally of the party.

After spending a week at the château, Monsieur Verneuil bade adieu to La Luc and his family; they parted with mutual regret, and the former promised that when he returned to Geneva, he would take Leloncourt in his way. As he said this, Adeline, who had for some time with much alarm observed La Luc's declining health, looked mournfully on his languid countenance, and uttered a secret prayer that he might live to receive the visit of Monsieur Verneuil.

Madame was the only person who did not lament his departure; she saw that the efforts of her brother to entertain his guest were more than his present state of health would admit of, and she rejoiced in the quiet that would now return to him.

But this quiet brought La Luc no respite from illness; the fatigue he had suffered in his late excursions seemed to have increased his disorder, which in a short time assumed the aspect of a consumption. Yielding to the solicitations of his family, he went to Geneva for advice, and was there recommended to try the air of Nice.

The journey thither, however, was of considerable length, and believing his life to be very precarious, he hesitated whether to go. He was also unwilling to leave the duty of his parish unperformed for so long a period as his health might require; but this was an objection which would not have withheld him from Nice, had his faith in the climate been equal to that of his physicians.

His parishioners felt the life of their pastor to be of the utmost consequence to them. It was a general cause, and they testified at once his worth and their sense of it by going in a body to solicit him to leave them. He was much affected by this instance of their attachment. Such a proof of regard, joined with the entreaties of his own family and a consideration that for their sakes it was a duty to endeavour to prolong his life, was too powerful to be withstood, and he determined to set out for Italy.

It was settled that Clara and Adeline, whose health La Luc thought required change of air and scene, should accompany him, attended by the faithful Peter.

On the morning of his departure, a large body of his parishioners assembled round the door to bid him farewell. It was an affecting scene; they might meet no more. At length, wiping the tears from his eyes, La Luc said, "Let us trust in God, my friends; he has power to heal all disorders both of body and mind. We shall meet again, if not in this world, I hope in a better. Let our conduct be such as to ensure that better."

The sobs of his people prevented any reply. There was scarcely a dry eye in the village; for there was scarcely an inhabitant of it that was not now assembled in the presence of La Luc.

He shook hands with them all. "Farewell, my friends," said he. "We shall meet again."

"God grant we may," said they, with one voice of fervent petition.

Having mounted his horse, and Clara and Adeline being ready, they took a last leave of Madame La Luc, and quitted the château. The greater part of the people, unwilling to leave La Luc, accompanied him to some distance from the village. As he moved slowly on, he cast a last lingering look at his little home, where he had spent so many peaceful years, and which he now gazed on perhaps for the last time, and tears rose to his eyes; but he checked them. Every scene of the adjacent country called up, as he passed, some tender remembrance. He looked toward the spot consecrated to the memory of his deceased wife; the dewy vapours of the morning veiled it. La Luc felt the disappointment more deeply, perhaps, than reason could justify; but those who know from experience how much the imagination loves to dwell on any object however remotely connected with that of our tenderness will feel with him. This was an object round which the affections of La Luc had settled themselves; it was a memorial to the eye, and the view of it awakened more forcibly in the memory every tender idea that could associate with the primary subject of his regard. In such cases fancy gives the stamp of reality to the illusions of strong affection, and they are cherished by the heart with romantic fondness.

His people accompanied him for near a mile from the village, and could scarcely then be prevailed on to leave him; at length he once more bade them farewell and went on his way, followed by their prayers and blessings.

La Luc and his little party traveled slowly on, sank in pensive silence—a silence too pleasingly sad to be soon relinquished, and which they indulged without fear of interruption. The solitary grandeur of the scenes through which they passed, and the soothing murmur of the pines that waved above, aided this soft luxury of meditation.

They proceeded by easy stages; and after traveling for some days among the romantic mountains and green valleys of Piedmont, they entered the rich country of Nice. The gay and luxuriant views which now opened upon the travelers as they wound among the hills appeared like scenes of fairy enchantment, or those produced by the lonely visions of the poets. While the spiral summits of the mountains exhibited the snowy severity of winter, the pine, the cypress, the olive, and the myrtle shaded their sides with the green tints of spring, and groves of orange, lemon, and citron spread over their feet the full glow of autumn. As they advanced the scenery became still more diversified; and at length Adeline caught a glimpse between the receding heights of the distant waters of the Mediterranean fading into the blue and cloudless horizon. She had never till now seen the ocean; and this transient view of it roused her imagination and made her watch impatiently for a nearer prospect.

It was toward the close of day when the travelers, winding round an abrupt projection of that range of alps which crowns the amphitheatre that environs Nice, looked down upon the green hills that stretch to the shores, upon the city and its ancient castle, and upon the wide waters of the Mediterranean, with the mountains of Corsica in the farthest distance. Such a sweep of sea and land, so varied with the gay, the magnificent, and the awful, would have fixed any eye in admiration. For Adeline and Clara, novelty and enthusiasm added their charms to the prospect. The soft and salubrious[92] air seemed to welcome La Luc to this smiling region, and the serene atmosphere to promise invariable summer. They at length descended upon the little plain where stands the city of Nice, and which was the most extensive piece of level ground they had passed since they entered the county. Here, in the bosom of the mountains, sheltered from the north and the east, where the western gales alone seemed to breathe, all the blooms of spring and the riches of autumn were united. Trees of myrtle bordered the road, which wound among groves of orange, lemon, and bergamot, whose delicious fragrance came to the sense mingled with the breath of roses and carnations that blossomed in their shade. The gently swelling hills that rose from the plain were covered with vines, and crowned with cypresses, olives, and date trees; beyond, there appeared the sweep of lofty mountains whence the travelers had descended, and whence rose the little river Paillon, swollen by the snows that melt on their summits and which, after meandering through the plain, washes the walls of Nice where it falls into the Mediterranean. In this blooming region Adeline observed that the countenances of the peasants, meagre and discontented, formed a melancholy contrast to the face of the country, and she lamented again the effects of an arbitrary government, where the bounties of nature, which were designed for all, are monopolized by a few, and the many are suffered to starve, tantalized by the surrounding plenty.

92. Healthful.

The city lost much of its enchantment on a nearer approach: its narrow streets and shabby houses but ill answered the expectation which a distant view of its ramparts and its harbour, gay with vessels, seemed to authorise. The appearance of the inn at which La Luc now alighted did not contribute to soften his disappointment; but if he was surprised to find such indifferent accommodation at the inn of a town celebrated as the resort of valetudinarians,[93] he was still more so when he learned the difficulty of procuring furnished lodgings.

After much search he procured apartments in a small but pleasant house situated a little way out of the town: it had a garden, and a terrace which overlooked the sea, and was distinguished by an air of neatness very unusual in the houses of Nice. He agreed to board with the family, whose table likewise accommodated a gentleman and lady, their lodgers, and thus he became a temporary inhabitant of this charming climate.

On the following morning Adeline rose at an early hour, eager to indulge the new and sublime emotion with which a view of the ocean inspired her, and walked with Clara toward the hills that afforded a more extensive prospect. They pursued their way for some time between high embowering banks till they arrived at an eminence, whence "heaven, earth, ocean, smiled!"[94]

They sat down on a point of rock overshadowed by lofty palm trees to contemplate at leisure the magnificent scene. The sun was just emerged from the sea, over which its rays shed a flood of light, and darted a thousand brilliant tints on the vapours that ascended the horizon and floated there in light clouds, leaving the bosom of the waters below clear as crystal, except where the white surges were seen to beat upon the rocks. The rays of light discovered the distant sails of the fishing boats, and the far distant highlands of Corsica, tinted with ætherial blue.

93. People with sickly constitutions.
94. James Beattie, *The Minstrel.*

La Luc in his walks met with some sensible and agreeable companions, who like himself came to Nice in search of health. Of these he soon formed a small but pleasant society, among whom was a Frenchman whose mild manners, marked with a deep and interesting melancholy, had particularly attracted La Luc. He very seldom mentioned himself, or any circumstance that might lead to a knowledge of his family, but on other subjects conversed with frankness and much intelligence. La Luc had frequently invited him to his lodgings, but he had always declined the invitation, and this in a manner so gentle as to disarm displeasure and convince La Luc that his refusal was the consequence of a certain dejection of mind which made him reluctant to meet other strangers.

The description which La Luc had given of this foreigner had excited the curiosity of Clara; and the sympathy which the unfortunate feel for each other called forth the commiseration of Adeline, for that he was unfortunate she could not doubt. On their return from an evening walk La Luc pointed out the chevalier, and quickened his pace to overtake him. Adeline was for a moment impelled to follow, but delicacy checked her steps, for she knew how painful the presence of a stranger often is to a wounded mind, and forbore to intrude herself on his notice for the sake of only satisfying an idle curiosity. She turned therefore, into another path; but the delicacy which now prevented the meeting, accident in a few days defeated, and La Luc introduced the stranger. Adeline received him with a soft smile but endeavoured to restrain the expression of pity which her features had involuntarily assumed; she wished him not to know that she observed he was unhappy.

After this interview he no longer rejected the invitations of La Luc but made him frequent visits, and often accompanied Adeline and Clara in their rambles. The mild and sensible conversation of the former seemed to soothe his mind, and in her presence he frequently conversed with a degree of animation which La Luc till then had not observed in him. Adeline too derived from the similarity of their taste and his intelligent conversation a degree of satisfaction which contributed, with the compassion his dejection inspired, to win her confidence, and she conversed with an easy frankness rather unusual to her.

His visits soon became more frequent. He walked with La Luc and his family; he attended them on their little excursions to view those magnificent remains of Roman antiquity which enrich the neighbourhood of Nice. When the ladies sat at home and worked, he enlivened the hours by reading to them, and they had the pleasure to observe his spirits somewhat relieved from the heavy melancholy that had oppressed him.

Monsieur Amand was passionately fond of music. Clara had not forgot to bring her beloved lute; he would sometimes strike the chords in the most sweet and mournful symphonies but never could be prevailed on to play. When Adeline or Clara played, he would sit in deep reverie, lost to every object around him, except when he fixed his eyes in mournful gaze on Adeline, and a sigh would sometimes escape him.

One evening when Adeline had excused herself from accompanying La Luc and Clara in a visit to a neighbouring family, she retired to the terrace of the garden which overlooked the sea, and as she viewed the tranquil splendour of the setting sun and its glories reflected on the polished surface of the waves, she touched the strings of the lute in softest harmony, her voice accompanying it with words which she had one day written.

Adeline ceased to sing when she immediately heard the last line repeated in a low voice, and turning her eyes whence it came, she saw Monsieur Amand. She blushed and laid down the lute, which he instantly took up, and with a tremulous hand drew forth tones "that might create a soul under the ribs of Death."[95]

Monsieur Amand paused; he seemed much oppressed, and at length, bursting into tears, laid down the instrument and walked abruptly away to the farther end of the terrace. Adeline, without seeming to observe his agitation, rose and leaned

95. John Milton, "Comus."

upon the wall, below which a group of fishermen were busily employed in drawing a net.

In a few moments he returned, with a composed and softened countenance. "Forgive this abrupt conduct," said he. "I know not how to apologise for it but by owning its cause. When I tell you, madam, that my tears flow to the memory of a lady who strongly resembled you, and who is lost to me forever, you will know how to pity me."

His voice faltered, and he paused. Adeline was silent.

"The lute," he resumed, "was her favourite instrument, and when you touched it with such melancholy expression, I saw her very image before me. But alas! why do I distress you with a knowledge of my sorrows! she is gone, and never to return! And you, Adeline—you—"

He checked his speech; and Adeline, turning on him a look of mournful regard, observed a wildness in his eyes which alarmed her. "These recollections are too painful," said she in a gentle voice. "Let us return to the house; Monsieur La Luc is probably come home."

"O no!" replied Monsieur Amand. "No—this breeze refreshes me. How often at this hour have I talked with her, as I now talk with you! Such were the soft tones of her voice— such the ineffable expression of her countenance."

Adeline interrupted him. "Let me beg of you to consider your health—this dewy air cannot be good for invalids."

He stood with his hands clasped, and seemed not to hear her. She took up the lute to go, and passed her fingers lightly over the chords. The sounds recalled his scattered senses; he raised his eyes, and fixed them in long unsettled gaze upon hers.

"Must I leave you here?" said she, smiling, and standing in an attitude to depart.

"I entreat you to play again the air I heard just now," said Monsieur Amand, in a hurried voice.

"Certainly," and she immediately began to play.

He leaned against a palm tree in an attitude of deep attention, and as the sounds languished on the air, his features gradually lost their wild expression, and he melted into tears. He continued to weep silently till the song concluded, and it was some time before he recovered voice enough to say, "Adeline, I cannot thank you for this goodness. My mind has recovered its bias, you have soothed a broken heart. Increase the kindness you have shown me by promising never to mention what you have witnessed this evening, and I will endeavour never again to wound your sensibility by a similar offence."

Adeline gave the required promise; and Monsieur Amand, pressing her hand with a melancholy smile, hurried from the garden, and she saw him no more that night.

La Luc had been near a fortnight at Nice, and his health, instead of amending, seemed rather to decline, yet he wished to make a longer experiment of the climate.

The air which failed to restore her venerable friend revived Adeline, and the variety and novelty of the surrounding scenes amused her mind though, since they could not obliterate the memory of past or suppress the pang of present affection, they were ineffectual to dissipate the sick languor of melancholy. Company, by compelling her to withdraw her attention from the subject of her sorrow, afforded her a transient relief, but the violence of the exertion generally left her more depressed. It was in the stillness of solitude, in the tranquil observance of beautiful nature, that her mind recovered its tone and, indulging the pensive inclination now become habitual to it, was soothed and fortified.

Of all the grand objects which nature had exhibited, the ocean inspired her with the most sublime admiration. She loved to wander alone on its shores, and when she could escape so long from the duties or the forms of society, she would sit for hours on the beach watching the rolling waves and listening to their dying murmur till her softened fancy recalled long-lost scenes, and restored the image of Theodore, when tears of despondency too often followed those of pity and regret. But these visions of memory, painful as they were, no longer excited that frenzy of grief they formerly awakened in Savoy; the sharpness of misery was passed, though its heavy influence was not perhaps less powerful. To these solitary indulgences generally succeeded calmness, and what Adeline endeavoured to believe was resignation.

She usually rose early, and walked down to the shore in the cool and silent hours of the morning to enjoy the cheering beauty of nature and inhale the pure sea breeze. Every object then smiled in fresh and lively colours. The blue sea, the brilliant sky, the distant fishing boats with their white sails, and the voices of the fishermen borne at intervals on the air were circumstances which reanimated her spirits.

During several days succeeding that on which Monsieur Amand had disclosed the cause of his melancholy, he did not visit La Luc. At length Adeline met him in one of her solitary rambles on the shore. He was pale and dejected, and seemed much agitated when he observed her; she therefore endeavoured to avoid him, but he advanced with quickened steps and accosted her.

He said it was his intention to leave Nice in a few days. "I have found no benefit from the climate," added Monsieur Amand. "Alas! what climate can relieve the sickness of the heart! I go to lose in the varieties of new scenes the remembrance of past happiness; yet the effort is vain; I am everywhere equally restless and unhappy."

Adeline tried to encourage him to hope much from time and change of place. "Time will blunt the sharpest edge of sorrow," said she. "I know it from experience." Yet while she spoke, the tears in her eyes contradicted the assertion of her lips.

"You have been unhappy, Adeline!—Yes—I knew it from the first. The smile of pity which you gave me assured me that you knew what it was to suffer." The desponding air with which he spoke renewed her apprehension of a scene similar to the one she had lately witnessed, and she changed the subject, but he soon returned to it. "You bid me hope much from time!—my wife!—my dear wife!"—his tongue faltered—"It is now many months since I lost her—yet the moment of her death seems but as yesterday."

Adeline faintly smiled.

[311]

"You can scarcely judge of the effect of time yet, you have much to hope for." He shook his head. "But I am again intruding my misfortunes on your notice; forgive this perpetual egotism. There is a comfort in the pity of the good such as nothing else can impart; this must plead my excuse; may you, Adeline, never want it. Ah! those tears—"

Adeline hastily dried them. Monsieur Amand forbore to press the subject, and immediately began to converse on indifferent topics. They returned toward the château, but La Luc being from home, Monsieur Amand took leave at the door. Adeline retired to her chamber, oppressed by her own sorrows and those of her amiable friend.

Near three weeks had now elapsed at Nice, during which the disorder of La Luc seemed rather to increase than to abate, when his physician very honestly confessed the little hope he entertained from the climate and advised him to try the effect of a sea voyage, adding that if the experiment failed, even the air of Montpellier appeared to him more likely to afford relief than that of Nice. La Luc received this disinterested advice with a mixture of gratitude and disappointment. The circumstances which had made him reluctant to quit Savoy rendered him yet more so to protract his absence and increase his expenses; but the ties of affection that bound him to his family and the love of life, which so seldom leaves us, again prevailed over inferior considerations, and he determined to coast the Mediterranean as far as Languedoc, where, if the voyage did not answer his expectations, he would land and proceed to Montpellier.

When Monsieur Amand learned that La Luc designed to quit Nice in a few days, he determined not to leave it before him. During this interval he had not sufficient resolution to deny himself the frequent conversation of Adeline, though her presence, by reminding him of his lost wife, gave him more pain than comfort. He was the second son of a French gentleman of family, and had been married about a year to a lady to whom he had long been attached when she died in

[312]

her lying-in. The infant soon followed its mother, and left the disconsolate father abandoned to grief, which had preyed so heavily on his health that his physician thought it necessary to send him to Nice. From the air of Nice, however, he had derived no benefit, and he now determined to travel farther into Italy, though he no longer felt any interest in those charming scenes which in happier days, and with her whom he never ceased to lament, would have afforded him the highest degree of mental luxury—now he sought only to escape from himself, or rather from the image of her who had once constituted his truest happiness.

La Luc, having laid his plan, hired a small vessel, and in a few days embarked, with a sick hope bidding adieu to the shores of Italy and the towering alps, and seeking on a new element the health which had hitherto mocked his pursuit.

Monsieur Amand took a melancholy leave of his new friends, whom he attended to the seaside. When he assisted Adeline on board, his heart was too full to suffer him to say farewell; but he stood long on the beach, pursuing with his eyes her course over the waters till tears dimmed his sight. The breeze wafted the vessel gently from the coast, and Adeline saw herself surrounded by the undulating waves of the ocean. The shore appeared to recede, its mountains to lessen, the gay colours of its landscape to melt into each other, and in a short time the figure of Monsieur Amand was seen no more. The town of Nice, with its castle and harbour, next faded away in distance, and the purple tint of the mountains was at length all that remained on the verge of the horizon.

She sighed as she gazed, and her eyes filled with tears. *So vanished my prospect of happiness,* thought she, *and my future view is like the waste of waters that surround me.* Her heart was full, and she retired from observation to a remote part of the deck, where she indulged her tears as she watched the vessel cut its way through the liquid glass. The water was so transparent that she saw the sunbeams playing at a considerable depth and fish of various colours glance athwart the current. Innumerable marine plants spread their vigorous leaves on the rocks below, and the richness of their verdure formed a beautiful contrast to the glowing scarlet of the coral that branched beside them.

The distant coast, at length, entirely disappeared. Adeline gazed with an emotion the most sublime on the boundless expanse of waters that spread on all sides. She seemed as if launched into a new world; the grandeur and immensity of the view astonished and overpowered her. For a moment she doubted the truth of the compass, and believed it to be almost impossible for the vessel to find its way over the pathless waters to any shore. And when she considered that a plank alone separated her from death, a sensation of unmixed terror superseded that of sublimity, and she hastily turned her eyes from the prospect, and her thoughts from the subject.

CHAPTER 19

Is there a heart that music cannot melt?
Alas! how is that rugged heart forlorn!
Is there who ne'er the mystic transports felt
Of solitude and melancholy born?
He need not woo the Muse—he is her scorn.

James Beattie, *The Minstrel*

Toward evening the captain, to avoid the danger of encountering a Barbary corsair, steered for the French coast, and Adeline distinguished in the gleam of the setting sun the shores of Provence, feathered with wood and green with pasturage. La Luc, languid and ill, had retired to the cabin, whither Clara attended him. The pilot at the helm, guiding the tall vessel through the sounding[96] waters, and one solitary sailor, leaning with crossed arms against the mast, and now and then singing parts of a mournful ditty, were all of the crew that remained upon deck—and Adeline silently watched the declining sun, which threw a saffron glow upon the waves and on the sails gently swelling in the breeze that was now dying away. The sun, at length, sank below the ocean, and twilight stole over the scene, leaving the shadowy shores

96. Resonant.

yet visible, and touching with a solemn tint the waters that stretched wide around.

As the shadows thickened the scene sank into deeper repose. Even the sailor's song had ceased; no sound was heard but that of the waters dashing beneath the vessel, and their fainter murmur on the pebbly coast. Adeline's mind was in unison with the tranquillity of the hour: lulled by the waves, she resigned herself to a still melancholy, and sat lost in reverie.

The present moment brought to her recollection her voyage up the Rhône when, seeking refuge from the terrors of the Marquis de Montalt, she so anxiously endeavoured to anticipate her future destiny. She then, as now, had watched the fall of evening and the fading prospect, and she remembered what a desolate feeling had accompanied the impression which those objects made. She had then no friends—no asylum—no certainty of escaping the pursuit of her enemy. Now she had found affectionate friends—a secure retreat—and was delivered from the terrors she then suffered—but still she was unhappy. The remembrance of Theodore—of Theodore who had loved her so truly, who had encountered and suffered so much for her sake, and of whose fate she was now as ignorant as when she traversed the Rhône, was an incessant pang to her heart. She seemed to be more remote than ever from the possibility of hearing of him. Sometimes a faint hope crossed her that he had escaped the malice of his persecutor; but when she considered the inveteracy and power of the latter, and the heinous light in which the law regards an assault upon a superior officer, even this poor hope vanished, and left her to tears and anguish.

She continued to muse till the moon arose from the bosom of the ocean and shed its trembling lustre upon the waves, diffusing peace, and making silence more solemn; beaming a soft light on the white sails, and throwing upon the waters the tall shadow of the vessel, which now seemed to glide along unopposed by any current. Her tears had somewhat relieved the anguish of her mind, and she again reposed in placid melancholy, when a strain of such tender and entrancing sweetness stole on the silence of the hour that it seemed more like celestial than mortal music—so soft, so soothing, it sank upon her ear, that it recalled her from misery to hope and love. She wept again—but these were tears which she would not have exchanged for mirth and joy. She looked round, but perceived neither ship or boat; and as the undulating sounds swelled on the distant air, she thought they came from the shore. Sometimes the breeze wafted them away, and again returned them in tones of the most languishing softness. The links of the air thus broken, it was music rather than melody that she caught, till, the pilot gradually steering nearer the coast, she distinguished the notes of a song familiar to her ear. She endeavoured to recollect where she had heard it, but in vain; yet her heart beat almost unconsciously with something resembling hope. Still she listened, till the breeze again stole the sounds. With regret she now perceived that the vessel was moving from them, and at length they trembled faintly on the waves, sank away at distance, and were heard no more. Their sweetness still vibrating on her fancy, she remained upon the deck a considerable time, unwilling to relinquish the expectation of hearing them again, and at length retired to the cabin oppressed by a degree of disappointment which the occasion did not appear to justify.

La Luc grew better during the voyage, his spirits revived, and when the vessel entered that part of the Mediterranean called the Gulf of Lyon, he was sufficiently animated to enjoy from the deck the noble prospect which the sweeping shores of Provence, terminating in the far distant ones of Languedoc, exhibited. Adeline and Clara, who anxiously watched his looks, rejoiced in their amendment; and the fond wishes of the latter already anticipated his perfect recovery. The expectations of Adeline had been too often checked by disappointment to permit her now to indulge an equal degree of hope with that of her friend, yet she confided[97] much in the effect of this voyage.

La Luc amused himself at intervals with discoursing and

97. Trusted.

pointing out the situations of considerable ports on the coast, and the mouths of the rivers that, after wandering through Provence, disembogue[98] themselves into the Mediterranean. The Rhône, however, was the only one of much consequence which he passed. On this object, though it was so distant that fancy, perhaps, rather than the senses beheld it, Clara gazed with peculiar pleasure, for it came from the banks of Savoy; and the wave which she thought she perceived had washed the feet of her dear native mountains. The time passed with mingled pleasure and improvement as La Luc described to his attentive pupils the manners and commerce of the different inhabitants of the coast, and the natural history of the country; or as he traced in imagination the remote wanderings of rivers to their source and delineated the characteristic beauties of their scenery.

After a pleasant voyage of a few days, the shores of Provence receded, and that of Languedoc, which had long bounded the distance, became the grand object of the scene, and the sailors drew near their port. They landed in the afternoon at a small town situated at the foot of a woody eminence, on the right overlooking the sea, and on the left the rich plains of Languedoc, gay with the purple vine. La Luc determined to defer his journey till the following day, and was directed to a small inn at the extremity of the town, where the accommodation, such as it was, he endeavoured to be contented with.

In the evening the beauty of the hour, and the desire of exploring new scenes, invited Adeline to walk. La Luc was fatigued, and did not go out, and Clara remained with him. Adeline took her way to the woods that rose from the margin of the sea, and climbed the wild eminence on which they hung. Often as she went she turned her eyes to catch between the dark foliage the blue waters of the bay, the white sail that flitted by, and the trembling gleam of the setting sun. When she reached the summit, and looked down over the dark tops of the woods on the wide and various prospect, she was seized

98. Flow.

with a kind of still rapture impossible to be expressed, and stood unconscious of the flight of time, till the sun had left the scene and twilight threw its solemn shade upon the mountains. The sea alone reflected the fading splendor of the West; its tranquil surface was partially disturbed by the low wind that crept in tremulous lines along the waters whence, rising to the woods, it shivered their light leaves, and died away.

Adeline quitted the heights, and followed a narrow path that wound to the beach below; her mind was now particularly sensible to fine impressions, and the sweet notes of the nightingale amid the stillness of the woods again awakened her enthusiasm.

The spreading dusk at length reminded Adeline of her distance from the inn and that she had her way to find through a wild and lonely wood; she bade adieu to the siren that had so long detained her, and pursued the path with quick steps. Having followed it for some time, she became bewildered among the thickets, and the increasing darkness did not allow her to judge of the direction she was in. Her apprehensions heightened her difficulties: she thought she distinguished the voices of men at some little distance, and she increased her speed till she found herself on the sea sands over which the woods impended. Her breath was now exhausted—she paused a moment to recover herself and fearfully listened, but instead of the voices of men, she heard faintly swelling in the breeze the notes of mournful music.

Her heart, ever sensible to the impressions of melody, melted with the tones, and her fears were for a moment lulled in sweet enchantment. Surprise was soon mingled with delight when, as the sounds advanced, she distinguished the tone of that instrument and the melody of that well-known air she had heard a few preceding evenings from the shores of Provence. But she had no time for conjecture—footsteps approached, and she renewed her speed.

She was now emerged from the darkness of the woods, and the moon, which shone bright, exhibited along the level sands the town and port in the distance. The steps that had followed now came up with her, and she perceived two men, but they passed in conversation without noticing her, and as they passed she was certain she recollected the voice of him who was then speaking. Its tones were so familiar to her ear that she was surprised at the imperfect memory which did not suffer her to be assured by whom they were uttered.

Another step now followed, and a rude voice called to her to stop. As she hastily turned her eyes, she saw imperfectly by the moonlight a man in a sailor's habit pursuing, while he renewed the call. Impelled by terror, she fled along the sands, but her steps were short and trembling—those of her pursuer's strong and quick.

She had just strength sufficient to reach the men who had before passed her and to implore their protection when her pursuer came up with them, but he suddenly turned into the woods on the left and disappeared.

She had no breath to answer the inquiries of the strangers who supported her, till a sudden exclamation and the sound of her own name drew her eyes attentively upon the person who uttered them, and in the rays which shone strong upon his features, she distinguished Monsieur Verneuil!

Mutual satisfaction and explanation ensued, and when he learned that La Luc and his daughter were at the inn, he felt an increased pleasure in conducting her thither. He said that he had accidentally met with an old friend in Savoy, whom he now introduced by the name of Mauron, and who had prevailed on him to change his route and accompany him to the shores of the Mediterranean. They had embarked from the coast of Provence only a few preceding days, and had that evening landed in Languedoc on the estate of Monsieur Mauron. Adeline had now no doubt that it was the flute of Monsieur Verneuil, which had so often delighted her at Leloncourt, that she had heard on the sea.

When they reached the inn they found La Luc under great anxiety for Adeline, in search of whom he had sent several people. Anxiety yielded to surprise and pleasure when he perceived her with Monsieur Verneuil, whose eyes beamed with unusual animation on seeing Clara. After mutual congratulations, Monsieur Verneuil observed and lamented the very indifferent accommodation which the inn afforded his friends, and Monsieur Mauron immediately invited them to his château with a warmth of hospitality that overcame every scruple which delicacy or pride could oppose. The woods that Adeline had traversed formed a part of his domain, which extended almost to the inn; but he insisted that his carriage should take his guests to the château, and departed to give orders for their reception.

The presence of Monsieur Verneuil and the kindness of his friend gave to La Luc an unusual flow of spirits; he conversed with a degree of vigour and liveliness to which he had long been unaccustomed, and the smile of satisfaction that Clara gave to Adeline expressed how much she thought he was already benefited by the voyage. Adeline answered her look with a smile of less confidence, for she attributed his present animation to a more temporary cause.

About half an hour after the departure of Monsieur Mauron, a boy who served as waiter brought a message from a chevalier then at the inn requesting permission to speak with Adeline. The man who had pursued her along the sands instantly occurred to her, and she scarcely doubted that the stranger was some person belonging to the Marquis de Montalt, perhaps the marquis himself, though that he should have discovered her accidentally, in so obscure a place, and so immediately upon her arrival, seemed very improbable.

With trembling lips and a countenance pale as death, she inquired the name of the chevalier. The boy was not acquainted with it. La Luc asked what sort of a person he was; but the boy, who understood little of the art of describing, gave such a confused account of him that Adeline could only learn he was not large, but of the middle stature.

This circumstance, however, convincing her it was not the Marquis de Montalt who desired to see her, she asked whether it would be agreeable to La Luc to have the stranger admitted. La Luc said, "By all means;" and the waiter withdrew.

Adeline sat in trembling expectation till the door opened, and Louis de la Motte entered the room. He advanced with an embarrassed and melancholy air, though his countenance had been enlightened with a momentary pleasure when he first beheld Adeline—Adeline, who was still the idol of his heart. After the first salutations were over, all apprehensions of the marquis being now dissipated, she inquired when Louis had seen Monsieur and Madame de la Motte.

"I ought rather to ask you that question," said Louis in some confusion, "for I believe you have seen them since I have; and the pleasure of meeting you thus is equalled by my surprise. I have not heard from my father for some time, owing probably to my regiment being removed to new quarters."

He looked as if he wished to be informed with whom Adeline now was; but as this was a subject upon which it was impossible she could speak in the presence of La Luc, she led the conversation to general topics, after having said that Monsieur and Madame de la Motte were well when she left them. Louis spoke little and often looked anxiously at Adeline, while his mind seemed labouring under strong oppression. She observed this, and recollecting the declaration he had made her on the morning of his departure from the abbey, she attributed his present embarrassment to the effect of a passion yet unsubdued, and did not appear to notice it.

After he had sat near a quarter of an hour, under a struggle of feelings which he could neither conquer nor conceal, he rose to leave the room and, as he passed Adeline, said in a low voice, "Do permit me to speak with you alone for five minutes."

She hesitated in some confusion, and then, saying there were none but friends present, begged he would be seated.

"Excuse me," said he, in the same low accent. "What I would say nearly concerns you, and you only. Do favour me with a few moments' attention."

He said this with a look that surprised her; and having ordered candles in another room, she went thither.

Louis sat for some moments silent, and seemingly in great perturbation of mind. At length he said, "I know not whether to rejoice or to lament at this unexpected meeting, though if you are in safe hands, I ought certainly to rejoice, however hard the task that now falls to my lot. I am not ignorant of the dangers and persecutions you have suffered, and cannot forbear expressing my anxiety to know how you are now circumstanced. Are you indeed with friends?"

"I am," said Adeline. "Monsieur de la Motte has informed you—"

"No," replied Louis, with a deep sigh, "not my father." He paused. "But I do indeed rejoice," resumed he, "O! how sincerely rejoice! that you are in safety. Could you know, lovely Adeline, what I have suffered!" He checked himself.

"I understood you had something of importance to say, sir," said Adeline. "You must excuse me if I remind you that I have not many moments to spare."

"It is indeed of importance," replied Louis, "yet I know not how to mention it—how to soften—this task is too severe. Alas! my poor friend!"

"Who is it you speak of, sir," said Adeline, with quickness.

Louis rose from his chair, and walked about the room. "I would prepare you for what I have to say," he resumed, "but upon my soul I am not equal to it."

"I entreat you to keep me no longer in suspense," said Adeline, who had a wild idea that it was Theodore he would speak of.

Louis still hesitated.

"Is it—O is it?—I conjure you tell me the worst at once," said she, in a voice of agony. "I can bear it—indeed I can."

"My unhappy friend!" exclaimed Louis. "O Theodore!"

"Theodore!" faintly articulated Adeline. "He lives then!"

"He does," said Louis, "but—" He stopped.

"But what?" cried Adeline, trembling violently. "If he is living you cannot tell me worse than my fears suggest; I entreat you, therefore, not to hesitate."

Louis resumed his seat and, endeavouring to assume a collected air, said, "He is living, madam, but he is a prisoner, and—for why should I deceive you? I fear he has little to hope in this world."

"I have long feared so, sir," said Adeline in a voice of forced composure. "You have something more terrible than this to relate, and I again entreat you will explain yourself."

"He has everything to apprehend from the Marquis de Montalt," said Louis. "Alas! why do I say to apprehend? His judgement is already fixed—he is condemned to die."

At this confirmation of her fears a death-like paleness diffused itself over the countenance of Adeline; she sat motionless, and attempted to sigh, but seemed almost suffocated. Terrified at her situation and expecting to see her faint, Louis would have supported her, but with her hand she waved him from her, and was unable to speak. He now called for assistance, and La Luc and Clara, with Monsieur Verneuil, informed of Adeline's indisposition, were quickly by her side.

At the sound of their voices she looked up, and seemed to recollect herself, when uttering a heavy sigh she burst into tears. La Luc rejoiced to see her weep, encouraged her tears, which, after some time, relieved her, and when she was able to speak, she desired to go back to La Luc's parlour. Louis attended her thither; when she was better he would have withdrawn, but La Luc begged he would stay.

"You are perhaps a relation of this young lady, sir," said he, "and may have brought news of her father."

"Not so, sir," replied Louis, hesitating.

"This gentleman," said Adeline, who had now recollected her dissipated thoughts, "is the son of the Monsieur de la Motte, whom you may have heard me mention."

Louis seemed shocked to be declared the son of a man that had once acted so unworthily toward Adeline, who, instantly perceiving the pain her words occasioned, endeavoured to soften their effect by saying that La Motte had saved her from imminent danger, and had afforded her an asylum for many months. Adeline sat in a state of dreadful solitude to know the particulars of Theodore's situation, yet could not acquire courage to renew the subject in the presence of La Luc; she ventured, however, to ask Louis if his own regiment was quartered in the town.

He replied that his regiment lay at Vaceau, a French town on the frontiers of Spain; that he had just crossed a part of the Gulf of Lyon and was on his way to Savoy, whither he should set out early in the morning.

"We are lately come from thence," said Adeline. "May I ask to what part of Savoy you are going?"

"To Leloncourt," he replied.

"To Leloncourt!" said Adeline, in some surprise.

"I am a stranger to the country," resumed Louis, "but I go to serve my friend. You seem to know Leloncourt."

"I do indeed," said Adeline.

"You probably know then that Monsieur La Luc lives there, and will guess the motive of my journey."

"O heavens! is it possible?" exclaimed Adeline."Is it possible that Theodore Peyrou is a relation of Monsieur La Luc!"

"Theodore! what of my son?" asked La Luc, in surprise and apprehension.

"Your son!" said Adeline in a trembling voice. "Your son!"

The astonishment and anguish depictured on her countenance increased the apprehensions of this unfortunate father, and he renewed his question. But Adeline was totally unable to answer him; and the distress of Louis, on thus unexpectedly discovering the father of his unhappy friend, and knowing that it was his task to disclose the fate of his son, deprived him for some time of all power of utterance, and La Luc and Clara, whose fears were every instant heightened by this dreadful silence, continued to repeat their questions.

At length a sense of the approaching sufferings of the good La Luc overcoming every other feeling, Adeline recovered strength of mind sufficient to try to soften the intelligence Louis had to communicate, and to conduct Clara to another room. Here she collected resolution to tell her, and with much tender consideration, the circumstances of her brother's situation, concealing only her knowledge of his sentence being already pronounced. This relation necessarily included the mention of their attachment, and in the friend of her heart Clara discovered the innocent cause of her brother's destruction.

Adeline also learned the occasion of that circumstance which had contributed to keep her ignorant of Theodore's relationship to La Luc; she was told the former had taken the name of Peyrou when an estate had been left him about a year before by a relation of his mother's upon that condition. Theodore had been designed for the church, but his disposition inclined him to a more active life than the clerical habit would admit of, and on his accession to this estate he had entered into the service of the French king.

In the few and interrupted interviews which had been allowed them at Caux, Theodore had mentioned his family to Adeline only in general terms, and thus when they were so suddenly separated had, without designing it, left her in ignorance of his father's name and place of residence. The sacredness and delicacy of Adeline's grief, which had never permitted her to mention the subject of it even to Clara, had since contributed to deceive her.

The distress of Clara on learning the situation of her brother could endure no restraint; Adeline, who only by a strong effort of mind had commanded her feelings so as to impart this intelligence with tolerable composure, was now almost overwhelmed by her own and Clara's accumulated suffering. While they wept forth the anguish of their hearts, a scene, if possible, more affecting passed between La Luc and Louis, who perceived it was necessary to inform him, though cautiously and by degrees, of the full extent of his calamity. He therefore told La Luc that, though Theodore had been first tried for the offense of having quitted his post, he was now condemned on a charge of assault made upon his general officer, the Marquis de Montalt, who had brought witnesses to prove that his life had been endangered by the circumstance; and who having pursued the prosecution with the most bitter rancour, had at length obtained the sentence which the law could not withhold but which every other officer in the regiment deplored.

Louis added that the sentence was to be executed in less than a fortnight, and that Theodore, being very unhappy at receiving no answers to the letters he had sent his father, wishing to see him once more, and knowing that there was now no time to be lost, had requested him to go to Leloncourt and acquaint his father with his situation.

La Luc received the account of his son's condition with a distress that admitted neither of tears or complaint. He asked where Theodore was, and desiring to be conducted to him, he thanked Louis for all his kindness and ordered post horses immediately.

A carriage was soon ready, and this unhappy father, after taking a mournful leave of Monsieur Verneuil and sending a compliment to Monsieur Mauron, set out for the prison of his son, attended by his family. The journey was a silent one; each individual of the party endeavoured, in consideration of each other, to suppress the expression of grief but was unable to do more. La Luc appeared calm and complacent; he seemed frequently to be engaged in prayer; but a struggle for resignation and composure was sometimes visible upon his countenance, notwithstanding the efforts of his mind.

CHAPTER 20.

And venom'd with disgrace the darts of Death.

Anna Seward, "Monody on Major André"

We now return to the Marquis de Montalt, who having seen La Motte safely lodged in the prison of D———y and learning the trial would not come on immediately, had returned to his villa on the borders of the forest, where he expected to hear news of Adeline. It had been his intention to follow his servants to Lyon; but he now determined to wait a few days for letters, and he had little doubt that Adeline, since her flight had been so quickly pursued, would be overtaken, and probably before she could reach that city. In this expectation he had been miserably disappointed; for his servants informed him that though they traced her thither, they had neither been able to follow her route beyond, nor to discover her at Lyon. This escape she probably owed to having embarked on the Rhône, for it does not appear that the marquis's people thought of seeking her on the course of that river.

His presence was soon after required at Vaceau, where the court-martial was then sitting; thither, therefore, he went, with passions still more exasperated by his late disappointment, and procured the condemnation of Theodore. The sentence was universally lamented, for Theodore was much beloved in his regiment; and the occasion of the marquis's personal resentment toward him being known, every heart was interested in his cause.

Louis de la Motte, happening at this time to be stationed in the same town, heard an imperfect account of his story, and being convinced that the prisoner was the young chevalier whom he had formerly seen with the marquis at the abbey, he was induced partly from compassion and partly with a hope of hearing of his parents to visit him. The compassionate sympathy which Louis expressed, and the zeal with which he tendered his services, affected Theodore, and excited in him a warm return of friendship. Louis made him frequent visits, did everything that kindness could suggest to alleviate his sufferings, and a mutual esteem and confidence ensued.

Theodore at length communicated the chief subject of his concern to Louis, who discovered with inexpressible grief that it was Adeline whom the marquis had thus cruelly persecuted, and Adeline for whose sake the generous Theodore was about to suffer. He soon perceived also that Theodore was his favoured rival; but he generously suppressed the jealous pang this discovery occasioned, and determined that no prejudice of passion should withdraw him from the duties of humanity and friendship. He eagerly inquired where Adeline then resided.

"She is yet, I fear, in the power of the marquis," said Theodore, sighing deeply. "O God!—these chains!"—and he threw an agonizing glance upon them.

Louis sat silent and thoughtful; at length starting from his reverie, he said he would go to the marquis, and immediately quitted the prison. The marquis was, however, already set off for Paris, where he had been summoned to appear at the approaching trial of La Motte. Louis, yet ignorant of the late transactions at the abbey, returned to the prison, where he endeavoured to forget that Theodore was the favoured rival of his love, and to remember him only as the defender of Adeline.

So earnestly he pressed his offers of service that Theodore, whom the silence of his father equally surprised and afflicted, and who was very anxious to see him once again, accepted his proposal of going himself to Savoy. "My letters I strongly suspect to have been intercepted by the marquis," said Theodore. "If so, my poor father will have the whole weight of this calamity to sustain at once unless I avail myself of your kindness, and I shall neither see him nor hear from him before I die. Louis! there are moments when my fortitude shrinks from the conflict, and my senses threaten to desert me."

No time was to be lost; the warrant for his execution had already received the king's signature, so Louis immediately set forward for Savoy. The letters of Theodore had indeed been intercepted by order of the marquis, who, in the hope of discovering the asylum of Adeline, had opened and afterward destroyed them.

But to return to La Luc, who now drew near Vaceau. His family observed him to be greatly changed in his looks since he had heard the late calamitous intelligence; he uttered no complaint, but it was too obvious that his disorder had made a rapid progress. Louis, who during the journey proved the goodness of his disposition by the delicate attentions he paid this unhappy party, concealed his observation of the decline of La Luc, and to support Adeline's spirits endeavoured to convince her that her apprehensions on this subject were groundless. Her spirits did indeed require support, for she was now within a few miles of the town that contained Theodore. While her increasing perturbation almost overcome her, she yet tried to appear composed. When the carriage entered the town, she cast a timid and anxious glance from the window in search of the prison, but passed through several streets without perceiving any building which corresponded with her idea of it, and the coach stopped at the inn.

The frequent changes in La Luc's countenance betrayed the violent agitation of his mind, and when he attempted to alight, feeble and exhausted, he was compelled to accept the support of Louis, to whom he faintly said, as he passed to the parlour, "I am indeed sick at heart, but I trust the pain will not be long."

Louis pressed his hand without speaking, and hastened back for Adeline and Clara, who were already in the passage.

La Luc wiped the tears from his eyes—they were the first he had shed—as they entered the room. "I would go immediately to my poor boy," said he to Louis. "Yours, sir, is a mournful office—be so good as to conduct me to him."

He rose to go but, feeble and overcome with grief, again sat down. Adeline and Clara united in entreating that he would compose himself and take some refreshment; and Louis, urging the necessity of preparing Theodore for the interview, prevailed with him to delay it till his son should be informed of his arrival, and immediately quitted the inn for the prison of his friend.

When he was gone, La Luc, as a duty he owed those he loved, tried to take some support, but the convulsions of his throat would not suffer him to swallow the wine he held to his parched lips, and he was now so much disordered that he desired to retire to his chamber, where alone and in prayer, he passed the dreadful interval of Louis's absence.

Clara yielded to the violence of her grief on the bosom of Adeline, who sat in calm but deep distress. "I shall lose my dear father too," said she; "I see it; I shall lose my father and my brother together." Adeline wept with her friend for some time in silence; and then attempted to persuade her that La Luc was not so ill as she apprehended.

"Do not mislead me with hope," she replied. "He will not survive the shock of this calamity—I saw it from the first."

Adeline, knowing that La Luc's distress would be heightened by the observance of his daughter's, and that indulgence would only increase its poignancy, endeavoured to rouse her to an exertion of fortitude by urging the necessity of commanding her emotion in the presence of her father. "This is possible," added she, "however painful may be the effort. You must know, my dear, that my grief is not inferior to your own, yet I have hitherto been enabled to support my sufferings in silence, for Monsieur La Luc I do, indeed, love and reverence as a parent."

Louis meanwhile reached the prison of Theodore, who received him with an air of mingled surprise and impatience.

"What brings you back so soon?" said he. "Have you heard news of my father?"

Louis now gradually unfolded the circumstances of their meeting, and La Luc's arrival at Vaceau.

A various emotion agitated the countenance of Theodore on receiving this intelligence. "My poor father!" said he. "He has then followed his son to this ignominious place! Little did I think when last we parted he would meet me in a prison, under condemnation!" This reflection roused an impetuosity of grief which deprived him for some time of speech. "But where is he?" said Theodore, recovering himself. "Now he is come, I shrink from the interview I have so much wished for. The sight of his distress will be dreadful to me. Louis! when I am gone—comfort my poor father."

His voice was again interrupted by sobs; and Louis, who had been fearful of acquainting him at the same time of the arrival of La Luc and the discovery of Adeline, now judged it proper to administer the cordial of this latter intelligence.

The glooms of a prison and of calamity vanished for a transient moment; those who had seen Theodore would have believed this to be the instant which gave him life and liberty. When his first emotions subsided, he said, "I will not repine, since I know that Adeline is preserved and that I shall once more see my father; I will endeavour to die with resignation." He enquired if La Luc was there in the prison; and was told he was at the inn with Clara and Adeline. "Adeline! Is Adeline there too!—This is beyond my hopes. Yet why do I rejoice? I must never see her more: this is no place for Adeline."

Again he relapsed into an agony of distress—and again repeated a thousand questions concerning Adeline, till he was reminded by Louis that his father was impatient to see him—when, shocked that he had so long detained his friend, he entreated him to conduct La Luc to the prison, and endeavoured to recollect fortitude for the approaching interview.

When Louis returned to the inn La Luc was still in his chamber. As Clara quit the room to call him, Adeline seized with trembling impatience the opportunity to enquire more particularly concerning Theodore than she chose to do in the presence of his unhappy sister. Louis represented him to be much more tranquil than he really was; Adeline was somewhat soothed by the account, and her tears, hitherto restrained, flowed silently and fast till La Luc appeared.

His countenance had recovered its serenity but was impressed with a deep and steady sorrow, which excited in the beholder a mingled emotion of pity and reverence. "How is my son, sir?" said he as he entered the room. "We will go to him immediately."

Clara renewed the entreaties to accompany her father that had been already rejected, who persisted in a refusal. "Tomorrow you shall see him," added he, "but our first meeting must be alone. Stay with your friend, my dear; she has need of consolation."

La Luc walked silently toward the prison, resting on the arm of Louis. It was now night: a dim lamp that hung above showed them the gates, and Louis rang a bell. La Luc, almost overcome with agitation, leaned against the postern till the porter appeared. He enquired for Theodore, and followed the man; but when he reached the second courtyard he seemed ready to faint, and again stopped. Louis desired the porter would fetch some water, but La Luc, recovering his voice, said he should soon be better, and would not suffer him to go. In a few minutes he was able to follow Louis, who led him through several dark passages and up a flight of steps to a door, which being unbarred, disclosed to him the prison of his son.

He was seated at a small table, on which stood a lamp that threw a feeble light across the place sufficient only to show its desolation and wretchedness. When he perceived La Luc he sprang from his chair, and in the next moment was in his arms.

"My father!" said he in a tremulous voice.

"My son!" exclaimed La Luc; and they were for some time silent, and locked in each other's embrace.

At length Theodore led him to the only chair the room afforded, and seating himself with Louis at the foot of the bed, had leisure to observe the ravages which illness and calamity had made on the features of his parent. La Luc made several efforts to speak but was unable to articulate. He laid his hand upon his breast and sighed deeply. Fearful of the consequence of so affecting a scene on his shattered frame, Louis, endeavouring to call off his attention from the immediate object of his distress interrupted the silence; but La Luc, shuddering and complaining he was very cold, sank back in his chair.

His condition roused Theodore from the stupor of despair. While he flew to support his father, Louis ran out for other assistance.

"I shall soon be better, Theodore," said La Luc, unclosing his eyes. "The faintness is already going off. I have not been well of late; and this sad meeting!"

Unable any longer to command himself, Theodore wrung his hand, and the distress which had long struggled for utterance burst in convulsive sobs from his breast. La Luc gradually revived, and exerted himself to calm the transports of his son; but the fortitude of the latter had now entirely forsaken him, and he could only utter exclamation and complaint. "Ah! little did I think we should ever meet under circumstances so dreadful as the present! But I have not deserved them, my father! the motives of my conduct have still been just."

"That is my supreme consolation," said La Luc, "and ought to support you in this hour of trial. The Almighty God, who is the judge of hearts, will reward you hereafter. Trust in him, my son; I look to him with no feeble hope, but with a firm reliance on his justice!" La Luc's voice faltered; he raised his eyes to Heaven with an expression of meek devotion while the tears of humanity fell slowly on his cheek.

Still more affected by his last words, Theodore turned from him and paced the room with quick steps. The entrance of Louis was a very seasonable relief to La Luc, who, taking a cordial he had brought, was soon sufficiently restored to discourse on the subject most interesting to him.

Theodore tried to attain a command of his feelings, and succeeded. He conversed with tolerable composure for above an hour, during which La Luc endeavoured to elevate the mind of his son by religious hope, and to enable him to meet with fortitude the awful hour that approached. But the appearance of resignation which Theodore attained always vanished when he reflected that he was going to leave his father a prey to grief, and his beloved Adeline forever.

When La Luc was about to depart, Theodore again mentioned her. "Afflicting as an interview must be in our present circumstances," said he, "I cannot bear the thought of quitting the world without seeing her once again; yet I know not how to ask her to encounter, for my sake, the misery of a parting scene. Tell her that my thoughts never, for a moment, leave her, that—"

La Luc interrupted, and assured him that since he so much wished it, he should see her, though a meeting could serve only to heighten the mutual anguish of a final separation.

"I know it—I know it too well," said Theodore, "yet I cannot resolve to see her no more, and thus spare her the pain this interview must inflict. O my father! when I think of those whom I must soon leave forever, my heart breaks. But I will indeed try to profit by your precept and example, and show that your paternal care has not been in vain. My good Louis, go with my father—he has need of support. How much I owe this generous friend," added Theodore, "you well know, sir."

"I do, in truth," replied La Luc, "and can never repay his kindness to you. He has contributed to support us all; but you require comfort more than myself—he shall remain with you—I will go alone."

This Theodore would not suffer, and La Luc no longer opposing him, they affectionately embraced, and separated for the night.

When they reached the inn, La Luc consulted with Louis on the possibility of addressing a petition to the sovereign in time enough to save Theodore. His distance from Paris and the short interval before the period fixed for the execution of the sentence made this design difficult; but believing it was practicable, La Luc, incapable as he appeared of performing so long a journey, determined to attempt it. Louis, thinking that the undertaking would prove fatal to the father without benefiting the son, endeavoured, though faintly, to dissuade him from it—but his resolution was fixed.

"If I sacrifice the small remains of my life in the service of my child," said he, "I shall lose little; if I save him, I shall gain everything. There is no time to be lost—I will set off immediately."

He would have ordered post horses, but Louis and Clara—who was now come from the bedside of Adeline, who, unable longer to struggle against the force of grief, had retired to her chamber and her bed—urged the necessity of his taking a few hours' repose. He was at length compelled to acknowledge himself unequal to the immediate exertion which parental anxiety prompted, and consented to seek rest.

When he had retired to his chamber, Clara lamented the condition of her father. "He will not bear the journey," said she. "He is greatly changed within these few days."

Louis was so entirely of her opinion that he could not disguise it, even to flatter her with a hope. She added, which did not contribute to raise his spirits, that Adeline was so much indisposed by her grief for the situation of Theodore and the sufferings of La Luc that she dreaded the consequence.

It has been seen that the passion of young La Motte had suffered no abatement from time or absence; on the contrary, the persecution and the dangers which had pursued Adeline awakened all his tenderness and drew her nearer to his heart. When he had discovered that Theodore loved her and was beloved again, he experienced all the anguish of jealousy and disappointment; for though she had forbade him to hope, he found it too painful an effort to obey her, and had secretly cherished the flame which he ought to have stifled. His heart was, however, too noble to suffer his zeal for Theodore to abate because he was his favoured rival, and his mind too strong not to conceal the anguish this certainty occasioned. The attachment which Theodore had testified toward Adeline even endeared him to Louis, when he had recovered from the first shock of disappointment, and that conquest over jealousy which originated in principle and was pursued with difficulty became afterward his pride and his glory.

When, however, he again saw Adeline—saw her in the mild dignity of sorrow more interesting than ever—saw her, though sinking beneath its pressure, yet tender and solicitous to soften the afflictions of those around her—it was with the utmost difficulty he preserved his resolution, and forbore to express the sentiments she inspired. When he further considered that her acute sufferings arose from the strength of her affection, he more than ever wished himself the object of a heart capable of so tender a regard, and Theodore in prison and in chains was a momentary object of envy.

In the morning, when La Luc arose from short and disturbed slumbers, he found Louis, Clara, and Adeline, whom indisposition could not prevent from paying him this testimony of respect and affection, assembled in the parlour of the inn to see him depart. After a slight breakfast, during which his feelings permitted him to say little, he bade his friends a sad farewell, and stepped into the carriage, followed by their tears and prayers.

Adeline immediately retired to her chamber, which she was too ill to quit that day. In the evening Clara left her friend and, conducted by Louis, went to visit her brother, whose emotions, on hearing of his father's departure, were various and strong.

CHAPTER 21

'Tis only, when with inbred horror smote
At some base act, or done, or to be done,
That the recoiling soul, with conscious dread,
Shrinks back into itself.

William Mason, *Caractacus*

We return now to **Pierre de la Motte, who, after** remaining some weeks in the prison of D———y, was removed to take his trial in the courts of Paris, whither the Marquis de Montalt followed to prosecute the charge. Madame de la Motte accompanied her husband to the prison of the Châtelet.[99] His mind sank under the weight of his misfortunes; nor could all the efforts of his wife rouse him from the torpidity of despair which a consideration of his circumstances occasioned. Should he be even acquitted of the charge brought against him by the marquis—which was very unlikely—he was now in the scene of his former crimes, and the moment that should liberate him from the walls of his prison would probably deliver him again into the hands of offended justice.

The prosecution of the marquis was too well-founded and its object of a nature too serious not to justify the terror of

99. A fortress and prison in Paris.

La Motte. Soon after the latter had settled at the Abbey of St. Clair, the small stock of money which the emergency of his circumstances had left him being nearly exhausted, his mind became corroded with the most cruel anxiety concerning the means of his future subsistence. As he was one evening riding alone in a remote part of the forest, musing on his distressed circumstances and meditating plans to relieve the exigencies which he saw approaching, he perceived among the trees at some distance a chevalier on horseback who was riding deliberately along and seemed wholly unattended. A thought darted across the mind of La Motte that he might be spared the evils which threatened him by robbing this stranger. His former practices had passed the boundary of honesty—fraud was in some degree familiar to him—and the thought was not dismissed. He hesitated—every moment of hesitation increased the power of temptation—the opportunity was such as might never occur again. He looked round, and as far as the trees opened saw no person but the chevalier, who seemed by his air to be a man of distinction.

Summoning all his courage, La Motte rode forward and attacked him. The Marquis de Montalt, for it was he, was unarmed, but knowing that his attendants were not far off, he refused to yield. While they were struggling for victory, La Motte saw several horsemen enter the extremity of the avenue, and rendered desperate by opposition and delay, he drew from his pocket a pistol, which an apprehension of banditti made him usually carry when he rode to a distance from the abbey, and fired at the marquis, who staggered and fell senseless to the ground. La Motte had time to tear from his coat a brilliant star, some diamond rings from his fingers, and to rifle his pockets before his attendants came up. Instead of pursuing the robber, they all in their first confusion flew to assist their lord, and La Motte escaped.

Before he reached the abbey he stopped at a little ruin, the tomb formerly mentioned, to examine his booty. It consisted of a purse containing seventy louis d'ors, a diamond star, three rings of great value, and a miniature set with brilliants of the marquis himself, which he had intended as a present for his favourite mistress. To La Motte, who but a few hours before had seen himself nearly destitute, the view of this treasure excited an almost ungovernable transport; but it was soon checked when he remembered the means he had employed to obtain it, and that he had paid for the wealth he contemplated the price of blood. Naturally violent in his passions, this reflection sank him from the summit of exultation to the abyss of despondency. He considered himself a murderer and, startled as one awakened from a dream, would have given half the world, had it been his, to have been as poor and, comparatively, as guiltless as a few preceding hours had seen him. On examining the portrait he discovered the resemblance, and believing that his hand had deprived the original of life, he gazed upon the picture with unutterable anguish.

To the horrors of remorse succeeded the perplexities of fear. Apprehensive of he knew not what, he lingered at the tomb, where he at length deposited his treasure, believing that if his offense should awaken justice, the abbey might be searched, and these jewels betray him. From Madame de la Motte it was easy to conceal his increase of wealth, for as he had never made her acquainted with the exact state of his finances, she had not suspected the extreme poverty which menaced him; and as they continued to live as usual, she believed that their expenses were drawn from the usual supply. But it was not so easy to disguise the workings of remorse and horror: his manner became gloomy and reserved, and his frequent visits to the tomb, where he went partly to examine his treasure, but chiefly to indulge in the dreadful pleasure of contemplating the picture of the marquis, excited curiosity. In the solitude of the forest, where no variety of objects occurred to renovate his ideas, the horrible one of having committed murder was ever present to him.

When the marquis arrived at the abbey, the astonishment and terror of La Motte—for at first he scarce knew whether he beheld the shadow or the substance of a human form—were quickly succeeded by apprehension of the punishment due to the crime he had really committed. When his distress had prevailed on the marquis to retire, he informed him that he was by birth a chevalier; he then touched upon such parts of his misfortunes as he thought would excite pity, expressed such abhorrence of his guilt, and voluntarily uttered such a solemn promise of returning the jewels he had yet in his possession, for he had ventured to dispose only of a small part, that the marquis at length listened to him with some degree of compassion. This favourable sentiment, seconded by a selfish motive, induced the marquis to compromise with La Motte.

Of quick and inflammable passions, he had observed the beauty of Adeline with an eye of no common regard, and he resolved to spare the life of La Motte upon no other condition than the sacrifice of this unfortunate girl. La Motte had neither resolution or virtue sufficient to reject the terms—the jewels were restored, and he consented to betray the innocent Adeline. But as he was too well acquainted with her heart to believe that she would easily be won to the practice of vice, and as he still felt a degree of pity and tenderness for her, he endeavoured to prevail on the marquis to forbear precipitate measures, and to attempt gradually to undermine her principles by seducing her affections. The marquis approved and adopted this plan: the failure of his first scheme induced him to employ the stratagems he afterward pursued, and thus to multiply the misfortunes of Adeline.

Such were the circumstances which had brought La Motte to his present deplorable situation. The day of trial was now come, and he was led from prison into the court, where the marquis appeared as his accuser. When the charge was delivered, La Motte, as is usual, pleaded not guilty, and the Advocate Nemours, who had undertaken to plead for him, afterward endeavoured to make it appear that the accusation on the part of the Marquis de Montalt was false and malicious. To this purpose he mentioned the circumstance of the latter having attempted to persuade his client to the murder of Adeline; he further urged that the marquis had lived in habits of intimacy with La Motte for several months immediately preceding his arrest, and that it was not till he had disappointed the designs of his accuser by conveying beyond his reach the unhappy object of his vengeance that the marquis had thought proper to charge La Motte with the crime for which he stood indicted. Nemours urged the improbability of one man's keeping up a friendly intercourse with another from whom he had suffered the double injury of assault and robbery; yet it was certain that the marquis had observed a frequent intercourse with La Motte for some months following the time specified for the commission of the crime. If the marquis intended to prosecute, why was it not immediately after his discovery of La Motte? and if not then, what had influenced him to prosecute at so distant a period?

To this nothing was replied on the part of the marquis; for as his conduct on this point had been subservient to his designs on Adeline, he could not justify it but by exposing schemes which would betray the darkness of his character and invalidate his cause. He, therefore, contented himself with producing several of his servants as witnesses of the assault and robbery, who swore without scruple to the person of La Motte, though not one of them had seen him otherwise than through the gloom of evening and riding off at full speed. On a cross examination most of them contradicted each other; their evidence was of course rejected; but as the marquis had yet two other witnesses to produce, whose arrival at Paris had been hourly expected, the event of the trial was postponed, and the court adjourned.

La Motte was reconducted to his prison under the same pressure of despondency with which he had quitted it. As he walked through one of the avenues he passed a man who stood by to let him proceed, and who regarded him with a fixed and earnest eye. La Motte thought he had seen him before; but the imperfect view he caught of his features through the duskiness of the place made him uncertain as to this, and his mind was in too perturbed a state to suffer him to feel an interest on the subject. When he was gone the stranger inquired of the keeper of the prison who La Motte was; on being told, and receiving answers to some further questions he put, he desired he might be admitted to speak with him. The request, as the man was only a debtor, was granted; but as the doors were now shut for the night, the interview was deferred till the morrow.

La Motte found Madame in his room, where she had been waiting for some hours to hear the event of the trial. They now wished more earnestly than ever to see their son; but they were, as he had suspected, ignorant of his change of quarters, owing to the letters which he had, as usual, addressed to them under an assumed name, remaining at the post-house of Auboine. This circumstance occasioned Madame de la Motte to address her letters to the place of her son's late residence, and he had thus continued ignorant of his father's misfortunes and removal. Madame de la Motte, surprised at receiving no answers to her letters, sent off another containing an account of the trial as far as it had proceeded and a request that her son would obtain leave of absence and set out for Paris instantly. As she was still ignorant of the failure of her letters and would not have known whither to have sent them had it been otherwise, she directed this as usual.

Meanwhile his approaching fate was never absent for a moment from the mind of La Motte, which, feeble by nature, and still more enervated by habits of indulgence, refused to support him at this dreadful period.

While these scenes were passing at Paris, La Luc arrived there without any accident after performing a journey during which he had been supported almost entirely by the spirit of his resolution. He hastened to throw himself at the feet of the sovereign, and such was the excess of his feeling on presenting the petition which was to decide the fate of his son that he could only look silently up, and then fainted. The king received the paper and, giving orders for the unhappy father to be taken care of, passed on. La Luc was carried back to his hotel, where he awaited the event of this his final effort.

Adeline, meanwhile, continued at Vaceau in a state of anxiety too powerful for her long-agitated frame, and the illness in consequence of this confined her almost wholly to her chamber. Sometimes she ventured to flatter herself with a hope that the journey of La Luc would be successful; but these short and illusive intervals of comfort served only to heighten, by contrast, the despondency that succeeded, and in the alternate extremes of feeling she experienced a state more torturing than that produced by either the sharp sting of unexpected calamity or the sullen pain of settled despair.

When she was well enough she came down to the parlour to converse with Louis, who brought her frequent accounts of Theodore, and who passed every moment he could snatch from the duty of his profession in endeavours to support and console his afflicted friends. Adeline and Theodore both looked to him for the little comfort allotted them, for he brought them intelligence of each other, and whenever he appeared a transient melancholy kind of pleasure played round their hearts. He could not conceal from Theodore Adeline's indisposition, since it was necessary to account for her not indulging the earnest wish he repeatedly expressed to see her again. To Adeline he spoke chiefly of the fortitude and resignation of his friend, not however forgetting to mention the tender affection he constantly expressed for her. Accustomed to derive her sole consolation from the presence of Louis, and to observe his unwearied friendship toward him whom she so truly loved, she found her esteem for him ripen into gratitude, and her regard daily increase.

The fortitude with which he had said Theodore supported his calamities was somewhat exaggerated. He could not sufficiently forget those ties which bound him to life to meet his fate with firmness; but though the paroxysms of grief were acute and frequent, he sought, and often attained in the presence of his friends, a manly composure. From the event of his father's journey he hoped little, yet that little was sufficient to keep his mind in the torture of suspense till the issue should appear.

On the day preceding that fixed for the execution of the sentence, La Luc reached Vaceau. Adeline was at her chamber window when the carriage drew up to the inn; she saw him alight and with feeble steps, supported by Peter, enter the house. From the languor of his air she drew no favourable omen, and almost sinking under the violence of her emotion, she went to meet him. Clara was already with her father when Adeline entered the room. She approached him but, dreading to receive from his lips a confirmation of the misfortune his countenance seemed to indicate, looked expressively at him and sat down, unable to speak the question she would have asked. He held out his hand to her in silence, sank back in his chair, and seemed to be fainting under oppression of heart. His manner confirmed all her fears; at this dreadful conviction her senses failed her, and she sat motionless and stupefied.

La Luc and Clara were too much occupied by their own distress to observe her situation; after some time she breathed a heavy sigh, and burst into tears. Relieved by weeping, her spirits gradually returned, and she at length said to La Luc, "It is unnecessary, sir, to ask the success of your journey; yet, when you can bear to mention the subject, I wish—"

La Luc waved his hand. "Alas!" said he, "I have nothing to tell but what you already guess too well. My poor Theodore!" His voice was convulsed with sorrow, and some moments of unutterable anguish followed.

Adeline was the first who recovered sufficient recollection to notice the extreme languor of La Luc and attend to his support. She ordered him refreshments, and entreated he would retire to his bed and suffer her to send for a physician, adding that the fatigue he had suffered made repose absolutely necessary.

"Would that I could find it, my dear child," said he. "It is not in this world that I must look for it, but in a better, and that better, I trust, I shall soon attain. But where is our good friend, Louis La Motte? He must lead me to my son."

Grief again interrupted his utterance, and the entrance of Louis was a very seasonable relief to them all. Their tears explained the question he would have asked; La Luc immediately inquired for his son and, thanking Louis for all his kindness to him, desired to be conducted to the prison. Louis endeavoured to persuade him to defer his visit till the morning, and Adeline and Clara joined their entreaties with his, but La Luc determined to go that night.

"His time is short," said he, "a few hours and I shall see him no more, at least in this world; let me not neglect these precious moments. Adeline! I had promised my poor boy that he should see you once more; you are not now equal to the meeting. I will try to reconcile him to the disappointment; but if I fail, and you are better in the morning, I know you will exert yourself to sustain the interview."

Adeline looked impatient, and attempted to speak. La Luc rose to depart, but could only reach the door of the room, where, faint and feeble, he sat down in a chair. "I must submit to necessity," said he; "I find I am not able to go farther tonight. Go to him, La Motte, and tell him I am somewhat disordered by my journey, but that I will be with him early in the morning. Do not flatter him with a hope; prepare him for the worst."

There was a pause of silence; La Luc, at length recovering himself, desired Clara would order his bed to be got ready, and she willingly obeyed. When he withdrew, Adeline told Louis what was indeed unnecessary, the event of La Luc's journey.

"I own," continued she, "that I had sometimes suffered myself to hope, and I now feel this calamity with double force. I fear too that Monsieur La Luc will sink under its pressure; he is much altered for the worse since he set out for Paris. Tell me your opinion sincerely."

The change was so obvious that Louis could not deny it, but he endeavoured to soothe her apprehension by ascribing this alteration, in a great measure, to the temporary fatigue of traveling.

Adeline declared her resolution of accompanying La Luc to take leave of Theodore in the morning. "I know not how I shall support the interview," said she, "but to see him once more is a duty I owe both to him and myself. The remembrance of having neglected to give him this last proof of affection would pursue me with incessant remorse."

After some further conversation on this subject Louis withdrew to the prison, ruminating on the best means of imparting to his friend the fatal intelligence he had to communicate. Theodore received it with more composure than he had expected, but he asked with impatience why he did not see his father and Adeline, and on being informed that indisposition withheld them, his imagination seized on the worst possibility, and suggested that his father was dead. It was a considerable time before Louis could convince him of the contrary, and that Adeline was not dangerously ill; when, however, he was assured that he should see them in the morning, he became more tranquil.

He desired his friend would not leave him that night. "These are the last hours we can pass together," added he, "I cannot sleep! Stay with me and lighten their heavy moments. I have need of comfort, Louis. Young as I am, and held by such strong attachments, I cannot quit the world with resignation. I know not how to credit those stories we hear of philosophic fortitude; wisdom cannot teach us cheerfully to resign a good, and life in my circumstances is surely such."

The night was passed in embarrassed conversation; sometimes interrupted by long fits of silence, and sometimes by the paroxysms of despair; and the morning of that day which was to lead Theodore to death at length dawned through the grates of his prison.

La Luc meanwhile passed a sleepless and dreadful night. He prayed for fortitude and resignation both for himself and Theodore; but the pangs of nature were powerful in his heart, and not to be subdued. The idea of his lamented wife, and of what she would have suffered had she lived to witness the ignominious death which awaited her son, frequently occurred to him.

It seemed as if a destiny had hung over the life of Theodore, for it is probable that the king might have granted the petition of the unhappy father had it not happened that the Marquis de Montalt was present at court when the paper was presented. The appearance and singular distress of the petitioner had interested the monarch, and instead of putting by the paper, he opened it. As he threw his eyes over it, observing that the criminal was of the Marquis de Montalt's regiment, he turned to him and inquired the nature of the offense for which the culprit was about to suffer. The answer was such as might have been expected from the marquis, and the king was convinced that Theodore was not a proper object of mercy.

But to return to La Luc, who was called, according to his order, at a very early hour. Having passed some time in prayer, he went down to the parlour, where Louis, punctual to the moment, already waited to conduct him to the prison. He appeared calm and collected, but his countenance was impressed with a fixed despair that sensibly affected his young friend. While they waited for Adeline he spoke little, and seemed struggling to attain the fortitude necessary to support him through the approaching scene. Adeline not appearing, he at length sent to hasten her, and was told she had been ill, but was recovering. She had indeed passed a night of such agitation that her frame had sunk under it, and she was now endeavouring to recover strength and composure sufficient to sustain her in this dreadful hour. Every moment that brought her nearer to it had increased her emotion, and the apprehension of being prevented from seeing Theodore had alone enabled her to struggle against the united pressure of illness and grief.

She now, with Clara, joined La Luc, who advanced as they entered the room, and took a hand of each in silence. After some moments he proposed to go, and they stepped into a carriage which conveyed them to the gates of the prison. The crowd had already began to assemble there, and a confused murmur arose as the carriage moved forward; it was a grievous sight to the friends of Theodore.

Louis supported Adeline when she alighted, for she was scarcely able to walk, and with trembling steps she followed La Luc, whom the keeper led toward that part of the prison where his son was confined. It was now eight o'clock; the sentence was not to be executed till twelve, but a guard of soldiers was already placed in the court, and as this unhappy party passed along the narrow avenues they were met by several officers who had been to take a last farewell of Theodore.

As they ascended the stairs that led to his apartment, La Luc's ear caught the clink of chains, and heard him walking above with a quick irregular step. The unhappy father, overcome by the moment which now pressed upon him, stopped, and was obliged to support himself by the banister. Louis, fearing the consequence of his grief might be fatal, shattered as his frame already was, would have gone for assistance, but he made a sign to him to stay. "I am better," said La Luc. "O God! support me through this hour!" and in a few minutes he was able to proceed.

As the warder unlocked the door, the harsh grating of the key shocked Adeline, but in the next moment she was in the presence of Theodore, who sprang to meet her and caught her in his arms before she sank to the ground. As her head reclined on his shoulder, he again viewed that countenance so dear to him, which had so often lighted rapture in his heart, and which though pale and inanimate as it now was, awakened him to momentary delight. When at length she unclosed her eyes, she fixed them in long and mournful gaze upon Theodore, who, pressing her to his heart, could answer her only with a smile of mingled tenderness and despair; the tears he endeavoured to restrain trembled in his eyes, and he forgot for a time everything but Adeline.

La Luc, who had seated himself at the foot of the bed, seemed unconscious of what passed around him and entirely absorbed in his own grief; but Clara, as she clasped the hand of her brother and hung weeping on his arm, expressed aloud all the anguish of her heart, and at length recalled the attention of Adeline, who in a voice scarcely audible entreated she would spare her father. Her words roused Theodore, and supporting Adeline to a chair, he turned to La Luc.

"My dear child!" said La Luc, grasping his hand and bursting into tears. "My dear child!" They wept together. After a long interval of silence, he said, "I thought I could have supported this hour, but I am old and feeble. God knows my efforts for resignation, my faith in his goodness!"

Theodore by a strong and sudden exertion assumed a composed and firm countenance, and endeavoured by every gentle argument to soothe and comfort his weeping friends.

La Luc at length seemed to conquer his sufferings; drying his eyes, he said, "My son, I ought to have set you a better example and practised the precepts of fortitude I have so often given you. But it is over; I know, and will perform, my duty."

Adeline breathed a heavy sigh, and continued to weep.

"Be comforted, my love, we part but for a time," said Theodore as he kissed the tears from her cheek; and uniting her hand with that of his father's, he earnestly recommended her to his protection. "Receive her," added he, "as the most precious legacy I can bequeath; consider her as your child. She will console you when I am gone, she will more than supply the loss of your son."

La Luc assured him that he did now, and should continue to, regard Adeline as his daughter. During those afflicting hours he endeavoured to dissipate the terrors of approaching death by inspiring his son with religious confidence. His conversation was pious, rational, and consolatory; he spoke not from the cold dictates of the head, but from the feelings of a heart which had long loved and practised the pure precepts of Christianity, and which now drew from them a comfort such as nothing earthly could bestow.

"You are young, my son," said he, "and are yet innocent of any great crime; you may therefore look on death without terror, for to the guilty only is his approach dreadful. I feel that I shall not long survive you, and I trust in a merciful God that we shall meet in a state where sorrow never comes; where the Son of Righteousness shall come with healing in his wing!" As he spoke he looked up; the tears still trembled in his eyes, which beamed with meek yet fervent devotion, and his countenance glowed with the dignity of a superior being.

"Let us not neglect the awful moments," said La Luc, rising, "let our united prayers ascend to Him who alone can comfort and support us!"

They all knelt down, and he prayed with that simple and sublime eloquence which true piety inspires. When he rose he embraced his children separately, and when he came to Theodore he paused, gazed upon him with an earnest, mournful expression, and was for some time unable to speak.

Theodore could not bear this; he drew his hand before his eyes, and vainly endeavoured to stifle the deep sobs which convulsed his frame. At length recovering his voice, he entreated his father would leave him. "This misery is too much for us all," said he, "let us not prolong it. The time is now drawing on—leave me to compose myself. The sharpness of death consists in parting with those who are dear to us; when that is passed, death is disarmed."

"I will not leave you, my son," replied La Luc. "My poor girls shall go, but for me, I will be with you in your last moments."

Theodore felt that this would be too much for them both, and urged every argument which reason could suggest to prevail with his father to relinquish his design. But he remained firm in his determination.

"I will not suffer a selfish consideration of the pain I may endure," said La Luc, "to tempt me to desert my child when he will most require my support. It is my duty to attend you, and nothing shall withhold me."

Theodore seized on the words of La Luc. "As you would that I should be supported in my last hour," said he, "I entreat that you will not be witness of it. Your presence, my dear father, would subdue all my fortitude—would destroy what little composure I may otherwise be able to attain. Add not to my sufferings the view of your distress, but leave me to forget, if possible, the dear parent I must quit forever." His tears flowed anew.

La Luc continued to gaze on him in silent agony; at length he said, "Well, be it so. If indeed my presence would distress you, I will not go." His voice was broken and interrupted. After a pause of some moments he again embraced Theodore. "We must part," said he, "we must part, but it is only for a time—we shall soon be reunited in a higher world!—O God! thou seest my heart—thou seest all its feelings in this bitter hour!" Grief again overcame him. He pressed Theodore in his arms; and at length, seeming to summon all his fortitude, he again said, "We must part—O! my son, farewell forever in this world! The mercy of Almighty God support and bless you!"

He turned away to leave the prison but, quite worn out with grief, sank into a chair near the door he would have opened. Theodore gazed, with a distracted countenance, alternately on his father, on Clara, and on Adeline, whom he pressed to his throbbing heart, and their tears flowed together. "And do I then," cried he, "for the last time look upon that countenance!—Shall I never—never more behold it?—O! exquisite misery! Yet once again—once more," continued he, pressing her cheek, but it was insensible and cold as marble.

Louis, who had left the room soon after La Luc arrived, that his presence might not interrupt their farewell grief, now returned. Adeline raised her head, and perceiving who entered, again sank on the bosom of Theodore.

Louis appeared much agitated.

La Luc arose. "We must go," said he. "Adeline, my love, exert yourself—Clara—my children, let us depart. Yet one last—last embrace, and then!"

Louis advanced and took his hand. "My dear sir, I have something to say; yet I fear to tell it."

"What do you mean?" said La Luc, with quickness. "No new misfortune can have power to afflict me at this moment. Do not fear to speak."

"I rejoice that I cannot put you to the proof," replied Louis. "I have seen you sustain the most trying affliction with fortitude. Can you support the transports of hope?"

La Luc gazed eagerly on Louis. "Speak!" said he, in a faint voice.

Adeline raised her head and, trembling between hope and fear, looked at Louis as if she would have searched his soul.

He smiled cheerfully upon her.

"Is it—O! is it possible!" she exclaimed, suddenly reanimated. "He lives! He lives!" She said no more, but ran to La Luc, who sank fainting in his chair, while Theodore and Clara with one voice called on Louis to relieve them from the tortures of suspense.

He proceeded to inform them that he had obtained from the commanding officer a respite for Theodore till the king's further pleasure could be known, and this in consequence of a letter received that morning from his mother, Madame de la Motte, in which she mentioned some very extraordinary circumstances that had appeared in the course of a trial lately conducted at Paris, and which so materially affected the character of the Marquis de Montalt as to render it possible a pardon might be obtained for Theodore.

These words darted with the rapidity of lightning upon the hearts of his hearers. La Luc revived, and that prison so lately the scene of despair now echoed only to the voices of gratitude and gladness. La Luc, raising his clasped hands to Heaven, said, "Great God! support me in this moment as thou hast already supported me! If my son lives, I die in peace."

He embraced Theodore, and remembering the anguish of his last embrace, tears of thankfulness and joy flowed to the contrast. So powerful indeed was the effect of this temporary reprieve, and of the hope it introduced, that if an absolute pardon had been obtained, it could scarcely for the moment have diffused a more lively joy. But when the first emotions were subsided, the uncertainty of Theodore's fate once more appeared. Adeline forbore to express this, but Clara without scruple lamented the possibility that her brother might yet be taken from them, and all their joy be turned to sorrow. A look from Adeline checked her. Joy was, however, so much the predominant feeling of the present moment, that the shade which reflection threw upon their hopes passed away like the cloud that is dispelled by the strength of the sunbeam; and Louis alone was pensive and abstracted.

When they were sufficiently composed, he informed them

that the contents of Madame de la Motte's letter obliged him to set out for Paris immediately; and that the intelligence he had to communicate intimately concerned Adeline, who would undoubtedly judge it necessary to go thither also as soon as her health would permit. He then read to his impatient auditors such passages in the letter as were necessary to explain his meaning; but as Madame de la Motte had omitted to mention some circumstances of importance, the following is a relation of the occurrences that had lately happened at Paris.

It may be remembered that on the first day of his trial, La Motte, in passing from the courts to his prison, saw a person whose features, though imperfectly seen through the dusk, he thought he recollected; and that this same person, after inquiring the name of La Motte, desired to be admitted to him. On the following day the warder complied with his request, and the surprise of La Motte may be imagined when, in the stronger light of his apartment, he distinguished the countenance of the man from whose hands he had formerly received Adeline.

On observing Madame de la Motte in the room, he said he had something of consequence to impart, and desired to be left alone with the prisoner. When she was gone, he told La Motte that he understood he was confined at the suit of the Marquis de Montalt. La Motte assented.

"I know him for a villain," said the stranger boldly. "Your case is desperate. Do you wish for life?"

"Need the question be asked!"

"Your trial, I understand, proceeds tomorrow. I am now under confinement in this place for debt; but if you can obtain leave for me to go with you into the courts, and a condition from the judge that what I reveal shall not criminate myself, I will make discoveries that shall confound that same marquis; I will prove him a villain; and it shall then be judged how far his word ought to be taken against you."

La Motte, whose interest was now strongly excited, desired he would explain himself; and the man proceeded to relate a long history of the misfortunes and consequent poverty which had tempted him to become subservient to the schemes of the marquis, till he suddenly checked himself, and said, "When I obtain from the court the promise I require, I will explain myself fully; till then I cannot say more on the subject."

La Motte could not forbear expressing a doubt of his sincerity, and a curiosity concerning the motive that had induced him to become the marquis's accuser.

"As to my motive, it is a very natural one," replied the man. "It is no easy matter to receive ill usage without resenting it, particularly from a villain whom you have served."

La Motte, for his own sake, endeavoured to check the vehemence with which this was uttered.

"I care not who hears me," continued the stranger, but at the same time he lowered his voice. "I repeat it—the marquis has used me ill—I have kept his secret long enough. He does not think it worthwhile to secure my silence, or he would relieve my necessities. I am in prison for debt, and have applied to him for relief. Since he does not choose to give it, let him take the consequence. I warrant he shall soon repent that he has provoked me, and 'tis fit he should."

The doubts of La Motte were now dissipated; the prospect of life again opened upon him, and with much warmth he assured the stranger, who was named du Bosse, that he would commission his advocate to do all in his power to obtain leave for his appearance on the trial, and to procure the necessary condition. After some further conversation they parted.

CHAPTER 22

Drag forth the legal monsters into light,
Wrench from their hands Oppression's iron rod,
And bid the cruel feel the pains they give!

James Thomson, *The Seasons*

Leave was at length granted for the appearance of du
Bosse, with a promise that his words should not criminate him, and he accompanied La Motte into court.

The confusion of the Marquis de Montalt on perceiving this
man was observed by many persons present, and particularly
by La Motte, who drew from this circumstance a favourable
presage for himself.

When du Bosse was called upon, he informed the court, that
on the night of the twenty-first of April, in the preceding year,
one Jean d'Aunoy, a man he had known many years, came to
his lodging. After they had discoursed for some time on their
circumstances, d'Aunoy said he knew a way by which du Bosse
might change all his poverty to riches, but that he would not
say more till he was certain he would be willing to follow it.

The distressed state in which du Bosse then was made him
anxious to learn the means which would bring him relief; he
eagerly inquired what his friend meant, and after some time
d'Aunoy explained himself. He said he was employed by a nobleman—whom he afterward told du Bosse was the Marquis de

Montalt—to carry off a young girl from a convent, and that she was to be taken to a house a few leagues distant from Paris.

"I knew the house he described well," said du Bosse, "for I had been there many times with d'Aunoy, who lived there to avoid his creditors, though he often passed his nights at Paris. He would not tell me more of the scheme, but said he should want assistants, and if I and my brother, who is since dead, would join him, his employer would grudge no money, and we should be well rewarded. I desired him again to tell me more of the plan, but he was obstinate, and after I had told him I would consider of what he said, and speak to my brother, he went away.

"When he called the next night for his answer, my brother and I agreed to engage, and accordingly we went home with him. He then told us that the young lady he was to bring thither was a natural daughter of the Marquis de Montalt and of a nun belonging to a convent of Ursalines; that his wife had received the child immediately on its birth, and had been allowed a handsome annuity to bring it up as her own, which she had done till her death. The child was then placed in a convent and designed for the veil; but when she was of an age to receive the vows, she had steadily persisted in refusing them. This circumstance had so much exasperated the marquis that in his rage he ordered that if she persisted in her obstinacy she should be removed from the convent, and got rid of any way, since if she lived in the world her birth might be discovered, and in consequence of this, her mother, for whom he had yet a regard, would be condemned to expatiate her crime by a terrible death."

Du Bosse was interrupted in his narrative by the council of the marquis, who contended that the circumstances alleged tending to criminate his client, the proceeding was both irrelevant and illegal. He was answered that it was not irrelevant, and therefore not illegal, for that the circumstances which threw light upon the character of the marquis affected his evidence against La Motte. Du Bosse was suffered to proceed.

"D'Aunoy then said that the marquis had ordered him to

dispatch her, but that as he had been used to see her from her infancy, he could not find in his heart to do it, and wrote to tell him so. The marquis then commanded him to find those who would, and this was the business for which he wanted us. My brother and I were not so wicked as this came to, and so we told d'Aunoy, and I could not help asking why the marquis resolved to murder his own child rather than expose her mother to the risk of suffering death. He said the marquis had never seen his child, and that therefore it could not be supposed he felt much kindness toward it, and still less that he could love it better than he loved its mother."

Du Bosse proceeded to relate how much he and his brother had endeavoured to soften the heart of d'Aunoy toward the marquis's daughter, and that they prevailed with him to write again and plead for her. D'Aunoy went to Paris to await the answer, leaving them and the young girl at the house on the heath, where the former had consented to remain, seemingly for the purpose of executing the orders they might receive, but really with a design to save the unhappy victim from the sacrifice.

It is probable that du Bosse, in this instance, gave a false account of his motive, since if he was really guilty of an intention so atrocious as that of murder, he would naturally endeavour to conceal it. However this might be, he affirmed that on the night of the twenty-sixth of April, he received an order from d'Aunoy for the destruction of the girl whom he had afterward delivered into the hands of La Motte.

La Motte listened to this relation in astonishment; when he knew that Adeline was the daughter of the marquis, and remembered the crime to which he had once devoted her, his frame thrilled with horror. He now took up the story, and added an account of what had passed at the abbey between the marquis and himself concerning a design of the former upon the life of Adeline; and urged, as a proof of the present prosecution originating in malice, that it had commenced immediately after he had effected her escape from the marquis. He concluded, however, with saying, that as the marquis had immediately sent his people in pursuit of her, it was possible she might yet have fallen a victim to his vengeance.

Here the marquis's council again interfered, and their objections were again overruled by the court. The uncommon degree of emotion which his countenance betrayed during the narrations of du Bosse and La Motte was generally observed. The court suspended the sentence of the latter, ordered that the marquis should be put under immediate arrest, and that Adeline—the name given by her foster mother—and Jean d'Aunoy should be sought for.

The marquis was accordingly seized at the suit of the crown, and put under confinement till Adeline should appear, or proof could be obtained that she died by his order, and till d'Aunoy should confirm or destroy the evidence of La Motte.

Madame, who at length obtained intelligence of her son's residence from the town where he was formerly stationed, had acquainted him with his father's situation, and the proceedings of the trial; and as she believed that Adeline, if she had been so fortunate as to escape the marquis's pursuit, was still in Savoy, she desired Louis would obtain leave of absence and bring her to Paris, where her immediate presence was requisite to substantiate the evidence, and probably to save the life of La Motte.

On the receipt of her letter, which happened on the morning appointed for the execution of Theodore, Louis went immediately to the commanding officer to petition for a respite till the king's further pleasure should be known. He founded his plea on the arrest of the marquis, and showed the letter he had just received. The commanding officer readily granted a reprieve, and Louis, who, on the arrival of this letter, had forborne to communicate its contents to Theodore, lest it should torture him with false hope, now hastened to him with this comfortable news.

CHAPTER 23

Low on his fun'ral couch he lies!
No pitying heart, no eye, afford
A tear to grace his obsequies.

Thomas Gray, "The Curse upon Edward"

On learning the purpose of Madame de la Motte's letter, Adeline saw the necessity of her immediate departure for Paris. The life of La Motte, who had saved more than hers, the life perhaps of her beloved Theodore, depended on the testimony she should give. And she who had so lately been sinking under the influence of illness and despair, who could scarcely raise her languid head, or speak but in the faintest accents, now reanimated with hope and invigorated by a sense of the importance of the business before her, prepared to perform a rapid journey of some hundred miles.

Theodore tenderly entreated that she would so far consider her health as to delay this journey for a few days, but with a smile of enchanting tenderness she assured him that she was now too happy to be ill, and that the same cause which would confirm her happiness would confirm her health. So strong was the effect of hope upon her mind now that it succeeded the misery of despair, that it overcame the shock she suffered on believing herself a daughter of the marquis, and every other painful reflection. She did not even foresee the obstacle that circumstance might produce to her union with Theodore, should he at last be permitted to live.

It was settled that she should set off for Paris in a few hours with Louis, attended by Peter. These hours were passed by La Luc and his family in the prison.

When the time of her departure arrived, the spirits of Adeline again forsook her, and the illusions of joy disappeared. She no longer beheld Theodore as one respited from death, but took leave of him with a mournful presentiment that she should see him no more. So strongly was this presage impressed upon her mind that it was long before she could summon resolution to bid him farewell; and when she had done so, and even left the apartment, she returned to take of him a last look. As she was once more quitting the room, her melancholy imagination represented Theodore at the place of execution, pale and convulsed in death; she again turned her lingering eyes upon him; but fancy affected her sense, for she thought as she now gazed that his countenance changed and assumed a ghastly hue. All her resolution vanished, and such was the anguish of her heart that she resolved to defer her journey till the morrow, though she must by this means lose the protection of Louis, whose impatience to meet his father would not suffer the delay. The triumph of passion, however, was transient; soothed by the indulgence she promised herself, her grief subsided, reason resumed its influence; she again saw the necessity of her immediate departure, and recollected sufficient resolution to submit. La Luc would have accompanied her for the purpose of again soliciting the king on behalf of his son, had not the extreme weakness and lassitude to which he was reduced made traveling impracticable.

At length, Adeline, with a heavy heart, quitted Theodore, notwithstanding his entreaties that she would not undertake the journey in her present weak state, and was accompanied by Clara and La Luc to the inn. The former parted from her friend with many tears and much anxiety for her welfare, but under a hope of soon meeting again. Should a pardon be granted to Theodore, La Luc designed to fetch Adeline from

Paris; but should this be refused, she was to return with Peter. He bade her adieu with a father's kindness, which she repaid with a filial affection, and in her last words conjured him to attend to the recovery of his health; the languid smile he assumed seemed to express that her solicitude was vain, and that he thought his health past recovery.

Thus Adeline quitted the friends so justly dear to her, and so lately found, for Paris, where she was a stranger, almost without protection, and compelled to meet a father who had pursued her with the utmost cruelty in a public court of justice. The carriage in leaving Vaceau passed by the prison; she threw an eager look toward it as she passed; its heavy black walls and narrow-grated windows seemed to frown upon her hopes—but Theodore was there, and leaning from the window; she continued to gaze upon it till an abrupt turning in the street concealed it from her view. She then sank back in the carriage and, yielding to the melancholy of her heart, wept in silence. Louis was not disposed to interrupt it; his thoughts were anxiously employed on his father's situation, and the travelers proceeded many miles without exchanging a word.

At Paris, whither we shall now return, the search after Jean d'Aunoy was prosecuted without success. The house on the heath described by du Bosse was found uninhabited, and to the places of his usual resort in the city, where the officers of the police awaited him, he no longer came. It even appeared doubtful whether he was living, for he had absented himself from the houses of his customary rendezvous some time before the trial of La Motte; it was therefore certain that his absence was not occasioned by anything which had passed in the courts.

In the solitude of his confinement the Marquis de Montalt had leisure to reflect on the past and to repent of his crimes; but reflection and repentance formed as yet no part of his disposition. He turned with impatience from recollections which produced only pain, and looked forward to the future with an endeavour to avert the disgrace and punishment which he saw impending. The elegance of his manners had so effectually veiled the depravity of his heart that he was a favourite with his sovereign; and on this circumstance he rested his hope of security. He, however, severely repented that he had indulged the hasty spirit of revenge which had urged him to the prosecution of La Motte, and had thus unexpectedly involved him in a situation dangerous—if not fatal—since if Adeline could not be found he would be concluded guilty of her death. But the appearance of d'Aunoy was the circumstance he most dreaded; and to oppose the possibility of this, he employed secret emissaries to discover his retreat and to bribe him to his interest. These were, however, as unsuccessful in their research as the officers of police, and the marquis at length began to hope the man was really dead.

La Motte meanwhile awaited with trembling impatience the arrival of his son, when he should be relieved, in some degree, from his uncertainty concerning Adeline. On his appearance he rested his only hope of life, since the evidence against him would lose much of its validity from the confirmation she would give of the bad character of his prosecutor; and if the parliament even condemned La Motte, the clemency of the king might yet operate in his favour.

Adeline arrived at Paris after a journey of several days, during which she was chiefly supported by the delicate attentions of Louis, whom she pitied and esteemed though she could not love. She was immediately visited at the hotel by Madame de la Motte: the meeting was affecting on both sides. A sense of her past conduct excited in the latter an embarrassment which the delicacy and goodness of Adeline would willingly have spared her; but the pardon solicited was given with so much sincerity that Madame gradually became composed and reassured. This forgiveness, however, could not have been thus easily granted had Adeline believed her former conduct was voluntary; a conviction of the restraint and terror under which Madame had acted alone induced her to excuse the past. In this first meeting they forbore dwelling on particular subjects; Madame de la Motte proposed that Adeline should remove from the hotel to her lodgings near the Châtelet, and

Adeline, for whom a residence at a public hotel was very improper, gladly accepted the offer.

Madame there gave her a circumstantial account of La Motte's situation, and concluded with saying that as the sentence of her husband had been suspended till some certainty could be obtained concerning the late criminal designs of the marquis, and as Adeline could confirm the chief part of La Motte's testimony, it was probable that now she was arrived the court would proceed immediately. She now learnt the full extent of her obligation to La Motte; for she was till now ignorant that when he sent her from the forest he saved her from death. Her horror of the marquis, whom she could not bear to consider as her father, and her gratitude to her deliverer, redoubled, and she became impatient to give the testimony so necessary to the hopes of her preserver. Madame then said she believed it was not too late to gain admittance that night to the Châtelet; and as she knew how anxiously her husband wished to see Adeline, she entreated her consent to go thither. Adeline, though much harassed and fatigued, complied.

When Louis returned from Monsieur Nemour's, his father's advocate, whom he had hastened to inform of her arrival, they all set out for the Châtelet. The view of the prison into which they were now admitted so forcibly recalled to Adeline's mind the situation of Theodore that she with difficulty supported herself to the apartment of La Motte. When he saw her a gleam of joy passed over his countenance; but again relapsing into despondency, he looked mournfully at her, and then at Louis, and groaned deeply. Adeline, in whom all remembrance of his former cruelty was lost in his subsequent kindness, expressed her thankfulness for the life he had preserved and her anxiety to serve him in warm and repeated terms. But her gratitude evidently distressed him; instead of reconciling him to himself, it seemed to awaken a remembrance of the guilty designs he had once assisted and to strike the pangs of conscience deeper in his heart. Endeavouring to conceal his emotions, he entered on the subject of his present danger, and informed Adeline what testimony would be required of her on the trial. After above an hour's conversation with La Motte, she returned to the lodgings of Madame, where, languid and ill, she withdrew to her chamber, and tried to obliviate[100] her anxieties in sleep.

The parliament which conducted the trial reassembled in a few days after the arrival of Adeline, and the two remaining witnesses of the marquis, on whom he now rested his cause against La Motte, appeared. She was led trembling into the court, where almost the first object that met her eyes was the Marquis de Montalt, whom she now beheld with an emotion entirely new to her, and which was strongly tinctured with horror. When du Bosse saw her he immediately swore to her identity; his testimony was confirmed by her manner, for on perceiving him she grew pale, and a universal tremor seized her. Jean d'Aunoy could nowhere be sound, and La Motte was thus deprived of an evidence which essentially affected his interest. Adeline, when called upon, gave her little narrative with clearness and precision; and Peter, who had conveyed her from the abbey, supported the testimony she offered. The evidence produced was sufficient to criminate the marquis of the intention of murder in the minds of most people present; but it was not sufficient to affect the testimony of his two last witnesses, who positively swore to the commission of the robbery, and to the person of La Motte, on whom sentence of death was accordingly pronounced. On receiving this sentence the unhappy criminal fainted, and the compassion of the assembly, whose feelings had been unusually interested in the decision, was expressed in a general groan.

Their attention was quickly called to a new object—it was Jean d'Aunoy who now entered the court. But his evidence, if it could ever, indeed, have been the means of saving La Motte, came too late. La Motte was reconducted to prison; but Adeline, who, extremely shocked by his sentence, was much indisposed, received orders to remain in the court during the examination of d'Aunoy. This man had been at length found

100. Forget.

in the prison of a provincial town where some of his creditors had thrown him, and from which even the money which the marquis had remitted to him for the purpose of satisfying the craving importunities of du Bosse had been insufficient to release him. Meanwhile the revenge of the latter had been roused against the marquis by an imaginary neglect, and the money which was designed to relieve his necessities was spent by d'Aunoy in riotous luxury.

He was confronted with Adeline and with du Bosse, and ordered to confess all he knew concerning this mysterious affair or undergo the torture. D'Aunoy, who was ignorant how far the suspicions concerning the marquis extended, and who was conscious that his own words might condemn him, remained for some time obstinately silent; but when the question was administered his resolution gave way, and he confessed a crime of which he had not even been suspected.

It appeared that in the year 1642 d'Aunoy, together with one Jacques Martigny and Francis Ballicre, had waylaid and seized Henry Marquis de Montalt, half brother to Phillipe, and after having robbed him and bound his servant to a tree, according to the orders they had received, they conveyed him to the Abbey of St. Clair in the distant forest of Fontanville. Here he was confined for some time till further directions were received from Phillipe de Montalt, the present marquis, who was then on his estates in a northern province of France. These orders were for death, and the unfortunate Henry was assassinated in his chamber in the third week of his confinement at the abbey.

On hearing this Adeline grew faint; she remembered the manuscript she had found, together with the extraordinary circumstances that had attended the discovery; every nerve thrilled with horror, and raising her eyes she saw the countenance of the marquis overspread with the livid paleness of guilt. She endeavoured, however, to arrest her fleeting spirits while the man proceeded in his confession.

When the murder was perpetrated d'Aunoy had returned to his employer, who gave him the reward agreed upon, and in a few months after delivered into his hands the infant daughter of the late marquis, whom he conveyed to a distant part of the kingdom, where, assuming the name of St. Pierre, he brought her up as his own child, receiving from the present marquis a considerable annuity for his secrecy.

Adeline, no longer able to struggle with the tumult of emotions that now rushed upon her heart, uttered a deep sigh and fainted away. She was carried from the court, and when the confusion occasioned by this circumstance subsided, Jean d'Aunoy went on. He related, that on the death of his wife, Adeline was placed in a convent, from whence she was afterward removed to another, where the marquis had destined her to receive the vows; that her determined rejection of them had occasioned him to resolve upon her death, and that she had accordingly been removed to the house on the heath. D'Aunoy added that by the marquis's order he had misled du Bosse with a false story of her birth. Having after some time discovered that his comrades had deceived him concerning her death, d'Aunoy separated from them in enmity; but they unanimously determined to conceal her escape from the marquis that they might enjoy the recompense of their supposed crime. Some months subsequent to this period, however, d'Aunoy received a letter from the marquis, charging him with the truth, and promising him a large reward if he would confess where he had placed Adeline. In consequence of this letter he acknowledged that she had been given into the hands of a stranger, but who he was, or where he lived, was not known.

Upon these depositions Phillipe de Montalt was committed to take his trial for the murder of Henry, his brother; d'Aunoy was thrown into a dungeon of the Châtelet, and du Bosse was bound to appear as evidence.

The feelings of the marquis, who in a prosecution stimulated by revenge had thus unexpectedly exposed his crimes to the public eye and betrayed himself to justice, can only be imagined. The passions which had tempted him to the commission of a crime so horrid as that of murder—and what, if possible, heightened its atrocity, the murder of one connected with him by the ties of blood, and by habits of even infantine association—the passions which had stimulated him to so monstrous a deed were ambition and the love of pleasure. The first was more immediately gratified by the title of his brother; the latter by the riches which would enable him to indulge his voluptuous inclinations.

The late Marquis de Montalt, the father of Adeline, received from his ancestors a patrimony very inadequate to support the splendour of his rank; but he had married the heiress of an illustrious family, whose fortune amply supplied the deficiency of his own. He had the misfortune to lose her, for she was amiable and beautiful, soon after the birth of a daughter, and it was then that the present marquis formed the diabolical design of destroying his brother. The contrast of their characters prevented that cordial regard between them which their near relationship seemed to demand. Henry was benevolent, mild, and contemplative. In his heart reigned the love of virtue; in his manners the strictness of justness was tempered, not weakened, by mercy; his mind was enlarged by science, and adorned by elegant literature. The character of Phillipe has been already delineated in his actions; its nicer shades were blended with some shining tints; but these served only to render more striking by contrast the general darkness of the portrait.

He had married a lady, who, by the death of her brother, inherited considerable estates, of which the Abbey of St. Clair and the villa on the borders of the forest of Fontanville, were the chief. His passion for magnificence and dissipation, however, soon involved him in difficulties, and pointed out to him the convenience of possessing his brother's wealth. His brother and his infant daughter only stood between him and his wishes; how he removed the father has been already related; why he did not employ the same means to secure the child seems somewhat surprising, unless we admit that a destiny hung over him on this occasion, and that she was suffered to live as an instrument to punish the murderer of her parent. When a retrospect is taken of the vicissitudes and dangers to which she had been exposed from her earliest infancy, it appears as if her preservation was the effect of something more than human policy, and affords a striking instance that Justice, however long delayed, will overtake the guilty.

While the late unhappy marquis was suffering at the abbey, his brother, who, to avoid suspicion, remained in the north of France, delayed the execution of his horrid purpose from a timidity natural to a mind not yet inured to enormous guilt. Before he dared to deliver his final orders he waited to know whether the story he contrived to propagate of his brother's death would veil his crime from suspicion. It succeeded but too well; for the servant, whose life had been spared that he might relate the tale, naturally enough concluded that his lord had been murdered by banditti; and the peasant, who a few hours after found the servant wounded, bleeding, and bound to a tree, and knew also that this spot was infested by robbers, as naturally believed him, and spread the report accordingly.

From this period the marquis, to whom the Abbey of St. Clair belonged in right of his wife, visited it only twice, and that at distant times, till after an interval of several years he accidentally found La Motte its inhabitant. He resided at Paris, and on his estate in the north, except that once a year he usually passed a month at his delightful villa on the borders of the forest. In the busy scenes of the court and in the dissipations of pleasure, he tried to lose the remembrance of his guilt; but there were times when the voice of conscience would be heard, though it was soon again lost in the tumult of the world.

It is probable that on the night of his abrupt departure from the abbey, the solitary silence and gloom of the hour, in a place which had been the scene of his former crime, called up the remembrance of his brother with a force too powerful for fancy, and awakened horrors which compelled him to quit the polluted spot. If it was so, it is however certain that the spectres of conscience vanished with the darkness; for on the following day he returned to the abbey, though it may be observed, he never attempted to pass another night there. But though terror was roused for a transient moment, neither pity or repentance succeeded, since when the discovery of

Adeline's birth excited apprehension for his own life, he did not hesitate to repeat the crime, and would again have stained his soul with human blood. This discovery was effected by means of a seal bearing the arms of her mother's family which was impressed on the note his servant had found and delivered to him at Caux. It may be remembered, that having read this note, he was throwing it from him in the fury of jealousy; but that after examining it again, it was carefully deposited in his pocketbook. The violent agitation which a suspicion of this terrible truth occasioned deprived him for a while of all power to act. When he was well enough to write he dispatched a letter to d'Aunoy, the purport of which has been already mentioned. From d'Aunoy he received the confirmation of his fears. Knowing that his life must pay the forfeiture of his crime should Adeline ever obtain a knowledge of her birth, and not daring again to confide in the secrecy of a man who had once deceived him, he resolved after some deliberation on her death. He immediately set out for the abbey, and gave those directions concerning her which terror for his own safety, still more than a desire of retaining her estates, suggested.

As the history of the seal which revealed the birth of Adeline is rather remarkable, it may not be amiss to mention that it was stolen from the marquis, together with a gold watch, by Jean d'Aunoy; the watch was soon disposed of, but the seal had been kept as a pretty trinket by his wife, and at her death went with Adeline among her cloths to the convent. Adeline had carefully preserved it because it had once belonged to the woman whom she believed to have been her mother.

CHAPTER 24

While anxious doubt distracts the tortur'd heart.

James Thomson, *The Seasons*

Wwe now return to the course of the narrative, and to Adeline, who was carried from the court to the lodging of Madame de la Motte. Madame was, however, at the Châtalet with her husband, suffering all the distress which the sentence pronounced against him might be supposed to inflict. The feeble frame of Adeline, so long harassed by grief and fatigue, almost sank under the agitation which the discovery of her birth excited. Her feelings on this occasion were too complex to be analysed. From an orphan, subsisting on the bounty of others, without family, with few friends, and pursued by a cruel and powerful enemy, she saw herself suddenly transformed to the daughter of an illustrious house, and the heiress of immense wealth. But she learned also that her father had been murdered—murdered in the prime of his days—murdered by means of his brother, against whom she must now appear, and in punishing the destroyer of her parent doom her uncle to death.

When she remembered the manuscript so singularly found, and considered that when she wept to the sufferings it described, her tears had flowed for those of her father, her emotion cannot easily be imagined. The circumstances attending the discovery of these papers no longer appeared to be a work of chance, but of a Power whose designs are great and just.

"O my father!" she would exclaim aloud, "your last wish is fulfilled—the pitying heart you wished might trace your sufferings shall avenge them."

On the return of Madame de la Motte Adeline endeavoured, as usual, to suppress her own emotions that she might soothe the affliction of her friend. She related what had passed in the courts after the departure of La Motte, and thus excited, even in the sorrowful heart of Madame, a momentary gleam of satisfaction. Adeline determined to recover, if possible, the manuscript. On inquiry she learned that La Motte, in the confusion of his departure, had left it among other things at the abbey. This circumstance much distressed her, the more so because she believed its appearance might be of importance on the approaching trial; she determined, however, if she should recover her rights, to have the manuscript sought for.

In the evening Louis joined this mournful party. He came immediately from his father, whom he left more tranquil than he had been since the fatal sentence was pronounced. After a silent and melancholy supper they separated for the night, and Adeline, in the solitude of her chamber, had leisure to meditate on the discoveries of this eventful day. The sufferings of her dead father, such as she had read them recorded by his own hand, pressed most forcibly to her thoughts. The narrative had formerly so much affected her heart and interested her imagination that her memory now faithfully reflected each particular circumstance there disclosed. But when she considered that she had been in the very chamber where her parent had suffered, where even his life had been sacrificed, and that she had probably seen the very dagger, seen it stained with rust, the rust of blood! by which he had fallen, the anguish and horror of her mind defied all control.

On the following day Adeline received orders to prepare for the prosecution of the Marquis de Montalt, which was to commence as soon as the requisite witnesses could be collected. Among these were the abbess of the convent who had received her from the hands of d'Aunoy; Madame de la Motte, who was present when du Bosse compelled her husband to receive Adeline; and Peter, who had not only been witness to this circumstance but who had conveyed her from the abbey that she might escape the designs of the marquis. La Motte and Theodore La Luc were incapacitated by the sentence of the law from appearing at the trial.

When La Motte was informed of the discovery of Adeline's birth, and that her father had been murdered at the Abbey of St. Clair, he instantly remembered and mentioned to his wife the skeleton he found in the stone room leading to the subterranean cells. Neither of them doubted, from the situation in which it lay, hid in a chest in an obscure room strongly guarded, that La Motte had seen the remains of the late marquis. Madame, however, determined not to shock Adeline with the mention of this circumstance till it should be necessary to declare it at the trial.

As the time of this trial drew near the distress and agitation of Adeline increased. Though justice demanded the life of the murderer, and though the tenderness and pity which the idea of her father called forth urged her to avenge his death, she could not without horror consider herself as the instrument of dispensing that justice which would deprive a fellow being of existence; and there were times when she wished the secret of her birth had never been revealed. If this sensibility was, in her peculiar circumstances, a weakness, it was at least an amiable one, and as such deserves to be reverenced.

The accounts she received from Vaceau of the health of Monsieur La Luc did not contribute to tranquillize her mind. The symptoms described by Clara seemed to say that he was in the last stage of a consumption, and the grief of Theodore and herself on this occasion was expressed in her letters with the lively eloquence so natural to her. Adeline loved and revered La Luc for his own worth and for the parental tenderness he had showed her, but he was still dearer to her as the father of Theodore, and her concern for his declining state was not inferior to that of his children. It was increased by the

reflection that she had probably been the means of shorten-
ing his life, for she too well knew that the distress occasioned
him by the situation in which it had been her misfortune to
involve Theodore had shattered his frame to its present infir-
mity. The same cause also withheld him from seeking in the
climate of Montpellier the relief he had formerly been taught
to expect there.

When she looked round on the condition of her friends, her
heart was almost overwhelmed with the prospect; it seemed
as if she was destined to involve all those most dear to her in
calamity. With respect to La Motte, whatever were his vices
and whatever the designs in which he had formerly engaged
against her, she forgot them all in the service he had finally
rendered her, and considered it to be as much her duty, as she
felt it to be her inclination, to intercede on his behalf. This,
however, in her present situation, she could not do with any
hope of success; but if the suit upon which depended the
establishment of her rank, her fortune, and consequently her
influence should be decided in her favour, she determined
to throw herself at the king's feet and, when she pleaded the
cause of Theodore, ask the life of La Motte.

A few days preceding that of the trial Adeline was informed
a stranger desired to speak with her, and on going to the room
where he was, she found Monsieur Vernueil. Her countenance
expressed both surprise and satisfaction at this unexpected
meeting, and she inquired, though with little expectation of
an affirmative, if he had heard of Monsieur La Luc.

"I have seen him," said Monsieur Vernueil. "I am just come
from Vaceau. But I am sorry I cannot give you a better account
of his health. He is greatly altered since I saw him before."

Adeline could scarcely refrain from tears at the recollection
these words revived of the calamities which had occasioned
this lamented change.

Monsieur Verneuil delivered her a packet from Clara; as he
presented it he said, "Besides this introduction to your notice,
I have a claim of a different kind, which I am proud to assert,

and which will perhaps justify the permission I ask of speaking upon your affairs."

Adeline bowed, and Monsieur Verneuil, with a countenance expressive of the most tender solicitude, added that he had heard of the late proceeding of the parliament of Paris, and of the discoveries that so intimately concerned her. "I know not," continued he, "whether I ought to congratulate or condole with you on this trying occasion. That I sincerely sympathise in all that concerns you I hope you will believe, and I cannot deny myself the pleasure of telling you that I am related, though distantly, to the late marchioness, your mother, for that she was your mother I cannot doubt."

Adeline rose hastily and advanced toward Monsieur Verneuil; surprise and satisfaction reanimated her features. "Do I indeed see a relation?" said she in a sweet and tremulous voice, "and one whom I can welcome as a friend?" Tears trembled in her eyes; and she received Monsieur Verneuil's embrace in silence. It was some time before her emotion would permit her to speak.

To Adeline, who from her earliest infancy had been abandoned to strangers, a forlorn and helpless orphan; who had never till lately known a relation, and who then found one in the person of an inveterate enemy; to her this discovery was as delightful as unexpected. But after struggling for some time with the various emotions that pressed upon her heart, she begged Monsieur Verneuil permission to withdraw till she could recover composure. He would have taken leave, but she entreated him not to go.

The interest which Monsieur Verneuil took in the concerns of La Luc, which was strengthened by his increasing regard for Clara, had drawn him to Vaceau, where he was informed of the family and peculiar circumstances of Adeline. On receiving this intelligence he immediately set out for Paris to offer his protection and assistance to his newly discovered relation, and to aid, if possible, the cause of Theodore.

Adeline in a short time returned, and could then bear to

converse on the subject of her family. Monsieur Verneuil offered her his support and assistance, if they should be found necessary. "But I trust," added he, "to the justness of your cause, and hope it will not require any adventitious[101] aid. To those who remember the late marchioness, your features bring sufficient evidence of your birth. As a proof that my judgement in this instance is not biased by prejudice, the resemblance struck me when I was in Savoy, though I knew the marchioness only by her portrait; and I believe I mentioned to Monsieur La Luc that you often reminded me of a deceased relation. You may form some judgement of this yourself," added Monsieur Verneuil, taking a miniature from his pocket. "This was your amiable mother."

Adeline's countenance changed; she received the picture eagerly, gazed on it for a long time in silence, and her eyes filled with tears. It was not the resemblance she studied, but the countenance—the mild and beautiful countenance of her parent, whose blue eyes, full of tender sweetness, seemed bent upon hers, while a soft smile played on her lips; Adeline pressed the picture to hers, and again gazed in silent reverie.

At length, with a deep sigh, she said, "This surely was my mother. Had she but lived, O my poor father! you had been spared."

This reflection quite overcame her, and she burst into tears. Monsieur Verneuil did not interrupt her grief but took her hand and sat by her without speaking till she became more composed.

Again kissing the picture, she held it out to him with a hesitating look.

"No," said he, "it is already with its true owner."

She thanked him with a smile of ineffable sweetness, and after some conversation on the subject of the approaching trial, on which occasion she requested Monsieur Verneuil would support her by his presence, he withdrew, having begged leave to repeat his visit on the following day.

101. Coming from an outside source.

Adeline now opened her packet, and saw once more the well-known characters of Theodore; for a moment she felt as if in his presence, and the conscious blush overspread her cheek; with a trembling hand she broke the seal and read the tenderest assurances and solicitudes of his love; she often paused that she might prolong the sweet emotions which these assurances awakened, but while tears of tenderness stood trembling on her eyelids, the bitter recollection of his situation would return, and they fell in anguish on her bosom.

He congratulated her with peculiar delicacy on the prospects of life which were opening to her; said everything that might tend to animate and support her, but avoided dwelling on his own circumstances, except by expressing his sense of the zeal and kindness of his commanding officer, and adding that he did not despair of finally obtaining a pardon.

This hope, though but faintly expressed, and written evidently for the purpose of consoling Adeline, did not entirely fail of the desired effect. She yielded to its enchanting influence, and forgot for a while the many subjects of care and anxiety which surrounded her. Theodore said little of his father's health; what he did say was by no means so discouraging as the accounts of Clara, who, less anxious to conceal a truth that must give pain to Adeline, expressed, without reserve all her apprehension and concern.

CHAPTER 25

Heav'n is just!
And, when the measure of his crimes is full,
Will bare its red right arm, and launce its lightnings.

William Mason, "Elfrida"

The day of the trial so anxiously awaited, and on which the fate of so many persons depended, at length arrived. Adeline, accompanied by Monsieur Verneuil and Madame de la Motte, appeared as the prosecutor of the Marquis de Montalt, and d'Aunoy, du Bosse, Louis de la Motte, and several other persons as witness in her cause. The judges were some of the most distinguished in France; and the advocates on both sides men of eminent abilities. On a trial of such importance the court, as may be imagined, was crowded with persons of distinction, and the spectacle it presented was strikingly solemn, yet magnificent.

When she appeared before the tribunal, Adeline's emotion surpassed all the arts of disguise, but adding to the natural dignity of her air an expression of soft timidity and to her downcast eyes a sweet confusion, it rendered her an object still more interesting; and she attracted the universal pity and admiration of the assembly. When she ventured to raise her eyes, she perceived that the marquis was not yet in the court, and while she awaited his appearance in trembling expectation, a confused murmuring rose in a distant part of the hall. Her spirits now almost forsook her; the certainty of seeing immediately, and consciously, the murderer of her father chilled her with horror, and she was with difficulty preserved from fainting. A low sound now run through the court, and an air of confusion appeared, which was soon communicated to the tribunal itself. Several of the members arose, some left the hall, the whole place exhibited a scene of disorder, and a report at length reached Adeline that the Marquis de Montalt was dying. A considerable time elapsed in uncertainty, but the confusion continued; the marquis did not appear, and at Adeline's request Monsieur Verneuil went in quest of more positive information.

He followed a crowd which was hurrying toward the Châtalet, and with some difficulty gained admittance into the prison; but the porter at the gate, whom he had bribed for a passport, could give him no certain information on the subject of his enquiry, and not being at liberty to quit his post, furnished Monsieur Verneuil with only a vague direction to the marquis's apartment. The courts were silent and deserted, but as he advanced a distant hum of voices led him on. Perceiving several persons running toward a staircase which appeared beyond the archway of a long passage, he followed thither, and learned that the marquis was certainly dying. The staircase was filled with people; he endeavoured to press through the crowd, and after much struggle and difficulty he reached the door of an anteroom which communicated with the apartment where the marquis lay, and whence several persons now issued. Here he learned that the object of his enquiry was already dead. Monsieur Verneuil, however, pressed through the anteroom to the chamber where lay the marquis on a bed surrounded by officers of the law, and two notaries, who appeared to have been taking down depositions. His countenance was suffused with a black and deadly hue, and impressed with the horrors of death; Monsieur Verneuil turned away, shocked by the spectacle, and on enquiry heard that the marquis had died by poison.

It appeared that convinced he had nothing to hope from

his trial, he had taken this method of avoiding an ignominious death. In the last hours of life, while tortured with the remembrance of his crime, he resolved to make all the atonement that remained for him, and having swallowed the potion, he immediately sent for a confessor to take a full confession of his guilt, and two notaries, and thus established Adeline beyond dispute in the rights of her birth; and also bequeathed her a considerable legacy.

In consequence of these depositions she was soon after formally acknowledged as the daughter and heiress of Henry Marquis de Montalt, and the rich estates of her father were restored to her. She immediately threw herself at the feet of the king on behalf of Theodore and of La Motte. The character of the former, the cause in which he had risked his life, and the occasion of the late marquis's enmity toward him were circumstances so notorious, and so forcible, that it is more than probable the monarch would have granted his pardon to a pleader less irresistible than was Adeline de Montalt. Theodore La Luc not only received an ample pardon, but in consideration of his gallant conduct toward Adeline, he was soon after raised to a post of considerable rank in the army.

For La Motte, who had been condemned for the robbery on full evidence, and who had been also charged with the crime which had formerly compelled him to quit Paris, a pardon could not be obtained; but at the earnest supplication of Adeline, and in consideration of the service he had finally rendered her, his sentence was softened from death to banishment. This indulgence, however, would have availed him little, had not the noble generosity of Adeline silenced other prosecutions that were preparing against him, and bestowed on him a sum more than sufficient to support his family in a foreign country. This kindness operated so powerfully upon his heart, which had been betrayed through weakness rather than natural depravity, and awakened so keen a remorse for the injuries he had once meditated against a benefactress so noble, that his former habits became odious to him, and his character gradually recovered the hue which it would probably always have worn had he never been exposed to the tempting dissipations of Paris.

The passion which Louis had so long owned for Adeline was raised almost to adoration by her late conduct; but he now relinquished even the faint hope which he had hitherto almost unconsciously cherished, and since the life which was granted to Theodore rendered this sacrifice necessary, he could not repine. He resolved, however, to seek in absence the tranquillity he had lost, and to place his future happiness on that of two persons so deservedly dear to him.

On the eve of his departure La Motte and his family took a very affecting leave of Adeline; he left Paris for England, where it was his design to settle; and Louis, who was eager to fly from her enchantments, set out on the same day for his regiment.

Adeline remained some time at Paris to settle her affairs, where she was introduced by Monsieur Verneuil to the few and distant relations that remained of her family. Among these were the Count and Countess D——— and Monsieur Amand, who had so much engaged her pity and esteem at Nice. The lady whose death he lamented was of the family of de Montalt, and the resemblance which he had traced between her features and those of Adeline, her cousin, was something more than the effect of fancy. The death of his elder brother had abruptly recalled him from Italy; but Adeline had the satisfaction to observe that the heavy melancholy which formerly oppressed him had yielded to a sort of placid resignation, and that his countenance was often enlivened by a transient gleam of cheerfulness.

The Count and Countess D———, who were much interested by her goodness and beauty, invited her to make their hotel her residence while she remained at Paris.

Her first care was to have the remains of her parent removed from the Abbey of St. Clair and deposited in the vault of his ancestors. D'Aunoy was tried, condemned, and hanged for the murder. At the place of execution he had described the spot where the remains of the marquis were concealed, which was in the stone room belonging to the abbey already mentioned.

Monsieur Verneuil accompanied the officers appointed for the search, and attended the ashes of the marquis to St. Maur, an estate in one of the northern provinces. There they were deposited with the solemn funeral pomp becoming his rank: Adeline attended as chief mourner; and this last duty paid to the memory of her parent, she became more tranquil and resigned. The manuscript that recorded his sufferings had been found at the abbey and delivered to her by Monsieur Verneuil, and she preserved it with the pious enthusiasm so sacred a relic deserved.

On her return to Paris, Theodore La Luc, who was come from Montpellier, awaited her arrival. The happiness of this meeting was clouded by the account he brought of his father, whose extreme danger had alone withheld him from hastening the moment he obtained his liberty to thank Adeline for the life she had preserved. She now received him as the friend to whom she was indebted for her preservation, and as the lover who deserved and possessed her tenderest affection. The remembrance of the circumstances under which they had last met, and of their mutual anguish, rendered more exquisite the happiness of the present moments. No longer oppressed by the horrid prospect of ignominious death and final separation, they looked forward only to the smiling days that awaited them when hand in hand they should tread the flowery scenes of life. The contrast which memory drew of the past with the present frequently drew tears of tenderness and gratitude to their eyes, and the sweet smile which seemed struggling to dispel from the countenance of Adeline those gems of sorrow penetrated the heart of Theodore.

The various and tumultuous emotions which the late events had called forth in the bosom of Adeline were now subsided; but the memory of her father still tinctured her mind with a melancholy that time only could subdue; and she refused to listen to the supplications of Theodore till the period she had prescribed for her mourning should be expired. The necessity of rejoining his regiment obliged him to leave Paris within the fortnight after his arrival, but he carried with him assurance of receiving her hand soon after she should lay aside her sable habit, and departed therefore with tolerable composure.

Monsieur La Luc's very precarious state was a source of incessant disquietude to Adeline, and she determined to accompany Monsieur Verneuil, who was now the declared lover of Clara, to Montpellier, whither La Luc had immediately gone on the liberation of his son. For this journey she was preparing when she received from her friend a flattering account of his amendment; and as some further settlement of her affairs required her presence at Paris, she deferred her design, and Monsieur Verneuil departed alone.

When Theodore's affairs assumed a more favourable aspect, Monsieur Verneuil had written to La Luc, and communicated to him the secret of his heart respecting Clara. La Luc, who admired and esteemed Monsieur Verneuil, and who was not ignorant of his family connections, was pleased with the proposed alliance; Clara thought she had never seen any person whom she was so much inclined to love; and Monsieur Verneuil received an answer favourable to his wishes, and which encouraged him to undertake the present journey to Montpellier.

The restoration of his happiness and the climate of Montpellier did all for the health of La Luc that his most anxious friends could wish, and he was at length so far recovered as to visit Adeline at her estate of St. Maur. Clara and Monsieur Verneuil accompanied him, and a cessation of hostilities between France and Spain soon after permitted Theodore to join this happy party. When La Luc, thus restored to those most dear to him, looked back on the miseries he had escaped and forward to the blessings that awaited him, his heart dilated with emotions of exquisite joy and gratitude; and his venerable countenance, softened by an expression of complacent delight, exhibited a perfect picture of happy age.

CHAPTER 26

Last came Joy's ecstatic trial:
. . . .
They would have thought who heard the strain,
They saw in Tempe's vale her native maids
Amidst the festal sounding shades,
To some unweary'd minstrel dancing.
While as his flying fingers kiss'd the strings,
Love fram'd with Mirth a gay fantastic round.

William Collins, "Ode to the Passions"

Adeline, in the society of friends so beloved, lost the impression of that melancholy which the fate of her parent had occasioned; she recovered all her natural vivacity, and when she threw off the mourning habit which filial piety had required her to assume, she gave her hand to Theodore. The nuptials, which were celebrated at St. Maur, were graced by the presence of the Count and Countess D———, and La Luc had the supreme felicity of confirming on the same day the flattering destinies of both his children.

When the ceremony was over he blessed and embraced them all with tears of fatherly affection. "I thank thee, O God! that I have been permitted to see this hour," said he. "Whenever it shall please thee to call me hence, I shall depart in peace."

"Long, very long, may you be spared to bless your children," replied Adeline.

Clara kissed her father's hand and wept. "Long, very long," she repeated in a voice scarcely audible.

La Luc smiled cheerfully, and turned the conversation to a subject less affecting.

But the time now drew nigh when La Luc thought it necessary to return to the duties of his parish, from which he had so long been absent. Madame La Luc too, who had attended him during the period of his danger at Montpellier and hence returned to Savoy, complained much of the solitude of her life; and this was with her brother an additional motive for his speedy departure. Theodore and Adeline, who could not support the thought of a separation, endeavoured to persuade him to give up his château and to reside with them in France; but he was held by many ties to Leloncourt. For many years he had constituted the comfort and happiness of his parishioners; they revered and loved him as a father—he regarded them with an affection little short of parental. The attachment they discovered toward him on his departure was not forgotten either; it had made a deep impression on his mind, and he could not bear the thought of forsaking them now that Heaven had showered on him its abundance.

"It is sweet to live for them," said he, "and I will also die amongst them." A sentiment also of a more tender nature— and let not the stoic profane it with the name of weakness, or the man of the world scorn it as unnatural—a sentiment still more tender attracted him to Leloncourt: the remains of his wife reposed there.

Since La Luc would not reside in France, Theodore and Adeline, to whom the splendid gaieties that courted them at Paris were very inferior temptations to the sweet domestic pleasures and refined society which Leloncourt would afford, determined to accompany La Luc and Monsieur and Madame Verneuil abroad. Adeline arranged her affairs so as to render her residence in France unnecessary; and having bade an affectionate adieu to the Count and Countess D——— and to

[385]

Monsieur Amand, who had recovered a tolerable degree of cheerfulness, she departed with her friends for Savoy.

They traveled leisurely, and frequently turned out of their way to view whatever was worthy of observation. After a long and pleasant journey they came once more within view of the Swiss mountains, the sight of which revived a thousand interesting recollections in the mind of Adeline. She remembered the circumstances and the sensations under which she had first seen them—when an orphan, flying from persecution to seek shelter among strangers, and lost to the only person on earth whom she loved—she remembered this, and the contrast of the present moment struck with all its force upon her heart.

The countenance of Clara brightened into smiles of the most animated delight as she drew near the beloved scenes of her infant pleasures; and Theodore, often looking from the windows, caught with patriotic enthusiasm the magnificent and changing scenery which the receding mountains successively disclosed.

It was evening when they approached within a few miles of Leloncourt, and the road winding round the foot of a stupendous crag presented them a full view of the lake and of the peaceful dwelling of La Luc. An exclamation of joy from the whole party announced the discovery, and the glance of pleasure was reflected from every eye. The sun's last light gleamed upon the waters that reposed in "crystal purity"[102] below, mellowed every feature of the landscape, and touched with purple splendour the clouds that rolled along the mountaintops.

La Luc welcomed his family to his happy home, and sent up a silent thanksgiving that he was permitted thus to return to it. Adeline continued to gaze upon each well-known object. Again reflecting on the vicissitudes of grief and joy, and the surprising change of fortune which she had experienced since last she saw them, her heart dilated with gratitude and complacent delight. She looked at Theodore, whom in these very scenes she had lamented as lost to her forever; who, when

102. Source unknown.

found again, was about to be torn from her by an ignominious death, but who now sat by her side her secure and happy husband, the pride of his family and herself. While the sensibility of her heart flowed in tears from her eyes, a smile of ineffable tenderness told him all she felt. He gently pressed her hand, and answered her with a look of love.

Peter, who now rode up to the carriage with a face full of joy and of importance, interrupted a course of sentiment which was become almost too interesting. "Ah! my dear master!" cried he, "welcome home again. Here is the village, God bless it! It is worth a million such places as Paris. Thank St. Jacques, we are all come safe back again!"

This effusion of honest Peter's joy was received and answered with the kindness it deserved. As they drew near the lake music sounded over the water, and they presently saw a large party of the villagers assembled on a green spot that sloped to the very margin of the waves, and dancing in all their holiday finery. It was the evening of a festival. The elder peasants sat under the shade of the trees that crowned this little eminence, eating milk and fruits, and watching their sons and daughters frisk it away to the sprightly notes of the tabor[103] and pipe, which was joined by the softer tones of a mandolin.

The scene was highly interesting, and what added to its picturesque beauty was a group of cattle that stood, some on the brink, some half in the water, and others reposing on the green bank, while several peasant girls, dressed in the neat simplicity of their country, were dispensing the milky feast. Peter now rode on first, and a crowd soon collected round him. Learning that their beloved master was at hand, they went forth to meet and welcome him. Their warm and honest expressions of joy diffused an exquisite satisfaction over the heart of the good La Luc, who met them with the kindness of a father, and who could scarcely forbear shedding tears to this testimony of their attachment. When the younger part of the peasants heard the news of his arrival, the general joy

103. A type of drum.

was such that, led by the tabor and pipe, they danced before his carriage to the château, where they again welcomed him and his family with the enlivening strains of music. At the gate of the château they were received by Madame La Luc, and a happier party never met.

As the evening was uncommonly mild and beautiful, supper was spread in the garden. When the repast was over, Clara, whose heart was all glee, proposed a dance by moonlight. "It will be delicious," said she. "The moonbeams are already dancing on the waters. See what a stream of radiance they throw across the lake, and how they sparkle round that little promontory on the left. The freshness of the hour too invites to dancing."

They all agreed to the proposal.

"And let the good people who have so heartily welcomed us home be called in too," said La Luc. "They shall all partake our happiness. There is devotion in making others happy, and gratitude ought to make us devout. Peter, bring more wine, and set some tables under the trees."

Peter flew, and, while chairs and tables were being placed, Clara ran for her favourite lute, the lute which had formerly afforded her such delight, and which Adeline had often touched with a melancholy expression. Clara's light hand now ran over the chords and drew forth tones of tender sweetness, her voice accompanying.

Peter, who could not move in a sober step, had already spread refreshments under the trees, and in a short time the lawn was encircled with peasantry. The rural pipe and tabor were placed, at Clara's request, under the shade of her beloved acacias on the margin of the lake; the merry notes of music sounded, Adeline led off the dance, and the mountains answered only to the strains of mirth and melody.

The venerable La Luc, as he sat among the elder peasants, surveyed the scene—his children and people thus assembled round him in one grand compact of harmony and joy—the frequent tear bedewed his cheek, and he seemed to taste the fullness of an exalted delight.

So much was every heart roused to gladness, that the morning dawn began to peep upon the scene of their festivity when every cottager returned to his home blessing the benevolence of La Luc.

After passing some weeks with La Luc, Monsieur Verneuil bought a château in the village of Leloncourt, and as it was the only one not already occupied, Theodore looked out for a residence in the neighbourhood. At the distance of a few leagues, on the beautiful banks of the lake of Geneva, where the waters retire into a small bay, he purchased a villa. The château was characterized by an air of simplicity and taste, rather than of magnificence, which however was the chief trait in the surrounding scene. The château was almost encircled with woods, which forming a grand amphitheatre swept down to the water's edge, and abounded with wild and romantic walks. Here nature was suffered to sport in all its beautiful luxuriance, except where, here and there, the hand of art formed the foliage to admit a view of the blue waters of the lake, with the white sail that glided by, or of the distant mountains. In front of the château the woods opened to a lawn, and the eye was suffered to wander over the lake, whose bosom presented an ever-moving picture, while its varied margin sprinkled with villas, woods, and towns, and crowned beyond with the snowy and sublime alps, rising point behind point in awful confusion, exhibited a scenery of almost unequalled magnificence.

Here, contemning the splendour of false happiness, and possessing the pure and rational delights of a love refined into the most tender friendship, surrounded by the friends so dear to them, and visited by a select and enlightened society—here, in the very bosom of felicity, lived Theodore and Adeline La Luc.

The passion of Louis de la Motte yielded at length to the powers of absence and necessity. He still loved Adeline, but it was with the placid tenderness of friendship, and when, at the earnest invitation of Theodore, he visited the villa, he beheld their happiness with a satisfaction unalloyed by any emotions of envy. He afterward married a lady of some fortune at Geneva, and resigning his commission in the French service, settled on the borders of the lake, and increased the social delights of Theodore and Adeline.

Their former lives afforded an example of trials well endured, and their present, of virtues greatly rewarded; and this reward they continued to deserve—for not to themselves was their happiness contracted, but diffused to all who came within the sphere of their influence. The indigent and unhappy rejoiced in their benevolence, the virtuous and enlightened in their friendship, and their children in parents whose example impressed upon their hearts the precepts offered to their understandings.

ABOUT THE AUTHOR

Ann Ward was born in London in 1764 and married William Radcliffe in 1787. She wrote to occupy herself (she remained childless) and published her first novel in 1789. *The Romance of the Forest*, her third novel, was published in 1791 and became her breakout novel.

Ann Radcliffe was a reserved and reclusive woman who left behind few personal writings that might reveal her thoughts and beliefs. To know her, one must read her novels, and there in the musings and favorite activities of her heroines one might discover the inner life of Ann Radcliffe the woman.

Her work influenced the great English Romantic poets—Wordsworth, Coleridge, Keats, Shelley, and Byron—as well as novelists such as Thackeray and Scott. Lesser novelists of the time copied her work outrageously, using the same place names in their titles and in some cases using even the same character names, in order to profit from her popularity.

Ann Radcliffe refined the Gothic into the form we know today: a heroine trapped by the prototype Byronesque villain in a Gothic setting filled with supernatural elements.

She died of pneumonia in 1823.

Made in the USA
Las Vegas, NV
22 February 2021